HISTORY OF THE MINISTRY OF MUNITIONS

VOLUME I

INDUSTRIAL MOBILISATION, 1914–15

Part I Munitions Supply 1914–15

Part II The Treasury Agreement

Part III The Armaments Output Committee

Part IV The Munitions of War Act 1915

D1476755

The Naval & Military Press Ltd

in association with

The Imperial War Museum
Department of Printed Books

Published jointly by

The Naval & Military Press Ltd

Unit 10 Ridgewood Industrial Park,

Uckfield, East Sussex,

TN22 5QE England

Tel: +44 (0) 1825 749494

Fax: +44 (0) 1825 765701

www.naval–military-press.com

www.military–genealogy.com

www.militarymaproom.com

and

The Imperial War Museum, London

Department of Printed Books

www.iwm.org.uk

Printed and bound by CPI Antony Rowe, Eastbourne

*In reprinting in facsimile from the original, any imperfections are inevitably reproduced
and the quality may fall short of modern type and cartographic standards.*

HISTORY OF THE MINISTRY OF MUNITIONS

VOLUME I

INDUSTRIAL MOBILISATION, 1914-1915

PART I

MUNITIONS SUPPLY

1922

VOLUME I

INDUSTRIAL MOBILISATION, 1914–1915

PART I

MUNITIONS SUPPLY

CONTENTS.

CHAPTER I.

Demand.

CHAPTER II.

The Machinery of Supply.

(6010) Wt. 33785/X4049 250 8/22 Harrow G.36

CHAPTER III.

Some Early War Contracts.

APPENDICES.

CHAPTER I.

DEMAND.

A narrative intended to review the administration of munitions supply during the first year of the war demands some comprehension of the character of the problem which the War Office was called upon to solve. It is necessary to realise clearly the nature and the limits of the preparatory measures which had been taken, and the complete collapse of the whole doctrine upon which these preparations were based. It is no less necessary to remember how obscure was the outlook; how scanty were the data upon which to establish a new war programme. It is, therefore, proposed in this chapter to consider what was involved in the formulation of a munitions programme and the steps by which that essential pre-requisite for a supply policy was in fact evolved.

I. The Size of the Army.

(a) THE SIX DIVISION STANDARD.

The task which confronted the War Office in the autumn of 1914, appears in the light of later experience no less formidable than when it was first envisaged under the stimulus of an overwhelming national emergency. Whatever may be the ultimate verdict upon the achievements of this period, the unexampled gravity and difficulty of the problems presented will not be questioned.

In speaking of the extent of the country's unpreparedness for participating in a European conflict on equal terms with other great Powers, it is not necessary to qualify the language employed, nor is it any reflection upon the old Army to emphasise its insignificant proportion relatively to the task in hand. " There is no Army," said Lord Kitchener. He might have put it more strongly. There was not only no Army on the Continental scale, but there was no provision for creating one.

This unpreparedness has two fundamental aspects, the one common to the experience of all combatants, the other attributable to the peculiar circumstances of Britain as an Island State and her traditional policy as determined thereby. The former of these has regard to the unanticipated character assumed by the conflict, the unprecedented scale upon which supplies were required and the progressive standard of equipment demanded. Neither foe nor ally had foreseen these developments though the initial standard set by the enemy outclassed our own.

" No previous experience," writes Lord ·French, " no conclusion I had been able to draw from campaigns in which I had taken part, or from a close study of the new conditions in which the war of to-day is waged, had led me to anticipate a war of positions. All my thoughts, all my prospective plans, all my possible alternatives of action, were concentrated upon a war of movement and manœuvre. . . . Judged by the course of events in the first three weeks of the war neither French nor German generals were prepared for the complete transformation of all military ideas which the development of operations inevitably demonstrated to be imperative for waging war in present conditions."[1]

The second characteristic of British unpreparedness is its deliberateness. Britain in 1914 was a naval power whose Army was intended for outpost duty. The strength of the land forces of the Empire was the faithful reflection of the national choice. The result of this policy was to limit the effective preparation permitted to the War Office to the equipment of a small Expeditionary Force. In Lord Kitchener's words :—

"The pre-war theory worked out by the General Staff on instructions from the Government of the day had been that, in certain eventualities, we should despatch overseas an Expeditionary Force of six divisions in all, or in round numbers, 150,000 men ; that the Territorial Force should take over the defence of these Islands ; and that the Special Reserve should feed the Expeditionary Force. On this basis, the business of the War Office, in the event of war, was to keep the Army in the field up to strength and to perfect the arrangements for Home Defence."[2]

Within the narrow limits imposed by this policy everything possible had been achieved. The prescribed supplies, exiguous and almost negligible as they appear in relation to the vast torrent which was presently to pour across the Channel, were faithfully provided and duly forthcoming to the last detail of equipment. It was this meagre provision which carried the Army through the famous days of the retreat from Mons ; and formed the nucleus of that rapidly growing armament which yet failed for weary months in succession to overtake the insatiable demand of the forces in the field.

Long before the retreat came to an end in the victory of the Marne, indeed, before the first six divisions had been despatched to France, the whole of the pre-war plan had been superseded. To the crisis that had to be met these arrangements were so grotesquely inadequate as to be merely inapplicable. The war formula had to be restated in unfamiliar and indeed as yet indefinable terms ; for the war was to be fought out between nations, and not between armies merely.

(b) ENLISTMENT FOR THE NEW ARMIES.

The strength of the Forces on mobilisation barely reached a total of 700,000 men, and this number included 250,000 men enrolled in the

---

[1] *1914*, by Field-Marshal Viscount French of Ypres.   Chapter I.
[2] Address to Members of Parliament, 2 June, 1916 ; *Life of Lord Kitchener*, Vol. III, p. 328.

Territorial Forces reserved for home defence, as well as about 100,000 men in India and other foreign stations.[1]

Thus, the first and the greatest task which confronted the Secretary of State for War was not that of filling the ranks of a skeleton force, not that of beating up an output of supplies according to a pre-arranged plan, but the work of creating an army and creating the machinery for supplying it at the very time when the urgent daily necessity of the Expeditionary Force was making demands of unforeseen dimensions on the pre-organised apparatus and arrangements for supply.

Lord Kitchener knew that miracles do not happen, but from the first moment his length of vision enabled him to lay his plans for the future and to foretell that even though her full weight could not be brought to bear upon the enemy, Britain's turn would come in time. Her rôle would be to grow stronger in the later stages of the struggle when the strength of combatants better prepared than she at the outset, would be waning.

Men were the first necessity ; and promptly after the declaration of war, there was issued the famous call for 100,000 recruits based upon the vote by the House of Commons of provision for 500,000 additional men on 6 August, 1914.[2] The terms of the appeal are historic, and in no respect more momentous than as the first revelation conveyed to the public by the " Terms of Service " announcement that the authorities contemplated at least the possibility of a long war.

YOUR KING AND COUNTRY NEED YOU.
A Call to Arms.

An addition of 100,000 men to His Majesty's Regular Army is immediately necessary in the present grave National Emergency. Lord Kitchener is confident that this appeal will be at once responded to by all who have the safety of our Empire at heart.

Terms of Service.

General Service for a period of 3 years or until the war is concluded.

Age of Enlistment, between 19 and 30.

How to Join.

Full information can be obtained at any Post Office in the Kingdom, or at any Military Depot.

GOD SAVE THE KING.[3]

Very shortly afterwards, on 25 August, Lord Kitchener was able to report that " the 100,000 recruits for which, in the first place, it has been thought necessary to call, have been already practically secured."

---

[1] The approximate total number of men mobilised at the outbreak of war, was :—

Regulars	234,000
Regular Reserve	145,000
Special Reserve	56,000
	435,000
Territorial Forces	256,000
	691,000

[2] *Parliamentary Debates* (1914), *H. of C.*, LXV, 2080.
[3] *The Times*, 7 August, 1914.

At the same time he foreshadowed a great extension in the demands that it would be necessary to make upon the manhood of the country. " I cannot at this stage say what will be the limits of the forces required, or what measures may eventually become necessary to supply and maintain them. The scale of the Field Army which we are now calling into being is large, and may rise in the course of the next six or seven months to a total of thirty divisions continually maintained in the Field. But if the war should be protracted, and if its fortunes should be varied or adverse, exertions and sacrifices beyond any which have been demanded will be required from the whole Nation and Empire, and where they are required we are sure they will not be denied to the extreme needs of the state by Parliament or the people."[1]

The actual response to these early appeals was so great that the limit of the numbers voted was soon in sight, and on 10 September, 1914, a second vote for 500,000 men was taken.[2]

A week later, on 17 September, the Secretary of State made the further significant announcement that "in response to the call for recruits for the new armies which it is considered necessary to raise we have had a most remarkable demonstration of the energy and patriotism of the young men of this country. We propose to organise this material into four new armies."[3] " But," he continued, " our chief difficulty is one of *matériel* rather than *personnel*,"[4] though strenuous endeavours were being made to cope with the unprecedented situation. This warning was prophetic of the troubles that were to follow, and showed that Lord Kitchener did not underestimate the difficulty.

By the end of September 1914, enlistment had reached a total of more than three quarters of a million men, and had thus doubled the numerical strength of the Regular Army at home, as it existed three months earlier. This first rush was moderated during succeeding weeks and it was nearly six months before a further total equal to that for August and September was reached. Still the numbers went on mounting in response to the now intensified recruiting campaign. On 16 November, the House of Commons voted another million men,[5] and on 10 February, 1915, the maintainance of land forces to the aggregate number of 3,000,000 men was authorised.[6] The million mark was in fact passed by the end of November 1914 ; by the end of July 1915, when the war had run a full year the total of 2,000,000 recruits had been reached.[7]

---

[1] *Parliamentary Debates* (1914), *H. of L.*, XVII, 504.
[2] *Parliamentary Debates* (1914), *H. of C.*, LXVI, 663.
[3] *Parliamentary Debates* (1914) *H. of L.*, XVII, 736.
[4] *Ibid*, 738.
[5] *Parliamentary Debates* (1914) *H. of C.*, LXVIII, 305.
[6] *Ibid*, LXIX, 601.
[7] *Enlistment during the First Year of the War.*   (Hist. Rec./R/322/12.)

1914 :	August and September	..	..	..	761,824
	October–December	..	..	..	424,533
1915 :	January–March ..	..	..	..	358,093
	April–June	..	..	..	369,029
	July	..	..	..	..	95,413

2,008,892

(c) THE SCALE OF NATIONAL EFFORT.

The work of extending the framework of the Regular Army by constituting what were known as the New Armies began on 21 August, 1914.[1] Each army was to consist of six divisions. Some of these armies were formed later by a grouping of the existing Territorial Divisions, these having been reduplicated so as to form reserve divisions; in this way the original 14 Field Divisions of the Territorial Force were extended to a total of 26. Other armies were built up from the new "Kitchener" divisions. Lord Kitchener's announcement on 25 August that the War Office was aiming at "a total of thirty divisions continually maintained in the Field" meant, as he said on 17 September, four new armies in addition to the original Regular Army. It would represent a field army of about 650,000 men.[2] The thirty division standard was thus definitely adopted as the aim of the War Office at the beginning of the war, and may be taken as the minimum programme of army strength which the War Office then hoped to achieve in 1915. This, however, was but a minimum, and, in view of the steady tendency towards enlargement of programme the basis of maximum requirements for the 1915 campaign, as envisaged in the autumn of 1914, may be put at 1,100,000 men,[3] or fifty divisions.

Even this figure, however, could not be taken as the final measure of requirements so far as equipment was concerned. Early in December, 1914, instructions were given that the measures necessary for the arming of a further 1,000,000 men should be taken in hand. But even an army of 2,000,000 enrolled men was not necessarily the limit of national effort. Mr. Lloyd George, at all events, held that three and a half millions was a practicable ambition. "I believe," he wrote in February, 1915, "we could, with a special effort, raise our 3,500,000 or, if that be found inconsistent with the turning out of the necessary equipment, we could certainly raise 3,000,000."[4] This figure went beyond the maximum which Lord Kitchener had contemplated,[5] and in view of the shortage of rifles and the length of time required for training, the proposal was not one which could be immediately adopted. The immediate task was to realise and make effective the 50 division standard. Efforts to this end continued throughout the spring and early summer of 1915, and it was not until the month of July that any further advance was definitely envisaged. Sir John French when formulating his demands for future supplies to the War Office on 25 June and 8 July, 1915, based his calculations upon a gradual increase in the forces under his command. The existing 22 divisions would, according to this plan, only reach the desired total of 50 divisions in France by March or April, 1916. In communicating[6] the first of these

---

[1] Note by Secretary of State for War, 31 May, 1915 (HIST. REC./R/1000/120).

[2] Ultimately there were five armies formed of "Kitchener" divisions; the sixth, seventh and eighth New Armies on the other hand were Territorial.

[3] HIST. REC./R/1000/120.

[4] Some further considerations on the conduct of the war. 25 February, 1915. (HIST. REC./R/170/22.)

[5] Ibid.

[6] 30 June, 1915 (D.M.R.S.30).

letters to the newly formed Ministry of Munitions for their action, the War Office increased the total demand to the figure required for the prospective equipment of 70 divisions. This higher standard was thus formally prescribed. Shortly afterwards it was tentatively announced by Lord Kitchener at the important Allied Conference held at Calais on 7 July, 1915, where the British and French Prime Ministers, attended by their principal advisers, reviewed the military position and prospects of the campaign as a whole. In the month of August the extent of the possible military effort came again under review before a strong Committee of the Cabinet where the desirability of adopting a standard of 100 divisions was powerfully advocated. This new standard did in fact become the measure of the efforts made by the Ministry of Munitions during the latter part of this year, and was accepted by Lord Kitchener as his ideal. He did not expect to see this total attained, but held that if it were possible it should be reached. Then he would say " England had done her duty and had no call to do any more."[1]

When the army actually attained its maximum strength two years later the number of its divisions still fell short of this total.

(d) Despatch of New Formations.

During the period now under review the strength of the forces in the field was steadily expanding. The original four divisions of the Expeditionary Force which took the field at the very outset, were reinforced by the fifth in time for the battle of le Cateau and by the sixth after the battle of the Marne. Including the cavalry this force may be reckoned as 150,000 men. After the battle of Ypres when the winter of trench warfare began, the total was about 225,000 or some 12 divisions ; by the end of February it was 407,000 and at the end of May the total of 600,000 had been reached. Thus, when the Ministry of Munitions was established, the strength of the British Forces in France under Sir John French consisted of 22 infantry divisions (Regulars, 12 ; Territorials, 6 ; " K " divisions, 3 ; Canadians, 1) ; and 5 Cavalry divisions, with a total strength of approximately 600,000 men.[2]

The garrison of Egypt between December and March consisted of the equivalent of 4 divisions ; one half being made up of Territorials (E. Lancs.) and troops from India and the other of contingents from Australia and New Zealand. The 29th Division was sent from England in March to take part in the land operations in the Dardanelles. The 2nd Territorial Mounted Division arrived in April, and another Territorial division (the Lowland) was sent out at the end of May, raising the total Dardanelles force to 125,000 men. The fighting forces in these two theatres of war thus amounted in all to 725,000 men. At the same time the total number of troops in England either preparing to go abroad, set aside for the supply of reinforcements, or doing garrison duty, numbered 1,500,000 men.

By the beginning of September, 1915, the strength of the army overseas had been raised to thirty-eight infantry divisions (say 800,000

---

[1] Hist. Rec./H/1000/3.   [2] Hist. Rec./R/1000/120.

men), thirty of which were in France. The whole Army at this time was being organised on a 70 division basis, its units being distributed[1] as follows :—

	Home.	France.	Dardanelles.	India.	Total.
Regulars	—	13	1	—	14*
Territorial Force	13	6	4	3	26
" K " Divisions	16	11	3	—	30
					70†

* Including the recently formed " Guards " Division.
† This total does not include the two Canadian, the two Australian divisions nor the Royal Naval Division.

The second half of the year 1915 is the period during which the great majority of the new Kitchener Divisions were able to take the field, the number of divisions in France being approximately doubled during this time.

By the end of the year the overseas army had actually attained a standard of approximately 50 divisions, or, in round numbers, 1,000,000 men.

II. The Calculation of Future Requirements.

(a)   PRE-SUPPOSITIONS OF A PROGRAMME.

The numbers we have so far been considering give, of course, the primary measure for gauging the volume of requisite supplies. But the achievements of the supply administration must be tested not so much by the sufficiency of the supplies actually forthcoming in relation to the momentary demand of the forces in the field, but rather by the degree of success attained in fulfilling the programme of requirements laid down from time to time in anticipation of future needs, such requirements being the official starting point of all programmes of supply. The necessity for this distinction arises from the inevitable instability of actual demand. Sudden extensions of demand can only be satisfied from reserves, that is from the proceeds of earlier demands ; and the possibility of procuring bulk output at short notice can in the nature of the case only be satisfied in very exceptional circumstances. Indeed, the average interval which must elapse between the formulation of demand and its satisfaction must be taken in the light of war experience as nearer six than three months. As the art of programme making was perfected during the latter years of the war the tendency to extend the period was pronounced. In general this elaboration took the form of following back the course of production from the finished article to its components and from these to their raw materials, with subsidiary programmes concerned with the provision of equipment (machine tools, etc.), transportation, and the like.

---

[1] HIST. REC./R/1000/121.

The length of the productive process is revealed to the supply administration primarily by the contractors' undertakings or contract delivery rates. Estimates of future output could, however not be based upon such promises with complete dependence on punctual performance. The degree of unpunctuality thus becomes the second important factor in programme making. In the first year of the war there was not only no accumulated experience to guide estimates as to attainable rates of delivery, but two further conditions were superimposed ; as the campaign developed the projected maximum scale of effort was itself rapidly enlarged, so that the maxima of one month became the minima of the next, while the unforeseen increase in the rate of consumption, especially in the case of gun ammunition, tended to widen the breach between output and immediate requirements.

It was not possible therefore in the circumstances of the autumn of 1914 for the Army Council to lay down a programme of supply or define the requirements for the Expeditionary Force during the campaign of the following year, with the careful elaboration and reliability of forecast that was achieved when the munitions movement reached its zenith. Much painful experience was required before even approximate bases for calculation were available, and during the period we are now considering kaleidoscopic changes followed one another with a rapidity which falsified the whole basis of the programme. Even now, were it desirable, it would be impossible to construct a single programme that would correspond to the task undertaken. A programme to meet the needs of the Army as known in August would be unrecognisable in October. The October programme in turn would need formulation in December. The nature of the problem must be clearly appreciated. It was the solution of an equation in which the Army's demand for each type of munitions for a stated period from six months to a year later could be measured and equated to the effective output at the same date. The demand factors were (a) the anticipated strength of the Army, month by month ; (b) the standard scale of armament equipment per unit ; (c) the estimated rate of consumption or of wastage. To these must be added, in the case of all non-standard stores (d) the process of standardisation, that is the translation of a generic demand, say for hand grenades, into the formal specification of type, pattern and design on which a manufacturer can base his preparations. Here were three unknown, mutually interacting factors.

On the supply side the principal considerations were (a) the normal capacity of the established and experienced War Office contractors, (b) the quantities of additional output procurable by expanding the premises and duplicating the equipment of these firms, (c) the further increase to be secured from untried firms either such as would undertake to work for armament firms as sub-contractors, or such as might be induced to launch out into an unfamiliar type of work on their own account, (d) the productiveness of extraneous sources of supply, particularly Canada and the United States. Only the first of these was known. The second could be estimated, but with small reliance upon the output dates. For the rest it was a matter of guess-work ; there was as yet no basis even for estimating the effects of the intensified demand for metals, for machinery, for gauges and above all for skilled labour.

In such circumstances the problem of a munitions programme tended to become inverted. A broad estimate of maximum output could be used to determine the probable dates at which the New Armies might be expected to take the field, though this maximum was itself indeterminate. The very conception of maximum output had to be modified under the stress of increasing urgency. The maximum of normal capacity reached in August and September became the minimum of the greatly augmented capacity the provision of which was demanded of manufacturers in October and November. These resources proving totally inadequate, a further reduplication of output from new sources of supply became necessary.

For these reasons only the most comprehensive formula can be used to indicate the actual demands envisaged in the autumn of 1914. We shall not, therefore, attempt any refinement on the proposition that the situation called for the equipment of a force of half a million men in the spring of 1915, rising to 1,000,000 before the close of that year's campaign.

(b) Divisional Artillery and other Equipment.

The strength of the Army is one of the three principal factors for measuring demand ; the other two are the scale of equipment and the rate of consumption. The former of these two may now be briefly examined. The scale of artillery equipment per infantry division had been, of course, precisely laid down for the old Army—54 18-pdr. guns, 18 4·5-in. howitzers and 4 60-pdr. guns ; the Horse Artillery used the 13-pdr.—6 guns to a battery. In Territorial divisions the corresponding figures were 36 15-pdr. B.L.C. guns, 8 5-in. howitzers and 4 4·7-in. guns. The Territorial Horse Artillery were armed with the 15-pdr. Q.F. gun.

The Territorial armament, though obsolescent was serviceable and considerable use was made of these weapons in the early stages of the campaign, and until output overtook the demand for the newer types. The 4·7-in. guns in particular were used as substitutes for 60-pdrs. and were reasonably effective.

The standard small arm equipment per division may be taken as 17,000 rifles. For machine guns the scale was 2 per battalion.

The earliest modification in these standards during the period under review was a change in the scale of 18-pdr. armament caused by the adoption of the 4-gun battery as the standard in place of the 6-gun unit. The effect of this change on the total armament was, however, small, since the number of batteries in a brigade was simultaneously increased from 3 to 4, the net reductions in guns per division being thus only 6— from 54 to 48.[1] In November, a more important innovation was adopted ; the scale of machine-gun equipment was doubled, and the new standard requirement became 4 guns per battalion. There was

---

[1] In 1916, the 6 gun standard for 18-pdr. batteries was restored. 121/Stores/8315.

also a most rapid development in special requirements dictated by the varying experience of the campaign such as siege ordnance for attacking entrenched positions, and trench ordnance and apparatus for the defence of forward positions. These highly significant extensions of the pre-conceived standard of equipment called in the main for supplies which had to be evolved before they could be placed on a manufacturing basis. Such stores will, therefore, be more conveniently considered in con-nection with the general question of design and standardisation.

(c) HEAVY ARTILLERY.

It had not been the view of the General Staff that the tendency of field operations to approximate towards siege warfare, as manifested under the exceptional conditions of the war in Manchuria, should be accepted as a general tendency. Nevertheless, it was the experiences of this time which led (1909) to the initiation of experiments with heavy howitzers.[1] These experiments eventuated a few weeks before the outbreak of war in the final approval of a 9·2in. howitzer. In the meantime, some slight experience had been gained with 6-in. B.L. howitzers.

At the outbreak of war, as soon as the need was evident, the War Office took up the question of providing heavy artillery. On 4 September, 1914, Messrs. Vickers were instructed to put in hand the manufacture of 16 9·2-in. howitzer equipments.[2] On 21 September, 1914, the Chief of the Imperial General Staff, Sir Charles Douglas, communicated to Lord Kitchener the first report of an expert Siege Committee which he had appointed some days earlier, the members being Maj.-Gen. Hickman, Col. Capper (succeeded by Col. Louis Jackson) and Maj. H. S. de Brett. The large programme which they put forward was finally approved by Lord Kitchener, with instructions to " proceed with all despatch," on 1 October, 1914, the advice of the French War Office having meantime been sought and the opinion elicited " Le Général en Chef des armées françaises juge très désirable que l'armée anglaise dispose le plus tôt possible des pièces de gros calibre . . . surtout en vue de l'attaque des positions fortifiées que les Allemands ont organisées." This programme involved doubling the order already given for 9·2-in. howitzers, bringing the number to 32, and, in addition, the provision of 32 12-in howitzers, a weapon of which the design was not yet settled, while some 6-in. guns were also converted into 8-in. howitzers.

With the conclusion of the battle of the Aisne and the end of the mobile phase of the war the question of siege artillery inevitably came to the front. On 29 September, 1914, Sir John French sent the following letter to the War Office[3] :—

" I have the honour to state that, in view of the heavy artillery used by the enemy, and the strongly fortified positions which may

---

[1] HIST. REC./R/1000/119.
[2] The contract was not signed until 7 October.
[3] Q/CR. No. 165 placed in 121/Stores/215.

have to be attacked by the Army during this campaign, it is essential that more heavy ordnance should be supplied.

" I recommend, therefore, that the following be sent out as soon as they can be made ready :—
       The 9·2-in. Howitzer.
       One 8-in. Gun B.L.C. with its transporter.
       One 10-in. High Angle Gun.

" A good supply of ammunition should accompany the guns, and the requisite means provided for transporting them, except such as must necessarily be provided locally."

As already explained the steps taken by the War Office looked far beyond this limited provision. The position at the moment is precisely defined in a memorandum addressed to G.H.Q. (France) by the Master-General of the Ordnance on 30 September, which in fact crossed in transmission the letter just quoted.[1] It ran as follows :—

I.

" I wired to you to-day saying that we had succeeded in making travelling carriages for 6-in. B.L. guns. We have made two and they have fired satisfactorily at the butts, but I am sending them to Shoeburyness to-day to try them for accuracy, and on conclusion of the practice they will be brought back by road drawn by a traction engine to see how they travel. I enclose some photographs showing the style of the thing. We can send two of these as soon as we have got the personnel and fittings together, probably the middle of next week, if you wire back and say you want them. Each gun probably would have a trailer carrying 100 rounds of ammunition, and both gun and trailer would be pulled by one traction engine.

" We are trying two different 6-in. guns, one Mark VII, the range of which is about 12,000 yards, and the total weight of gun and carriage will be about 14 tons. The 6-in. Mark VI is two tons lighter but the range is only 10,000 yards. It rests with you to say whether you would like the longer range, accepting the heavier weight. If these guns are found to be of use we could send you out six more after a short time, and even make up the total number to sixteen eventually.

" As regards the ammunition, at present we have 8,000 rounds, making 1,000 rounds for each of the first eight guns sent out. It would take some little time to manufacture more, but we shall proceed. Before getting these carriages ready, I had contemplated sending out these 8,000 shell to you for your 6-in. howitzers, as they are the 100 lb. shell and I have already told you we have no other 100 lb. shell available just yet for your howitzers, further supplies being 120 lb. shell, which lose some 1,500 yards in range.

" You will realise that my change of attitude about the 6-in. guns is entirely due to the production by the Arsenal of this new

---

[1] Q/CR. No. 165 placed in 121/Stores/215.

carriage, and I think that very likely Sir John French would like
to have at his command guns firing up to ranges of either 10,000
yards or even slightly more in case he wishes to use them."

II.

" To-day we are firing the 9·2-in. gun on a railway truck
mounting, which fires a 380 lb. shell to a range of 1,300, and we
could provide three more within two or three weeks if, as I say
again, you wire and say you would like them.

" You would probably have to lay a loop line for them to fire
off, the line being made slightly on a curve so as to give latitude,
the gun itself not being able to fire more than 5 deg. on either side
of the fore and aft line. I gather that you would leave such guns
well down the line at a siding, and only bring them up for some
special purpose."

III.

" I am busy trying to get you a gun firing 12½-lb. shrapnel
shell, mounted either on a field carriage or else on a motor lorry,
to deal with aircraft, but I cannot speak with any certainty of its
success for the moment."

IV.

" I am waiting to hear whether you want the single 9·2-in.
howitzer, mentioned in that table I forwarded you, sent out. We
hope to have four more ready during January."

In reply to this communication G.H.Q. asked on 4 October for two
6-in. B.L. guns Mark VII, to be sent at once and the remaining six
to be held ready. Sir John French also intimated that he would like
the 9·2-in. guns got ready, " but I do not see at present any call for
this nature of railway borne ordnance. Future contingencies might,
however, render the employment of this type of gun necessary."[1]
The two 6-in. guns and the 9·2-in. howitzer were despatched
accordingly on the following day, 5 October. They were consigned to
Antwerp but were diverted to Havre at the wish of G.H.Q. Their
despatch, so Sir John French reported, had relieved him of very
considerable anxiety, since " if heavy ordnance is not forthcoming
when required, future operations may be seriously handicapped and
protracted and increased loss of life may result."[2]
Some of the existing 6-in. howitzers had arrived at the front in time
to take part in the battle of the Aisne, and Lord French tells how he
watched (24 September) the battle from the mouth of a great cave
opposite the village of Missy, then held by the 5th Division, and saw
for the first time with his own eyes the havoc created by the H.E. shells
from these guns.[3]   A day or two later Sir Charles Haddon, President of

[1] 121/Stores/215.   [2] *Ibid.*   [3] *1914*, p. 149.

the Ordnance Board, visited the Commander-in-Chief, who then urged upon him the necessity of providing more heavy guns and ammunition for them.[1]

On 28 December, 1914, Sir John French again drew attention to the provision of heavy artillery.[2] The equipment provided for the 12 divisions of the Expeditionary Force (including the 28th Division) was :—

60 pdr. gun batteries	6
4·7-in. gun ,, ...	10
6-in. howitzer ,, ...	6
6-in. gun ,, ...	2
9·2-in. howitzer	1

Of these the 4·7-in gun was inconvenient in action and cumbersome in traction, while the 6-in. gun was inaccurate and the 6-in. howitzer deficient in range. The War Office replied on 12 January, that a large number of heavy howitzers had been ordered.

32	9·2-in howitzers—range	10,500 yds,	290lb. shell.
24	8-in. ,, ,,	11,000 yds,	200lb. ,,
32	12-in ,, ,,	12,000 yds,	750lb. ,,

It was hoped that 8 of the 9·2-in. would be ready to go out by 1 March, and 4 of the 12-in. by 1 April, further deliveries following fairly quickly. In addition the Admiralty was providing 8 15-in. howitzers, firing a 1,400lb. shell, and possibly five of these would go out in February. The War Office added that " no steps had been taken to provide a howitzer to replace the 6-in. howitzer beyond getting designs, as manufacturers are so full of work none could be completed for five months at least."[3]

On 30 January, 1915, Sir John French put forward a special plea for an adequate supply of 6-in. howitzers on the ground that "the experience of the war has proved this weapon to be one of the most effective in the field," and it was specially necessary for the purpose of replying to the German 15-cm. howitzers which formed the backbone of the German artillery.[4] The British had only 24 of these weapons in the field or 1 battery per corps as against 4 batteries (or 16 howitzers) per corps on the German side. Sir John French therefore asked that two more batteries should be sent at once, being satisfied that the question of ammunition supply was no longer an adequate reason for withholding them, since stocks had accumulated somewhat. Finally, he urged that the production of an up-to-date 6-in. howitzer should be pressed forward, the existing type being really obsolescent. Lord Kitchener, to whom these matters were referred, at once gave orders for the despatch of the two additional batteries asked for. He also approved the placing of a trial order for 6-in. howitzers of the new type. Sir John French was informed accordingly. On 24 February, a further two batteries were asked for and these were sent on 5 March. The War Office intimated that it was only possible to supply ammunition with the guns sufficient to fill their vehicles—152 rounds per gun. All

---

[1] *1914*, p. 162.				[3] 121/Stores/1204.
[2] O.A.W. 70, in 121/Stores/1204.		[4] *Ibid.*

further supplies would have to be drawn from the stocks on Lines of Communication.[1] Sir John French in reply (19 March), again emphasised the importance of these weapons, and expressed the hope that the ammunition supply would improve sufficiently to justify a further despatch of howitzer batteries.

The German preponderance in heavy guns became more pronounced as the winter wore on, but the French, whose reserves enabled them to supply their armies more adequately than the British, had by the month of May, 1915, been able to supply heavy artillery in proportion to field guns in the ratio of 1 to 2·3, while the corresponding British proportion was 1 to 20. Sir John French's heavy artillery at this time consisted of 12 9·2-in. and 40 6-in. howitzers, together with 8 6-in. guns, his medium and light guns numbered 268 and 971 respectively. On 10 June, the Commander-in-Chief emphasised to the War Office the necessity for supplementing the supply of heavy guns as a condition precedent to a successful offensive, the possibility of which the enemy had demonstrated in Galicia. It was, he said, necessary " to make adequate provision for the reinforcements of heavy guns that are necessary to enable the Army to deliver the crushing blows that are essential for a successful offensive on a scale capable of producing important strategical results."[2]

The scale of heavy artillery equipment was one of the principal matters considered at the Boulogne Conference[3] between Mr. Lloyd George and .M. Albert Thomas, the two Ministers responsible for munitions supply in Britain and France respectively, which took place at the instance of the former[4] on 19 and 20 June, 1915. Both Ministers were accompanied by technical advisers and artillery experts from G.H.Q. " There were French military officers from the Front —all artillery—and French artillery officers from Headquarters. We had General du Cane and other officers." (Mr. Lloyd George). An entirely new standard in heavy gun equipment was advocated by the French, namely, that the number of heavy guns and howitzers to be provided for each army corps engaged in trench warfare should be equal to the number of field guns supplied. All these weapons were to be of 6-in. calibre and upwards. The French had already nearly attained this ideal as far as the provision of guns was concerned, though the output of ammunition was still deficient. Field howitzers (4·5-in.) were not thought by them to be of material assistance owing to the small powers of the projectile. When, a week later, the British G.H.Q. submitted their requirements to the War Office[5] the above recommendations were adopted as the basis, except that the French view as to the field howitzer was definitely rejected. As far as heavy weapons were in question, Sir John French recommended that 6-in. howitzers should be supplied at the rate of one battery per division. In addition, heavy howitzers were asked for in the proportion of eight

---

[1] Letter of 13 March, 1915 (121/Stores/1204)
[2] Hist. Rec./R/1300/122.
[3] Memorandum on Supply of Heavy Guns, October, 1915.
[4] Hist. Rec./R/1000/11.
[5] D.M.R.S. 30.

8-in. or 9·2-in. howitzers (two batteries) for each army corps of three divisions and four very heavy howitzers, 12-in. or 15-in. for each army of three corps. These, however, were minimum and not full requirements, and the War Office was asked to increase its efforts with a view to securing double this equipment by the spring of 1916, when the scale would be :—[1]

13 pdr. A.A. guns	2 per division.
18 pdr. guns	48 ,, ,,
4·5-in. howitzers	16 ,, ,,
60 pdr. guns	8 ,, ,,
6-in. howitzers	8 ,, ,,
8-in. or 9·2-in. howitzers	16 per army corps.
12-in. or 15 in. howitzers	8 per army.

These were the requirements which, as will elsewhere be narrated in greater detail,[2] formed the foundation of the first programme adopted by the new Ministry of Munitions.

(d) Ammunition Ration : Rounds per Gun.

The reserves of artillery ammunition available when war broke out were limited to a fixed scale of rounds per gun :—

13 pdr.	1,900 rounds per gun.
18 pdr.	1,500 ,, ,, ,,
4·5-in.	1,200 ,, ,, ,,
60 pdr.	1,000 ,, ,, ,,

This scale was based upon the anticipation that the campaign would be one in which general engagements were occasional, and in which intervals of movement or readjustment of position would obviate the need for continuous expenditure. The actual consumption should, on this hypothesis, have been readily made good within the estimated period of six months over which the expenditure would be spread, and it was laid down that provision should be made within this period for securing additional supplies on the scale of 500 rounds for each field gun and 400 rounds for each field howitzer.[3] The falsification of this hypothesis was, of course, absolute, and the miscalculation was incomparably most serious for the British, who had assumed the task of equipping and maintaining forces out of all proportion with their pre-war Army. Even for the combatants who were better prepared the situation was grave enough. As Mr. Lloyd George put it, speaking in April, 1915 :—[4]

" In this war more ammunition has been expended than any army ever anticipated. That is not a miscalculation confined to us. There is not an army in the field at the present moment that ever dreamt there would be such an expenditure of ammunition

---

[1] This standard involved the gradual elimination of the 15 pdr. B.L.C. and the 4·7-in. gun. (Hist. Rec./R/1000/8.)

[2] See below, p. 42.

[3] Hist. Rec./R/1000/119, p. 10.

[4] *Parliamentary Debates* (1915), *H. of C.*, LXXI, 313.

as has taken place. I had the privilege of seeing one of the great French generals when I was over there on this very question of ammunition . . . and he said to me :—' The surprise of the war has been the amount of ammunition which we have had to expend. . . . The ordinary ideas of strategy were that after three or four weeks of manœuvring you would have a great battle, and that that battle might occupy a fortnight or three weeks, and, of course there would be a very great expenditure of ammunition, and we thought that after that one or the other of the parties would have been defeated. There would have been a retreat, a reconstruction, and the other army would have advanced, and perhaps after a month's time we would have another great fight. But for seventy-nine days and nights my men have been fighting, and firing has gone on almost night and day by these great cannons.' ''[1]

No one ever dreamt, as he said, of the expenditure of ammunition at that rate, and it is perfectly clear that the Germans also were taken by surprise. ' By mid-September,' says Falkenhayn, ' the spectre of the shortage of munitions was already apparent . . . Consumption exceeded peace time estimates many times over.'[2]

At this time Sir John French also was finding great difficulty in maintaining his stocks, since the expenditure was constantly outrunning receipts. His 18-pdr. guns, he records, on 28 September, were firing 14 rounds per day, receipts being only 7 rounds per gun per day, while the few 60-pdr. guns and the 4·5-in. howitzers fired more than 40 rounds per gun per day.[3] The War Office took anxious counsel with General Deville, the head of the French Ordnance who came over on 22 October.[4] The Expeditionary Force was at this time being reformed on the Flanders front, and was preparing for the intensified fighting incidental to the first battle of Ypres. The anxieties of the moment were greatly increased by the pronounced shortage of ammunition supplies. On 29 October, Sir John French reported that he had been compelled to restrict the expenditure to a ration of 20 rounds per gun per day, and that even that rate could not be maintained unless better supplies were received.[5] Lord Kitchener was, of course, fully alive to the gravity of the position. " The supply of ammunition," he wrote on 31 October, " gives me great anxiety . . . at the present rate of expenditure we are certain before long to run short."[6] And this shortage of supply continued to hamper the campaign and restrict its advantageous development. The situation was but aggravated by the increased number of guns which were added from time to time to Sir John French's command. Early in January, 1915, Lord Kitchener addressed

---

[1] This was realised by the French as early as September, 1914, when they found during the battle of the Marne, that " les canons de 75 devoraient en quelque jours des stocks de projectiles qui paraissaient suffisants pour des semaines, peut-être des mois." Rapport de M. Perchot, Senate Document 284 (1916), p. 3.
[2] *Memoirs* (Morning Post, 10 November, 1919).
[3] 121/Stores/216.
[4] Hist. Rec./R/1000/120.
[5] 121/Stores/216.
[6] *Life of Lord Kitchener*, III, 74.

to Sir John French a memorandum embodying the conclusion of a War Council presided over by the Prime Minister on 7 and 8 January, which dealt primarily with Sir John French's plan for an advance along the Belgian Coast. This memorandum contained the following passage :—

" It is impossible at the present time to maintain a sufficient supply of gun ammunition on the scale which you considered necessary for offensive operations. Every effort is being made in all parts of the world to obtain an unlimited supply of ammunition ; but as you are well aware, the result is still far from being sufficient to maintain the large number of guns which you now have under your command adequately supplied with ammunition for offensive purposes."[1]

But the Commander-in-Chief needed more and yet more artillery to enable him to carry out his plans. " In order," he wrote on 3 January, 1915, " to attain the double object of relieving the French troops and thus strengthening the Allied forces at the decisive points, and of undertaking a vigorous offensive to effect the capture of Ostend and Zeebrugge, it is absolutely necessary that I should have more troops, a liberal supply of artillery ammunition of all kinds, but especially high explosives, and a sufficient number of heavy guns."[2]

Though the need for " a liberal supply of artillery ammunition " had been urgent for many weeks it had not been precisely formulated. The possibilities of maintaining supply at a definite prescribed rate of expenditure which experience had dictated was now formally challenged. On the last day of 1914, Sir John French forwarded to the War Office a statement of his estimated requirements expressed as a scale of income supply per gun per day :—

REQUIRED OUTPUT OF AMMUNITION.[3]

					Rounds per Gun per day.
13 pdr.	..	..	..	..	50 (25 H.E.)
18 pdr.	..	..	..	..	50 (25 H.E.)
4·5-in. Howitzer	..	..	..	40 (35 H.E.)
60 pdr.	..	..	..	..	25 (15 H.E.)
4·7-in.	..	..	..	..	25 (15 H.E.)
6-in. Howitzer	..	..	..	25 (all H.E.)
6-in. Gun	..	..	..	..	25 (all H.E.)
9·2-in. Howitzer	..	..	..	12 (all H.E.)

Such a scale of supply would allow of the accumulation of reserves during periods of less active fighting.

These standards were far in excess of any scale of supply hitherto contemplated, and when translated into total requirements per month for all guns present and prospective made a most alarming aggregate. Lord Kitchener again appealed to the French for advice as to what number of rounds per gun per day they regarded as necessary in the light of their experience during the autumn campaign.

The reply he received was as follows :—[4]

---

[1] *1914.* Chapter XV.
[2] HIST. REC./R/1000/72.
[3] *1914,* Chapter XVIII.
[4] *Life of Lord Kitchener,* III, 276.

Le Ministre de la Guerre de France, répondant à la question que vous m'avez prié lui poser, me prie de faire connaître à Votre Excellence ce qui suit :

" 1. Le chiffre de 25 coups par pièce et par jour a été admis pour assurer le coefficient indispensable, en se basant sur la consommation atteinte pendant plusieurs mois, et notamment en Flandre où les corps engagés ont tiré du 25 octobre au 23 novembre, 33 coups par pièce et par jour en moyenne.

" 2. Il estime cependant que l'armée anglaise pourrait se contenter d'un chiffre moindre, car elle a, dans l'offensive, des procédés un peu differents des nôtres, et garde toujours des forces. importantes en seconde ligne, pour les besoins de la relève."

It may be noted that the conclusions drawn from this pronouncement by the War Office did not apparently convince G.H.Q. " According to the experience of the French Army," the Army Council wrote, " based on a much larger number of troops and guns over a much longer line than that occupied by the British Army, a figure of 20 rounds a gun has been accepted by them as being sufficient, and this, they remark, may be more than sufficient for our requirements." " So far," replied the British Commander-in-Chief, " from a large Army with many guns acting on a very extended front requiring a larger number of rounds per gun per day than a small army, the contrary is the case. . . . It stands to reason that a small force is more likely to find a larger proportion of its troops engaged in severe fighting than a large one." Therefore, as the Army increased in strength it should prove possible to make a reduction in the scale of requirements for field artillery.

The Army Council in communicating the French opinion (quoted above) to Sir John French on 19 January 1915, pointed out[1] that the French authorities were hoping to work up their own output to 20 rounds per gun per day. They stated that they were " thoroughly alive to the urgent importance of increasing gun ammunition for the Expeditionary Force, and have spared, and will spare no effort to secure this end." Success was imperilled by the shortage of available labour ; but " the Council desire to emphasise the fact that the orders for manufacture are not being limited by what they think it necessary to supply, but are entirely conditioned by the highest possible output of the ordnance factories throughout the Empire and the trade of England and the allied and neutral countries of the world." The Army Council further undertook that ·" if and when the figure of 20 rounds a day for every gun in the field is attained " they would not relax their efforts but would aim at whatever further increase experience should indicate as necessary. The provision of 20 rounds per gun per day was thus formally accepted as the objective, though the standard actually adopted by the War Office as the effective minimum scale of requirements gave 17 rounds per gun to the field guns. This figure was accepted as a minimum standard at a meeting between the British and French

[1] Hist. Rec./R/1000/119, p. 28.   Mr. Asquith's Speech of 3 June, 1919. Hist. Rec./R/1300/109.

War Ministers and Commanders-in-Chief, which took place at the French Army Headquarters later in the spring of 1915.[1] It was then agreed that in order to render more effective the co-operation of the British Army in the contemplated French offensive it was necessary that ammunition supply should reach the scale of 17 rounds per gun per day for the field gun and other natures in proportion. No lesser quantity would be adequate for a sustained offensive. Thus the War Office standard during the spring of 1915 was : 17 rounds for field guns and field howitzers, (18 pdr., 15 pdr., 4·5-in., 60 pdr.) ; 10 rounds for the 4·7-in. gun ; 5 rounds for heavy howitzers (6-in., 8-in., 9·2-in., 12-in.).[2] This, of course, was a minimum scale necessitated by the actual shortage ; and in at least one important nature, the 6-in. howitzer, did not cover the prevailing rate of expenditure.[3] In a memorandum sent to Mr. Lloyd George on 10 May, 1915, Sir John French reaffirmed his need for a more generous allowance per field gun with proportionate rations for other guns.[4]

" We have found by experience " he wrote, " that the field guns actually engaged in offensive operations such as Neuve Chapelle, fire about 120 rounds per gun per day. Heavy guns and howitzers according to their calibre fire less in proportion. The guns of the whole army are, of course, never equally heavily engaged at the same time, but the number of guns available and the amount of ammunition are the limiting factors when a plan of attack is being considered. There is, therefore, scarcely any limit to the supply of ammunition that could be usefully employed. The more ammunition the bigger the scale on which the attack can be delivered, and the more persistently it can be pressed."

Demands must, however, be reasonable, and the position would be materially improved if the supply reached the standard of 24 rounds per field gun per day (50 per cent. H.E.) and other guns in proportion.

A month later, the Commander-in-Chief communicated to the War Office an elaborate memorandum[5] reviewing the whole subject of the past and future supply and requirements of artillery ammunition, and enclosing an estimate of requirements in rounds per gun per day. These rations were accordingly adopted by the War Office and were set before the newly-created Ministry of Munitions as the basis on which future supplies should be calculated.[6] Twenty-five rounds per gun per day was the new scale for light guns (18 pdr., 15 pdr., 13 pdr.) ; 20 rounds for 4·5-in. howitzer and 60 pdr. gun ; 15 rounds for 4·7-in. gun, 5-in. howitzer, 6-in. howitzer and 8-in. howitzer ; 12 rounds for the 9·2-in. howitzer and 5 for the 15-in. howitzer. A ration of 10 rounds was also asked for for trench mortars, the first time a regular scale had

---

[1] 121/Stores/2765. Lord Kitchener's memorandum of 31 May, 1915 speaks of the " 17 rounds that Sir John French and General Joffre have decided as being the amount that they require." HIST. REC./R/1000/120, p. 5.

[2] HIST. REC./R/172/7.

[3] *Ibid.*

[4] *1914*, p. 358. HIST. REC./R/1000/119, p. 45.

[5] Dated 10 June, 1915. (121/Stores/2765).

[6] HIST. REC./R/1300/6.

been put forward. The result of these successive formulations may be set out in comparative form, concluding with the maximum scale attained in 1916.

Scale of Rounds per gun per day Requested or Approved at Various Dates.

	Commander-in-Chief 31.12.14	War Office. 13.4.15.	Commander-in-Chief 10.5.15.	Commander-in-Chief 10.6.15.	Maximum.
18 pdr. Q.F. ..	50	17	24	25	50 (1916)
15 pdr. B.L.C. ..	—	17	24	25	—
13 pdr. Q.F. ..	50	—	24	25	—
4·5-in. Howitzer ..	40	17	20	20	38 (1917)
5-in. Howitzer ..	—	—	15	15	—
60 pdr. ..	25	17	16	20	37½ (1917)
4·7-in. Howitzer ..	25	10	16	15	—
6-in. Howitzer ..	25	5	12	15*	43½ (1918)
6-in. Gun	25	—	—	12	30 (1918)
8-in. Howitzer ..	—	5	—	15	33 (1917)
9·2-in. Howitzer ..	12	5	12	12	30 (1916)
12-in. Howitzer ..	—	5	—	5†	10 (1916)
15-in. Howitzer ..	—	5	—	5	7 (1916)

* Raised to 20 on 15/7/15.　　　　† Raised to 8 on 31/7/15.

The standards of June–July, 1915, were in all important cases largely increased the following year, when Sir John French's original standard of 50 rounds per gun was prescribed. The final scales adopted in later years receded somewhat from this maximum.[1]

(e) High Explosives versus Shrapnel.

Demand for ammunition has to do not alone with the volume of supply, but with the nature of product. In particular, the difficulties of supply 1914–1915, were concerned not alone with the general shortage of output, but in a special degree with the deficient supply of high explosive shell, which the conditions imposed by a war of position rendered a matter of extreme urgency.

At the outbreak of war the standard types of ammunition and the relative proportions of shrapnel supplied were as follows :—

Royal Field Artillery	..	..	18 pdr. (Shrapnel only).
Royal Horse Artillery	..	..	13 pdr.　　,,　　　,,
Field howitzers	..	..	4·5 in. howitzer (70 per cent. Shrapnel, 30 per cent. H.E.).
Heavy field guns	..	..	60 pdr. (70 per cent. Shrapnel, 30 per cent. H.E.).
Heavy howitzers	..	..	6-in. 30 cwt. (H.E. only.)

---

[1] See Vol. X, Part II, Chap. I. Hist. Rec./H/1300/16.

The decision to rely exclusively upon shrapnel ammunition for the field gun was taken at the time when the 15 pdr. gun was superseded by the 18 pdr. It was then thought that the provision of a proportion of high-explosive ammunition for field howitzers would adequately meet the need.[1] In 1912 the Serbians employed high explosive field-gun ammunition against the Turks with good results.[2] The adoption of the new type of ammunition by the French Army was already an accomplished fact. Steps had also been taken to produce for the British Army a shell of the universal type such as had been introduced by Germany, this being a combination of the H.E. and shrapnel principles. The conclusion of the experimental stage had hardly been reached, however, when war broke out.

On 31 August, 1914, the Master-General of the Ordnance, Major-General Sir Stanley von Donop, wrote to Major-General Lindsay, the General Officer Commanding, Royal Artillery in France, asking if the provision of high explosive shell for field and horse artillery should be taken up. The reply was given on 4 September. "If you have safe explosives for field guns by all means proceed to manufacture." On receipt of this communication the Master-General of the Ordnance re-stated his offer to the Chief of the General Staff. "If you want some high explosive common shell—not high explosive shrapnel—for your field guns I could probably send you out some for the 13-pdr. and later, if you wished it, I could probably make you some high explosive shrapnel or high explosive common for the 18 pdr. But the former has only just completed its experimental stage, and I do not want to hamper the manufacture of the service ammunition until I have ample reserve." On 15 September the Chief of the General Staff, Sir Archibald Murray, replied in conclusive terms stating that Corps Commanders had so far as possible been consulted, and that the general opinion in which the Commander-in-Chief concurred, was that high explosive ammunition for field guns "should be supplied as soon as possible."[3]

Even before this message arrived the matter was being actively investigated, and experimental filling of 18 pdr. shell with T.N.T. was in progress at the Royal Laboratory. The chief difficulty was the detonating system, but a makeshift method of fusing was found practicable by using a combination of the existing direct action fuse No. 44 with the ordinary time fuse No. 80. An order for 20,000 rounds was placed with the Ordnance Factory on 5 October,[4] and issues of completed ammunition to France began on 22 October, the whole order being discharged by February, 1915. By the latter date very extensive arrangements for future supply had been completed.

---

[1] HIST. REC./R/1000/119, p. 24.

[2] Sir C. E. Callwell, K.C.B., *Morning Post*, 16 June, 1919. Sir John French at this time was Chief of the Imperial General Staff.

[3] HIST. REC./R/1000/119, p. 26.

[4] HIST. REC./R/1122.11/16.

Issues of 18 *pdr. H.E. Cartridges to France.* *Extract L.47/322.*

22 October, 1914	.. ..	.. 1,000
2 November, ,,	.. ..	.. 912
4 ,, ,,	.. ..	.. 64
6 ,, ,,	.. ..	.. 176
11 ,, ,,	.. ..	.. 280
16 ,, ,,	.. ..	.. 728
17 ,, ,,	.. ..	.. 560
19 ,, ,,	.. ..	.. 168
22 ,, ,,	.. ..	.. 112
27 ,, ,,	.. ..	.. 680
2 December ,,	.. ..	.. 408
4 ,, ,,	.. ..	.. 60
7 ,, ,,	.. ..	.. 284
6 ,, ,,	.. ..	.. 568
12 ,, ,,	.. ..	.. 652
13 ,, ,,	.. ..	.. 480
15 ,, ,,	.. ..	.. 108
17 ,, ,,	.. ..	.. 420
20 ,, ,,	.. ..	.. 468
22 ,, ,,	.. ..	.. 700
30 ,, ,,	.. ..	.. 164
		8,992
3 January, 1915 ..	.. ..	.. 1,000
10 ,, ,, ..	.. ..	.. 1,946
14 ,, ,, ..	.. ..	.. 52
18 ,, ,, ..	.. ..	.. 1,000
25 ,, ,, ..	.. ..	.. 1,996
2 February ,, ..	.. ..	.. 1,952
10 ,, ,, ..	.. ..	.. 448
15 ,, ,, ..	.. ..	.. 600
22 ,, ,, ..	.. ..	.. 1,014
18 ,, ,, ..	.. ..	.. 1,000
		11,008
	Grand Total	20,000

Such was the trickle which was destined to become a torrent—but only after many delays and disappointments.

The day when the first consignment was dispatched, 22 October, 1914, was also the occasion of the visit of General Deville to the War Office to discuss the ammunition problem with the Secretary of State. He was able to explain to the War Office the policy adopted by the French of abandoning shrapnel for field guns and substituting high explosive shells fused with delay action so as to burst in the air on ricochet.[1]

There was as yet no graze fuse available. Consequently this new ammunition could not be employed so effectively on wire as could the French shell, and its utility against fortified posts became less as the original shallow trenches were succeeded by systems of deep and well-protected shelters.

A favourable report on the first issues was made by G.H.Q. on 6 November, 1914, and about this time it was requested that future

[1] Hist. Rec./R/1000/119, p. 26.

supplies of 18 pdr. ammunition should include 25 per cent. high explosive shell. This demand was reiterated on 31 December, 1914, when in addition it was further asked that the 4·5-in howitzer ration should contain 35 per cent. H.E. and the heavy howitzers 100 per cent. The 60 pdr. and 4·7-in. gun, on the other hand, were to be reduced to 15 per cent. H.E.

The question of the relative value of high explosive and shrapnel shell continued to be a matter for investigation. Trials carried out under Sir John French's direction in January, 1915, showed that rather better results could be obtained in clearing wire entanglements by the use of 18 pdr. shrapnel than with the high explosive, and at Neuve Chapelle good results were realised from the use of the former.[1] Sir John French's demands for high explosive ammunition, however, became increasingly urgent. On 18 March, 1915, he drew attention to the dangerous inadequacy of his supplies, and made an emphatic demand that steps should be taken to improve the supply of high explosive ammunition for the 18 pdr., 4·5-in. and 6-in. howitzer.[2] When formulating his requirements in June, Sir John French again pressed for an allowance of 50 per cent. high explosive for his field guns, as justified by recent experience. "Shrapnel is invaluable for beating off attacks, forming barrages of fire to prevent the intervention of fresh hostile troops in the fight, cutting wire and exploding communication trenches. H.E. cuts wire equally well, and, in addition, will destroy earthworks and buildings and generally fulfil functions for which shrapnel is unsuitable." A particularly liberal allowance was asked for in the case of 4·5-in. howitzer (80 per cent.), while for the Territorial weapons—15 pdr. and 5-in. howitzer—a proportion of 75 per cent. and 100 per cent. respectively was recommended, on the ground that this form of ammunition was most suitable for less highly trained troops. For the 4·7-in., 60 pdr. and 6-in. guns 50 per cent. was desired, and 100 per cent. for all howitzers of 6-in. or larger calibre. As regards the 6-in. howitzer ammunition in particular, Sir John French had reported in January, 1915, that the lyddite shell was proving more useful, and that shrapnel would no longer be required.[3] It was even suggested that available 6-in. lyddite ammunition should be diverted from the guns to the howitzers ; the long-distance shrapnel fire of the 6-in. guns, on the other hand, was becoming increasingly valuable. As was made clear when these proposals were considered at the Boulogne Conference on 20 June, 1915, the importance of the high explosive question was no longer exclusively or mainly concerned with the provision of 18 pdr. H.E. The French view urged upon this occasion brought about the recognition of the vastly greater significance of heavy artillery, and this artillery, they urged, should be provided with H.E. ammunition exclusively, and fused partly with delay and partly with direct action fuses.[4] Thus the question took on

---

[1] Hist. Rec./R/1000/119, p. 29.
[2] 121/Stores/1214.
[3] Letters of 17 and 26 January (121/Stores/1392).
[4] Lord Kitchener's Memorandum, Oct. 1915. (Hist. Rec./R/1200/56.)

a new aspect. It was no longer primarily a matter of ammunition supply, but was now a question of the provision of heavy guns.

Owing to the formidable difficulties which had been experienced in evolving an effective method of detonating the 18 pdr. H.E. ammunition—a problem which was governed and complicated by the necessity for adopting for the bursting charge an amatol 40/60 mixture which was only sanctioned in May, 1915—and the fact that after fuse No. 100 came into supply in the summer, it became necessary to re-design the gaine in order to counteract the proclivity towards " blinds " or, worse still, " prematures," it was not until the spring of 1916 that a thoroughly reliable bulk supply of this ammunition was available. By this time, however, the need for it had become far less urgent. As early as January, 1916, doubts began to be expressed by the Ministry's advisers as to the need for maintaining output in equal proportions between shrapnel and H.E.[1] Shrapnel was definitely preferred for wire cutting, and for these, and other reasons, the experience of the winter pointed to a marked tendency for the consumption of shrapnel to outrun that of high explosive. This view was confirmed by a letter from G.H.Q. in April asking for the proportion of shrapnel to be maintained at 70 per cent., and this remained the predominant rate for the remainder of the war.

(f) NOVEL EQUIPMENT : DESIGN AS PRE-REQUISITE TO SUPPLY.

We have dealt so far with stores with which the old Army was familiar, and which had been definitely prescribed as necessary to the equipment of the Expeditionary Force. We have now to consider the measurement of demand in the case of those additional munitions, the need for which was demonstrated by the experience of the campaign. In such circumstances requirements were primarily generic rather than specific, qualitative rather than quantitative. Thus the Army found itself from time to time in urgent need of the means both of defence against and of reply to forms of attack which their existing equipment was not calculated to deal with. First it was the heavy German howitzers flinging their " Black Marias " or their " Coal Boxes " against troops who had to rely on their field-gun shrapnel and their light howitzers. And simultaneously there developed an even more imperious need for high explosive projectiles for use both in attack and defence. With November, 1914, came a whole set of novel requirements for the purpose of the stationary warfare which supervened after the first battle of Ypres. The cry was now for hand grenades, rifle grenades, trench mortars and ammunition, periscopes, catapults, barbed-wire entanglements, trench helmets and special appliances of other and very various kinds. In April, 1915, after the second battle of Ypres, it became necessary to provide all the apparatus—defensive and offensive—for gas warfare. Similarly, new demands again were necessitated by the development of aerial warfare. Indeed, every arm of the service underwent a similar transformation.

---

[1] See HIST. REC./H/1300/16, Vol. X, Part II, Chap. I.

All these new demands have one feature in common, that the general demand was followed after a very brief experimental stage, if good results were attained or even promised, by demands for bulk supply long before the pattern had been standardised. But bulk supply involves mass production, and mass production is only possible after stability of design and fixity of pattern have been arrived at. Inevitable loss, delay and disappointment are the consequences entailed by the premature organisation of an extensive manufacturing unit with its series of processes carefully balanced in sequence and velocity, which is then subject to a compulsory readjustment at a single stage in order to conform to a modification of design. That stage is practically certain at least to constitute a " bottle neck," which will delay the flow of materials from machine to machine or process to process and the efficiency of the whole organisation will thus be impaired. It is a commonplace of mechanical industry, that the full momentum of output can only be attained after a lengthy period of tuning up, even when the design of the article to be manufactured is settled and the accessories and special forms of equipment, such as tools, jigs, and gauges, are at hand. When, as was often the case during the first year of war, orders were given for articles the design of which was merely provisional and the drawings and gauges for which were not available, there could be no real programme of supply. Thus, the war imposed upon British manufacturing ingenuity the severest of all possible tests ; the need for perpetual readjustments in process while maintaining or increasing output. There was no way of evading the necessity which demanded that the development of design should proceed *pari passu* with the development of manufacture. The munitions themselves had first to be evolved, and all the time that this process was laboriously and painfully progressing every nerve had to be strained to increase to a maximum the output of such weapons as were already standardised and authorised.

A comparison of the equipment of the Expeditionary Force with that of the armies which took part in the first battle of the Somme will be sufficient to emphasise this contrast. Rifles and small arms ammunition, light and heavy field guns and field howitzers (18 pdr., 60 pdr., and 4·5-in.) as well as 13 pdr. guns for the Royal Horse Artillery were available, but there was an inadequate equipment of modern machine guns. There was, as has been seen, no high explosives ammunition for the 18 pdr. or 13 pdr. guns and only a small proportion of lyddite shell for the 4·5-in. and 60 pdr. guns, There was no authorised fuse suitable for adoption with the newer form of high explosive which was itself an innovation, and the output of which had consequently to be organised. There were no grenades, no trench mortars, or other forms of short range projector. There were no helmets or other devices for personal protection of troops. Of the weapons which later played the most prominent part—the heavy howitzers, the long range guns, to say nothing of the aeroplane in its developed form, or the tank—there were virtually none, the solitary exception being a single experimental 9·2-in. howitzer and such heavy ordnance as had previously been provided for purposes of coast defence or as siege artillery. There were, of course, no preparations for gas or chemical warfare. By the summer of 1916, on the other hand, not only was the equipment of the greatly enlarged Army maintained on the original scale, but the troops enjoyed the support of a large number of heavy howitzers with a generous supply of ammunition, an increased equipment of machine guns, a supply of trench mortars of light and medium weight, and an abundant provision of hand grenades and helmets.

It will be worth while to review with more particularity the evolution of design for one or two representative supplies during the first year of war.

High Explosives.—The high explosive bursting charge for artillery projectiles in use at the beginning of the war was picric acid. At this time it was about to be superseded by T.N.T., a less sensitive though equally powerful explosive. The principal obstacle to making this change was the difficulty of securing satisfactory detonation. Two special D.A. fuses for this purpose had been introduced, adapted to large and small shell respectively, but there was, as yet, no graze fuse for securing detonation on ricochet.

The use of T.N.T. was approved in September, 1914, and some 18 pdr. H.E. shells were loaded with it experimentally. These shells formed part of the first consignment of shells issued from Woolwich to France on 22 October, 1914. They were detonated by a combination fuse No. 44/80. The supply of the new explosive was, however, very limited and at this time involved a wasteful use of oleum which was also required for propellant manufacture. Lord Moulton, who was called in to advise in November, 1914, promptly reported that the maximum procurable amount of both picric acid and T.N.T. would prove altogether inadequate, and that mixed explosives must be substituted for plain T.N.T.

The use of Schneiderite and ammonal, as alternative fillings, had been investigated in consultation with the French, and both forms of filling were tested, but with inconclusive results. On 10 March, 1915, the Research Department put forward a fresh proposal—the use of a mixture in which plain ammonium nitrate served to dilute the T.N.T. On 15 April, the Ordnance Board agreed to approve the use of such a mixture (55 per cent. of ammonium nitrate) for land service shell of calibre not exceeding 6-in. Owing to difficulties in filling shell with this mixture, the proportion of ammonium nitrate was reduced to 40 per cent. and this 40/60 mixture was approved on 11 May, 1915, for small shell, though approval was withheld in the case of heavier natures until August. In April, experiments with an 80/20 mixture by pressing instead of melting had been carried to a successful conclusion and was approved for loading straight walled 13 pdr. and 18 pdr. shells. But serious detonation difficulties remained to be overcome. The new graze fuse (No. 100) was produced in August. Both this and the provisional fuses No. 80/44 required a gaine, and to this minor accessory the unsatisfactory results obtained in the field were attributed, both prematures and blinds being reported. By March, 1916, satisfactory trials with a modified fuse No. 101 and a new type of gaine showed that the problem of using the 80/20 nature had at last been solved. Picric acid remained in use for particular types of shell until 1918.

The evolution of artillery equipment was the work of skilled experts. There existed no body of technical experts whose primary function was the development of other novel classes of munitions. Hence the development of the comparatively simple weapons employed in trench warfare was at first subject to delays as lengthy as those which attended the evolution of the far more complex high explosive shell.

Mills Grenade.—The Mills grenade may be selected as a typical example of the new trench warfare requirements. Urgent demands were received early in December, 1914, for large quantities of grenades. The first request was for 2,000 rifle grenades and 4,000 hand grenades per week ; in January the demand for hand grenades became 10,000 per week ; that for rifle grenades was raised to 5,000 in March. In June the total was raised from 15,000 to 42,000 for France alone. In July the demand for a single type (Mills) was 500,000 weekly, and a year later this became 1,000,000.

At the outbreak of war a few Service patterns of grenades existed, but these were of such complexity that rapid or bulk supply was unattainable. Improvisation was, therefore, resorted to both by manufacture in the field and by contract production of experimental types of grenades at home. Many of these emergency patterns, however, proved to be dangerous and unreliable, so that the troops lost confidence in them. Large quantities of the " Ball " grenade, for example, were available for the battle of Loos, but their utility was destroyed by the prevalent wet weather.

The pattern of the Mills grenade was first submitted about January, 1915, and the experimental stage was complete by April. Output began in July. By the end of the year it had reached 800,000 a week, and 4½ millions were supplied during the last quarter. But even in September, 1915, or ten months after the original need for such supplies was formulated the Army was still equipped principally with stop-gap patterns (" Ball " and " Pitcher " principally), including in all, eleven varieties. These were the supplies with which the battle of Loos was fought.[1] The limiting factor in the output of the Mills grenade up to this time (September, 1915) was the provision of detonator sets.

Comparison may be made with the case of a demand for a special anti-tank grenade in May, 1918, when the accumulated experience of three and a half years of war was available. Manufacture was facilitated by the use of important components secured by breaking up another type of grenade, and bulk supply began in August.[2]

Trench Mortars.—The supply of special trench ordnance was first proposed by the War Office Siege Committee on 25 September, 1914. A month later (20 October) G.H.Q. put forward a general request for

---

[1] The case of trench mortars is closely parallel, as the Army was still obliged to rely upon the emergency 3·7-in. " pipe gun," the only weapon for which ammunition in appreciable quantities was available.

[2] In the case of the Liven's projector first improvised in July, 1916, and finally approved in December, manufacturing difficulties were not serious and bulk supply was available from April, 1917. This may be counted an instance of very rapid supply.

supplies of this kind. By January there had been supplied twelve
4-in. mortars made by boring out a 6-in. shell, and a score of 3·2-in.
mortars of a pattern which had been devised by the Indian Corps.
In January a design of a 1·57-in. trench howitzer introduced by
Messrs. Vickers was approved, and 127 were issued by the end of June.
In March, 1915, the 2-in. mortar was reported on as acceptable to
G.H.Q., and 25 were issued by the end of June. By the beginning of
April, 1915, there were 106 trench howitzers in France, a figure which
was trebled during the next three months. This latter total comprised
127 of the 1·57-in., 25 of the 2-in., 125 of the 3·7-in., and 40 of the
4-in. weapons.[1]

At this time, therefore, the Army was supplied with small numbers
of four different types, two of which were improvisations or stop gaps.[2]
The output of ammunition was, however, even more unsatisfactory,
since nearly every design authorised by the War Office involved the
use of fuses even more urgently needed for artillery ammunition.
Two of them threw a shell less than 10 lb. in weight, and only 50,000
rounds in the aggregate had been manufactured by June, 1915.

III. Evolution of the Programme.

(a) HAND TO MOUTH DEMAND.

The earliest munition orders that were given on the outbreak of
war were of a prescribed character, intended to provide for the replacement of ammunition that would be consumed by the Expeditionary
Force during the first six months of the war. These demands, it must
be remembered, represented the full scale of supply capacity, the need
for which had been definitely anticipated. But even before they had
been completely translated into contracts instructions were issued
(10 August) for the provision of equipment required by the first New
Army,[3] and as has been related above, the scale of demand grew
from this time in volume and intensity with almost uninterrupted
continuity.

The rate of expenditure raised a problem of the first magnitude.
It is sufficient to recall the fact, for example, that when the war began
the total available supply of 18 pdr. gun ammunition, including
108,000 rounds subsequently received from India, was only 654,000
rounds, part of this being held in the form of components which had
to be built into complete rounds. By 1 November 385,000 rounds
had been expended.[4] The total amount was, in fact, not expended
until February, 1915, and was thus spun out over the prescribed period
of six months, though at a cost to the Expeditionary Force which is

---

[1] HIST. REC./R/1000/39.
[2] The 4-in. and 3·7-in. were withdrawn in the spring of 1916.
[3] HIST. REC./R/1000/119, p. 5.
[4] HIST. REC./R/1000/120.

now clearly recognised.[1] The corresponding amounts of 4·5 in. ammunition (129,600 rounds) and 60 pdr. ammunition (24,000 rounds) were exhausted by mid-December and the end of November, 1914, respectively.[2] By March, 1915, 2,000,000 rounds of all natures had been issued to the front, less than half of which aggregate had been in existence when war broke out.

The War Office was concerned not only with these current deficiencies, but at least equally with the prospects of securing the output prospectively required for the equipment of the New Armies. As we have already seen it was impossible in the autumn of 1914 to draw up a formal programme of future supplies at specific dates. The only form which a supply forecast could take at this time was a tabular statement of aggregate output promised by contractors. Such returns were compiled, and indicated month by month ahead the output which contractors were pledged to produce. It was not yet realised how utterly unreliable *as regards early deliveries* these promises were likely to prove. But even had they been trustworthy, it would only have been the first step in the calculation ; for the contracts were placed in the main for components and not for complete ammunition. The business of adjusting and balancing the flow of these components and securing a rapid and uninterrupted output involved many other factors, the incidence of which could not as yet be estimated.

A forecast of such a character with or without elaboration and refinement takes the form of a supply programme. It is totally different from an estimate of requirements based on an assumed number of rounds per gun per day for a force of a postulated size such as was submitted by the Commander-in-Chief from time to time. The latter may be called a demand programme. A complete programme is one which includes both aspects. This will be clear when some examples have been examined.

(b) A Supply Programme.

The work of recording and tabulating contractors' promises of output was of course one of the regular duties of the Contracts Department, though the fact that the Master-General of the Ordnance was not responsible for this part of the contracts work until January 1915, presumably weakened the contact between that branch and the technical advisers of the Director of Artillery. The first time such estimates were officially put forward appears to have been unfortunate in its failure to guard against the failure of paper pledges. The Army Council when replying to Sir John French's despatch of 31 December, 1914, enclosed a forecast of monthly output up to May, 1915, containing the following anticipations.[3]

---

[1] The number of 18 pdr. guns in the field at this latter date was approximately double that on which the pre-war estimates of ammunition required had been based.

[2] Hist. Rec./R/1300/49.

[3] Hist. Rec./R/1300/122.

Estimated Approximate Output of Ammunition.

1915.			January.	February.	March.	April.	May.
18 pdr.	..	.. S.	134,000	170,000	260,000	460,000	490,000
,,	..	.. H.E.	6,000	10,000	50,000	100,000	120,000
13 pdr.	..	.. S.	11,000	12,000	15,000	24,000	28,000
,,	..	.. H.E.	—	1,500	3,000	10,000	12,000
4·5-in.	..	.. S.	14,000	17,000	20,000	24,000	24,000
,,	..	.. H.E.	14,000	18,000	26,000	32,000	32,000
60 pdr.	..	.. S.	12,000	12,000	13,000	14,000	14,000
,,	..	.. H.E.	12,000	12,000	14,000	14,000	14,000
4·7-in.	..	.. S.	6,000	6,000	6,000	6,000	6,000
,,	..	.. H.E.	6,000	6,000	7,000	7,000	7,000
6-in. How.		.. S.	2,000	500	1,000	1,000	1,000
,,		.. H.E.	3,000	3,500	5,000	5,000	5,000
6-in. Gun ..		.. S.	*	500	1,000	—	—
,,		..	*	1,500	2,000	2,000	2,000
9·2	..	.. H.E.	200	1,200	2,000	4,000	6,000
			220,200	271,700	425,000	703,000	761,000

* Included in 6-in. Howitzer.

Immediately on receipt of this statement, apparently on 19 January, 1915, G.H.Q. telegraphed to enquire whether the 18 pdr. and 4·5-in. ammunition promised for the current month would in fact be forthcoming.[1] The critical character of the situation makes it worth while to give the War Office reply (21 January) in full.

" The estimated approximate output (not promises) for the month of January was given as 140,000 rounds 18 pdr. ; and 28,000 rounds 4·5-in. Up to date (19 January) 65,000 rounds 18 pdr. have been despatched to the Lines of Communication, made up as follows :—

45,998   direct to Lines of Communication.
19,008   with 28th Division.
──────
65,006
──────

" The Canadian Division is expected to leave at an early date and in order gradually to equip it, 4,000 rounds have been appropriated. In addition it is proposed to put aside 1,000 rounds a day towards completion of its equipment ammunition (i.e., 4,000 + 11,000 = 15,000). This leaves a balance of 60,000 rounds to complete the 140,000 estimated approximate output, and it is hoped to send 50,000 rounds to Lines of Communication by the end of January.

[1] 121/Stores/1417.

" The Army Council wish to point out that the fitting out of new formations—27th, 28th and Canadian Divisions—has seriously reduced the number of rounds available for Lines of Communication, and further that a request from you (your O.A.W.18) has now been received to carry out experiments with shrapnel and H.E. against wire entanglements, and this will occasion a further reduction.

" Ammunition for 4·5-in. Q.F. howitzer: up to date (19 January, 1915) 5,858 lyddite and 2,270 shrapnel have been sent to Lines of Communication. There will probably be a shortage of about 8,000 rounds on the estimated 28,000 ; but the first week in February it is hoped to send out (including ammunition with the three Batteries you have asked for) 10,000 rounds (7,000 lyddite and 3,000 shrapnel)."

True the statement communicated by the Army Council had been qualified by the explanation that it represented the amounts which contractors had undertaken to produce and that it was not to be taken as a precise and definite estimate, but no qualification can blunt the sharpness of the contrast between the hope of output thus dangled before the eyes of G.H.Q. and the actual figures of issues to France at corresponding dates.[1]

Issues of Completed Gun Ammunition to France.[2]

1915.	March (5 weeks ending 3 April).	April (4 weeks ending 1 May).	May (4 weeks ending 29 May).
18 pdr. S. and H.E. ...	193,762	180,396	285,642
13 pdr. ,, ..	14,500	15,560	12,600
4·5-in...	29,708	23,550	35,032
60 pdr.	14,950	10,000	16,000
4·7-in...	12,598	18,224	11,878
6-in. How.	5,573	6,446	7,000
6-in. Gun	650	200	950
9·2-in. How.	1,350	1,919	1,900
	273,091	256,295	371,002

(c)   DEMAND PROGRAMME.

The second type of programme—the demand programme—was that derived from the requirement factor—rounds per gun per day. A good example is found in the statement included in the memorandum which Sir John French prepared on 10 May, 1915, and sent home for the personal information of Mr. Lloyd George and other Ministers of the Crown.[3]

---

[1] HIST. REC./R/1300/78.
[2] These figures include issues with units, such quantities not constituting a supply for the replenishment of exhausted reserves.
[3] *1914*, p. 239.

Table Accompanying Memorandum of 10 *May,* 1915.[1]
[*Wanted Three Months Hence, say* 1 *August.*]

Nature.	Guns now in Country.	Rounds per Gun per day.		Total Rounds required daily.*	
		Shrapnel.	H.E.	Shrapnel.	H.E.
18 pdr.	700	12	12	8,500	8,500
13 pdr.	125	12	12	1,500	1,500
15 pdr. B.L.C.	200	12	12	2,500	2,500
4·7-in. gun ·	80	8	8	650	650
60 pdr.	28	8	8	250	250
5-in. Howitzer	50	—	15	—	750
4·5-in. Howitzer..	130	4	16	500	2,000
6-in. Howitzer	40	—	12	—	500
9·2-in. Howitzer..	12	—	12	—	150
Total				13,900	16,800

Grand Totals	{ Daily			30,700
	{ Monthly			921,000

* Round numbers are given. Expansion must be provided for at a similar rate. We need more guns and a correspondingly large amount of ammunition.

This gave an aggregate requirement for August of 921,000 rounds of all natures, more than half of which was to be high explosive. The actual issues overseas during the 4 weeks ending 28 August, 1915, were 480,052 rounds of all natures, less than a third of which was of the high explosive variety. Moreover, by the date mentioned the actual number of guns in the field was almost double the number early in May upon which the estimate was based.

(d) The Boulogne Programme.

The full development of the demand programme is seen in a statement submitted by Sir John French to the War Office on 8 July, 1915.[2] At the Boulogne Conference on 19 June, Mr. Lloyd George had handed to General Du Cane a written question : " Given an army of 1,000,000 men what would your requirements be in guns and ammunition in order to deliver a decisive and sustained attack to enable you to break through the German lines ? "[3] Accordingly, a statement was drawn up exhibiting the requirements for an army of 1,000,000 men or 54 divisions in guns, and ammunition reserves required before such an army could take the field (approximately 3,750,000 rounds) and the scale of weekly supply required, the figures working up to a total of 675,000 rounds per week. The July programme was an elaboration of these estimates. The latter programme consists of two portions—a gun programme showing the number of additional guns required month by month between June, 1915 and April, 1916, in order to secure the

[1] *1914*, p. 359.
[2] Hist. Rec./R/1000/8.
[3] Hist. Rec./R/1200/56.

proper equipment on the new scale of an army of 50 divisions by the latter date ; and secondly, an ammunition programme based upon the foregoing, in which the rounds per gun per day were gradually raised from the existing level up to the desired standard at the same time that provision was made for the supply of the rapidly increasing number, of guns.

The table may be reproduced in abbreviated form :—

AMMUNITION.

Suggested weekly output month by month.

Gun.	July, 1915.		October, 1915.		January, 1916.		April, 1916.	
	Weekly output.	Rounds per gun per day.	Weekly output.	Rounds per gun per day.	Weekly output.	Rounds per gun per day.	Weekly output.	Rounds per gun per day.
13 pdr.								
Shrapnel	3,400	} 9	7,750	} 15	12,000	} 21	16,000	} 25
H.E.	3,400		7,750		12,000		16,000	
18 pdr.								
Shrapnel	52,000	} 11	75,000	} 17	135,000	} 22	170,000	} 20
H.E.	18,000		76,000		135,000		170,000	
15 pdr. B.L.C.								
Shrapnel	10,000	} 7	13.500	} 12	3,000	} 18	—	—
H.E.	—		3,500		9,000			
4·5-in. Howitzer								
Shrapnel	2,500	} 7	5,000	} 15	9,000	} 19	10,000	} 20
H.E.	7,500		28,000		53,000		75,000	
5-in. Howitzer.	1,700	5	4,000	12	5,000	15	5,000	15
4·7-in. Q.F.								
Shrapnel	2,000	} 7	2,000	} 13	—	—	—	—
H.E.	2,000		2,000					
60 pdr.								
Shrapnel	2,500	} 12	7,000	} 16	19,000	} 20	28,000	} 20
H.E.	2,500		7,000		19,000		28,000	
6-in. Howitzer	4,500	10	12,000	14	35,000	17	56,000	20
6-in. B.L.C.								
Shrapnel	175	} 6	300	} 11	400	} 15	400	} 15
H.E...	175		300		400		400	
8-in. Howitzer	800	7	4,000	13	8,500	15	13,000	15
9·2-in. Howitzer	1,000	7	4,000	10	7,500	12	11,000	12
12-in. Howitzer	100	4	550	7	1,500	8	1,800	8
15-in. Howitzer	100	4	100	5	100	5	200	5
TOTAL	114,350		259,750		464,400		600,800	

The aggregate output on this basis was to grow from 114,000 rounds per week in June, 1915, to 600,000 rounds per week in April, 1916. This programme was not that actually adopted by the War Office and Ministry of Munitions, since, among other reasons, a larger number of divisions was legislated for and provision for other theatres of war than France had to be made.

(e) Master-General of the Ordnance's Programme, April, 1915.

Three months before the Boulogne programme saw the light the Master-General of the Ordnance had put forward a statement which well exemplifies what we have referred to as a complete or balanced programme, which reflects simultaneously estimates of output and anticipated requirements, the former being based on contractors' promises, the latter on the scale of output—rounds per gun per day—required to meet the needs of the Army as reinforced from time to time. This, the first true supply programme, is the prototype of those which were to serve as the point of departure for the successive waves of industrial energy directed and controlled by the Ministry of Munitions on an ever-increasing scale and with a steadily gathering momentum. The elaboration of this most pregnant statement was due to instructions received from the Cabinet Committee on Munitions of War, known as the " Treasury Committee," a body appointed by Mr. Asquith to take in hand the examination of the difficult position which had arisen. Mr. Lloyd George was chairman, a position to which he had established his claim by his indefatigable insistence on the need for wider views and a maximum policy in munition matters. A chief obstacle to the effectiveness of such criticism had been the secrecy with which the plans of the War Office were enshrouded, a secrecy based primarily upon military considerations, but rendered increasingly baffling by the technical character of the data. Since, then, it was essential, before the significance of the manufacturing problem could be fully comprehended, to examine the statistical basis or programme, it was decided at the first meeting of the Committee which was held on 12 April, 1915, that the Committee's initial task was to ascertain the position in regard to the supply of the more important types of artillery and ammunition. The Master-General of the Ordnance, who was a member of the Committee, undertook to prepare statements showing, in respect of the 18 pdr. and other important guns, the number that would be required and the numbers expected to be delivered under existing arrangements ; with corresponding figures for the output of ammunition anticipated at the end of April, and subsequent months.[1]

The result is illustrated in the tables which follow.[2] The basis of the estimate appears to have been the assumption that a new army would join the Expeditionary Force every month from May to August

---

[1] Minutes of First Meeting M.C.1. Hist. Rec./R/172/1.

[2] Hist. Rec./R/172/7. The statement contained similar tables for the 4·7-in. 60 pdr., 6-in. howitzer, 8-in. howitzer, 9·2-in. howitzer and 12-in. howitzer.

inclusive. The Estimates were prefaced by a cautionary statement to the effect that "the estimates of deliveries are the best available but no responsibility for their ultimate correctness can be taken."

18 pdr.

	1 April.	1 May.	1 June.	1 July.	1 Aug.
1. Number of guns required	625	913	1,201	1,489	1,777
2. Number of guns expected to be ready.	990	1,100	1,225	1,525	2,000*
3. Number of rounds per week at 17 per gun per day required for guns as at 2.	74,375	108,587	142,800	177,291	211,463
4. Rounds expected per week—					
(a) From Home	38,750	51,250	62,500	65,000	75,000
(b) From Abroad	26,250	38,750	57,500	85,000	140,000
5. Rounds per week promised by contractors when orders were placed.	271,000	271,000	271,000	393,000	420,000

* 2,600 promised.

Each army will require at least one month's supply at 20 rounds a gun a day equipment before going into the Field.

4·5-in. Howitzer.

	1 April	1 May.	1 June.	1 July.	1 Aug.
1. Number of armies	2	3	4	5	6
2. Number of guns required..	116	212	308	404	500
3. Number of guns expected to be ready.	186	208	268	360	450
4. Number of rounds per week at 17 per gun per day required for guns as at 2.	13,800	25,600	36,600	48,000	59,500
5. Rounds expected per week—					
(a) Home	8,000	10,000	14,000	16,000	16,000
(b) Abroad	—	2,000	4,000	8,000	10,000
6. Rounds per week promised by contractors when orders were placed.	18,000	20,000	38,000	48,000	48,000

There is considerable difficulty in getting the particular size of cordite required for this gun.

The salient features of this programme so far as ammunition is concerned, may be brought out by examining its validity in the light of subsequent experience. We may take the figures for the month of August, 1915, and compare the programme figures with the output actually obtained.

Weekly Ammunition Output in August, 1915. Actual output realised as compared with forecast contained in the Master-General of the Ordnance's Programme dated 13 April, 1915. (Principal Natures Only.)

	Contractors' Promises.	War Office Anticipation.	Requirements.	Actual Issues.[1]
18 pdr.	420,000	215,000	211,463	108,000
4·5 in. howitzer	48,000	26,000	59,500	14,600
4·7-in.	8,400	8,000	6,020	1,600
60 pdr.	8,000	7,500	11,900	1,825
6-in. howitzer ..	14,000	4,000	2,240	2,333
8-in. howitzer ..	2,000	1,800	840	735
9·2-in. howitzer ..	3,200	1,600	1,120	492
	503,600	263,900	293,083	129,585

This concise statement contains the essence of the munitions problem as it was in the summer of 1915. It will be noticed that the War Office anticipation, to the correctness of which they explicitly refused to be committed, discounted contractors' promises approximately 50 per cent. The actual output, however, was only approximately half this reduced figure.

(*f*) THE FIRST MINISTRY OF MUNITIONS PROGRAMME, JULY, 1915.

This survey may be fitly concluded by a summary of the earliest gun and ammunition programme formulated by the Ministry of Munitions. This will exhibit the essential continuity of the future series of such programmes with those which had already been developed. It may also serve to bridge the transition between the period of War Office responsibility and that of the Ministry of Munitions.

As already explained, the basis of this programme is to be found in the Du Cane statement of requirements for heavy guns and ammunition, as expanded by the War Office from a 50 to a 70 division scale. In the tables given below the figures of the original programme have been supplemented so as to show the quantities due from contractors after the further orders contemplated by the Ministry had been placed ; the actual output as measured by issues overseas has also been set against the requirements, in order to exhibit the final outcome of these efforts during the period ending with midsummer, 1916.

The statement of the programme may be prefaced by some comments which will elucidate the character of the demands entailed thereby. Thus in the matter of guns the War Office had asked for an additional output by March, 1916, in excess of numbers already ordered, of 641 60 pdrs., 458 6-in. howitzers, 300 8-in. or 9·2-in. howitzers and 16 12-in. howitzers.

Enquiries showed that such an achievement was impossible by the date named.[2] The fresh output implied that creation of capacity as its prior condition and new buildings equipped with fresh plant and

---

[1] Average weekly issues overseas of completed ammunition during 4 weeks to 28 August, 1915.

[2] HIST. REC./R/1000/57.

machinery must be provided before productive work could begin. It was also necessary, as bitter experience had proved, to discount the promises or sanguine estimates of the manufacturer based upon this development of productive capacity. After a critical review of the situation the Gun Department on 23 July, 1915, put forward the following tentative estimate showing the dates when the additional guns would be forthcoming.

	March, 1916.	June, 1916.
60 pdr.	339	519
6-in. how.	198	362
8-in. or 9·2-in.	120	184
12-in. or 15-in.	60	60

The figures finally accepted as the basis of the gun and ammunition programme " B " receded still further. They were as follows :—

Anticipated output of Guns after 30 June, 1915.

End of	Sept., 1915	Dec., 1915.	March, 1916.	June, 1916.
60 pdr.	49	139	271	451
6-in. how.	8	32	112	276
8-in. or 9·2-in.	14	37	78	148
12-in. or 15-in.	16	32	47	47

Thus the anticipated deficits at the end of March, 1916, the crucial date when supplies for the new campaign would be required to be ready in the field, would be 370 60 pdrs., 346 6-in. howitzers, 222 8-in. or 9·2-in. howitzers. There would be a surplus of 12-in. howitzers. These figures assumed moreover that all outstanding War Office orders would be punctually executed.

Additional light field guns and howitzers were also required, but these it was expected would be supplied, if not by March, 1916, at all events by June. The full list of principal types, the expected output and the actual deliveries attained by March, 1916, were as follows :—

Gun Programme " B " (July, 1915): Position in March, 1916.

	Outstanding on War Office Orders.	Additional Deliveries expected.	Actual Deliveries.
18 pdr.	2,826	2,680	2,507
13 pdr.	218	130	28
4·5-in.	611	667	700
60 pdr.	115	271	250
6-in. how.	16	112	45
8-in. how.	8	28	1
9·2-in. how.	30	50	44
12-in. how.	27	47	27
15-in. how.	—	—	1
Total	3,851	3,985	3,603

Thus in the case of the heavier natures the programme fell seriously short of realisation at this date.

The 1915 shell and ammunition programme gave the requirements that would have to be satisfied if the anticipated number of guns were forthcoming, these requirements being based as usual upon the accepted ration or allowance per gun per day.

The results of the programme are shown in detail in the appended statement which gives the position in March, 1916.

Completed Ammunition. It will be seen that in the case of light ammunition the output had attained only 57 per cent. of the requirements figure in March, 1916. By June, however, output was actually in excess of requirements for this group of natures, thanks to the outpouring of the belated deliveries of 18 pdr. shrapnel and H.E. from Canada and the United States which came to hand in great abundance at this time. In heavy natures which were now of primary importance the deliveries reached only 27 per cent. of the requirements in March, 1915, rising to 55 per cent. in June. This improvement was due to the fact that the new filling factories established by Mr. Lloyd George came into full bearing in this quarter.

Shell Manufacture.—Turning next to the recorded weekly output of shell in comparison with contract promises it will be seen that home contractors show a progressive improvement in attainment, reaching 42, 52, 74, and 81 per cent. respectively, in September, 1915, December, 1915, March, 1916, and June, 1916. Contract promises had, however, long since been realised to be useless as the basis of a military programme and departmental estimates of anticipated output had been substituted. How much nearer these estimates approached the actual results obtained inspection of the tables will show.

In the case of deliveries from abroad the task of forecasting actual receipts was more baffling than in the case of British supplies, though in view of the great importance which this output from Canada and the United States had already attained it was vital that the best estimates possible should be secured. The results as shown prove that the revised expectations realised a fair degree of accuracy even in this case, though in the last period shown, owing to the influence of the factor already referred to—the late delivery of accumulated arrears—the deliveries actually exceeded expectations.

This table also exhibits the relation between the orders placed by the War Office and the total realised output under the administration of the Ministry of Munitions. It will be noticed that the former totals were not surpassed before the first quarter of 1916.

Finally, a comparison should be made between the volume of orders given and the requirements as laid down. It was an obvious corollary from the fact that contract performances were in the aggregate uniformly behind promises that the ordering of *excess* quantities should be adopted. The War Office shell orders were nearly double the required quantity of ammunition (184 per cent. for September deliveries). The augmented Ministry of Munitions orders for shell were equivalent to more than twice the quantity of finished ammunition required.

FIRST MINISTRY OF MUNITIONS GUN AND AMMUNITION PROGRAMME (JULY, 1915).

Summary of Position in March, 1916.

Calibre.	Guns.	Guns, Additional Output.			Completed Ammunition (Weekly).		Shell Manufacture (Weekly).				
	Stock on 30.6.15[1]	Outstanding on War Office Orders[2]	Expected (July 1915) Programme B.[3]	Delivered.[4]	Required (5.10.15)[5]	Issued.[6]		Due from Contractors, War Office Orders.[7]	Due from Contractors, Total.[8]	Anticipated Deliveries.[9]	Actual Deliveries.[10]
Light.											
18 pdr.	1,700	2,826	2,680	2,507 { H.E	233,400	98,012	{ Home	138,500	383,400	309,400	331,374
							{ Abroad	289,500	356,000	334,000	276,202
				{ S.	233,400	202,322	{ Home	94,000	127,500	104,000	104,126
							{ Abroad	295,000	451,500	288,000	336,805
13 pdr.	114	218	130	28 { H.E	12,950	4,454	{ Home	1,000	50,250	17,400	22,633
							{ Abroad	7,500	10,000	8,500	8,468
				{ S.	12,950	7,579	{ Home	6,940	17,500	15,000	11,277
							{ Abroad	1,250	7,150	1,000	218
4·5-in.	334	611	667	700 { H.E	135,000	58,673	{ Home	22,900	135,200	68,600	74,920
							{ Abroad	103,050	181,500	101,500	94,364
				{ S.	5,000	4,381	{ Home	7,900	6,850	6,500	4,779
							{ Abroad	—	—	—	—
5-in.	80	—	—	— H.E	8,400	1,277	{ Home	—	—	—	—
							{ Abroad	1,900	24,000	10,000	16,935
60 pdr.	68	115	271	250 { H.E	23,100	7,656	{ Home	3,450	15,400	10,450	11,655
							{ Abroad	14,000	25,000	2,000	1,788
				{ S.	23,100	2,889	{ Home	3,260	17,600	6,400	9,235
							{ Abroad	—	—	—	—
				{ H. E	4,620	3,703	{ Home	5,350	3,100	2,550	3,170
							{ Home	500	2,500	1,300	1,147
				{ S.	4,620	877	{ Abroad	400	1,385	100	2,594
Total (light)	2,384	3,770	3,748	3,485 { H.E	417,400	173,775	{ Home	171,200	587,350	408,400	443,752
							{ Abroad	417,750	603,450	460,200	400,863
				{ S.	279,000	217,048	{ Home	112,600	161,950	133,200	130,564
							{ Abroad	296,650	460,035	289,100	339,617
Heavy.											
6-in. Howitzer	86	16	112	45 H.E	39,200	9,000	{ Home	9,800	39,750	13,700	12,593
							{ Abroad	7,800	82,970	12,700	10,180
8-in. Howitzer	24	8	28	1 H.E	11,200	3,753	{ Home	3,500	9,100	5,070	4,500
							{ Abroad	900	33,800	1,900	1,707
9·2-in. Howitzer	18	30	50	44 H.E	6,300	2,689	{ Home	2,930	3,350	2,700	2,746
							{ Abroad	1,000	23,560	1,480	1,382
12-in. Howitzer	1	27	47	27 H.E	2,450	361	{ Home	1,200	1,270	670	740
							{ Abroad	400	2,650	450	124
15-in. Howitzer	4	—	—	1 H.E	420	60	{ Home	—	195	120	107
							{ Abroad	—	350	100	119
Total (heavy)	133	81	237	118 H.E	59,570	15,863	{ Home	17,430	53,665	22,260	20,686
							{ Abroad	10,100	143,330	16,630	13,512
GRAND TOTAL	2,517	3,851	3,985	3,603 { H.E	476,970	189,638	H.E	616,480	1,387,795	907,410	815,813
				{ S.	279,000	217,048	S.	409,250	621,985	422,300	470,181

[1] Hist. Rec./R/1000/123/1.
[2] Hist. Rec./H/1200/14.
[3] Hist. Rec./R/1000/123/2
[4] Hist. Rec./R/1000.1/3.
[5] Hist. Rec./R/1000/123/4.
[6] Hist. Rec./R/1300/49.
[7] Hist. Rec./R/1000/123/5.
[8] Hist. Rec./R/1000/123/6.
[9] Ibid.
[10] Ibid.

c *

CHAPTER II.

THE MACHINERY OF SUPPLY.

I. Organisation existing at the Outbreak of War.

Before reviewing the steps taken by the War Office to secure the supplies required by the Army, it is desirable to understand the administrative organisation at the War Office for dealing with these matters and its development during the first year of the war.

The organisation of the War Office, in June, 1914, in its main outline, dated from the Esher Committee, appointed in 1903. On the recommendation of that Committee the War Office was reorganised and an Army Council was constituted by Letters Patent,[1] consisting of the Secretary of State, six other members, and a Secretary. The four Military Members were : the Chief of the Imperial General Staff, the Adjutant-General, the Quartermaster-General, and the Master-General of the Ordnance. The Civil Member was the Parliamentary Under Secretary for State. The Finance Member replaced the former Financial Secretary. The Secretary to the War Office was also the Secretary to the Army Council. All existing duties within the War Office were distributed among these seven members of the Council ; but the Directorate of Military Aeronautics, created in September, 1913, was made immediately responsible to the Secretary of State.

The actual composition of the Army Council at the beginning of the war was as follows :—

Secretary of State for War ..	Earl Kitchener.
Chief of the Imperial General Staff.	General Sir C. W. H. Douglas, G.C.B. (First Military Member).
Adjutant-General to the Forces.	Lt.-General Sir H. C. Sclater, K.C.B. (Second Military Member).
Quartermaster-General to the Forces.	Major-General Sir J. S. Cowans, K.C.B. (Third Military Member)
Master-General of the Ordnance.	Major-General Sir S. B. von Donop, K.C.B. (Fourth Military Member).
Parliamentary Under Secretary of State.	Mr. H. J. Tennant, M.P. (Civil Member).
Financial Secretary	Mr. H. T. Baker, M.P. (Finance Member).
Appointed 18.12.14	Sir G. S. Gibb (Additional Civil Member (Temporary) for Armament Contracts).

Secretary.

Sir R. H. Brade, K.C.B.	(Secretary of the War Office).

---

[1] 6 February, 1904.

The members of the Council principally concerned with supply in its various aspects were the Quartermaster-General, the Master-General of the Ordnance and the Finance Member. The respective spheres of these three may be briefly indicated.

(a)　Department of the Quartermaster-General.

The third Military Member, the Quartermaster-General, shared with the Master-General of the Ordnance, the chief responsibility for providing supplies required by the Army, the province of the latter being confined, in the main, to artillery supplies and technical munitions. The Quartermaster-General was responsible for the administration of sea and road transport ; for Remount, Veterinary, Ordnance, Supply and Barrack Services ; for the organisation, administration and training of personnel employed in these services ; for the custody and issue of all military stores including those provided by the Master-General of the Ordnance ; for reserves and mobilisation stores. In particular, the Director of Equipment and Ordnance Stores was responsible for clothing and personal equipment and certain technical supplies not falling within the province of the Master-General of the Ordnance, together with the preparation of mobilisation store tables.

(b)　Department of the Master-General of the Ordnance.

The duties of the Master-General of the Ordnance were primarily concerned with armaments and fortifications ; with the determination of scales of reserves of arms and ammunition ; with patents and inventions ; with patterns, provision and inspection of guns, small arms, ammunition, R.A. and R.E. technical stores and vehicles ; with technical committees on war *matériel*, with the administration of Royal Ordnance Factories. In addition the Master-General was responsible for the construction and maintenance of fortifications and works, and for the administration of the Ordnance College. The principal branches of this department were the Directorate of Artillery, the Directorate of Fortifications and Works, and the Directorate of Barrack Construction.

At the outbreak of war the work of the Director of Artillery, Brig.-General H. Guthrie Smith, was divided between four sections known as A1, A2, A3 and A4. *A*1 dealt with fixed armaments and naval ordnance and all questions relating to coast defence. *A*2 was the branch to which fell the responsibility for the most onerous and anxious section of supply. It dealt with field armaments, both horse, field, heavy siege and mountain equipments ; with movable armaments (other than machine guns) ; with patterns, estimates, manufacture and inspection of these stores, and with all technical questions relating thereto.

*A*3 dealt with small arms and vehicles, and with equipments, patterns, manufacture and provision of the same ; with explosives (other than artillery ammunition), with optical instruments (other than those special to artillery), and with bicycles. In November, 1914, this branch was divided and an additional section *A*5 was created to deal exclusively with ·303 in. rifles and small arms ammunition.

*A*4 dealt with questions of personnel in the departments for which the Director of Artillery was responsible ; with questions relating to patents and inventions ; with correspondence relating to the administration of the Ordnance Factories, the Inspection Department, the Experimental Establishments, the Ordnance College and Artillery Institution.

*A*6 was created on 1 January, 1915, to supervise the supply of high explosives and ingredients in conjunction with Lord Moulton's Committee on the Supply of High Explosives.

*A*7 was established in April, 1915, by the transfer to the Director of Artillery of the branch known as Contracts I.A which had previously been responsible under the Director of Army Contracts for all contract business relating to warlike stores.

The total personnel of these various sections only amounted to some 52 persons.

The Ordnance Board, Woolwich, under the Master-General of the Ordnance, was a body of expert artillerists whose duty was to direct research work in connection with the introduction or development of guns, ammunition and explosives and similar questions referred to them by the Admiralty or War Office (Chairman, Major-General Sir Charles F. Hadden, K.C.B.).

The Small Arms Committee, under the Master-General of the Ordnance, undertook similar research and experimental work in connection with small arms and ammunition.

Royal Ordnance Factories.—The Ordnance Factories at Woolwich, Waltham Abbey, and Enfield Lock were under the general superintendence of a Chief Superintendent of Ordnance Factories (Sir H. Frederick Donaldson, K.C.B.). These Factories included the Royal Laboratory, Woolwich Arsenal, the Royal Gun and Carriage Factories, Woolwich Arsenal, the Royal Gunpowder Factory, Waltham Abbey and the Royal Small Arms Factory at Enfield Lock, besides a Building Works Department, a Mechanical Engineering Department, and a Medical Department, all at Woolwich.

The Deputy Director of Ordnance Stores (D.D.O.S.), responsible to the Quartermaster-General, was also located in Woolwich Arsenal. He dealt with the receipt and issue of warlike stores.

The Chief Inspector, Woolwich (C.I.W.), and his staff were at the Royal Arsenal, Woolwich. He was responsible to the Master-General of the Ordnance for seeing that supplies satisfied all prescribed tests.

The Superintendent of Experiments at Shoeburyness was under the Master-General of the Ordnance. Artillery and ammunition tests were carried out on these ranges.

The *Research Department*, Woolwich, was also under the Master-General of the Ordnance and contained laboratories where chemical and mechanical research work was carried on.

(c) Department of the Finance Member.

The Finance Member acted as Financial Secretary to the War Office, assisted by an Assistant Financial Secretary and a Director of Army

Contracts as his principal officers. On the recommendation of the Esher Committee, a Director-General of Army Finance had been appointed in 1904, assisted by two Directors, one for Financial Services, the other for Army Accounts. But the office of Director-General of Army Finance was replaced in 1909 by that of the Assistant Financial Secretary. In the same year the Contracts Department was separated from the Finance Branch, and the Director of Contracts became immediately responsible to the Finance Member as regards discipline and general policy, though no order could be placed without the concurrence of the Military Branch concerned. A small Finance Branch for estimates and financial advice was administered through the Director of Financial Services. A considerable part of the duties of the old Finance Department was amalgamated with those of the old Army Pay Department, and the whole entrusted to a new civil branch, called the Army Accounts Department, administered through the Director of Army Accounts. A Finance Section, known as M.G.O.F., under Mr. (later Sir Sigmund) Dannreuther was attached to the Department of the Master-General of the Ordnance and served as a link between the administration of armament supply and the higher financial authority. This branch became responsible for granting or securing approval for expenditure on munitions, for accountancy and for general financial supervision of contracts placed. By the beginning of December, 1914, the Contracts Department's operations had assumed a scale which was thought to require the whole attention of a Member of the Army Council. Accordingly, Sir George Gibb was appointed an additional member of the Army Council, and assumed responsibility for the Contracts Branch which was thus removed from the control of the Finance Member.[1]

II. The Duties of the Director of Army Contracts.

The Contracts Branch of the War Office was created during the Crimean War, the first Director being appointed in June, 1855. It was then laid down that all stores required for all the departments of the Army should be purchased by the Contracts Branch, and that the normal method of making contracts should be by public competition. Special authority was required for departing from this procedure.

In the early history of the branch, an excessive use was made of brokers and middlemen, and much of the work was carried on on old-fashioned lines. These methods, however, were gradually discarded and the procedure modernised under the third Director (Sir Evan Nepean) 1877–1891.

So far the purchases for all the departments of the Army had been centralised in the Contracts Branch ; this principle of centralisation has, however, been questioned twice recently, the second time with a temporary success. The first occasion was in 1901, when a Committee (Sir Clinton Dawkin's) was appointed to enquire into War Office

---

[1] See below, p. 71.

organisation. The third paragraph of the terms of reference directed the Committee to report :—

> " Whether the Office of the Director of Contracts should deal with all the business now transacted there, or whether the making of contracts could be, in whole or part, transferred to the Military Districts or to the Military Departments of the War Office."

After taking evidence not only from the military officers and officials of the War Office, but from representatives of railway companies and other large companies, as to the method of purchasing employed by them, the Committee reported in favour of the retention of a Central Purchasing Branch. They criticised, however, the existing relations between the supply departments and the Contracts Branch, and suggested a number of changes, many of which were adopted.

Not long afterwards, however (in February, 1904), the general principle of centralisation was again called into question by Lord Esher's War Office (Reconstitution) Committee, and this time it was discarded in favour of a new system, as defined in the following paragraph :—

> " Each Military member of Council will administer a specific vote or votes of the Army estimates, and each branch will be provided with a civil finance section charged with the work of accounting and of furnishing such financial advice as the member may require. The two great providing branches under the third and fourth Military members will each be equipped with a contract or buying section whose head may be civil or military. All contracts above a certain amount will be independently registered and reviewed by the Financial Secretary."

This new system did not, however, work well in practice. It resulted in competition in the same markets by the sections dealing with contracts for the different directorates, and in other ways as well, the absence of a single purchasing authority led to difficulties. The Army Council, therefore, decided in 1907 to re-establish the post of Director of Army Contracts, and to combine the various sections performing contract duties into a directorate under the Financial Secretary. In 1913, however, the purchase of aeroplanes and aeronautical stores, as being highly technical and to a large extent experimental in character, was transferred from the Director of Army Contracts to the Director-General of Military Aeronautics.[1]

The normal administrative procedure in regard to army contracts is clearly indicated in the instructions formulated for the guidance of the Director when the Department of Army Contracts was reconstituted in 1907,[2] extracts from which may be here reproduced.

> " The Director of Contracts will, in concert with the Directors administering Votes, be responsible for contracts made at the War Office for the purchase and sale of supplies, stores, machinery, clothing, and for other services required for the Army, including

---

[1] The above sketch is taken from a Memorandum on War Office Contracts by Mr. U. F. Wintour, February, 1916. (HIST. REC./R/170/25).

[2] War Office Notice 541 (29 November, 1907).

the erection and maintenance of works. He will also, in concert with the Directors concerned, deal with labour and wages questions arising on Army contracts. He will report upon the cost of production in the manufacturing departments as compared with purchase from the trade, and upon proposals for the allocation of orders, and will be present at allocation meetings."

" *The List of Contractors*.—In order to secure the satisfactory quality of supplies, and the due observance of the House of Commons' resolution in regard to fair wages and sub-letting, and to safeguard the public from possible loss arising from a contractor's failure to carry out his covenants, care will be taken to place orders only with persons or firms of good reputation, not necessarily to the exclusion of those in a small way of business. Transactions with agents and middlemen will be avoided as far as possible, and orders for manufactured articles limited to actual manufacturers."

" Applications from persons or firms desirous of being placed on the lists of those eligible to compete for contracts will be carefully considered. If satisfactory evidence is obtained that their means of production are sufficient, and that their reputation, both financially and for quality of manufacture, and as employers of labour is good, the request should be granted, after reference to the Director administering the Vote, but as a rule they should only be entrusted with small trial orders in the first instance."

" Before firms are placed on the list their works should, as a rule, be inspected. When inspection by an officer of a technical department is necessary the Director concerned will be asked to arrange accordingly."

" *Requisition upon Contract Department*.—Requisitions for purchase will be accompanied by full particulars as to pattern, make, descriptions and quality of the articles demanded, and where patterns, specifications or drawings exist they will either be attached or will be referred to by identification numbers. When the article is of a new design or special character, carefully prepared specifications and such drawings as may be necessary will be furnished for the guidance of manufacturers."

" The responsibility for pattern, specification and nomenclature of stores rests with the Director administering the Vote. It will, however, be open to the Director of Contracts to bring to notice any case in which a pattern or specification appears to be of such a standard as to be impossible of fulfilment without great additional cost."

" *Tenders*.—All tenders will be addressed in sealed covers to the Director of Contracts, and placed in the tender box provided for the purpose at or before the hour indicated in the invitation, after which time no tender will be received, except in special circumstances. One key of the tender box will be kept in the custody of the Principal of the Contract Department and the other by some responsible official of another department.

"At the appointed hour, the tender box will be unlocked in the presence of the principal (or other authorised officer). All tenders due on that day will be opened and the numbers of those received, and the names of the firms tendering, will be recorded then and there, and initialed by the officers present. Tenders (and acceptances) are to be treated as strictly confidential."

"The tenders will afterwards be tabulated and considered. The basis of consideration should be the most favourable prices ; but attention should be paid to the record and character of the firms tendering, their competence to perform orders satisfactorily and punctually, the necessity for maintaining or widening the area of supply and any other special circumstance which may affect the case."

"The Director of Contracts will use his discretion in submitting for higher sanction the acceptance of a contract, always remembering that the established principle of public purchase is competition and the acceptance of the lowest offer, and that good reasons are necessary to justify a departure from this rule."

"Purchases by single tender, by direct negotiation on an emergency, or by broker, will be reported to higher authority, if over £200 in amount."

"*Execution of Contracts.*—All questions as to deliveries under a contract or as to time of delivery will be dealt with, in the first instance, by the receiving department concerned, but any proposal which involves a change in the pattern or specification governing the contract or any departure from the terms of the contract, will be referred to the Director of Contracts, who will conduct any further correspondence on the subject, and if necessary, obtain such higher War Office or Treasury authority as may be prescribed.

"The receiving department will correspond direct with firms in regard to the quantity, quality and punctuality of their deliveries and generally on all questions of detail (not involving changes in pattern) that may arise during the execution of a contract.

"If the receiving department should find serious difficulty in securing the satisfactory fulfilment of a contract, full particulars will be given to the Director of Contracts, who will then take such action as he may deem desirable to secure delivery and more satisfactory results in future.

"In the event of failure to complete a contract on the proper dates, a report will be made to the Contracts Department, and special returns as to progress on contracts will be prepared from time to time, as may be arranged."

"It will be open to Directors administering Votes to consider a contract completed if there should be short deliveries not exceeding 5 per cent. in quantity, or to accept surplus deliveries within the same limit, notifying their action to the Contracts Department. Any case in which these limits are exceeded will be referred to the Contracts Department for concurrence in the proposed action. If the limits are seriously exceeded, the approval of the Financial Secretary will be obtained."

III. Normal Contract Procedure.[1]

(a) Contracts Demands.

The size of the Army being determined by Parliament, and the scale of equipment being approved, the formulation of definite requirements was a straight-forward matter. It was the duty of the Master-General of the Ordnance and his officers to prescribe what equipments should be supplied and the duty of the Contracts Department was limited to procuring from the armament firms such portions as might be definitely requisitioned. In the case of gun ammunition, for example, the Master-General of the Ordnance, through the Director of Artillery, was the approval authority and the supply authority. Two sources of supply were available, the Ordnance Factories, which were under the direct control of the Master-General of the Ordnance, and trade contractors, with whom the Contracts Department placed orders subject to the Master-General of the Ordnance's approval. Thus the responsibility of the Contracts Department commenced with the receipt of a " Contracts Demand " or instruction to place contracts for a specified quantity.

(b) System of Tendering.

Having received a contracts demand, it was the duty of the Contracts Department to issue tenders, the normal system of buying for Government in peace time being by means of a system of competitive tender, confined in general to a limited number of approved suppliers.

The rules laid down for the regulation of competitive tendering required :—[2]

(a) That purchases should as a general rule be made by competitive tendering and not by private treaty ;

(b) that all tenders should be delivered at a certain place by a given hour ;

(c) that if requirements were modified after the receipt of tenders all firms should be given an equal chance of amending their offers.

These rules were designed to secure absolute fairness as between rival firms, and to avoid the suspicion of anything like favouritism or collusion. In normal times, reasonable prices were secured by the competition of several firms for a limited order which all were anxious to obtain, and the allocation of orders could usually be readily made on the basis of the lowest offers which were satisfactory as regards delivery.

The defects of the method of purchase by tender when applied to the wholesale requirements of war time were formulated with lucidity by Mr. U. F. Wintour after 18 months' experience as head of the Army Contracts Department. Though these criticisms have reference primarily to non-munition supplies, such as barbed wire,

---

[1] Based on History of P.M.3, by Mr. C. Burrage, July 1917. (Hist. Rec. H./500/10) ; Memorandum on the Contracts Branch and its Functions, by Mr. U. F. Wintour, November 1914. (Hist. Rec./R/500/64).

[2] Memorandum on War Office Contracts, by Mr. U. F. Wintour, February, 1916. (Hist. Rec./R/170/25).

textile or leather goods, they are equally applicable to armament supplies and may therefore be reproduced here.[1]

" 1. Where all or most offers have to be accepted there is no effective competition to keep prices down to a reasonable level.

" 2. As the demands of the War Office are not only large but in nearly every case extremely urgent, there is no possibility of adopting the waiting policy of refusing high tenders in the hope that disappointed firms will reduce their prices at the next invitation to tender.

" 3. The principle of inviting offers from all manufacturers at the same moment has several vicious consequences. In the first place it means that the total requirements of the War Office are known to everyone in the trade, and the relation of such demand to the probable supply can therefore be pretty accurately gauged by all concerned.

" 4. Attempts have been made to remove this objection (a) by inviting tenders for a smaller quantity than that actually required, or (b) by asking for all that firms can offer by a certain date. But the result of (a) is that firms often do not quote for their full possible production, and the impression conveyed by (b) is that the total demands of the War Office are probably even greater than the maximum output of the industry within the time stated. Neither of these alternative methods is, therefore, satisfactory.

" 5. The second consequence is that all firms able to tender go into the market at the same time for the raw materials or partly manufactured goods that they will require if they get the order. The inevitable result is that the net demand is multiplied several times over in the market for raw materials or for semi-manufactured goods such as yarn, cloth, etc. Where 20 firms may eventually receive orders for say 2,000 tons weight of goods, 200 firms or more will have been obtaining options for 20,000 tons of raw material, yarn or cloth. This causes complete chaos in the market for these goods, and the competition for options forces the price up to a quite fictitious and unwarranted level.

" 6. Further disadvantages incidental to the tendering system at a time of pressure are due to the inevitable delays involved in dealing with a numerous list of offers all at the same time. First there is the scheduling of the offers in the prescribed form. Where there are two hundred or more firms quoting, this alone may occupy twenty-four hours. It is then necessary to refer the scheduled offers to Pimlico or through the military branch of the War Office, to Woolwich, for reports on the samples submitted by the firms, and recommendations as to the allocation of orders on the basis of the deliveries offered. Delay frequently occurs because firms have not submitted samples at the time the tender was sent in. At other times, owing to insufficient marking or labels being torn off, samples go astray, and further samples have to be obtained.

---

[1] Memorandum on War Office Contracts, by Mr. U. F. Wintour, February, 1916. (Hist. Rec./R/170/25).

The result is that a period of ten days or a fortnight normally lapses before a large tender is returned to the Contracts Branch for the acceptances to be made out.   In the meantime, owing to the fluctuations of the market, firms will be compelled to withdraw their offers owing to their options having expired.   They will then be asked to renew their offers, and further samples will require to be submitted.   In many cases manufacturers are dependent on an uncertain source of supply, and can only offer subject to immediate acceptance, and tenders are often sent in headed by the words 'without engagement.'   Such offers cannot properly be dealt with by the usual routine of the tendering system.

" 7.   The tendering system in normal times is generally based on the supposition that all firms are quoting for the same article and to the same specification.   Where this is the case the allocation of orders according to the price and rate of delivery offered is simple and fair.

" During the war, however, the standard specifications drawn up in times of peace are continually being departed from, owing to the necessity of taking reasonable substitutes to secure the quantities required in a short time.   Trade patterns are more and more taking the place of regulation patterns, and great difficulty is found in revising specifications so as to make them both sufficiently wide and sufficiently definite.   When tenders are received for a great variety of patterns for one or more articles, there is no real competition between the tendering firms, and the allocation of orders according to price—which is a single and satisfactory method in times of peace—no longer necessarily secures that the Department gets the best value for its money.

" 8.   Competitive tendering may have an adverse effect on the prices, not only by setting up undue competition for a limited supply of raw material, but by encouraging undue competition for a limited supply of labour in the same industry.   Competition for labour leads to increased wages, just as competition for raw material leads to higher market prices.   In both cases the increase in the cost of manufacture is reflected in the price quoted on the tendering."

(c)   Delivery and Inspection.

The duty of receiving deliveries was not part of the work of the Contracts Department.   Each contract specified the receiving officer to whom stores were to be delivered, usually the Deputy Director of Ordnance Stores, Royal Arsenal, Woolwich, to whom, for example, all consignments of gun ammunition or components would be made. Delivery, however, did not imply acceptance, since the articles had to be submitted to an inspection test to show whether they were as required, " of the qualities and sorts described, and equal in all respects to the patterns, specifications, drawings and samples specified."[1]   It was laid down that " the articles before being received into store shall be examined, and if found inferior in quality to or differing in form or material from the patterns, specifications, drawings or samples specified

---

[1] Conditions of Contract (Army Form K. 1271.)   See Appendix I.

in the schedule, may be rejected.   Such rejected articles shall not be considered as having been delivered under the contract, but the contractor shall, if required to do so by the Secretary of State for War, replace the same at his own expense, without any allowance being made to him." The Chief Inspector, Royal Arsenal, Woolwich, was the principal of the inspection authorities. In the case of a shell contract, for example, the contractor was dependent upon him for all technical information to guide manufacture, usually contained in a drawing and specification, and naturally turned to him on matters of technical difficulty. The Chief Inspector was, however, not in a position to sanction any relaxation of the conditions or tests without reference to the military branch, which was in turn advised, where necessary, by the body of experts known as the Ordnance Board and by the Superintendent of Research. If the work of inspection was in arrears, or if any doubtful question arose, the interval between delivery to the Deputy Director of Ordnance Stores and acceptance by the Chief Inspector, Woolwich, was likely to be considerable, and the contractor might in such circumstances be seriously hampered. His situation was not made easier by the fact that the Contracts Department, with whom he normally corresponded, could exercise no control over the receiving officer or the inspecting officer.

(d)   PENALTIES FOR DELAY.

Under the standard conditions of contract applied to War Office purchases of stores and materials the contractor was liable to penalties in respect of overdue deliveries.

" (a) *Damages for Delay*.—Should the articles or any portion thereof not be delivered within the period or periods stipulated in the schedule, whether by reason of the exercise by the Secretary of State for War of his power of rejection under Clause 2 or otherwise, the contractor shall be liable by way of liquidated damages for delay for a sum equal to 1 per cent. on the value of the articles deficient if the delay does not exceed thirty days, for 2 per cent. if the delay exceeds thirty days but does not exceed sixty days, and for 3 per cent. if the delay exceeds sixty days ; such sum may at any time be deducted from any sum or sums then due, or which at any time thereafter may become due to him under this or any other contract with this Department, or may be demanded of him to be paid within fourteen days to the Paymaster-General for credit to Army Funds.

" (b) *Purchase in Default*.—In addition to the above, if and whenever there may be any articles or any portion thereof deficient, the Secretary of State for War shall be at liberty to purchase other articles of the same or similar description from other persons to supply such deficiency ; and in the event of any excess cost being incurred by reason of any difference between the price paid for the same and the contract price, to charge the amount of such excess cost to the contractor, and the sum so charged shall, at the option of the Secretary of State for War, be deducted and paid in like manner as the liquidated damages hereinbefore mentioned.

" (c) *Termination of Contract.*—The Secretary of State for War shall also be at liberty to terminate the contract at, or after, any one of the specified periods at which default shall have been made, either wholly or to the extent of such default, without prejudice to his remedies under paragraphs (a) and (b) of this Clause,"

If deliveries were delayed, the Receiving Officer could send a " default report " to the Contracts Department, who then communicated with the firm. This process was repeated until either the goods were received or the delays became so serious that it was necessary to purchase the goods elsewhere.[1] In normal times no attempt was made to get into personal touch with the firm or to ascertain and remedy the causes of delay.

On the completion of a contract, the Receiving Officer reported to the Contracts Branch on the extent of any delay and the amount of liquidated damages incurred under the terms of the contract. The contractor having been asked to show reasons why the penalty should not be enforced, the case was submitted to the Military Branch (or where damages exceeded £100 to the Finance Member), with a recommendation whether the penalty should be imposed or not—the penalty was in fact insisted on only in very exceptional cases.

(e)   List of Contractors.

In peace time the Contracts Branch published in all the leading newspapers and trade journals an "Annual Notice of Army Contracts."[2] This stated that " tenders for specified quantities of the undermentioned manufactured goods are invited from time to time as required." The principal articles bought were enumerated under the following heads :— Metal trades, etc. ; Textile trades, etc. ; Electrical and Scientific Instruments trades ; General trades. Manufacturers were further invited to apply to be placed on the War Office lists. It was not, however, the custom to invite firms to apply to be placed on the list for warlike stores. Firms properly equipped for this purpose were expected to approach the War Office, since they would be more or less dependent on Government orders, and as a rule they could not get foreign Government orders until they were on the War Office list.

Most of the lists of approved firms were adequate to meet peace requirements.[3] In September 1914, when Mr. Wintour was appointed,

---

[1] Under condition 4 (b) of the contract form in use (Army Form K. 1271) which provides for purchase· in default. A copy of this form is given in Appendix I.

[2] 94/Gen. No./35.

[3] The following are the lists of firms which were formally invited to tender for shell :—

Lyddite or H.E. Shell.	*Shrapnel Shell.*
Messrs. Armstrong.	Messrs. Armstrong.
,, Cammell Laird.	,, Beardmore.
,, Firth.	,, Cammell Laird.
,, Hadfields.	,, Firth.
,, Projectile Co.	,, Hadfields.
,, Vickers.	,, King's Norton Metal Co.
	,, Projectile Co.
	,, Vickers.
	,, Watson Laidlaw.

the lists were found to be insufficient to meet the then demands, and were very largely increased.

When new firms were required it was the function of the Contracts Branch to find them, with the assistance of the Inspection and Factory Branches at Woolwich and sometimes of the Military Branches. After the formal enquiries as to financial status, etc., the works of the new firms were usually inspected by representatives of the Contracts Branch and the Inspection Department, Woolwich. With the concurrence of the Military Branch concerned, the firm could then be noted.[1]

Once a year each list of firms to be invited to tender for a particular article was revised. Firms who had six times consecutively failed to respond to an invitation to tender were removed. The remainder were retained with the approval of the Military Branch. In a few cases firms were classified according to past performances, and considerable orders were entrusted only to Class I firms. The others had to prove their worth by executing small orders before being promoted to Class I. As a rule, firms were removed from the list only for very serious offences.

(f) ALLOCATION OF ORDERS.

At the beginning of each financial year the Board of Admiralty and the Army Council drew up a programme of requirements for the year. The items were provisionally allocated by the Contracts Branch between the Ordnance Factories and the trade, after taking into consideration their relative capacities and costs of manufacture. The allocation was finally approved by a committee consisting of Admiralty representatives, the Master-General of the Ordnance, the Director of Artillery, the Chief Superintendent of the Ordnance Factories, the Finance Member, and the Director of Army Contracts.

Whenever the orders for munitions were not sufficient to keep all the regular makers busy, the Contracts Branch, as trustees of the trade, were careful that orders should be allocated in such a way as to keep both the Royal Factories and the trade firms from shutting down. The general principle observed was, so far as possible, to keep a constant minimum number of hands employed at the Royal Factories, allowing a margin for sudden expansion in emergency, and to throw the fluctuations on the trade. Orders were occasionally placed with trade firms, e.g., for certain natures of shell, even though the tender price might be in excess of the Ordnance Factory estimate, on the ground that the firms might be unable to supply shell of that nature on mobilisation if they were not given orders in time of peace.

(g) CONTROL OF COSTS.

The section known as Contracts T.R. (i.e., Trade Records) kept records showing how the costs of production of the several classes of munitions in the Ordnance Factories (as shown in the annual accounts published by the Chief Superintendent of Ordnance Factories) compared with the average prices paid to contractors for the articles in the same

---

[1] Mr. Wintour's evidence before the Public Accounts Committee, 1916 (115 of 1916).

period. These records were of considerable value in keeping down contract prices. They would have been more useful if the Ordnance Factory system of costing had been more in line with trade custom, and if the costs could have been more quickly produced. It should be understood that the great number and complexity of the manufactures made these Ordnance Factory accounts very elaborate, and, as they were primarily designed for purposes of parliamentary accounting, the cost results were arrived at only some six months after the end of the financial year. Further, the accounts dealt only with expenditure actually incurred by the Government, and accordingly did not embrace such elements as profits, interest on capital, or rent of Government lands, in any form. Another disturbing factor was that the Ordnance Factories were not run purely on commercial lines, but were governed by the above-mentioned order to maintain a fixed nucleus of staff with a view to expansion in time of war. The result was that, in comparing the costs with a contractor's selling price, certain allowances had to be made. In spite of these impediments, the War Office was able to use these accounts as giving a standard of costs for warlike stores. Thus in some cases, such as rifles and machine guns, where effective competition by tender could not be secured, contract prices were settled by negotiation on the basis of Ordnance Factory costs.[1]

IV. Financial Control.

The control of the Treasury over naval and military expenditure in time of peace is normally exercised in three principal ways :—

(1) The total sums to be provided for the Army and Navy respectively are approved by the Chancellor of the Exchequer, and detailed estimates working up to the approved total are submitted to the Treasury for approval before being laid before Parliament.

(2) Treasury sanction is required for material deviations from the Parliamentary estimates, and for meeting excesses on one vote from savings on another vote within the total sum granted by Parliament to the Department concerned.

(3) Prior Treasury sanction is also granted for all Royal Warrants, Orders in Council, and other regulations which affect expenditure, and (with certain exceptions) for establishments, scales of personal remuneration, permanent works, payments outside the terms of contracts, and losses or fruitless payments.

In so far as considerations of finance affect military policy in the larger sense, the machinery by which they operate comes under the first two headings above. To take a simple illustration : if the Army Council desired in time of peace largely to increase the artillery, that would presumably involve, if not an excess on Army votes as a whole, certainly an excess on one or another vote or sub-head, with the result that the increase could not be made without Treasury approval in the course of any financial year. If the increase were proposed to take effect in the following financial year, it would affect the total of the Army

---

[1] *Report from the Committee of Public Accounts*, 31 July, 1917, p. 214 (123 of 1917). The work of the Trade Records Section was dropped at the outbreak of war, the staff being required for more urgent duties.

estimates for the following year, and again would require Treasury sanction.

Under the conditions of the war, the machinery described under the headings (1) and (2) was not in operation. No detailed estimates were submitted to Parliament or to the Treasury, and there was no Parliamentary limit of an operative kind to the sums which the Army and Navy could expend.

Under heading (3) there was comparatively little deviation from peace procedure. The Treasury, however, gave a larger measure of general authority to the War Office under several of the principal divisions of expenditure, and by the Treasury Minute of 8 December 1914, provided a " safety valve," waiving the requirement of Treasury sanction for expenditure certified by the Secretary of State as vitally necessary and urgent. This procedure was made use of by the War Office almost solely in connection with building works.[1]

This relaxation was extended by a Treasury Minute of 29 January, 1915, which dealt particularly with Admiralty and War Office contracts for munitions of war. It was pointed out that the general principle that spending Departments are responsible for their own contracts would not in ordinary times cover the cases of contracts containing unusual financial provisions, such as specific capital advances to contractors for plant, etc. In the present emergency, however, it was not possible to insist on this requirement. The Chancellor of the Exchequer had, therefore, agreed that throughout the war such contracts should be concluded without reference to the Treasury. Responsibility for controlling expenditure was thus thrown back upon the Department, and especially upon the officials who occupied the posts of Assistant Financial Secretary and Director of Army Contracts, the former being primarily concerned as Accounting Officer, the latter as responsible for fixing prices.

The division of responsibility for contract expenditure in normal times may be described as follows : The three main points in a contract are (1) the quantity, (2) the conditions as to inspection, delivery, payment, etc., (3) the price. (1) The main questions of quantity, such as how many rifles or uniforms are wanted, are not, either in peace or war, subject to Treasury control ; but in peace they are governed by the limitation imposed by the Committee of Supply on the estimates. The estimates are drawn up by the Finance Department and the Military Department in conjunction, so that the Finance Department is aware of what quantities of stores are represented by the sums of money in the estimates. In that sense the quantity ordered is normally liable to financial control. (2) The conditions of contracts in peace time are usually what may be called sealed pattern conditions which have been considered by all the branches concerned. If any departure from those conditions is contemplated, the Director of Contracts customarily consults the Finance Department. (3) The price paid is not subject to financial control. It depends upon a special knowledge of markets, of contractors, and of all sorts of business considerations with which the

---

[1] *First and Second Reports from the Committee of Public Accounts*, 8 August, 1916, p. 206 (115 of 1916).

CH. II]   MACHINERY OF SUPPLY.   61

Accounting Officer of a large Department could not be expected to be conversant. Accordingly, under peace conditions, the Accounting Officer has no direct responsibility for prices. His duties as laid down by Order in Council are to act as deputy and assistant to the Finance Member of Council, and to advise the administrative officers at the War Office and in commands on all questions of Army expenditure. " As the Accounting Officer of Army votes, funds and accounts, he shall be charged with the allowance and payment of all monies for Army services ; with accounting for and auditing all cash expenditure and preparing the annual accounts of such expenditure for Parliament ; and with auditing all manufacturing, expense, supply, and store accounts."

Under war conditions, the situation was very largely changed. The Accounting Officer was still not responsible for prices in contracts of the ordinary type ; but a very large number of contracts were made on abnormal conditions, and in these cases the Finance Department shared the responsibility with the Director of Contracts.

The prices paid under the early contracts with the armament firms were high. The Government did not wish to commit itself for more than a few months in advance, and at the same time new fixed capital had to be provided by the firms, who may have shared the popular opinion that the war might be over in a few months. In these circumstances the manufacturers were naturally unwilling to undertake the work except for high prices.

At the expiration of the first contract, the firm, if its performance had been reasonably satisfactory and further supplies were needed, was normally offered a continuation order at its full output subject to three months' notice to discontinue.[1] The opportunity was then taken to attempt a reduction of price ; but the manufacturers usually pleaded that rises in wages and in the cost of materials made any reduction out of the question. It was not possible to cut down prices substantially before the winter of 1915, when cost returns could be obtained from the National Shell Factories, which showed that the prices still being paid to armament firms were unjustifiable. A considerable number of running contracts were then terminated, and drastic reductions were effected, which will be described in a later volume.[2]

V. Contract Administration under War Conditions.

(a) ORGANISATION OF THE CONTRACTS BRANCH.

The actual work of the Contracts Branch was distributed among several sections under the supervision of the Director of Army Contracts with an Assistant Director of Army Contracts.[3]

Contracts 1.—Purchases and sales of warlike stores (including Indian and Colonial orders) ; scientific instruments ; electrical

---

[1] It was explained in a letter of 30 May, 1916, from the Director of Munitions Contracts to Messrs. Armstrong, that "three months' notice" meant "that shells will only be accepted which can be completely finished and actually despatched within three months of receiving notice to stop." (94/Gen. No./440).

[2] Vol. III, Part II.

[3] *War Office Administrative Directory, 1914.*

stores ; timber, chemicals, oils and medicines ; leather, harness and saddlery, furniture ; earthenware, glass and miscellaneous manufactured articles in metal and wood.

Contracts 2.—Purchases and sales of supplies ; fuel ; building materials ; clothing ; textiles ; india-rubber goods (except tyres) ; boats ;

Contracts for works, barrack services, transport and advertisements. Review of all contracts accepted locally.

Contracts 3.—Purchases and sales of mechanical transport and other vehicles ; bicycles ; metals ; machinery.

Contracts : Trade Records.—Inspection of works of contractors, and local investigation of industrial conditions. Supervision of trades' records, investigation of questions of labour and wages connected with army contracts.

Issue and receipt of tenders.

The two sections of the Contracts Branch with which this review is specially concerned, are the Armament Contracts Section of Contracts 1, known as " Contracts 1A," and " Contracts 3." The Armament Contracts Section underwent certain administrative changes, which must here be reviewed. This section, Contracts 1A, purchased " warlike stores " and scientific and optical instruments. " Warlike stores " included guns, gun ammunition, small arms, small arms ammunition, explosives and ingredients. With the exception of high explosives and ingredients, these stores continued to be in the charge of this section up to the formation of the Ministry of Munitions.

After the abrogation about 1906, of the old practice by which this section purchased all supplies of the above stores for the Navy as well as for the Army, the Admiralty and the War Office continued to exchange copies of all contracts for similar classes of munitions, in order that the prices paid might be compared. In spite of this precaution, however, the interests of the two Departments frequently clashed, and competition between them was not eliminated. The practice continued in force between the Admiralty and the Ministry of Munitions.

When war broke out, the staff of the section consisted of one staff clerk, three second division clerks (one of whom was removed almost at once), one assistant clerk, and three copyists. The head of the Contracts Branch was Mr. de la Bère, Director of Army Contracts, an experienced administrator accustomed to the elaborate procedure which obtained between the Contracts Department and the Department of the Master-General of the Ordnance. On 26 September, 1914, Mr. de la Bère left the War Office and was succeeded by Mr. U. F. Wintour from the Board of Trade, who brought to his task width of outlook and familiarity with the industrial organisation, acquired during his service in the Exhibitions Branch of his former Department.[1] Among

---

[1] " On the outbreak of war we developed what may be called a new organisation. A very valuable public servant, and one who has rendered great public service, was compelled by ill-health to withdraw from the work of the Contracts Branch. He was replaced by a man who came from the Board of Trade . . . . where he had the great advantage of studying the general industrial conditions of the country." (Mr. Harold Baker, M.P., Financial Secretary to the War Office). *Parliamentary Debates* (1914), *H. of C.*, LXVIII., 1447.

the assistants whom Mr. Wintour brought in was Mr. P. Hanson, who was put in charge of Section 1A.

Mr. Wintour, from the outset, took up the position that a contracts department could not properly fulfil its duties unless it acted as a supply department. In the case of the supplies (food, clothing, etc.) belonging to the province of the Quartermaster-General, Mr. Wintour, was able, with some exceptions, to put his theory into practice. The position as regards the Master-General of the Ordnance stores was different ; the functions of supply remained with the Master-General of the Ordnance and his deputy, the Director of Artillery. Mr. Wintour accordingly withdrew his personal attention to a great extent from this department and left it to the control of Mr. Hanson, the latter was thus in the position of making such bargains as he could with firms selected by, and receiving instructions from, the Director of Artillery. Section 1A thus began to act more and more as a branch of the Master-General of the Ordnance's Department.

The dependence of Contracts Section 1A on the Department of the Master-General of the Ordnance, which had been made effective in January, 1915, was formally recognised at the beginning of April, 1915, by the transfer to the Master-General of the Ordnance of the contract business relating to warlike stores (other than high explosives) and scientific instruments, including purchases for the Indian and Colonial Governments.[1] The section previously known as Contracts 1A accordingly reported henceforth to the Director of Artillery, and was known as A7.

The personnel of the section at this time consisted of Mr. P. Hanson, Civil Assistant to the Director of Artillery ; Mr. W. G. West, Acting Assistant Principal ; Messrs. W. M. Foster, R. H. Carr, C. J. Phillips and A. M. Samuel, Personal Assistants to Mr. Hanson ; and Mr. C. C. W. Burrage, Staff Clerk ; together with eight second division clerks, five assistant clerks, four copyists and nine temporary men clerks. The duties of A7 were limited to the purchase of the stores above mentioned ; statistical records of such purchases ; and the allocation of orders between the Ordnance Factories and the trade. In order to secure continuity of contract procedure and policy, other questions were to be referred to, or dealt with, in consultation with the Director of Army Contracts.

On 1 January, 1915, the provision of high explosives was put into the charge of a new branch (A6) of the Directorate of Artillery.[2] The duties of A6 included the supervision of all contracts for high explosives and ingredients, and a small staff for financial and accounting duties was detached from M.G.O.F. At the same time, Lord Moulton, as chairman of the Committee on High Explosives,[3] was given executive authority from the Master-General of the Ordnance, in conjunction

---

[1] War Office Memorandum 801 (5/4/15) ; 1/Gen. No./1508.

[2] Contracts/T/4920. War Office Memorandum 795.

[3] Appointed in November, 1914, "to consider and advise as to the steps which should be taken to ensure an adequate supply of high explosives for the British and Allied Governments, and of the materials and products necessary for their manufacture."

with the newly-appointed Assistant Director of Artillery, Brigadier-General Savile, who joined the Committee as the War Office representative.

From April, 1915, accordingly, the War Office contracts business so far as it related to warlike stores and aircraft, was allocated as follows :—

A.6 (M.G.O. Department) High explosives (Propellants were transferred to A.6 in June, 1915).

A.7 (M.G.O. Department) Warlike stores, other than explosives and scientific instruments.

Director of Military Aeronautics, M.A.3. Contracts for aeronautical supplies.

This arrangement lasted until A.6, A.7, together with Contracts 3, the section responsible for mechanical transport supplies and metals, were transferred to the Ministry of Munitions.

(b) STAFF.

We have seen that at the outbreak of war the staff dealing with the supply of munitions at the War Office consisted of about 52 persons serving under the Director of Artillery, and about eight persons in the Armament Section of the Contracts Department, 60 in all. At the time when it was transferred to the Master-General of the Ordnance the C ntracts Branch had increased to 33. The Director of Artillery's staff had also expanded, and an independent organisation under Lord Moulton was growing up at Storey's Gate. The expansion was rapid during the succeeding months, a new organisation, known as the War Office Armaments Output Committee, being instituted by Lord Kitchener in April to supplement the work of the Director of Artillery.

The Ministry of Munitions took over large sections of the existing staff engaged on supply and rapidly multiplied their number. On 1 July, 1915, the total staff of the Ministry was 688, of whom 385 were engaged on work directly related to the production of warlike stores, including trench warfare material and explosives. On 1 October this total had reached 2,350, of whom, perhaps, 1,400 were employed on supply matters.[1] The number in the Department of Munitions Contracts alone was 127.

The following summary by an official of the Contracts Department indicates some of the difficulties under which the work of the staff was carried on during the early months of the war :—[2]

1. The failure to provide staff adequate in either numbers or competence.

2. The chaos caused by the contempt for " red tape " of the men with commercial experience who were brought in.

3. The ordinary Civil Servant's ignorance of commercial matters and consequent incapacity for transacting business with contractors.

4. The difficulty of making full use of the experienced junior members of the staff who could not be placed in charge of officials of higher grade introduced from elsewhere.

---

[1] HIST. REC./R/263.3/27.   [2] HIST. REC./H/500/10.

5. The difficulty of finding time to train new comers.

6. The inadequacy and overcrowded character of the accommodation and the long 14-hour day had an injurious influence upon the efficiency of the staff.

(c) Number of Contracts Placed, 1914–15.

The significance of the foregoing hindrances to efficient administration will be realised when they are considered in the light of the volume of work for which the Contracts Department was responsible. In this connection attention may be directed to the appended statement[1] which exhibits the number of orders for warlike stores placed with trade contractors during the 12 months immediately preceding the war in comparison with those for the 12 months ending July, 1915.

When the war broke out the existing procedure was at first maintained, but step by step modifications were introduced, which resulted in a considerable relaxation of checks and speeding up of decisions. Had the demand for supplies sprung suddenly to great heights it might have led to an early recasting of the machinery ; but, as it was, the inception of the new system was gentler than might have been expected. The moratorium, of course, caused some abnormality, and the general disturbance of business upset calculations. But on the other hand, there was a breathing space before the Expeditionary Force was in contact with the enemy ; moreover the growth of that Force and— more important still—the growth of the plans for extending and reduplicating the Army in the field, were gradual and unforeseeable.

Throughout August and September, therefore, orders for shells, for example, were passed from the Master-General of the Ordnance to the Contracts Department in the form of individual demands for fixed quantities, and it was left for the latter to issue tender forms to approved firms and allocate the orders in the usual manner. The Master-General also arranged for the Royal Ordnance Factories to produce to capacity.

(d) Sub-Contracting.

One of the first directions in which relief was sought from the pressure of new orders was in a relaxation of the regulation regarding sub-contracting.[2]

By the terms of the Fair Wages Clause, incorporated in the standard form of War Office contract, the contractor was prohibited from " transferring or assigning, directly or indirectly, to any person or persons whatever, any portion of his contract without the written permission of the Department." Subletting other than that which might be customary in the trade concerned was prohibited ; and the contractor was held responsible for the observance of the Fair Wages Clauses by the sub-contractor.

It was clearly sound policy on the part of the War Office, who had no expert staff available for training new firms, to allow these to accept orders from experienced contractors who thus became responsible for aiding during the most difficult period. The alternative plan of placing

---

[1] Appendix II.   [2] Hist. Rec./H/500/10.

direct contracts with untried firms and leaving them unaided to find
out by hard experience the best way of producing an acceptable article,
would have resulted in an enormous waste of time, labour and material,
and in the swamping of the inspector's department with masses of
material which had to be rejected. By allowing the experienced firms to
sublet, and holding them responsible for the quality of the product, the
work of training was spread among all those who were capable of
teaching.

Accordingly, when inexperienced firms applied for work on
munitions, they were classified according to the class of work which they
offered to undertake, and lists compiled in this manner were circulated
to firms from whom tenders were invited. These lists would have been
even more valuable if they had been verified by a competent inspecting
staff of skilled engineers such as was subsequently established by the
Ministry of Munitions. Some assistance in this direction was in fact
rendered by the Board of Trade, who reported upon the capacity of
applicant firms in certain cases, but these reports were not always
based upon adequate knowledge of the technicalities of munition
making. The Trades Records Branch, the one branch of the War
Office whose duties included the local investigation of industrial
conditions, had been abolished upon the outbreak of war.

The Inspection Department at Woolwich was the natural authority
to provide the help required. But here again there was no reserve of
skilled man-power, and the inadequate and overdriven staff could not
be spared to inspect the plant of potential contractors. The most
effective assistance in their power was the advice they were able to
give to contractors who visited Woolwich. Here samples and drawings could be examined and difficulties discussed. Unfortunately, since
the Inspection Department was not the supply authority, it was not
in a position to know the relative urgency of different components or
supplies. Moreover, its resources were restricted, its supply of drawings and specifications very limited, and even in the matter of gauges
it could give little practical assistance to a firm not already equipped.

Early in 1915 a step forward was taken by the appointment of
Major-General R. H. Mahon, C.B., as the Master-General of the Ordnance's representative, to visit and report upon untried firms offering
their services as contractors for munitions. This resulted from an
enquiry addressed by Mr. Hanson, the officer in charge of armament
contracts, to the Director of Artillery, on 22 January, 1915.[1]

Mr. Hanson anticipated that the campaign undertaken by the Board
of Trade about this time would be likely to result in a flood of enquiries
from contractors whose productive capacity was unknown. The
Director of Artillery suggested that such enquiries should be referred to
the Inspection Department at Woolwich, where specimens of components required could be inspected, and that the Chief Inspector
should arrange to inspect the works of promising firms. The Chief
Inspector, however, reported that while he was prepared to arrange
for visitors, he had no staff to act as travelling inspectors, and this

---

[1] 94/Gen. No./7.

latter function was therefore assumed by Major-General Mahon, who continued to act in this capacity during the following critical months. He was also responsible under the Master-General of the Ordnance for the issue of war service badges to firms employed on munitions manufacture who wished to secure exemption from recruiting for their indispensable workers.

(e) The Utilisation of Expert Commercial Knowledge.

The administration of War Office contracts did not escape Parliamentary criticism during the autumn of 1914. Such criticism rested for the most part upon a growing feeling that military officialism imposed a barrier between the commercial community and the War Office ; that the War Office was ignorant of commercial usage, and that its procedure was cumbersome and tortuous and unfavourable for securing the immediate and large scale results which the crisis demanded ; that, on the other hand, the administration was extravagant, and that contractors were reaping undue advantages. It was frequently suggested that a civilian committee should be appointed to supervise the placing of War Office contracts, and so relieve the pressure upon the officials and secure that administration was guided by sound technical knowledge. Mr. Wintour, as we have seen, was fully alive to the desirability of better commercial control. A proposal made to the War Office in October by Mr. George Booth had resulted in the appointment of certain consultative trade experts, Mr. McClellan for the steel trade, Mr. J. S. Oliver, of Messrs. Debenham & Freebody, for the clothing trade, and Mr. Cecil Baring for American orders.[1] On 26 October, Mr. George Duckworth laid before Sir Reginald Brade a memorandum drawn up in consultation with the Rt. Hon. Charles Booth and Mr. George Booth, which contained proposals for establishing a system of consultative trade committees for each of the principal trade groups linked up to the Contracts Department by means of an expert adviser. A small beginning was made in this direction and the House of Commons was assured on 23 November that all was well :—

> " I should be very glad," said Mr. Harold Baker, M.P., Financial Secretary to the War Office, " to have any help that could be given by anyone ; but I would ask the House to remember that the Contracts Branch of the War Office is a machine that is very well organised in peace and which is served by great devotion and ability by the officials at the War Office. I believe that it has been re-organised to work well in war also. It is by no means composed solely of soldiers and of permanent civilians who were there before the war broke out. A vast quantity of expert civilian assistance has been brought in which has been of the very greatest possible value to us, and I do think that, with this civilian assistance already incorporated in that portion of the work, it might hinder the work very seriously indeed if you had an inquisitorial Committee standing over them and scrutinising every contract which they had to make."[2]

---

[1] Hist. Rec./R/500/1.
[2] Parliamentary Debates (1914), *H. of C.*, LXVIII, 852.

Three days later Mr. Baker further stated :—

"We have had at the War Office for some time buyers, and besides buyers, advisers . . . . men of wide experience whose knowledge is of great value, men who do not give and do not accept contracts, but men who furnish just that element of special business experience which it is said we need so much."[1]

Public uneasiness in regard to this matter was, however, not easily allayed, and much pointed advice was offered on points affecting War Office contract administration. Attention was drawn to matters affecting clothing, barbed wire, building, bedding and furniture, food, timber supplies and hutting, but little, if any, reference was made to matters affecting the output of essential munitions, such as rifles, guns or ammunition, except from the standpoint of labour supply and recruiting.[2]

Sir John Harmood-Banner, speaking on the 9 February, 1915,[3] complained of the want of accessibility of the War Office where contractors were concerned, and suggested that the scale of business had grown to a point beyond the capacity of the old system, "There are plenty of able men quite ready to give their services in the purchase of stores and to assist the War Office in any way they can." (In this connection reference was made to an advisory committee which dealt with clothing, though it was not empowered to intervene in contract questions.)[4] A few weeks later,[5] Mr. Baker again defended the War Office from the charge of ignoring industrial assistance and said that

"for hon. Members, and even the Leader of the Opposition, to continue to suppose, as he appears to suppose, that the War Office is still acting without considerable and valuable advice from business men drawn from outside is a great mistake. . . . . We have almost from the beginning of the war been continually helped by people with full knowledge of the particular branch of trade as to which their advice has been asked. We have not widely advertised the fact, but we have taken care to choose men whose advice we knew we could trust, who we know to be disinterested, and who had a single mind and patriotic purpose in coming to our aid. That has been going on continually."

He hoped, however, that this system would be extended and that these advisers would be organised in a committee. There had been no failure to get the best possible civilian advice whatever branch of trade might be concerned.

The employment of expert buyers did not, in fact, overcome the difficulty inherent in the division of responsibility between the Contracts Branch and the Military Inspection Branch. Consequently the buyer was seldom authorised to settle offers on the spot, all he was able to

[1] Parliamentary Debates (1914), *H. of C.*, LXVIII, 1448.
[2] *Parliamentary Debates* (1915), *H. of C.*, LXIX. Mr. Tennant's speech on the Army Estimates of 8 February, 1915, and subsequent debate.
[3] *Ibid.*, p. 508.
[4] *Ibid.*, pp. 634 and 658.
[5] *Ibid.*, LXX, pp. 1092–3.

do was to bring pressure to bear upon firms able to tender, the contract being dealt with in the usual way.[1] Moreover, the employment of men directly engaged in trade as Government agents gave rise to many difficulties.[2] Only the exceptional man was wanted, and such a man was certain to be fully occupied. Even the best man is likely to be an object of suspicion, if not of open attack, on the ground of the unfair advantages which he secures over competitors, while on the other hand, it is essential that the agent selected should enjoy in the fullest measure the confidence of the trade with which he has to deal.

VI. Conclusion.

It will be realised from the foregoing that the organisation of the Contracts Department did not expand as rapidly as might have been anticipated under the stress of war conditions. Probably one of the principal hindrances was the tendency to regard the work of a civilian branch as of secondary importance, and the opposition aroused by any proposal which seemed to give authority to such a branch which might conflict with the military departments. Mr. Wintour when appointed Director of Army Contracts at the end of September, found himself in the position of a supply officer with only a partial and limited authority over the processes by which supplies were procured.[3] The military departments were responsible for estimates of requirements, for prescribing quality, for the allocation of contracts, for accepting deliveries, for inspection, and for administering the Ordnance Factories. The Contracts Department were only called upon to find contractors willing to provide what was required and to draw up and negotiate terms and ensure the reasonableness of prices. The manufacturer, accustomed to negotiate a deal throughout with a single customer, found himself dealing with an inspection authority and a contracts authority, neither of whom were competent to treat a bargain as a whole ; and as the Contracts Department did not administer the contract when made, they had no first hand knowledge of the relative reliability of performance by different firms. Neither were they authorised to facilitate the placing of contracts or extension of supply where this involved any departure from specification or substitution for materials difficult to procure. Their ignorance of future, as distinct from present requirements, made it impossible to plan for increase of capacity, the demand for which was not yet formally registered.

Realising that these deficiencies were inherent in the system, Mr. Wintour, who had been invited by the Secretary to the Army Council to formulate proposals for re-organising the Contracts Department, submitted a scheme based upon the principle of making one authority responsible for the whole business of providing Army supplies, including negotiations as to price and the duty of watching and stimulating deliveries.

---

[1] Memorandum on War Office Contracts (February, 1916), Part IV (Copy in Hɪsᴛ. Rᴇᴄ./R/170/24).

[2] *Ibid.*, Part VI.

[3] Hɪsᴛ. Rᴇᴄ./R/500/64.

" It must be constantly borne in mind," said Mr. Wintour, " that the problem of securing supplies which now confronts the War Office is of an entirely different nature from any which it has previously met.   In time of peace there is seldom any difficulty in obtaining any articles which the military authorities desire. The resources of the whole world are at the disposal of the War Office, and there is no lack of manufacturers to compete for the privilege of supplying all that is needed.

" The present case is otherwise.   In many branches of trade the ordinary resources of the country are insufficient to produce all that is required.   Manufacturers must be assisted in every way, their difficulties of labour and the supply of raw materials must be smoothed out and great care and thought must be devoted to the task of organising them to produce to the utmost capacity of their trade.   If the new armies are to be equipped in time the co-operation of every available manufacturer and worker must be secured.

" It is in these circumstances useless to attempt to adhere rigidly to standard patterns and specifications, and it is essential to give greatly increased attention to such considerations as the comparative speed at which articles of slightly different types can be produced, the available supplies of raw materials, and the most fruitful use of labour and machinery."

*   *   *   *   *   *   *   *

" The important part played by industry in fitting out an army has not been sufficiently recognised.   The war is a war of organisation in which the raising of men is one very important item.   It is equally important that they should be equipped, clothed, fed, and provided with guns, arms and ammunition. For the provision of these necessaries industry, and industry alone, has to be relied upon, and the rapidity and effectiveness with which industry can be organised to meet the emergency cannot but have an enormous influence upon the issue of the struggle."

*   *   *   *   *   *   *   *

" Under the present system it has been difficult in many cases to obtain even an approximate idea of the extent of the orders which have to be placed in the future, and it is essential in any new scheme that provision should be made for preparing estimates showing probable requirements for three months, six months, and a year ahead.   It is, of course, realised that rapid change of military plans makes it impossible to furnish any final estimates, but this in itself is no valid reason why rough estimates should not be prepared which would afford a sufficiently good working basis."[1]

This was a noteworthy formulation of what may be called the civilian aspect of the war, and might be taken as expressing the essential principles upon which the Ministry of Munitions relied for its inception and development.   But whatever its prophetic significance, its immediate effect was not great ; the time was not yet ripe.

---

[1] Hist. Rec./R/500/64.

One of the innovations proposed by Mr. Wintour was, however, adopted in part, namely, the appointment of an additional member on the Army Council, whose duty should relate particularly to supply. On 18 December, 1914, Sir George S. Gibb was appointed additional Civil Member (temporary) for artillery contracts.[1] This appointment did not, of course, fulfil Mr. Wintour's proposal, which had aimed at co-ordinating responsibility for supply. Carried out in this form, it merely added another spoke to the wheel, and valuable and important as Sir George Gibb's experience and advice were in the handling of important negotiations and dealing with different problems of supply policy, the framework of the existing organisation remained practically unaltered. The full scheme was not realised until in May, 1917, a Surveyor-General of Supply was appointed, who was further made a Member of the Army Council, and whose duties embraced all " such functions as relate to the commercial side of the business of supplying the Army."[2]

This new authority not only assumed the responsibility of the Director of Army Contracts, but also took over executive supply duties from the military departments. Long before this came to pass, however, the business of munitions supply had been transferred to the new Ministry of Munitions.

---

[1] War Office Memorandum 792.
[2] War Office Memorandum 929.   See also Vol. VII, Part I, Supplement.

CHAPTER III.

SOME EARLY WAR CONTRACTS.

I. The Difficulties of Supply : Orders for Small Arms Ammunition.

It is not necessary to emphasise the handicap with which the War Office entered upon its task. But it may, perhaps, be worth while to trace in a little detail the actual course of supply negotiations for a representative military supply during the first two months of the war, in order to exhibit the characteristic feature of this period, the hand-to-mouth scramble for supplies in a market whose output capacity was in the nature of the case severely restricted.

We may select for this illustrative purpose the organisation of output for small arms ammunition, both as being the primary military requirement for the maintenance of an army in contact with an enemy, and also as having been, in fact, a principal pre-occupation of the supply authorities at this time.

(a) THE POSITION AT THE OUTBREAK OF WAR.

The situation when war broke out was this. There were stocks in the hands of the Deputy Director of Ordnance Stores amounting to 29,000,000 rounds.[1] The maximum trade capacity of five regular contractors on 1 August, 1914, was $3\frac{1}{2}$ millions a week under normal arrangements, but was capable of being raised to six millions a week if nightwork, the suspension of Factory Acts, and an abundant supply of material were secured.[2] The theoretical maximum capacity of Woolwich was $3\frac{1}{2}$ millions.[3] Some three months earlier orders had been placed with the Birmingham Metal & Munitions Company, Messrs. Eley Bros., Greenwood and Batley, Kynoch, and the King's Norton Metal Company. The total order was for 27 millions,[4] but 22 millions were still outstanding, and completion was not expected for many months.[5]

(b) THE FIRST WAR CONTRACTS.

Instructions were at once given to accelerate deliveries on these orders. Tenders for further supplies were called for on 4 August, and, after an interview at the War Office, the firms submitted their

---

[1] HIST. REC./R/1440/2. By 2 October this quantity had shrunk to three million rounds.
[2] Contracts/C/7963. In 1900, working at full pressure, these same firms had given an average output of $3\frac{1}{4}$ millions a week (75/3/1033).
[3] 75/3/2357 (October, 1913)
[4] Contracts/C/7749.
[5] Contracts/C/7963.

TRADE CONTRACTS FOR .303 AMMUNITION MARK VII. [1]

Position at end of August, 1914.

Firm	Contract	Date	Quantity	Rate for Delivery	Due for Completion by†	Price per 1000	Maximum Rate of Output per week
Birmingham Metal & Munitions Co.	C/7749	15.5.14	3 million	per month 500,000	18.9.14	103/–	2,500,000
	C/8134	21.8.14	48 million	per week 2,500,000	5.2.15	108/6	
Messrs. Greenwood & Batley	C/7749	15.5.14	7 million	per month 875,000	25.9.14	99/– 108/6*	1,000,000
	C/8134	21.8.14	18 million	per week 1,000,000	30.1.15	108/6	
King's Norton Metal Co., Ltd.	C/7749	15.5.14	4 million	per month 750,000	25.9.14	101/4	1,800,000
	C/8134	21.8.14	32 million	per week 1,800,000	30.1.15	108/6	
Messrs. Eley Bros.	C/7749	15.5.14	6 million	per week 158,000	27.3.15	91/6–106/6*	550,000
	C/8134	21.8.14	8 million	per week 375,000	13.2.15	106/6	
Messrs. Kynoch Ltd.	C/7749	15.5.14	7 million	per month 2,000,000	12.9.14	99/3	2,400,000
	C/8134	21.8.14	48 million	1,100,000 in 4 weeks then per week 2,400,000	7.2.15	108/6	

* Increase in price for rise in cost of material, etc.

† The contracts placed 15/5/14 were originally due for completion as follows :—Birmingham Metal & Munitions Co. on 26/11/14 ; Messrs. Eley Bros., 27/3/15 ; Messrs. Greenwood, 9/3/15 ; Messrs. Kynoch, 17/10/14 ; King's Norton Metal Co., 10/12/14. An order for 20 million cartridges had also been placed specially with the Canadian Government for completion by 22/1/15.

[1] 57/Gen. No./3595.

proposals jointly in a letter of 6 August, 1914.[1] They indicated the rate of output they could attain if the Factory Acts were suspended, and suggested a Government embargo on dealings in essential materials, such as electrolytic copper, zinc, nickel, lead, and mercury. They quoted a standard basis price of 105s. per thousand cartridges, but stipulated that the price should vary according to the monthly variation in the basic price of materials, including cordite and fulminate. They asked for an advanced payment, equal to one-third of the value of the total order. The moratorium was at this time creating some temporary uncertainty and want of confidence, and the contractors had not yet felt their feet. The following extract from a letter to the Director of Army Contracts from the King's Norton Metal Company, dated 5 August, 1914, will serve to illustrate this passing phase :—

re War.

" Sir,—Now that the above has commenced, you will readily understand that the whole of the conditions of supplies are altered for all classes of metals. We are now asked for cash against documents. I believe that the ammunition makers could procure their supplies without any difficulty if the payment were guaranteed by His Majesty's Government. . . ."

A fresh demand for 100 millions was issued, 21 millions being undertaken by Woolwich. The remaining 79 millions were allocated to the trade contractors, but before the formal contracts were placed it was decided to arrange for a second 100 millions, of which total the Ordnance Factory took 25 millions, leaving 75 millions, or 154 millions in all, for the new trade orders.[2] The annexed statement[3] gives the allocation of these orders and the prospective rate of output. Practically the whole quantity was due for completion by February, 1915, the maximum rate of delivery to be attained being 8¼ million cartridges a week.

(c) THE POSITION AT THE END OF AUGUST, 1914.

Great as was the expansion of pre-war supply thus initiated, it was barely sufficient to cover the requirements already in sight. A programme drawn up on 27 August, 1914, which compared the supply available and in sight with the requirements of the Army at home and overseas, showed a serious deficit in prospect for January, 1915, on the assumption that the first New Army might then be sent to the Front. The aggregate output for the first six months would be 458 million cartridges, against requirements of 499 million. Moreover, no provision was made in these calculations for the Territorial Division of the Naval Brigade, nor for any New Army subsequent to the first.

Important, and indeed formidable, as were the total requirements on British account, this was not the whole of the problem. Before the end of August Lord Kitchener received an urgent appeal for assistance

---

[1] Contracts/C/7963.
[2] 57/3/4287 ; Contracts/C/7963 and 8134.   [3] See above, p. 73.

from the Belgian Army, which in consequence of the invasion of that country, and the stoppage of industry, was very short of raw material. There were no stocks which they could purchase, and orders for the British Government made it impossible for manufacturers in this country to satisfy the additional requirements. It was, therefore, arranged by the War Office, on 27 August, that Messrs. Kynoch should give priority to an order on Belgian account for 20 million cartridges, which it was hoped to procure in ten weeks time. The same day the Master-General of the Ordnance reported to Lord Kitchener on the position of British supplies affected by this arrangement, and pointed out that all available sources, including America and Canada, were now being tapped,[1] but that he would be hard put to it to provide for the expanded requirements of the New Army in addition to those of Colonial and Territorial Divisions. Lord Kitchener insisted that Belgium must have her 20 million cartridges ; but he went much further. He gave peremptory instructions for " all manufacturers of small arms ammunition to provide themselves with fresh plant sufficient to enable their present output to be doubled in six months time or less." Expense was not to interfere.

Prompt measures were taken. The Chief Superintendent of Ordnance Factories was instructed to increase his Woolwich plant to provide an output of 10 million cartridges a week, and representatives of the principal contractors, Messrs. Kynoch, Greenwood & Batley, the King's Norton Metal Company, Messrs. Nobel and the Birmingham Metal & Munition Company (Messrs. Eley Bros. were not represented), met the Master-General of the Ordnance on 28 August, when the latter invited the firms to submit proposals for largely extending their output. Messrs. Kynoch were asked for an additional one million cartridges per week, and Messrs. Greenwood & Batley, Messrs. Nobel and the Birmingham Metal & Munitions Company (jointly) for a similar addition to their output. The King's Norton Company offered an increase after six months. In due course the firms formulated definite proposals. All of them contemplated a substantial advance in prices— amounting to about 20s. per thousand—which in the view of the Contracts Department was an excessive charge. The average price in the pre-war contracts had been about 100s. per thousand, and in the August contracts, 108s. 6d. per thousand. The subsequent negotiations may be briefly summarized.[2]

(d) Negotiations with Individual Firms.

Messrs. Greenwood & Batley.—This firm offered to accept an order for an additional 20 million rounds output at the rate of 500,000 per week, the price to be 129s. 6d. per thousand, their total output being thus raised to 1,500,000 per week. This price it was intimated would cover an anticipated increase in the cost of cordite which they had to

---

[1] An American firm, the Remington Arms Union, began to give deliveries before the end of 1914 on an order placed in August with the Canadian Government.

[2] See 57/Gen. No./3595.

buy. The firm were instructed to proceed (2 September, 1914), and in reply to the remonstrance of the Contracts Department in respect of the price asked, replied:

" We note that you consider the price quoted for this ammunition is high, but we would ask you kindly to bear in mind . . . that in times of peace the existing plant of the various factories is capable of dealing with approximately four or five times the amount of cartridges ordered. That in view of the present urgent demand all manufacturers are increasing their plant very considerably, and that, therefore, when normal conditions again prevail the large increases made to the now existing plant will become useless.

" We may further add that we understand it is the intention of H.M. Government largely to increase the cartridge plant at Woolwich, which will further prejudice the chance of orders being secured by contractors in time of peace.

" In view of these temporary and abnormal conditions, we trust it will be recognised that it is necessarily incumbent on contractors to protect themselves against probable heavy loss of capital by asking rather higher prices than they would otherwise be ready to accept. The further conditions of the rise in the price of metal and of cordite, the enhanced cost of plant and a considerable rise in working expenses owing to overtime, etc., etc., have also a very direct bearing on the increase of price."

The price was by subsequent negotiation reduced from 129s. 6d. to 128s. 6d., at which price the formal contract was completed on 2 October, 1914. The firm entered a protest against the insertion of a penalty clause under which failure to complete deliveries by the specified date would entail reduction of price by 20s. per thousand rounds.

King's Norton Metal Company, Ltd.—This company submitted a proposal for building and equipping a complete plant capable of dealing with every stage of production, from the casting and rolling of the metal up to the final processes, and giving an additional output of from 2 to 2½ million cartridges per week, raising their total weekly output to 4 millions. They asked for a contract for the supply of 4 millions a week from March, 1915, to March, 1916, or a firm order for 100 millions. The terms asked were 128s. 9d. per thousand, together with a cash advance of £65,000. In a further communication the firm asked for some assurance as to their post-war position, having especially in view the presumption that the Woolwich plant would also be greatly extended. They maintained that " if in the past the various contractors had been subsidised, or kept going with regular orders for ammunition, the present emergency would not have occurred." The firm was told in reply that "on the conclusion of the war, orders for small arms ammunition will naturally contract to the peace scale, and no undertaking as to their extent can possibly be given."

On 8 September the firm were instructed to proceed in anticipation of a contract for an additional quantity of 45,000,000 cartridges, the price to be settled later. The firm, in acknowledging this order, took the opportunity of " directing attention to the fact that we cannot be responsible for the work of other people, and, as we are in the hands of several for supplies, should they fail we must make it a condition that the contract should not be cancelled through such causes or delays."

The order was accepted on 21 September at 125s. per thousand, but the firm demurred to the application of the penalty clause under which cartridges delivered after completion date would be paid for at the rate of 108s. 6d. only, if such delays should be due to causes beyond their control. The War Office undertook that such circumstances should be given due consideration, provided that an output of 4 million cartridges per week had been attained.

In the event, only 9,400,000 cartridges were delivered within the specified time limit, the balance, 35,600,000, becoming liable under the penalty clause to liquidated damages amounting to £5,150.[1] The firm stated that among the causes of delay the excavating contractor had been two months behind time, that the plant was delivered late, that labour supply had been inadequate, and that appeals to the Government for assistance in securing toolmakers had met with little result. The claim was accordingly waived.

Messrs. Kynoch, Ltd.—Messrs. Kynoch pointed out (31 August, 1914) that in order to fulfil the instructions of the Master-General to increase output up to 3½ million cartridges per week the firm would be obliged to incur a very heavy capital outlay, and that both the existing contract for 48 millions and the contemplated order for 52 millions would be increased in cost. In the circumstances it would be best to cancel the previous contract and place an inclusive new order for 100 millions at 117s. 6d. per thousand, instead of an additional contract at 125s. per thousand, these two alternatives giving equivalent aggregates. The firm added that the prices proposed would fairly meet the added cost and risk, and no more. The War Office objected that the price proposed was very high, to which the firm responded that they were unable to accept this view.

> " We are constantly being brought up by things we had not allowed for, and which are the cause of additional capital or revenue expenditure. We do not think any other firm could have promised so large an addition to their regular output in anything like so short a time, nor do we think they would have been able to quote so low a price had they been able to produce the cartridges."

A formal contract for an additional 52 million cartridges at 125s. per thousand, with a clause reducing payments on late deliveries to 108s. 6d., was accepted by the firm on 28 September, 1914, with the following qualifications :—

> " You will notice that we have struck out from this tender the clause providing for reduced prices in the case of failure to submit the full quantities to time. Our Chairman pointed out to the Assistant Director of Army Contracts that we should not

---

[1] 94/C/1011.

be able to accept any clause such as this. The increased cost to us will be incurred practically in full, whether the exact output is attained or not. Consequently it is not fair to suggest that the price should be reduced for a slight failure· in delivery which, should it occur, will not be due to any fault or lack of attention on our part. Before promising these deliveries we made every calculation for difficulties and contingencies, and you may confidently rely on our keeping our promises, but we cannot accept a fine greater than your usual one in case of the unlikely event which your additional clause provides for."

The War Office refused to accept the deletion of the clause, but agreed to make it inapplicable if the contractor could show that the delay was due to causes beyond his control, and that he had in fact reached the prescribed rate of output.

Nobel's Explosives Company, Ltd. and the Birmingham Metal and Munitions Company, Ltd.—Messrs. Nobel had been asked to equip their sporting ammunition factory at Waltham Abbey for the production of service ammunition at a rate of 1,000,000 rounds per week, these deliveries to be supplementary to the 2½ million per week ordered from the Birmingham Metal and Munitions Company. They calculated that the new equipment would cost 20,000*l.* including " a substantial premium for prompt delivery." They estimated that manufacture ·at Waltham Abbey would be much more costly than at Birmingham, by reason of the training of fresh workers which was involved. They quoted 126s. per thousand for an order of 48 millions, a quantity identical with that already contracted for with the Birmingham Metal and Munitions Company. Instructions to commence manufacture were given on 2 September, the joint output to work up to 3½ million rounds per week.

As in the cases already reviewed, Messrs. Nobel declined to accept the penalty clause for late delivery :

" We consider that in view of the exceptional circumstances surrounding this contract, the price of 126s. per thousand should apply to this order . . . . whether or not delivery is effected by 1 May, 1915. You are aware that we are equipping ourselves with plant for the manufacture of Mark VII ammunition for you and the price which we quoted to you for these cartridges was calculated upon a certain capital outlay which we had made upon the plant for the manufacture of the ammunition being recouped to us on the order for 48 millions. This being so we are being penalised if by any chance our deliveries to you are not completed by the 1 May, 1915, and we regret we cannot accept the· first condition in the schedule attached to your contract form, which provides that cartridges not delivered by that date shall only be paid for at the rate of 108s. 6d. per thousand . . . . We feel sure that you do not desire to penalise us in view of the fact that you have accepted the principle of allowing us an increased price on this order to compensate us for the plant which is required specially for its execution."

As in other cases the War Office declined to delete the clause, but relaxed it to allow of extraneous causes of delay to be pleaded together with a concession of a period of grace.   The contract was amended accórdingly and was formally executed on 27 October, 1914, though in further correspondence the firm secured some further concession in regard to the application of the ordinary penalty clause imposing a fine for late delivery which formed part of the standing conditions of War Office contracts.   The following clause was added as a common form clause applicable to contracts when the cost of plant was borne by the War Office.

> " This contract is placed on the understanding that the additional plant provided at the expense of His Majesty's Government will be held at the disposal of the War Office for the duration of the war.   At the end of the war Messrs. Nobel's Explosives Company undertake to maintain the plant and keep it in good order.   Should, however, Messrs. Nobel's Explosives Company desire to dismantle the plant or to use it for any other purpose which would render it unfit for the manufacture of small arms ammunition they undertake to give the Secretary of State for War one year's notice in writing before taking any such steps."

On 7 January, 1915 a further contract for 200 million was placed involving a fresh extension of the Birmingham Metal and Munitions Company's plant.   These additional deliveries were to reach 5 million per week by the end of June, 1915.[1]   At the end of March, 1915, on an order for 75 million, yet another extension was arranged, which was to yield an output of 4 million a week.[2]   Thus by the end of the year these firms alone would be giving a weekly output of $1+2\frac{1}{2}+5+4$ millions, $12\frac{1}{2}$ millions in all.

Messrs. Eley Bros. Ltd.—Negotiations for doubling the contract previously placed by an additional order for 8 million rounds were opened on 7 September.   The firm replied in these terms :—

> " We have already accelerated deliveries as promised, and up to the 4th September we had made deliveries amounting to 896,800 cartridges.   We shall complete this contract within the time specified.

> " Further than this, by putting down some additional machines, and provided the Home Office will give us permission to work our women from ten at night until six in the morning (application for this permission has already been made), we could accept your order for a further eight million cartridges for delivery at the rate of one million per month, deliveries to commence in from five to six weeks from receipt of contract.

> " To cover the cost of putting down these additional machines and to meet the additional cost of the all night work, our price for this additional order for (say) eight million cartridges is 120s. per thousand."

---

[1] Contracts /C/9101A.   [2] 15/Contracts/36.

This offer was conditional on success in procuring supplies of metal, cordite, etc. The firm were also prepared to report on the possibility of further increases to their plant, enquiries to this end having been already initiated by the Admiralty.

Instructions to proceed were promptly given and a draft contract sent, inclosing a penalty clause imposing reduction of price to 106s. 6d. in case of failure to reach the deliveries specified by the contract in any individual month. This severe condition was not unnaturally rejected by Messrs. Eley, who pointed out that it would be disadvantageous to the War Office also, since it would compel them to hold back surplus output in order to make good accidental deficiencies in any month's deliveries. A contract in modified terms was executed by the firm on 21 September, 1914.

(e) Significance of the Foregoing Examples.

The foregoing negotiations have been traced in detail, not on account of any exceptional or crucial features revealed therein, but rather, for the opposite reason, as a fair sample of the difficulties with which the War Office was confronted at every turn, and as an account which might be paralleled from the record of the supply administration of any other type of warlike stores. It is worth while, therefore, to follow this small episode in the history of munitions supply with some particularity, in order to realise the prevailing character of the activities of this period.

There is, however, a further justification for this study, the prophetic and symptomatic indications of the future developments contained therein. For there is hardly a single form of serious difficulty or hindrance subsequently experienced which is not plainly indicated in these early weeks of the war ; the difficulties of establishing fresh capacity, of multiplying labour force, of procuring plant and of organising a complex productive unit in great haste ; the inadequacy of the powers and experience required for a proper control of prices and the resulting mutual suspicion and difficulty in regard to terms, the War Office emphasising the extortionate character of the contractors' proposals and taking every opportunity to throw on the latter the fullest measure of contingent financial responsibility—in particular the loss of post-war capital valuation ; the contractors wishing to safeguard themselves and secure exemption from penalties, etc., while allowing generously in their quoted prices, not only for the costs of immediate production, but more or less for hypothetical increases in wages and cost of materials.

II. Artillery Supplies during the first Months of the War.

During the first weeks of the war there was no clear indication of the probable length of the conflict, and Lord Kitchener's pronouncement on 25 August, 1914, that the terms of enlistment would be for three years or the duration of the war, was interpreted as being rather a measure of ample insurance than a deliberate judgment of probabilities. In any case, it was inevitable that the first steps in the provision of munitions should be modest in extent.

It had been laid down that the reserves held under the Mowatt scheme would require supplementing within six months from the outbreak of war, and the earliest requisitions were based upon this principle being rapidly expanded to meet the necessity of supplying the augmented forces, which it was at once decided to raise. Thus, as early as 10 August, instructions were given for the provision of equipment and ammunition for the first new army.

Before proceeding to describe briefly the steps taken during the first two months of the war to provide guns, it will be well to give some account of the stocks in existence on the outbreak of war.

(a) Guns available at the Outbreak of War.

The pre-war production of British service guns from 1905-1914, including those manufactured on account of the Dominion and Indian Governments, had been as follows :—18-pdr. Q.F. gun for the Royal Field Artillery, 1,126 ; 13-pdr. Q.F. for the Royal Horse Artillery, 245 ; 4·5-in. field howitzer, 182 ; 60-pdr. B.L. heavy field gun, 41.

The distribution of these totals was as follows :—

	Home.	Canada.	South Africa.	Aus-tralia.	New Zea-land.	India.	Total.
Field Artillery 18-pdr. Q.F.	797	136	16	104	24	49	1,126
Horse Artillery 13-pdr. Q.F.	174	24	28	—	—	19	245
Field howitzer 4·5-in. ..	139	14	—	—	8	21	182
Heavy field gun 60-pdr. B.L.	28	12	—	—	—	1	41

In addition to the above there had been manufactured in India 99 18-pdr. and 21 13-pdr. guns.

The scale of equipment laid down by the war establishments for the six divisions of the field army was as follows :—

	Guns.		Ammunition.	
	Batteries.	Total Guns.	Rounds per Gun.	Total Number.
18-pdr.	54	324	1,500	486,000
13-pdr.	6	36	1,900	68,400
4·5-in.	18	108	1,200	129,600
60-pdr.	6	24	1,000	24,000

The above represented the standard of equipment for the Expeditionary Force. Provision was, however, made for other batteries, either stationed abroad or unallocated, training brigades, and reserve stores :—

	18-pdr.	13-pdr.	4·5-in.	60-pdr.
Field Army :—				
Batteries..	54	6	18	6
Guns	324	36	108	24
Colonies :—				
Batteries	3	1	—	—
Guns	18	6	—	—
Unallocated :—				
Batteries	15	7	—	—
Guns	90	42	—	—
Reserve Stores :—				
Batteries..	15	3	3	1
Guns	90	18	18	4
Total :—				
Batteries..	87	17	21	7
Guns	522	102	126	28

In addition to the above there was a certain number of guns on hand in charge of training brigades and other units, raising the total number of guns available in Great Britain at the outbreak of war to 624 18-pdr. guns ; 126 13-pdr. guns ; 128 4·5-in. howitzers, and 28 60-pdr. guns.

Further, guns which were in the possession of Dominion and other overseas forces at the outbreak of war were brought over and became available during the winter of 1914–15. As will be seen from the following table, this does not completely exhaust the manufactured output ; the balance presumably represents guns condemned for wear, or otherwise unfit for service.

18-pdr.	India	240
	Canada	84
	Australia	36
	New Zealand	12
		372
13-pdr.	India	47
	Canada	12
		59
4·5-in.	India	12
	New Zealand	4
		16
60-pdr.	Canada	10

The total numbers accounted for were thus :—18-pdr., 996 ; 13-pdr., 185 ; 4·5-in., 144 ; 60-pdr., 38.

The equipment of the Territorial artillery was an armament of obsolescent guns which had been displaced in the case of the regular army by the equipments specified above. These earlier types of weapon were, however, serviceable, and substantial use was made of them in minor theatres of war during the interval which elapsed before they could be replaced by modern weapons. The numbers in existence and those subsequently utilised were as follows :—

	In existence.[1]	Actually employed.[2]
Territorial Horse Artillery :—		
15-pdr. Q.F.	85	20
Territorial Field Artillery :—		
15-pdr. B.L.C.	623	228
5-in. Howitzer	150	80
Heavy Field Artillery :—		
4·7-in.	164	88

A few siege guns were also available at the outbreak of war or subsequently were adapted for service in the field, the most important being :—

6-in. B.L. Mk. VII Guns	18
6-in. 30-cwt. B.L. Howitzers Mark I*	24
9·2-in. B.L. Howitzer	1

These were semi-mobile equipments, and a certain number were subsequently adapted for service in the field and sent to the front. The 6-in. Mark VII guns were those taken from coast defences, where they were erected on concrete platforms, and were placed on extemporised field mountings, the first eight being sent to France in January, 1915. They were very heavy and their lives were short, but they were at that time the only means of satisfying the demand for a long range weapon. They could fire a 100-lb. shell over 17,000 yards. Of the 6-in. howitzers a single brigade was in existence at the outbreak of war. In addition to these, a number were collected from various garrisons and colonial stations and were converted to fire a 100-lb. shell and put in the field. They were subsequently replaced by the new 6-in. 26-cwt. howitzer. They did extremely good service, but they were cumbersome and their range with 120-lb. shell was only 4,800 yards, and even with the light 100-lb. shell was limited to 6,500 yards.

The only effective and utilisable gun of really heavy calibre was the solitary 9·2-in. howitzer, which could throw a 300-lb. projectile a distance of 10,000 yards.[3] This howitzer had passed its tests in June,

---

[1] Note by Secretary of State for War, 31 May, 1915, Appendix III (Hist. Rec./R/1000/120).

[2] Hist. Rec./R/1000.3/9.

[3] The 15-in. howitzers ordered in November, 1914, by Mr. Churchill, then First Lord of the Admiralty, had a similar range but fired a projectile weighing 1,450 lb. The 12-in. howitzer of improved design supplied some years later had a range of 14,500 yards. By the time of the Armistice the 60-pdr. gun could fire 15,000 yards and the 12-in. gun gave a range of 33,000 yards.

1914, and possessed outstanding value as an up-to-date model. This weapon was sent to France in November, 1914, as soon as service ammunition could be got ready for it, and served as prototype and precursor of a numerous family, being universally known in the Army by the name of " Mother."

There were available in the country, in addition to the foregoing, a certain number of obsolescent heavy guns intended for fixed emplacements, to which recourse might be had in case of necessity. Of these the 6-in. B.L. howitzers Mark I (with platform) were of importance, since they could be converted to Mark I (with carriage and limber). There were 24 converted howitzers and 36 unconverted in hand, making a total of 60 available, exclusive of those otherwise appropriated. There were also 16 6-in. B.L.C. guns, with a range of 12,000 yds., and capable, in spite of their weight, of being travelled in lorries. There was less possibility of utilising the 18 10-in./9-in. R.M.L. guns, which weighed 12 tons each, and their mountings 17 tons 10 cwt. each, though their employment in the field (siege train) was at first contemplated. The four 9·45-in. howitzers were weapons of lighter weight, acquired during the South African War, but of very unsatisfactory accuracy and range. Finally there were eight 8-in. R.M.L. howitzers, but these weapons were also unsuitable.[1]

(b) The First Orders for Guns.

During August and September, 1914, arrangements were made for a large output of field guns from the Ordnance Factories and the trade. On 8 August the Deputy Director of Ordnance Stores, Woolwich, was asked to give an " urgent extract " for 18 18-pdr. complete equipments, and by the end of the month the number had been increased to 68, for delivery by the middle of 1915.[2] Tenders were also called for from the armament firms, and on 25 August Messrs. Armstrong and Vickers were instructed to proceed with 78 18-pdrs. each. The 4·5-in. howitzer was also ordered at once, the Ordnance Factories on 13 August promised 30 complete equipments,[3] arranging with railway companies for assistance with the carriages, and on 25 August an order for 60 was given to the Coventry Ordnance Works,[4] the firm from which the first howitzers had been ordered in 1908.

During the following weeks these early orders were by successive stages greatly increased, in the hope of securing earlier and larger deliveries. By the first week in October Messrs. Vickers had undertaken to deliver 360 18-pdrs. before August, 1915, and Messrs. Armstrong 450,[5] while the Coventry Ordnance Works' order for 4·5-in. howitzers had been doubled, the whole number being promised by the end of June, 1915.[6] Thus, during the first two months of the war

---

[1] Memorandum prepared by A2, 17 September, 1914 (Hist. Rec./R/170/25).
[2] 57/3/4247.
[3] 57/3/4259 ; 73/4/6500.
[4] Contracts/G/1599.
[5] A2 Returns and Order and Supply Lists.
[6] Contracts/G/1653.

orders were placed for a total of 878 18-pdrs. and 150 4·5-in. howitzers, the bulk of the deliveries being expected during the first six months of 1915. The further expansion in orders for field guns which took place during October will be described below.[1]

In the meantime the first steps had also been taken towards the provision of heavy howitzers. At the end of August inquiries had been made of Messrs. Vickers as to the possibilities of bulk production of 9·2-in. howitzers, and on 4 September the firm were instructed to proceed with 16 complete equipments, promising first deliveries in seven months' time.[2]

In September important developments took place with regard to heavy howitzers. In the middle of the month an expert committee, known as the Siege Committee,[3] under Major-General Hickman, was called together to consider what steps should be taken to supply the artillery which might be required " in the event of the Allies being brought face to face with the fortresses on the Rhines." On 19 and 23 September the committee urged the supply of

(a) 32 heavy howitzers, firing shell of 750 lbs. or more ;

(b) 48 medium howitzers, firing shell of 300–400 lbs. or more ;

(c) 60 light howitzers (6-in.).

A certain number of the howitzers called for by this programme were already in existence. The light (6-in.) howitzers were available in sufficient numbers, though many of them would need to be converted to take a lighter shell. Towards the desired number of medium howitzers there were understood to be 18 10/9-in. R.M.L. guns which could be used, while the 17 9·2-in. howitzers (16 being on order) would also fall into this class. With regard to the very heavy howitzers, eight 15-in. howitzers, firing 1,000-lb. shell, were, it was understood, about to be ordered by the Admiralty, and these might be adopted for land service.

Additional guns would be required as well as the howitzers, ranging from 9·2 in. guns on railway mountings to 60-pdrs. Anti-aircraft guns also " would be most valuable, and as many as possible should be supplied," as well as " light armament for use in trenches,"[4] together with dial sights and instruments for the observation of fire, particularly stereoscopic telescopes.

Upon receiving the committee's report, Lord Kitchener immediately authorised the carrying out of the programme laid down. Preliminary estimates were submitted by the Master-General of the Ordnance, which placed the cost at over £3,000,000, and indicated that the outlook for delivery was unpromising. He asked for a further ruling as to " the desirability and necessity of providing on the scale recommended," and hesitated to embark on these big orders until it was definitely clear that the policy outlined was to be adopted. The principal

---

[1] See below, p. 93.
[2] Contracts/G/1624 and 1711.
[3] See above, p. 16.
[4] Such as 10-pdr. or 2·75-in. B.L. guns equipped with overhead and frontal shields.

difficulties were the uncertainty of the period required for delivery, not only of guns but still more of ammunition, which was likely to lag behind the guns. " All the manufacturers of big shell are busily engaged in supplying the wants of the Navy as well as ourselves, and it may have to be a matter for the Cabinet to decide whether any of the naval requirements can possibly be delayed in order to give us the ammunition for these siege artillery." On 1 October Lord Kitchener, having ascertained that the French Minister for War thought it very advisable for the British Army to secure such equipment with a view to attacking the fortified positions then being organised by the Germans, gave peremptory instructions for the ordering of all the necessary material " to proceed with all dispatch." Orders were promptly given for 32 12-in. B.L. howitzers and mountings,[1] and the existing order for 16 9·2-in. B.L. howitzers and mountings was doubled.[2]

On the same day (5 October) Messrs. Armstrong and Vickers were each instructed to proceed with 36 60-pdr. complete equipments, an order for 18 having already, in September, been given to the Ordnance Factories.

Subsequent developments with regard to heavy howitzers may be briefly outlined here. In addition to the placing of orders, investigations were made into the possibilities of providing heavy guns immediately, it being understood that G.H.Q. would welcome any long-range weapons which could be provided in anticipation of the output from new orders. Early in October the Chief Superintendent of Ordnance Factories suggested that 9·2-in. guns might be cut down into 12-in. howitzers,[3] and this course was provisionally approved, but on 14 October the Siege Committee recommended the conversion of 6-in. guns into 8-in. howitzers, and at the beginning of November the Ordnance Factories were asked to alter one gun and manufacture a carriage. Subsequently, following a decision of the Siege Committee to use 8-in. howitzers instead of the 10-in./9-in. guns previously contemplated, arrangements were made for the conversion of 23 6-in. guns which were immediately available, without awaiting the completion of the experimental equipment, and in December the Ordnance Factories were instructed to proceed with 12 guns, the trade undertaking the remaining 11.[4] All these converted howitzers had been delivered by May, 1915, and more were put in hand.

By the beginning of 1915 urgent demands were being received from G.H.Q. for long-range weapons to keep down the enemy's artillery fire, and by arrangement with the Admiralty the 15-in. howitzers ordered by the latter, the first of which was proved at the end of 1914, were put into the field as rapidly as possible. Two had been issued to service by the end of February, 1915, one was delivered in March, one in April, and one in June. The first deliveries of 9·2-in. howitzers took place in February, and of 12-in. howitzers in May.[5]

---

[1] Contracts/A/1608 (5/10/14).   [4] 75/3/8015, 8019, 8024, 8027, 8037.
[2] Contracts/G/1746 (31/10/14).   [5] Hist. Rec./R/1000/73 ; H/1200/7.
[3] Ordnance Board Minutes, 11593.

In the autumn of 1914 a design had been called for 'of a mobile howitzer to replace the 6-in. 30 cwt. The essential requirements for the new howitzer were a range of 10,000 yards and a weight not exceeding that of the 60-pdr. gun. In answer to this demand Messrs. Vickers produced the design of the 6-in. 26 cwt. howitzer, which was approved. The manufacture of one trial equipment was hurried on, and early in February an order for four was given, twelve more being promised in April.[1]

III. Supplies of Ammunition.

(a) STOCKS AVAILABLE AT THE OUTBREAK OF WAR.

During the years immediately preceding the outbreak of war the manufacture of gun ammunition was on the minimum scale of peace requirements. The prescribed war reserves were assumed to be adequate for the purpose of keeping the field army supplied during a short campaign, or until manufacturing resources sufficient for the replacement of wastage could be developed. The actual distribution of these reserves was approximately as follows :—

| | Rounds per Gun. | | | |
	With Units.	For Lines of Communication.	Mowatt Stores.	Total.
13-pdr.	546	230	1,124	1,900
18-pdr.	528	250	742	1,520
4·5-in.	280	520	400	1,200
60-pdr.	250	250	500	1,000

The ammunition shown under the head of Mowatt stores, unlike the supplies carried by units or reserved for lines of communication, was not entirely held as filled ammunition, but, as regards three-quarters of the total amount, as empty components, ammunition for columns not formed being held in the form of components.

The amount of ammunition available was, in fact, in the case of the 13-pdr. and 18-pdr. ammunition, somewhat larger than that here indicated, since provision was made for batteries in the Colonies and for unallotted batteries.

The 18-pdr. and 13-pdr. ammunition consisted exclusively of shrapnel. In the case of the 4·5 in. and 60-pdr., approximately one-third of the total consisted of lyddite shell.

---

[1] HIST. REC./R/1000/118 ; 94/G/128.

The total·supplies of available ammunition on the above basis were as shown in the following statement :—[1]

	Filled	Empty	Total
18-pdr. Q.F.—			
Shrapnel	332,919	213,561	546,480
Additional rounds subsequently received with Divisions from India ..	108,000	—	108,000
13-pdr. Q.F.—			
Shrapnel	60,456	34,944	95,400
4·5-in. Q.F. Howitzer—			
Shrapnel	64,800	21,600	86,400
Lyddite	32,400	10,800	43.200
60-pdr. B.L.—			
Shrapnel	10,500	6,300	16,800
Lyddite	4,500	2,700	7,200
Total—			
Shrapnel	576,675	276,405	853,080
Lyddite	36,900	13,500	50,400
	613,575	289,905	903,480

For the heavy ordnance the following ammunition was immediately available.[2]

6-in. Howitzer—		
Lyddite		
Light Shell	800	
Heavy ,, ...	18,400	
Shrapnel	1,800	
	21,000	
6-in. B.L.C. gun—		
Lyddite	2,400	
Shrapnel	5,600	
	8,000	
6-in. B.L. Mark VII—		
Lyddite	1,800	

[1] Hist. Rec./R/1200.1/3.
[2] Statements by A1 and A2, dated 17 September, 1914 (Hist. Rec./R/170/25).

(b) The First Shell Orders.

During the first two months of the war large orders were placed for shell for the new types of field guns—13-pdr., 18-pdr. and 60-pdr. guns and 4·5-in. howitzer—and some supplies were also arranged for the older types with which the Territorial Army was equipped—the 15-pdr. and 4·7-in. guns and 5-in. howitzer. Small orders were also given for 6-in. and 9·2-in. lyddite shell, but heavy shell were not ordered on a large scale until October.

During this early period, orders for the various components of a shell were placed separately, and though some firms made fuses and cartridge cases as well as shell bodies, the minor components were as a rule ordered from firms who did not undertake shell cases. The shell were assembled at Woolwich, and the correlation of the supply of components in itself presented a formidable problem. There were, however, a few British firms who had made " complete rounds " of shell before the war, and in the late autumn of 1914 a few orders for complete rounds of 18-pdr. shell were arranged.

On the outbreak of war immediate provision was made for increased output from the Ordnance Factories. Deliveries were still outstanding on orders for 18-pdr. shrapnel given in April 1913 and April 1914, and by the end of August an additional 200,000 of this nature had been promised, as well as 11,000 15-pdr. and 6,000 13-pdr. shell. Orders were also given for 4,600 4·5-in. H.E. and 9,500 shrapnel and for 2,800 60-pdr. shrapnel.

On 5 August, demands were passed to the Contracts Department for the following quantities of shell :—408,000 18-pdr. shrapnel, 12,000 13-pdr. shrapnel, 5,600 60-pdr. shrapnel, 2,400 60-pdr. lyddite, 47,000 4·5-in. shrapnel and 9,400 4·5-in. lyddite. On 11 August, demands were made for 21,800 15-pdr. shrapnel and 20,000 5-in. shrapnel, and on 14 August for 7,800 9·2-in. lyddite or H.E. The original demand for 4·5-in. lyddite was increased on 16 August, those for 15-pdr. and 5-in. shrapnel on 28 August, and for 13-pdr., 4·5-in. and 60-pdr. shrapnel on 1 September.

Tenders were immediately called for from the recognised War Office contractors for shell, and during August and the early part of September the following quantities were ordered :—22,000 13-pdr. shrapnel ; 119,800 15-pdr. shrapnel ; 620,000 18-pdr. shrapnel ; 11,500 60-pdr. shrapnel ; 2,400 60-pdr. lyddite ; 91,500 4·5-in. shrapnel ; 45,400 4·5-in. lyddite or H.E. ; 30,000 5-in. howitzer shrapnel ; 7,800 9·2-in. H.E. ; and 33,770 6-in. lyddite. Orders were also placed for 9·2-in. and 6-in. A.P. shell ; 4-in. lyddite or H.E. ; 2·75-in. shrapnel ; 12 and 14-pdr. lyddite ; and 10-pdr. shrapnel.

These orders, which were for the most part due for completion by the end of 1914 or the early months of 1915, were distributed among the following contractors :—Messrs. Firth, Hadfield, Vickers, Armstrong, Watson Laidlaw, Cammell Laird, Beardmore, and the Projectile Company. Of these firms Messrs. Hadfield undertook only 9·2-in. and 6-in. A.P. shell, Messrs. Watson Laidlaw only 5-in. shrapnel,

Messrs. Beardmore only 60-pdr. shrapnel, and Messrs. Firth 9·2-in. and 6-in. A.P., 4·5-in. and 60-pdr. shrapnel; but Messrs. Vickers, Armstrong, Cammell Laird and the Projectile Company each accepted large orders for several different types of shell. Messrs. Armstrong, for instance, undertook 9·2-in. A.P. and H.E., 6-in. lyddite, 5-in. shrapnel, 4·5-in. lyddite, 4-in. lyddite, 60-pdr. lyddite, 18-pdr. shrapnel, 15-pdr. shrapnel and 10-pdr. shrapnel. Their total orders amounted to 415,000 shell, of which 346,700 were light shrapnel shell (below 4-in.), and of their 13 contracts 4 only were due for completion later than March 1915.

This brief review serves to indicate the way in which demands for shell were piled up during the first weeks of the war, necessitating rapid multiplication of orders with the few British firms capable of giving an early output.

At the same time the possibility was not neglected of supplementing the output of these firms by supplies from overseas. On 12 August, 1914, the Bethlehem Steel Company of America offered to supply guns or shell to the War Office, and shortly afterwards a representative of the company, Mr. Schwab, came over to England at Lord Kitchener's request to discuss the matter. Negotiations proceeded for some weeks, and in the middle of October contracts were concluded for 100,000 18-pdr. shrapnel shell and 30,000 4·7-in. shrapnel and 30,000 H.E.[1]

Before this, arrangements had been made for supplies from Canada. At the end of August enquiries had been made as to the possibility of obtaining empty 18-pdr. shrapnel from Canada, or through the Canadian Government from the United States, and on 2 September, as a result of a meeting of manufacturers, an offer to make shell in Canada was cabled to the War Office.[2] On 19 September, a contract for 100,000 18-pdr. shrapnel and 100,000 15-pdr. shrapnel shell was concluded with the Canadian Shell Committee, which had been set up to obtain supplies from the Dominion.[3] The shell were to be without bursting charges or fuses, and delivery was to begin in November and be complete by February, 1915. Towards the end of the year further large contracts were given to Canada for 18-pdr. shrapnel, a proportion being promised in the shape of complete rounds, and later on 18-pdr. H.E. and 4·5-in. H.E. were also ordered, over 10,000,000 shell having been ordered from Canada at the time of the establishment of the Ministry of Munitions.

At the beginning of October, 1914, also, the War Office accepted an offer from India to send home monthly consignments of 13-pdr. and 18-pdr. shrapnel shell. This contribution, though small in quantity, was particularly valuable, for the Indian Ordnance Factories were able to produce complete rounds of shell.[4]

---

[1] Contracts/Firms B/3394, Contracts /S/7022, 6972.
[2] 57/Gen.No./3588.
[3] HIST. REC./H/1142/7.
[4] Contracts/S/16332. 121/Stores/230.

IV. The Supply of Small Arms.

(a) MACHINE GUNS.

On the outbreak of war the only machine guns which were available were Maxim and Vickers. Of the former a small number could be produced or converted at the Royal Small Arms Factory, Enfield. The gun was, in fact, obsolescent, but those in service were retained, and spare parts and accessories were produced at Enfield, where a small number of new guns were also made during the first two years of the war.[1] Messrs. Vickers had a monopoly of their type of gun, which could only be made at their Erith works. In August, 1914, the Lewis gun was in process of development, and the Birmingham Small Arms Company were making experimental guns for the Armes Automatiques Lewis, and were contemplating production on a manufacturing scale.

During August and September, 1914, a total of 1,792 guns were ordered from Messrs. Vickers.[2] The first order, dated 11 August, was for 192 guns ; the second, on 10 September, for 100, full deliveries on both being due by the end of the year. On 19 September a larger order for 1,000 guns was given. These were to be delivered at the rate of 50 a week, to be completed in April, 1915, and by a further order given on 26 September, this production was to be followed by an output of 500 guns at the same rate, deliveries continuing until June, 1915. In October permission was given the firm to lay down plant for making 50 guns a week for the French Government, provided that the output for the War Office should not thereby be delayed.[3] Proposals for continuation orders were under consideration from December onwards, but no definite arrangement was made until after the establishment of the Ministry of Munitions.[4] Messrs. Vickers were considerably in arrears on their contracts. The first contract for 192 guns was due for completion by 19 November, but 21 guns were then undelivered[5] ; their second contract was a fortnight late in completion. At the beginning of June, 1915, 468 guns were overdue on the third contract for 1,000.

With regard to Lewis guns, 10 had been purchased just before the war broke out, and a further 45 were ordered in August for the Air Service.[6] In September supplies were also arranged for the general service. On 5 September telegraphic inquiries were sent by the War Office to the Birmingham Small Arms Company asking them to quote for 100 Lewis guns. The enquiry was referred to the Armes Automatiques Lewis, the number required was verbally amended to 200, and delivery of 100 in October and 100 in November was promised, the manufacture

---

[1] HIST. REC./H/1122/101.

[2] Contracts/G/1566, 1609, 1669 ; 94/G/7, 11.

[3] HIST. REC./R/1000/119.

[4] At the end of May, 1915, a contract was arranged through Messrs. Vickers with an American firm, Messrs. Colt, but was subsequently cancelled in favour of a Russian order.

[5] Contracts/G/1766.

[6] 77/6/4420.

being undertaken by the Birmingham Small Arms Company.[1] Subsequently, orders on a larger scale were arranged. Before the end of 1914 an additional 400 had been promised, and another 400 were ordered in March, 1915, while in May negotiations began for the production of 2,000 guns, a contract for which was placed in June, 1915.[2] In the case of these guns also there was considerable delay in reaching the anticipated rate of delivery. The Birmingham Small Arms Company had hoped to be producing 100 guns a week by May, 1915, but their deliveries during that month averaged only 36 a week.

(b) Rifles.

The sources of supply for rifles at the outbreak of war were three— the Enfield Royal Small Arms Factory, the Birmingham Small Arms Company, and the London Small Arms Company. Instructions were immediately given for the maximum output to be worked up to as rapidly as possible. The full capacity of Enfield was about 3,000 a week. The Birmingham Small Arms Company had just before the war been producing about 700 a week ; by working night shifts they hoped, on existing plant, to give a weekly output of nearly 4,000 by December, 1914. The London Small Arms Company had been turning out 250 a week, and they estimated their maximum capacity with night shift at 1,200 a week.

Instructions were at once given to the Birmingham Small Arms Company to increase their plant in order to give an output of 6,000 a week by May, 1915, and shortly afterwards a further expansion was arranged for to give 8,000 a week by July. The London Small Arms Company also undertook to lay down new plant and increase their output to 1,500 a week by January, 1915.[3]

These orders were all for the standard rifle, the R.S.M.L.E. Mark III, sighted for use with Mark VII ammunition. There were also in existence, in the hands of Territorial troops, a number of rifles sighted for Mark VI. ammunition, and in September, 1914, when it was realised that it was necessary at once to increase to the maximum limits the number of service rifles available for the Expeditionary Force, the Birmingham Small Arms Company undertook to convert 150,000 of these to take Mark VII ammunition. The firm had already undertaken to convert 40,000 of the original short rifle, known as M.L.E. Mark I, most of the rifles of this type in existence having already been converted to a pattern known as Mark I***. The supply of rifles to the firm for conversion was never maintained at the full rate,[4] and in April, 1915, the issue of rifles for re-sighting was suspended.

A large expansion in the orders for new rifles took place in the late autumn of 1914, and again in the spring of 1915. Some account of these developments will be given elsewhere.[5]

---

[1] Contracts/G/1634.

[2] Contracts/G/1634, 2303.

[3] Hist. Rec./R/1000/119.

[4] In November, 30,000 were diverted to Enfield, as the B.S.A. Co.'s deliveries were in arrears and the rifles were urgently needed to equip troops under orders to proceed to France (Contracts/R/2159).

[5] See below, p. 97.

CHAPTER IV.

SUPPLY POLICY AND ADMINISTRATION, AUGUST TO DECEMBER, 1914.

I. The Cabinet Committee on Munitions.

(a) APPOINTMENT OF THE COMMITTEE.

The gravity of the whole question of munitions supplies was recognised by the Government at a very early date, and steps were taken to give all possible Ministerial support to the War Office in the discharge of this task. A Cabinet Committee, consisting of :—

The Secretary of State for War (Lord Kitchener),
The Lord Chancellor (Lord Haldane),
The Chancellor of the Exchequer (Mr. Lloyd George).
First Lord of the Admiralty (Mr. Churchill),
The Home Secretary (Mr. McKenna),
The President of the Board of Trade (Mr. Runciman),
The President of the Board of Agriculture (Lord Lucas),

was appointed to supervise the steps taken in regard to munitions supply. This Committee met six times between 12 October and 1 January, and took the initiative in the more important questions of policy and procedure which arose.

In giving some account of the various questions dealt with by the Committee it will be convenient to indicate also the developments which followed their decisions.

(b) MEETINGS OF 12 AND 13 OCTOBER : THE SUPPLY OF FIELD GUNS.

At the first meeting on 12 October the Committee considered the extended provision of guns for the use of the New Armies, and at the suggestion of Mr. Churchill and Mr. Lloyd George decided upon the ordering of 3,000 18-pdr. guns, to be produced before the month of May, 1915. Orders had already been placed for 892 guns, the bulk of which were anticipated to be available by June, 1915. Mr. Lloyd George considered that the armament firms might be called upon to extend their operations by sub-contracting, or that, if necessary, the entire works of large engineering firms should be taken over and converted to munitions production. Representatives of the gun-making firms were summoned, therefore, to attend on the following day.

At the same time a message was despatched to an officer in America, instructing him to ascertain the maximum output which could be secured from firms capable of manufacturing field guns or rifles to a total of 1,500 18-pdr. guns, and half a million rifles. A reply to this enquiry showed that there was little hope of securing additional output from that source before September, 1915.

The campaign thus opened for securing a single type of gun was to be regarded as a test case.   Should it be found possible to place orders on the scale indicated and within the period mentioned, other supplies, including shells and fuses, could be secured in like manner.

On 13 October, Sir Frederick Donaldson, Chief Superintendent of Ordnance Factories, Mr. Saxton Noble (Messrs. Armstrong), Sir Trevor Dawson (Messrs. Vickers), Admiral Bacon (Coventry Ordnance Works), and a representative of Messrs. Beardmore, met the Committee. On receiving the Government's promise that the capital required for extension would be found, and that they would be fully compensated for any consequential loss, they undertook to extend their output by every practicable means.

The results of this meeting are indicated below.

Aggregate Orders Before and After the Cabinet Committee's Meetings.

		Before.	After.
12-in. How.	Vickers ..	8	8
	Armstrong	24	24
		32	32
9·2-in. How.	Vickers ..	16	32
60-pdr. ..	Ordnance Factories	18	36
	Vickers ..	36	36
	Armstrong	36	36
		90	108
4·5-in. How.	Ordnance Factories	30	80
	Coventry Ordnance Wks.	120	300
		150	380
18-pdr. ..	Ordnance Factories	68	168
	Vickers ..	360	640
	Armstrong	450	700
	Beardmore	Nil.	100
		878	1,608

Deliveries on these orders were in all cases to be completed not later than August, 1915.

Under the auspices of the Cabinet Committee attempts were made to carry still further the promised expansion of output, particularly in the case of 18-pdr. guns.   By the end of October, Messrs. Vickers had agreed to undertake a total of 1,010 18-pdrs., and to do their best to produce 1,000 before 1 July, 1915.   They would not, however, quote rates of delivery for any guns in excess of the 640 they promised at the conference on 13 October.   Messrs. Armstrong promised 850

18-pdr. guns by the end of June, 1915, and a further 150 during July. In the middle of November also a contract was concluded with the Bethlehem Steel Company, of America, for 200 18-pdrs., delivery to be completed by 30 June, 1915.[1] At the end of October, the Coventry Ordnance Works were induced to undertake a further 150 4·5-in. howitzers. They were urged to promise the whole 450 for which they had contracted by the end of June, 1915, but they refused to guarantee more than 300 by that date. No further orders for 18-pdr. guns or 4·5-in. howitzers were given until, at the end of 1914, the continuation of the firms' output on the conclusion of their existing orders was arranged for. These continuation orders arose from a decision early in December to make provision for the equipment of an additional million men over and above the number required for the six New Armies. The position with regard to guns is indicated by the following minute addressed by the Master-General of the Ordnance to the Director of Artillery and the Director of Contracts on 14 December.[2]

" With reference to further orders for all natures of guns in the Field.

Taking the 18-pdr. first. Including the eight Divisions of Expeditionary Force, two Indian Divisions, the 27th, 28th and 29th [Divisions] and six new Armies, we shall require 2,386 guns. Of these 702 were provided without touching the new orders, leaving 1,684 required out of the 2,478 new orders. Thus there will be 794 spares, just about enough to act as a reserve.

We must now begin to prepare for 7th and subsequent New Armies. I spoke to Secretary of State to-day, he decided that 1,000 more 18-pdr. guns should be legislated for, *i.e.*, the orders should be placed in time for the present manufacture to continue at the rate of production, which will be in force next June. Would you please consider the best means of doing this, not only for 18-pdr. guns but also for the other natures."

Letters were accordingly addressed on 18 December to Messrs. Armstrong and Vickers, the Coventry Ordnance Works and Messrs. Beardmore, enquiring whether they would be willing to continue output of 18-pdr. 4·5-in. and 60-pdr. B.L. equipment after the existing orders had been completed.

Some anxiety was expressed by the Contracts Department as to the possibility of finding additional firms to assist with the necessary work. The Assistant-Director of Artillery reported, however, that there were no other firms capable of undertaking these orders and that the firms already employed were keeping " fairly well " up to date with deliveries. Accordingly on 11 January 1915, telegraphic instructions were sent to Messrs. Armstrong and Vickers to proceed with 450 18-pdr. equipments each, delivery to follow on that of existing orders, while 70 18-pdrs. were also ordered from Messrs. Beardmore and 200 4·5-in. from the Coventry Ordnance Works.

---

[1] A second order for 50 18-pdrs. and 100 13-pdrs. was given to the Bethlehem Company in June, 1915. Hist. Rec./H/1141/6.

[2] Contracts/G/2031.

(c) MEETING OF 20 OCTOBER : PROPELLANT SUPPLIES.

At the third meeting of the Cabinet Committee on 20 October, 1914, the question of cordite supplies was discussed. It was reported that on the outbreak of war the Admiralty had instructed the seven regular trade contractors to increase output up to the maximum possible from their existing plant. The rifle cordite plant at the Royal Gunpowder Factory was being extended under orders given in September. Of this increased supply, 1,000 tons due for delivery between November, 1914, and March, 1915, together with deliveries due on pre-war orders, was allocated to the Army. This arrangement had been sanctioned by Mr. Churchill on 14 October on grounds of general policy, since it was recognised that this concession would interfere with the long prepared plans of the Admiralty. After March, 1915, the War Office would have to rely on output from the contemplated extensions at Waltham Abbey and at contractors' works, as the Admiralty claimed the whole of the trade output from existing plant from that date. Negotiations had already been initiated at the War Office with Messrs. Nobel with a view to the erection of a new self-contained and State-aided factory at a cost of £400,000. Sir Frederic Nathan, who had previously served as a superintendent at Waltham Abbey, was present to represent the firm. He was questioned as to the possibility of expediting increase of output from the new factory, the anticipated date being given as September, 1915. He explained that everything possible was being done to expedite the installation of the new plant, but that at best it would require from six to nine months to secure output, a complete unit, including an acid plant, being necessary.

On 26 October, 1914, in view of the unsatisfactory character of the situation, the cordite manufacturers were summoned to a conference with Lord Kitchener. Representatives of Messrs. Nobel's Explosives Company, Chilworth Gunpowder Company, Curtis's and Harvey, the National Explosives Company, the New Explosive Company and Messrs. Kynoch attended—the latter not having been engaged on Government orders for some years prior to the war—and gave undertakings as to the additional output for which they would be responsible, subject to the provision of increased capacity. The Secretary of State undertook to assist in meeting capital expenditure involved in such extensions.

As a result of the above conference all firms were instructed to lay down new plant, and in the case of Messrs. Kynoch two further extensions were subsequently authorised in 1915, the last of these extensions not being expected to fructify before January, 1916.

In view of the steady expansion in the requirements of the two Services, the situation continued to cause anxiety. It was recognised not only that it would be necessary for the Admiralty to erect a national factory, but to arrange for further particular extensions unless the War Office were able to provide additional supplies.

Accordingly, Mr. Churchill, on 15 December, authorised negotiations for further extensions from Messrs. Curtis's and Harvey, Nobel's Explosives Company, the Cotton Powder Company and Messrs.

Nobel's, and a meeting with War Office representatives was held in the First Lord's room on 24 December, 1914.

Four days later Lord Moulton, who was then organising the supply of high explosives,[1] was called into conference in order to prevent the proposed extension of Messrs. Nobel's from interfering with the increased output of high explosives which was being organised by that firm. The matter was further discussed on 1 and 6 January, and on 25 January, 1915, Mr. Churchill gave instructions that proposals should be submitted for the erection of a naval cordite factory, and on 22 February discussed with Lord Moulton the question of unifying production for the two Services. On the same day he wrote to Lord Kitchener suggesting that Lord Moulton should take over propellants of all kinds as well as high explosive : " and let us have a large and guaranteed scheme of action."

On the following day Lord Moulton informed the Master-General of the Ordnance that arrangements had been made for him to take over derelict works at Queen's Ferry, Cheshire, and it was decided on Lord Kitchener's authority that Lord Moulton should do what he could to provide increased output for the Army in addition to naval requirements.

Shortly afterwards the Admiralty appointed Sir Frederic Nathan to advise on naval cordite production, and it was decided early in March to erect a cordite factory for naval supplies at Poole. The raw material for this factory (guncotton) would be temporarily manufactured at Queen's Ferry, and upon Mr. Churchill's authority the Admiralty secured the Queen's Ferry site on 27 March, 1915. It was anticipated that the Poole factory would be in full working order at the beginning of 1916.

In addition to these British supplies orders had been placed with the Hercules Powder Company of the United States of America for an output rising to 500 tons per month from January, 1916. The Japanese Government had promised a small supply from stock in May, 1915, and the Indian Government a small monthly output from April, 1915. An order for nitro-cellulose powder was also placed with an American firm, Messrs. du Pont de Nemours, in order to make good the deficiency in cordite supply, an extended agreement being executed in March, 1915.[2]

(d) MEETING OF 21 OCTOBER : THE SUPPLY OF RIFLES.

The Cabinet Committee met for the fourth time on 21 October and discussed the supply of rifles. The Master-General of the Ordnance stated that on the orders already placed 781,000 rifles were promised by 1 July, 1915. The Committee decided that steps should be taken to increase this total by 400,000. The chairman of the Birmingham Small Arms Company, Sir Hallewell Rogers, who was present at the meeting was asked if his increased rate of output could not be accelerated. He replied that the chief difficulty was the shortage of skilled labour required to make fixings, jigs and gauges.

---

[1] See below p. 110.　　[2] For further details, see Vol. X, Part IV.

In order to carry out the instructions of the Cabinet Committee, extensions of plant were arranged at Enfield to increase the weekly output to 5,750 ; the London Small Arms Company were induced to promise an increase from 1,500 to 2,000 a week by June, 1915 ; Messrs. Vickers, who had been considering the manufacture of rifles before the war and had put forward a new model, were given an order, promising 2,000 a week in July, 1915 and 3,000 in November ; and a new firm, the Standard Small Arms Company, was given financial assistance to enable it to start rifle manufacture, promising 1,250 a week in June, 1915.

The lárgest new orders, however, were those placed in America. An order had already, in September, been given to the Ross Rifle Company of Canada for 100,000 rifles, while early in October inquiries had been made in the United States. In November, agreements were concluded with the Winchester Arms Company and the Remington Arms Union Metallic Cartridge Company for 200,000 rifles each, first deliveries at the rate of 1,000 a day being promised for about July, 1915. A further contract was later arranged with the Winchester Company for an increase of 300 a day from March, 1916; and in February, 1915, the Remington Company received a second order for 200,000, deliveries at the rate of 500 a day to begin in November, 1915. In April, 1915, an order for 1,500,000 was placed with the Remington Arms Company, a separate company organised by the Remington Arms Union Metallic Cartridge Company, first deliveries being promised for February, 1916.

These American orders represented the principal expansion during the first part of 1915. A proposal put forward in March, to extend Enfield to produce 12,000 a week was dropped owing to labour shortage and housing difficulties. The Birmingham Small Arms Company, however, in April, promised an increase of 4,000 a week, bringing their total weekly output up to 12,000.[1]

(e) MEETING WITH ARMAMENT FIRMS, 23 OCTOBER : PROPOSALS FOR CO-OPERATION.

At the meeting of the Cabinet Committee on 21 October, it was decided that Lord Kitchener should see representatives of the armament firms and ascertain whether they would be willing to form a committee similar to the Railway Executive Committee, possibly with the addition of members of other engineering firms.

On 23 October the Committee met again and discussed the whole question of the organisation of trade resources. It was reported that representatives of the armament firms had agreed to act as a committee. The question whether the Government should take over the commercial control of the firms was under consideration, but it was decided that for the time being all that was necessary was for the allocation of orders to be arranged by the firms' representative committee, but that prices and finance would be arranged individually and confidentially as hitherto.

---

[1] For further details, see Vol. XI, Part IV.

(f) MEETINGS OF 23 DECEMBER AND 1 JANUARY, 1915.

The Committee did not meet again until 23 December. The discussion on that day dealt with the position of Lord Moulton's Committee on High Explosives,[1] the co-ordination of Army and Navy requirements, and the supply of labour. The last point arose in connection with the report of a conference on shell supplies held on 21 December, and the recommendations of the Committee are dealt with below.[2]

The last meeting of the Committee was held on 1 January, to discuss the proposed appointment of Messrs. Morgan as Purchasing Agents in the United States. The terms to be arranged with the firm were provisionally agreed to at this meeting, and a formal agreement was signed on 15 January.[3]

II. The Supply Policy of the War Office.

In the preceding pages an attempt has been made to outline the principal developments connected with the administration of the supply of munitions from the outbreak of war to the end of 1914 ; to show the kind of difficulties with which the War Office had to contend, as instanced by the supply of small arms ammunition ; to describe the steps which were taken to secure supplies of the principal stores upon the outbreak of war, and the subsequent expansion under the auspices of the Cabinet Committee on Munitions. The story is mainly concerned with the supply of guns and ammunition, because the problems raised by the necessity of providing, on an unprecedented scale, artillery and shell of old and new types were the most formidable by which the War Office were faced. Moreover, it was primarily the breakdown of the War Office arrangements for supplying ammunition which led, through the movement for the organisation of local resources, to the establishment of the Ministry of Munitions.

At this point, before proceeding to give some account of the breakdown of supply in the spring of 1915, it will be well to pause and consider in greater detail what was the policy upon which the War Office had acted in regard to the supply of munitions.

(a) RELIANCE UPON THE ARMAMENT FIRMS.

It has been seen that during the first two months of the war orders for gun ammunition were placed on a large scale with the armament firms, and supplies from overseas were also arranged.

During this early period, moreover, the Contracts Department of the War Office was inundated with offers of assistance from British firms, and there was a general desire throughout the country that additional firms should be allowed to compete for the privilege of supplying the Army. The eagerness of these applications was naturally accentuated by the extent of dislocation of normal industry

---

[1] See below, p. 110.
[2] See below, p. 125.
[3] For details of the Morgan Agreement, see Vol. II, Part III.

caused by the outbreak of war. The War Department was very ready
to utilise such assistance, with the proviso that the firms were competent
to satisfy the normal contract conditions; in other words, that they
were prepared to tender on equal terms with the expert armament
firms. Firms whose equipment was not adequate for the production
of complete munitions in the normal way could thus not obtain direct
contracts for any of the more important types of munitions. They
were, therefore, virtually restricted either to the supply of subsidiary
munitions and accessories or to sub-contracting for the firms able to
undertake the principal contracts.

In October, when the Cabinet Committee in considering the question
of munitions supply decided on a large expansion of gun orders, it
became clear that an enormous extension of the shell manufacturing
capacity of the country would be required, and that this extended
demand would involve the mobilisation of a large number of firms
which had not hitherto had experience of munitions production, and
which would require assistance, not only with equipment and buildings,
but still more with technical advice and supervision.

How was this supervision to be secured? There was at that time
a small expert staff under the Chief Inspector at Woolwich fully competent to advise on manufacturing requirements, but this staff was
already overwhelmed in the endeavour to cope with its immediate
work in connection with output from existing sources. The Chief Superintendent of Ordnance Factories equally found his staff overburdened
with current production, and the most that he could undertake was to
facilitate visits of inspection by representatives of contracting firms.

It was thus decided to adopt the policy of utilising the resources
and knowledge of the armament firms themselves to the uttermost, and
to rely upon them to arrange for the allocation of work among inexperienced firms, and for the consequent co-ordination in the flow of the
products of manufacture, and thus to decentralise a task which
threatened to overwhelm the capacity of the War Office or the Royal
Ordnance Factories.

" It was decided that in the first instance it was best to place
orders with the usual armament firms to the extent of which their
managers thought they were capable. It was most necessary,
especially in connection with the fuses, that the requisite supervising staff with its experience should be not only fully utilised,
but utilised to the best advantage. The system more or less
followed was to take the most difficult component, viz. the fuse,
first, and when orders had been placed for the fuses, then orders to
balance up the remaining components were entered into. The full
output of the armament firms having been taken up, further orders
were given for such components of ammunition to such other firms
as had works which were considered capable of undertaking them
and financial assistance was given them for providing necessary
plant.

" The necessity of organising all the trade resources for supplying our wants was fully recognised at this period, but it was
considered that instead of attempting to organise centrally from

the War Office it was much better that the main orders should be given to the Ordnance Factories and the large armament firms, and that they should themselves organise and expand to supplement what they could do with existing buildings and machinery."[1]

The policy of relying upon the armament firms in the matter of expanded output was not adopted without deliberation. A Cabinet mission was sent to France to enquire into the measures adopted for the organisation of private industry in that country for the manufacture of gun ammunition and artillery. On 18 October, Mr. Lloyd George, Sir John Simon and Lord Reading conferred with General St. Clair Deville, the inventor of the 75-mm. gun, and Captain Cambefort, a Lyons manufacturer. It was found that the French had been enabled to extend production among private firms by reason of their extensive initial resources in the possession of numerous arsenals and technical personnel. The plan which had been adopted at the end of September was to divide France into districts, each under the direction of a prominent engineering employer. The district undertook a contract collectively, and the work was distributed among the firms according to their capacity. By the middle of October some private firms were already turning out shell, and a rapid increase of production was expected. These developments afforded a valuable and suggestive example of the expansion of output that might be secured by decentralised organisation. The lead thus given was of importance as stimulating the movement for local area organisation. The weight of expert opinion was, however, unfavourable at this time, on the ground that the established armament manufacturers alone possessed the requisite technical capacity, and that the introduction of new firms could best be achieved under their tutelage by means of sub-contracts. Thus the project was suffered to remain in abeyance until the beginning of 1915.

On 21 April, 1915,[2] Mr. Lloyd George describing the results of this investigation, said :—

" At the beginning of October the problem was realised by France as well as by ourselves. . . We had a committee to consider what should be done to extend our machinery for the purpose of turning out cannon, rifles, and ammunition. I had a report from France of what had been done there. That report was presented to the War Office, and there was a committee appointed to organise the resources of this country to the best of their ability.

" The experts advised that the best method of doing that was, in the first instance, to extend sub-contracting. That was the experts' opinion, as it was undoubtedly the opinion of the armament firms, and I think they gave a perfectly honest opinion. I do not believe they were doing it merely in their own interests. There was a good deal to be said for that view, because it is highly technical work, it is very difficult work, and it is skilled work.

---

[1] Memorandum by the Master-General of the Ordnance (HIST. REC./R/1000/ No. 119, p. 8).

[2] *Parliamentary Debates* (1915), *H. of C.*, LXXI, 315.

Although there are no better engineers in the world than you have in this country, these firms were without any experience at all of the kind of work the War Office required to be done. So it was thought better that the armament firms, who had got men accustomed to this class of work, should parcel out, as it were, the parts of the work which could be done even by inexperienced firms, leaving to themselves the more difficult and more delicate work, and also leaving to themselves the putting together of the various parts."

The policy adopted by the War Office thus falls under two heads :— (1) the expansion of the regular armament work by means of subsidies granted by the Government ; and (2) the extension of the usual system by which the chief armament contractors gave sub-contracts for single parts or processes to ordinary engineering firms.

(b) SUBSIDISED EXPANSION OF ARMAMENT WORKS.

Some idea of the nature of the demand made upon the armament firms, and of the successive stages by which that demand was increased, can be gained from a study of the early orders for a single nature of shell—the 18-pdr.—placed with one of the principal firms, Messrs. Armstrong, Whitworth.

At the outbreak of war, a contract for 18-pdr. shrapnel shell had just been placed with this firm (31 July, 1914). Their first war order was placed on 18 August, and was for 162,000 shrapnel shell. This was superseded on 30 August by a contract for 300,000 shell,[1] earlier orders for cartridge cases and No. 80 fuses being correspondingly increased.[2] The weekly output was to work up to 15,000 by December, 1914, and the whole quantity was due for delivery by March, 1915. In October, the Assistant Director of Artillery made verbal arrangements with the firm to proceed with a further 400,000 shell, cartridge cases and fuses, for delivery on completion of the earlier order. The weekly output of 15,000 already promised was to be increased to 35,000 by March, the contract being due for completion in May. The contract[3] for 400,000 shell was signed on 10 November, and on the same day the firm were instructed to continue deliveries at the maximum rate (35,000 a week) on the conclusion of their contracts in May.[4] Four days later, as the result of further communications with the Master-General of the Ordnance, Messrs. Armstrong agreed to increase their weekly output to 55,000 within four months. At the end of November they were instructed to divide the output into 42,500 shrapnel, with No. 80 fuse, making an increase of 7,500 a week[5] over the earlier contracts, and 12,500 H.E. The fuse first ordered for the H.E. shell was the No.80/44, but this was replaced early in 1915 by the No. 100 graze fuse. The whole output

---

[1] Contracts/S/6507.
[2] Contracts/C/8050 and Contracts/F/2288.
[3] Contracts/S/7007.
[4] 57/S/4441.
[5] No deliveries of shrapnel were made on this contract (Contracts/S/7436) nor on a contract for a further 20,000 a week arranged in January (Contracts/S/7777).

of 55,000 a week was to be in the form of completed rounds, the War Office supplying the H.E.[1] In December, the firm was instructed to continue manufacture at the rate of 12,500 H.E. shell a week, until three months' notice to discontinue was given, and in May a contract was placed for an additional 30,000 a week[2], bringing the weekly total of H.E. up to 42,500. The first instalment on this last contract was expected at the beginning of June. In May, also, it was arranged that 150,000 H.E. shell should be substituted for an equal quantity of shrapnel, which was in arrears, and the War Office agreed to the firm's sub-letting a contract for the number in question to the Pennsylvania Steel Company.[3]

Obviously, expansion of output on this scale could only be obtained by laying down new plant, and even in the earliest orders, some allowance was usually made in the prices quoted on account of extensions. In Messrs. Armstrong's order of 18 August mentioned above, for instance, the price quoted per shell (17s. 6d.) included 2s. for new plant.

In October, 1914, the War Office invited the armament firms to submit proposals for increasing their output by extending their plant. Under an arrangement with the Treasury, financial assistance was promised to enable them to carry out approved extensions. Most of the firms engaged in the manufacture of ammunition, explosives, guns, and small arms submitted schemes and received grants to cover the expenditure. Attempts were made to induce the firms to borrow the money for these extensions from the Government ; but at the outset most of the armament firms refused to consider any repayment of the capital advanced, and the grants were, in effect, gifts to the contractors. These arrangements constituted the earliest type of "assisted contract."

The first plant subsidies were paid to the shell-making firms in November, 1914, and subsidies for increased plant for guns, rifles, and small arms ammunition followed in quick succession.

(c) Sub-contracting.

It has been said that offers of assistance in munitions manufacture were made to the War Office from the very beginning of the war. The list of new firms asking for orders grew rapidly ; during August and September, 1914, 70 applications were received for work on shell, 54 for shell parts, 38 for fuses or parts, 13 for cartridge cases, 13 for gun parts, 12 for gun mountings, 7 for parts of gun mountings, 4 for machine guns or parts, 4 for rifles and 4 for rifle parts.

The greater number of the applicants, however, could only offer to undertake work of a limited character. In accordance with the general policy such firms as could not undertake direct contracts were encouraged to accept subcontracts from the principal contractors.

---

[1] The contract for assembling 42,500 rounds of shrapnel and an equal quantity of H.E. was not signed until 21 May, 1915 (Contracts/Firms A/1797).

[2] 94/S/404.

[3] 57/3/4579.

In order to put the armament firms in touch with possible sub-contractors when tenders for a particular munition were invited, a list of firms who had applied for work that might be useful in the production of that munition was issued with the tender forms. The utility of these lists would have been greater, if a larger and more technical staff could have been employed in drawing them up. The Board of Trade helped by inspecting firms and reporting on the capabilities of their plant ; but the staff available for this work were too ignorant of the technicalities of munitions manufacture for their reports to be of much value.

As an example of this procedure reference may be made to invitations to tender[1] which were sent to 37 firms on 19 October, 1914, for shells of various types (4,500 common lyddite 12-pdr. and 14-pdr. Q.F., 300 common lyddite 4-in. Q.F., 2,350 H.E. heavy 9·2-in. gun B.L., 1,300 common lyddite light 9·2-in. gun B.L., 19,750 common lyddite 6-in. gun B.L. or Q.F.). The only tenders received were from six regular armament contractors. With the tender form was circulated a list of 129 firms who had offered their services to the War Department for the supply of parts of shells or for carrying out some of the processes of manufacture.

The usual method of sub-contracting was thus that armament firms sub-let the making of parts to new firms, and themselves assembled the parts and finished the article. Less often the armament firms sub-let the whole contract for the complete article. There is no doubt, however, that this practice led to abuses, and unfair profits were made in some cases through firms taking advantage of the ignorance of new makers. In one instance, a case came to light in which a whole contract had been sub-let at a much lower price than that paid to the main contractor, and a large sum thus was obtained for teaching a new firm what was only a simple job.[2] Such an abuse might have been checked earlier if a more adequate liaison system had existed between the Inspection Staff and the Contracts Branch.

The variety of the work undertaken by sub-contractors is illustrated by a list of sub-contractors for War Office contracts drawn up in July, 1915, by one of the smaller armament firms (Messrs. Firth), who were then employing sub-contractors as follows :—Steel, 3 firms ; punching and drawing, 2 ; machining, 17 ; copper bands and tubes for same, 8 ; nose bushes and metal for same, 5 ; shrapnel components (discs, bullets, tin cups, felt washers, heads, screws, metal tubes, sockets), 13.[3]

Similar endeavours to extend the area of supply by means of sub-contracts during the autumn months were made by the Royal Ordnance Factories, the general policy being to place out with sub-contractors the simpler portions of manufacture involved in the production of supplies for which they were responsible.[4]

[1] Contracts/S/7129 with 94/S/994.   [2] Hist. Rec. H/500/10.
[3] 94/S/659.
[4] e.g., invitations to tender for machining 60-pdr. shrapnel and making 15-pdr. H.E. shell were issued on 18 November to a number of important firms (Contracts/S/7588 with 94/S/2870).

(d) Spreading of Contracts.

So far we have considered sub-contracting in regard to the production of gun ammunition components only, this being the field in which there was the greatest room for multiplication of production and that which presented the fullest scope for firms of ordinary engineering capacity and experience. It was not to be expected that the same degree of success would attend the efforts to extend sub-contracting in directions which were less favourable. In the case of gun manufacture, for example, which necessarily involved very special plant and great technical difficulties as regards control of forging operations required for the manufacture of gun bodies, and no less difficulty and delicacy in the engineering work for the manufacture of breech mechanisms, sub-contracting could not readily be carried on to any great extent.

Nevertheless, endeavours were made to this end. The possibility of field artillery being manufactured by outside firms was raised by the President of the Board of Trade in an interview with Mr. Morcom, of Messrs. Belliss & Morcom on 14 October, 1914.[1] The number mentioned was about 1,200 18-pdr. guns. Mr. Morcom suggested that the British Electrical and Allied Manufacturers' Association might render collective assistance. At a meeting of the Council of this Association on 15 October all the members present expressed their willingness, but they were doubtful if the work were not of too special a character. An Emergency Committee was appointed. Mr. Morcom, accompanied by several engineers, visited Woolwich on 16 October. He reported on the 21st to Mr. Runciman that the Association could do the work, but it would need close organisation, considerable assistance from steel works, machine tool makers, gaugemakers, and ordnance experts. He proposed the formation of a committee, representing the principal trades involved and the ordnance experts, which he thought might be a good agency for distributing the orders for emergency work and securing the assistance of the less-known firms.

Mr. Alfred Herbert and Mr. Dumas (British Thomson-Houston Company, Rugby), who had also been consulted, were opposed to the project, and considered that all that a committee could usefully accomplish would be the development and co-ordination of the resources of private firms to assist the armament companies. Sir Frederick Donaldson held the same opinion. The proposal was dropped, and the matter ended in a list of fourteen firms belonging to the Association being sent to the Arsenal. A number of these firms undertook work for Woolwich and for the armament firms.

The highly technical character of gun manufacture would certainly have presented very serious difficulties to any experiments in production by untried firms. There was a strong case for meeting the fresh demands by expanding the resources of the regular makers. Considerable subsidies were granted to Messrs. Armstrong, Messrs. Beardmore, the Coventry Ordnance Works, and Messrs. Vickers.

---

[1] Hist. Rec./H/1121/1.

Similar difficulties did not, of course, apply in the case of gun carriages and vehicles. From the first weeks of the war the Chief Superintendent of Ordnance Factories drew largely on the resources of private firms for assistance in this respect, and the expansion of output which he promised in October was conditional on this assistance being continued.

WORK OF RAILWAY COMPANIES.

The railway companies in particular were utilised by the Royal Ordnance Factories in this way, and special mention should be made of their munitions work. The companies were approached by the Factories shortly after the outbreak of war for assistance in various work : their help was asked, for instance, in the manufacture of carriages for 4·5-in. howitzers ordered from the Ordnance Factories on 13 August, and a few months later it was proposed that they should make the carriages for certain 6-in. guns which the Ordnance Factories were to convert to 8-in. howitzers. They also, at the request of the War Office, took up the manufacture of shell components and of shell, being asked to associate themselves particularly with the manufacture of 6-in. H.E. shell.

On the first request for assistance from Woolwich, the Railway Executive Committee appointed a sub-committee to consider the matter. This sub-committee was later enlarged to include representatives of the principal railway companies, the War Office, and ultimately of the Ministry of Munitions and the Admiralty, and, as the Railway War Manufactures Sub-Committee, continued throughout the war to deal with applications for assistance from the Government in munitions work.[1]

In addition to the work undertaken directly for the Government, the railway companies sub-contracted to a large extent to munition making firms. In the autumn of 1914, for instance, the North Eastern Railway Company undertook the manufacture of 18-pdr. shell for Messrs. Armstrong, and erected a building for the purpose adjacent to their works at Darlington.[2] In other cases large quantities of shell components were supplied to War Office contractors. To assist these activities, sub-committees of the Railway War Manufactures Sub-Committee were appointed in various areas.

In the case of these sub-contracts to firms, precautions had to be taken against the main contractor buying at a low rate from the railway companies, which were financed by the Government, and making an undue profit by selling to the Government. The financial arrangements agreed to between the War Office and the Railway Executive Committee[3] accordingly provided that

" so far as practicable work done by a Railway Company as sub-contractor to a firm holding a contract at fixed prices with the

---

[1] Sec./Gen./2028.

[2] This factory was subsequently transferred to the direct control of the Government and was classed as a National Projectile Factory.

[3] As embodied in a memorandum drawn up in June, 1915 (94/Gen. No./312).

Government, will be excluded from the contract of the Government with the firm.

" Where this is not possible, Railway Companies will assess their charges on the basis fixed for direct work for the Government, and will add a further charge of 10 per cent. to the cost of the work as profit. This percentage, as in the case of the shop costs and supervision charges, will be credited to the revenue account."

The " basis fixed for direct work for the Government " was that charges should be made up as follows :—

(i) *Materials* : if bought specially, at cost price plus usual charges for carriage and handling ; if used out of stock, at replacement prices plus usual charges for carriage and handling.

(ii) *Labour* : at cost price.

(iii) *Workshop Expenses* : as usual in the shop.

(iv) *Supervision and Establishment charges* : calculated at 12½ per cent. on the total of (i), (ii) and (iii).

Search for New Contractors.

It has already been said that as early as the beginning of September, 1914, tender forms for some of the simpler natures of shell had been issued to engineering firms who had never before made complete shell. It was, however, practically impossible for such firms, even if they could obtain drawings and specifications without delay, to prepare estimates of the probable cost of manufacture within the few days that were customarily allowed before tenders had to be sent in. Consequently, it not infrequently happened that the only tenders received were from armament firms, and even where new firms could formulate an offer, the contract usually went to an experienced contractor who was able to quote lower prices and earlier deliveries.

For instance, on 6 September, invitations were issued to a number of firms to tender for the supply of 5,600 60-pdr. shrapnel shell, 12,000 13-pdr. shrapnel and 34,500 4·5-in. shrapnel. Twelve of the firms communicated with made no tender ; 7, of whom 5 were armament firms, tendered for the 60-pdr. ; 8 (6 armament firms) for the 13-pdr. ; and 8 (6 armament firms) for the 4·5-in. The new firms who tendered were Messrs. J. & P. Hill, Messrs. Rolls Royce, and the James Cycle Company, and none of them received a contract, orders for 60-pdrs. being given to Messrs. Beardmore and Messrs. Firth, for 13-pdr. to the Projectile Company and Messrs. Vickers, and for 4·5-in. to the Projectile Company, Messrs. Vickers and Messrs. Firth.[1]

The endeavours of the Contracts Branch to discover new sources of supply were severely handicapped by the difficulty of giving applicants ready access to samples, drawings and specifications. The branch had no sample room of its own ; firms had to be sent to the inadequate sample room at Woolwich, where no one knew which of the articles were most required. Drawings and specifications were issued only by Woolwich on the request of the Contracts Branch,

---

[1] Contracts/S/6724 (94/S/51).

and then after considerable delay. The stock of copies was insufficient. These obstacles discouraged many firms who might have been useful.

As the result, however, of the efforts to extend sub-contracting which have been described above, a considerable number of firms of ordinary engineering capacity were able to acquire experience of shell manufacture and in certain instances subsequently developed into contractors on a large scale. In other cases the growth of the miscellaneous demands of the Army enabled firms to obtain work more in accordance with their normal industrial activities. This may be illustrated by the following list of orders placed with certain firms who, in March, 1915, were stated to have recently informed the Contracts Branch of the War Office that they were open to receive orders for various kinds of engineering and machine work. Of the total of 50 firms, 21 received no direct orders from the War Office or Ministry of Munitions. Four had already received orders, one for pull-throughs, rifle parts and cleaning rods, one (the Austin Motor Company) for shell, one for oil bottles and pull-throughs, and one for optical instruments. During the remainder of 1915 nine more received contracts, of whom one undertook 4·5-in. H.E. shell, four shell components (adapters, plugs or gaines), one small petrol bombs, one aeroplane bombs, and one rifle components. In 1916 contracts were placed with fourteen more, two undertaking shell, seven shell components, one petrol engines, one Temple silencers for trench howitzers, one acetylene generators, one hauling chains, and one director stands. One more firm on the list was given an order in 1917 for explosives machinery, and one in 1918 for A tubes for 18-pdr. guns.

Up to the end of 1914 the direct contracts for shell placed by the War Office with new firms were few in number. In October a contract was arranged with Messrs. Dick Kerr, and in November with Messrs. J. & P. Hill, for 6-in. H.E. shell, and Messrs. Hill also undertook 4·7-in. H.E. On 26 December, the Rees Roturbo Manufacturing Company, who, as has already been mentioned, were represented at the shell conference on 23 December, received the first contract which was placed for 8-in. shell. This firm subsequently developed a large capacity for shell making, and some details of the negotiations with them may be given, as an illustration of the conditions under which new firms undertook shell manufacture.

On 17 November, Messrs. Rees Roturbo wrote informing the War Office that they were "seriously contemplating the installation of a plant for the manufacture of the larger sized projectiles." An interview was arranged with a representative of the firm, Mr. Brindley, who stated that he had himself acquired experience of shell manufacture in Messrs. Firth's works at Sheffield, and that he had designed various types of presses. The firm were considering putting down plant at an expenditure of £5–6,000, the output contemplated being 2,500 6 in. shell a week. Mr. Brindley was asked to consult his directors also on the subject of 8 in. and 9·2 in. shell, and at the end of November, having found that additional plant and tools would be required, he submitted a revised estimate of expenditure in this respect (£11,800) for an output of 2,000 a week of 6 in. shell or other sizes *pro rata*.

During the first week of December there was further discussion as to prices and the terms of a War Office loan, and on 7 December the firm were instructed to proceed with the erection of plant for 8 in. shell, delivery of which would begin in March at 600 a week and continue subject to three months' notice. The alternative manufacture of 6 in. or 9·2 in. was still under consideration.

Before the end of the month, the situation was altered by the acquisition by the firm at a cost of £10,000 of premises at Ponder's End, containing powerful hydraulic presses. They were thus able to offer an increased output, but they required financing in respect of the necessary purchases of steel, which was already rapidly rising in value. New proposals were accordingly discussed by the Master-General of the Ordnance with Sir George Gibb, Colonel Bingham and Mr. Hanson, and it was agreed that the War Office should advance capital sums for expenditure on works and provision of plant up to 80 per cent. of expenditure incurred, but not exceeding £80,000 ; while a further capital sum of £137,000, to be advanced for the provision of materials[1] and wages, was to be recoverable by the deduction of 50 per cent. from payments for shell. The deliveries now promised were 600 8 in. a week from the middle of March, and 600 6 in. from the middle of April, both rising to 3,000 by the middle of June and continuing at that rate till notice to terminate was given. The Secretary of State, however, reserved the right to instruct the company to change over from 8 in. to 9·2 in. at two months' notice. The price of the shell, £9 15s. for 8 in. and £4 8s. 6d. for 6 in., was to be reduced to £9 3s. 4d. and £4 2s. 6d. for shell delivered after 1 July, 1915. A contract embodying these terms was signed on 26 December : it was modified in April to provide that, since the firm had experienced great difficulty in obtaining plant, notice to discontinue should not be given before 31 July.

Messrs. Dick Kerr, J. and P. Hill and the Rees Roturbo Company remained, until the establishment of the Ministry of Munitions, the only contractors outside the armament group to make heavy shell, but orders for H.E. shell of the lighter types were more widely distributed. During the first five months of 1915 orders for 4·5 in. H.E. shell were given to Messrs. Dick Kerr and Messrs. Harper Sons and Bean, the latter also undertaking 4·5 in. shrapnel. New contractors for 18-pdr. H.E. included the Austin Motor Company and Messrs. Dorman Long in February, the Ebbw Vale Steel Iron and Coal Company in March and Messrs. Craven Brothers in May.

(e) THE BEGINNINGS OF THE CONTROL OF INDUSTRY.

At the conference with gun makers on 13 October, the Cabinet Committee authorised the Chief Superintendent of Ordnance Factories, to take whatever steps were necessary to secure an additional output

---

[1] In January, 1915, in view of the increased price of steel, the company asked for compensation for actual increase above a basis price of £20 per ton, and this was agreed to subject to its not becoming operative until after delivery of 24,000 6-in. and 42,000 8-in. shells.

of 100 18-pdr. complete equipments, 50 4·5 in. howitzer equipments and 18 60-pdrs. On the following day the Chief Superintendent communicated to the Master-General of the Ordnance his requirements in regard to labour,[1] machinery,[2] and assistance from outside sources.[3]

With regard to this last point he wrote :—

" As regards the work which it is hoped to get done by private firms, I may have to ask for powers to oblige firms who undertake work to give absolute preference to our orders over those of any other clients, and of course in saying this I contemplate that the firms so employed would not be otherwise engaged on War Department or Admiralty work, or at any rate that any other War Department or Admiralty work would not suffer. On both these points I should like to be assured of official approval and support."

The question of compelling firms to give preference to War Department orders over those of private clients, which subsequently became the basis of the elaborate system of control known as priority regulation, here makes its appearance for the first time. The suggestion was referred to the War Office Secretariat in order to ascertain whether there was power to enforce such control. The view taken was that " the legal question had better not be raised. This course has been taken with regard to firms making motor lorries, and there is no doubt as to the powers of the Government to give such orders and to enforce them."[4] The Chief Superintendent of Ordnance Factories was accordingly informed that action on these lines would receive official support. No further steps were, however, taken immediately, but in November the question of the powers of the Government in relation to industry was raised again, this time from the point of view of the supply of high explosives.

High explosives were not manufactured at the Royal Gunpowder Factory, and it had been the practice of the War Office to rely upon the trade supply for picric acid. The same procedure was at first adopted in regard to trinitrotoluene (T.N.T.), but in the month of October it became apparent that an adequate output of trinitrotoluene would not be obtainable from this source.

On 10 November, 1914, the Board of Trade was invited to co-operate, and Lord Moulton's Committee on High Explosives was constituted on 16 November, to advise as to the methods which should be adopted to secure an adequate supply of the products in question. The line of action to be followed was formulated in a memorandum[5] drawn up by Lord Moulton towards the end of the month, in which he revealed the alternative sources of supply and indicated the policy to be followed :—

" The plan of action set out in this Memorandum is based on the principle that, at all events, for some weeks, if not months, the policy to be pursued is to develop in every practicable way the production in England of high explosives suitable for use in warfare. The enormous expenditure of such explosives on the

---

[1] See below, p. 123.   [3] 73/Gen. No./1561.
[2] See below, p. 125.   [4] 24/10/14 (Contracts 1130).
                    [5] Memorandum dated 27 November, 1914.

part of our foes since hostilities began, has shown that no calculations of the quantities required can be based on the experience of previous wars. The only safe line of action, therefore, is to develop the production of these explosives to the utmost in every direction until the danger of a shortage is removed. . . .

"The conclusion is, therefore, that for the moment we ought not to think of working to specific needs, but to aim at developing our productive power in high explosives to the greatest possible extent. Even this will, unfortunately, not be adequate to prevent the possibility of shortage until many weeks, and perhaps several months, have passed, but much can be done in that time."

In the first place it was necessary to face the prospective shortage in the supply of trinitrotoluene. It was evident that the view adopted shortly after the outbreak of war, that this explosive alone could be relied upon to satisfy all requirements, must be abandoned. All available supplies of picric acid (lyddite) must also be stimulated in every practicable way. The fundamental difference between picric acid and trinitrotoluene was the strict limitation on the supply of the raw material (toluene) for the latter. In the case of lyddite, there was no similar limitation upon the quantity of raw material, phenol, which could be obtained by synthetic process from benzene or some derivative of that substance. The primary question was, therefore, to secure for the Government the whole of the toluene produced in the country, and arrange for its conversion into trinitrotoluene without leakage. This would involve the control of gas undertakings and coke oven undertakings having recovery plant for the distillation of toluene from tar.

On 20 November, Lord Moulton's Committee decided that special powers should be asked for in order to carry out these proposals, since it would be necessary to requisition both stocks and output of toluol. It would also be necessary to supervise closely the manufacture of these essential supplies and dealings therein. The urgency of this need was recognised, and steps were taken to give effect to the committee's wishes by means of an amendment to the Defence of the Realm Act, then under consideration in Parliament.

The primary purpose of this enactment was to strengthen and codify the powers already granted by Parliament under the Defence of the Realm Act and the Defence of the Realm (No. 2) Act, passed on 8 and 28 August respectively, and the regulations instituted therein. The former Act gave power to make regulations to prevent communication with the enemy and for the better security of means of communication—railways, docks, and harbours. The latter Statute had extended this authority to cover the spreading of reports likely to cause disaffection, and had given power to deal with areas in which troops were concentrated, or to suspend restrictions on acquisition or user of land.

The new Statute gave wide powers for the making of regulations for these various purposes, or "otherwise to prevent assistance being given to the enemy, or the successful prosecution of the war being endangered."

The Bill was introduced on 23 November, 1914. In order to deal with the difficulty above indicated, the addition of the following clause was proposed by Mr. McKenna during the Committee stage on 25 November :—

" (a) To require that there shall be placed at their disposal the whole or any part of the output of any factory or workshop in which arms, ammunition, or warlike stores or equipment, or any articles required for the production thereof, are manufactured ;

" (b) To take possession and use for the purpose of His Majesty's Naval or Military Service, any such factory or workshop, or any plant thereof, and Regulations under this Act may be made accordingly."[1]

The purpose of the clause, as announced by Mr. McKenna, was " to secure that the Government can obtain the highest maximum possible output of the factories or workshops in which arms, ammunition, warlike stores, or equipment, are manufactured. I am sure that the Committee will agree that it is most desirable that every step should be taken which will assist the Government in securing as abundant a supply of arms and ammunition as the country is capable of producing."[2]

On the following day, Mr. Harold Baker, the Financial Secretary to the War Office, described[3] the object more specifically as intended to give the War Office full authority to acquire supplies from contractors :—" What we have done is to take powers under the Defence of the Realm Act yesterday to commandeer at a fair price the whole of the output of any factory, or, in a further stage of necessity, to take over that factory and work it ourselves. We have taken that step in order to secure the power of applying a check to any tendency to squeeze the War Office by charging excessive prices."

The Act received the Royal Assent on 27 November, 1914, and the powers conferred by it were immediately put into effect, in connection with the supply of explosives. On 28 November, the War Office took over the Rainham Chemical Works from the Synthetic Products Company, the works being utilised for the purification of crude T.N.T. Messrs. Coley and Wilbraham were placed in control[4] of the factory, as the agents of the Government. On 25 and 27 November, circulars had been issued by the Director of Army Contracts to certain coal tar producers, notifying them of the Government's intention to requisition stocks of toluol, and on 3 December, a further circular to all coal tar producers and distillers informed them that they were required to place at the disposal of the Government, for the period of the war, their whole output of toluol, or substances containing toluol.[5]

[1] *Parliamentary Debates* (1914), *H. of C.*, LXVIII, 1274.
[2] *Ibid.*, 1275.
[3] *Ibid.*, 1449.
[4] Vol. VIII, Part II, p. 75.
[5] Vol. VII, Part IV, pp. 13 and 89. An account of the work done by Lord Moulton's Committee on High Explosives will be found in Vol. X, Part IV.

CHAPTER V.

THE NEED FOR REINFORCEMENT OF THE SUPPLY ORGANISATION.

I. The Shell Conference, 21 December, 1914.

The increases in the gun programme in October, 1914, involved a corresponding expansion in supplies of shell. It has been seen that only a few experimental orders had been given to untried contractors before the end of 1914, and it follows that heavy demands had to be made on the armament firms, not only for field gun ammunition, but also for shell for the heavy howitzers ordered in accordance with the Siege Committee's recommendations.

This expansion in the volume of their orders of course greatly aggravated the difficulties of the task undertaken by the armament firms. Not only had they now, at the urgent instruction of the Government, undertaken to expand to its utmost limits the existing and potential capacity of their respective works, but the discharge of their undertaking was conditional upon the successful negotiation and supervision of sub-contracts with inexperienced firms. This latter fact did, as the sequel showed, introduce a factor of uncertainty which was, perhaps, the principal cause of the failure to deliver within the contract time, and rendered unreliable the best estimates which the armament firms could frame, based upon a knowledge of their own resources.

Similar efforts were made at this period to increase the output of the Ordnance Factories and to expand the volume of contracts placed overseas. Orders placed with the Shell Committee at Ottawa were increased to a very large total, and on 14 October the first large American contract was placed, an order being given to the Bethlehem Steel Company for 1,000,000 complete rounds of 18-pdr. shrapnel ammunition, the contract being based on an agreement arrived at on 28 October.

By the end of the year the total orders for shell had reached a figure of ten millions, distributed as follows :—

Ordnance factories	812,000
Armament firms	6,210,000
American firms	1,280,000
Canadian Shell Committee	1,700,000
Indian Government	52,000
	10,054,000

A comparison of the orders for the principal natures of field artillery included in this aggregate with the total reserves on hand at the

outbreak of war gives some measure of the new scale of supplies which
contract negotiators had now to envisage :—

		Stocks at Outbreak of War.		Total Ordered 31.12.14.
18-pdr.—Shrapnel..		654,480	..	6,580,923
H.E.	..	—	..	758,000
13-pdr.—Shrapnel..		95,400	..	283,000
H.E.	..	—	..	50,000
4·5 in.—Shrapnel ..		86,400	..	347,500
H.E.	..	43,200	..	476,500
60-pdr.—Shrapnel..		16,800	..	123,100
H.E.	..	7,200	..	137,450

As already indicated, Sir George Gibb was appointed an additional
member of the Army Council early in the month of December, with a
view to strengthening the internal administration of the War Office in
respect of munitions contracts.

On 12 December the Master-General of the Ordnance sent him a list
of outstanding requirements for munitions, inviting his help in securing
contractors from whom deliveries could be obtained by the summer of
1915. It was understood that these additional orders were not in any
way to interfere with existing contracts, either as regards manufacture,
raw materials, or labour. The list included the following items :—

No. 80 T. & P. fuses	100,000	a week.
No. 82 ,, ,, ,, ...	10,000	,,
No. 83 ,, ,, ,, ...	5,000	,,
No. 65A ,, ,, ...	7,500	,,
D.A. Fuse No. 44	35,000	,,
Complete rounds of 18-pdr. ammunition without fuses	85,000	,,
Complete rounds of 13-pdr. ammunition without fuses	15,000	,,
4·5 in. lyddite shell cases* and primers	10,000	,,
4·5 in. shrapnel shell cases and primers	10,000	,,
60-pdr. lyddite shell*	3,000	,,
60-pdr. shrapnel shell	3,600	,,
6 in. gun lyddite shell	(No quantity stated)	
8 in. lyddite shell	1,000	a week
·303 in. rifles, short, Lee-Enfield III...	10,000 or 20,000	,,
Small arms ammunition	10,000,000	,,

* Including filling.

By this time all the principal manufacturers were congested with
work, and it was highly desirable to open out new sources of supply
rather than to overload any further the capacity of the armament firms.
In these circumstances it was thought advisable to take counsel with
representatives of the manufacturers " in order to ascertain how the
industrial resources of the country could best be organised to meet
still further demands for artillery ammunition." This conference was

held on 21, December, 1914, at the War Office.[1]   The Master-General
of the Ordnance and Sir George Gibb, accompanied by Mr. Wintour
Mr. Hanson and Mr. Dannreuther, met representatives of :—[1]
Messrs. Sir W. G. Armstrong, Whitworth & Company (A.B.D.), Messrs.
W. Beardmore and Company (A), Messrs. Coventry Ordnance Works
(B.D.), Messrs. Cammell, Laird & Company (A), Messrs. Dick
Kerr & Company (A), Messrs. The Electric & Ordnance Accessories
Company (B.C.), Messrs. T. Firth & Sons (A), Messrs. Harper,
Sons & Bean (A), Messrs. Hadfields, Ltd. (A), Messrs. Head,
Wrightson & Company (A), Messrs. The King's Norton Metal Company
(B.C.D.), Messrs. The Projectile Company (1902) Ltd. (A), Messrs. Rees
Roturbo Manufacturing Company (A), Messrs. Vickers, Ltd. (A.B.C.D.).
Messrs. J. & P. Hill (A) and Messrs. Watson Laidlaw & Company (A)
were invited, but were unable to send representatives.

It will be interesting to notice that the above list includes two
firms—Messrs. Rees Roturbo Manufacturing Company and Messrs.
Head, Wrightson & Company—which were the first firms outside the
circle of the armament firms proper to undertake shell production on
a comprehensive scale.

Sir George Gibb said that it was essential to ascertain what the
present contractors could do to increase their output ; when the
increase would commence ; what additional labour they would require ;
and what prospects there were of obtaining it.   He assumed that
manufacturers could not make more fuses without extending their
works, and said that he was prepared to discuss some fair financial
arrangement in connection with such extensions, his idea being to
assure them a fair profit.   He presumed also that it would be necessary
to go to America to obtain the extra machinery and plant, or at least
some of part it.   He urged that the contractors should pool their
requirements in order to avoid unnecessary competition and to make
it easier to get the machinery.   Each firm would send out experts to
select the machines and to be responsible for their suitability, while
the War Office would, so far as possible, arrange for the purchase.

The manufacturers, with practical unanimity, drew attention to
the increasing scarcity of labour.   This meeting, in fact, marks a
turning point, for from this moment labour questions predominated
over all other issues.   The firms' representatives made it clear that,
in almost every case, they could not promise an increase of output

---

[1] The letters A. B. C. D. indicate the type of contracts held by the firm at
the date :—
    A. Contractors for *Shell*.—Messrs. Douglas Grant, Ltd. (Kirkcaldy) and the
        James Cycle Co. also had contracts for iron shell.
    B. Contractors for *Fuses*.—Contracts for fuses were also held by
        Messrs. G. Kent, Ltd. (London), Raleigh Cycle Co. (London and
        Nottingham), Sterling Telephone Electric Co. (London), and Vauxhall
        Motors (1914), Ltd., (Bedford).
    C. Contractors for *Primers*.—Contracts also held by the Birmingham Metal
        and Munitions Co., Messrs. Kynoch, Ltd., and Messrs. Eley Bros.
    D. Contracts for *Cartridge Cases*.—Contracts also held by the Birmingham
        Metal and Munitions Co., Kynoch, Ltd., and Messrs. Allen Everitt
        and Sons.

unless they were furnished with additional labour, which they could not find themselves. This question will be referred to below.[1]

Apart from general considerations, the conference gave particular attention to requirements for fuses and shell. With regard to fuses, increased output was offered by Messrs. Armstrong, the Coventry Ordnance Works, and the King's Norton Metal Company, while Messrs. Beardmore were prepared to put down new shops for the purpose. All the offers, however, were contingent on the necessary labour being found, and in any case no increase in output was to be expected for some five or six months.

The additional orders for shell provisionally accepted amounted to a total of 60,500 lyddite shell and 8,000 shrapnel, made up as follows :—

13-pdr :—
    Lyddite, 5,500 (2,500 possibly 15-pdr. or 18-pdr.).
18-pdr. :—
    Lyddite, 37,000.
4·5-in. or 5-in. :—
    Lyddite, 11,500 (3,000 possibly 6-in.).
    Shrapnel, 7,000.
60-pdr. :—
    Lyddite, 2,000.
    Shrapnel, 1,000.
6-in. :—
    Lyddite, 3,500.
8-in. :—
    Lyddite, 1,000.

Most of the firms made their offer conditional on the supply of labour, while new buildings or plant were stated to be necessary by Messrs. Hadfield, Armstrong, Firth, Harper Sons & Bean, and the King's Norton Metal Company. In spite of the failures that the firms were experiencing among their sub-contractors,[2] nothing said at this conference revealed any apprehensions about the soundness of the. general policy that had been adopted. Though offers made by the firms (notably those for the smaller natures of shell) did not cover the requirements stated on the Master-General of the Ordnance's list, it was still hoped that, by means of further sub-contracting and subsidised extensions, the growing needs of the Army could be met. The crucial difficulty put forward was the shortage of labour ; and the general impression left was that, if this could be overcome, all would be well.

II. Placing of Long-dated and Continuation Orders for Shell in the first Months of 1915.

Thus the shell conference, while it gave rise to important developments in connection with the supply of labour, led to no immediate modification of the existing arrangements for obtaining supplies.

---

[1] See below p. 124.   [2] See below p. 126.

During the first weeks of 1915, renewed attempts were made to secure increased output from the armament firms and their sub-contractors, and when these sources of supply proved obviously inadequate the capacity of overseas contractors was drawn on to an ever-increasing extent.

In the middle of January a circular was sent to all firms holding contracts for warlike stores urging them to make still further efforts. The letter issued ran as follows :—[1]

"I am directed to inform you that, in spite of the great efforts which have been made by the manufacturing firms of this country to meet the requirements of the Naval and Military services, the supplies of ammunition and other warlike stores promised for delivery, are not so great as the Secretary of State would wish to see provided for the troops, which it is contemplated to place in the field. I am, accordingly, to enquire whether it is within your power still further to increase the output of the various munitions of war which you are producing under War Office contracts. If so, I shall be glad if you will let me have, at the earliest possible date, particulars of the further supply which you think you could produce, stating at what time you could begin to deliver the increased output. It should be very clearly understood in this connection that the Secretary of State does not desire that any contractor should promise more than he can perform, or enter upon fresh engagements, which would imperil the due performance of those already made.

If the provision of an increased supply of any article would necessitate the construction of new plant, the fact should be mentioned, but it is not necessary in your immediate reply to go into details of the scheme, or to give an estimate of cost, which must, of course, depend upon the amount to be produced.

The Secretary of State understands that it is rather the shortage of skilled labour and of men qualified to undertake duties of superintendence and management than any lack of material, which is likely to limit the ability of contractors to undertake further extensions. He would be glad to have this view confirmed or corrected in your case."

The replies received to this letter were disappointing. To take a single example, Messrs. Dick Kerr, who had recently accepted orders for 6-in., 4·7-in., and 13-pdr. H.E., could not promise any increase in delivery until August. They could then deliver an additional 1,000 a week of 13 or 18-pdr. H.E., while from September they could make additional deliveries of either 1,000 4·5-in. or 4·7-in. per week, or 500 6-in. They could not undertake further extensions, because the space at their works was limited, and they anticipated difficulties in obtaining enough labour.[2]

As a further encouragement to increased shell production, the practice was adopted of giving running contracts, *i.e.*, a contractor

---

[1] Contracts/1281/1A.   [2] *Ibid.*

was instructed to continue delivery at his maximum rate on the completion of his existing contracts, until three months' notice should be given him to discontinue. A number of contracts of this type had been placed with armament firms in the last two months of 1914, and by January, 1915, the placing of these continuation orders had been adopted as the general policy in regard to all contractors whose orders terminated at an early date.[1]

The shell contracts placed up to the end of 1914 had, for the most part, provided for increasing deliveries during the summer and autumn of 1915 ; the new type of running contract formed a means of making provision further ahead. Similar considerations were taken into account in arranging the enormous overseas orders placed during the first half of 1915, which provided in the main for 1916 deliveries.[2] Some hesitation was felt at the War Office as to the desirability of some of the later American and Canadian orders, but by the middle of March, Lord Kitchener had decided that an effort must be made to secure a large additional output of field gun ammunition for the British Army during 1916, and as he took the view that it was impossible to have too much, the orders in question were proceeded with.[3] Since the supply of shell was, in fact, the outstanding problem of this period, and since overseas sources of supplies formed the only apparent means of meeting the anticipated demands for 1916, it is worth while to give some indication of the huge dimensions assumed by orders with American firms and the Canadian Shell Committee.

Before the end of 1914, the Bethlehem Steel Company, who, as has been seen, had received their first order in October, had undertaken in addition to deliver 1,000,000 complete rounds of 18-pdr. shrapnel by October, 1915,[4] and contracts had also been placed, through Messrs. Firth and Messrs. Vickers, with the Washington Steel and Ordnance Company and Messrs. E. W. Bliss, the former undertaking 13-pdr. and 18-pdr. H.E. and 6-in. lyddite, and the latter 5-in. howitzer lyddite. In February, 1915, the Bethlehem Company were given another contract[5] for 18-pdr. shrapnel complete rounds, and on 9 March, as the result of enquiries by Messrs. J. P. Morgan, who had recently been appointed Purchasing Agents in the United States, an offer was made for the supply by the Bethlehem Company and its associates of 4,500,000 18-pdr. complete rounds. This output was originally offered to the Russian authorities, but being refused by them it became available for the British War Office. Orders already placed for 18-pdr. ammunition would give an output of more than 1,800,000 a month, but in view of Lord Kitchener's plans for 1916 this additional output was accepted, for delivery at the rate of 250,000 a month from January, 1916.[6]

---

[1] Contracts/S/7275/1A ; 7958.
[2] Similar long-dated orders were placed in the United States for rifles during this period. See above p. 98.
[3] 94/S/128.
[4] Contracts/C/9104, 9724.
[5] Contracts/S/8079.
[6] RSC/S/37, 94/S/128.

Other important long-dated orders placed with American firms during the earlier months of 1915 were two in January, one with the Trayler Engineering and Manufacturing Company[1] for 1,000,000 18-pdr. H.E. (delivery April, 1915, to January, 1916), and one with Messrs. Bliss[2] for 2,000,000 18-pdr. shell and components (delivery April, 1915, to April, 1916) ; and a third in April with the American Locomotive Company[3] for 5,000,000 18-pdr. complete rounds, in equal proportions of shrapnel and H.E. (delivery September, 1915, to August, 1916). Orders were also placed during this period for 4·5-in., 6-in., 9·2-in., and 12-in. shell.

During the first half of 1915 similar large orders were given to Canada. By the end of 1914 the Shell Committee had undertaken to produce 1,600,000 18-pdr. shrapnel shell, of which over 1,000,000 were to be complete rounds.[4] Early in 1915 running contracts were arranged for a monthly output of 200,000 18-pdr. H.E. and 150,000 shrapnel complete rounds,[5] and orders for 4·5-in. H.E. shell, 60-pdr. H.E. shell, and 13-pdr. H.E. complete rounds were also given. In April, an offer of a further 4 or 5 million complete rounds of 18-pdr. was made, and though the Shell Committee's existing orders would, at the end of the year, be giving a weekly output of 100,000 of this nature, the offer was accepted, after the matter had been referred to the Secretary of State. The contract concluded at the end of April was for 5,000,000 rounds, in equal quantities of 18-pdr. shrapnel and H.E. and 4·5-in. H.E., for delivery by March, 1916.[6]

During the early part of 1915, in fact, overseas contractors assumed a place of the utmost importance, since upon them the War Office was forced to depend for the bulk of the shell supplies required for the 1916 campaign. The proportion of overseas to home orders may be illustrated by taking the nature for which there was the greatest demand—the 18-pdr. Of a total of nearly 16,000,000 18-pdr. shrapnel ordered up to the end of May, 1915, nearly 11,000,000 were to come from abroad, while of the H.E. type, 10,000,000 out of a total of 14,000,000 had been ordered from overseas contractors.

These large orders, however, since they were mainly for 1916 delivery, could be of no assistance in meeting the immediate demand from the front, which during the spring of 1915 was growing ever more urgent, while at the same time it became more and more obvious that supplies were not coming forward at the expected rate. In point of fact, the deliveries which should. have been coming in during this period from the earlier overseas orders were almost as much in arrears as those from home contractors, thus still further widening the gap between estimated and actual supplies.[7]

---

[1] Contracts/S/8023.
[2] Contracts/S/8057. The Bethlehem Company subsequently undertook to assemble the components.
[3] RSC/S/118.
[4] Without the fuse, which Canada could not supply at this time.
[5] Contracts/S/7970, 8243.
[6] 94/S/182.
[7] See below p. 128.

III. The Breakdown of Supply.

(a) INTRODUCTORY.

The failure of the main shell contractors at home to make good their promised deliveries was already an established fact at the end of 1914. By the time of the Shell Conference it had become clear that the output arranged for under the programme of subsidised extensions and increased sub-contracting was not materialising at the anticipated rate. This can be seen from the table given in Appendix III, which shows the position with regard to deliveries, on 31 December, 1914, and on 29 May, 1915.

Similar examples of delayed deliveries might be quoted in the case of other stores: the machine guns ordered from Messrs. Vickers early in August were considerably in arrears; gun contractors, though the bulk of their deliveries were not yet due, were already finding themselves unable to live up to their promises. It was, however, on the shortage of ammunition that the issue in the spring of 1915 turned, and it is not necessary to seek for further illustrations outside the story of shell supply.

For some weeks past signs had been multiplying that contractors would be unable to keep to their promised rate of delivery. A good illustration is found in a letter written by Messrs. Cammell Laird on 5 October, 1914,[1] which gave reasons for the necessity of revising in a downward sense the estimates of delivery placed before the War Office on 19 August when the first orders for shell were being settled. During the intervening six weeks, as the firm explained, the conditions had materially altered so that the prospects were no longer as favourable as had been hoped for. The three dominant factors were (1) labour supply, (2) machinery, (3) the assistance to be obtained from sub-contractors.

(1) *Labour Shortage.*—This had not been reckoned on in August but already its incidence was serious.

" From our own Shell Department many of the younger men, thoroughly trained and skilled in shell manufacture, enlisted; and other works being similarly placed efficient substitutes cannot be found within the district. We are in constant communication with the various Labour Bureaux, and have sent our own officials round Manchester, Leeds and Derby, but there seems no doubt that the demand for skilled workmen, such as are required for the manufacture of shell, exceeds the supply. Even when good mechanics are obtained from other trades they require special instruction before they are capable of performing useful work. This shortage has another retarding effect as unfortunately men are disinclined to work during Saturday afternoon and Sunday, and so far as we can judge, any attempt on our part to force them would result in their leaving our employment."

---

[1] Contracts S/6980.

(2) *Supply of new machinery.*—Messrs. Cammell further drew attention to the difficulty experienced in procuring the necessary supplies of additional machinery :—

"At the time our letter was written it was thought that no special difficulty would be experienced in obtaining machines. We may regard ourselves as fortunate in having procured 26 high-class machines during the past two months ; but the manu-facturers' stocks of suitable machines appear to be nearly exhausted, and some time must elapse before we can make extensive additions to our plant."

(3) *Failure of Sub-contractors.*—Finally the hopes and expectations of assistance from the sub-letting of work had to be revised. With regard to those assisting with special machine work, Messrs. Cammell had now realised that

"in spite of precautionary advice on our part they were too optimistic of their powers of production with regard to initial as well as continuous delivery. The conversion of machines, designing and making special tools and instructing men has taken longer than they anticipated : and furthermore they would not be convinced that the manufacture of shell had difficulties different from those they had been accustomed to meet. We believe that with many firms their powers of production will continuously improve, but in estimating their first deliveries we regret that sufficient allowance was not made for their want of experience."

With regard to contractors supplying fittings and component parts required to complete various types of shell it was realised that the demand on their resources had increased so suddenly that they too were failing to fulfil delivery promises ; but it was hoped that there would be an improvement as soon as supply became better regulated to meet the demand—a wish whose fulfilment was unfortunately still a very long way away.

Shortage of labour and machinery and the failure of sub-contractors were in fact the principal causes of the breakdown of supply in the spring of 1915, and it is therefore worth while to consider each of these points in some detail.

(b) Labour for Armament Work.

The outbreak of war brought in its train the menace of serious unemployment, in consequence of the dislocation of continental trade and the breakdown of international credit. Emergency steps for the provision of employment were, therefore, necessary at the very time when the first recruiting campaign was opened, and the manufacture of armaments was calling for additional labour.

Time was required for the absorption of even skilled men into munitions work. The extension of the scale of operations was neces-sarily gradual, and involved local concentration and transfer of labour before it could be effective. It was inevitable in these circumstances that an apparent surplus of unemployed skilled men should be found in many engineering centres, even while the private and public arsenals of the country were preparing to absorb additional labour of this essential type. Meanwhile, many of these men were being enrolled for military service. By October, 1914, the engineering trade group lost by enlistment 12·2 per cent. of its male workers as compared with the period three months earlier. By February, 1915, this proportion had increased to 16.4 per cent. and by July, 1915, to 19·5 per cent., though this exodus was partially counteracted by the immigration of workers from other trade groups.

Already in September, 1914, many of the principal armament works were experiencing difficulties due to the recruitment of their skilled employees, and there arose a general demand for some form of protection or special inducement. In response to a request by an important firm for permission to issue a recognised badge to their men, replies were sent on 8 September, 1914, both by Lord Kitchener and by the Master-General of the Ordnance, the latter of whom suggested that a ticket should be issued to each employee " indicating that he is engaged in the manufacture of munitions of war and that therefore he is unable to serve his country in any other manner." Six weeks later action was initiated at the Admiralty by the First Lord, who, on 27 October, caused inquiries to be made of important Admiralty contractors " as to how far their operations have been hampered by the withdrawal of workmen to fight." At the same time he ordered a badge to be designed, bearing the words " Admiralty service," for issue to all men employed on Admiralty work of a necessary character. This proposal was referred to the War Office, who, however, adhered to their preference for a ticket as making personal identification easier and thus diminishing the liability to misuse.

In November, 1914, a memorandum couched in similar terms, being in substance a reproduction of Lord Kitchener's letter of 8 September, was circulated by the War Department[1] and the Admiralty[2] to the armament firms respectively employed by them. The purport of these documents, which bore the signatures of the First Lord and the Secretary of State respectively, was to impress upon the employees of such establishments " the importance of the Government work upon which they are engaged," and to assure them that " in carrying on the great work of providing for the requirements of the Royal Navy (providing the Army with supplies and equipment) they are doing their duty for their King and country equally with those who have joined H.M. Forces for active service afloat or ashore (joined the Army for service in the field)."

The proposed issue of badges by the Admiralty was temporarily suspended owing to Treasury objections to the expenditure, but the question was again raised and referred to the Cabinet, who decided in favour of the scheme. The issue of badges by the Admiralty was sanctioned on 26 December. The policy of the War Office in the matter was also revised, and in March, 1915, a new branch in the Department of the Master-General of the Ordnance was set up to deal with the issue of badges, contracting firms being classified for this

---

[1] 27/Gen. No./2750.   [2] P. 2511.

purpose according to the importance and urgency of the work undertaken.[1]

In the meantime, however, the shortage of skilled men was having serious results. The importance which the labour question had assumed by the autumn of 1914 can be clearly seen from the position at Woolwich Arsenal in October, when the Chief Superintendent of Ordnance Factories was asked to make arrangements for an increased output of field guns and ammunition. On 12 October, in reporting the results of his preliminary enquiries, Sir F. Donaldson wrote :—

" I think it is necessary to refer to a difficulty which we may anticipate, and this is the requisite labour of a skilled nature to man these machines when we get them. Such men are coming forward very slowly, much more slowly than we had hoped for, and we already suffer from this dearth."

On the day following the conference between the Cabinet Committee and gun makers (13 October) the Chief Superintendent, as already mentioned, sent a memorandum[2] to the Master-General of the Ordnance in which he dealt, among other matters, with his labour requirements.

" I should like it to be very clearly understood that any success to be attained in making this exceptionally large output will depend almost entirely upon our being able to secure the requisite labour of suitable type. This, as I pointed out, is a present very great difficulty, and how it is to be overcome is not readily seen, otherwise it would have been overcome already. The only way in which improvement may be possible would be that we should give a guarantee to suitable men of employment, or its equivalent, for two years, or, if necessary, three years ; the effect of this would be that men engaged on these terms would, on the completion of the war, previous to the expiration of the guaranteed period and the cessation of excessive urgency, have to be dispensed with, with a bonus for the unexpired period of the guarantee. It is suggested that this might be half day-rates in a lump sum for the unexpired period. This, I am aware, can hardly be regarded as a very sound business proposition, but none the less under present special circumstances we shall have to do something of the sort if we are to ensure getting the men we want. Even so, it is not certain that success will be attained by this means. One of the great difficulties to it undoubtedly will be that it will be hard to resist giving similar guarantees to other men engaged, though it may be possible to restrict the concession to men of a particular class.

" I must again emphasise the statement already made that unless men can be got, and got readily, it will be impossible to carry out the programme."

It was not enough to secure the provision of additional labour for the Arsenal, since a certain amount of the work had already been placed

---

[1] An account of the steps taken with regard to protection and limitation of recruiting will be found in Vol. I, Part II, Chap. I.
[2] 75/Gen. No./1561.

with private firms, to the number of 25, on gun carriages alone. The Chief Superintendent wished to have powers to compel firms to give preference to War Department orders over those of private clients.[1]

The labour problem was thus raised for the first time in acute form, and the radical proposals put forward by the Chief Superintendent of Ordnance Factories raised important questions of policy, which were discussed at a conference between War Office and Board of Trade representatives on 5 November, 1914.

It was then agreed that in order to secure the transference of the necessary men it would be enough to guarantee one year's employment without special rates of pay. The power to give this guarantee was approved by the Master-General of the Ordnance on 7 November, 1914, but was not put into operation, since the Chief Superintendent reported on 10 November that the action taken was bearing good fruit, and that it might not be necessary to make use of the guarantee.

As has already been mentioned, the increasing shortage of labour was the most important point revealed by the Shell Conference of 21 December, 1914, and the promises of increased output made at that conference were conditional on the necessary labour being forthcoming. In the discussion which took place on the labour question, various suggestions were made. Sir Trevor Dawson, representing Messrs. Vickers, thought that the labour deficiency might be largely mitigated by using Belgians, but he recounted various difficulties, official and otherwise, which he had met in his efforts to obtain skilled Belgian labour through Holland. He also suggested that women might be trained, and that the Government should authorise all workmen to remain in their present employment, and commandeer men, to be sent from factories engaged on private work, to the large armament firms.

This last proposal, it was pointed out, had been considered some time before and dismissed, but a memorandum had been issued to contractors by Lord Kitchener, and recruiting officers had been instructed not to enlist workmen from specified firms without the employers' permission.

In reply to a statement that Messrs. Armstrong could put their hand on 500 skilled workmen serving with the colours, who would not return unless they were ordered to do so, the Master-General of the Ordnance promised to take the matter up with the Adjutant-General.

With regard to labour stealing, Sir George Gibb said that he would arrange for a new clause to be inserted in contracts, to the effect that the contractor would not employ men who came from other contractors holding simultaneous contracts for the War Office.[2] He thought that the only means of increasing labour supply at the present time was to arrange for the transfer of men from less important trades.

The results of the Shell Conference were reported to the Cabinet Committee, which assembled on 23 December, 1914.

---

[1] See above p. 110.
[2] It did not prove possible to take this action.

In view of the serious aspects of the labour situation thus revealed, the Board of Trade was instructed through Mr. Runciman to take energetic action for the purpose of securing an adequate supply of labour for armament contractors.

The Cabinet Committee suggested the following measures : (1) to co-ordinate the supply of labour ; (2) to substitute Belgians for British workmen ; (3) to divert labour from less urgent or unnecessary industries (*e.g.*, railway construction works, etc.) ; (4) where employers in the less necessary trades were reluctant to part with their men, to put pressure upon them, first by persuasion, and then, if that failed, by refusal of railway facilities, etc., and by publicity for unpatriotic action ; (5) any other means for obtaining enough men for all the armament companies.

This new departure marks a turning point in the story of industrial mobilisation. It leads at first away from the War Office to the Board of Trade campaign for the transfer of labour, to the steps taken to deal with the correlative problem of securing relaxation of restrictive practices by trade unions, and so to the work of the Committee on Production, appointed early in February, 1915, and subsequent events, which finally resulted in the Treasury Conferences of March 18 and 25, 1915. The full narrative of these events will be found elsewhere.[1]

(c) Shortage of Machinery.

The provision of the machine tools required for the equipment of extensions to factories became a matter of concern early in the war. It was, for instance, one of the points raised by Sir Frederick Donaldson in October, in his memorandum summarising the steps necessary to secure an increased output of field guns.

In consequence of the limited capacity of the home industry and the scale of requirements, it was necessary to have recourse to the United States of America, and the failure of American deliveries of machine tools to come to hand at the anticipated dates, proved a prime cause for the breakdown of the programme of ammunition output arranged by the War Office, the shortage of machinery being one of the excuses most frequently urged by contractors for their delayed deliveries. The following are typical statements made by firms in reply to " hasteners " from the War Office.

Messrs. Armstrong.—

    15-pdr. shrapnel (Contract/S/6676). Deliveries not begun owing to non-receipt of machinery. (Letter, 17 February, 1915).

    9·2-in. lyddite (Contract/S/6386). Machinery for 9·2-in. and 12-in. howitzer much overdue. (Interview, 1 February, 1915).

    4·7-in. lyddite (Contract/S/6834). Delay due to non-receipt of machinery. (Letter, 28 April, 1915).

---

[1] Vol. I, Part II.

Messrs. Vickers.—

    4·5-in. lyddite (Contract/S/6993). Work prevented by delay in delivery of machinery from United Kingdom and United States of America. (General Mahon's Report, 22 May, 1915).

    18-pdr. shrapnel (Contract/S/6507). Output held up for want of 38 screw milling machines. (General Mahon's Report, 12 March, 1915).

(d) The Failure of Sub-Contractors.

From the correspondence between the War Office and the main contracting firms it does not appear that the latter were, in the early months of the war, feeling the effects of labour shortage so acutely as was the case with the subsidiary contractors. The tide of surplus labour was, in fact, setting strongly towards the principal armament contractors in response to the general publicity given to their requirements, stimulated as this was by individual appeals and by the currency of reports as to the high earnings obtainable, and possibly, in some measure also, by the belief that such work would afford protection from the importunity of the recruiting sergeant. The subsidiary contractors had not the same advantages, either in the general recognition of the national character of the work they undertook or in the terms they were able to offer. It was, at least, a common complaint, that while the armament firms, as direct contractors, had *carte blanche* in the matter of expenditure and were able to name their own price, the contracts that were sublet—doubtless, for the most part, confined to the easier and, therefore, cheaper processes—were given on terms which left a very moderate margin of profit. The sub-contractors were further hampered by the difficulty in securing deliveries of machine tools. Many of them, moreover, were new to their work and did not appreciate the high degree of accuracy required in shell manufacture, or the strictness of inspection, with the result that their products failed to pass the tests. They also suffered from the delays already mentioned in obtaining samples, drawings, and specifications ; and it is probable that the difficulty of obtaining immediate supplies of machinery and raw material bore more hardly upon them than upon the large firms.

For these various reasons the sub-contractors did not find their position wholly satisfactory, for the cumulative weight of the economic and technical difficulties of their undertaking seemed to concentrate upon them without any countervailing compensation, and this discontent, doubtless, encouraged them to give the first place wherever possible to direct orders, and to complaints that undue preference was given by the War Office to the armament firms.

The cumulative result of the above-mentioned difficulties was, that the sub-contractors commonly disappointed the expectations of the principal contracting firm, and this was, perhaps, the most general form of excuse given by the latter to the War Office in response to complaint as to overdue deliveries.

The difficulties experienced with sub-contractors may be illustrated by following in some detail the fortunes of a particular contract for

4·5-in. H.E. shell, placed with Messrs. Cammell Laird on 2 September, 1914.

Tenders for 14,600 4·5-in. howitzer common lyddite shell were issued on 17 August. Messrs. Cammell explained on the following day that they were making special provision for the manufacture of shell of 6-in. calibre and over by increasing the equipment of their own shops, but that they had come to an arrangement with the Sheffield Simplex Motor Car Company whereby their works, which were thoroughly equipped with tools suitable for machining shell below 6-in. had been placed at their disposal.[1] A few days later Messrs. Cammell stated that they had accepted Admiralty orders for approximately 65,000 shell below 6-in., and that it would be difficult to estimate deliveries of 4·5-in. or other land service shells without knowing the sequence of requirements. If they were permitted to allocate their machinery in the proportion required between the Departments, they could promise prompt delivery.[2]

On 26 August this suggestion was referred to the Admiralty, asking that the output of the firm should be shared as proposed. The Admiralty accordingly undertook to diminish their orders with the firm to the extent of 30,000 12- and 14-pdr. common shell in order that Messrs. Cammell might be in a position to give half their capacity for shell below 6-in. to land service and still complete their essential naval orders within the necessary time. An order was therefore placed on 2 September for 14,600 4·5-in. lyddite shells. On 4 September the firm were asked to quote for a further 5,400 as a contribution towards a further requirement of 12,000, and this amount was added to the original order,[3] the deliveries to follow its completion, which was due at the end of 1914.

First deliveries on the original order were expected on 23 September, but on 30 September Messrs. Cammell were unable to promise deliveries before November.[4] They had trusted entirely to sub-contracts with the Hardy Patent Pick Company and the Sheffield Simplex Company and the former had altogether failed. They were considering the possibility of making these shells in their own shops, but this would entail some further relaxation of Admiralty work. The question was referred to the Admiralty on 4 October, the War Office pointing out that " the expenditure of 4·5-in. ammunition has been considerably more than was expected and we are in difficulties." The Admiralty replied on 20 October[5] expressing their inability to assist in a way which would entail delay in the supply of naval 6-in. shell. Messrs. Cammell's contracts were admitted to be in a very unsatisfactory condition and it was clear that the firm were not in a position to satisfy the requirements of both Departments for lyddite shell concurrently.

---

[1] Contracts/FirmsC/2367.

[2] Messrs. Hadfield who had also been invited to tender, had declined on the ground of " extreme pressure of Admiralty work " (Contracts/S/6573).

[3] The contract (Contracts/S/6573) was dated 9 September. The balance of the 12,000 was ordered from Messrs. Armstrong and the Projectile Company.

[4] Contracts/S/6924.

[5] G./19866/14 in Contracts/S/7113.

On 11 November the War Office enquired of Messrs. Cammell whether their revised promise of delivery in November would be made good, but the firm could only hold out the hope that the shell would be forthcoming " unless sub-contractors fail " ; and on 12 December the War Office was informed that " we are finishing these shell ourselves as our sub-contractor (the Sheffield Simplex Motor Works) have failed to do so." On 10 December a telegraphic inquiry as to why the shell had not been delivered as promised elicited the fact that deliveries were beginning. A week later the firm stated that they proposed, in order to place the work on a better footing, to extend their own shops, and on 5 January, they were instructed to proceed with their output of 4·5-in. shell at the rate of 600 a week, and to put down plant for an additional 1,000 a week, the maximum of 1,600 a week to be reached by 1 July, 1915.

(a) The Failure of Overseas Supplies.

The result of the shortage of labour and machinery and the failure of sub-contractors was, as has been indicated, to falsify the estimates on which the War Office had relied and to bring about a serious actual and prospective shortage of shell. It must not be forgotten, moreover, that by the spring of 1915, deliveries should have been coming in from overseas on a considerable scale, but here again expectations were not fulfilled. The orders which had been placed during the autumn of 1914 in both Canada and the United States had by May, 1915, produced a comparatively small output.

Canadian deliveries of shell were particularly disappointing. The Shell Committee had to contend with all the difficulties of organising manufacture among a large number of inexperienced firms, and as a large proportion of their promised output was to be in the form of complete rounds, they had also to arrange for the various components to come forward at corresponding rates. It is not surprising that they failed to secure co-ordination in this respect, with unfortunate results. The manufacture of shell bodies outran that of other components and by the end of May the arrears of 18- and 15-pdr. shrapnel shell were comparatively small, but though 800,000 complete rounds of 18-pdr. shrapnel were due only 21,000 had been delivered, and these were without primers, the manufacture of which had presented particular difficulties, as well as fuses. They had not at that date succeeded in producing any complete rounds of 18-pdr. H.E. or any 4·5-in. shell.

The greater part of the American shell orders, as has been seen, were placed in 1915, and were not due for delivery till the second half of the year. A considerable output, however, was due by the middle of the year from the Bethlehem Steel Company, who were then in arrears on their 4·7-in. contract, but practically up to date with 18-pdr. shrapnel shell. Their large contract for complete rounds of 18-pdr. was an outstanding contribution; owing to a strike at the works. although the contract rate was not passed till September, the whole quantity was delivered within contract time.

Deliveries of shell from other American firms were considerably behind the contract rate. At the end of May, 1915, for instance, 245,000 18-pdr. H.E. shell were due from three firms, but only 27,500 had been delivered, the bulk of these coming from one firm, the Washington Steel and Ordnance Company. The delay was in part due to the unexpected difficulties sometimes encountered owing to lack of familiarity with British specifications and methods of manufacture. For example, in the case of the Bethlehem Company's first contract for 4·7-in. H.E. shell, arranged in October, 1914, a month elapsed between the signing of the contract and the decision as to the Mark of shell to be made, and when the firm finally received the specification they found that the method of manufacture required involved processes, such as boring the shell internally, which they had never contemplated when fixing the price, the misunderstanding being due to the difference between American and English technical expressions. In effect the firm had " quoted for an entirely different article to that which they are expected to supply. The English were ignorant of the American methods and the Americans were ignorant of English methods." In view of the interruptions and difficulties experienced, the firm had by the end of 1915 found this contract unremunerative.[1]

IV. The Need for Complete Industrial Mobilisation.

It has been seen that by the end of 1914 delays in shell deliveries had assumed a sufficiently serious aspect, and the prospects for the future were such as to cause serious concern to the authorities concerned with munitions supply. Even so, no drastic revision of the policy hitherto followed was as yet considered necessary. The appointment of Sir George Gibb in December as an additional member of the Army Council marked an important departure in supply administration, but the first steps which he took towards improving the supply position followed the familiar line of ·consultation with the established contractors ; and the conference to which those contractors were summoned, by pointing to the labour shortage as the crucial problem, did little to shake the faith of the War Office in the policy of organising industrial resources through the armament firms.

On the last day of 1914 the Board of Trade was called in to assist the War Office to find the labour required for munitions work. The most hopeful course was considered to be the diversion of labour from firms engaged on private work to the armament firms. Owing to the wide extent of the sub-contracting system a campaign on these lines was beset with many difficulties, and, in addition, firms outside the armament group were more disposed to ask for contracts for themselves than to part with their men. As has been seen,[2] it was not easy for untried firms to obtain direct War Office contracts,

---

[1] 94/S/176. The price originally quoted by Bethlehem (£3 per shell) was as low as the lowest British price at that time.

[2] See above p. 107.

and the process by which direct contractors evolved from sub-contractors was bound to be a gradual one. Nevertheless, a few of the larger engineering firms had obtained shell contracts before the end of 1914, and it is significant that their representatives were included among the delegates to the Shell Conference.

In the first months of 1915 the demand from engineering firms for direct contracts, stimulated by the danger of losing workmen, grew steadily. The possibilities thus opened up were recognised by the Board of Trade as soon as they began their preparations for the campaign for diverting labour and under the auspices of the Board there sprang up a powerful movement for the local organisation of munitions production, independent of the armament firms. The steps taken to provide labour for munitions work and the development of the movement for industrial mobilisation are described in the succeeding parts of this volume. It is only necessary to point out here that demands for a revision of the War Office supply policy in the direction of a further spreading of contracts were being made by the engineering industry some weeks before public attention was attracted to the shortage of munitions and before the beginning of the accusations launched against the War Office in the House of Commons and in the Press in the spring of 1915.

As has been shown in an earlier chapter, repeated demands were received from the front from the end of 1914 onwards for a more liberal supply of ammunition. To these appeals, the War Office could only reply that they were fully aware of the importance of increasing supplies and were sparing no efforts to secure the highest possible output from every available source.[1] By March, 1915, however, it was no longer possible to conceal the fact that so far as the immediate future was concerned, an adequate supply of ammunition could not be assured.

In the middle of March the seriousness of the position was revealed by Lord Kitchener, when, in speaking in the House of Lords on the 15th he admitted that supplies were not coming up to expectations and that there was great cause for anxiety. The main theme of his speech was the improvement which the Government hoped to effect by means of the Defence of the Realm Amendment No. 2 Act, the second reading of which was later moved by Lord Crewe. The provisions of this Act and the terms come to with Labour at the end of March are discussed elsewhere, but a portion of the speech may be quoted here, because of its importance as an official pronouncement on the shortage of munitions.

" The work of supplying and equipping new Armies depends largely on our ability to obtain the war material required. Our demands on the industries concerned with the manufacture of munitions of war in this country have naturally been very great, and have necessitated that they and other ancillary trades should work at the highest possible pressure. The armament firms have promptly responded to our appeal, and have undertaken orders

---

[1] See above p. 23.

of vast magnitude. The great majority also of the employees have loyally risen to the occasion and have worked, and are working overtime and on night shifts in all the various workshops and factories in the country.

" Notwithstanding these efforts to meet our requirements, we have unfortunately found that the output is not only not equal to our necessities but does not fulfil our expectations, for a very large number of our orders have not been completed by the dates on which they were promised.

" The progress in equipping our new Armies and also in supplying the necessary war material for our forces in the field has been seriously hampered by the failure to obtain sufficient labour and by delays in the production of the necessary plant, largely due to the enormous demands, not only of ourselves but of our Allies. While the workmen generally, as I have said, have worked loyally and well, there have, I regret to say, been instances where absence, irregular timekeeping, and slack work have led to a marked diminution in the output of our factories. In some cases the temptations of drink account for this failure to work up to the high standard expected. It has been brought to my notice on more than one occasion that the restrictions of trade unions have undoubtedly added to our difficulties, not so much in obtaining sufficient labour as in making the best use of that labour. I am confident, however, that the seriousness of the position as regards our supplies has only to be mentioned and all concerned will agree to waive for the period of the war any of those restrictions which prevent in the very slightest degree our utilising all the labour available to the fullest extent that is possible.

" I cannot too earnestly point out that unless the whole nation works with us and for us, not only in supplying the manhood of the country to serve in our ranks but also in supplying the necessary arms, ammunition, and equipment, successful operations in the various parts of the world in which we are engaged will be very seriously hampered and delayed. I have heard rumours that the workmen in some factories have an idea that the war is going so well that there is no necessity for them to work their hardest. I can only say that the supply of war material at the present moment and for the next two or three months is causing me very serious anxiety, and I wish all those engaged in the manufacture and supply of these stores to realise that it is absolutely essential, not only that the arrears in the deliveries of our munitions of war should be wiped off, but that the output of every round of ammunition is of the utmost importance and has a large influence on our operations in the field."

*   *   *   *   *   *   *   *

" Labour may very rightly ask that their patriotic work should not be used to inflate the profits of the directors and shareholders of the various great industrial and armament firms, and we are therefore arranging a system under which the important armament firms come under Government control, and we hope that workmen who work regularly by keeping good time shall reap some of the benefits which the war automatically confers on these great companies.   I feel strongly, my Lords, that the men working long hours in the shops by day and by night, week in and week out, are doing their duty for their King and country in a like manner with those who have joined the Army for active service in the field. They are thus taking their part in the war and displaying the patriotism that has been so manifestly shown by the nation in all ranks."[1]

Before this speech was made, the first criticisms of the War Office supply policy had been heard in the House of Commons.   On 1 March Mr. Asquith made a speech on the Supplementary Vote of Credit for 1914–15 and the Estimates for 1915–16, in which he compared the rate of expenditure on army services with the cost of great wars in the past. In the debate which followed Mr. Bonar Law urged that further utilisation of the industrial resources of the country was both possible and necessary.

" I do ask, not by way of criticism, but by way of suggestion, Are we doing everything that we can to end this war?   I think, as regards the Army and the Navy, we are doing everything we can, but what about utilising the industrial resources of this country.   One of the lessons which our enemy ought to have taught us is that their preparation for war meant just as much the organisation of the civilian population as the organisation of those who are actually bearing arms.   That is comparatively easy in a State of governed like Germany, for in war, as each form of government has its advantages and disadvantages, a despotic Government has the advantage that it can more easily control these things ; but we have seen from what happened in France that it is possible for a democratic country too.   When the war broke out France mobilised the whole of her industry in precisely the same way in which she mobilised her troops.   Have we done, and are we doing, the same ?   The Government know that both this House and the country will give them all the power they ask. We are the greatest manufacturing country in the world.   This war has been going on for seven months, and if—I do not say that it is so, for I do not know—after seven months there is a shortage of ammunition, or of the necessary munitions of war, then, in my belief, we have not utilised to the utmost the industrial resources of this country, and I say to the Government now that to bring this war to a close nothing that they can do would be more effective than to look at the industrial position of the country and to consider, though business as usual is wise from the point of view of stopping panic, though business is necessary, that the first necessity is to provide what we need for this war, and it should be done, and other business must wait until the needs of the State have first been met.   I hope that is being done, and I am sure that it ought to be done."[2]

---

[1] *Parliamentary Debates* (1915) *H. of L.*, XVIII, 721–724 (15/3/15).
[2] *Parliamentary Debates* (1915) *H. of C.*, LXX, 606-7.

Mr Bonar Law reiterated this view a week later : " I do think that we have not mobilised the industries of the country in the way in which it was possible to mobilise them for the purposes of the war."[1]

On 1 March, Mr. Bonar Law could say that he did not know whether there was in fact a shortage of ammunition. A fortnight later the position was made clearer by Lord Kitchener's speech in the House of Lords, and this was followed by a Press campaign for better organisation.

Towards the end of March, *The Times* published two or three articles on the subject of the shortage of ammunition.

" Evidence has recently been accumulating from the seat of war to prove that the only thing which is now delaying the active progress of operations. . . is the inadequate supply of ammunition. The publicly expressed opinion of the highest authority on the spot coincides with much other information to establish the fact beyond the possibility of doubt. . . the problem of the moment is to increase the supplies and it is an industrial, not a military problem."[2]

During the next fortnight the criticisms of the Government's arrangements for supplying munitions grew more and more pointed. The campaign against drink was at this time at its height, and on 6 April, *The Times* pointed out that public attention was being diverted from the business of producing war material to the drink question :—

" The thing wants handling in a large way. The national resources in men, premises and plant capable of turning out the material required should be pooled, and the items redistributed to the best advantage. The need has not been realised before, and no doubt the authorities have been overwhelmed with work : but it is certain that the national resources have not been utilised to the full. Indeed, no attempt has been made to do so."

At the end of March, Lord Kitchener had appointed an Armaments Output Committee, to assist in the provision of labour for munitions work. Its formation was announced in the Press on 7 April, and commenting on it on the following day, *The Times* wrote :—

" A great deal has been said of late about the shortcomings of certain sections of workmen. We believe far stronger things might be said, with far more justice, about the extraordinary failure of the Government to take in hand in business-like fashion during the early stages of the war the matter of providing a full and adequate supply of munitions. They talked as though they were organising miracles of output, but in point of fact there was no proper organisation at all. The War Office has sought to do too much. It has been jealous of civilian aid. . . the War Office should chiefly devote itself to the task of organising its armies. It should state its requirements as to supplies and leave to others the far more complex task of organising industry."

Two days later (10 April) the charge was reiterated : —

" The primary reason why Sir J. French is unduly short of munitions is not drink at all. It is that in our previous wars the War Office has been accustomed to rely for all such supplies

[1] *Parliamentary Debates* (1915) *H. of C.*, LXX, 1275.   [2] *Times*, 31 March, 1915.

upon the Master-General of the Ordnance, who was wont to figure as a sort of Universal Provider. In this unprecedented war the Government ought to have insisted upon the instant organisation of the whole of our national resources, leaving the War Office to state its requirements and raise its armies."

The critics of the War Office failed, as was natural, to take into account the circumstances which had brought about the breakdown of supply, which, since they arose from the unprecedented and unforeseen scale of the demand, must have been encountered in some degree by the men who undertook to organise the supply of munitions during the first year of the war, whether those men had been officials of the War Office or had held, from the first, an independent status. The policy, deliberately adopted, of organising the resources of the country through the armament firms, had much in its favour. The fact remains that the armament firms were at the outbreak of war the only firms with actual experience of munitions manufacture ; ordinary engineering firms could not take up such work at a moment's notice when there was little or no organisation at headquarters for instructing and supervising them ; and it was to a great extent the education in shell making which such firms received as sub-contractors to the armament firms which enabled them in the summer of 1915 to organise their own resources on a wider and more independent basis. Thus it does not follow, because the country in the summer of 1915 was ripe for industrial mobilisation on the lines followed by the Armaments Output Committee and the Ministry of Munitions, that such industrial mobilisation could have been successfully carried out in August, 1914.

Moreover, the shortage of ammunition—the primary reason for the handing over of supply to a new Department—since it was brought about by arrears of deliveries rather than by lack of orders was to a certain extent remedied by time alone. The real achievement of the War Office was the creation of capacity to meet the demands of the 30-division standard contemplated in the autumn of 1914 ; the true results of their labours are more fairly represented by the supply position of December, 1915, than by that of May, 1915.[1] The time needed for the creation of new capacity, though uniformly disappointing the expectations of those responsible, differed little in fact from that which the large experience of the Ministry of Munitions showed to be the normal time required for the development of bulk output from new sources of supply.

None the less, the view of the public, as indicated in the above extracts, reflected an instinctive appreciation of the facts. The existing machinery of supply was strained to breaking point, despite the strenuous and unremitting labours of the Master-General of the Ordnance and his staff. The armament contractors were in arrears with their deliveries ; their sub-contractors had been unable to give the expected assistance. The Royal Ordnance Factories were thus compelled to carry a disproportionate share of the load of bulk supply, a situation which was bound to react injuriously upon their other vital duties

---

[1] See Appendices III and IV.

in regard to experimental and specialised manufacture and the balancing and co-ordination of output as a whole. Moreover, they were ill-equipped for certain classes of work which now became of outstanding importance, such as the filling of heavy shell with new kinds of high explosive. Every branch of the Arsenal's activities had become intolerably congested in consequence of the fact that it was the chief national munitions factory as well as the headquarters of all work connected with stores, inspection and experimental manufacture. Geographical limitations made further extension difficult, while the long piecemeal development of bygone years was a heritage full of embarrassments.

A new departure was necessary. All the indications pointed to the need for vesting the responsibility for the supply of munitions in a new separate authority, for entrusting the task of mobilising the industrial resources of the country as a whole to a department specially equipped and unhampered by precedent. Only so could the development of new sources of supply, whether by the creation of new arsenals or the organisation of private industry, be effectively secured.

By the second week in April the first steps in this direction had already been taken. On 31 March, as has been seen, Lord Kitchener had appointed the Armaments Output Committee, the original functions of which were, it is true, confined to the provision of labour for munitions work but which in fact took the leading part in the organisation of local resources for shell manufacture. On 8 April the appointment of a second committee was announced—the Munitions of War or Treasury Committee, under the chairmanship of Mr. Lloyd George, then Chancellor of the Exchequer. A week later, Mr. Asquith, in announcing the names of the members in the House of Commons, stated that the decision to appoint such a committee had in fact been taken a month before, but that the ground had had to be prepared for its activities. He explained that its functions were " to ensure the promptest and most efficient application of all the available productive resources of the country to the manufacture and supply of munitions of war for the Navy and the Army."

The work of this committee and of the Armaments Output Committee, the adoption of a scheme for organising production on new lines, and the development of a central department for supplying munitions form the subject of a separate part.[1] The Munitions of War Committee was in fact an embryo Ministry of Munitions. With its appointment the end of the administration of supply by the War Office was in sight ; and on 26 May the announcement was made that the Government had decided to create a new Department of State to take over from the War Office the duty of supplying munitions to the Army.

---

[1] Vol. I, Part III.

APPENDICES.

APPENDIX I.

(CHAPTER II, p. 55.)

Form of Contract and Schedule as issued in August, 1914.

(Army Form K. 1271.)

STORES AND MATERIALS.

Messrs. ....

Notices and Instructions to Persons Tendering.

1. *Lowest Tender not necessarily to be accepted.*—The Secretary of State for War does not bind himself to accept the lowest or any Tender.

2. *Power to accept portion of Tender.*—The Secretary of State for War reserves the power, unless the Contractor expressly stipulates to the contrary in his Tender, of accepting such portion thereof as he may think fit.

3. *Delivery of Tender.*—This Tender is to be delivered at the War Office by 12 *o'clock noon,* on .... in the enclosed envelope, addressed to " The Director of Army Contracts, War Office, Whitehall, London, S.W.," and marked on the outside, " Tender for.........
...."

4. *Prices.*—The prices quoted should be " net," all discounts being allowed for in the quotations.

5. *Schedule not to be altered by Contractor.*—The Schedule issued with this Form of Tender must not be altered by the Contractor. Any modification of the Schedule considered expedient by the Contractor should form the subject of a separate letter to accompany the Tender.

6. *Incomplete Tenders.*—Tenders may not be considered if complete information be not given at the time of tendering, or if the particulars and data (if any) asked for in the Schedule be not fully filled in.

7. *Rendering of Accounts, &c.*—Upon receipt of a notification that articles have been accepted, the Contractor is to put forward his Account or Bill. Payment will, as a rule, be made within 16 days after the receipt of a correct Bill.

Application for the necessary invoice and bill forms, or for instructions as to delivery or as to rendering of claims, should be made to the Receiving Officer at the place named in the Schedule.

8. *Notification of result of Inspection.*—Unless otherwise provided in the Specification or Schedule, the examination of the articles will be made as soon as practicable after receipt, and the result of the examination will be notified to the Contractor.

9. *Sample deliveries.*—Small sample deliveries, if specially so marked and submitted in separate parcels, together with invoice, will be inspected within a few days of receipt, and the result of the inspection will be notified immediately to the Contractor.

10. *Samples.*—When practicable, samples will, on application, be lent to the accepted Contractor for his general guidance ; the cost of carriage both ways must be borne by the Contractor.

11. *Port of London Dues.*—Goods entering or leaving the Port of London in the course of delivery under a War Office contract are exempt from Port Dues.

To secure such exemption the Contractor should obtain from the Port of London Authority the proper forms of certificate of exemption, and send them *in duplicate* to the consignee with the necessary particulars duly filled in.

If the transaction is in order, the consignee will sign and return the certificate to the Contractor, who should present it to the Port of London Authority.

12. *Port of London Wharfage and Porterage charges.*—In the case of stores delivered under a War Office contract, f.o.b. London, the Port of London Authority allow a rebate of one-third of the wharfage and porterage charges made by them ; this rebate should be allowed for in the tender price.

To His Majesty's Principal Secretary of State for the War Department.

Sir,—

We, the undersigned (hereinafter styled " the Contractor "), do hereby engage to provide and deliver the several articles enumerated in the Schedule hereunto annexed, to which we have affixed prices (or such portion thereof as, in accordance with the power reserved by you, you may determine), at the price or prices therein stated, and upon the Conditions herein and in the Specification set forth. The work to be performed under this Contract will be carried out at our premises situated at ....

Dated this .... day of 19

Witness.....................   Signature of } ....
                              Contractor }

Address.....................   Address ....

....

CONDITIONS OF CONTRACT.

1. *Description and delivery of the Stores.*—The articles required shall be of the qualities and sorts described, and equal in all respects to the Patterns, Specifications, Drawings and Samples specified in the Schedule ; and shall be delivered by the Contractor, at his own expense, at the time or times specified, into the charge of the Officer at the place named in the Schedule. An Invoice (*see* Instruction No. 7 above) shall be sent to the Officer as soon as any articles have been despatched.

2. *Inspection and Rejection.*—(a) The articles, before being received into Store, shall be examined, and if found inferior in quality to, or differing in form or material from the Patterns, Specifications, Drawings or Samples specified in the Schedule, may be rejected. Such rejected articles shall not be considered as having been delivered under the Contract, but the Contractor shall, if required to do so by the Secretary of State for War, replace the same at his own expense without any allowance being made to him.

(b) Articles so rejected shall be removed by the Contractor at his own expense, within eight days of the date of the notification of the rejection. In the event of the Contractor failing to remove them, or any of them, within such period, the Secretary of State for War at his sole discretion shall be at liberty either to return the rejected articles, carriage forward, by such mode of transit as he may select, or to sell them by public auction or by private contract on the Contractor's behalf, and to retain such portion of the proceeds as may be necessary to cover any loss or expenses incurred by the War Department in connection with the said sale.

3. *Payment.*—Payment will be made direct to the Contractor, or to an Agent or Attorney, duly authorised to receive payment by the Contractor in writing or by a revocable power of attorney. The Secretary of State for War will not recognise any assignment other than is before mentioned of moneys due or to become due under this Contract, and neither Section 25 (6) of the Judicature Act, 1873, nor Section 28 (6) of the Supreme Court of Judicature (Ireland) Act, 1877, shall apply to this Contract or to moneys due or to become due thereunder.

4. (a) *Damages for Delay.*—Should the articles or any portion thereof not be delivered within the period or periods stipulated in the Schedule, whether by reason of the exercise by the Secretary of State for War of his power of rejection under Clause 2 or otherwise, the Contractor shall be liable by way of liquidated

I*

damages for delay for a sum equal to 1 per cent. on the value on the articles deficient if the delay does not exceed thirty days, for 2 per cent. if the delay exceeds thirty days but does not exceed sixty days, and for 3 per cent. if the delay exceeds sixty days ; such sum may at any time be deducted from any sum or sums then due, or which at any time thereafter may become due to him under this or any other Contract with this Department, or may be demanded of him to be paid within fourteen days to the Paymaster-General for credit to Army Funds.

(b) *Purchase in default.*—In addition to the above, if and whenever there may be any articles or any portion thereof deficient, the Secretary of State for War shall be at liberty to purchase other articles of the same or similar description from other persons to supply such deficiency ; and in the event of any excess cost being incurred by reason of any difference between the price paid for the same and the Contract price, to charge the amount of such excess cost to the Contractor, and the sum so charged shall, at the option of the Secretary of State for War, be deducted and paid in like manner as the liquidated damages hereinbefore mentioned.

(c) *Termination of Contract.*—The Secretary of State for War shall also be at liberty to terminate the Contract at, or after, any one of the specified periods, at which default shall have been made, either wholly or to the extent of such default, without prejudice to his remedies under paragraphs (a) and '(b) of this Clause.

5. *Contractor's responsibility for Government Property.*—The Contractor guarantees the due return of all Government property issued to him, and will be responsible to the full value of such property, to be assessed by the Secretary of State for War, for all loss or damage from whatever cause happening thereto while in the possession or control of himself, his servants or agents.

6. *Principals or Partners to be notified.*—The Contractor shall furnish within seven days after the notification to him of the acceptance of the Tender, to the Secretary of State for War, unless such information shall have been given previously, the names of all the persons who are at the time principals to the contract or partners in the Contracting Firm, or, in the case of a Company with limited liability, the names of all the Directors. In case of any change occurring in such principals, partners or directors, during the currency of the Contract, the Contractor shall notify such change to the Secretary of State for War within fourteen days from the date thereof. In the event of any breach of this clause the Secretary of State for War may terminate the Contract forthwith, and may recover from the Contractor any loss resulting from such termination.

7. (a) *Fair Wages, Transfer of Contract, and Sub-letting.*—The Contractor shall, in the execution of this Contract, observe and fulfil the obligations upon contractors specified in the Resolution passed by the House of Commons on the 10 March, 1909, namely :—

" The Contractor shall . . . pay rates of wages and observe hours of labour not less favourable than those commonly recognised by employers and trade societies (or, in the absence of such recognised wages and hours, those which in practice prevail amongst good employers) in the trade in the district where the work is carried out. Where there are no such wages and hours recognised or prevailing in the district, those recognised or prevailing in the nearest district in which the general industrial circumstances are similar shall be adopted. Further, the conditions of employment generally accepted in the district in the trade concerned shall be taken into account in considering how far the terms of the Fair Wages Clauses are being observed. The Contractor shall be prohibited from transferring or assigning, directly or indirectly, to any person or persons whatever, any portion of his contract without the written permission of the Department. Sub-letting, other than that which may be customary in the trade concerned shall be prohibited. The Contractor shall be responsible for the observance of the Fair Wages Clauses by the sub-contractor."

(b) *Exhibition of Notice at Works.*—The Contractor shall cause the preceding condition to be prominently exhibited for the information of his workpeople, on the premises where work is being executed under the contract.*

---

* Forms of Notice for exhibition may be obtained on application to the Director of Army Contracts, War Office, London, S.W.

(*c*) *Inspection of Wages Books, etc.*—The Contractor shall keep proper wages books and time sheets, showing the wages paid, and the time worked by the workpeople in his employ in and about the execution of the Contract, and such wages books and time sheets shall be produced whenever required for the inspection of any officer authorised by the Department.

8. *Bribery.*—Any bribe, commission, gift, loan or advantage given, promised or offered by, or on behalf of, the Contractor, or his partner, agent, or servant, in relation to the obtaining or to the execution of this or any other Contract for His Majesty's service, or given, promised, or offered by, or on behalf of, the Contractor, or his partner, agent, or servant, to any officer or person in the service or employ of the Crown, who shall be in any way connected with the obtaining or the execution of this or any other Contract, subjects the Contractor to cancellation of this Contract, and also to payment of any loss resulting from any such cancellation. Where any · such bribe, commission, gift, loan, or advantage, has been given or promised in relation to the obtaining or the execution of this Contract, or to any officer or person in the service or employ of the Crown who shall be in any way connected with the obtaining or the execution of this Contract, the Contractor shall also be liable to pay by way of liquidated damages a sum equal to 10 per cent. of all the sums which become payable to him under this Contract. Any question or dispute as to a breach of this Article, or the sums to be paid, is to be settled by the Secretary of State for War, in such manner, on such evidence or information, as he thinks fit, and his decision is to be final.

9. *Bankruptcy.*—The Secretary of State for War, in addition to any power which he may have under this Contract of terminating the same, may also at any time terminate the Contract if, under any present or future Bankruptcy Act, any receiving order or order for administration shall be made in respect of the Contractor's estate, or if the Contractor shall enter into, make or execute any deed of arrangement as defined by the Deeds of Arrangement Act, 1887, or other composition or arrangement with, or assignment for the benefit of, his creditors, or purport so to do ; or if (in Scotland) he become insolvent or notour bankrupt, or application be made under any present or future Bankruptcy Act for sequestration of his estate, or application be made by him or any of his creditors for cessio bonorum against him, or a trust deed be granted by him for behoof of creditors ; or in the case of a Company (in any part of the United Kingdom) in the event of the passing of any effective resolution or the making of any order for winding up, whether voluntary or otherwise.

10. *Members of the House of Commons.*—In pursuance of the House of Commons (Disqualification) Act, 1782 (22 Geo. III., cap. 45), and under the pain of the penalties therein mentioned, no member of the House of Commons shall be admitted to any part or share of this Contract, or to any benefit to arise therefrom, contrary to the true intent and meaning of the said Act.

APPENDIX II.

(Chapter II, p. 65.)

Orders placed with the Trade 1913-14, and August, 1914-July, 1915.[1]

Description of Store.	Number Ordered.	
	1913–1914.	Aug. 1914–July 1915.
Guns :—		
12 in. Howitzers	—	40
9·2 in. Guns	—	4
9·2 in. Howitzers	—	36
8 in. Howitzers	—	11
6 in. Guns	4	—
6 in. Howitzers..	—	16
4·5 in. Howitzers	—	650
3 in. Guns	—	12
60-pdr. Guns	—	72
18-pdr. ,,	—	3,380
13-pdr. ,,	—	18
1-pdr. ,,	—	27
Mortars	—	200
Bomb-throwers	—	200
Gun Carriages and Mountings :—		
12 in. Howitzer Mountings	—	40
9·2 in. ,, ,,	—	36
4·5 in. Equipments ..	—	650
18-pdr. ,,	—	3,380
13-pdr. ,,	—	18
Gun Equipment :—		
Springs, Running out	976	21,123
Wheels, Artillery	—	5,116
Poles, Draught	—	12,157
Bars supporting Draught Poles	—	9,044
Miscellaneous Items	£923	£273,227
Optical Munitions :—		
Sights, Dial No. 7	456	3,602
,, ,, No. 1.	—	2,150
,, Rocking Bar	—	591
Adapters, Dial Sight	—	750
Carriers, ,, ,,	24	3,820
Indicators, Fuse	—	5,140
Gun Ammunition :—		
Shell 12 in. H.E.	—	40,400
,, 9·2 in. A.P.	991	7,901
,, 9·2 in. H.E.	806	139,886
,, 8 in. H.E.	—	188,300
,, 6 in. A.P.	—	10,300
,, 6 in. H.E.	—	767,420
,, 6 in. Shrapnel	—	12,300
,, 6 in. C.P.	—	150
,, 5 in. H.E.	—	202,524
,, 5 in. Shrapnel	—	40,500
,, 4·7 in. H.E.	—	356,200
,, 4·7 in. Shrapnel	—	54,500
,, 4·5 in. H.E.	(a)459	(a)3,266,250

Orders for warlike stores placed by A6 and A7. (Hist. Rec. R 170 15).

APPENDIX II—*contd.*

Description of Store.	Number Ordered.	
	1913–1914.	Aug. 1914–July 1915.
Shell 4·5 in. Shrapnel	650	420,000
,, 4·5 in. Common	500	372
,, 4 in. H.E.	—	6,900
,, 2·95 in. Double	—	4,500
,, 2·75 in. H.E.	—	99,000
,, 2·75 in. Shrapnel	22,950	9,000
,, 60-pdr. Shrapnel	—	156,300
,, 60-pdr. H.E.	—	388,850
,, 18-pdr. ,,	(a)—	(a)5,887,000
,, 18-pdr. Shrapnel	(a)—	(a)4,565,783
,, 18-pdr. Common	—	9,000
,, 15-pdr. H.E.	—	180,000
,, 15-pdr. Shrapnel	—	898,800
,, 13-pdr. H.E.	(a)—	(a)190,000
,, 13-pdr. Shrapnel	(a)—	(a)234,500
,, 12-pdr. and 14-pdr. Lyddite	—	24,800
,, 10-pdr. Shrapnel	—	700
,, 2-pdr. N.T.	—	500
Total Shell	26,356	18,113,636
Proof Shot, 9·2 in.	—	600
,, ,, 6 in.	—	6,900
,, ,, 4·7 in.	—	5,000
,, ,, 4·5 in.	—	23,000
,, ,, 4 in.	—	2,250
,, ,, 60-pdr.	—	5,100
,, ,, 18-pdr.	—	92,700
,, ,, 13-pdr.	—	7,900
,, ,, 12-pdr. 12 cwt.	—	6,500
Proof Shell, 6 in.	—	2,600
,, ,,· 4·5 in.	—	3,750
,, ,, 60-pdr.	—	4,500
,, ,, 18-pdr.	—	14,000
,, ,, 15-pdr.	—	10,000
,, ,, 13-pdr.	—	1,500
Practice Projectile :—		
9·2 in.	500	—
6 in.	200	—
5 in.	—	960
4·7 in.	—	6,500
4·5 in.	500	1,000
12-pdr. and 14-pdr.	—	1,000
Cartridges, Complete Rounds :—		
4·5 in. Howitzer	—	1,866,000
3 in.	—	6,000
18-pdr. Shrapnel	2,400	11,067,000
18-pdr. H.E.	—	8,417,000
13-pdr. H.E.	—	100,000
13-pdr. Shrapnel	7,320	—
2-pdr.	—	1,500
1-pdr.	—	21,000
Total. Complete Rounds	9,720	21,478,500

(a) See also complete rounds below.

APPENDIX II—*contd.*

Description of Store.	Number ordered.	
	1913–1914.	Aug. 1914–July 1915.
Bombs :—		
Aeroplane	—	14,370
Trench Mortar	—	151,000
Signal	—	7,715
Cartridge Cases :—		
6 in. short	—	1,000
4·7 in.	—	286,950
4·5 in.	1,100	4,088,200
4 in.	—	2,800
18-pdr.	—	9,305,900
12-pdr. 12 cwt.	—	10,150
2-pdr.	—	500
Fuses :—		
No. 17	—	205,300
No. 44	—	1,697,000
No. 63	11,000	—
No. 65A	4,000	1,725,000
No. 80	38,600	8,707,533
No. 82	10,000	397,000
No. 83	—	5,400
No. 85	—	200,000
No. 86	—	175,000
No. 100	—	9,427,800
Primers	82,350	10,046,549
Gaines	—	12,524,400
Tubes, Friction	—	1,603,750
,, Vent Sealing	—	201,900
Machine Guns :—		
Vickers ·303 in.	41	3,792
Lewis ·303 in.	2	3,052
Machine Rifles	—	500
Rifles :—		
·303 in.	42,500	3,045,062
,, altered	—	162,000
Converted to 22 in.	5,860	9,329
Pistols	1,159	70,400
Rifle Stocks :—		
Butts	3,000	94,450
Fore Ends	15,000	102,108
Handguards, Front	120,300	109,900
,, Rear	76,000	36,000
Longstocks	94,500	198,477
Lances	—	1,050
Swords, Cavalry	—	40,250
Tulwars	—	5,550
Swords, Artillery	—	2,000
,, Practice	—	1,500
Bayonets	—	3,286,800
Small Arms Ammunition :—		
·303 in. Ball	53,085,527	2,307,360,000
·303 in. Blank	19,585,700	12,360,000
Japanese	—	16,000,000
Snider	59,000	—
7·9 mm.	—	1,315,000
Aiming Tube	1,100,000	1,100,000
·22 in.	34,888,300	572,500,000

APPENDIX II—*contd.*

Description of Store.	Number ordered.	
	1913–1914.	Aug. 1914–July 1915.
Small Arms Ammunition.—contd		
Pistol Ammunition	849,936	39,465,735
Cartridge Chargers	11,000,000	432,772,500
Detonators for Fuse	41,785	1,906,872
Grenades, Hand	—	4,722,625
,, Rifle	100	363,650
Pistols, Signal	120	18,545
Explosives, etc. :—		
*Ballistite	—	460 tons
*Cordite	455 tons	14,430 ,,
*Gun Cotton	—	2,310 ,,
*Gun Powder	74,100 lbs.	1,940,000 lbs.
*Nitrocellulose Powder	—	14,702 tons
*Acetone	280 tons	10,915 ,,
*Glycerine	168 ,,	750 ,,
*Nitric Acid	—	1,500 ,,
*Sulphuric Acid	2,000 ,,	42,120 ,,
*Benzol	—	79,300 galls.
*Dimethyl Analine	—	117 tons
*Mineral Jelly	100 ,,	260 ,,
*Saltpetre	—	1,650 ,,
*Soda Nitrate	2,270 ,,	22,730 ,,
*Soda Ash	175 ,,	150 ,,
*Sulphur Grough	—	350 ,,
*Toluol	—	270,860 galls.
*Cotton Waste	600 ,,	8,644 tons
		Aug. 8, 1914–Dec. 12, 1914.
*Picric Acid	139 ,,	3,454 tons
*Trinitrotoluene	239 cwt.	118,711 cwt.
		Aug. 1914–July 1915.
Scientific Instruments, etc. :—		
Fire Control Apparatus	—	18
Observation of Fire Apparatus	16	50
Barometers	—	1,112
Binoculars, Prismatic	3,082	58,375
,, Galilean	—	6,578
Clinometers	264	18,105
Compasses	2,987	54,544
Directors	175	3,980
Heliographs	143	4,828
Angle of Sight Instruments	95	796
Levels	—	3,575
Mekometers	1,376	2,600
Periscopes	—	26,325
Plotters	15	2,370
Artillery Rangefinders	129	592
Infantry ,,	157	5,058
Telemeters	—	224
Telescopes	835	14,297
Theodolites	1	100
Thermometers	622	2,402

* From December, 1914, these stores were transferred to the Explosives Department.

APPENDIX III.

(CHAPTER V, p. 134.)

Number of Shell ordered by the War Office for use in the Field[1] and position with regard to delivery on 31 December, 1914, and 29 May, 1915.

Note.—The following table deals with the principal types of service shell only, and does not include proof shot, common shell, etc., or shell intended for fixed armaments. A number of the orders placed from January, 1915, onwards were standing orders for a fixed monthly or weekly output ; in these cases the total due for delivery to the end of 1915 has been taken. The figures for both orders and arrears are in some cases approximate only. The terms of delivery were not always precisely formulated when orders were given, subsequent modifications were frequently made and orders were sometimes postponed in favour of others. It is, therefore, not always possible to estimate exactly the total quantity ordered, or the quantity due for delivery at a given date.[2]

Nature.	Position on 31/12/14.			Position on 29/5/15.		
	Total ordered.	De-livered.	Arrears.	Total ordered.	De-livered.	Arrears.
12-*in. How.*—						
H.E.—Trade	32,000	–	–	32,000	–	7,500
U.S.A.	–	–	–	10,000	–	–
Total	32,000	–	–	42,000	–	7,500

[1] In addition to the orders placed by the War Office, by 29 May, 1915, orders had been arranged by the Armaments Output Committee with Local Munitions Committees and National Shell Factories as follows :—

Maker.			*Total Ordered.*		*Weekly Output.*
18-*pdr.*—					
Birmingham	..	..	30,000	..	1,000
Huddersfield	..	..	56,000	..	2,000
Dundee	..	..	150,000	..	5,000 to 10,000
Keighley	..	..	105,000	..	5,000
Derby	..	..	105,000	..	5,000
Coventry	..	..	100,000	..	10,000
		Total	546,000		
4·5-*in.*—					
Leicester	..	..	23,000	..	500 to 1,000
Birmingham	..	..	275,000	..	13,000
Leeds	..	..	105,000	..	3,000 to 5,000
Hull	..	..	40,000	..	2,000 to 5,000
Bradford	..	..	60,000	..	2,000 to 4,000
Coventry	..	..	10,000	..	500
		Total	513,000		

It is not possible to estimate accurately the total amount of these orders, most of them being dependent upon the creation of capacity, working up to a given weekly output, the date of which was indeterminate. A number of schemes in addition to those here shown were under negotiation at the end of May, 1915.

[2] The figures are taken mainly from the *Lists of Orders for all Natures of Ammunition used in the Field* (A.2. War Office) and from *Gun Ammunition, Components, Accessories, etc., ordered by War Office from the Trade* (A. 7. War Office).

APPENDIX III—*contd.*

Nature.	Position on 31/12/14.			Position on 29/5/15.		
	Total ordered.	De-livered.	Arrears.	Total ordered.	De-livered.	Arrears.
9·2-*in. How.*—						
H.E.—Trade	63,200	548	1,052	85,775	7,082	18,993
U.S.A. ..	–	–	–	42,000	–	–
Total	63,200	548	1,052	127,775	7,082	18,993
8-*in. How.*—						
H.E.—Trade	94,800	–	–	149,300	118	7,082
U.S.A. ..	–	–	–	39,000	–	2,700
Total	94,800	–	–	188,300	118	9,782
6-*in. How.*—						
H.E.—Trade	248,400	–	1,500	313,400	123	50,077
U.S.A. ..	52,000	–	–	277,000	6,720	31,280
Total	300,400	–	1,500	590,400	6,843	81,357
Shrapnel—Trade ..	12,000	–	240	12,000	–	8,280
5-*in. How.*—						
H.E.—Trade	400	–	–	400	–	400
U.S.A. ..	20,000	–	–	95,000	1,752	–
Total	20,400	–	–	95,400	1,752	400
Shrapnel—Trade	30,000	–	9,900	30,000	4,573	25,427
60-*pdr.*—						
H.E.—O.F.	20,200	5,213	–	20,200	5,278	–
Trade ..	117,250	5,145	11,079	207,850	37,804	76,796
Canada ..	–	–	–	300,000	–	–
U.S.A. ..	–	–	–	60,000	–	–
Total	137,450	10,358	11,079	588,050	43,082	76,796
Shrapnel—O.F. ..	21,800	7,156	–	31,300	22,325	3,175
Trade ..	101,300	6,792	11,908	156,300	45,065	49,936
Total	123,100	13,948	11,908	187,600	67,390	53,111
4·7-*in.*—						
H.E.—Trade	235,400	390	1,900	235,400	2,546	69,304
U.S.A. ..	30,000	–	–	120,800	–	30,500
Total	265,400	390	1,900	356,200	2,546	99,804
Shrapnel—Trade	24,500	–	–	24,500	–	9,750
U.S.A. ..	30,000	–	–	30,000	14,548	13,452
Total	54,500	–	–	54,500	14,548	23,202
4·5-*in.*—						
H.E.—O.F.	49,600	14,745	–	76,600	34,509	3,791
Trade ..	426,900	4,469	21,080	1,010,400	57,430	182,413
Canada ..	–	–	–	700,000	–	50,000
U.S.A. ..	–	–	–	575,000	–	45,000
Complete Rds.—						
Canada ..	–	–	–	1,866,666	–	–
Total	476,500	19,214	21,080	4,228,666	91,939	281,204

APPENDIX III—*contd.*

Nature.	Position on 31/12/14.			Position on 29/5/15.		
	Total ordered.	De-livered.	Arrears.	Total ordered.	De-livered.	Arrears.
4·5-in.—cont.						
Shrapnel—O.F. ..	54,540	648	–	54,540	1,417	–
Trade	313,000	17,360	14,290	400,000	45,703	134,447
Total ..	367,540	18,008	14,290	454,540	47,120	134,447
18-pdr.—						
H.E.—O.F. ..	50,000	–	–	122,000	30,981	13,019
Trade	238,000	–	–	3,373,000	8,152	111,848
Canada	–	–	–	125,000	–	–
U.S.A.	–	–	–	2,050,000	27,492	217,508
Total ..	288,000	–	–	5,670,000	66,625	342,375
Complete Rds.—						
O.F.	20,000	8,992	–	20,000	19,990	–
Trade	400,000	–	–	400,000	–	100,000
Canada	–	–	–	3,266,666	–	200,000
U.S.A.	–	–	–	4,750,000	–	–
Total ..	420,000	8,992	–	8,436,666	19,990	300,000
H.E. Total (incl. complete Rds.) ..	708,000	8,992	–	14,106,666	86,615	642,375
Shrapnel—O.F. ..	538,440	46,815	–	638,440	124,345	8,766
Trade	2,734,283	143,996	197,003	3,139,283	608,375	625,908
Canada	500,000	3,294	76,706	625,000	389,966	60,034
U.S.A.	100,000	–	–	100,000	69,684	–
Total ..	3,872,723	194,105	273,709	4,502,723	1,192,370	694,708
Complete Rds.—						
Trade	600,000	–	–	600,000	–	100,000
Canada	1,100,000	–	–	3,466,666	21,132	778,868
U.S.A.	1,000,000	–	–	7,250,000	165,884	184,116
India	60,000	15,000	–	60,000	22,500	37,500
Total	2,760,000	15,000	–	11,376,666	209,516	1,100,484
Shrapnel Total (incl. complete Rds.) ..	6,632,723	209,105	273,709	15,879,389	1,401,886	1,795,192
15-pdr.—						
H.E.—Trade ..	–	–	–	180,000	–	25,000
Shrapnel—O.F. ..	11,000	–	–	11,000	–	5,500
Trade	598,800	–	46,000	598,800	9,207	259,593
Canada	100,000	–	50,000	300,000	62,292	37,708
Total ..	709,800	–	96,000	909,800	71,499	302,801
13-pdr.—						
H.E.—Trade ..	–	–	–	40,000	–	4,500
U.S.A.	50,000	–	–	150,000	15,394	74,606
Complete Rds.—						
Canada	–	–	–	100,000	–	–
Total	50,000	–	–	290,000	15,394	79,106

149

APPENDIX III—*contd.*

Nature.	Position on 31/12/14.			Position on 29/5/15.		
	Total ordered.	De-livered.	Arrears.	Total ordered.	De-livered.	Arrears.
13-pdr.—cont.						
Shrapnel—O.F. ..	94,000	17,643	–	194,000	75,212	–
Trade	182,000	3,079	11,921	182,000	23,153	137,755
Complete Rds.—						
India	7,000	–	7,000	14,000	7,500	6,500
Total	283,000	20,722	18,921	390,000	105,865	144,255
2·75-in.—						
H.E.—Trade ..	21,000	–	–	82,500	–	16,000
Shrapnel—O.F. ..	3,260	965	–	3,260	1,676	–
Trade	4,000	450	3,550	9,000	2,629	1,371
Total	7,260	1,415	3,550	12,260	4,305	1,371
Total H.E.—						
O.F.	139,800	28,950	–	238,800	90,758	16,810
Trade	1,877,350	10,552	36,611	6,110,025	113,255	669,913
Canada	–	–	–	6,358,332	–	250,000
U.S.A.	152,000	–	–	8,168,800	51,358	401,594
India	–	–	–	–	–	–
Total	2,169,150	39,502	36,611	20,875,957	255,371	1,338,317
Total Shrapnel—						
O.F.	723,040	73,227	–	932,540	224,975	17,441
Trade	4,599,883	171,677	294,812	5,151,883	738,706	1,352 467
Canada	1,700,000	3,294	126,706	4,391,666	473,390	876,610
U.S.A.	1,130,000	–	–	7,380,000	250,116	197,568
India	67,000	15,000	7,000	74,000	30,000	44,000
Total	8,219,923	265,835	428,518	17,930,089	1,717,187	2,488,086
Total H.E. and Shrap-						
nel—O.F.	862,840	102,177	–	1,171,340	315,733	34,251
Trade	6,477,233	182,229	331,423	11,261,908	851,960	2,022,380
Canada	1,700,000	3,294	126,706	10,749,998	473,390	1,126,610
U.S.A.	1,282,000	–	–	15,548,800	301,474	599,162
India	67,000	15,000	7,000	74,000	30,000	44,000
Grand Total ..	10,389,073	302,700	465,129	38,806,046	1,972,558	3,826,403

APPENDIX IV.

(CHAPTER V, p. 134.)

Aggregate Deliveries of the Principal Natures of Shell to 31 December, 1915, distinguishing those on War Office and Ministry of Munitions Orders.[1]

Nature of Shell.	Deliveries on W.O. Account.	Deliveries on M.M. Account.	Total Deliveries.
15-in. How. H.E.	426	—	426
12-in. How. H.E.	8,846	—	8,846
9·2-in. How. H.E.·	50,677	1, 040	51,717
8-in. How. H.E.	71,278	—	71,278
6-in. Gun or How. H.E. ..	220,988	2, 475	223 ,463
5-in. Howitzer—			
H.E.	155.192	—	155,192
Shrapnel	11, 939	—	11,939
4·7-in.—			
H.E.	88,596	—	88,596
Shrapnel	25,215	—	25,215
60-pdr.—			
H.E.	102,421	115,305	217,726
Shrapnel	181,957	6,940	188,897
4·5-in. Howitzer—			
H.E.	1,127,062	147,140	1,274,202
Shrapnel	264.989	3,163	268,152
18-pdr.—			
H.E.	3,861,478	568,498	4,429,976
Shrapnel	6,855,790	1,774,284	8,630,074
15-pdr.—			
H.E.	103,560	63,000	166,560
Shrapnel	147,037	—	147,037
13-pdr.—			
H.E.	182,864	32,623	215,487
Shrapnel	270,674	—	270,674
2·75-in.—			
H.E.	11,034	—	11,034
Shrapnel	4,410	—	4,410
Total[2] ..	13,746,433	2,714,468	16,460,901

[1] HIST. REC./H/1300/6 and 12.

[2] As will be seen by a comparison with the table in Appendix III, the total deliveries at this date did not by any means equal the total of the War Office orders (38,806,046). This figure was, however, practically reached by the end of April, 1916, when the total deliveries on all orders amounted to 38,475,900.

Contents of Volume I.

Note.—The contents of this issue are subject to revision
and must be regarded as provisional.

HISTORY OF THE MINISTRY OF MUNITIONS

VOLUME I

INDUSTRIAL MOBILISATION, 1914-15

PART II

THE TREASURY AGREEMENT

x

PART II

THE TREASURY AGREEMENT

CONTENTS.

CHAPTER I.

The Supply of Armament Labour.

(474) Wt 3643/A.P.5036 10/18 250 D.St.

CHAPTER II.

The Relaxation of Trade Union Restrictions, August, 1914, to February, 1915.

CHAPTER III.

The Control of Industry and the Limitation of Profits.

CHAPTER IV.

The Treasury Agreement.

APPENDICES.

INDEX.

CHAPTER I.

THE SUPPLY OF ARMAMENT LABOUR.

I. The Demand for Armament Labour.

At the outbreak of war no general shortage of labour was anticipated. Within the first week, the Cabinet Committee on the Prevention and Relief of Distress invited the Mayors and Provosts throughout the Country to form local committees to provide against unemployment. The Local Government Board urged local authorities to expedite public works and to frame schemes which might be put in hand if serious distress should arise. The Executives of the Engineering Employers' Federation and of the Amalgamated Society of Engineers met on 19 August, 1914, " to discuss ways and means whereby the unemployment contingent upon the national crisis may be minimised." The employers proposed to reduce overtime, to introduce night shifts, and to work short time in preference to discharging workmen. Even the Director of Army Contracts drew up a *Memorandum as to minimising Unemployment during the War*,[1] copies of which were attached to some of the tender forms issued in August for articles other than warlike stores.

As early as mid-September, however, the information received by the Board of Trade showed that the total unemployment was not very great. On the other hand, a considerable and increasing dislocation of labour had already been caused by enlistment. At that time there was a strong demand for labour both in country districts where recruiting had been specially heavy, and on the part of contractors to public Departments who had just received fresh contracts.[2]

For armament work alone, some indication of the extent of the demand is given by the fact that some 18,000 workpeople of all classes were supplied through the Labour Exchanges to the Royal Factories and chief armament firms in the first five months of war (August-December, 1914).[3] In November there was an unsatisfied demand for 6,000 armament workers.[4]

At the Shell Conference of 21 December,[5] the outstanding fact which came to light was the grave shortage of skilled engineering labour that threatened to prevent nearly all the great firms from offering a substantial increase of production. Up to this time it does not appear

[1] See Appendix I.

[2] L.E. Department, C.O. Circ. 1607 (14/9/14).

[3] Large numbers of shipyard workers were also placed.

[4] L.E./48688.

[5] An account of this conference, at which the chief armament contractors were invited largely to increase their capacity and output of shells and fuses, is given in Part I.

that the principal armament contractors had had serious difficulty in finding enough skilled labour to man their existing plant. To a large extent they had been able to make good the losses due to enlistment by attracting men from smaller establishments. But by the end of the year, when the subsidised extensions of their works already in hand were beginning to mature, and they were asked at the Shell Conference still further to enlarge their capacity, one after another of their representatives intimated that any fresh offers they could make were conditional upon the supply of another 400, 500, or 600 skilled mechanics, besides much larger numbers of unskilled men and women. Nearly all of them said that they could not find this additional labour for themselves. For two of their establishments alone, Messrs. Armstrong stated their requirements in round numbers at 4,150 (1,950 at Alexandria, 2,200 at Elswick)[1] ; Messrs. Vickers demanded 633 skilled men for Crayford, 133 for Erith, 814 for Barrow, 96 for Sheffield.[2]

At the Royal Factories, it had for some years been the settled policy to keep a reserve of producing capacity ready for immediate expansion in time of emergency, and to avoid large fluctuations in the numbers employed by allowing the surplus of orders to be taken up by the trade makers. At Woolwich, for example, it was laid down that the number of hands employed in the productive departments should lie between 7,700 and 8,300, as a sufficient nucleus to keep the shops in thorough working order. At the end of June, 1914, 8,500 were actually employed. The number required to keep all the machinery going on the basis of a normal day's work was estimated at 16,000. The same policy was pursued at Enfield. Thus the immediate requirements of the Royal Factories on the outbreak of war would be considerable.[3]

On 6 January, 1915, Sir Frederick Donaldson gave the following estimate of the numbers of men and boys that would be required in the Ordnance Factories at the Royal Arsenal in the next six months.[4]

	Jan.	Feb.	Mar.	April.	May.	June.
Skilled Workmen :						
Fitters	162	116	86	80	—	—
Turners	80	70	20	—	—	—
Machine hands ..	100	400	500	500	500	500
Others	51	46	25	—	—	—
Labourers	100	200	300	300	300	300
Boys	120	600	600	220	220	240

The Superintendent of the Royal Torpedo Factory at Greenock, on 13 January, stated that 700 skilled workmen were required to deal with urgent work on order for the Fleet, apart from labourers and

---

[1] L.E. Department, C.O. Circ. 1701 (5/1/15). These figures probably largely exceed the numbers that could have been actually employed, and were merely estimated in view of future extensions.

[2] C.O. Circ. 1707 (9/1/15).

[3] See Report of the Select Committee on the Estimates (5/8/14), pp. 215, 257.

[4] L.E. 1965/12A.

boys who could be found locally.[1]   For the Government Dockyards and for shipbuilding firms employed on Government work the December returns showed an unsatisfied demand for nearly 8,000 men.

The actual shortage of labour and the difficulty of meeting additional demands for expansion were due mainly to the unrestricted enlistment of skilled workmen.   Before considering the extraordinary measures taken by the Board of Trade in January, 1915, to meet the demand, some account will be given of the operation of this factor and of the earlier attempts to check the outflow of men from the engineering and shipbuilding industries into the Army.

II. The Enlistment of Skilled Workmen and the Problem of Man-power.

The effect of enlistment upon the engineering trades can be traced in the successive Board of Trade reports on employment.   By October, 1914, the trades in this group had lost by enlistment 12·2 per cent. of their pre-war male workers.   By February, 1915, the percentage had risen to 16·4 ; by July to 19·5.[2]   It is true that against this gross loss must be set a rapidly increasing percentage of replacement by transference from other trades, shown in October, 1914, as 0·2 per cent. of the total number occupied before the War ; in February, 1915, as 7·4 ; in July, as 16·3.   These offsets, however, so far from making up the extra numbers required to meet the expanding demand, did not suffice to keep the employment figure stationary.   At the time of the formation of the Ministry, the number of engineers working had fallen below the figure for July, 1914, by 48,000, while the outstanding demand at two Government factories and sixteen firms doing munitions work amounted to nearly 14,000.

In the light of later experience, the problem of this drain into the Army of men taken from the industry most vital to munitions production has come to be regarded as only one aspect of the wider question of the distribution of man-power in general.   Another aspect is presented by the conflicting claims of the Army and munitions production together as against the maintenance of commercial work, especially for export trade.   A satisfactory solution implies a distinction between essential and unessential industries or products ; and Government intervention was needed alike to direct the flow of skilled labour towards armament work and to check the enlistment of the most responsible and intelligent, and therefore the most skilled, workmen.

Although, however, it may now be clear that the fundamental connection between these problems requires that they should be handled together, in the less stringent conditions which prevailed at the end of 1914 they were dealt with separately by distinct authorities, whose interests threatened to conflict.   It was part of the duty of the Board of Trade to maintain production for export at a level high enough to keep up necessary imports and to secure the credit

---

[1] L.E. 1965/50.

[2] Tables showing the effect of enlistment on the industrial population are given in Appendix II.

of the Country. Enlistment was in the province of the Adjutant-General's department at the War Office, which had started by thinking of the new armies in hundreds of thousands, and, before the year 1914 was out, was beginning to think of them in millions. Munitions production was the concern of the Master-General of the Ordnance, whose department worked independently of the Adjutant-General's, both being subordinate only to the Secretary of State. The War Office at once looked with a jealous eye on schemes for protecting any industry from enlistment, and expected the Board of Trade to find skilled labour in ever increasing quantities for armament work.

Apart, however, from the divergent interests and rivalries of Departments, it is certain that forces were at work which would have defeated the closest co-operation of Government officials, not yet armed with powers of either military or industrial compulsion. Nor can it be altogether a matter for regret that a voluntary system of enlistment automatically selected for the first new armies the most spirited and adventurous men, rather than those who could best have been spared from the factory, the shipyard, or the mine.

Co-operation with regard to enlistment was established between the Board of Trade and the War Office towards the end of August, 1914, when the use of the Labour Exchanges was offered for recruiting purposes.[1]   Posters and leaflets on the subject of recruiting the second Army of 100,000 were issued to managers on 2 September, and others were forwarded later. As early as the beginning of September, however, complaints had begun to flow in from employers whose works were being disorganised by the loss of pivotal men.

The proposal to issue badges was at first discountenanced by the War Office, and alternative expedients were considered. In response to a request from Messrs. Vickers for permission to issue a recognised badge to their men, Lord Kitchener replied on 8 September with the following letter :—

" I wish to impress upon those employed by your Company the importance of the Government work upon which they are engaged. I fully appreciate the efforts which the employees are making, and the quality of the work turned out. I trust that everything will be done to assist the Military Authorities by pushing on all orders as rapidly as possible.

" I should like all engaged by your Company to know that it is fully recognised that they, in carrying out the great work of supplying munitions of war, are doing their duty for their King and Country equally with those who have joined the Army for active service in the field."

The Master-General of the Ordnance also replied, suggesting that a ticket should be issued to each employee, " indicating that he is engaged in the manufacture of munitions of war and

---

[1] L.E. Department, C.O. Circular 1601.

that therefore he is unable to serve his country in any other manner."

In December the Admiralty circulated to firms on their list of contractors samples of badges, which were to be restricted to employees whose services were absolutely indispensable for the execution of work on His Majesty's ships and armaments.   The War Office had not gone further than instituting a list of firms whose men were not to be accepted for enlistment without the written consent of a responsible member of the firm.   Both Departments kept such lists ; but, so far as warlike stores were concerned, the slight measure of protection they afforded extended only to the leading armament firms. It was natural that the War Office, bent upon its task of finding men for the new armies, should in this matter lag behind the Admiralty, whose principal concern was the enormous material requirements of the Fleet and of new construction.   Up to December, 1914, neither Department showed any interest in the protection of industries other than those most directly concerned with the production of war material.

At the end of the year, however, the earliest attempts were made to take in hand the general problem of man-power.   It is due to the War Office to record that the first move in this direction was made by the recruiting authorities.   Two days after the Shell Conference of 21 December, Colonel Strachey of the Adjutant-General's department put forward proposals which recognise the need of considering recruitment in connection, not only with the protection of the armament firms, but with the claims of the whole range of industry [1]

Colonel Strachey suggested that the help of the Board of Trade should be invoked in order to make such a classification of industries as might be the basis of instructions to recruiting officers.   He pointed out that in certain industries (*e.g.*, war material, food, power and light, transport, public corporations' services) only a small proportion of men of recruitable age should be taken ; others (*e.g.*, building and allied trades) should not be barred to recruiting on considerations of general prosperity.   The question had arisen, how to decide what numbers could be taken from particular firms without injury to vital requirements.   The great variety of local conditions made it impossible to deal with trades as wholes.   The sound way would be to decide first what trades should be entirely, or almost entirely, barred ; and as regards others, falling within the line of partial exemption, to consider each case on its merits.

The entirely, or almost entirely, barred trades were being dealt with by instructions to recruiting officers to enlist no man from armament or food-producing firms, etc., and a list of individual protected firms had been issued.   The cases for partial exemption were scattered and various, and called for local knowledge.   The responsibility for decision must rest with local recruiting officers ; but, as the difficulties

---

[1] *Memorandum on Recruiting from Certain Industries* (23/12/14).

would increase, these officers would need some general guidance. This might be given in a table under three heads :—

(a) Industries, etc., barred, except with special permission.

(b) Occupations, etc., whose services to the country were such that the numbers taken must be limited.

(c) All other occupations, etc., to be recruited from freely.

The help of the Board of Trade would be needed to enumerate occupations under (b). They might also be able to suggest local officials who could assist the recruiting officers.

This memorandum reached the Board of Trade on 28 December, and led to a conference on 31 December, at which representatives of the Board met Sir Reginald Brade and Colonel Strachey. It was agreed, as a provisional arrangement, that employers' applications for the exemption of their men from recruiting should be referred by the War Office to the Board of Trade for consideration under two points of view : (1) the national importance of the industry concerned ; (2) the scarcity of labour for that industry and the possibility of replacing it. As will presently appear, this scheme of co-operation was held up by the War Office.

At the same moment the whole question was taken up by the Committee of Imperial Defence. On 1 January, 1915, Mr. A. J. Balfour wrote for this Committee a *Note on the Limits of Enlistment.*[1]

Mr. Balfour said that the very success of Lord Kitchener's appeal for men raised the question whether there was " any limit beyond which, *in the interests of the country as a fighting power,* enlistment ought not to be carried." What he had to say referred solely to fighting efficiency, not to private interests, however legitimate, or to the general convenience of the public.

Certain limitations were obvious and unquestioned. Not a man could be spared from the production of war material (in the widest sense of the term), which was required in excess of any powers of output possessed by the Allies. No man really required for the railways, mercantile marine, or collieries, or for the Civil Service, could be spared. In other words, in order that as a nation we might fight well, there were many citizens physically fit to fight, who must not be allowed to fight. Were there other classes to which these remarks applied ?

For convenience' sake he would omit, in the first instance, all reference to anything beyond our immediate material requirements, for example, public order and national credit. We *must* import food, raw material, probably gold, and probably munitions of war. We *must,* therefore, although a creditor country, make immense foreign payments, which could only be done either by borrowing abroad, or selling securities, or exporting goods. Of these expedients, borrowing was undesirable and perhaps impracticable ; to sell securities was undesirable. Only the export of goods deserved consideration. It followed

---

[1] Copy in HIST. REC./R/180/2.

that any enlistment which crippled industries either producing commodities for export or producing commodities at home (such as foodstuffs) which, if not made at home, must be imported, must diminish our fighting efficiency.

Accordingly, the general principles to be kept in mind were :—

(1) We could send to the Front, without national loss, every man of suitable age engaged in producing luxuries for home consumption. If, for example, every flower gardener, manservant, or gamekeeper were to join the Army, no loss of any kind would be inflicted on the community *as a fighting organism*. The same might be said of teachers, lawyers, ·writers, artists, of many employees of local authorities, and of all who were not engaged in any trade or profession.

(2) We could not send abroad, without further consideration, producers of luxuries for foreign consumption. It was necessary to consider whether the country would gain more by increase of its fighting numbers than it would lose by diminution of purchasing power.

These limitations were largely increased when moral or psychological elements were considered. Money was almost as necessary as men ; and most of the money must be borrowed. We should have to finance our Allies to some extent ; to pay our troops and their dependants ; and to buy arms and munitions in part for our Allies, as well as for ourselves. Also, those who were not, directly or indirectly, paid for fighting, must earn their living or be supported by the community. Our credit depended largely on two things : first, the maintenance of trade and commerce, and secondly, the healthy state of the country— the fighting spirit, and the absence of widespread distress and of any symptom of discouragement or disorder. To secure these conditions, recruiting must not be pressed too far. We should not find willing lenders if great sums of public money were being spent in relief of distress ; or if the War were bringing our economic machinery to a standstill ; or if discontent should become prevalent. We might go on fighting, but we should find it difficult to borrow.

It was assumed that the War would not be over in a few weeks. If an early peace were probable, national industry might be left to take care of itself. But, in the actual conditions, the Board of Trade should consider the situation, not from the point of view of national wealth, present or prospective, but from that of national production considered merely as an instrument of military success *in this War*.

The following Propositions suggested, not what could be done in practice, but what ought to be done in theory :—

1. No man should be encouraged to enlist whose labours are required to provide needful transports or fuel, or to produce armaments and equipment for us or our Allies.

2. Enlistment should not be allowed to hamper those industries which produce necessaries for home consumption.

3. Nor should it be allowed to hamper those industries which produce either luxuries or necessaries for foreign consumption, *so far as these are required to pay for our necessary imports.*

4. Every fit man, on the other hand, should be encouraged to enlist who is engaged either in producing nothing at all, or in producing luxuries for home consumption. But this proposition must be taken with a proviso. In cases where the enlistment of the physically qualified would throw out of employment a large number of those, who, by reason of sex or age, cannot serve in the Army, enlistment may conceivably be a source of weakness rather than strength. For it may diminish public confidence, and therefore also public credit, and thus destroy our powers of borrowing largely and cheaply. How many Army Corps would be required to compensate us for such a loss?

Having read Mr. Balfour's *Note*, Sir H. Llewellyn Smith addressed a memorandum to the President of the Board of Trade.[1] After mentioning the interim arrangements made for advising the War Office on employers' applications for the exemption of their employees, he stated that, at the request of the War Office, the Department was then examining the possibility of classifying industries and occupations in such a way as to afford some guidance to recruiting officers. The task was difficult as soon as it went beyond a very few groups of industries, about which there could be no two opinions. It was hoped that the examination of individual cases referred by the War Office might lead to the formulation of some general principle.

It was possible that occupations might be grouped as :—

(*a*) Barred to recruiting till further notice ;

(*b*) Barred to recruiting except through, or after consultation with, a Labour Exchange ;

(*c*) Freely open to recruiting.

As regards (*b*) a large amount of recruiting had been done through the Labour Exchanges. If it were laid down that, in border-line industries, applicants for enlistment must be passed through the Exchanges, instructions to managers might be varied from time to time according to the state of the labour market and military needs. As regards (*c*), recruiting could be encouraged in particular industries, such as the building trade, by appeals to employers and Trade Unions ; and the Labour Exchanges might be used to bring applicants for employment to the notice of recruiting officers.

In settling a classification, the Board of Trade and the War Office could give any desired degree of weight to each of Mr. Balfour's general considerations, especially maintenance of exports. It was doubtful, indeed, whether that consideration alone should be a ground for putting

---

[1] Copy in HIST. REC./R/180/2.

an occupation in class (a), in view of the notorious difficulty of distinguishing between luxuries and necessaries, and of separating luxuries for home consumption from those intended for export. The consideration might, however, weigh in the decision of border cases between (b) and (c). Mr. Balfour's memorandum was of value as emphasising the need to keep in view, not only the direct supply of naval and military material, but also the maintenance of exports sufficient to enable us to import, and of trade activity sufficient to enable us to borrow.

Sir H. Llewellyn Smith's memorandum was followed by a *Statistical Supplement*, estimating the number of recruits available and the proportions that might, without seriously crippling industry, be drawn from various groups of trades, classified in two lists.[1] List A contained essential occupations, in which labour not already occupied on war work should not be recruited, but diverted to war work. Under this head, the unenlisted balance of men physically capable of military service was estimated at 952,000. List B contained occupations which might spare a certain proportion of the balance for the Army. The outside limit of numbers that could be recruited without seriously crippling industry was about 1,100,000, in addition to the 2,000,000 already with the Colours, though the withdrawal of so large a number would greatly hamper industry, since the margin of unemployment (whether in the form of short time or of total unemployment) among men physically fit for service in all industries did not exceed 100,000. If the same figures were taken for unemployment in non-industrial occupations, the probable number of recruits available without any curtailment of production would be 200,000. Thus the ideal additional enlistment figure would be between 200,000 and 1,100,000. Production could be considerably curtailed with little harm,[2] and, if occupations were judiciously selected both for propaganda and for exemption, the limit might be put not far below 1,000,000.

A small inter-departmental committee of the Board of Trade and the War Office Recruiting department was formed to give effect to these proposals. Instructions had already been given to suspend recruiting in the case of armament workers, railway employees and woollen workers. The object of the committee was to examine applications from employers for similar exemption on the ground that their industries were essential to the armament firms.

In the debate on Army Reinforcements in the House of Lords on 8 January, Lord Midleton[3] called attention to the high percentage of recruits drawn, in the first three months of the War, from the mainly

---

[1] The lists are given in Appendix III.

[2] With regard to curtailment of production and Mr. Balfour's argument against reducing exports too far, it was estimated that, having regard to our position as a creditor country, to the export of capital before the War, and to other considerations, exports might fall at least 50% without danger, and perhaps considerably further. The recorded decline since the beginning of the War was 45% (as compared with 1913) and for December alone 40%.

[3] *Parliamentary Debates* (1915), *H. of L.*, XVIII., 351.

industrial, as contrasted with the mainly agricultural, districts. He quoted the official figures supplied to the Parliamentary Recruiting Committee as follows :—

ENLISTMENT OF MEN RECRUITED BY ALL SOURCES, 4 AUGUST, 1914, TO 4 NOVEMBER, 1914.

	Number of recruits per 10,000 of the population.
Mainly Industrial Counties—	
S. District of Scotland	237
Warwickshire and Midland Counties	196
Lancashire, etc.	178
London and Home Counties	170
Yorkshire, Durham, Northumberland	150
Cheshire, part of Lancs., and neighbouring Welsh Counties	135
N. of Ireland	127
Nottinghamshire and Derbyshire	119
Mainly Agricultural Counties—	
North of Scotland	93
West of England	88
East of England	80
South and West of Ireland	32

Lord Lucas, replying on behalf of the Government, acknowledged the need of protecting industries essential to the production of war material. He said :—

" We have at any rate under our system, though it may be uneven and may fall heavily on some districts and lightly on others, avoided the enormous dislocation of industry which has followed the mobilisation of large conscript armies in the belligerent countries. The information which has reached us with regard to that, where they have had to call up men because they fell into certain categories or were of a certain age, and so on, has gone to show that the effect on the various trades has been of the very worst kind ; and in certain cases we know that special measures have had to be taken to enable men who occupy leading and important positions in their industries to go back. The noble Viscount (Lord Midleton) says that certain industries have suffered more than others. For this purpose you can divide industries into only two classes :—(1) industries which are essential to the turning out of war material and (2) all other industries ; and I think you can only say that, while it is of the utmost importance to prevent industries which turn out war material from being in any way crippled by recruiting, with regard to other industries, always speaking within limits, the first duty of any man is, if possible, to serve his country, and the second to continue his industry."

Mr. Balfour's *Note* and Sir H. Llewellyn Smith's Memorandum were considered by the Committee of Imperial Defence on 27 January, but no decision was reached. Lord Kitchener feared that the demands of labour in satisfaction of Mr. Balfour's propositions or of others like them might, directly or indirectly, prejudice recruiting more than seemed likely at first sight. He objected to any system which entailed the rejection of any willing recruit. Instead of approving any scheme for protecting industry from enlistment, the Committee passed a Conclusion which aimed merely at replacing recruited men by ineligibles. The Conclusion was as follows :—

> " Employers of labour and trade unions should be appealed to to co-operate as far as possible, having regard to the special conditions of particular trades, to secure the employment of men ineligible through age or other reasons to become recruits, and of women in place of eligible men who may be taken as recruits."

In consequence of Lord Kitchener's attitude, the scheme of co-operation between the War Office and the Board of Trade was suspended. The Board of Trade still offered the help of the Labour Exchange organisation in any attempt to concentrate the active propaganda of recruiting agents upon unessential trades, leaving the others alone. It was, however, for the War Office to make a move.

Co-operation with the Board of Trade having thus been ruled out, the natural result was that during the next few months the matter was handled at the War Office, not as a broad question of the general distribution of man-power between military service and essential or unessential industries, but on the old principle, established by the Admiralty, of according the minimum of protection, by means of badges, to direct contractors for war material. At the end of 1914 it was no longer possible for the War Office to resist the emphatic representations of the great armament firms that they were losing men whose services they considered indispensable for the prompt execution of their orders. The principle of issuing official badges was adopted, and the work was organised in January and February by a new branch (M.G.O.L.) of the Master-General of the Ordnance's department, under Major-General Mahon.[1]

Under the scheme brought into operation in March, 1915, contractors were classified according to the importance and urgency of their work. Recognised armament firms holding contracts for war-like stores and certain manufacturers of explosives and aircraft were supplied with certificates for issue to all their employees, stating that the holder's services were urgently required, and with badges for technical workers whose services were " important for the manufacture of armament material for use in the field." The further steps taken in this direction after the appointment of the Armaments Output Committee at the end of March will be described later.[2]

In the first seven or eight months of the War, before the War Office scheme of badging was brought into working order, enthusiasm for enlistment had been at its height and the most vital industries had

---

[1] The formation of this Branch was announced in War Office Memorandum 801 of 5 April, 1915.

[2] See Part III, Chap. V., Section VII.

suffered losses which no subsequent efforts could altogether repair. When once a man had joined the Colours, no power could make him return to civil work against his will, and the influence of all his military superiors, from the General Officer to the platoon sergeant, was exerted to keep him in the Army, if he promised to make a useful soldier. Employers were constantly making attempts to reclaim valuable workmen ; but no arrangements for Release from the Colours were made till January, 1915. On the 13th of that month the Master-General of the Ordnance stated at a conference that engineering firms had been asked to supply lists of their men serving with the Colours ; but that no steps had yet been taken for their release. An Army Council letter was addressed, on 22 January, to the Commander-in-Chief of the British Army in the Field and to the General Officers Commanding-in-Chief, Commands at Home, directing the release of certain men. A further step was taken in March, when telegrams were sent to all the Commands in the United Kingdom, giving instructions that men of a few specified trades were to be picked out and sent to certain selected armament works. But no considerable numbers were actually released until the late summer.

The general result was that the activity of the recruiting officer during the first year of the War was subject to no effective check. Every outside influence was in his favour ; above all, the patriotism of the workman, who often could not be persuaded that his work was indirectly necessary to the equipment of the Army, and who, if he remained at his post, was insulted in the streets and taunted in the vulgar press as a coward. The need for a great increase of munitions production did not become known to the newspapers or to the public until long after it was appreciated by the Government, with the natural consequence that the Army filled its ranks with men who could never be replaced at the bench or in the shipyard.

III. The Board of Trade Programme for the Supply of Armament Labour and the Relaxation of Trade Union Restrictions, 30 December, 1914.

On 22 December, 1914, the large demands for additional labour made at the Shell Conference on the previous day were reported to the Cabinet Committee on Munitions. Instructions were immediately given by the President of the Board of Trade to Sir H. Llewellyn Smith to take the question in hand, in conjunction with Sir George Gibb and a representative of the Admiralty.

The Cabinet Committee suggested the following measures : (1) to co-ordinate the supply of labour ; (2) to substitute Belgians for British workmen ; (3) to divert labour from less urgent or unnecessary industries (*e.g.* railway construction works, etc.) ; (4) where employers in the less necessary trades were reluctant to part with their men, to put pressure upon them, first by persuasion, and then, if that failed, by refusal of railway facilities, etc., and by publicity for unpatriotic action ; (5) any other means for obtaining enough men for all the armament companies.

In pursuance of these instructions, on 30 December representatives of the Army Council and of the Board of Trade conferred with representatives of some of the chief armament firms and of the Royal Arsenal.[1] The meeting laid down the lines along which the efforts of the Board should be directed. The programme falls under three heads :

A. Fresh labour was to be provided from the following sources : (1) unemployed engineering workmen, to be supplied through the Labour Exchanges ; (2) Belgian refugees in this country (so far as these were suitable for armament work) ; (3) Belgian refugees in Holland, to be recruited by special agents sent by the Board of Trade.

B. An endeavour was to be made through the Labour Exchange organisation to induce engineering employers engaged on commercial contracts to spare some of their skilled workmen for employment at the armament firms' works.

C. Efforts were to be made to promote arrangements with the engineering Trade Unions whereby the existing supply of labour might be more economically and productively used.

The present chapter will deal with the measures taken by the Board of Trade under the first two heads of this programme, (A) for the drawing in of fresh labour, and (B) for the diversion of labour already employed from commercial to armament work. The former of these undertakings came properly within the functions of the Labour Exchange organisation and was pursued uninterruptedly throughout this preliminary period. The latter involved Government intervention in regions normally left open to the free play of bargaining between employer and employed, and soon encountered obstacles which could only be overcome by a series of measures establishing control over both parties.

IV. The Preference List of Royal Factories and Armament Firms.

It was decided by the Master-General of the Ordnance on 9 January that British skilled labour should be sent to the Royal Factories and the four armament firms on the following preference list :—

Royal Arsenal, Woolwich ;
Royal Small Arms Factory, Enfield ;
Royal Torpedo Factory, Greenock ;
Armstrong (Alexandria and Elswick) ;
Vickers (Crayford, Erith, Barrow, and Sheffield) ;
Coventry Ordnance Works ;
Birmingham Small Arms.

Belgians were to be sent only to the armament firms.

---

[1] Sir H. Llewellyn Smith, *Supply of Armament Labour, Preliminary Note* (23/1/15). HIST. REC./R/180/8.

Instructions[1] were issued, accordingly, that the circulation, through the Central Clearing House, of orders for engineering labour should be limited to these factories and firms and certain Admiralty contractors, who were to be added later. Employed workpeople whom their employers promised to release, were to be submitted only for vacancies at the firms and factories on the list.

On 8 April, in view of the urgent need for armament workers at Woolwich and Greenock, these factories were given the first refusal of all applicants, and four aircraft firms were added.[2] Other armament firms were included in the list from time to time.

V. The Supply of Fresh Labour for Armament Work.

(a) Unemployed British Skilled Workmen.

On 4 January the managers of Labour Exchanges were instructed[3] to bring the armament vacancies systematically to the notice of all suitable men signing an unemployed register or drawing benefit. If a man judged to be suitable declined to consider such a vacancy, his benefit was to be refused. The terms offered to unemployed men were identical with those offered to men whom their employers undertook to release from commercial employment.[4]

It was clear that the supply that could be drawn from the reserve of unemployed would not approach the figure of the total demand. A return of the numbers of unemployment books lodged on 18 December in the United Kingdom gave the following figures for the three groups of Trades specially concerned :—

Shipbuilding	4,011
Engineering	12,420
Construction of Vehicles	3,448

It was, however, believed that in Engineering the number of unemployed men was really far below the large figures given above. It was stated, for instance, that half the unemployed members of the Amalgamated Society of Engineers in this winter were in Canada.

There were several definite difficulties in the way of making available for armament work the reserve of labour apparently existing in the engineering trades. The men who were out of work at a moment when the demand was so keen were naturally the least skilled and efficient, whereas the armament firms generally asked for highly skilled labour. Some attempt was made to induce employers to take less skilled hands on trial ; but the campaign for what was later known as " Dilution " had yet to be begun, and the barrier of Trade Union rules to a large extent excluded the unskilled from the higher forms of work. Again, a large number were non-unionists, while many of the employers asked for union men and employed

---

[1] L.E. Department, C.O. Circ. 1719 (22/1/15).   [2] C.O. Circ. 1788 (8/4/15).
[3] C.O. Circ. 1700 (4/1/15).   [4] See below, p. 24.

hardly any others. This was another point of conflict with Trade Union rules. It was proposed that the Unions should be asked to withdraw their objection to working with non-unionists, on condition that all men should be paid the Trade Union rates and that men taken on after this arrangement was made should be the first to be affected by reductions of staff after the War. A third difficulty was that the men were, for the most part, scattered in small numbers all over the country. They would have to travel considerable distances to the armament works, and the majority, being married, could not easily move.

The effect of these difficulties and of the continued recruiting of skilled engineers for the Army was that, while the demands for labour rapidly rose, the supply gradually decreased during the first three months of 1915. The result of the first fortnight of the Board of Trade's campaign was that 1,493 unemployed British skilled engineers were submitted through the Labour Exchanges to the armament firms and Royal Factories ; the yield of the next three weeks (to 13 February) was only 1,178 ; and a month later (13 March) the total result of the special measures taken at the beginning of the year was that 4,003 British skilled workmen had been submitted— a figure which included a small proportion of men diverted from commercial work—and of these only some 2,000 were known to have been actually engaged and to have started work. The weekly figures, moreover, were steadily falling. It was now evident that, even if the demand had remained stationary, it could not be met from the reserve of unemployed, and that it would be necessary to take some drastic action in the direction of compelling employers to release men engaged on private work.[1]

(b) BELGIAN REFUGEES.

As early as September, 1914, the Labour Exchanges were dealing with applications for Belgian and other refugee labour.[2] On 10 November a notice was issued in the Press stating that the Local Government Board and the Board of Trade had decided to act on a resolution transmitted to them by the Departmental Committee on Belgian Refugees, to the effect that it was desirable that Belgian labour should be engaged only through the Labour Exchanges, since these organisations alone were in a position to give priority to suitable British labour. Admiralty and War Office contractors were instructed to abide by this rule. Arrangements were accordingly made for lists of vacancies and applications for refugee labour to pass through the Labour Exchange organisation, and for obtaining a live register of Belgians. Two Belgian officials were employed in investigating the *bona fides* of any Belgians whom it might be desired to employ in Government contractors' works, or who were already so engaged. Rules of procedure for dealing with applications and

---

[1] See Sir H. Llewellyn Smith, *Supply of Armament Labour* (15/3/15). HIST. REC./R/180/8.

[2] L.E. Department, C.O. Circulars, 1620, 1649, 1658, 1665, 1686.

placings were issued to Labour Exchange managers on 15 December ; and on 28 January they were instructed to secure a register of employable Belgian men and women, with a view to placing those who were either not of military age or exempt from service. The wages and conditions of employment were to be as good as those offered to British labour, and British labour was not to be displaced.[1]

On 4 January the Board of Trade also sent special agents to recruit Belgian refugees in Holland.[2] Up to 11 February, 1915, 434 armament workers were registered at the London Camp Exchanges as having been forwarded by these agents. About the end of January, it was decided that the work of the Board of Trade in Holland should be supplemented by agents of private firms selected by the Admiralty and the War Office. Letters were issued on 5 February to the firms concerned, stating the conditions laid down by the Board.

In spite of these efforts, however, the weekly figures indicated that this source of recruitment also was steadily drying up.[3] The numbers of Belgian workmen known to have been engaged through the Labour Exchanges and to have started work in the weeks ending at the undermentioned dates were as follows :—

January	9	..	..	..	..	..	525
,,	16	..	..	..	..	..	466
,,	23	..	..	..	..	..	477
,,	30	..	..	..	..	..	229
February	6	..	..	..	..	..	231
,,	13	..	..	..	..	..	386
,,	20	..	..	..	..	..	394
,,	27	..	..	..	..	..	203
March	6	..	..	..	..	..	235
,,	13	..	..	..	..	..	136

By 17 April the total number engaged was estimated at 4,094.

(c) Unskilled and Female Labour.

The figures so far given refer only to skilled male labour in the engineering trades, supplied in pursuance of the special arrangements initiated by the Board of Trade in January, 1915. They do not include the men and women supplied direct by local Exchanges. When these are added, the total number of workpeople of all classes supplied for armament work in the first ten weeks of 1915 amounts to 12,000, as compared with 18,000 in the previous five months.

The demand for female labour was, at the end of 1914, rather a prospective than a present one. Women would be needed to staff factories which were to be in working order in two or three months' time or later. The total prospective demand was then estimated roughly at from 10,000 to 15,000.[4]

---

[1] L.E. Department, C.O. Circulars, 1690, 1694, 1726.
[2] L.E. 1965/3.
[3] Sir H. Ll. Smith, *Supply of Armament Labour* (15/3/15). Hist. Rec. R/180/8.
[4] L.E. 48688.

The Board of Trade returns for December, 1914, showed the total contraction of women's employment as 34,000. The great bulk of this (30,000) occurred in the Lancashire Cotton Trade and ancillary occupations. It was considered that some of this free labour could be attracted into armament work if a wage of 20s. a week, together with the other terms allowed to men brought from a distance, were offered to women who had to leave their homes, and special care were taken in providing housing accommodation.

From the outbreak of war to 15 March, 1915, not less than 2,000 women were supplied for armament work, especially at Elswick and Alexandria. But in December, 1914, it was already clear that, since the great mass of unemployed women skilled in machine-minding were clustered in the Lancashire Textile area, female labour could be used with much greater ease and economy if new armament factories could be placed, not (as was proposed) in such centres as Coventry or Newcastle, but in existing buildings adapted for the new purpose in one or another of the Lancashire towns. This consideration was one of those which pointed to the alternative policy of spreading armament contracts over centres of industry hitherto devoted to peaceful trades.

The first systematic attempt to enrol women to replace male labour was made by the Board of Trade, which issued on 16 March, 1915, a notice to the Press and a poster inviting women prepared to undertake employment of any kind, with or without previous training, to register at the Labour Exchanges[1]. With regard to wages for substituted women, the general principle which Government contractors were required to observe was that for piece-work the same rate should be paid as to men.

The following table[2] shows the number of women enrolled by 15 May on the Special War Register for Women for work connected with munitions :—

Class of work desired.	Number registered.	With previous experience in their own trades.	Placed.
Armament Work	13,780	269	34
Engineering	450	360	0
Construction of Vehicles	13	60	0
Miscellaneous Metal Trades	389	1,265	26

The total number of women enrolled by June 4 for all classes of work was 78,946, of whom 1,816 had been engaged. The smallness of the second figure was officially explained[3] as partly due to the fact that in filling vacancies the supply of suitable labour on the ordinary

[1] L.E. Department, C.O. Circ. 1766.
[2] Intelligence Section Report, 20/5/15.
[3] *Parliamentary Debates* (1915), *H. of C.*, LXXII., 347.

Labour Exchange register was first exhausted before the resources of the War Service Register were drawn upon. But it is probable that the 13,000 would-be armament workers with no previous experience included a large proportion of persons whom no employer would have thought it worth his while to train. It must also be remembered that the numerous obstacles which Trade Union customs and rules presented to " Dilution " had still to be overcome.

(d) Shipyard Labour.

With respect to the shortage of shipyard labour, steps were taken as the result of a conference held on 14 January at the Board of Trade with representatives of the Admiralty and of the principal shipbuilding contractors, and a joint conference with the Admiralty and the War Office. The December returns had shown the total demand for all classes of labour at the Government Dockyards and for shipbuilding firms employed on Government work as about 8,000.[1] Although on the same date there was, at various places in Yorkshire, a reserve of about 4,000 shipyard hands working short time or not engaged on Government work, discussion at the conference revealed that there was little chance of the shipbuilders' requirements being satisfied. There was very little unemployment, except in ship-repairing, a trade in which employment is casual and highly paid, involving therefore a considerable loss to the workmen transferred to regular shipyard work. Objection was taken to the employment of Belgians, on the ground that few Belgians were trained for this class of work. The shipbuilders accordingly had to look for fresh supplies mainly to the diversion of labour from private work ; and, as this prospect was not very hopeful, their attention was rather focussed on increasing output by securing the relaxation of Trade Union rules.

(e) Importation of Colonial Labour.

As soon as it became clear that all the above-mentioned expedients for securing fresh labour were not likely to meet the demand, proposals for importing colonial and foreign labour were taken into consideration.

On 13 December, 1914, Mr. A. C. Johnson, of Alberta, Canada, had written to the Chancellor of the Exchequer a letter in which he stated that there were in Canada some 100,000 unemployed, of whom at least a considerable portion were ex-employees of Woolwich Arsenal, Government Dockyards, or armament firms. From among these the Canadian contingents for the new armies had been largely recruited. Mr. Johnson said that thousands more would willingly come to England to form an industrial reserve, as they had been hard hit by the collapse of industry. The terms suggested were : passage money, and a guarantee of steady work at a rate duly proportioned to the high rates prevalent in Canada. Mr. Johnson thought that

---

[1] L.E. 48688.

such a plan would be enthusiastically received even as far west as Alberta. This letter was forwarded by Mr. Hanson to the Board of Trade on 14 January, 1915.

The Master-General of the Ordnance' Committee on Armaments at its second meeting on 8 January, considered proposals both for sending skilled men to Canada to increase the munitions output there and for importing men from Canada to be trained by the Ordnance Factories or the armament firms in England. The latter proposal was negatived in view of the large orders already placed in Canada by the War Office.

It was revived by Sir H. Llewellyn Smith at a conference with representatives of the Admiralty and the War Office on 12 February. The Board of Trade then had reason to believe that there was considerable unemployment in Canada, and suggested that an agent might be sent to investigate the situation. The Admiralty and War Office representatives were not unfavourable, provided that due steps should be taken to see that only men of the right type were brought over.[1]

A cable[2] was accordingly addressed on 20 February to the Dominion Government, inquiring whether suitable men were available, and stating that passages could probably be paid both ways and that wages would be at standard rates with abundant overtime. A reply came on 23 February to the effect that a considerable number of suitable men could be found, and the despatch confirming the cable stated that there were " probably some hundreds of machinists at present (3 March) unemployed in Canada, the unemployment being found chiefly in the Western portions of the Dominion."

As soon as this confirmation had been received, the interested parties in this country were asked to state the numbers of men they would require and the conditions of employment. It then appeared that neither Woolwich Arsenal and the Government Dockyards nor private firms who were consulted (notably Messrs. Armstrong and Messrs. Vickers) favoured the proposal. The grounds of opposition were : (1) that the introduction of this labour would be likely to cause trouble with their employees ; (2) the difficulty of securing suitable men, since the best would probably have gone to the United States ; (3) a preference for placing further orders in Canada instead of withdrawing labour. For the moment, accordingly, no further steps were taken.

On 9 April the Chief Industrial Commissioner reported[3] that he had had conversations on the subject with Sir George Gibb and several employers, and that all united in thinking that, with the improvement in work likely to ensue from recent agreements, the uncertain value of the Canadian labour, and the large orders for the

---

[1] M.C. 201.   [2] Copy in L.E. 1965/92.   [3] M.C. 201.

Allies lately placed in Canada, a mission to collect labour there would not be advisable at the present time.[1]

The question of importing Colonial labour came before the Munitions of War Committee[2] on 26 April. Before the meeting, the Secretary prepared a memorandum[3] in which, after reviewing the abortive proposals for the importation of Canadian labour which have been described above, he said that the question had recently been revived by a number of communications from both employers and men in Canada, recommending importation to relieve unemployment in Canada, and to increase output in this country. Taken together, these communications, which came from Vancouver, Winnipeg, Hamilton and Toronto, afforded evidence of unemployment sufficient to call for investigation ; and the Dominion Government were pressing for some answer from the Home Government. Messrs. Armstrong appeared now to favour the introduction of properly tested Canadian labour, and several prominent shipbuilders in the North were pressing for it. If the Committee should decide that labour trouble was not to be feared, and that substantial numbers of men were available, who might better be imported than employed locally, there might be a case for a detailed local inquiry.

The Committee decided that a mission should be sent to Canada, and the Board of Trade were instructed on 26 April to send representatives to make inquiries and, if a sufficient supply were found, to arrange for their transport, for the conditions of employment, and for testing the fitness of the men before they embarked. The mission was despatched early in May. It was under the charge of Mr. Windham (Board of Trade), and included Mr. G. N. Barnes, M.P., and technical officers from the Royal Arsenal and Dockyards. It was proposed to test the selected men in the workshops of the Grand Trunk and Canadian Pacific Railways.[4] The following were the conditions offered :—

    (a) The standard British rate of wages, including war bonus, etc. ;

    (b) A guarantee of work to suitable men for a minimum of six months, for which time the men were to undertake to remain ;

---

[1] Messrs. Vickers appear to have changed their minds on this question. The management at Barrow wrote on 10 May to the Head Office in London that they had already made arrangements with the A.S.E. to send through their agents in Canada a considerable number of workmen. Two consignments, of 16 and over 100 men, had been received, and a third of 52 men was then crossing.

[2] The " Treasury Committee," under the Chairmanship of Mr. Lloyd George, appointed at the beginning of April, 1915.

[3] M.C. 201

[4] The Canadian Pacific Railway refused facilities on the ground that the better policy would be to entrust more orders to Canada (Letter to Mr. Barnes, 31 May).

(c) Fares to be paid by the employer, and return fares to men who remained so long as they were needed for Government work during the war ;

(d) £1 to be paid by the employer for incidental expenses[1] ;

(e) No families to be brought over.

In the first fortnight of July the Board of Trade imported 1,000 skilled men from Canada, and others were then on the way over. The field, however, was limited, owing to the number of Government contracts placed in Canada.

Proposals were also considered in April and May for bringing labour from the United States. A firm on the Clyde had tried the experiment of importing American labour and had succeeded in overcoming the initial difficulties. In April our Ambassador at Washington had reported numerous inquiries from American workmen who wished to come. The Munitions of War Committee, however, decided on 7 May that no action could be taken.

Offers of skilled men were received from New Zealand, Australia, and South Africa. The Committee at first resolved to accept these offers, but later came to the conclusion that the difficulties connected with transport, distance, and the testing of the applicants made it necessary to decline them.

VI. The Diversion of Labour from Commercial to Armament Work.

The activities of the Board of Trade in its campaign to increase the supply of armament labour, as above described, did not go beyond an unusual extension of the normal functions of the Labour Exchanges. The rest of the programme laid down in January involved Government intervention, to be justified (as was then considered) only by the emergency of war, in the field where hitherto the services, conditions, and rewards of labour had been the subject of free bargaining between employers and employed. In particular, the second head of the programme—the diversion of labour from commercial to Government work—meant an interference, on the one hand, with the freedom of the workman to take his services to the best market, and on the other, with the employer's freedom to undertake or to carry out whatever contracts might promise him the highest profit, without regard to the general needs of the Country.

The campaign in this direction had not been under way for a fortnight before it became evident that little progress could be made without compulsory powers. This part of the story is the preface to the whole series of measures by which the Government secured control over the operations of the employer and over the movement of labour.

---

[1] In July, however, it was arranged that the firms engaging Canadians would not be required to pay fares or subsistence.

THE TRANSFER OF LABOUR ON MOBILISATION.   ALDERSHOT AND
ADMIRALTY TERMS.

The Board of Trade scheme for diverting labour from private to armament work was, with some modifications, modelled on the procedure put in practice at the outbreak of war in connection with the mobilisation of the Expeditionary Force and the strengthening of the staff of the dockyards and shipyards engaged on Admiralty work. It will, therefore, be convenient to give here some account of these emergency arrangements. The terms, moreover, which were offered to the men transferred were used by Labour representatives as a lever in bargaining with private employers who sought to attract labour from a distance.

The mobilisation of the Expeditionary Force involved the instantaneous release of a relatively small number of men for short periods. A scheme known as the " Aldershot Scheme "[1] had been drawn up in March, 1914, and agreed upon between the G.O.C.-in-C. Aldershot Command and the Board of Trade Divisional Officer for the S.W. Division. When the scheme was approved by the War Office, the Managers of Labour Exchanges were informed that the rates offered for men transferred would be (according to the statement of the officer notifying the order) either the normal rates or the special " Aldershot terms," which were as follows :—

(1) Employers to receive 10s. a week for every man released for the duration of the emergency, provided that the man were re-employed at the end of that time.

(2) The workman to receive : (a) return fares, and, if he were not engaged on his arrival and were receiving no wages, a subsistence allowance till his return, on the basis of 5s. for 24 hours or less, and 2s. 6d. for every additional 12 hours or less ; (b) wages at the London rate for ordinary and overtime work ; (c) free food and lodging, or an allowance of 10s. a week ; and (d) a bonus, at the end of the emergency, if he stayed in War Office employment so long as he was wanted, at the rate of 50% of his entire wages for the first week, 20% for the second week, and 10% for each subsequent week.

Mobilisation being complete on 8 August, the special terms were withdrawn. A War Office letter[2] of 19 August stated that it had not been intended that labour should be taken on under the scheme for any other purpose than to expedite mobilisation, and that such labour should not be retained after this object was fulfilled.

It had been arranged with the Board of Trade in 1910 that the Admiralty should obtain through the Labour Exchanges all the additional skilled labour needed for the Dockyards, Victualling yards,

[1] L.E. 40540, L.E. 26387/7.
[2] 79/5027 (M). L.E. Department, C.O. Circ. 1603 (12/9/14).

and Naval Ordnance and Naval Stores Depôts, in times of war or other emergency. The final arrangements were approved by the Admiralty on 2 August, 1914.

The terms for emergency employment at the Dockyards were as follows :—

    (a) Travelling expenses ; fares to be paid and, failing engagement, a subsistence allowance (as in the military scheme).

    (b) Wages : the rates generally applicable in the Dockyards.

    (c) Food and lodging to be free, or, in lieu of them, a subsistence allowance of 20s. a week, for 3 months at least, if the employment should last so long, and the man were not taken on the regular staff. This allowance was to be given only to men brought from other districts.

    (d) Regular engagement or bonus. If the man were not taken on the staff at the end of the emergency, he was to receive a bonus, provided he stayed as long as he was required, at the rate of 10% of his entire wages for the first three months, and 5% for any subsequent period of emergency employment.

In the case of Admiralty work, the emergency of course did not cease with mobilisation, and consequently the Admiralty terms were not withdrawn. Though it had been originally intended that the subsistence allowance should be paid only for a short time, in fact it continued to be paid indefinitely. This practice naturally gave rise to a claim on the part of men whom private employers wished to transfer from a distance to their shipyards that they should receive the "Admiralty terms." As will be seen, this became the principal point of contention between the Shipbuilders and the Unions.

Men required for work in the military camps, and those transferred from private shipbuilding yards to yards engaged on Admiralty work were moved by the Labour Exchanges in the ordinary way with no special terms, except that, as a rule, railway fares were paid by the employers. Altogether, in the first fortnight of war, over 30,000 men were transferred by the Exchanges to urgent war work, principally in the dockyards and shipyards.

The Canvass of Employers in January, 1915.

The circular[1] issued by the Board of Trade on 4 January, 1915, contains instructions for the canvass of employers " not having Government contracts, who are likely to be able or willing to release men for armament work." Two lists were attached, one showing the classes of labour required, the other showing the firms in each Division who were working short time or reporting slackness of work on Form Z 8,

---

[1] C.O. Circ. 1700 (4/1/15).

and might therefore be expected to have men to spare.[1] The employers were to be asked on patriotic grounds to release, so far as possible, their best qualified workmen, since a high degree of skill was required. An undertaking was to be given that, if a man's services should be required by his present employer at the end of the War, the employer to whom he was transferred would release him. The terms offered to the men were as follows:—

(a) The standard rate of wages for the area in which the man was engaged;

(b) A guarantee of work for a minimum time of six months to suitable men;

(c) Free railway fares to the work, and return fares if the man were discharged by the employer as unsuitable within the guaranteed period of work.[2]

The schedule enclosed with the circular enjoined that, in the search for labour suitable for armament firms, every possible source, no matter how small, should be examined. Besides the general engineering and motor firms, many other classes of engineering concerns were suggested, including cycle manufacturers, textile engineers, electrical plant engineers, etc., and firms making objects from metal and using any of the machines for turning, boring, slotting, etc. Men of the high degree of skill required for armament work might be " looked for anywhere."

This circular was considered at the second meeting of the Master-General of the Ordnance' Committee on Armaments, held on 8 January. It was agreed that the Board of Trade should be asked to prepare a letter to engineering firms, pressing them to transfer men to other firms engaged on urgent war work.

This letter was issued about 15 January by the President of the Board of Trade, who, after referring to the urgent need for an immediate increase of production, continued:—

" At the request of H.M. Government, steps are being taken by the Board of Trade to obtain the large numbers of additional

---

[1] Since the outbreak of the War a very large number of short time applications had been received at the Board of Trade under Section 96 of the Act, and rulings had been granted in a good many cases. Many of the firms were now working full time again, but reports from Divisional Officers showed as working short time : 5 general engineering firms employing about 2,000 men, 7 textile machinery manufacturers (about 1,500 men), 6 printing machinery makers in Yorkshire (about 1,000 men). (L.E. 48688.)
Firms chiefly employed on Government work and Railway Companies were reserved to be dealt with separately. Enquiries addressed to the chief Railway Companies soon showed that little could be expected from this source.

[2] These terms were suggested in a memorandum by Mr. Beveridge of 29/12/14 (L.E. 48688) with the following additional terms :—(d) a subsistence allowance of 5s. a day up to 3 days to be paid to the man, if not engaged, by the Labour Exchange and charged to the employer who had applied for the man ; (e) a bonus of £3 or £2 to be paid by the employer to a man who left with his previous employer's written consent to take armament work through the Labour Exchange.

workmen required for this purpose. In doing this, the Board desire, as far as possible, to approach men now in employment only through and with the co-operation of their present employers, with a view to causing the minimum of disturbance to the course of ordinary industry. It is possible that some of the workmen now employed by you would be suited for this work and willing to take it. If this is so, I hope it may be possible for you to assist the Government by releasing these men for such employment.

" I realise of course that in view of your own requirements, the releasing of men may cause you difficulty or inconvenience, but I can only ask you, in view of the urgent national need, to give such help as you are reasonably able to give. Mr. Churchill and Lord Kitchener have intimated to me that they attach the greatest possible importance to the success of the efforts now being made by the Board of Trade. No greater service can be rendered at the present time by the employers of workmen qualified for such work as I have mentioned than by making men available for this work, or by the workmen themselves than by undertaking it."

By the middle of January preliminary reports received by the Board of Trade from several Divisions on the results of their canvass of employers had brought to light the obstacles which threatened to prevent any wholesale transference of labour from private work.[1]

(1) A strong and widespread demand was put forward by ordinary engineering firms that, instead of surrendering their men to the armament firms, they should be allowed themselves to tender directly for Government contracts. This was, in effect, to challenge the whole policy, then being pursued, of concentrating the flow of labour from the outside engineering trade upon the armament firms. The Board of Trade appreciated the economic advantages of bringing the work to places where labour could be found and existing premises and plant converted to the new purpose. They accordingly lost no time in setting about an examination of the possibilities of devolution and spreading of armament work. The history of the measures taken will be given later.[2] They prepared the ground for the activities of the Armaments Output Committee in April and May, and laid the foundation on which the whole structure of " Area Organisation " was afterwards to be reared.

(2) Some employers complained that their men were already being stolen from them by rivals who, in their anxiety to complete urgent contracts, attempted to abstract labour by advertisement or by canvassing agents empowered to offer higher wages, regardless of whether such labour was already employed on Government contracts or sub-

---

[1] See Sir H. Ll. Smith, *Supply of Armament Labour, Preliminary Note* (23/1/15). HIST. REC./R/180/8.
[2] Part III., Chap. I.

contracts. This grievance was ultimately remedied by the promulgation, on 29 April, 1915, of Regulation 8 B, under the Defence of the Realm Act.[1] The immediate effect of the complaints was to make it clear that any attempt to take men from private work, over their employers' heads, by advertisement or enticement, would incur the fierce hostility of the whole engineering industry outside the armament firms, and would render many firms unable to complete their contracts.

(3) Another objection frequently advanced by employers was that they could not, except under *force majeure*, set aside or postpone their existing contracts with their customers, in order to release their men for armament work. Several employers represented that they would welcome such compulsion. It is a point of some interest that this suggestion should have come from the employers' side, because in the sequel this limited proposal for Government control soon came to be linked with wider and vaguer schemes for the " taking over " of engineering concerns, including those exclusively engaged on armament work. It marks the beginning of that movement for the official direction of industry which finally led to the powers exercised by the Government over the " controlled establishment."

The Board of Trade was not slow to realise that some form of compulsion would be necessary, if labour was to be transferred in any but negligible numbers. Sir H. Llewellyn Smith, as early as 23 January, foreshadowed the provisions subsequently embodied in the Defence of the Realm (Amendment) No. 2 Act of March, 1915, which gave protection to employers prevented by Government interference from fulfilling their obligations.[2]

(4) Not the least of the difficulties encountered was that a much larger number of firms than had been anticipated were found to be doing, either directly or indirectly, Government work. This was the main ground of opposition reported, for instance, by the Divisional Officer of the West Midlands Division.[3] Before the end of January, his staff had visited 272 employers, of whom only 25 had promised to release men, while, out of the 75 men offered, no more than 28 had actually been secured. Even where Government work occupied only a substantial fraction of a firm's capacity, the margin could not be lopped off without dislocating the economy of the works and impairing the efficiency and output of what remained. The question how to make the best use of this immovable surplus of machinery and men was to become in the next few months the central problem of local organisation.

The upshot was that neither employers nor employed felt that sufficient inducement had been offered. It will be noted that no subsistence allowance, such as had been given to labour transferred on mobilisation, was included in the terms offered to the men. Without such a provision, it was difficult to persuade married men either to take

---

[1] See Part III., Chap. V.   [2] See below, Chap. III.
[3] L.E. 1965/66.

work at a distance from their homes or to bear the expense of moving their families. The reason for the omission of any provision for subsistence allowances was that, at two conferences held on 13 and 14 January, the representatives of the War Office and of the Admiralty agreed with all the armament and shipping employers present in opposing the suggestion, when it was put forward by the Board of Trade. It was argued that such allowances caused trouble with the local workmen, and were used as a lever for raising wages.

VII. Results of the Board of Trade Campaign for the Supply of Labour.

The main results achieved by the Board of Trade campaign for supplying the armament firms with labour, whether unemployed or diverted from private work, may now be reviewed.

The following table[1] shows the results obtained up to 31 January :—

Firm and place of employment.	Belgians started work.	British workpeople submitted (including re-submissions).		British reported as having started work.
		Unemployed.	Released by employers.	
Armstrong, Alexandria ..	47	251	91	45
Elswick ..	—	601	116	265
Coventry Ordnance ..	118	113	26	27
Vickers, Crayford	1	233	58	11
Erith	306	110	62	33
Barrow	601	913	273	179
Sheffield	—	200	83	23
Manchester ..	3	—	—	—
Birmingham S.A.	8	128	128	4
Other armament firms ..	620	—	—	—
The Arsenal, Woolwich ..	—	273	85	34
Royal Factory, Enfield ..	—	90	38	5
Torpedo Factory, Greenock	—	342	82	12
Totals	1,704	3,253	942	638

A fortnight later the demands of the Royal Factories and the four armament firms on the preference list amounted to 9,103.[2]

---

[1] L.E. 1965/77.   [2] L.E. 1965/8.

By the end of the first 10 weeks (up to March 15) some 4,000 skilled British workmen had been submitted to the Royal Factories and the armament firms, and about 2,000 of them had been actually engaged. To these must be added about 3,300 Belgians, making the total of men actually engaged 5,300, out of a total of 7,300 submitted. The balance of 2,000 submitted, but not engaged, included workmen who were rejected as unsuitable, or who refused the terms offered, or who changed their minds and stayed in their previous employment, or who were still awaiting definite engagement.[1]

A month later the supply was continuing, but at a much reduced rate. In the four weeks from 15 March to 10 April, another 1,000 skilled men were engaged, raising the total to 6,300. In addition, very large numbers of unskilled men, boys, and women were supplied. When the labour supplied to the shipbuilding trades is added to the above figures for armament workers, the total of men placed through the Labour Exchanges in the three months ending 16 April was 55,000, of whom 30,000, representing an average of nearly 400 a day, were in occupations reckoned as skilled. These, however, would not necessarily all be for Government work, since the Exchanges could of course only urge, not compel, men to take such work.[2] In any case the figures fell far below the demand.

It should be added, however, that, although the numbers of transfers declined for a time, by the first week of June they were mounting. During eight weeks in May and June the increase of men employed on war work in three Government works and private works belonging to six firms reached a total of 13,467.[3] This increase was probably due to the special efforts made by local munitions committees from April onwards.

On 10 June Mr. Runciman[4] stated in the House of Commons that in the preceding four months the Labour Exchanges had filled over 400,000 vacancies, of which more than 80,000 were in the engineering and shipbuilding trades, including 46,000 in skilled trades. Vacancies were now being filled at the rate of 4,000 a day.[5] Since the outbreak of war not less than 100,000 workpeople had been transferred through the Labour Exchanges to engagements on national work in other districts ; and the total number of transfers from one district to another had been not less than 187,000.

In spite of these efforts, however, the demand continued to outstrip the supply. At the same date returns compiled by the Intelligence

---

[1] Sir H. Ll. Smith, *Supply of Armament Labour* (15/3/15). Hist. Rec./ R/180/8. The return of placings through the Central Clearing House for this period is given below in Appendix IV.

[2] Sir H. Ll. Smith, *Memorandum on Labour for Armaments* (9/6/15). Hist. Rec./R/320/1.

[3] Hist. Rec./R/200/10.

[4] *Parliamentary Debates* (1915), H. of C., LXXII., 428.

[5] The increases in the numbers employed in the Government Factories and 12 private armament works in the quarter ending 3 July are shown in Appendix V.

Section of the Ministry showed that the labour requirements at Woolwich, Enfield, and 16 firms doing munitions work amounted to 13,966 workpeople.[1]

Writing on 9 June, Sir H. Llewellyn Smith[2] observed that the acute shortage was practically confined to the skilled trades ; demands for unskilled men could be satisfied locally.   The shortage was particularly marked in regard to certain types of workmen essential for setting up and equipping new factories and machines, men in the tool department, millwrights, etc.   The ordinary economic control over the individual workman had broken down.   " The question is whether some exceptional form of control or motive not of a purely economic character can be effectively substituted."

The answer to this question was the Munitions of War Act.

---

[1] M.W. 4591. A table given in Appendix VI., shows the demand at the National Clearing House on 1 July at a little over 14,000.
[2] *Memorandum on Labour for Armaments* (9/6/15). Hist. Rec./R/320/1.

CHAPTER II.

THE RELAXATION OF TRADE UNION RESTRICTIONS, AUGUST, 1914, TO FEBRUARY, 1915.

I. Introductory.

Under the third and last head of the programme adopted on 30 December, 1914, the Board of Trade undertook to make " efforts to promote arrangements with the engineering Trade Unions, whereby the existing supply of labour might be more economically and productively used." These efforts were directed mainly to two objects : (a) the settlement of disputes, by means of some agreed procedure of arbitration, without stoppage of work by strike or lockout ; (b) the temporary suspension, for the duration of the War, of such Trade Union rules and practices as tended to restrict output, and, in particular, of those rules of Demarcation which parcel out the whole field of a highly organised industry into close compartments, dividing one class of skilled work from another, and excluding the semi-skilled or unskilled man or woman from the skilled man's job. The second of these objects was by far the more intricate and revolutionary of the two. The suspension of restrictive rules and customs was justly regarded by the workman as imperilling the most highly valued and hardly won safeguards of his standard of living. It meant the surrender of a system of defences built up, piece by piece, through the struggles of a century ; and it entailed a sacrifice for which no compensation could be offered. It would be hard to name a more perilous field for even the most delicate advance of Government intervention.

The movement by which this question passed from the region of voluntary negotiation and agreement to the region of compulsory legislation falls into four stages :—

(1) During the first five months of war (August to December, 1914) it was debated at conferences of the normal type between the employers' Federations and the Unions. The discussions led to no agreement within that period, and tended rather to prejudice the chances of success in the following months.

(2) In January, 1915, the Board of Trade was invoked ; and in February a Committee under the chairmanship of the Chief Industrial Commissioner reached a settlement of some minor points and formulated a programme for Government action.

(3) At the Treasury Conference in March, all the forces of the Government were brought into play. A direct appeal from the Cabinet

to all the Trade Unions connected, even remotely, with munitions production, resulted in a treaty, known as the Treasury Agreement, which, if it had proved effective, would have secured the suspension for the war period both of strikes and lock-outs and of restrictions upon output.

(4) Finally, when in the course of the next three months it had become clear that the Agreement was little more than a dead letter, negotiations between the Government and the Unions were re-opened, and the terms of the treaty were embodied in the first Munitions of War Act (2 July, 1915).

The present chapter will cover the first two stages only. Before the Treasury Conference can be discussed, it will be necessary to take account of a new factor—the proposed " taking over " of engineering establishments and the limitation of their profits—which emerged in February and March and had a decisive influence on the successful negotiation of the treaty.

II. Conferences of Shipbuilding and Engineering Employers and Workmen, August to December, 1914.

In response to an appeal issued by the Admiralty and the War Office in the first few days of war, joint meetings of employers and workmen were held to arrange what was called the Truce with Labour. Thus, on 4 August, representatives of the Clyde Shipbuilding and Engineering employers and employees " unanimously agreed to recommend to their respective constituents to assist in every possible way, as specially asked by the Admiralty and War Office, all firms employed on Government work urgently wanted during the present national crisis, in order to complete at the earliest possible date all such work." A resolution in similar terms, passed on 10 August by the Shipbuilding, Engineering, and Ship-repairing employers and workmen on the Tyne, explicitly included a recommendation " that all working restrictions be removed." Two clauses were added : " It is understood that the employers will endeavour to employ all men available, and arrange for night shifts where practicable in preference to excessive overtime. All existing machinery between employers and Trade Unions will continue, and be requisitioned when necessary."

The first step towards a suspension of strikes and lock-outs was taken on 25 August at a joint meeting of the Parliamentary Committee of the Trades Union Congress, the Management Committee of the General Federation of Trades Unions, and the Executive Committee of the Labour Party. The meeting resolved—

> " That an immediate effort be made to terminate all existing trade disputes, whether strikes or lock-outs, and whenever new points of difficulty arise during the war period, a serious attempt should be made by all concerned to reach an amicable settlement before resorting to a strike or lock-out."[1]

---

[1] *Parliamentary Debates* (1915), *H. of C.*, LXXII., 1572.

That this resolution represented the general feeling of the rank and file of trade unionists is sufficiently proved by the rapid decline in the numbers of strikes known to the Board of Trade during the first six months of war. In August the figure fell from about 100 to 20, in which some 9,000 workpeople were concerned. By the beginning of 1915 it had fallen to 10. The numbers of industrial male workpeople on strike were estimated in mid-July, 1914, at 72,000 ; in February, 1915, as " practically nil."[1]   In February the curve began to rise again. These first six months were a time of peace in the labour world such as had never existed before and has not existed since.

(a) SHIPBUILDING CONFERENCES.

Although the terms above quoted of the resolution passed at the North-East Coast meeting show that the shipbuilding trades shared the common apprehension of unemployment, very soon afterwards there was a marked shortage of shipbuilding labour on Tyne and Clyde and in the Barrow and Birkenhead districts. Efforts to find fresh skilled labour were unfruitful, and suggestions began to be put forward that demarcation rules should be relaxed so as to admit of one class of workmen supplementing another, and of the introduction of semi-skilled and unskilled workmen. On the Clyde, to obviate the scarcity of drillers, the Shipbuilders' and Engineers' Association made proposals to this effect in October. They were rejected by the Union to which the bulk of the drillers belonged. The Association then issued a letter stating that large numbers of workmen were still needed. The merchant shipbuilders had surrendered many of their hands to the warship-builders, and thousands had lately enlisted. Merchant ship-building was threatened with disorganisation and the closing of some of the yards. There was a special shortage of ironworkers, of drillers, and of apprentices. The Association urged that these vacancies should be filled at once, and emergency arrangements made for using other workmen, skilled and unskilled, in every suitable way. A joint meeting, to secure the co-operation of the Unions, was suggested. Though this letter referred only to the needs of merchant shipbuilders, the shortage was also felt at the Government Dockyards and by the Admiralty contractors. At this time, when the submarine was thought of chiefly, if not solely, as a danger to ships of war, the building and owning of the mercantile marine was not regarded as a national concern ; and, since it was carried on for private profit, the employers were in a much weaker position, when it came to bargaining for the suspension of restrictions, than the contractors who could claim that their work was vitally necessary to the Fleet.

At the series of conferences which followed[2] it will be seen that the employers emphasised both the urgent need of obtaining more men

---

[1] *Board of Trade Supplementary Report on the State of Employment*, Feb., 1915, p. 9.
[2] Confidential Reports of the Conferences at York (3 November), Glasgow (9 and 16 November), Newcastle (19 November), and Carlisle (9 December), printed for the Ship-constructors and Shipwrights' Association, I.C. 71.

for Admiralty and for private work and the necessity of suspending Trade Union restrictions and particularly demarcation rules. The men, on their side, demanded for the transference of labour terms which the employers would not grant, and believed that the labour could be provided, if sufficiently attractive conditions were offered, without the sacrifice of Trade Union practices.

The proposed Conference " to consider the necessary steps for the acceleration of Government work due to the War " was held between the Shipbuilding Employers' Federation, the Standing Committee of Shipbuilding Trade Unions, and the Boilermakers' Society, at York on 3 November, 1914. The Union representatives suggested for consideration the following resolution :—

> " That the representatives of the various trades, having considered the position put before them by the Shipbuilding Employers' Federation, are willing to assist where possible to accelerate all Admiralty work in the present national crisis. In view, however, of the imperative necessity of the members in the various localities being consulted, the representatives suggest that, in those districts where urgent Admiralty work is being executed, the local representatives of the Unions and employers involved should meet with a view to agreeing on a method to accelerate such Admiralty work on an organised basis."

The employers objected that the resolution made no reference to merchant work. The opinion was expressed that that might follow.

The employers replied by handing in a resolution, in the form of a proposed joint finding, to the following effect :—

> That in view of the urgency of Admiralty work and the shortage of labour, due largely to the enlistment of nearly 13,000 workmen and apprentices, the representatives of employers and workmen, after full discussion, agree to the following special arrangements during the emergency :—(1) A general relaxation of Trade Union rules. (2) In view of the shortage of certain classes of men (especially drillers) occasioning the dislocation of the work of other trades and the suspension from time to time of other workmen, the employers shall be at liberty to add from any source such numbers of suitable workmen as may be needed. (3) In view of the shortage of apprentices (of whom one-third had joined the Colours and many would not return to their trades), all necessary steps should be taken and facilities given for filling such vacancies as soon as possible.

The Union representatives could not see their way to put such a proposal before their members. They undertook, as an alternative, first to attempt to find the men needed in any locality ; failing that, to relax their rules so that one class of workmen should supplement another ; and failing that again, to hold local meetings and consider the numbers required, there being still a certain amount of unemployment.

After this meeting local conferences were summoned at Glasgow and Newcastle.

I–2

At Glasgow the Clyde Shipbuilders' Association met the representatives of the shipbuilding trades on 9 November. The chairman stated that the Clyde firms needed 1,038 men at once, and fully double that number in the next three months. Difficulties were raised with regard to the wages of unskilled men, whom it was proposed to put on skilled work. It was also stated that some firms had refused to pay fares and subsistence allowances to transferred men.

After retiring, the Union representatives said they were prepared to assist in finding the men wanted for Admiralty work, and to that end put the following questions to the employers for the information of the various societies :—" (1) Will fares be paid to men coming from a distance ? (2) What lodging allowance will be paid to such men ? (3) How long will the job last ? "

An adjourned Conference was held at Glasgow on 16 November. The Admiralty had meanwhile been consulted about travelling allowances and had replied that, if they were paid, they must be paid by the firms, not by the Admiralty. The employers were not prepared to pay them. The Union representatives said that they could not pay the fares, and they required a guarantee of three months' employment. Local officials were not prepared to recommend their men to relax demarcation rules. They would do all they could to supply men locally.

At Newcastle the local conference between the Tyne Shipbuilders' Association and the representatives of the Shipyard Trades was held on 19 November. The questions as to travelling allowances and a guarantee of duration of work and of a minimum rate of pay were raised. The employers' chairman said that the employers could pay fares, provided the man stayed for three months. They would not pay subsistence allowances, or guarantee the duration of the job. The standard rate of the district would be paid ; but no minimum wage would be guaranteed.

On 3 December the Shipbuilding Employers' Federation addressed a letter to the Shipyard Trades stating that the results of the efforts of local Union officials to supply men had been disappointing. Very few additional workmen had been furnished. They invited the Unions to meet them in further conference at Carlisle on 9 December.

At this meeting the employers put forward the same terms for men transferred from other districts that had been offered at Newcastle. They further proposed that on warship work, electricians, joiners, and shipwrights should be allowed to drill any holes required for their own work, and that demarcation between joiners and shipwrights should be suspended. They were willing to discuss with the shipwrights piece-work, premium bonus systems, or other measures for expediting work. They intended to appeal to the War Office to get men released from the Colours.

After this conference negotiations by correspondence were carried on with the Boilermakers on the subject of broken squads,[1] and with

---

[1] Riveters in shipyards work in squads, which are so constituted that, if one member of the squad is absent, the rest cannot begin work. The squad is then described as " broken."

Mr. Wilkie on behalf of the other shipyard trades. With regard to broken squads the employers accepted some of the Boilermakers' proposals, but rejected others, thereby making the scheme, in the Society's opinion, unworkable. They also failed to agree about subsistence allowances and other terms to be offered to men brought from a distance. The correspondence dragged on till February without any agreement being reached.

In a letter addressed to Mr. Wilkie after the Conference, the Federation confirmed the employers' proposals to the other Shipyard Trades. Mr. Wilkie replied on 22 December, stating the men's objections. (1) They objected to the restrictions attached to the offer to pay railway fares. (2) Employers could not expect men to come from a distance and keep up two homes, unless a subsistence allowance, such as was paid by the Admiralty, were given. (3) If employment was to be for a considerable period, there should be no difficulty in guaranteeing the length of the job. Without such a guarantee it was much harder for the Unions to persuade men to leave one district for another. (4) Piece-work rates had been arranged in certain cases, but on warship work such rates could not cover all work, and there was therefore a large volume of work for which the prices must be left to arrangement between the men's representatives and the manager, as was now the custom. (5) The question of piece-work and premium bonus for shipwrights was left to each district. Some arrangement might be made by individual firms with the district representatives. (6) The shortage of drillers could better be met by drafting 10% or 15% from merchant work. (7) Suspension of demarcation rules must be dealt with locally.

On 22 January the Federation replied, adhering to their proposals and expressing regret that no progress had been made in two and a half months.

Meanwhile, the Admiralty authorities decided that the matter was so urgent as to call for their intervention. On 15 December Dr. Macnamara interviewed the Standing Committee of the Shipyard Trades at Newcastle. The Chairman of the Committee referred to the conferences at York and Carlisle. He believed that with proper organisation the men required could be obtained ; but men would not now go to shipyard work unless the shipbuilders would offer a subsistence allowance. The Secretary of the Boilermakers' Society quoted the employers' proposals made at the Carlisle Conference, and said that the Admiralty and other employers had granted all the terms refused by the shipbuilders. He accused the shipbuilders of exploiting the crisis to do private work for which there was no urgency, while they asked the Unions to remove their restrictions.

Dr. Macnamara summed up the men's proposals as follows :— (1) The employers should state their absolute requirements precisely and offer reasonable inducements ; if that were done, the Unions would try to find the men. (2) The employers might fairly be asked to turn over 10% or 15% of their men from private to Government work. (3) Fares and subsistence allowances should be paid to men brought from a distance. (4) Three months' employment should be guaranteed.

Later on the same day, Dr. Macnamara met the Newcastle Shipbuilders. The employers stated that the Unions could not supply the men. They also complained that the percentage of time lost had increased during the War. They suggested a reversion to the old practice under which the whole of shipwright work was done as piece-work, and pressed for the abolition of demarcation. One speaker said that the difficulties could largely be met by adopting piece-work, by riveters working full time, and by some relaxation of rules as to apprentices. The additional payments demanded by the men would only have the effect of drawing labour from one district to another, and the firms could not afford them. To divert labour from private work would involve breaches of contract. The ship-repairers complained that many of their men had been attracted away by the Admiralty terms.

It was evident that the negotiations had reached a deadlock, neither party being willing to give way. The Government decided that the mediation of the Board of Trade should be invoked, and Dr. Macnamara reported the results of his enquiries to the Secretary of the Board.

(b) ENGINEERING CONFERENCES.

At the same time, similar negotiations were going on with regard to the relaxation of restrictions in the Engineering trades. Two special conferences were held at Sheffield on 10 and 17 December between the Engineering Employers' Federation and the Amalgamated Society of Engineers and kindred organisations, to discuss the shortage of labour. After discussion, the employers tabled proposals : " That in consequence of the Unions' inability to supply the requisite amount of labour, they agree to remove certain trade restrictions, without prejudice, during the continuance of the War." The employers asked for :—(1) more freedom to employ semi-skilled and unskilled men ; (2) freedom to put turners and other machine men on two machines ; (3) removal of all overtime restrictions ; (4) removal of all demarcation restrictions. These concessions were to be for the duration of the War only, with adequate safeguards for the return to existing conditions.

The majority of the workmen's delegates appeared favourable, but feared they could not carry their members with them, if (as was likely) a hostile minority should start an agitation. Accordingly no decision was reached.

At the second meeting on 17 December the Unions' counter-proposals were put forward. These included the payment of subsistence allowances to transferred men. The employers rejected the proposals as inadequate. They offered to resume discussion, if the Unions would agree to remove the restrictions specified in the employers' scheme. The Unions declined these terms, but it was arranged that a further conference should be held at Sheffield on 13 January.

Meanwhile, in the last days of December, the parties to this controversy also came into touch with the Board of Trade.

III. The Intervention of the Board of Trade.

Sir H. Llewellyn Smith, writing on 23 January, described the relaxation of trade union restrictions as " the most difficult and delicate of all the matters with which the Board of Trade have undertaken to deal." He added that the situation had been prejudiced by injudicious action and fruitless conferences between employers and trade unions. " The men are full of suspicion as to the real motives of the employers and the ultimate result of any concessions that they may make."[1]

The correspondence between the two parties in the shipbuilding trade had, in fact, been marked by a tone of increasing exasperation ; and labour troubles of a serious cast were already brewing on the Clyde. In the engineering trade the relations were not as yet so strained. Mr. Brownlie and Mr. Young, of the A.S.E. Executive, co-operated with Mr. Allan Smith, of the Engineering Employers' Federation, in seeking a solution. On the other hand, the Union leaders felt by no means sure of carrying the rank and file with them. The Labour world took alarm at proposals made in the House of Lords on 8 January that preparations should be made for the introduction of compulsory military service, if the voluntary system should fail. On that occasion the Lord Chancellor declared that compulsory service, though a bad thing in itself, was not foreign to the Constitution and might be resorted to as a last necessity.[2] The suppression of strikes in foreign countries by means of the mobilisation laws was not forgotten ; and the hatred of conscription was doubled by the fear that it would be used as a lever for industrial compulsion. Something of this apprehension may be read between the lines of the following passage summarised from the editorial notes written by the General Secretary of the A.S.E. in the *Monthly Journal and Report* for January :

> In order to accelerate production every reasonable means must be adopted to make the best use of the skilled workmen available. If the employers and the Unions could not agree, the Government would probably intervene in the interests of the men at the Front and what the Government might consider to be the interests of the nation as a whole. This opened up a way for compulsory orders from the War Office and the Admiralty, which in turn might ultimately pave the way for compulsory legislation not favourable to the workers. The writer was not opposed to the principle of national control over all armament factories and shipyards, but he felt that such an economic change would be more for the workers' benefit if carried out under peace conditions. He hoped that some *via media* might be arranged with the employers, with guarantees to safeguard the trade. Nothing must be done that would lower their future standard of living. The first essential, however, to maintain this was complete victory

---

[1] *Supply of Armament Labour, Preliminary Note* (23/1/15). HIST. REC./ R/180/8.

[2] *Parliamentary Debates* (1915), H. of L., XVIII., 378.

for the Allies. Failing agreement with the employers, assurances must be obtained from the Government, if they should intervene, that innovations should be only temporary. Otherwise the outlook for peace in the industrial world, after the War, would be black indeed.

The tone of this passage suggests that the Executive recognised the necessity of relaxation, but felt no less keenly that any bargain they could make must be one-sided and might easily be denounced as a traitorous surrender.

The embarrassments which beset the overtures of official intervention were expressed by Mr. I. H. Mitchell, of the Industrial Commissioner's department, in a memorandum dated 29 December. He pointed out that a request for the general suspension of restrictions would be met by the question how Trade Union interests were to be safeguarded after the War. Mere assurances would be of little value. Opposition, perhaps of national extent, might be aroused, and conducted by the rank and file, who could not be interviewed and conciliated. He thought it inadvisable to offer inducements to the Unions to make concessions ; it would be better to leave them to formulate demands. On the other hand, negotiations with the Employers' Federation might raise other difficulties. An alternative would be to deal with individual firms ; to induce the A.S.E. to relax their restrictions in particular shops ; and gradually to extend the process to others. The Society would then not appear as making any universal concessions ; rather it would connive at these local arrangements. Whatever was done, differences must occur, which would have to be settled without a stoppage of work.

It was arranged that a deputation of the Executive Council of the A.S.E. should confer with Sir H. Llewellyn Smith on 29 December. At this meeting several important suggestions were considered.

(a) Work to which Relaxation should apply.

It was urged that restrictions could not be relaxed for Government work and retained for commercial work in the same establishment. If this principle were accepted, it was evidently necessary to draw the line between establishments, rather than between the two classes of work. It was proposed that relaxation should be applied to any establishment, as a whole, certified by the Board of Trade, on the employers' application, as one in which Government work (or a " substantial amount " of such work) was done. As a compensation to the Unions, a 10% increase of wages in such establishments was suggested.

The Board of Trade later pointed out that this scheme would leave to the employer the option of paying the increased wages for the advantage of having no restrictions, or going on as at present. No legal sanction existed to enforce the proposed settlement on employers. To announce it as compulsory would involve the risk of having a Government decree openly flouted. If it were left optional, employers short of hands would probably adopt it, on pain of losing men to other firms who offered the higher wages. The ambiguous proposal for a 10% increase on wages would be best interpreted as a 10% increase, in relaxed shops, on ordinary district rates at any time. This would mark the connection of the increase with relaxation, and would lead to a simpler settlement after the War. The settlement might be perpetuated and other shops levelled up ; or there might be a return to present conditions at a sacrifice of 10% on wages.

In the later negotiations this method of compensation by increase of wages was dropped ; nor did it prove possible to discover any other. All that could be offered to the Unions was the undertaking to limit the employers' profits, and the best possible security for a return to existing conditions after the War. Only the latter of these two conditions was discussed on 29 December.

(b) The Employers' Guarantee of Restitution.

It was at this meeting that the first definite formula was put forward by Sir H. Llewellyn Smith for an undertaking binding the employer to restore after the War the practices which the Unions were asked to sacrifice. It ran as follows :—

> " Messrs.   being unable to obtain sufficient skilled engineers and being, as a consequence, prevented from meeting the urgent needs of the Country during the present national emergency, hereby undertake that any departure from present practice which it may be necessary to resort to in such matters as the working of machines, overtime, greater utilisation of semi-skilled, unskilled, or other labour, shall only be for the period of the War or until such time as sufficient skilled mechanics can be obtained, whichever period is the shorter.

> " Any difference arising under this undertaking shall be referred to the Board of Trade for settlement."

As will be seen later, this formula was considerably expanded before it was embodied in the Treasury Agreement and transferred from that Agreement into the Munitions of War Act, 1915.

(c) Proposed direct Appeal by the Government to the Unions.

As early as 23 December, Mr. Brownlie and Mr. Young had suggested to Mr. Mitchell that, in lieu of further negotiations on the old lines between the Union and the employers, some member of the Government should address both parties in a joint conference and impress upon them that in the interests of the nation it was imperative that the fullest use should be made of the workpeople and the machines. The suggestion was considered on 29 December, and again pressed by Mr. Brownlie and Mr. Young at an interview with Mr. Mitchell on 31 December. They believed that to such an appeal the men would respond loyally ; but they thought it better that employers and men should be approached jointly. Mr. Brownlie suggested that an address from Mr. Churchill would have a great effect.

This proposal, taken up later by the Chief Industrial Commissioner, bore fruit in the Treasury Conference of 17-19 March. It is a point of considerable interest, and not publicly known, that it came in the first instance from the side of the Trade Unions. It is probable that the Union leaders were prompted by a consciousness that their unaided influence would not carry the Societies with them. The sacrifice which was called for undoubtedly involved great risk of compromising the whole Trade Union position, and that in a manner which, so long as profits were not limited, meant a very large increase of private gain to the employers. In advocating it, the leaders preferred to confront their members as the ambassadors of higher powers ; and they might justly feel that so great a sacrifice could only be demanded by those who could pronounce with authority that it must be made in the interest of the Country.

At the request of Mr. Brownlie and Mr. Young, this proposal was left in abeyance till a final attempt should have been made to reach a settlement at the Sheffield Conference already arranged for 13 January. Meanwhile Mr. Brownlie and Mr. Allan Smith waited on the War Office and procured the issue of the following letter :—

LETTER FROM THE WAR OFFICE TO THE AMALGAMATED SOCIETY
OF ENGINEERS.

WAR OFFICE,
2 *January*, 1915.

Dear Sir,—

I am desired by the Secretary of State for War to inform you that, while he fully appreciates the efforts of both employers and workmen to maintain adequate supplies for the Army in the field, the present requirements are such as render it necessary that further and greater efforts should be made.

The Secretary of State is aware of the difficulty due to a shortage of various classes of the workpeople required, but he is of opinion that temporary arrangements could be made to overcome this shortage, and that a greater output than at present could be attained.

Lord Kitchener believes that the call of the present national emergency is fully appreciated by the representatives of both employers and workmen, and that they will make arrangements to meet the requirements of the crisis and to secure the safety of the nation. He does not desire even to suggest what steps should be taken, but he does express the hope that these important matters may have your immediate attention.

A letter in similar terms has been sent to the Chairman, the Engineering Employers' Federation.

Yours sincerely,
HAROLD BAKER.

The General Secretary,
The Amalgamated Society of Engineers.

A letter in similar terms was issued on the same day by the Admiralty.

The third Conference between the Engineering Employers' Federation and the Amalgamated Society of Engineers and kindred Unions was held at Sheffield on 13 January.

The Employers submitted proposals as follows :—

" *Supply of Workpeople.*

" The Admiralty and War Office having requested the Federation and the Unions to take steps to secure an increased output ;—

" It is mutually agreed :—

" 1.   The following arrangements shall have effect during the War, and shall in no way prejudice any of the parties on any of the points covered, and the parties shall, at the termination of the War, as the Federation and the Unions now undertake, revert to the conditions which existed in the respective shops on the outbreak of hostilities.

" 2.   The Unions agree :—

That they shall not press the following questions to an issue, but shall confine themselves to noting any such by way of protest for the purpose of safeguarding their interests—

    (*a*) Manning of machines, including lathes and the number to be worked by one operator ;

    (*b*) Manning of hand operations ;

    (*c*) Demarcation of work between trades ;

    (*d*) Employment of non-union labour ;

    (*e*) Employment of female labour ;

    (*f*) Limitation of overtime.

" 3.   The Employers agree :—

    (*a*) The provisions of paragraph 2 hereof shall be subject to the continued inability of the Unions to supply suitable workpeople of the classes desired by the employers at district rates.

    (*b*) That with regard to demarcation of -work the employers shall, as far as they can, having regard to the urgency of the work and the trades available, observe the demarcation fixed by local agreement or in practice observed.

    (*c*) That workpeople shall receive the rates of wages and work under the conditions recognised in the shop in question for the trade at which they are for the time engaged.

    (*d*) That this agreement shall not warrant an employer making such arrangements in the shops as will effect a permanent restriction of employment of any trade in favour of semi-skilled men.

" 4. The Unions further agree :—

To recommend Unions not here represented that they should also adopt the foregoing attitude with regard to demarcation questions."

The Unions' representatives sent the following reply :—

" Supply of Workpeople.

" The Unions represented have given careful consideration to the proposals made by the Engineering Employers' Federation. The Unions regard these proposals as calculated to hinder production by introducing factors inevitably leading to friction in the workshops of the country, and as unlikely to meet the situation as stated by the employers. The Unions are, therefore, unable to agree to the abrogation of their established trade rights embodied in these proposals, and again direct the attention of the Engineering Employers' Federation to the proposals and suggestions made by the Unions."

This reply was signed on behalf of the A.S.E., the Steam Engine Makers' Society, the Amalgamated Toolmakers' Society, the United Machine Workers' Association, and the Scientific Instrument Makers.

The Unions' counter-proposals were as follow :—

" (*a*) Firms not engaged in the manufacture of war goods to be given such work.

" (*b*) Firms that are at present working short time to transfer their workmen to firms engaged on Government work.

" (*c*) Joint representations to be made to the Government to pay subsistence allowance money to men working in places at a distance from their homes.

" (*d*) That the Government draft skilled engineers from Australasia, Canada, and South Africa.

" (*e*) In view of the fact that 10,000 skilled engineers have recently enlisted, thus reducing the supply of skilled labour, the Government should withdraw from military duties all those available for industrial purposes."

The Unions' representatives held that these measures would furnish sufficient labour without encroachment upon Trade Union customs. The employers, on the other hand, considered them inadequate, and no agreement was reached. The engineering trades were now in the same deadlock that the shipbuilding trades had come to in December.

After the failure of the Sheffield Conference, Mr. Allan Smith proposed that Lord Kitchener should be asked to make a personal appeal to the Unions to suspend their restrictions. The suggestion was forwarded by the Board of Trade to the War Office. Lord Kitchener, however, declined to intervene. He considered that the Board of Trade, as the Department to which the War Office had referred the question of labour supply for armament purposes, should communicate with the parties and seek a settlement. It was then decided (about 19 January) that the whole range of questions in dispute with the engineers and with the shipwrights and boilermakers should be dealt with by the Chief Industrial Commissioner, Sir George Askwith. Sir H. Llewellyn Smith wrote on 23 January in his memorandum to the Cabinet Committee on Munitions : " I have considerable hope that by the exercise of patience and tact a successful result may yet be achieved. I am strongly of opinion that nothing but disaster would attend any attempt to rush the position by a frontal attack on Union policy, or by any Government action which would give the Unions the impression that the Government in this matter were acting as the mouthpiece of the employers."[1]

The Board of Trade was in fact disinclined to resort to the policy of a direct appeal from the Cabinet, until the chances of conciliation by means of departmental intervention should have been exhausted. The needs of the country were paramount ; but it was unquestionable that, on the broad issue considered merely as a bargain between employers and employed, the employers had everything to gain, the workmen everything to lose. As such a bargain the matter had hitherto been treated ; and the too sudden descent of even the most tactful god from the Cabinet machine must strike Labour as, on the face of it, no better than a reinforcement of the enemy's ranks.

IV. Appointment of the Committee on Production.

Sir G. Askwith began his enquiries by interviewing Major-General Mahon, Sir Frederick Donaldson, a representative of Sir James Marshall, Sir Frederick Black, and Mr. Allan Smith. Officers of his department were sent to make local investigations at Newcastle and Glasgow.

A memorandum sent by Major-General Mahon to Sir George Askwith on 28 January is of interest as expressing the point of view of the M.G.O. department. Major-General Mahon began by stating the figures for the shortage of deliveries of projectiles as compared with contractors' undertakings. The shortage was attributed partly to the inexperience of subcontractors ; partly to lack of material and delay in obtaining material and machinery ; partly to delay due to bad weather, in completing new shops. But it was also caused to some extent by shortage of labour and bad time-keeping.

In addition to the efforts already being made, the following suggestions were offered :—

(1) Unskilled and female labour could be brought in for the less skilled classes of work. Learners should be attached to every machine now at work. Private workshops might be closed compulsorily in order to set free their labour.

A good deal had been done towards spreading contracts, but not with much success. All armament work required close expert supervision and could be better done in large shops than in small ones. The labour should be brought to the work, not the work to the labour.

(2) Loss of time was partly due to overstrain. There should be a compulsory rest from, say, 1 p.m. on Saturday to Sunday morning.

---

[1] *Supply of Armament Labour, Preliminary Note* (23/1/15). HIST. REC. R/180/8.

A " civil " service decoration might be offered for deserving workmen, to be given when the War was over.[1]

(3) Some form of compulsory training, not necessarily amounting to military service, might be useful to give the employer more power over men who were slack at their work. But the country was opposed to this. The hours of closing public-houses should be considered.

(4) Competition for labour between employers in the same district should be checked. Advertisement for men at a distance should be stopped.[2] No form of maintenance or separation allowance for imported workmen should be allowed.

After a week spent in collecting information, Sir George Askwith mapped out a programme of action.[3] He began by remarking that there was little chance of progress being made, if the employers and the Union leaders were allowed to continue their dilatory negotiations. The Union leaders were hindered from accepting the removal of restrictions partly by distrust of the employers, partly by the fear that their own members would repudiate them. The Shipbuilding Employers' Federation was still making strenuous efforts, prompted no doubt by a desire to avoid the whole matter being taken up by the Government ; but the essentials to useful negotiation were wanting—confidence, trust in each other, and good faith. In such matters organisation of either party was a hindrance, since the officials on both sides, though eager to help in the national emergency, were hampered by their regard for the safety of their associations, and by the delay and difficulty of talking over their local branches.

Two methods of settlement were suggested, the second only in case the first should fail :—

(1) The ideal settlement would be to induce both sides to accept an agreement, by which the employers would undertake—

> " That any departure from present practice now ruling in their shops which may be necessary shall only be for the period of the War, or until circumstances should admit of existing practice being resumed. Departures from present practice contemplated would cover the attendance on machines, overtime restriction, greater utilisation of semi-skilled, unskilled, or other labour. Any difference arising from this undertaking shall be referred to the Board of Trade for settlement."

Such an agreement would leave the employers free to settle with their own men ; and, since in most instances the departure from present practice would mean more money for the men, it might be assumed

---

[1] This suggestion was adopted at the War Office. The institution of the decoration was announced by Lord Kitchener in the House of Lords on 15 March, 1915.

[2] The measures taken for this purpose by a Defence of the Realm Regulation prohibiting Enticement will be described below, Part III., Chap. V.

[3] Memorandum on *Shortage of Labour : Shipbuilding and Engineering* (28/1/15). Hist. Rec./R/180/3.

that, if they were assured by their leaders that the Trade Union position was secured and that any departure was only temporary, the men directly concerned would not be averse from coming to an agreement with their foremen.

(2) The prospects of such an agreement being very doubtful, there remained in reserve a direct appeal to be made by representatives of the Government, who might put a prepared scheme before both parties ; hear and, if they chose, adopt any amendment suggested by either side ; and then give a decision, intimating that that decision must be taken as a final settlement, at least until the parties could come to a satisfactory arrangement among themselves. A schedule of definite terms, to be put before the two parties, was given in the memorandum. It enumerated in detail the restrictions which it was desired to suspend on Government work, and included the employers' undertaking to restore existing conditions. There was also a provision that " in view of the necessity to avoid stoppages of work, on any difference arising which fails to be settled by the parties, work should be continued and the matter in dispute referred to the Government." In the Shipbuilding trades habitual time-losers were to be reported to the Trade Unions, fined, and if necessary expelled ; and men so expelled were not to be re-employed. The vexed question of subsistence allowances was to be dealt with by leaving it to the men employed at a distance from their homes to arrange conditions with their new employers.

In a " General Introduction " to this schedule it was suggested that the Government should recommend, as the most satisfactory arrangement, " a complete suspension of activity by both employers' and workmen's organisations," allowing individual employers to settle with their workmen the conditions under which departures from practice might be introduced in order to accelerate production, on the understanding that workmen would not be put in a worse position and that any increased responsibility they were asked to undertake would be recognised.

This second part of Sir George Askwith's programme was, in its main idea, carried out at the Treasury Conference in March, though on that occasion it was departed from in one important respect, namely, that only the Unions, not both parties jointly, were invited to be present.

Meanwhile, in the course of February, Sir George Askwith and his colleagues on the Committee on Production sought to effect an agreement on the lines of the first part.

On 4 February Sir George Askwith submitted the outlines of his programme to the President of the Board of Trade, who expressed his approbation. It was considered that, since the Admiralty and the War Office were vitally concerned, it would be preferable that the Chief Industrial Commissioner should be assisted at the conferences by representatives of those Departments. The Prime Minister accordingly appointed the Committee on Production in Engineering and Shipbuilding Establishments, consisting of Sir George Askwith as chairman, Sir Francis Hopwood (Admiralty) and Sir George Gibb (War Office). The Secretary was Mr. H. J. Wilson. The appointment was announced to the Engineering and Shipbuilding employers and to the Trade Unions connected with those industries.

The terms of reference were as follows :—

" To enquire and report forthwith, after consultation with the representatives of employers and workmen, as to the best steps to be taken to ensure that the productive power of the employees in engineering and shipbuilding establishments working for Government purposes shall be made fully available, so as to meet the needs of the nation in the present emergency."

The Committee received instructions that, failing agreement, they should report to the Government, adding, if they pleased, statements of what they thought would be a satisfactory arrangement. They accordingly drew up four Reports, dated (1) 16 February ; (2) 20 February ; (3) 4 March ; and (4) 5 March.[1]

Invitations were at once issued for two conferences, one for Shipbuilding, the other for Engineering. To each of these the associations of the employers and of the workmen concerned were invited, and individual firms on the Admiralty and War Office Lists were also asked to send representatives. It will be convenient to take these conferences in connection with the several Reports issued by the Committee as a result of them.

V. First Interim Report on Loss of Time and Broken Squads.

The Committee dealt first with the Shipping Trades. The complaints of the employers were set forth in a memorandum sent by the Secretary of their Federation (Mr. Biggart) to Sir George Askwith on 26 January.

(1) The increase of labour supply for shipbuilding was being checked by Trade Union rules limiting the manning of machines to their own members in cases where unskilled labour could be used, and by the refusal of Union men to work with non-unionists.

(2) Increase of output on the part of men already employed was hindered by lost time, which was attributed to high wages and drink ; by sectional strikes and stoppages for higher wages ; by demarcation rules ; by limitation of overtime ; by opposition to piece-work and to the premium bonus system ; and by objections to the employment of journeymen for certain operations.

A Conference was fixed for 9 February, to which the following were invited :—

Employers.   The Shipbuilding Employers' Federation.
             The principal shipbuilding firms.
Workmen.   The Boilermakers' Society.
             The Shipwrights' Association.

---

[1] The first two Reports were published at once. The Third Report was printed along with the first two in the Board of Trade Labour Gazette for March, 1915 (published 15 March). The fourth was never published.

·Before the Conference met, a letter was received from the Employers' Federation objecting to meeting the Unions in presence of the Committee. The Conference was accordingly adjourned ; but the Committee met the representatives of the Unions at a later hour on 9 February. The adjourned Conference met two days later. The Employers' Federation stayed away ; but sent in a memorandum ·on the history of the previous conferences and negotiations.[1] Representatives of eleven firms, however, attended, and a joint meeting was held, followed by separate interviews with both sides.

The discussion centred round Lost Time and Broken Squads.

The question of travelling and subsistence allowances was also raised. The representatives of the Shipwrights' Association stated once more the case they had put forward in the earlier negotiations in 1914. They said that they would be in a better position to obtain labour, if the firms doing Admiralty work would give a definite assurance on the following points :—(1) railway fares to be paid to men from a distance ; (2) lodging or subsistence allowances for such men ; (3) some guarantee as to the length of the job.

They further suggested :—(a) that 10% of the men employed on merchant work should be drafted on to urgent Admiralty work ; (b) that shipwrights and drillers who had enlisted and were still in the country should be brought back to the yards.

Mr. Carter, of Cammell, Laird & Co., wrote to Sir G. Askwith on 12 February, suggesting the following scheme for lodging allowances, designed to secure that only those men would be paid who would be put to the inconvenience of leaving or moving their homes in the public interest :—(a) Lodging allowance at 17s. 6d. a week (the amount regularly paid by engineers and shipbuilders, and agreed between the engineering contractors and the Amalgamated Society of Engineers) to be paid to men leaving one district for another for urgent Admiralty work. The Tyne, Clyde and Mersey to be treated each as one district. (b) No allowance to be paid unless the man produced a ticket from the Labour Exchange in the district he was leaving. The Labour Exchange officials, before giving such a ticket, to ascertain that he left with his previous employer's consent and (in some cases) to be satisfied that the man was not wanted in his own district.

The Committee, however, did not see its way to a settlement of this question. The only point on which there was a prospect of immediate agreement was the question of the loss of time occasioned by Broken Squads. The Committee decided to present without further delay an *Interim Report* (16 February) confined to this subject.[2]

In this Report the Committee pointed out that the methods of dealing with Broken Squads, which varied in different yards, could be considerably improved. The parties directly concerned, being acquainted with local conditions, should be charged with the duty of making the first efforts ; but the matter was so urgent that the Government should intimate that it must be dealt with effectively

---

[1] Hist. Rec./R/180/4.   [2] Hist. Rec./R/242. 3/1.

within ten days. Failing agreement within that time, they recommended that the Committee should forthwith be called in to settle
finally any outstanding differences. The employers should report
the results of the proposed new arrangement to the Committee, who
would then be able to consider what further steps were necessary.

This ultimatum led to an agreement for the making-up of Broken
Squads, concluded between the Shipbuilders' Federation and the
Boilermakers' Society on 13 March. This particular problem was
thus for a time settled ; but on 3 May the Executive Committee of
the Boilermakers' Society, acting on the advice of the National Labour
Advisory Committee, reported to the Committee on Production that
the agreed arrangement had failed through an alleged lack of
co-operation on the part of the employers.

The more important and general questions of relaxation, in which
the Engineers were equally concerned, remained outstanding.

VI. Second Interim Report.

The Second Report of the Committee dealt, in the first place,
with the special question of the relaxation of certain restrictions
with a view to increasing the output of shells and fûses. This was
the subject of contemporary negotiations between the Engineering
Employers and Unions which led to the Shells and Fuses Agreement
of 5 March.[1] As the Engineers were specially concerned in this question,
the conferences with their Societies may be taken here. The rest
of the Report dealt with general questions. It provided for the
reference of all trade disputes to arbitration without stoppage of work ;
and it proposed a formula for the employers' guarantee to workpeople
that suspended trade practices should be restored at the end of the
War.

The first Conference of the Committee with the Engineers was
summoned for 10 February. The following bodies were invited :—

> *Employers.* The Engineering Employers' Federation.
> The principal engineering firms.
> *Workmen.* The Amalgamated Society of Engineers.
> The Steam Engine Makers' Society.
> The Amalgamated Toolmakers' Society.
> The United Machine Workers' Association.
> The Scientific Instrument Makers' Society.

Like the Shipbuilders, the Engineering Employers' Federation
declined, as a body, to meet the Unions. They thought that their
position had been sufficiently defined in the earlier negotiations, and
that there was no prospect of an agreement being reached by joint
discussion. They suggested that the Committee should interview
the two parties separately. When the Conference met on 10 February,
the representatives of the Federation withdrew, but individual employers remained and the enquiry was opened. The workmen handed

---

[1] See below, p. 51.

in their proposals, which the Committee discussed with them separately. The Committee also interviewed the employers and asked them to draw up a Memorandum.

This Memorandum[1] was a revised version of the proposals debated at the Sheffield Conference on 13 January. The most important addition was an express provision that the agreement should cover private work :—

> " 9. In order to secure the maximum output for national requirements, these proposals shall apply to the industry as a whole and not to Government work only, and shall apply to workpeople employed in the shops or on board ships or elsewhere away from the factory."

The Committee's *Second Interim Report* (20 February)[2] contained very important proposals. It may be summarised as follows :—

A. Production of Shells and Fuses.

In view of the pressing and continuously increasing need of shells and fuses, the Committee urged that restrictive rules and customs should be suspended during the period of the War, with proper safeguards and adjustments to protect the interests of the workpeople. Two methods of increasing output were suggested :

(1) Workmen at present confined their earnings, on the basis of the existing piece rates, to " time-and-half," or whatever the local standard might be, partly with the object of protecting piece rates. The Committee agreed that the present circumstances should not be used as a means to lower these rates ; but they could be protected by other means than restriction of earnings and output. The men could be asked to produce to their fullest capacity, if the following recommendation were adopted. The firms engaged in producing shells and fuses " should give an undertaking to the Committee on behalf of the Government to the effect that in fixing piece-work prices the earnings of men during the period of the War shall not be considered as a factor in the matter, and that no reduction in piece rates will be made, unless warranted by a change in the method of manufacture, *e.g.*, by the introduction of a new type of machine."

(2) The employment of female labour should be extended.

Any differences under these two heads that could not be settled by the parties should be referred as suggested in the recommendation under (B).

B. Avoidance of Stoppage of Work.

During the present crisis nothing could justify a resort to strikes and lock-outs which were likely to impair the productive power of establishments engaged on Government work and to diminish the output of ships, munitions, or other commodities required by the Government for war purposes. The Committee submitted for the con-

---

[1] Hist. Rec./R/180/30   [2] Hist. Rec./R/242. 3/1

sideration of the Government that the following recommendation to Government contractors and sub-contractors and to Trade Unions should be at once published, and their adhesion requested :—

" *Avoidance of Stoppage of Work for Government Purposes.*

" With a view to preventing loss of production caused by disputes between employers and workpeople, no stoppage of work by strike or lock-out should take place on work for Government purposes. In the event of differences arising which fail to be settled by the parties directly concerned, or by their representatives, or under any existing agreements, the matter shall be referred to an impartial tribunal nominated by His Majesty's Government for immediate investigation and report to the Government with a view to a settlement."

C.   Guarantee to Workpeople.

It was recommended that each contracting firm should give an undertaking, to be held on behalf of the Unions, in the following terms :—

" To H.M. Government—

" We hereby undertake that any departure during the War from the practice ruling in our workshops and shipyards prior to the War shall only be for the period of the War.

" No change in practice made during the War shall be allowed to prejudice the position of the workpeople in our employment or of their trade unions in regard to the resumption and maintenance after the War of any rules or customs existing prior to the War.

" In any readjustment of staff which may have to be effected after the War, priority of employment will be given to workmen in our employment at the beginning of the War who are serving with the colours or who are now in our employment."

" Name of Firm ....
" Date........................"

Disputes which might arise under this head to be referred as suggested under (B).

On the recommendation contained in Section (B) of the Committee's Report the Government took immediate action. On 21 February a Notice was issued to the Press, headed : *Avoidance of Stoppages of Work on Contracts for His Majesty's Government.* This notice embodied the recommendation in Section (B) of the Report, prefaced by the reasons the Committee had given for it. The Government expressed their concurrence, and, with a view to providing the necessary tribunal, they extended the present reference to the Committee by empowering them " to accept and deal with any cases arising under the above recommendation."

This Notice was sent on 22 February to the War Office and the Admiralty, who were requested to issue it to their contractors with an intimation that arrangements should be made for the procedure indicated for settling disputes. It was also communicated to the employers' associations and to the principal Trade Unions throughout the country.

Under the new extension of their terms of reference the Committee now undertook arbitration. This ultimately became their principal function, under the Treasury Agreement and the Munitions of War Act.

On 1 March Sir George Askwith sent copies of the *Second Report* to the War Office and the Admiralty for distribution to their contractors, with a letter calling attention to the Employers' Guarantee and requesting the contractors to give the undertaking recommended. The Admiralty at once took action accordingly. At the War Office the issue of similar notices was delayed by a misunderstanding which was not cleared up until 12 March.[1]

VII. The Shells and Fuses Agreement.

The negotiations which had been simultaneously carried on between the Engineering Employers' Federation and the A.S.E. and allied organisations led to a conference at Sheffield on 5 March, at which a memorandum known as the Shells and Fuses Agreement was accepted by both parties. The principal points may be summarised as follows[2] :—

1. The making of tools and gauges and the setting up of machines was to be done by skilled or competent men. Such men might be drawn from other branches of the industry, provided they should be qualified and receive at least the standard district rate, and should be the first to be affected by reductions of staff.

2. Semi-skilled or female labour might be substituted for skilled labour in suitable cases, provided that skilled employment in the same department were found for the men displaced, and that the substituted workpeople should be paid at the usual district rates, and be the first to be affected by reductions of staff.

3. The Employers' Federation undertook—

(a) That the temporary relaxation should not ultimately prejudice the workpeople or the Unions ;

(b) That pre-war working conditions should be reinstated at the end of the War, unless the Government should notify that the emergency continued ;

(c) That men serving in the Forces should so far as possible be re-employed ;

---

[1] The Treasury Memorandum of 19 March, as will appear later, contained a fuller form of Employers' Guarantee. The Committee on Production, after the issue of that Memorandum, decided that the formula contained in it should be substituted for the one given in their own Second Report. See below, Chapter IV., Section III., p. 95.

[2] The text of the Agreement is given in Appendix VII.

(*d*) That work should not be so re-adjusted as to restrict employment permanently to semi-skilled or female labour ;

(*e*) That the Agreement should not be used, after the War, to decrease wages, premium bonus times, or piece-work prices (unless warranted by new methods or means of manufacture), or to break down established conditions. The proposals were to be adopted only to increase output in the present extraordinary circumstances.

4. The employers agreed to do all they could to ensure distribution of Government work throughout the kingdom.

5. The employers agreed to reduce overtime where this was possible and consistent with national requirements, and, in any case, to distribute it as widely as practicable.

6. No employer was to take advantage of these proposals unless he intimated to the local representatives of the Union his acquiescence in all the provisions.

The result of the ballot taken among the Trade Union members early in April was favourable.

VIII. Third Interim Report. Demarcation and Utilisation of Semi-skilled or Unskilled Labour.

Meanwhile, the Committee on Production continued to deal with the question of restrictions. Further conferences on the subject of demarcation were held with the representatives of the Trade Unions concerned, including the Emergency Committee of the Federation of Engineering and Shipbuilding Trades and the Shipbuilding Joint Trades Standing Committee. The Committee also heard the employers' views on the matter.

At a Conference held on 15 February with the Shipping Trades Unions, to which the Amalgamated Society of Engineers were also invited to send a representative, the Chairman proposed the suspension of demarcation restrictions subject to the following safeguards :— (1) That the men usually employed on the work required should not be available ; (2) that urgency of execution should be essential ; (3) that difficulties arising from departure from practice, if not settled by the parties, should be referred to the Board of Trade, and that, pending such reference, there should be no stoppage ; (4) that the employers should give a guarantee that departure " shall only be for the period of the War or until circumstances (before the termination of the War) admit of existing practice being resumed."

After retiring to consider the proposal, the Trade Union representatives put certain points to which the Committee subsequently replied. (1) It was agreed that the present discussion was confined to the relaxation of demarcation rules in the skilled trades there represented. It did not, therefore, leave an opening for the introduction of semi-skilled labour. (2) The Unions wished it to be understood that the arrangement should apply only to Government work. The Committee stated that they were aiming at separating Government from merchant work, but were not sure how far the distinction was practicable in certain yards. (3) The Committee accepted the principle that any substituted labour should be paid at least the ordinary rate of wages for the work. (4) It was agreed that disputes should be referred " within seven days." (5) The Unions proposed that, in the case of piece-work, where a departure from practice caused loss of wages to individual men, the wage should be made up to the average wage before the change. This proposal was recast by the Committee, who suggested that differences as to loss of wages due to departures from practice should be adjusted between the men's representatives and the employers, and, failing adjustment, should be referred, the principle being that, where possible, the average wages of the men should be taken into account. (6) Departures from practice were to be recorded by the Board of Trade. (7) The Unions believed that many skilled men would come from a distance, if travelling allowances on the lines of the Admiralty terms were offered. This the employers had refused. On this point the Committee would not make any definite statement.

The Chairman remarked that the Committee would be in existence to impress upon the Government the necessity of restoring the pre-war status. The intention was that there should be no prejudice after the emergency. The Union representatives undertook to report at once to their Society.

A few days later the Executive Council of the Amalgamated Society of Engineers at their quarterly meeting considered a report of the proceedings on 15 February, and " unanimously agreed to endorse the recommendation of the workmen's representatives to afford the Government every possible facility for the output of work intended for the naval and military forces during the present national crisis."

The Shipping Trades Unions, on the other hand, adhered to their old position. The Ship-constructors' and Shipwrights' Association wrote on 2 March to the Committee on Production. Their Executive Committee had decided that any departure from past custom, so far as the allocation of work was concerned, must be after consultation with the men involved. Without the men's cordial co-operation work would only be retarded, as had already happened. They urged that their suggestions, as made at the Conference, were the only practicable means of accelerating work. They undertook that where firms required skilled men of their trade, if the firm would apply to their district representatives, and fares and lodging allowances were given, they' would endeavour to find the men. Failing that, then, in consultation with the firm and the men involved, the district representative would arrange, in accordance with the Committee on Production's suggestions, for the work to proceed.

The Shipbuilding Trades Standing Committee wrote to Sir G. Askwith that they had agreed to recommend to their affiliated societies the suggestion put before them by the Committee on Production. At the same time they reiterated the propositions laid down in the above letter of 2 March.

The *Third Interim Report* of the Committee (4 March)[1] may be summarised as follows :—

(a) DEMARCATION OF WORK.

The Committee recommended that demarcation restrictions should at once be suspended in Government establishments, where they were understood to be less numerous than in private yards and workshops. In private establishments they considered that " on work required for Government purposes or affecting the same, the demarcation restrictions which at present exist in regard to the work of the different skilled trades in the Engineering and Shipbuilding industries should be suspended during the continuance of the War," subject to certain safeguards :—(1) That the men usually employed on the work required were not available ; (2) that men might be brought from a distance, under certain conditions ; (3) that the relaxation should not lower the customary rates ; (4) that a record of the nature of the departures from the *status quo* should be kept ; (5) that differences which could not be settled between the parties should be referred to the Board of Trade within seven days, and meanwhile there should be no stoppage ; (6) that the guarantee to workpeople suggested in the Second Report should be adopted.[2]

(b) UTILISATION OF SEMI-SKILLED OR UNSKILLED LABOUR.

It was recommended that the employers should be allowed greater freedom to use unskilled or semi-skilled labour, subject to proper safeguards, which were held to be sufficiently provided for in the Employers' Guarantee.

Disputes which could not be amicably adjusted should be referred to the Committee.

The above Report was sent on 8 March to the Admiralty, to the Army Council, and to the Unions and the Employers. Before discussing the Report and, if possible, coming to an agreement upon it and upon methods of carrying it out, both parties waited till the Amalgamated Society of Engineers' ballot on the Shells and Fuses Agreement of 5 March should be complete.

IX. Results achieved by the Board of Trade and the Committee on Production.

By the end of February it was seen that Sir George Askwith was justified in his original forecast that the first of the two methods he had proposed would fail. The only tangible results achieved by conference and conciliation were :—The Boilermakers' Agreement for the making-up of Broken Squads ; the Engineers' Shells and Fuses Agreement ; the issue to War Office and Admiralty contractors of a request that they would give the Employers' Guarantee ; and the erection of the Committee on Production into an arbitration tribunal, to which the Government had given instructions (of no binding force) that

---

[1] HIST. REC./R/242. 3/1.

[2] It will be noted that these safeguards combine some of the Committee's original proposals put forward on 15 February with some of the workmen's proposals on the same occasion.

differences should be referred without stoppage of work.   Valuable as these results were, they went but a little way towards effecting a really substantial increase of production.   The wider proposals for a general relaxation of restrictive trade practices were not accepted by the Unions, but stood as mere recommendations in the Committee's Reports to the Government.

It was unfortunate that the Committee's efforts should have coincided with a sudden and marked outbreak of industrial unrest, which was caused in the month of February by the rise in the cost of food and of other necessaries.   In a debate on this subject in the House of Commons on 11 and 17 February, several members asserted that exorbitant prices were being exacted, and that the food markets were rigged by speculators.   Mr. Bonar Law made the first of his honest confessions that " well-managed ships to-day are making simply enormous profits, and that these profits come from the very'cause for which the people of this country are making sacrifices in every direction and even giving their lives "[1]—a statement not calculated to allay the agitation then being conducted on the Clyde.   Extravagant accusations of profiteering and cornering had been current in the Press since the last weeks of 1914.   The sudden effect in February of the rise in prices outstripping any advance in wages, may be illustrated by the following figures of the numbers of disputes involving stoppage of work, known to the Board of Trade[2]:—

1 January, 1915	..	..	..	10	
February	..	..	..	47	fresh disputes
March	..	..	..	74	,, ,,
April ..	..	..	..	44	,, ,,
May ..	..	..	..	63	,, ,,

If the situation was grave in February, it became more menacing during the next four months.   Reviewing this period in June, 1915, Mr. I. H. Mitchell, of the Industrial Commissioner's Department, wrote :—

> " I am quite satisfied that the labour difficulty has been largely caused by the men being of opinion that, while they were being called upon to be patriotic and refrain from using the strong economic position they occupied, employers, merchants and traders were being allowed perfect freedom to exploit to the fullest the Nation's needs.   This view was frankly submitted to me by the leaders of the Clyde Engineers' strike in February last.   As soon as Labour realised that nothing was being done to curtail and prevent this exploitation by employers, it let loose the pent-up desire to make the most they could in the general scramble.   This has grown until now many Unions are openly exploiting the needs of the Nation.   If the work is· Government work, it is the signal for a demand for more money.   Trade Union·leaders who, from August last year until February this year, loyally held their members back from making demands, are now with them in the rush to make the most of the opportunity."

[1] *Parliamentary Debates* (1915), *H. of C.*, LXIX., 793.
[2] *Ibid.*, LXXII., 1257.

Mr. Mitchell's statement points to the fundamental opposition which lay at the root of these troubles. On the employers' side was the demand for the wholesale removal of restrictions which tended to limit output. On the men's part, besides the doubt whether restrictions, once removed, could ever be restored, there arose about this time the counter-demand for some security that this sacrifice should benefit, not the employer, but the Nation—in a word, for limitation of profits, if not for complete Government control of production.

By the beginning of March two things had become evident. In the first place, the time had come to have recourse to the second of Sir George Askwith's methods—a direct appeal from the Government to the Unions. This appeal was made at the Treasury Conference of 17 March. In the second place, no further headway could be made until the Government should have taken some steps towards limiting employers' profits, and shown some intention of controlling the employer as well as the workman. The measures adopted to this end will be the subject of the next chapter.

CHAPTER III.

THE CONTROL OF INDUSTRY AND THE LIMITATION OF PROFITS.

I. Introductory.

In March, 1915, the Government embarked on two undertakings which, partly owing to the fact that they were pursued concurrently and partly because the ambiguous phrase, " taking over," was applied to both, were inextricably confused in the public mind. One was the passing of the Defence of the Realm (Amendment) No. 2 Act, which extended the power, already possessed by the Government, of taking possession of munitions works so as to include any factories or workshops whatsoever, and also gave them power to control the use of works and plant, of which they did not " take possession," with the object of increasing war production. The other was a scheme for securing some control over the principal armament and shipbuilding firms, analogous to the control exercised over the railways—a scheme which was soon narrowed down to the limitation of their profits, and was finally realised in the controlled establishment clauses of the Munitions of War Act, 1915. These two measures were alike in so far as they both aimed at establishing Government control over engineering concerns ; but there the resemblance ends. In origin, method, and purpose they differ widely.

The control exercised by the Government over the controlled establishment under the Munitions of War Act principally means : (1) that the profits are limited, and (2) that restrictive Trade Union practices are suspended, the employers giving a guarantee of restoration after the War. This has now become so familiar that it is, perhaps, forgotten that originally the idea of " taking over " factories (other than the regular armament works) for munitions production was not associated either with the relaxation of restrictions or with the limiting of employers' profits. This is true not only of the relevant section of the Defence of the Realm Consolidation Act, 1914, but also of the amendment of that section which was embodied in the Act of March, 1915. The history of this Act goes back to January of that year. At its inception the sole object in view was to facilitate the extinction of private work in favour of munitions production, either by converting fresh engineering factories to war purposes or by transferring the plant and labour from them to armament works. The Bill was prepared because it was found impossible, without compulsory powers, to divert engineering plant and (above all) labour from private to Government work. From beginning to end, there is not a word in it that even hints at limiting profits or removing restrictions on output.

The powers obtained under this Act were not required for the other scheme of " taking over " the armament firms ; the necessary powers already existed under the principal Act, though, as it turned out, they were not exercised. All that came of this second enterprise was some negotiations for limiting the profits of the chief contractors, which could not be carried through until the Munitions of War Act had been passed in July.

The confusion which arose between the two undertakings was increased by the circumstance that the amending Act was passed on the very eve of the day when the bargain between the Government and the Trade Unions, that restrictions should be sacrificed if profits were limited, took shape at the Treasury Conference ; and the powers which the new Act gave the Government to " take over " engineering works were then pointed to as providing the means of limiting profits. In the last weeks before the Bill was introduced on 9 March, the failure of conciliation to secure the removal of restrictions had become apparent. The rock in the path was the profits of the employer, who stood to gain all the pecuniary benefit accruing from the suspension of Trade Union rules. Hence the policy of " control " took a new orientation, directed towards limiting the profits of the chief War Office and Admiralty contractors, and negotiations were opened with Messrs. Armstrong and Messrs. Vickers, with the ulterior purpose of inducing the Trade Unions to ratify the bargain struck at the Treasury Conference. The accidental fact that, at the same moment, an Act was passed which, though totally different in scope and intention, dealt with the " taking over " of engineering works, undoubtedly influenced the Unions to give their consent and created confusion in the minds, not only of the Unions, but of Members of Parliament and of the general public.

II. The Defence of the Realm (Amendment) No. 2 Act, 1915.
Origin of the Bill.

The Board of Trade campaign for the diversion of suitable labour from commercial to Government work had been blocked in the first weeks of 1915 by several obstacles, which have been described in an earlier chapter.[1] These proved so serious that Sir H. Llewellyn Smith wrote on 23 January : " It is feared that not much more can be expected under this head."[2] In face of this immobility of labour, the course favoured by the Board of Trade was to take the work to the labour and plant by spreading munitions contracts as widely as possible over the whole engineering industry ; and measures were at once taken to explore these possibilities. It was, however, clear that this process, even if it should prove a success, might not by itself set free from private work enough labour and plant to absorb the new contracts. At the same time that Sir H. Llewellyn Smith recommended it, he added :—

" It is, however, probable that we shall ultimately find some form of compulsion necessary in order to ensure both that

---

[1] See above, p. 25.

[2] *Supply of Labour for Armament Work, Preliminary Note* (23/1/15). Hist. Rec./R/180/8.

effective priority shall be given to Government work on existing contracts and sub-contracts, and also that new Government contracts (and sub-contracts) shall be accepted and given priority as compared with private orders already booked. Nothing but compulsion could relieve the contractors from the obligations of their private contracts, and in many cases, therefore, they would welcome such compulsion. It should, therefore, be carefully considered whether the matter can be dealt with by existing regulations under the Defence of the Realm Act or whether new legislation or new regulations would be necessary for this purpose."

Legal advice having been taken, it was found necessary to proceed by way of fresh legislation. The outcome was the Defence of the Realm (Amendment) No. 2 Act.

The problem was discussed in all its bearings at an interdepartmental conference on 12 February, to which the Board of Trade invited Dr. Macnamara and Sir Frederick Black, representing the Admiralty, and General von Donop, Mr. Harold Baker, and Sir George Gibb, representing the War Office. Proposals were put forward for the direct recruiting of labour for the armament firms, that is to say, taking men from employment on private work without their employer's consent. Sir H. Llewellyn Smith urged against this suggestion that it would excite much resentment ; that there would be a risk of withdrawing men from what was indirectly work for Government purposes ; and that all the possibilities of spreading armament contracts ought first to be exhausted. Another point considered was the compulsory postponement of private contracts to Government work, and the relief of the contractor from such obligations by *force majeure*.

It was decided that the proper course would be to draft a Bill amending Section 1 (3) of the Defence of the Realm Consolidation Act, 1914, which empowered the Admiralty or the Army Council

" (*a*) to require that there shall be placed at their disposal the whole or any part of the output of any factory or workshop in which arms, ammunition, or warlike stores or equipment, or any articles required for the production thereof, are manufactured ;

" (*b*) to take possession of and use for the purpose of His Majesty's naval or military service any such factory or workshop or any plant thereof."

In moving the addition of this clause on 25 November, 1914, Mr. McKenna had said :—" These powers are desired to secure that the Government can obtain the highest maximum possible output of the factories or workshops in which arms, ammunition, warlike stores, or equipment are manufactured. . . . These powers may not have to be used. In other cases we have similar powers, and I do not think, except in the case of railways, they have been put into operation ; but it is very necessary to have some reserve power of this kind in order to secure the maximum output."[1]

---

[1] *Parliamentary Debates* (1914), *H. of C.*, LXVIII., 1275.

It will be seen that under this Section the Government already had power to "take over" not merely the armament firms, but any establishment doing munitions work. The Amending Act was not required for this purpose. Its first object was to extend the powers of paragraph (b) to cover engineering establishments where no such work was done, and possibly also shipbuilding establishments. Accordingly a clause was drafted extending this power

> "to factories and workshops other than those in which arms, ammunition, or warlike stores or equipment, or articles required for the production thereof are manufactured, and accordingly the said paragraph (b) shall have effect as if the word 'such' were omitted therefrom."[1]

In the second place, after paragraph (b) two new paragraphs, (c) and (d), were to be added, which would empower the Government to exercise control over factories and workshops which were not taken over :—

> "(c) to require any factory or workshop or any plant therein to be used for the purposes of His Majesty's naval or military service in such manner as the Admiralty or Army Council may direct."

In the Bill as introduced and passed this paragraph reads as follows :—

> "(c) to require any work in any factory or workshop to be done in accordance with the directions of the Admiralty or Army Council given with the object of making the factory or workshop, or the plant or labour therein as useful as possible for the production of war material."

In the next paragraph an important change, which will be mentioned later, was made before the Bill was introduced. In the first draft it read as follows :—

> "(d) to prohibit or restrict the employment in any factory or workshop of any workman or class of workman whose services may be required for or in connection with the manufacture by or on behalf of the Admiralty or Army Council of any arms, ammunition, or warlike stores or equipment, or any articles required for the production thereof."

These three paragraphs constituted the first printed draft of the Bill, dated 19 February. A further paragraph, which had been accidentally omitted, was added in the second draft (23 February). It dealt with a difficulty which had been discussed at the conference on 12 February, namely the acute shortage of housing accommodation at armament centres such as Newcastle and Barrow. It had been proposed to take powers to billet workmen compulsorily, like soldiers. The Board of Trade representatives questioned the possibility of this, and recommended a more moderate provision, giving powers to take possession of unoccupied premises. Accordingly, the following paragraph was added :—

> "(e) to take possession of any unoccupied premises for

---

[1] This paragraph was verbally amended before the Bill was introduced.

the purpose of housing workmen employed in the production, storage, or transport of war material."

The relief of the contractor from actions for breach of contract was provided for in a second Sub-section, which declared that

"where the fulfilment by any person of any contract is interfered with by the necessity on the part of himself or any other person[1] of complying with any requirement, regulation, or restriction of the Admiralty or the Army Council" under the Defence of the Realm Acts and regulations, "that necessity is a good defence to any action or proceedings taken against that person in respect of the non-fulfilment of the contract so far as it is due to that interference."

The Bill ended with a definition of "War material":—

"(3) In this section the expression "war material" includes arms, ammunition, warlike stores and equipment, and everything required for or in connection with the production thereof."

It will be observed that this very wide definition would cover coal mines, the whole iron and steel industry, the machine-tool trade, and many other industries not directly producing "war material" in the ordinary sense.

The powers of interference with the management of factories, as defined by the Bill, are sweeping and vague. A more detailed statement of the ways in which it was desired to exercise them was given in a memorandum prepared by Sir George Gibb for Lord Kitchener at the end of February. He suggested that the powers to be obtained should cover the following:—

(1) Power to take possession of and remove from any factories or workshops any machinery, tools, or stores capable of being used for Government work.

(2) Power to enter any works to inspect the machinery, tools, or stores, and the work which is being executed.

(3) Power to compel manufacturers to undertake the production of any articles which they are able to produce and which are required by the Government, in priority to any other work.

(4) Power to require manufacturers engaged on Government work to stop any private work on which they may be engaged and to give priority to Government work.

(5) Power to require manufacturers to stop any private work on which they may be engaged for the purpose of releasing the men employed on such work.

(6) Protection to be given against any claim on manufacturers under private contracts for any breach of contract attributable to compliance with Government requirements.

(7) Power to require from employers returns showing the names and occupations of men and women in their employment.

---

[1] The words "on the part of himself or any other person" were inserted at the Committee stage, with a view to extending the protection of this clause to sub-contractors who might be indirectly affected.—*Parliamentary Debates* (1915) *H. of C.* LXX., 1475.

III. The Proposal to take over Shipbuilding.

On 12 February Mr. Churchill, then First Lord of the Admiralty, discussed with Sir Francis Hopwood, who represented the Admiralty on the Committee on Production, the negotiations that were being carried on by that Committee for the removal of Trade Union restrictions. He afterwards wrote a Memorandum[1] (dated 13 February) which is peculiarly interesting in that the " taking over " of private establishments, so far from being regarded as a means to securing relaxation, was recommended as an alternative to meddling further with that problem.

Mr. Churchill urged that energy should not be diverted into the labyrinth of difficulties concerning the frontiers between different classes of Trade Union labour. Such negotiations touched deep interests and prejudices and offered a comparatively small gain for work for war purposes. It would be far more fruitful to concentrate the whole forces of labour on Government work, as opposed to merchant work. He suggested that the principle successfully applied to the railways should be extended, for the war period, to shipping and shipbuilding.

He proposed, in the first place, that the Government should take over the whole British mercantile marine for national purposes, and thus prevent the rise of freights, while leaving the fullest incentive to trading.

Secondly, the same should be done for shipbuilding. Power should be taken to requisition, for use or suspension, all shipbuilding work then in progress. All hulls within (say) three months of completion should be finished for national purposes ; all others should be left, when it should be convenient to divert labour from them, the shipbuilder being held free from actions for breach of contract.

The transfer of labour to Government work could be effected by offering a subsistence allowance of £1 a week to men moving to a new district, and guaranteeing three or six months' employment. The Trade Union leaders believed that such a transference from merchant work would fully meet the deficiency of labour for shipbuilding ; and, since shipbuilding was the key to many minor industries, a similar transference from those industries to corresponding employments where the War Office needed labour would be effected.

The first of Mr. Churchill's proposals, namely, the taking over of the mercantile marine, was negatived on grounds which were explained by Mr. Runciman in the House of Commons on 17 February.[2] The taking over of shipbuilding, on the other hand, was contemplated by the Government, and was independently recommended in the Fourth Report (5 March) of the Committee on Production for the same reasons which applied to engineering.[3] The project, however, was dropped ; the Bill does not provide for it, and no reference was made to the subject in the debates.

---

[1] Hist. Rec./R/180/38.
[2] *Parliamentary Debates* (1915), *H. of C.*, LXIX., 1184.
[3] See below, p. 69.

IV. Provisions with Regard to Labour.

In the first draft the only explicit reference to labour was contained in paragraph (d), which gave power " to prohibit or restrict *the employment* in any factory or workshop *of any workman or class of workmen whose services may be required* " for the production of war material. Before the end of February the state of feeling in the Labour world was such that it was thought politic to remove from the Bill this expression, which might be construed as implying the intention to forbid workmen to remain in employment on private work, and so indirectly to compel them to seek an engagement on Government work, perhaps at a distance from their homes, without at the same time offering them those travelling or subsistence allowances which were at the moment being demanded by the Unions as the condition of any such arrangements.

On 4 March the Cabinet decided that the paragraph should be redrafted as follows :—

" (d) to prohibit or restrict the use of any factory or workshop or of any plant therein for purposes other than those of His Majesty's naval or military forces."

In the Bill as introduced and passed this has undergone further amendment as follows :—

" (d) to regulate or restrict the *carrying on of work in* any factory or workshop, or *remove the plant therefrom, with a view to increasing the production of war material in other factories or workshops.*"

The effect of this change was to shift from the Government to the management of the factory the onus of any dismissal of workmen which might follow upon an exercise of the power.[1]

An addition of much greater importance was made in a draft of the Bill dated 26 February, prepared upon Mr. Lloyd George's instructions. Clauses were framed which prohibited strikes and lock-outs and incitement thereto, and enacted the compulsory reference of disputes to arbitration. They ran as follows :—

" 2—(1) An employer of persons employed on or in connection with the production of war material shall not declare or cause a lock-out ; and if he does so, he shall be liable, in respect of each offence, to a fine not exceeding　　　pounds for each day or part of a day on which the lock-out continues.

" (2) A workman employed on or in connection with the production of war material shall not strike, or, in connection with his work, act in a manner prejudicial to the speedy and proper production of war material ; and if he does so, he shall be liable for each offence to a fine not exceeding　　　pounds for each day or part of a day on which he is on strike.

" (3) A person shall not incite or encourage in any manner any person to act in contravention of this section or aid in any manner any person who is so acting.

---

[1] The provision of the original draft was restored when this paragraph was amended by Section 10 of the Munitions of War Act, 1915, by the addition of the words : " or other premises, or the engagement or employment of any workman or all or any classes of workmen therein."

" If any person acts in contravention of this provision, he shall be liable in respect of each offence to a fine not exceeding   pounds ; and if the person so acting in contravention of this provision is a body corporate or a trade union, every officer thereof shall be liable to the same penalty.

" 3—(1) If any difference as to rate of wages, hours of work, or otherwise as to terms of employment exists or is apprehended between any employer or employers of persons employed on or in connection with the production of war material and persons so employed, that difference shall be referred, on application made on behalf of the employers or persons employed, to the arbitration of the Board of Trade, and the Board of Trade shall make an award in respect of it.

" (2) The award of the Board of Trade shall be binding on both employers and employed ; and if any employer or person employed acts in contravention of, or fails to comply with the award, he shall be liable in respect of each offence to a fine not exceeding   pounds.

" (3) The Arbitration Act, 1889, shall not apply to the settlement by arbitration of any difference under this section, but the proceedings on such an arbitration shall be conducted in accordance with rules made by the Board of Trade.

" 4—(A section interpreting the meaning of ' lock-out and ' strike.').

The inclusion of these clauses would have given a completely new turn to a Bill ostensibly dealing with the extinction of commercial work ; and they strikingly illustrate the change in the underlying purpose of the promoters of the measure.   Mr. Lloyd George's mind was already bent upon the bargain with Labour which was to be concluded, immediately after the hurried passage of the Bill, at the Treasury Conference.   From one point of view the enactment of compulsory arbitration was recommended as an alternative method of meeting the agitation against excessive profits.   It was urged that excessive profits which employers were found to be making in particular cases would be shared with the workmen in the form of awarded increases of wage.   The proposed clauses were, however, cancelled, as likely to embarrass the negotiations then in progress with the workmen on the Clyde and elsewhere.   It was hoped that, if the Government should decide to take control of the armament firms, their power to prevent stoppages of work would be greatly increased.   In the meantime, provisions for the settlement of disputes without stoppage of work were included in the Treasury Agreement.

This shift in the current of official policy naturally led to a considerable degree of obscurity about the Government's intentions, which was not removed by the ministerial speeches on the Bill in either House.   The Government was, in fact, in the position of introducing a very drastic measure for the control of private industry which had only an indirect bearing on the policy immediately in view at the moment. It must further be remembered that the general public as yet knew nothing as to the shortage of munitions.   The Bill was described by the Parliamentary correspondent of the *Times* (10 March) as " taking the

House of Commons by surprise." On 9 March Mr. Bonar Law said he had no knowledge " whether we had a shortage of ammunition or of other munitions of war."[1] On this question the Government had every reason to maintain its reserve, and no official speaker went further than Lord Kitchener's statements on 15 March that " the output is not only not equal to our necessities, but does not fulfil our expectations," and that " the supply of war material at the present moment and for the next two or three months is causing me very serious anxiety."[2]

Besides these motives for reticence, it was still uncertain whether industry could not better be developed by the Board of Trade's alternative scheme for spreading contracts.[3] The exhibitions of sample shells and fuses which had been arranged in various industrial centres to test the capacities and willingness of untried engineering firms, were not opened until the day after the Bill was introduced. If the results were good, this policy, which ran counter to the wholesale transference of plant and labour to armament works contemplated by the Bill, might be ultimately preferred.

All these reasons account for the vagueness of the ministerial speeches. It was impossible for the Government to take Parliament into their confidence.

V. The Passage of the Bill.

The Bill was passed very rapidly. It went through all stages in the House of Commons in two days (9 and 10 March), and occupied another two days (15 and 16 March) in the House of Lords, receiving the Royal Assent on 16 March.

In introducing the Bill, Mr. Lloyd George threw the emphasis on the provision for relieving contractors from their obligations. The Government was seeking to extend their powers under the Act, so as to include firms and factories which were not now producing war material, but which " we hope to use, and use very soon."

> " We are not doing so because we have experienced any difficulty with any individual employer or workman, but, at the moment, when we propose a very considerable extension on these lines, we think it is better even for the employers that it should be done in obedience to an Act of Parliament rather than at a request from the Government, because those that are limited liability companies especially have to consider their shareholders . . . and they have also to consider their trust deeds and articles of association." It was also necessary to exonerate them from breaches of contract.[4]

---

[1] *Parliamentary Debates* (1915), *H. of C.*, LXX., 1275. This statement must be interpreted in the light of Mr. Bonar Law's words on 21 April : " It is common knowledge—I knew it not as guess-work, but as knowledge—that we were short of ammunition months ago. I ventured to touch on it very gingerly in the House of Commons, from fear of doing harm, but suddenly the thing is shouted from the housetops by Ministers themselves." (*Ibid.*, LXXI. 326).

[2] *Parliamentary Debates* (1915), *H. of L.*, XVIII., 721, 722.

[3] An account of these measures will be given in Part III., Chapter I.

[4] *Parliamentary Debates* (1915), *H. of C.*, LXX., 1271.

On the Second Reading, Mr. Lloyd George outlined the method of procedure and the organisation contemplated, in the following words :—

> " It certainly is not proposed to run this without full consultation with all manufacturers. The idea is that they should be summoned together . . . in their district, and that we should take them into consultation. It is possible that we could get a business man at the head of the organisation. We are on the look out for a good, strong business man with some go in him, who will be able to push the thing through and be at the head of a Central Committee.[1] Then we propose to take all the manufacturers concerned into full consultation. . . . We propose to organise the whole of the engineering community for the purpose of assisting us in increasing the output, and I am perfectly certain we are going to get . . . the willing assistance of them all. . . . When we point out to them that it is not a matter of profit, but a matter of urgent need of their country, I am sure they will render every assistance in their power."[2]

The debate turned chiefly on the question of compensation to the employers interfered with. Mr. Lloyd George said that this question could not be included in the terms of the Bill, but would be dealt with by an impartial tribunal.[3]

On 10 March Mr. Tyson Wilson, speaking for the Labour Party, asked for an assurance that, in " taking over the labour," the Government would see that the wages of men taken from skilled work to do semi-skilled work should not be lowered, and that men transferred from one town to another should receive a subsistence allowance. Mr. Lloyd George replied that the Government were " quite prepared to meet the point by dealing with it on exactly the same basis as they now deal with workmen who are transferred from the dockyards."[4]

Mr. Hewins said that he could not find in the Bill itself or in Mr. Lloyd George's words that the Government had worked out any plan of an organisation to administer it. On this point Mr. Lloyd George would not say more than : " We must have a Central Committee."[5]

---

[1] According to the Parliamentary correspondent of the *Times*, over 2,000 candidates for this position, ranging from commercial travellers to a Peer of the Realm, applied to the Treasury in the next few weeks.

[2] *Parliamentary Debates* (1915), *H. of C.*, LXX., 1277.

[3] The Defence of the Realm Losses Commission was accordingly appointed under Royal Warrant of 31 March, 1915. The Commissioners were :—Mr. Duke, chairman, Sir James Woodhouse, and Sir Matthew Wallace. The terms of reference were :—" To enquire and determine, and to report what sums (in cases not otherwise provided for) ought in reason and fairness to be paid out of public funds to applicants who (not being subjects of an enemy state) are resident or carrying on business in the United Kingdom, in respect of direct and substantial loss incurred and damage sustained by them by reason of interference with their property or business in the United Kingdom, through the exercise by the Crown of its rights and duties in the Defence of the Realm."

[4] *Parliamentary Debates* (1915), *H. of C.*, LXX., 1459.

[5] *Ibid.*, 1467.

Mr. Aneurin Williams expressed the hope that, in taking over industries, the Government would be able to establish better relations between Capital and Labour. " The necessary preparations for the victorious carrying on of this War are very much interfered with by the fact that in many cases the workmen employed find that they are suffering hardships by the diminished purchasing power of their wages, while they also see, or believe that they see, certain employers or contractors getting increased profits." He supposed that industries would be taken over on some such basis as the railways ; and he had seen it stated that it was intended to pay previous owners one-fourth of the profits above the average profit of the last three years. " If that is so, I hope there will also be some plan by which a part of the profits shall be paid to or made over for the benefit of the employees."[1]

On this point the Parliamentary Secretary to the Board of Trade, speaking some days later, said :—

" As regards the possibility of undue profits being made by certain classes of firms, I can only say that I trust that the action of the Government under the latest Defence of the Realm Act may do something to reassure the workers as to their extra services and toil in the interests of the nation. . . . The workers of the country are ready to make any sacrifice and undergo any toil, if they can be satisfied that the nation will get the good of it."[2]

On 15 March, before the Second Reading of the Bill was moved in the Upper House, Lord Kitchener made a speech in which he referred to its provisions. He said that the enormous output required could " only be obtained by a careful and deliberate organisation for developing the resources of the country." The regular armament firms had undertaken enormous contracts, vastly in excess of their normal engagements. Orders had also been spread, both in direct contracts and in sub-contracts, over a large number of subsidiary firms not accustomed in peace to this kind of work. " It will, I am sure, be readily understood that, when new plant is available for the production of war material, those firms that are not so engaged should release from their own work the labour necessary to keep the machinery fully occupied, ... as well as to supply sufficient labour to keep working at full power the whole of the machinery which we now have."[3]

Lord Crewe, in moving the Second Reading, described the Bill as " rather a measure of organisation than of the actual displacement of industry." In bringing it into operation, the Government desired to consult the manufacturers and also representatives of the workmen. He denied that manufacturers generally were thinking only of profits or that workmen generally were guilty of bad time-keeping and drunkenness. But suspicion existed on both sides.

---

[1] *Parliamentary Debates* (1915), *H. of C.*, LXX., 1489.   [2] *Ibid.*, 1838.
[3] *Parliamentary Debates* (1915), *H. of L.*, XVIII., 722. It will be noticed that the War Office still had in view the original purpose of the Bill, namely, the reinforcement of the armament firms by labour diverted from commercial work. See Part III., Chap. II., Section I.

" We hope that the general system of consultation and discussion which will take place as the result of the passing of this measure will do much to dispel on both sides those suspicions, unfounded in the main as we believe them to be, so far as they exist. Therefore, my Lords, even if it should prove as some have prophesied—I think Mr. Bonar Law made the statement in another place—that the actual transactions under a measure of this kind are not very numerous—and I think it is exceedingly difficult to say how numerous the actual transactions are likely to be—yet at the same time I venture to think that no small amount of solid national benefit may come from the passage of this measure."[1]

The official speeches on the Bill appear to have left the impression that the Government had not yet decided on any definite line of policy or planned any system of administrative organisation.   Such was in fact the case.   The last sentences quoted above from Lord Crewe's speech amount to an admission that the Act was passed, not solely for its ostensible purpose, but for the indirect use that might be made of it in settling the dispute between employers and Labour.

Lord Crewe's forecast that the actual transactions under the measure might not be very numerous proved true to this extent, that it was seldom found necessary to put the new powers formally into force.   The mere fact of their existence, however, was of great service in the ensuing months, as providing a lever for the coercion of recalcitrant employers whose plant it was desired to turn over to munitions work.

VI. The Limitation of Profits.   Fourth Report of the Committee on Production.

At the same time that the Government were securing their new powers over that part of the engineering industry which was not yet engaged in munitions production, they were seeking to obtain some sort of control over the principal armament and shipbuilding firms on the War Office and Admiralty lists.   This undertaking in no way involved the new Act, but lay altogether outside its scope. There are three outstanding features of this scheme :—

(1) The works of which it was proposed to " take possession " under the Defence of the Realm Consolidation Act and Regulations were only those of the chief contractors for " armaments "—some forty firms in all.[2]

(2) It was at first intended that the control should be exercised through a Central Committee, analogous to the Railway Executive Committee.   This form of administration had been suggested in Mr. Churchill's memorandum of 13 February, and it was again proposed

---

[1] *Parliamentary Debates* (1915), *H. of L.,* XVIII., 724.
[2] These lists of contractors are given in Appendix VIII.

in the Fourth Report of the Committee on Production, which will be summarised below.

(3) With regard to profits, the original notion was, not so much to attach for the Exchequer all profits in excess of a certain standard, as to " compensate " the firms for interference with their business by guaranteeing them a minimum profit and a proportion of any excess.   It was under this light that the question of dealing with profits was looked at in the earliest stages, when the operation contemplated could still be properly described as " taking over " or assuming control of the concerns.

The emphasis is for the first time shifted from " compensation " to limitation of profits in a memorandum entitled *A Note on Labour Unrest*, which Sir George Askwith sent to Sir H. Llewellyn Smith on 24 February.   This document reflected the experience gained by the Committee on Production in its endeavours to secure the removal of restrictions on output.   Sir George Askwith wrote that, throughout the country, Labour men were interpreting the Prime Minister's speech of 11 February on the rise of food prices as an intimation that little could be done to curtail the large profits which contractors were believed to be making.   They were drawing the inference that Labour was entitled to higher wages, which were, in fact, in many cases being received.   Unless something were done to correct the view that contractors were entitled to unlimited profits, the workmen would claim corresponding freedom ; and they had never been in a stronger position to enforce their demands.   They might lower their claims, if they could be satisfied that some control was being exercised over contractors to minimise their profits.

In forwarding this memorandum to the President of the Board of Trade, Sir H. Llewellyn Smith wrote : " The situation is serious, but the remedy is not obvious unless we are prepared for wholesale commandeering of armament works ; and I fear that that would not necessarily give us the command of skilled management."

The same incidence of emphasis on the need for limiting profits is noticeable in the *Fourth Report* (5 March) of the Committee on Production, which is further remarkable in that it adumbrates the use which might be made of a Government pledge to limit profits in securing the consent of the Unions to a suspension of their restrictive rules.   It thus contains all the essentials of the bargain with Labour which was to be made a fortnight later at the Treasury Conference.

The Committee proposed that the Government should assume control of the principal armament and shipbuilding firms.   They pointed out that the general Labour unrest of the previous few weeks was accompanied by a widespread belief among workpeople that abnormal profits were being made, particularly on Government contracts.   There were consequent demands for higher wages.   It seemed to be thought that limitation of profits might be decided to be impracticable, and the men were claiming the freedom to ask the maximum price for their labour.   The unrest would prevail while these ideas were abroad.

They recommended that the Government should at once issue a pronouncement, stating clearly that they did not acquiesce in the view that employers and contractors must be left to secure maximum prices and profits.

The control of profits could be effected by the following means : that under the Defence of the Realm Act, with necessary amendments, " the Government should assume control over the principal firms whose main output consists of ships, guns, equipment, or munitions of war, under such equitable financial arrangements as may be necessary to provide for the reasonable interests of proprietors, management and staff."

An Executive Committee, on the lines of the Railway Executive Committee, should be established (a) to search for new sources of supply, and (b) to exercise continuous and responsible supervision with representatives of the firms concerned. The executive conduct of each business should be left to the existing management.

Besides the removal of the suspicion above indicated, other advantages would accrue. (1) Trade Union restrictions might be more readily removed, when it was known that the Government, not private employers, would benefit. (2) The existence of a central executive with wide authority over the sources of supply, would make possible the control over the output of the various works, the supervision and co-ordination of sub-contractors' work according to relative urgency, and some general regard to efficient and co-ordinated utilisation of labour on private and Government work. (3) Some private establishments would spare labour, if assured that it would be for the direct benefit of the nation.

Such control would enable a confident appeal to be made to work-people, and would restore national unanimity. It would also impress on the nation that the country was at war and industrial resources must be mobilised.[1]

The recommendations of this Report were adopted by the Cabinet, and Mr. Runciman was entrusted with the task of opening negotiations with the chief contractors.

A preliminary scheme had been outlined by Sir H. Llewellyn Smith in a memorandum dated 1 March.[2] His proposals referred not only to armament firms but, *mutatis mutandis*, to shipyards.

It was pointed out that possession could be taken of the armament firms under Regulation 8 of the Defence of the Realm

---

[1] This Report was sent to the Prime Minister on 8 March, and first printed as a Cabinet Memorandum. It was decided to delay publication until after the Treasury Conference of 17–19 March. Mr. Lloyd George then again postponed the publication. On 15 April the Committee on Production wrote to the Prime Minister recommending that the Report should be published ; but further delay was thought to be desirable. Sir George Gibb again recommended it in a Memorandum to Mr. Lloyd George on 2 June. The Report, however, has never been published, and its contents must be regarded as confidential.

[2] Hist. Rec./R/360/1.

Consolidated Regulations, 1914.[1] Notification of the intention to take possession should go to Messrs. Armstrong, Messrs. Vickers, the Birmingham Small Arms Co., and the Coventry Ordnance Co., at least, and to any other firms the War Office might think necessary. An early date (*e.g.*, 8 March) should be fixed for the operation, with an intimation that the Government would be prepared, shortly after the taking over, to discuss terms of compensation. It was suggested that Government control might last for six months, renewable at their option for six-monthly periods.

Under Regulation 8, every director, officer, and servant of the Companies would be bound to obey the directions of the Army Council. It was suggested that instructions should be given that the work of the various undertakings was to be carried on exactly as at present, subject to any future instructions by the supreme controlling authority. Existing contracts might continue, unless and until modified by mutual arrangement ; and future contracts might be arranged, as hitherto, between the War Office and the various controlled Companies.

It was proposed that the control, ultimately vested in the Army Council, should be administered through an Executive Committee, on the lines of the Railway Executive Committee, consisting of representatives of the armament firms with the Secretary of State as nominal chairman and ultimate referee.

The memorandum finally dealt with a method of " compensation " to be based on the rate of profit distributed in the last complete financial year before the War. The ascertainment of the net distributable income promised to be a very intricate matter. It was suggested that the amount should be determined by arrangement between the Company's auditors and an auditor appointed by the Treasury, with a referee in case of disagreement. Pending the determination of the net distributable income, the Companies might be allowed to distribute an interim dividend of 10%. If the net distributable income should fall below 10% the Government should make up the deficit. If it should be more than 10% but less than $12\frac{1}{2}$% (assuming $12\frac{1}{2}$% to be the rate of profit distributed in the last pre-war year), the Government should make up three-quarters of the deficit. If it should exceed $12\frac{1}{2}$%, the Government should take three-quarters of the surplus. An arrangement on these lines would preserve the necessary incentive to economy and good management.

With regard to the basis of compensation, it was decided to

---

[1] Regulation 8 read as follows : " The Admiralty or Army Council may take possession of any such factory or workshop as aforesaid (*i.e.*, in which arms, ammunition, or any warlike stores or equipment, or any articles required for the production thereof are manufactured) . . . and may use the same for His Majesty's naval or military service at such times and in such manner as the Admiralty or Army Council may consider necessary or expedient, and the occupier, and every officer and servant of the occupier, and, where the occupier is a company, every director of the company shall obey the directions of the Admiralty or Army Council as to the user of the factory or workshop . . . and if he fails to do so he shall be guilty of an offence against these regulations."

consult Sir William Plender, who put forward the following suggestions[1] :—

(1) *Guarantee of minimum profit.*—There were various possible ways of " compensating a Company for the temporary taking over of its undertaking " :

" (*a*) Guaranteeing to the ordinary shareholders the same rate of dividend as that paid in respect of the last year, or the average during the past three or five years.

" (*b*) Guaranteeing the profit, during the control period, as equalling the profit of the last year, or the average of a series of years, proportionate to the length of the control period.

" (*c*) Guaranteeing the same percentage of profit earned on the turn-over during the control period, as was earned on the turn-over during the last year or average of a series of past years.

" (*d*) Guaranteeing the same ratio or percentage of net earnings on the capital employed during the control period, as was earned in the preceding financial year or average of a series of past years. (By ' capital employed ' is meant share capital, debentures, reserves, and undistributed profits ; and by ' net earnings ' is meant profits before charging interest on debentures and loans forming part of the capital employed.)"

Of these arrangements Sir William Plender recommended (*d*) as the most equitable. It would obviate many controversial questions and give the owners the full ratio of benefits on the capital employed, as above defined, which they had enjoyed in the past.

(2) *Disposal of excess profits.*—Besides the percentage so determined, it might be thought reasonable that the owners should obtain some additional advantage because of the War, since a war between continental powers only would have benefited them greatly, and war directly promotes their business. It was suggested that, if in the control period the profits should exceed the percentage as determined under (*d*), the excess should be divided equally between the Companies and the Government, and that the Companies should, out of their share of the extra profits, consider the claims of their workpeople for greater devotion to duty, and also take full responsibility for settling claims for possible breach of contract with their ordinary customers. To announce that a defined part of the extra profits should pass to the workpeople might create difficulties at Woolwich and other Government works, since the treatment of employees should, so far as the Government was concerned, be as uniform and consistent as possible. It was desirable also to avoid saddling on the Government claims for compensation for breach of contract ; but, if the Companies faced this responsibility, they would need an Insurance Fund, which would be provided by the suggested 50% of the extra profits.

---

[1] *Memorandum to the President of the Board of Trade* (14/3/15).   Hist. Rec./R/360/1.

(3) *Special capital expenditure.*—If the Company should incur special capital expenditure at the instance of the Government, it should be entitled to claim for any loss that might arise owing to the assets being unremunerative after the control period.   If the Government incurred such expenditure or advanced money, such expenditure or advances would not, so far as the Company was concerned, form part of the capital employed, and interest thereon should be charged against the profits and credited to the Government.   The expenditure (*i.e.*, the value of the assets at the end of the period) and advances should be repayable when the control terminated.

(4) *Compensation for losses after the control period.*—It might be necessary to consider whether the Government should make good a proportion of any possible deficiency in profits arising after the control period, but attributable to the intervention.

The memorandum also contained suggestions on minor points, such as the exclusion of part of the Company's undertaking (*e.g.*, Messrs. Armstrong's Italian Company), valuation of stock, and certification of accounts.

It will be seen that Sir William Plender assumed that the Government intended to " take possession " of the armament companies' works under the Defence of the Realm Regulations, and that the management, though remaining the same, would be " controlled somewhat by Government supervision."   He accordingly treated the financial arrangements as a question of " compensation " for this interference.   But from the outset of the negotiations with the armament companies, begun by Mr. Runciman on 12 March, this intention was abandoned.   The companies barred any interference with their direction or management.   The idea of control exercised through an Executive Committee was consequently dropped, and the unhappy phrase " taking over," though it continued to be used in reference to these negotiations, ceased to have any meaning in this connection.[1]   Since there was to be no interference, there could be no further question of compensation.   The issue was thus narrowed down to a purely financial scheme for the limitation of excess profits.

This had, in fact, become the primary object of the Government from the moment when they adopted the Fourth Report of the Committee on Production.   The transformation of the scheme was really due to that Committee, which was led by its negotiations with the Unions to see that limitation of profits, with or without any executive control, was the essential condition on which the Unions could be

---

[1] As late as 21 April the impression was still current that the Government might be intending to control the armament firms in the same way as the railways. On this day, Mr. Samuel Roberts in the House of Commons, speaking as " the only member of the House who is on the Board of one of the large armament companies," and professing to state their position, said : " I do not know what the plan of the Government is, but I gather that they wish—and, if so, we shall not oppose it—to have a certain control during the time of the War.   I do not know whether the kind of control is going to be the same as with regard to the railways.   But whatever the Government say is necessary, we of the armament firms shall not oppose it." (*Parliamentary Debates* (1915), *H. of C.*, LXXI., 309, 310.)

induced to sacrifice their restrictive practices.   The Committee on Production may, therefore, be regarded as the first parent, not only of the Treasury Agreement, but of the controlled establishment.

VII.   Negotiations with Messrs. Armstrong and Messrs. Vickers.

Mr. Runciman held a series of meetings on 12, 15, 16, 23 and 26 March, with Sir G. Murray, Mr. Falkner and Mr. Gladstone, representing Messrs. Armstrong's, and Sir Vincent Caillard and Mr. Barker, representing Messrs. Vickers.   Mr. Carrington (Armstrong's) was present on 16 March.[1]

After the first meeting on 12 March, Mr. Falkner addressed to Mr. Runciman a letter summarising the suggestions made as a basis for discussion :—

(1) There was no intention of interfering with the direction or management of the Companies.   The duties and rights of the directors and management were to remain as at present.

(2) The Companies were prepared to discuss limiting dividends during the War and for a certain period after its close.

(3) To eliminate any suggestion of abnormal profits, all new contracts after 1 March, 1915, should be on the following basis :—

(a) The profits on such contracts to bear the same ratio to turnover (selling value) as the profits for the years bore to the turnover of those years.

(b) Before arriving at profit, the usual charges for depreciation and other provisions, management and operating expenses, etc., to be made.

(4) Returns from existing contracts, investments, and all rents, royalties, and the like, to be excluded from the arrangement.

(5) The ratio on the above basis to be certified by the Companies' Auditors.

At subsequent interviews these proposals, taken *seriatim*, underwent the following modifications :—

(1) It was confirmed that the direction and management of the Companies should not be interfered with.

(2) The proposal to limit dividends was subsequently incorporated in the next clause, in the form of a provision that the net divisible profit should be limited.

(3) *Meaning of new contracts.*—The basis proposed for new contracts was the subject of further discussion.   At the second interview on 15 March, it was agreed that the " new contracts " to be covered by the arrangements should include extensions of existing contracts ; and that, in order to make this clear, the words : " new orders or extensions of existing orders " should be substituted.   It

---

[1] Copies of the Papers relating to these negotiations, Hist. Rec./R/360.

was later agreed that the firms should arrange with the War Office the precise meaning of " new orders."

(a) *Calculation of Profit.*—The Companies argued strongly in favour of the profits on new orders being allowed to bear the same ratio to turnover as in normal years.

Mr. Runciman criticised this suggestion and pointed out that the turnover would be treble that of normal years.   He called attention to the three other methods suggested by Sir William Plender, and expressed his preference for guaranteeing the same ratio or percentage of net earnings on the capital employed as in previous years.   Special arrangements could be made as regards the large additional capital expenditure contemplated.

(b) *Charges for Special Depreciation.*—It was proposed to add to provision (3) (b) of the above scheme the following words :—

> " and after taking off depreciation on the customary scale plus special depreciation for extra wear and tear during the War and special depreciation for such capital expenditure as has been incurred by the companies for the output of war material on an accelerated scale required by the War Office and Admiralty."

It was later (16 March) agreed that the firms should arrange with the War Office the precise definition of the amount which might be written off for depreciation.

On 23 March Mr. Runciman proposed to substitute, for the provision relating to capital expenditure, the following :—" Any capital expenditure specially incurred by the Companies for the execution of Government work shall be allowed for, with due regard to its value to the Company at the end of the war period."   This was accepted.

On 26 March the Companies renewed their objection to basing the calculation of profit on capital employed.   All their calculations in making contracts were based on turnover.   The formula now proposed by the Companies provided—

(a) That the profit should be limited so that it should bear the same ratio to output as in the last year or series of years ; and that after deducting the usual charges debited to the accounts before arriving at the profit, and charging for special depreciation due to war work, the surplus remaining should be the final balance of net profit for the year ;

(b) That the final balance of net profit for the year must not exceed 20% over and above that shown in the two previous years' balance sheets, after taking account of all the other above provisions.

In the last clause Mr. Runciman suggested that 15% should be substituted for 20%, *i.e.*, that the final balance of net divisible profit should not exceed £1,150,000 for Vickers and £960,000 for Armstrong's.

On 23 March the Companies held out for 20% ; and this percentage was finally agreed upon.

(4) *Disposal of Surplus.*—As methods of disposing of any surplus over the net divisible profit, Mr. Runciman suggested—

(*a*) reduction of prices ; *or*
(*b*) payment of bonus to the men ; *or*
(*c*) a return of it to the Exchequer ; *or*
(*d*) any combination of these methods.

On 23 March the Companies objected to (*b*) as likely to lead to trouble with the men.   The clause was dropped.

(5) Mr. Runciman agreed to accept the Auditors' certificate that, in arriving at the net divisible profits, the Companies had not departed from the method and principles followed in calculating such profits in previous years.

The preliminary discussions resulted in a draft being drawn up, which was sent to both firms, after the meeting on 23 March.   The heads of the draft, as finally amended, may be summarised as follows : —

(1) There was to be no interference on the part of the Government with the direction or management of the Companies.

(2) In arriving at the net divisible profit, the principles followed in previous years were to be observed.

(3) The final balance of net divisible profit must not exceed the average of the two previous years by more than 20%.

(4) Before arriving at the profit, besides the usual allowances for depreciation and expenses of management, etc., charges were to be made for special depreciation for the extra wear and tear during the War, and allowance made for such capital expenditure as the firms had specially incurred for Government work, with due regard to its value to the Company at the end of the War.

(5) The surplus (if any) over the net divisible profit was to be dealt with by—

(*a*) rebate of price, *or*
(*b*) return of it to the Exchequer.

The amended draft was sent to both firms, and both sent a reply accepting it.   It was agreed that the arrangement should date from 1 January, 1915, and terminate at the end of the War.   The Companies asked for confirmation of the promise that no other firm should be more favourably treated, and requested that no publication should be made till a definite settlement with the Government Departments had been reached.

The heads of the agreement drawn up at the above-mentioned meetings served as a basis for Mr. Runciman's interviews with the other firms concerned. By 22 May the following firms had been interviewed :—

> T. Firth & Sons.
> Hadfield's, Limited.
> Cammell, Laird.
> King's Norton Metal Company.
> Coventry Ordnance Works.
> Birmingham Metal and Munitions Company.
> Birmingham Small Arms Company.
> Greenwood & Batley.
> London Small Arms Company.
> Eley Brothers.
> John Brown & Co.
> Palmer's Shipbuilding & Iron Company.[1]

VIII. The Proposal that Workmen should receive a Share in Excess Profits.

Something further must be said about one important point in these negotiations, namely, Mr. Runciman's proposal that a proportion of the surplus profits should be made over as a bonus to the workmen. This part of the scheme fell to the ground in consequence of the opposition of the firms. Meanwhile, however, expectations of some such arrangement had been aroused by a passage in Lord Kitchener's speech in the House of Lords delivered on 15 March, three days after Mr. Runciman's first meeting. Referring definitely to these negotiations, Lord Kitchener said :—

> " Labour may very rightly ask that their patriotic·work should not be used to inflate the profits of the directors and shareholders of the various great industrial and armament firms, and we are therefore arranging a system under which the important armament firms will come under Government control, and we hope that workmen who work regularly by keeping good time shall reap some of the benefits which the war automatically confers on these great companies."[2]

On the motion for the Adjournment of the House of Commons on 12 May, Mr. Peto called attention to these words.[3] He complained that no arrangements for profit-sharing had been made, and challenged the President of the Board of Trade to say whether Lord Kitchener's statement was unauthorised and could not be carried into effect because the Secretary of State had no authority over private firms.

In reply Mr. Runciman stated that he thought that nearly all the principal firms had already been interviewed. They had been informed

---

[1] Mr. Runciman decided that it was not necessary to interview Beardmore & Co. (since they were controlled by Vickers) or the Projectile Company ; they, like the Coventry Ordnance Co., had (he understood) been working at a loss during recent years, and some special arrangement with the War Office might be needed in both these cases. The seven explosives manufacturing firms on the War Office List were not approached.

[2] *Parliamentary Debates* (1915), *H. of L.*, XVIII., 723.

[3] *Parliamentary Debates* (1915), *H. of C.*, LXXI., 1766, *ff.*

of the Government's intentions, in so far as they could be vaguely outlined at the present time, and in a short time he hoped that it might be possible for the Army Council and the Board of Admiralty to make formal communications to the large firms, showing the directions in which their profits must be limited. The Government had not been able to dictate to the big firms as to the use to be made of the surplus, beyond requiring that it should either be for reduction of price or for return to the Exchequer. That, however, did not relieve the firms from the obligation of treating their workmen well and generously ; nor was it inconsistent with Lord Kitchener's statement on 15 March, that workmen should reap some benefit from regular work and attendance. Lord Kitchener's language had been carefully chosen with the object of not binding him to any system of profit-sharing. " In our conferences with the employees of the armaments companies[1] we had discovered that, so far from profit-sharing being regarded by the Trade Unions themselves as a solution of many of the problems by which they were faced, they could not waive any of their demands for the remuneration of labour on profit-sharing lines ; that they were not prepared to divert their claims for extra remuneration to those lines ; that they themselves did not put forward any demand for profit-sharing ; and that the one condition they made, when they agreed with us to restrict some of their Trade Union regulations, was that the profits of these firms should be limited." The Amalgamated Society of Engineers had made no demands for any profit-sharing system. The principle of limitation of profits could not be applied to all the many thousands of firms doing Government work ; and it had been agreed at the Treasury Conferences that it would be unreasonable to apply it to firms not wholly or mainly so engaged.

Other speakers asserted that a widespread impression had been created by Lord Kitchener's words that some part of the profits made by the armament companies was to be distributed to their workmen, quite apart from any bargain made at the Treasury Conferences, or any general scheme of profit-sharing. The impression was well-founded, for this had been part of the Government scheme when Lord Kitchener spoke. The proposal was defeated by the armament companies, and it was not revived when the limitation of profits was imposed upon the " controlled establishment " under the Munitions of War Act.

IX. The Outcome of the Negotiations.

The abandonment of the Government's original intention to " take possession " of the armament and shipbuilding works, and the narrowing down of the issue to a mere limitation of profits, led to two curious consequences.

In the first place, it came to light, after the negotiations with the firms had reached the stage above described, that the Government, though they had ample power to " take over " the concerns, had not the power to complete, by way of voluntary agreement, their undertaking to limit profits. The firms, though not for the most part adverse

---

[1] The reference is to the Treasury Conferences of 17–19 March and 25 March, described below in Chapter IV.

to the agreement, represented that they could not bind their shareholders unless they were themselves bound by the Defence of the Realm Act. For this purpose the Government were advised that an amendment of the Act would be required. The result was that the matter could go no further until the necessary powers had been obtained in those clauses of the Munitions of War Act which institute the " controlled establishment."

In the second place, there now remained no sufficient reason for confining the limitation of profits to the chief War Office and Admiralty contractors. So long as it was a question of " taking possession " of works, it was obvious that the Government could not take over every concern that was making excessive war profits. But from the moment when this intention was given up, the only logical course was to institute a general Excess Profits Tax. It was commonly believed that undue profits were being made, not merely by armament and shipbuilding firms, but in many other industries. The complaints that came from the representatives of Labour were mainly directed against shipping freights and the producers and distributors of food and coal. In comparison with these, the armament firms in particular could plead that they had made enormous efforts in the national emergency, and that a time of war was precisely the time when they counted upon making exceptional profits. Nor could the widespread unrest which had followed upon the rise in cost of living be allayed by reducing the dividends of a handful of companies producing war material for the Army and Navy. Nothing but the extreme urgency of the need for munitions and the pre-occupation of the Cabinet with the immediate measures for meeting it will account for the Government handling the question of excessive war profits on what appears to be so partial, and even inequitable, a basis.

The suggestion of a general tax upon all excessive war profits had been in the air since the time of the debate on Food prices in February. On 3 March Mr. Anderson asked the Chancellor of the Exchequer whether he would cause an examination to be made of the books of Government contractors, and of the ship-owning, farming, food, and coal firms, with a view to ascertaining the present and prospective profits that such interests were making out of the War, and whether he had considered the question of levying a special tax upon profits obtained from the war emergency. Mr. Lloyd George replied that, though the Income Tax authorities did not possess the power to examine books, Mr. Anderson might " rest assured that the profits he mentioned would be fully assessed."[1]

The Budget introduced by Mr. Lloyd George in May, however, contained no proposal of this nature. Towards the end of May the Coalition Government was formed, and Mr. McKenna, immediately after his acceptance of the office of Chancellor of the Exchequer, drew up an outline scheme for the Excess Profits Tax.[2] On 16 June the Government's intention to introduce such a tax was announced by

---

[1] *Parliamentary Debates* (1915), *H. of C.*, LXX., 780.
[2] *Ibid.*, LXXXII., 1760.

Mr. Montagu.[1]   Finally the tax was proposed in Mr. McKenna's Budget speech of 21 September.[2]   Mr. McKenna afterwards explained that he could not introduce it earlier, because in May, June and July he had still to carry through his predecessor's Budget.[3]   The tax was thus not imposed until after the limitation of profits in controlled establishments had been enacted by the Munitions of War Act.

Meanwhile, the tangible outcome of Mr. Runciman's negotiations in March was that the declared intention to limit the profits, at least, of the chief War Office and Admiralty contractors had considerable influence in inducing the Trade Unions to accept their part of the bargain—the relaxation of restrictive practices—at the Treasury Conference.

---

[1] *Parliamentary Debates* (1915), *H. of C.*, LXXII., 729.
[2] *Ibid.*, LXXIV., 356.   [3] *Ibid.*, LXXXII., 1760.

CHAPTER IV.

THE TREASURY AGREEMENT.

I. Treasury Conference of 17-19 March, 1915.
The Treasury Agreement.

The decision of the Cabinet to call a representative meeting of Trade Unionists, with a view to reaching some general understanding with them about the suspension of restrictive rules and practices was taken on 11 March. Invitations were sent out from the Offices of the Board of Trade, in the names of the Chancellor of the Exchequer and of the President of the Board of Trade, for a Conference to be held at the Treasury on 17 March. The form of letter sent to the Trade Unions invited them to send representatives

> " to consult with the Chancellor of the Exchequer and the President of the Board of Trade on certain matters of importance to labour arising out of the recent decision of the Government, embodied in the Defence of the Realm (Amendment) Act, to take further steps to organise the resources of the country to meet naval and military requirements."

The Conference met on 17-19 March. The Government was represented by the Chancellor of the Exchequer (Mr. Lloyd George), the President of the Board of Trade (Mr. Runciman), Mr. Montagu, and Dr. Macnamara. Mr. Arthur Balfour represented the Opposition. Rear-Admiral Tudor represented the Admiralty, and Lieutenant-General Sir J. Wolfe-Murray took the place of Lord Kitchener, who was unavoidably absent. There were also present :—Mr. D. J. Shackleton, Sir George Askwith, Sir Francis Hopwood, Sir George Gibb, Sir Charles Harris, Sir H. Llewellyn Smith, Mr. Harold Baker, M.P., Mr. Beveridge, Mr. Isaac Mitchell, Mr. Cummings, Mr. H. P. Hamilton, and Mr. J. T. Davies.[1]

A list of the Unions represented is given in the *Memorandum of Proposals* drawn up by the Conference.[2] At the first two meetings (17 and 18 March) two representatives of the Miners' Federation of Great Britain attended, but they withdrew at the final meeting on 19 March, and this Federation was not a party to the Agreement. Mr. J. H. Thomas, M.P., representing the National Union of Railwaymen, joined the Conference on 19 March.

---

[1] Verbatim Report of the proceedings at the Conference, HIST. REC./R/180/17.

[2] Printed below, p. 85.

At a preliminary meeting of the workmen's representatives the following Committee of seven was appointed to conduct the negotiations :—

Mr. Arthur Henderson, M.P., Ironfounders, President.

Mr. William Mosses, Pattern-makers, Secretary.

Mr. Alex. Wilkie, M.P., Shipwrights.

Mr. John Hill, Boilermakers.

Mr. J. Brownlie, Amalgamated Society of Engineers.

Mr. Frank Smith, Cabinetmakers.

Mr. C. W. Bowerman, M.P., representing the Parliamentary Committee of the Trade Union Congress.

This Committee was engaged during the three days of the Conference in considering the terms of the Agreement, and held several discussions at various stages with the general body of delegates. The Committee, as will be seen, afterwards became the National Advisory Committee on War Output, appointed under the Agreement drawn up at the Conference.

In opening the proceedings, Mr. Lloyd George said that those present were invited to consider the need for a larger output of munitions and the steps which the Government proposed to take to organise industry to that end. Every belligerent country had found that the expenditure of war material exceeded all anticipations.

He referred to the very drastic powers taken by the Government under the Defence of the Realm Acts " to assume control or to take over any works in this country which are either turning out munitions of war or which are capable of being adapted for that purpose."

" That is what I want to consult you about. Although we have the power, we cannot exercise it unless we have the complete co-operation of employers and workmen. What does it mean ? I do not want to use the term ' taking over ' without explaining that it is capable of an interpretation which I do not wish to put upon it. By ' taking over ' a works we do not mean to establish an Admiral or a General in command of the works, turning adrift those who are managing them at the present moment ; that is an impossible task. . . . We mean to assume control of works which are now being exclusively devoted to that purpose. There are certain works which are not adapted for that kind of control, but there are others which are ; and the great works which are now being used for the purpose of the production of munitions of war are eminently works of that kind.

" Above all we propose to impose a limitation of profits, because we can quite see that it is very difficult for us to appeal to Labour to relax restrictions and to put out the whole of its strength, unless some condition of this kind is imposed. The workmen of the country, I am perfectly certain, are prepared to put their whole strength into helping the War, so long as they know that it is the State that is getting the benefit of it, and that it does not merely inure to the benefit of any particular individual or class.

" If we are merely to take over the works and assume control and guarantee profits within that limit, you will realise that means that the employer has not quite the same interest as he has now in limiting expenditure. Therefore, we might be face to face, not merely with the employees making demands upon the State which we for the moment might regard as unreasonable, but we might find the employers in combination with them, and therefore we should have employers and employed combining to bring pressure upon the State, and we should not be in a position to deal with it unless we had a complete understanding in advance. . . .

" What understanding can be asked for ? The understanding we must get with the employers is an understanding with regard to the limitation of profits ; that we must get, and an understanding, of course, that the works will be completely under the control of the State, to the extent that whatever the State wants done there shall be done. I do not dwell upon these two points ; those are matters which I shall have to put before the employers when the time comes."[1]

Mr. Lloyd George then passed to the other side of the bargain, which affected the workmen : (1) that there should be no stoppage of work pending the settlement of disputes ; and (2) that Trade Union restrictions should be suspended.

(1) The Government did not say that workmen ought never to complain, or to ask for an increase of wages. " Our point is that during the time the questions at issue are being adjudicated upon, the work shall go on. . . . We want to get some kind of understanding with you about that before we undertake the control of these works. The first proposition, therefore, which I shall put before you for your consideration is this :—

> " With a view to preventing loss of production caused by disputes between employers and workpeople, no stoppage of work by strike or lock-out should take place on work for Government purposes.—

" All this is purely during the continuation of the War, and does not bear on anything that might happen after the War.—

> " In the event of difficulties arising which fail to be settled by the parties directly concerned, or by their representatives, or under any existing agreement, the matter shall be referred to an impartial tribunal, nominated by His Majesty's Government, for immediate investigation and report to the Government with a view to a settlement."[2]

Three forms of tribunal were suggested :—

(a) A single arbitrator agreed upon by the parties or appointed by the Board of Trade ;

(b) The Committee on Production ;

(c) A court of arbitration on which labour and employers should be equally represented.

---

[1] It had been intended to call a conference of employers, but in the event no general meeting of employers was summoned.

[2] This proposition is textually identical with the Government Notice, *Avoidance of Stoppages of Work on contracts for H.M. Government,* published on 21 February in pursuance of the Second Report of the Committee on Production. See above, Chap. II., Section VI., p. 50.

(2) " The second proposition is the suspension, where necessary, during the War, of all restrictions on output. Here I want to make it perfectly clear that I am only discussing this suspension during the War. . . . There is the question of the number of machines which one man is permitted to attend to. There is the question of the employment of semi-skilled labour where under normal conditions you could not assent to it ; and there is the question of the employment of female labour." In France these rules had been suspended.

Mr. Lloyd George then dealt with "the effect which excessive drinking amongst a minority of the workmen, in some districts, has upon the output," and appealed to Labour leaders to support any action which the Government might think necessary.

In conclusion, he said that the Government would not have summoned the Conference if the situation had not been very grave ; but it was "difficult to talk about it without creating an impression which is not very helpful for the moment."

Mr. Arthur Henderson said that, while all the representatives present were exceedingly anxious to assist the Government with regard to output, they desired an assurance that the management of concerns under Government control would be prepared to meet the Unions in negotiation. The Railway Companies, which were already controlled, had all either refused to meet the skilled Unions in conference or had ignored requests for such a meeting to discuss an application for an advance of 5s. in wages to meet the increased cost of living. " Something different to the treatment the skilled Unions have received from the Railway Companies will have to be meted out to all the Unions represented here to-day, if we are going to give effect to the Chancellor's desire, so that we can help the Government to keep the peace and to secure the output."

In reply to this point, Mr. Lloyd George pointed out that, if the employers should refuse to confer with the Unions, the machinery for arbitration, which he had proposed, would come into play.

Mr. Brownlie (A.S.E.) referred to the Shells and Fuses Agreement,[1] and to an arrangement made by his Society with the Engineering Employers' Federation that no stoppage of work should take place without discussion at local and central conferences, with a view to reaching an amicable settlement and avoiding open rupture. The point about which his Society felt concern was, not the settlement of disputes, but the introduction into the engineering industry of unskilled and semi-skilled labour which might oust skilled labour at the end of the War. He also urged that the powers under the Defence of the Realm Acts should be administered, not by Government officials and employers, but by some Board of Control on which Labour should be represented.

In answer to a question as to the restoration of the *status quo*

---

[1] See above, Chap. II., Section VII. and Appendix VII.

after the War, Mr. Lloyd George said it was the intention to make every firm taking Government work sign a guarantee on the lines of that proposed in the Second Report of the Committee on Production, which he quoted.[1]

The members and representatives of the Government having retired, the Committee of workmen's representatives prepared a draft, which was discussed and explained at a further conference in the evening. This draft contained a proposal that the Government should appoint an Advisory Board, with equal representation of employers and workmen, to assist in securing acceleration of output ; to act as an informal court of arbitration ; and to exercise control over the conditions of employment.[2] It will be observed that the Agreement in its final form does not provide for the appointment of a Committee with these executive powers. The Advisory Committee mentioned in clause (3), and afterwards known as the National Advisory Committee on War Output, consisted only of workmen's representatives, and its functions were confined to consultation.

The Conference met again on 18 March, but was adjourned to the following day, in order that the draft might be more fully discussed and amended.

On 19 March Mr. Arthur Henderson presented a document which had been accepted with only two dissentients. This Memorandum was signed on behalf of the Government by Mr. Lloyd George and Mr. Runciman, and on behalf of the workmen's representatives by Mr. Henderson and Mr. Mosses. Mr. Lloyd George undertook that each Union should receive enough copies to enable it to send one to each of its members.

The following is the text of the Agreement :—

ACCELERATION OF OUTPUT ON GOVERNMENT WORK.

Memorandum of proposals which the Workmen's Representatives agreed to recommend to their members at a Conference with the Chancellor of the Exchequer and the President of the Board of Trade, held at the Treasury, on March 17th-19th, 1915.

The following workmen's organisations were represented :—

> Friendly Society of Ironfounders.
> British Steel Smelters' Association.
> Amalgamated Society of Engineers.
> Federation of Engineering and Shipbuilding Trades.
> Electrical Trades Union.
> Associated Blacksmiths and Ironworkers.
> Associated Ironmoulders of Scotland.
> National Amalgamated Cabinetmakers.

---

[1] See above, Chap. II., Section VI., p. 50.

[2] The account of the contents of this draft is taken from a statement issued to the Press Association and published in the *Times* of 19 March.

Steam Engine Makers' Society.
General Union of Carpenters and Joiners.
United Patternmakers' Association.
National Transport Workers' Federation.
General Union of Textile Workers.
Amalgamated Society of Carpenters and Joiners.
Boilermakers and Iron and Steel Shipbuilders' Society.
Ship-constructors and Shipwrights' Association.
National Amalgamated Sheet Metal Workers.
United Operative Plumbers' Association.
Gasworkers' and General Labourers' Union.
United Machine Workers' Association.
Associated Iron and Steel Workers of Great Britain.
National Amalgamated Union of Labour.
Workers' Union.
Amalgamated Society of Woodcutting Machinists
Amalgamated Toolmakers' Society.
National Amalgamated Furnishing Trades Association.
National Amalgamated House and Ship Painters and
    Decorators.
National Union of Railwaymen.
National Union of Boot and Shoe Operatives.
General Union of Braziers and Sheet Metal Workers
Scottish Painters' Society.
Sheet Iron Workers and Light Platers Society.
Shipbuilding Trades Agreement Committee.
General Federation of Trade Unions.
Parliamentary Committee of the Trade Union Congress.

The Workmen's Representatives at the Conference will recommend to their members the following proposals with a view to accelerating the output of munitions and equipments of war :—

(1) During the war period there shall in no case be any stoppage of work upon munitions and equipments of war or other work required for a satisfactory completion of the War :

All differences on wages or conditions of employment arising out of the War shall be dealt with without stoppage in accordance with paragraph (2).

Questions not arising out of the War should not be made the cause of stoppage during the war period.

(2) Subject to any existing agreements or methods now prevailing for the settlement of disputes, differences of a purely individual or local character shall unless mutually arranged be the subject of a deputation to the firm representing the workmen concerned, and differences of a general character affecting wages and conditions of employment arising out of the War shall be the subject of Conferences between the parties.

In all cases of failure to reach a· settlement of disputes by the parties directly concerned, or their representatives, or under existing agreements, the matter in dispute shall be dealt with under any one of the three following alternatives as may be mutually agreed, or in default of agreement, settled by the Board of Trade.

(a) The Committee on Production.

(b) A single arbitrator agreed upon by the parties or appointed by the Board of Trade.

(c) A court of arbitration upon which Labour is represented equally with the employers.

(3) An Advisory Committee representative of the organised workers engaged in production for Government requirements shall be appointed by the Government for the purpose of facilitating the carrying out of these recommendations and for consultation by the Government or by the workmen concerned.

(4) Provided that the conditions set out in paragraph (5) are accepted by the Government as applicable to all contracts for the execution of war munitions and equipments the workmen's representatives at the Conference are of opinion that during the war period the relaxation of the present trade practices is imperative, and that each Union be recommended to take into favourable consideration such changes in working conditions or trade customs as may be necessary with a view to accelerating the output of war munitions or equipments.

(5) The recommendations contained in paragraph (4) are conditional on Government requiring all contractors and subcontractors engaged on munitions and equipments of war or other work required for the satisfactory completion of the War to give an undertaking to the following effect :—

Any departure during the War from the practice ruling in our workshops, shipyards, and other industries prior to the War, shall only be for the period of the War.

No change in practice made during the War shall be allowed to prejudice the position of the workpeople in our employment, or of their trade unions in regard to the resumption and maintenance after the War of any rules or customs existing prior to the War.

In any readjustment of staff which may have to be effected after the War priority of employment will be given to workmen in our employment at the beginning of the War who are serving with the colours or who are now in our employment.[1]

Where the custom of a shop is changed during the War by the introduction of semi-skilled men to perform work hitherto performed by a class of workmen of higher

[1] These first three clauses are taken from the form of undertaking proposed in the Second Report of the Committee on Production. See above. p. 50.

skill, the rates paid shall be the usual rates of the district for that class of work.[1]

The relaxation of existing demarcation restrictions or admission of semi-skilled or female labour shall not affect adversely the rates customarily paid for the job. In cases where men who ordinarily do the work are adversely affected thereby, the necessary readjustments shall be made so that they can maintain their previous earnings.

A record of the nature of the departure from the conditions prevailing before the date of this undertaking shall be kept and shall be open for inspection by the authorised representative of the Government.

Due notice shall be given to the workmen concerned wherever practicable of any changes of working conditions which it is desired to introduce as the result of this arrangement, and opportunity of local consultation with men or their representatives shall be given if desired.

All differences with our workmen engaged on Government work arising out of changes so introduced or with regard to wages or conditions of employment arising out of the War shall be settled without stoppage of work in accordance with the procedure laid down in paragraph (2).

It is clearly understood that except as expressly provided in the fourth paragraph of clause 5 nothing in this undertaking is to prejudice the position of employers or employees after the War.

(*Signed*)

D. LLOYD GEORGE.

WALTER RUNCIMAN.

ARTHUR HENDERSON,

(*Chairman of Workmen's Representatives*).

WM. MOSSES,

(*Secretary of Workmen's Representatives*).

March 19th, 1915.

---

[1] A point not provided for in this paragraph was the question whether the semi-skilled worker should also receive the guarantee (given according to the practice of some shops to the skilled worker) of his minimum time rate when he was employed on piece-work. The reason of the omission was probably that the practice was not general before the War.

II. Treasury Conference of 25 March. Agreement with the Amalgamated Society of Engineers.

Although the Amalgamated Society of Engineers appears in the list of Unions at the head of the Agreement, the Executive Council of that Society had instructed the representatives not to sign any agreement or to commit themselves to recommending any scheme until the whole report should have been presented to the Council for consideration and endorsement.[1] When it became known that the Society was not pledged to the Memorandum, the Chancellor of the Exchequer, on 20 March, sent an urgent request to the Executive Council that they would summon their local representatives to a further conference.

This second conference was held at the Treasury on 25 March. The Government was represented, as before, by Mr. Lloyd George, Mr. Runciman, Mr. Montagu, and Dr. Macnamara ; and Mr. Arthur Balfour was present, as well as representatives of the Admiralty, the War Office, and the Board of Trade. The Amalgamated Society of Engineers was represented by its Executive Council and District Delegates.[2]

MR. LLOYD GEORGE, in opening the proceedings, followed the lines of his speech on 17 March. He appealed to the Society, which had it in its power to make any arrangement impossible, to render its assistance.

MR. BROWNLIE said that the Society was not oblivious of the exigencies of the War, but was also conscious of its responsibilities to its members.

" We number in our organisation something between 178.000 and 180,000 members ; of those members, between 150,000 and 160,000 are located in the United Kingdom. And if, as custodians of the trade rights of our fellow craftsmen, it should appear to you that we are somewhat stubborn, obstinate, and indifferent to the needs of the Nation, I can assure you that such is not the case. We are just as jealous and just as anxious that the Nation should come out of this great world struggle triumphant, and that we shall kill Prussian militarism for all time, as anybody can be. But our spirit in this problem may be likened to the attitude taken up by the Barons of old, who were called upon to forgo what they considered to be their rights and privileges within the Kingdom. The Government has taken over, or, at all events, is contemplating taking over, workshops, factories, and shipyards. But there was a time in the history of the country when the Government did not control the Army, or Navy, and when, to some extent, the armed forces of the Nation were under the control of private individuals, who were great and mighty Barons. And, Sir, just as these people fought strenuously and tenaciously against the relaxation of any of their rights, or forgoing what they considered to be the heritage handed down to them by their forefathers for untold generations in the interests of the Nation, we on the other hand have to view

---

[1] A.S.E. *Monthly Journal and Report,* April, 1915, pp. 17, 19.
[2] Verbatim Report, HIST. REC./R/180/18.

the problem in a somewhat similar manner, as we are relaxing trade rights which have been won at much sacrifice by our forefathers."

Mr. Brownlie explained that no decision had yet been reached with regard to the Memorandum drawn up at the previous conference. The Executive Council had neither rejected it nor decided to recommend it.

MR. BUTTON claimed that, so far as the production of ammunition was concerned, the Society had already met the case by the Shells and Fuses Agreement of 5 March. So soon as a similar need should arise in any other branch of the industry, the Society was willing to meet the Government. "But to ask us, as your Agreement does ask us, to allow the introduction of semi-skilled and female labour into all branches of the engineering trade, is something which, at the moment, we are not prepared to agree to." In what other branch were relaxations required ? Torpedoes were out of the question. In the rifle trade, fully skilled men were employed only in the higher branches, and the conditions required practically prevailed there already. In gun manufacture, the Agreement already operated in the roughing stages ; in the later stages a high degree of skill was essential to good workmanship. It was for the Government to prove that any further extension of the Shells and Fuses Memorandum was necessary.

Mr. Button also demanded that, for the satisfaction of the Society's members, the definite terms of any agreement reached with the employers as to limitation of profits should be laid before them.

MR. LLOYD GEORGE said in reply that he agreed with Mr. Button's main proposition. "I want a general agreement with you upon principles. I quite agree that you should not be called upon to sweep away all the safeguards which protect your industry and your order, and give us a blank cheque, as it were, in the matter . . . We simply want exactly what Mr. Button has said he is prepared to concede. We want from you that, whenever we can demonstrate to you that it is necessary, in order to increase the output of munitions of war in any particular direction, for the moment to introduce semi-skilled and female labour, you will agree. That is all we ask you.

"In regard to the second proposition that you should have a guarantee that you will not be doing these things merely in order to benefit individual companies, or firms, or shareholders, that we are now seeing to, and we are now negotiating upon that basis. It is true that we shall probably have to employ individual firms to assist in the output without taking them over. We cannot undertake, for instance, to take over every firm that we employ. I will tell you what I mean. There are certain firms which turn out munitions of war exclusively. So far as they are concerned, we propose to impose these restrictions upon their profits. That bears upon the bulk of your trade as far as munitions are concerned. But there may be another firm which is turning out something else in the main, which we employ to assist us. We cannot undertake to control a business in which we are not for the moment concerned. Supposing it is motor-cars ; or let us take another case, which is even better for our purpose. Supposing you have a very considerable concern, which is turning out mining machinery or repairing mining machinery. We might say : ' We do not want to stop all your mining machinery, and we do not want to stop your repairing mining machinery, nor do we want to take over the business of making or repairing mining machinery ; therefore, you carry on your business as far as that is concerned ; but we do ask you to give us 50,000 shells a month.' I will take that figure for the sake of argument. We should not take over a concern of that kind ; you could not expect us to take it over, because the bulk of the business would still be something which we cannot really control, or undertake to control. In that case, you could not impose the same restrictions, because there you would be entering upon a part of the business with which we have nothing whatever to do. But so far as we take over works and confine them exclusively to this purpose—I am now talking about your trade—in that case, we are not merely intending to restrict the profits, but we are at the present moment negotiating for the purpose of doing so."

The points raised in the discussion which followed may be grouped under several heads.

(a) The Restriction of the Agreement to War Work.

Referring to the Chancellor s speech last quoted, Mr. Kaylor[1] said: " In your explanation in regard to mining machinery, you said that if four-fifths of the work done was in making mining machinery, you could not interfere with the profits arising from the production of that mining machinery. Then I take it that we should not be called upon to relax any conditions in regard to the four-fifths of the work, but would be asked only to relax conditions in regard to the one-fifth which belongs to the category of war munitions ? "

Mr. Lloyd George : " You may make any conditions you like with the employers with regard to the part of their business with which the Government is not concerned. You must make your own fight in regard to that. We only want relaxations for the purpose of turning out munitions of war. In regard to other work, any question that arises is between you and the employers."

Mr. Hutchinson[2] later put a question on paragraph (4) of Clause 5 (" Where the custom of a shop is changed during the War by the introduction of semi-skilled men to perform work hitherto performed by a class of workmen of higher skill, the rates paid shall be the usual rates of the district for that class of work "). Mr. Hutchinson asked : " Are we to understand . . . that this shall not apply to any commercial work, and that it will only apply to work which is wanted specifically by the Government for war purposes ? "

Mr. Lloyd George : " Yes."

Mr. Hutchinson : " And only in the shops which the Government are taking over for the War ? "

---

[1] *Report*, p. 18.   [2] *Report*, p. 24.

MR. LLOYD GEORGE : " No ; it will apply in the shops the Government are not taking over, for war work."

MR. HUTCHINSON : " But it is for war work only ? "

MR. LLOYD GEORGE : " Yes ; otherwise we could not extend our operations."

(b) SAFEGUARD FOR THE RESTORATION OF CONDITIONS IN THE CASE OF NEW INVENTIONS INTRODUCED DURING THE WAR.

MR. RYDER[1] raised a question which had been overlooked in earlier discussions. In connection with some new invention, unskilled or semi-skilled labour might be introduced on what would normally be skilled work. In this case there would be no pre-war practice to appeal to, and the employers would be likely to continue with unskilled labour after the War.

This point was dealt with in the Agreement drawn up after this Conference.

(c) THE GOVERNMENT TO CERTIFY THAT WORK IS FOR WAR PURPOSES.

MR. JAMES[2] asked that the Government should certify whether work in which it was proposed that conditions should be changed was work for war purposes.

This point also was dealt with in the Agreement.

After adjournment, MR. BROWNLIE reported that the assent of the Society's representatives would depend upon the answers to four points, which were stated as follows :—

" (1) Profits which may accrue as a result of any relaxation of trade restrictions or trade practice.

" (2) Whether the relaxation of any trade practice, as suggested in the Memorandum, is only applicable to the production of work for war, and during the war period only.

" (3) Whether, in the case of any introduction of new inventions which were not in existence in the pre-war days, which call for the operation of skilled workmen, such work will be considered as the work of skilled workmen ; and, if it is necessary that semi-skilled workmen be called upon to do such work, that also will be viewed in the light of pre-war days.

" (4) That the Government Department shall endorse any application for relaxation of trade practices or customs in connection with war work during the war period."

MR. LLOYD GEORGE replied to these points in the following terms :—

" (1) I adhere to the statement I made before, that, with regard to any relaxation that you consent to, we shall make arrangements to the best of our power that these shall not inure to the financial advantage of the employing firms and companies, but entirely to the advantage

---

[1] *Report*, p. 26.   [2] *Report*, p. 28.

of the State. . . . We are already negotiating upon that basis. . . . I think that is a perfectly fair demand."

" (2) We are only urging you to make these relaxations in respect of the war work. It is in order to increase the output of war munitions, and we have no concern, as a Government, with the arrangements which you make with the employers in respect of other work."

" (3) It is perfectly true . . . that you have no rule, at the present moment, which is applicable to any absolutely new invention ; but still it is analogous to something which is done at the present moment, and therefore the same rule would apply."

" (4) I understand it is . . . for the purpose of enabling the workmen to feel that the Government undertake the responsibility to see that the *status quo* is restored. As I understand, they want to bring us in, I think, quite rightly. They say : ' We cannot trust the individual employers and firms, and therefore we must feel that the Government realise it is also their responsibility to support us in restoring the *status quo*.' I think that is perfectly fair.

" I have had an opportunity during the interval of consulting with Mr. Balfour upon this subject. I need hardly tell you that is a very important matter, because Governments come and go, and it is rather important you should have a distinguished and dominant personality of the other great party of the State express his views on that point. He feels that quite as strongly as I do."

MR. BALFOUR : " That is a matter of honour."

MR. LLOYD GEORGE : " It does not mean that any rules and regulations are going to be like the laws of the Medes and Persians. But that is a matter you will have to fight among yourselves at a future time. Our business is to see, if you press it, that the *status quo ante bellum* is restored ; and Mr. Balfour takes exactly that view. You have relaxed your rules for the purpose of the War, and during the War, and you have done it at the request of the Government. You have done it for the benefit of the State, for a particular purpose, and during a particular period. Therefore, we feel that, if, at the end of that period, you are of opinion that the pre-war conditions should be restored, it is an obligation of honour on our part to support your claim in that respect."

After the termination of the meeting, the following memorandum was signed on behalf of the Government and the Engineers' Society :—

ACCELERATION OF OUTPUT ON GOVERNMENT WORK.

At a meeting held at the Treasury on 25 March, 1915, between the Chancellor of the Exchequer and the President of the Board of Trade and the Executive Council and Organising District Delegates of the Amalgamated Society of Engineers, the Chancellor of the Exchequer explained the circumstances in which it had become essential for the successful prosecution of the War to conclude an agreement with the Trade Unions for the acceleration of output on Government work. After discussion the representatives of the Amalgamated Society of Engineers resolved that, in the light of the Chancellor of the Exchequer's statement and explanations, the agreement be accepted by the Union, and expressed a desire that the following statements by the Chancellor of the Exchequer in answer to questions put to him as to the meaning of various clauses in the Memorandum agreed upon at a Conference with Workmen's Representatives on 17-19 March, be put on record :—

(1) That it is the intention of the Government to conclude arrangements with all important firms engaged wholly or mainly upon engineering or shipbuilding work for war purposes, under which their profits will be limited, with a view to securing that benefit resulting from the relaxation of trade restrictions or practices shall accrue to the State.

(2) That the relaxation of trade practices contemplated in the agreement relates solely to work done for war purposes during the war period.

(3) That in the case of the introduction of new inventions which were not in existence in the pre-war period the class of workman to be employed on this work after the War should be determined according to the practice prevailing before the War in the case of the class of work most nearly analogous.

(4) That on demand by the workmen the Government Department concerned will be prepared to certify whether the work in question is needed for war purposes.

(5) That the Government will undertake to use its influence to secure the restoration of previous conditions in every case after the War.

> D. Lloyd George.
>
> Walter Runciman.
>
> Jas. T. Brownlie (Chairman of Executive Council of Amalgamated Society of Engineers).
>
> Wm. Harold Hutchinson (Member of Executive Council).
>
> George Ryder (Organising District Delegate).
>
> Robert Young (General Secretary).

The importance of this Memorandum lies chiefly in two points. It contains the first written pledge that the profits of " all important firms engaged wholly or mainly upon engineering and shipbuilding work for war purposes " should be limited. Secondly, it for the first time bound the Government to use its influence in securing the " restoration of the previous conditions in every case after the War." This clause does not include the proviso contained in Mr. Lloyd George's verbal pledge at the meeting : " *if at the end of that period you are of opinion that the pre-war conditions should be restored* " ; but, in any case the mention or omission of this qualification makes no practical difference. From this moment the Government was bound in honour to see that, where the fulfilment of the pledge was claimed by the Unions, the conditions varied under the Agreement should be restored as they were before the War.

In the Amalgamated Society of Engineers' *Journal* for April (p. 67), the General Secretary wrote as follows :—

" To avoid even the possibility of defeat (in the War) the Government has been urging the relaxation of Trade Union restrictions. These restrictions are necessary, and have been imposed to safeguard the standard of life of skilled workers. Any relaxation of these economic safeguards must be jealously controlled in the interests of the workers. The interests of the engineers are probably more affected than those of any other trade. Yet, when the interests of the State are involved, relaxations may become necessary.

" The policy of your officials has been : no relaxation of trade regulations until good and satisfactory cause is shown for its necessity. It is because good and definite reasons have been given that the ballot on shells and fuses became necessary.[1] It is because good cause has been shown that the memorandum arising out of the Conference with the Chancellor of the Exchequer has been signed. The best safeguards possible have been got. The members should, therefore, follow the lead of their officials. The work must be done. We believe the work will be done. The nation cannot afford to wait. Men and masters, if need be, will be wise to accept the Government's arrangement. If we abide by the arrangements, our safeguards will be respected. If the arrangement is disregarded, penal statutes may become operative. It is, therefore, in the interests of the men employed on munitions of war, as well as in the interests of the nation, that no stoppage of work should take place, that losing time should be avoided, and that differences *re* wages and other conditions of employment should be settled by the machinery created for the war period."

Subject to the additional pledges and explanations given in the Memorandum of 25 March, the Executive Council of the A.S.E. recommended their members to accept the Treasury Agreement.[2] It was confirmed by ballot of the whole Society, but not until 16 June, 1915 The voting was : 18,078 for ; 4,025 against.

III. The Form of Guarantee given by Government Contractors.

Shortly after the Conference, Sir George Askwith addressed a letter to the Admiralty and the War Office with reference to the form of the employers' undertaking.

He said that the question had been raised whether the guarantee

---

[1] See above, Chap. II., Section VII. and Appendix VII.

[2] A.S.E. *Monthly Journal and Report*, May, 1915, p. 5.

in the Treasury Memorandum was to be substituted for the form given in the Second Report of the Committee on Production.[1] The Shipbuilding Employers' Federation were not signing the latter, pending a decision on this question. The Committee on Production thought that the Treasury formula should be adopted. They had been informed that contractors to the War Office and the Admiralty had been asked, some time ago, to sign the guarantee in the Committee's Report, and that some of them had done so ; and further, that the War Office had since asked their contractors to sign the Treasury form. The Committee thought that those contractors who should not reply or sign should not be pressed to do so. It would suffice if contractors and sub-contractors were informed, as occasion arose, that the Treasury guarantee was an implied condition of all contracts.

In accordance with the suggestion contained in the above letter, the following Notice was issued to Admiralty Contractors :—

" ACCELERATION OF OUTPUT ON GOVERNMENT WORK.

" It is hereby notified that all work performed for the Admiralty during the period of the War, whether under direct contract with the Admiralty or by sub-contractors, is regarded as work within the scope of the arrangements contained in the enclosed Memorandum of 19th March. In view of the national necessity for accelerating the output of work for the Admiralty, the undertaking required by paragraph 5 of the Memorandum will be regarded by the Admiralty as accepted by all employers concerned in the case of contracts and sub-contracts now current, and will be a condition of all future contracts entered into by the Admiralty during the War.

" This announcement is made by the Admiralty in full confidence that all employers will be willing in the national interest to conform to this requirement."

On 29 March the War Office issued a circular agreed upon between Sir Charles Harris and Mr. Lloyd George, requesting their contractors to sign a printed form of undertaking which was enclosed. This embodied all the conditions laid down in paragraph 5 of the Agreement.[2]

IV. The National Advisory Committee on War Output.

The Treasury Agreement of 19 March provided in clause (3) for the establishment of an Advisory Committee, representative of the organised workers engaged in production for Government requirements, to facilitate the carrying out of the recommendations and for consultation by the Government or by the workmen.

On 31 March the members of the Committee of workmen's representatives which had been appointed to negotiate the Agreement, were summoned to the Offices of the Chief Industrial Commissioner.

---

[1] See above, Chap. II., Section VI., p. 50.

[2] 94/Gen. No./34. Copies of the Circular and Undertaking are given in Appendix IX.

Sir G. Askwith announced that all the members of the Committee had been invited, and had consented, to serve on the National Advisory Committee on War Output.

It was decided by this Committee on 31 March that local Advisory Committees should be appointed in the chief engineering centres, the nucleus being formed by the local district Committees of the Federation of Engineering and Shipbuilding Trades, with representatives co-opted from societies which were not represented on those bodies, but whose members were engaged in the production of war material. These enlarged Local Committees were to be requested to appoint sub-committees for their own and adjacent districts, whose function would be to collect information as to impending labour difficulties, to co-operate with their central Committees and the National Advisory Committee in preventing stoppages or curtailment of work, and to facilitate in every way the output of war material.[1]

The Executive Council of the Amalgamated Society of Engineers at first refused to recognise the National Advisory Committee. Later however, on the initiative of the Committee, these differences were adjusted on the following basis :

> " In all cases where the National Advisory Committee on War Output find it necessary to send a deputation to any district with a view to a settlement of any difficulty in which engineers are involved, it is agreed that the Executive Council of the Amalgamated Society of Engineers be invited to elect a member of the deputation to visit the district concerned along with the Committee's representatives and at its expense."

On these terms the Amalgamated Society of Engineers promised its co-operation.[2]

V. The Failure of the Treasury Agreement.

The document signed on 19 March, though commonly known as the " Treasury Agreement," was, strictly speaking, a " Memorandum of Proposals." It bound the workmen's representatives at the Conference to recommend these proposals to their members ; but, until a favourable ballot of each Society should have been taken, no Union was committed. Even when any particular Union had expressed its assent, paragraph (4) only bound it " to take into favourable consideration " such changes of working conditions or trade customs as might be necessary for the acceleration of output. It was not committed to the suspension of any given rule or practice—to enumerate these, varying as they do from trade to trade, would of course have been impossible—and further, in every case, the question whether a particular change was necessary for the purpose specified might be open to dispute. There was evidently much room for the play of obstructive

---

[1] The Armaments Output Committee issued in April a circular laying down a constitution for local Advisory Committees. See Part III., Chap. IV. Section IV.

[2] The correspondence confirming this agreement was laid before a meeting of the National Advisory Committee on 8 June.

forces between the signing of the document on March 19 and the actual suspension of a single restriction by any one society.

The event proved that it was one thing to draw up the Treasury Memorandum on paper, another thing to induce the general mass of workmen to pay attention to its provisions. Three months passed before the Government's pledge to limit profits was given legislative sanction in the Munitions of War Act of 2 July, 1915. There was a corresponding delay on the side of the Unions. On 9 June, a deputation from the Emergency Committee of the Shipbuilding Employers' Federation, was received at the Board of Trade. The Executive Board of this Federation had itself agreed, on 26 May, that all the federated firms engaged on Government work should accept the Treasury Agreement ; but the deputation stated that " in most cases " the workmen's organisations represented at the Treasury Conference " had not approached their members in the matter at all." The Amalgamated Society of Engineers had by that date submitted the proposals of the two Memoranda, but the men's vote was not to be taken till 16 June. The Shipwrights' Society had attached to the Memorandum of 19 March a supplementary agreement of their own, which they demanded that the employers should sign before they would allow their men to accept any work. The deputation summed up the position in the statement that the Agreement of 19 March had " practically never become operative."

The principal cause of this failure is clearly stated in the concluding paragraphs of a *Memorandum on Labour for Armaments* by Sir H. Llewellyn Smith, dated 9 June, 1915,[1] as follows :—

" The difficulty, as it has been expressed both by workmen's representatives at " the two Treasury Conferences " and by employers themselves (as in the Shipbuilding Employers' deputation received to-day) is that the workmen, though engaged on armament work, still feel themselves to be working essentially for private employers, with whom they have only a ' cash nexus,' and that in the present circumstances a ' cash nexus ' is quite inadequate to secure control. . . .

" So long as contractors' profits are not brought under control, the workmen feel that any sacrifice they may make of their rules and restrictions will directly increase the profits of private persons, and their unwillingness to make the sacrifice is made almost insuperable by this suspicion."

A subsidiary cause, which the same Memorandum illustrates, was that the men were by this time " to a very considerable extent out of the control both of the employers and of their own leaders." During these months Labour had been more and more rapidly escaping from all the influences of economic circumstance and disciplined organisation which tend to control it in normal times. Almost any workman of any pretensions to skill in the engineering and shipbuilding trades had so little difficulty in finding work the moment he wanted it, that he had

---

[1] Hist. Rec./R/320/1.

little motive left for remaining with his employer, if he was in any way dissatisfied, whether with good reason or without.   This economic freedom of the individual workman tended, of course, to remove also the normal motives for submitting to Trade Union discipline and to the guidance of the Labour leader.   The men were becoming more than commonly impatient of the moderation of Union officials, and inclined to ignore or to repudiate any compacts they might make with Government Departments or federations of employers.   Throughout these three months, employer and Labour leader alike more and more found themselves left in the air, while the rank and file, whose suspicion that the employers had the best of the bargain could be fired by any spark of irresponsible agitation, went as they pleased, or put forward demands, backed by threats of stoppage, either for better terms or for the perpetuation of restrictions which their leaders, but not themselves, had bargained away.   In some cases, such demands were supported by the leaders of Unions which were not finally committed to the Agreement.   The attempt of the employers to obtain the removal of restrictions was resolving itself into a long struggle to get them surrendered piecemeal.

The Memorandum of 9 June cited above records that threats of stoppage were then common, and actual stoppage by no means rare. The elaborate machinery for arbitration set up in the Treasury Memorandum was in some cases ignored, in others rejected.[1]

It must be borne in mind that this Memorandum is based chiefly on employers' evidence, and naturally puts forward the points still calling for remedy, without reviewing the more successful aspects of the situation   Nor must it be forgotten that, while profits and prices were left free to rise, the burden of sacrifice was thrown wholly on the workman, who knew that the fruits of that sacrifice, to a large extent, were reaped by private capitalists, and that nothing but an undertaking of doubtful value stood between the temporary surrender of cherished rights and a permanent deterioration of his standard of living. It would probably be impossible to obtain any complete evidence as to the extent to which relaxation of restrictions had been actually secured by this date as a consequence of the Agreement.   But the mere fact that it was necessary to embody the bargain for removal of restrictions on the one side, and limitation of profits on the other, in the Munitions of War Act, is sufficient proof that the early voluntary negotiations had failed to secure their object.

---

[1] Further evidence on this subject will be given in Part IV.

APPENDICES.

APPENDIX I.

(CHAPTER I., p. 1.)

Memorandum as to Minimising of Unemployment during the War.

In order to assist as far as possible in minimising the evils of unemployment which must in some districts arise as a result of the War, it is particularly desired that, in the execution of Army orders, Contractors shall act upon the following suggestions to such extent as they reasonably can, *viz.* :—

(1) Rapid delivery to be attained by employing extra hands, in shifts or otherwise, in preference to overtime, subject always to the paramount necessity of effecting delivery within the times requisite for the needs of the Army.

(2) Subletting of portions of the work to other suitable manufacturers situated in districts where serious unemployment exists, although contrary to the usual conditions of Army Contracts, is admissible during the present crisis, and it is desired to encourage such subletting on the following conditions, *viz.* :—

(*a*) The main Contractor to remain solely responsible for due execution of the contract as regards quality, dates of delivery, and in every respect.

(*b*) The Fair Wages clause to apply strictly, with the exception of the passage prohibiting subletting. The main Contractor to be responsible for subletting only to manufacturers who will undertake to observe the other provisions of the Fair Wages clause.

(*c*) Names and addresses of all Firms to whom it is proposed to sublet work to be submitted for approval before work is actually given out to them.

(*Signed*) H. DE LA BERE,
Director of Army Contracts.

War Office,
August, 1914.

APPENDIX II.

(CHAPTER I., p. 3.)

The Effects of Enlistment on the Industrial Population.

TABLE I.

The total effect of enlistment is shown in the following table of the state of employment in April and July, 1915, compared with employment before the War (*Board of Trade Report on the State of Employment in the United Kingdom in July*, 1915, Part I., p. 3) :—

Trade Groups.	Approximate industrial population (Census, 1911).	Percentage of Numbers employed in July, 1914.					
		Contraction (−) or expansion (+) of numbers employed.		Known to have joined the Forces.		Net displacement (−) or replacement (+)	
		April	July	April	July	April	July
Shipbuilding ..	164,000	+ 6·5	+10·8	15·3	16·5	+21·8	+27·3
Engineering ..	588,000	− 7·3	− 3·2	17·5	19·5	+10·2	+16·3
Electrical Engineering ..	77,000	− 5·9	− 5·8	20·5	23·7	+14·6	+17·9
All trades ..	6,373,000	−10·8	−11·8	17·3	20·2	+ 6·5	+ 8·4

TABLE II.

EFFECT OF ENLISTMENT ON SMALL ENGINEERING FIRMS.

Number of small firms.	Number of males employed, July, 1914.	Number enlisted		Total enlisted by 15 April.
		Up to Feb., 1915.	February– 15 April.	
985	33,451	5,500 (16·4%)	599 (1·8%)	6,099 (18·2%)

NOTE.—On 6 May, Mr. Layton, in reporting these figures, stated that in the case of both large and small engineering firms the increase (since February) in the percentage of enlistment was over 2 per cent. in London and Scotland ; for small firms, over 2 per cent. in the Midlands ; for large firms, small in the Northern, West Midlands, and South-Eastern (including Enfield, Erith, Ipswich, etc.) Divisions.

TABLE III.

Percentage and amount of enlistment since the outbreak of War, and from 16 April to 16 July, 1915, in the metal trades, exclusive of the work of any such trades undertaken by railway companies :—

Trade.	Total enlistment up to 16 July, 1915.		Enlistment between 16 April and 16 July, 1915.	
	Percentage on Service.	Numbers on Service.	Percentage known to have joined the Forces.	Numbers known to have joined the Forces.
Iron and Steel ..	18·2	47,800	1·8	4,121
Wire-drawing ..	18·1	7,800	1·9	675
Hardware, etc. ..	20·9	15,400	3·3	2,091
Engineering ..	19·5	90,700	1·9	7,279
Electrical Engineering	23·5	12,000	3·2	1,408
Shipbuilding ..	16·5	24,700	1·2	1,615
Cycles and Motors	23·6	20,700	3·2	2,428
Railway Carriages	20·0	3,900	2·6	448
Carriage, Cart, etc.	19·8	2,500	3·8	422
Cutlery, etc. ..	17·3	7,300	2·1	791
Small Arms ..	16·9	750	1·1	45
Scientific Instruments	17·4	2,600	2·3	298
Other metals ..	20·9	13,400	2·4	1,325
Totals ..		249,550		26,450

APPENDIX III.
(CHAPTER I., p. 9.)

Lists given in the Statistical Supplement to Sir H. Llewellyn Smith's Memorandum on the Limits of Enlistment, January, 1915.

LIST A.

Essential occupations from which practically no further labour could be drawn.

	Unenlisted balance physically capable of military service (in thousands).
Iron and Steel	99
Shipbuilding	46
Engineering	179
Woollen and Worsted	44
Boots and Shoes	64
Leather, etc.	29
Chemicals	36
Hosiery	6
Food	62
Cycles, Motors, and Railway Carriages	38
Central Government	56
Railways and Docks	213
Add for salaried persons, etc., in these trades	80
Total	952

LIST B.

Occupations that might spare a certain proportion of the balance.

These were divided into three categories, according to the proportion of labour of military age and capacity that might be drawn from them, namely—

(1) one-fifth ;
(2) a quarter to one-third ;
(3) a half.

		Unenlisted balance of men physically capable of military service (in thousands)	
Category 1	Mining	375	
	Agriculture and Fishing	539	
	Clothing	70	
	Local Government	46	
			1,030
Category 2	Furniture, Timber, etc.	72	
	Glass and Pottery	25	
	Cotton and other textiles	96	
	" Other " Metal	167	
	" Other " Transport	270	
	Other Miscellaneous	46	
			676
Category 3	Building	239	
	Brick, Stone and Quarries	60	
	Brewing and Tobacco	38	
	Paper and Printing	78	
	Professional	125	
	Domestic	151	
	Commercial	250	
	Dealers, etc.	361	
			1,302

APPENDIX IV.

(CHAPTER I., p. 28.)

Labour for Armament Firms.

BOARD OF TRADE LABOUR EXCHANGES CENTRAL CLEARING HOUSE.

RETURN OF PLACINGS FOR THE PERIODS,

1/8/14 TO 13/3/15 AND 1/1/15 TO 13/3/15.

Firm or Factory.	For Period 1 August, 1914, to 13 March, 1915.				For Period 1 January, 1915, to 13 March, 1915.			
	British.		Belgian.		British.		Belgian.	
	Men and Boys.	Women and Girls.	Men and Boys.	Women and Girls.	Men and Boys.	Women and Girls.	Men and Boys.	Women and Girls.
Armament Firms* ..	10,843	2,146	609	41	4,216	795	199	—
Woolwich, Enfield and Greenock	14,086	—	†	†	3,899	—	†	†
Grand Totals	24,929	2,146	609	41	8,115	795	199	—

* The firms supplied were : Armstrong's (Alexandria, Elswick), Coventry Ordnance, Vickers (Crayford, Erith, Barrow, Sheffield), B.S.A., Babcock & Wilcox (Renfrew), Beardmore (Glasgow), Hadfield (Sheffield), Firth (Sheffield).

† Areas to which Belgians had not been sent.

APPENDIX V.

(CHAPTER I., p. 28.)

Table of increases in numbers employed in Government Factories and Armament Works, 3/4/15 to 3/7/15.

The following table, compiled from weekly returns of increases in the numbers employed in the Government Factories and 12 private works, shows the increase during the quarter ending 3 July, 1915 (I. and R. Department, *Weekly Report*, II. (15/7/15), App. A).

Firm or Works.	Total No. employed. April 3.	Total No. employed. July 3.	Increase in 13 weeks. No.	Increase in 13 weeks. Per cent.
O.F., Woolwich ..	28,280	32.138	3,858	13·6
S.W.E. R.S.A.F...	6,008	6,756	748	12·5
,, R.G.P.F.	1,909	2,484	575	30·3
,, B.W.D. ..	196	315	119	59·5
Vickers, Barrow ..	3,650	6,243	2,593	72·0
,, Sheffield	3,935	4,520	585	15·0
,, Erith ..	6,112	7,251	1,139	18·7
,, Crayford	1,851	2,556	705	31·1
,, Dartford	702	788	86	12·3
,, E. & O.A. ..	1,193	3,991	2,798	233·2
, Wolseley Motors	2,612	3,184	572	22·0
Armstrong ..	25,531	32,697	7,166	28·1
Coventry Ordnance, Main Works	4,879	5,605	726	14·8
T. Firth ..	3,169	3,726	557	17·4
Greenwood & Batley ..	2,244	3,536	1,292	58·7
B.S.A. ..	7,046	7,786	740	10·5
TOTALS :				
Government Works	36,393	41,693	5.300	14·6
12 Private Works ..	62,924	81,883	18,959	30·1
COMBINED TOTAL	99,317	123,576	24,259	24·4

APPENDIX VI.

(CHAPTER I., p. 29.)

Demands for Labour at the Royal Factories and Armamen. Firms on the Preference List.

BOARD OF TRADE NATIONAL CLEARING HOUSE

1 *July*, 1915.

ERECTORS, FITTERS, AND TURNERS—
General—Fitters	2,500
Turners	2,000
Marine Engine Fitters	150
Millwrights	900
Toolmakers	450
Machine Tool Makers	500
Tool Fitters	250
Tool Turners	369
Tool Setters	800
Steam Engine Fitters	350
Guns and Mountings Fitters	1,300
Motor Fitters	50
Motor Turners	50
Marine Engine Turners	50
Aeroplane Fitters	150
Setters-Up	550

COPPERSMITHS—
Ship Work	100

METAL MACHINISTS—
Planers	300	
Slotters	200	
Shapers	20	
Borers	220	
Millers, Universal	400	
Millers, Others	700	*Highly Skilled*
Vertical Drillers	100	*Men only.*
Radial Drillers	70	
Other Drillers	300	
Grinders, Universal	50	
Capstan Hands	150	
Machinists	800	

SHEET METAL WORKERS—
General	210

TOTAL	14,030

APPENDIX VII.

(CHAPTER II., p. 51.)

The Shells and Fuses Agreement, 5 March, 1915.

MEMO. OF SPECIAL CONFERENCE

BETWEEN

THE ENGINEERING EMPLOYERS' FEDERATION

AND

AMALGAMATED SOCIETY OF ENGINEERS

(Executive Council and District Delegates),

STEAM ENGINE MAKERS' SOCIETY,

UNITED MACHINE WORKERS' ASSOCIATION,

AMALGAMATED SOCIETY OF TOOLMAKERS, ETC.

Held within ROYAL VICTORIA STATION HOTEL, SHEFFIELD, on 5 March, 1915.

Production of Shells and Fuses.

The Government having represented that there is a present and continuously increasing need for shells and fuses for use by both Naval and Military services and that it is necessary for the existing production to be increased rapidly in order to meet the demand and that the numbers of men required for this purpose are not at present available :

IT IS MUTUALLY AGREED to recommend that the following provisions shall have effect during the War :—

1. Men engaged in the making of tools and gauges shall be skilled men. Men engaged in setting up machines shall be fully qualified for the operations they undertake.

2. Such men may be drawn from other Branches of the Engineering industry provided they possess the necessary qualifications and shall be paid, at least, the standard rate of the district, for the operation on which they are for the time engaged.

3. Lists of men employed in terms of the foregoing provisions shall be furnished to the Local Representatives of the Unions concerned.

4. Such men shall first be affected by any necessary discharges either during or after the period of the War.

5. Where skilled men are at present employed they shall in no case be displaced by less skilled labour unless other skilled employment is found for them in the same department.

6. Operations on which skilled men are at present employed, but which, by reason of their character, can be performed by semi-skilled or female labour, may be done by such labour during the War period.

Where semi-skilled or female labour is employed in place of skilled labour the rates paid shall be the usual rates of the districts obtaining for the operations performed.

7. The Federation undertakes that the fact of the restrictions being temporarily removed shall not be used to the ultimate prejudice of the workpeople or their Trade Unions.

8. Any Federated Employer shall at the conclusion of the War, unless the Government notify that the emergency continues, reinstate the working conditions of his factory on the pre-War basis, and as far as possible afford re-employment to his men who are at present serving with His Majesty's Forces.

9. These proposals shall not warrant any Employer making such arrangement in the shops as will effect a permanent restriction of employment of any trade in favour of semi-skilled men or female labour.

10. The Employers agree that they will not, after the War, take advantage of this Agreement to decrease wages, premium bonus times, or piecework prices (unless warranted by alteration in the means or method of manufacture), or break down established conditions, and will adopt such proposals only for the object of increasing output in the present extraordinary circumstances.

11. The Employers agree to take all possible steps to ensure distribution of Government work throughout the Kingdom.

12. So far as consistent with the National requirements regarding output, the Employers undertake to reduce overtime wherever possible, and in any event to distribute it over as large a number of workpeople as practicable.

13. In the event of semi-skilled or female labour being employed as per the foregoing clauses, they shall first be affected by any necessary discharges either before or after the War period.

14. The liberty of any employer to take advantage of these proposals shall be subject to acquiescence in all the provisions thereof, and to intimation of his acquiescence to the Local Representatives of the Unions through his local association.

APPENDIX VIII.

(CHAPTER III., p. 68.)

Lists of Chief War Office and Admiralty Contractors for Armaments, March, 1915.

WAR OFFICE LIST.

Armstrong, Whitworth & Co.
Vickers, Limited
Firth & Son
Hadfields, Limited
Projectile Company
W. Beardmore & Co.
Dick, Kerr & Co.
Cammell, Laird & Co.
King's Norton Metal Company
Coventry Ordnance Works
Birmingham Metal & Munitions Co.
Kynoch's, Limited
Birmingham Small Arms Co.
Greenwood & Batley
London Small Arms Co.
Eley Bros.
Nobel's Explosives Co.
Cotton Powder Co
Curtiss & Harvey
New Explosives Co.
Chilworth Powder Co.
National Explosives Co.
British Explosives Syndicate

ADMIRALTY LIST.

Armstrong, Whitworth & Co.
W. Beardmore & Co.
J. Brown & Co.
Cammell, Laird & Co.
Denny & Brothers
Fairfield Shipbuilding & Engineering Co.
Hawthorn, Leslie & Co.
Palmer's Shipbuilding & Iron Co.
Parsons Marine Steam Turbine Co.
Scott's Shipbuilding Co.
Swan, Hunter & Wigham Richardson, Ltd
Thornycroft & Co.
Vickers, Ltd.
White, J. S., & Co.
Wallsend Slipway Company
Yarrow & Co.

APPENDIX IX.

(CHAPTER IV., p. 96.)

War Office Circular to Contractors and Form of Employers' Undertaking.

WAR OFFICE,

LONDON, S.W.,

94/G. No./34.   29th March, 1915.

SIR,

I am commanded by the Army Council to send you the enclosed Memorandum of proposals relating to the acceleration of output on Government work during the war, drawn up at a conference between the Chancellor of the Exchequer, the President of the Board of Trade, and representatives of workmen's organisations.

You will observe that under Clause 5 of the memorandum due notice is to be given wherever practicable to the workmen concerned before any changes are introduced, and it is desirable that full opportunity should be given in each case for adequate consultation, either local or central, between employers and men.

You are requested to sign and return to this Department the enclosed copy of the form of Undertaking.

If you have sub-contracted with any firms for any work for this Department, you are requested to forward a copy of this Circular, and the Undertaking for signature to each firm to which, in your judgment, these documents apply. Further copies may be had on application to this Department.

I am, Sir,

Your obedient Servant,

R. H. BRADE.

94/Gen. No./34.

To His Majesty's Government.

In respect of any work on munitions or equipments of war, or other work required for the satisfactory completion of the war, now in our hands or hereafter placed with us, we undertake as follows : —

1. Any departure during the war from the practice ruling in our workshops, shipyards, and other industries prior to the war, shall only be for the period of the war.

2. No change in practice made during the war shall be allowed to prejudice the position of the workpeople in our employment, or of their trade unions in regard to the resumption and maintenance after the war of any rules or customs existing prior to the war.

3. In any readjustment of staff which may have to be effected after the war priority of employment will be given to workmen in our employment at the beginning of the war who are serving with the Colours or who are now in our employment.

I-2   I

4. Where the custom of a shop is changed during the war by the introduction of semi-skilled men to perform work hitherto performed by a class of workmen of higher skill, the rates paid shall be the usual rates of the district for that class of work.

5. The relaxation of existing demarcation restrictions or admission of semi-skilled or female labour shall not affect adversely the rates customarily paid for the job. In cases where men who ordinarily do the work are adversely affected thereby, the necessary readjustments shall be made so that they can maintain their previous earnings.

6. A record of the nature of the departure from the conditions prevailing before the date of this undertaking shall be kept and shall be open for inspection by the authorised representative of the Government.

7. Due notice shall be given to the workmen concerned wherever practicable of any changes of working conditions which it is desired to introduce as the result of this arrangement, and opportunity of local consultation with men or their representatives shall be given if desired.

8. All differences with our workmen engaged on Government work arising out of changes so introduced or with regard to wages or conditions of employment arising out of the war will be settled without stoppage of work in accordance with the following procedure :—

Subject to any existing agreements or methods now prevailing for the settlement of disputes, differences of a purely individual or local character shall unless mutually arranged be the subject of a deputation to the firm representing the workmen concerned, and differences of a general character affecting wages and conditions of employment arising out of the war shall be the subject of conferences between the parties.

In all cases of failure to reach a settlement of disputes by the parties directly concerned or their representatives, or under existing agreements, the matter in dispute shall be dealt with under any one of the three following alternatives as may be mutually agreed, or in default of agreement, settled by the Board of Trade :—

(a) The Committee on Production.
(b) A single arbitrator agreed upon by the parties or appointed by the Board of Trade.
(c) A court of arbitration upon which Labour is represented equally with the employers.

9. It is clearly understood that, except as provided under clause 3 of this undertaking, nothing in this undertaking is to prejudice the position of employers or employees after the war.

Signature......................

Date......................1915.

INDEX.

CONTENTS OF VOLUME I.

NOTE.—The present issue is subject to revision,
and must be regarded as provisional.

HISTORY OF THE MINISTRY OF MUNITIONS

VOLUME I

INDUSTRIAL MOBILISATION, 1914-15

PART III

THE ARMAMENTS OUTPUT COMMITTEE

a

Volume I

INDUSTRIAL MOBILISATION, 1914–15

PART III

THE ARMAMENTS OUTPUT COMMITTEE

CONTENTS.

CHAPTER I.

The Beginnings of Local Organisation.

CHAPTER II.

The Armaments Output Committee.

(474) Wt. 3643/A.P. 5036 10/18 250 D.St

CHAPTER II

Local Organisation, 31 March to 28 April.

CHAPTER IV.

Local Organisation, 28 April to 26 May.

CHAPTER V.

Central Organisation under Sir Percy Girouard and Mr. Booth, 28 April to 26 May.

CONTENTS vii

APPENDICES.

CHAPTER I.

THE BEGINNINGS OF LOCAL ORGANISATION.

I. The Engineering Employers' Demand for Direct Contracts.

The preceding chapters have traced the outcome of the Board of Trade's activity along the lines of the programme laid down, in consultation with representatives of the Army Council, of the Royal Arsenal, and of the armament firms, on 30 December, 1914.

The scope of this campaign, in so far as it has yet been considered, had been entirely governed by the immediate aim of increasing the output of the recognised and established armament makers. The means to be taken were the reinforcement of these firms with fresh supplies of labour and the intensification of the productive power of labour already employed by obviating stoppage of work and securing the removal of Trade Union restrictions. At the outset, in fact, the sole object in view had been a great expansion of the system of munitions production which had prevailed before the War. The War Office Contracts department was still to deal, as it had always dealt, directly with a small group of well-known and expert manufacturers ; only, the scale of these dealings was to be immensely increased. The armament firms, in their turn, were to draw into the system fresh resources from the general engineering industry, by enlisting new sub-contractors, to whom they would pass on such work as, while their own new factories were building, they could not themselves absorb. And, at the same time, the Board of Trade was to call upon other employers to sacrifice their private contracts and to surrender some of their skilled staff to man those factories. Finally, when certain objections were raised to this part of the scheme, the Government took powers under the Defence of the Realm (Amendment) No. 2 Act, not merely to protect the willing employer from proceedings for breach of contract entailed by the disorganisation of his business, but to coerce the unwilling by taking away his men or his plant, or even by closing down his works altogether.

The principles of this December programme had been dictated by a previous decision, taken nearly three months earlier, on the general question, how best to bring the reserve forces of the engineering industry to bear on the production of armaments. Were the firms who came fresh to munitions work to be drawn into the old system, and either grouped, as sub-contractors, round the armament firms in which that system centred, or treated as a reservoir from which men and machines could be transferred to them ? Or were they, whether singly or in co-operative groups, to contract directly with the War

Office for stores of the simpler kinds that might be within their capacities, and so enter the field as independent competitors and set up what would be, in effect, new centres of armament work ?

The problem was put in this form in October, 1914, when the Cabinet mission to France reported on the French system of co-operative production, and the suggestion was made that it should be adopted in this country.[1] The opinion of the military authorities and of their expert advisers, the armament firms, was adverse to such a course. To judge this decision fairly, it is necessary to bear in mind that no one at that moment could possibly foresee either the length of the War or the enormous expansion of the military establishment. Until Lord Kitchener, on 4 December, in one of the very few interviews he granted to the Press, spoke of the possibility that the War would last for three years, it may be doubted whether more than a very few of the men recruited in the previous four months had taken seriously the terms of their enlistment : " Three years or the duration of the War." The new armies were being enrolled by a hundred thousand men at a time ; but the total numbers that were ultimately to be reached by voluntary enlistment were beyond the purview of the most prudent calculation. In October, the need for a large increase in the daily allowance of gun ammunition had only just become apparent. In these circumstances, the task of supplying the Expeditionary Force, and of equipping the new units with munitions, did not appear likely to exceed the powers of the regular contractors, provided they could be reinforced by subsidised extensions of their works and by a wide expansion of sub-contracting. The first duty of the military authorities was to develop production on lines that should secure the greatest possible rapidity and efficiency. They naturally looked to the expert firms, who understood every detail of manufacture, were accustomed to work up to the severe limits of the inspection tests prescribed for safety, and alone could provide fully qualified supervision and management.

The decision reached on these grounds was momentous : it governed the general trend of War Office policy until the end of March, 1915. Some time necessarily passed before it was possible to form any estimate of the prospects of success. The schemes of expansion could not be carried out in a week or a month. The new buildings at the armament works had to be erected ; the new machinery to be purchased ; the new labour to be recruited ; and the new sub-contractors to be put in the way of unfamiliar work. When it was discovered in December that the deliveries of gun ammunition promised by the main contractors were not coming forward, it was not inferred that the scheme in itself was in fault. The contractors' estimates had been too sanguine ; the sub-contractors had broken down over unforeseen difficulties. This failure might be taken as pointing to the fundamental soundness of the position that the technical difficulties of armament work were likely to defeat the inexpert manufacturer, and that the War Office should put its faith

---

[1] See Part I.   Details of the French system will be given below, p. 10 and Appendix IV.

more than ever in the established makers.   Accordingly, when the help of the Board of Trade was invoked in the last days of 1914, the focus of its programme was entirely on the armament firms.   Its efforts were all to be directed to the interests of the October policy, which the War Office saw no reason to abandon.

On the other hand, one of the proposed methods of remedying the shortage of skilled labour depended for its success on the attitude of the ordinary engineering employer.   If the necessity had not arisen for the Labour Exchange organisation to go beyond its normal functions and attempt to persuade employers to surrender their skilled men to the armament firms, the voice of the outside manufacturer might have remained unheard.   He had not been consulted in October on the general question that has been stated above, though it was a question which concerned him nearly, and to which he might be expected to return an answer different from that of the armament firms who advised the War Office.   Now, however, when the Board of Trade officials came to him on their mission in the first weeks of 1915, it was soon brought home to them that a scheme which involved disorganising his establishment and depleting it of skilled men for the equipment and expansion of other private factories, would not be accepted without examination or demur   The most important result of the canvass was, not the somewhat meagre numbers of men released for transfer, but the opportunity it gave to the employer of claiming, as an alternative, that he should be allowed to tender for direct armament contracts.

This suggestion occurs, as early as 7 January, in a preliminary report to the Board of Trade from the Divisional Officer of the N.W. Division.   Enquiries in his district had shown that a very large number of textile engineers were making shell cases, and other firms were sub-contracting for machinery needed for Government work. Apart from this reason against parting with their men, the employers objected to surrendering them to private firms like Armstrong's and Vickers.   The writer suggested that some engineering works, for instance in Manchester, should be allowed to contract for some preparatory processes that were then done by the armament firms. Otherwise they would refuse to release their men

In London, where visits to 2,619 firms had yielded by 23 January no more than 225 men for transfer, seven firms offered to take armament work.

In South Wales, again, a deputation of the Welsh Engineers and Founders' Association, received at Cardiff on 13 January, explained that the five firms they represented were already engaged on sub-contracts for metal work and ship-repairing for the Government, and were also doing work on which other sub-contractors depended.   They had lost men through enlistment and the attraction of higher wages offered elsewhere.   In order to keep the men still left to them and avoid closing down, they asked for an opportunity of taking Government contracts themselves, arguing that their men would be bette

off, even on lower wages, if they were not transferred to a distance
from their homes.

These are only a few instances out of many. Such claims were
supported by the strong argument that the ramifications of sub-
contracting were so intricate as to make it hardly possible to pick out
men from any given engineering establishment without dislocating work
that was connected. at however many removes, with some contract
for Government. Behind the employers' opposition, moreover, lay a
lively jealousy of the armament firms, who were generally believed
to squeeze their sub-contractors, and had already, by the high wages
which their large profits enabled them to offer, robbed the outside
engineering industry of many of its skilled men. The employer who
had suffered in either of these ways was not too ready to part with
more of his hands to swell still further the dividends of private
companies.

The Board of Trade was impressed by these considerations. Sir
H. Llewellyn Smith, reviewing the results of the canvass of employers
n the first fortnight of January, wrote[1] :—

> " The effort to divert labour from ordinary engineering
> work to armament work by persuading employers voluntarily
> to release workmen to be transferred to armament firms has been
> much less productive " (than the measures taken to recruit
> unemployed labour), " and it is feared that not much more can
> be expected under this head.
>
> " The difficulties encountered are many. A very large
> number of engineering firms are doing sub-contracting work for
> armament firms or are making machinery for armament work ;
> many others think that they ought to have Government
> contracts or sub-contracts, and express a strong preference for
> spreading the work as a mode of increasing the amount of labour
> employed for armament purposes, as compared with the
> diversion of their work-people to earn high profits for Armstrong
> or Vickers. . . .
>
> " I have therefore been led to the conclusion that, if a large
> amount of labour in addition to what can be obtained from
> among the unemployed British and Belgian workpeople is
> required for armament purposes, it is necessary in the first place
> to ascertain precisely how much additional work can be devolved
> on other engineering firms by the armament firms, or given to
> them direct, and to distribute this work judiciously so as to take
> advantage to the fullest extent of the plant and labour available.
>
> " While there are obvious limitations to the extent to which
> this method can be applied, it is evident that, so far as it is found
> practicable to adopt it, it presents many economic advantages
> over the alternative method of transferring the workmen, both
> because it makes additional premises and plant, as well as

---

[1] *Supply of Armament Labour, Preliminary Note* (23/1/15). HIST. REC.
R/180/8.

additional labour, available for Government purposes, and because it does not give rise to the housing and other difficulties which have already been encountered in the case of the transference of labour to Barrow."

Thus, in the reaction of the employers against the diversion of their labour to armament firms, emerged the demand for the opposite policy of spreading direct munitions contracts over a wider field. Through stages which will be traced in the following chapters, the movement led to results of the greatest importance. Alongside of the established system of armament production, which went on as before, independent local organisations were formed by the enthusiasm and enterprise of smaller engineering firms all over the country. First came the Co-operative Group ; later, the National Factory. At the end of March, Mr. Booth's Committee, appointed by Lord Kitchener, took up the central direction of this work, and itself developed, in the course of the following three months, into the Ministry of Munitions.

If the original impetus came from the employers, the merit of seeing the possibilities of the movement, of encouraging it, and of preparing the way for its progress in the first quarter of 1915, belongs solely to the Board of Trade. During those months all the active sympathy and support which the employers received from the Government came from this Department, working through the Labour Exchange organisation and through such influence as it was able to exercise upon the War Office. In the history of the War, this action will rank high among the services which the Board of Trade has rendered to the country.

II. Survey of Engineering Firms Proposed by the Board of Trade.

After no more than a fortnight's experience, it would have been imprudent to abandon the campaign for the diversion of labour and to adopt exclusively the alternative policy of spreading contracts, even if the War Office could have been induced to change its attitude. Divergent as the two methods were, the Board of Trade wisely pursued both concurrently. The measures taken to facilitate the transfer of labour have already been reviewed.[1] Such obstacles as legislation could remove were dealt with by the Defence of the Realm (Amendment) No. 2 Act. In the other direction, the Department at once set to work to discover what actual resources could be turned to account on the lines of the employers' demand. This promptitude saved three months which would otherwise, for these purposes, have been lost.

Any such action, of course, required the concurrence of the Master-General of the Ordnance. It happened that a suitable mode of procedure was already in working order. Co-operation had been established between the Army Contracts department and the Board of Trade as early as September, 1914. It had arisen out of the duty of the Board to maintain employment so far as possible during the War ; but, owing to the serious shortage of supplies occurring in several classes

---

[1] Part II., Chap. J.

of stores (other than destructive munitions), the Board had also been asked to undertake the discovery of new firms capable of making the articles required, and the inspection of such firms in order to ascertain their status and capacity before they were included in the War Office lists.[1] What was now required was an extension of this system to firms which might offer to undertake armament work.

On 9 January, two representatives of the Board of Trade interviewed the Master-General of the Ordnance, and suggested that firms should be informed through the Labour Exchange organisation that requests on their part for contracts which they could undertake would be considered by the War Office. The Master-General of the Ordnance gave his sanction, and it was agreed that instructions in this sense should be issued to Divisional Officers, after reference to him.[2]

Action was immediately taken on this agreement. On 12 January, a letter was sent to the N.W. Divisional Officer, who was to hold a meeting of engineering employers at Manchester on the following day. This letter (which was sanctioned by the Master-General of the Ordnance) stated that the War Office could not, of course, promise contracts until they knew the capabilities of the firms. Some work was of too technical a character, and for this work men must be obtained for the armament firms and the Arsenal. If, however, employers would release their men generously, the War Office would consider requests for direct contracts or sub-contracts. It was left to the employers to tender. The Government would probably not subsidise firms to enable them to manufacture new commodities. If they wished to tender, they would have to provide the machinery.[3]

On 14 January, Mr Rey, Mr. Wolff, and Mr. Davison of the Board of Trade agreed in recommending that the Board should undertake a survey of the engineering trade.[4] It was proposed that the War Office should furnish a brief description of stores which were needed and which could be made by inexperienced firms. With this description managers of Labour Exchanges could call on firms in their districts with a form of report containing two questions : (a) whether the firm was now, directly or indirectly, engaged on Government work ; and (b) whether it was prepared to do such work or to increase the amount it was already doing. The names of firms who replied " Yes " to question (b) would then be sent to the War Office, which could examine their capabilities and pass on the names of any that proved suitable to the armament firms with a view to sub-contracts. From firms which answered " No," the Board of Trade would then be free to take men (if they had the necessary powers) with or without the employers' consent. The proposed survey would thus prepare the way both for spreading contracts and for transferring men compulsorily, if they could be authorised to do so.

This plan was submitted by a representative of the Board to the Master-General of the Ordnance and the Director of Army Contracts

---

[1] About 11,000 firms were inspected through the Labour Exchange organisation in the first 18 months of the War.

[2] L.E. 1965/15.   [3] L.E. 1965/40.   [4] L.E. 1965/30.

at an interview on 18 January. A series of questions to be put to likely firms was drawn up. In view of the great variety and complication of specifications, it was considered that the best way to estimate the capacity of a firm was to obtain information as to its machinery. The War Office, accordingly, was to furnish a list (A) of the machines, gauges, etc., that would be required for the manufacture of the stores. They were also to provide a list (B) of articles that could be made in ordinary engineering works. These arrangements were confirmed on the following day by the Master-General of the Ordnance' Committee on Armaments, and Messrs. Vickers, who were represented on that Committee, were requested to prepare the list of machinery.[1] The questionnaire, drawn up by Mr. Beveridge for the inspectors' report, was printed.[2] A third list (C) of classes of labour was prepared, to accompany the questionnaire. The inspector was to report what numbers of men of each class were employed by the firm, and to what extent they were engaged on private work.

The Board of Trade had completed its arrangements for the survey by 26 January. The actual work, however, could not be put in hand until the lists of articles and of machines were received from the War Office. This occasioned a delay of some weeks.

Meanwhile, on 26 January, Mr. Beveridge wrote on this subject to the Secretary of the Engineering Employers' Federation, who asked that, as regards the federated firms, the Federation should be allowed to send out the enquiry. A circular was accordingly drawn up, which stated that the enquiry was directed to the discovery of—

"(1) Any additional firms whose machinery is suitable for the manufacture of certain armaments or parts of them ;

"(2) Any firms already engaged on work of this character, but capable of undertaking further orders, if all their private work could be set aside ;

"(3) The number of workpeople belonging to the classes set out in List C but not at present engaged on Government work."

The circular continued :—

"It must be understood that this enquiry in no way indicates that your firm will receive a Government contract or sub-contract, or even an opportunity of tendering for specific articles. It must be regarded as a preliminary to any further enquiries by the Board of Trade which may be necessary in order to ascertain the capacity of your firm for work connected with armaments in the event of the possible future needs of the Government "

When the draft circular was submitted to the Federation for approval, they took objection to the absence of any specific informa-

---

[1] L.E. 1965/49. It was also decided to compile a list of War Office contractors and sub-contractors, to the third degree. The Board of Trade representatives, however, thought it would be impossible to make a comprehensive list and that other measures for surveying industry would make such a list superfluous.

[2] See Appendix I. Owing to the change of plan described below, this form was never issued.

tion as to the types of contract that might be offered by the War Office. They declined to issue the circular, and the matter dropped.[1]

Owing to the adoption of another method presently to be described, the original plan of the Board of Trade was not carried out. It was arranged instead that the Home Office should undertake a Census of Machinery.[2] This was conducted in March by the Factory Inspectors, and took some three weeks. The results were communicated to the War Office in reports, the form of which is given in Appendix II.

III. Exhibitions of Samples at Labour Exchanges.

While the Board of Trade was waiting for the War Office to supply the lists of articles and machines required for the survey, another method of approaching the engineering firms was suggested on 29 January by the Divisional Officer of the N.W. Division. He proposed that sample articles should be exhibited in important centres, such as Manchester, Sheffield, Glasgow, and Birmingham. Employers should be invited to inspect them and to tender for any articles they thought they could make, stating a price, the quantity they could offer, and the time of delivery.

By a coincidence, a similar plan had just been adopted independently by the War Office.[3] As a consequence of the canvass of employers early in January, the Master-General of the Ordnance Contracts Branch had begun to receive offers from firms who described the machinery they possessed and asked for specifications and drawings of any work that could be done on their machines. On 26 January, it was agreed between the Director of Artillery and Mr. Hanson that the best procedure would be that representatives of such firms should see specimens of ammunition in the Inspection Department at Woolwich, and that then, if they considered themselves able to manufacture any particular type, their works and plant should be inspected. The Chief Inspector, Woolwich, reported that he could arrange for the visits to Woolwich, but could not provide a staff to undertake the inspection. It was, accordingly, decided on 18 February that Major-General Mahon, of the Master-General of the Ordnance staff, should be responsible for the inspection, and this procedure continued in being till May.

These arrangements appear to have been initiated without consulting the Board of Trade. The Board, however, took up their Divisional Officer's suggestion, as providing a better method of testing the possibilities than their original plans for the survey.

On 9 February, Mr. Davison interviewed Major-General Mahon, who welcomed the proposal that samples should be displayed in Liverpool, Manchester, Glasgow, Leeds, Coventry, Sheffield, Birmingham

---

[1] L.E. 1965/62A.

[2] In pursuance of the following conclusion of a Conference of Ministers held on 5 March, 1915 : " The Home Office to obtain information as to the number of machines at present available for the production of various kinds of war material, the number lying idle, and the present rate of production compared with the maximum." HIST. REC./R 170/22.

[3] See 94/GEN. No /17.

and London. He agreed that, except in the case of Liverpool,[1] the
local arrangements should be made by the Divisional Officers. He also
agreed that the Board of Trade officials, guided by the list of machines
which had been now supplied by Messrs. Vickers, should inspect all
suitable firms and report to the War Office. It was to be made clear
to the firms that they were to judge their capacity for armament work
only on the basis of their existing plant and labour. Major-General
Mahon undertook to edit the list of machines, and to obtain from the
armament firms information as to the articles of which they stood most
in need at any time, so as to be able to put any suitable firms discovered
by the Board of Trade into communication with the main contractors.[2]

Preliminary instructions were issued on 24 February by the Board
of Trade in a circular to Divisional Officers,[3] the terms of which
were agreed with Major-General Mahon. As soon as these officers
should be informed that all the samples were ready for exhibition, they
were to issue to employers in their Division a letter (a copy of which
was enclosed) inviting them to examine the samples and accompanying
specifications. Firms who thought they could undertake any of the
work were to inform the Divisional Officer what stage or stages of work
they contemplated, and state the number and class of machines they
had at their disposal. The circular also enclosed two memoranda,
drawn up by Major-General Mahon, on plant required for the manufacture of (1) Steel Shells, (2) Simple Fuses. These were for the guidance
of the Board of Trade officials, who were to inspect the works of such
firms as should offer to tender. The inspectors' reports were to be
made for the War Office on the form given in Appendix III.

When the samples had been obtained, the exhibitions were opened
on 10 March by the Labour Exchanges in London, Birmingham,
Coventry, Leeds, Sheffield, Manchester, Liverpool, Newcastle and
Glasgow. A very large number of invitations were issued, and the
response was good. The articles exhibited were—(1) *Shells*: 13-pdr.,
15-pdr., 18-pdr., 4·5-inch ; (2) *Fuses*: No. 100.

A general review of the results obtained in the first fortnight
during which the exhibitions were open was given in a report by
Mr. Davison on 25 March.

(*a*) A certain number of firms had been discovered who were
completely unable to assist in the manufacture of shells, although they
might be employing classes of labour which were urgently required by
the armament firms. It was suggested that it should now be possible
to attempt to persuade these firms to release a certain proportion of
this labour.

(*b*) A considerable number of firms were unable to undertake the
manufacture of shells, but willing to assist in making other articles
required by the War Office. Their offers were reported to the War
Office.

---

[1] At Liverpool, Major-General Mahon specially suggested that the samples
should be exhibited at Mr. E. C. Given's, the Civic Service League, 17, Water Stree .
[2] Note by Mr. Davison (9/2/15). HIST. REC./R/170/17.
[3] C.O. Circ. 1741 (L.E. 1965/59).

(c) In all parts of the country firms were found who were willing and anxious to make shells or parts of them. Some of these firms had, after seeing the samples, put themselves into direct communication with the armament firms, with the result that sub-contracts for machining work or other processes were placed with them. Cases of this character were reported from Yorkshire.

(d) A small number of firms offered to undertake the manufacture of the complete shell. Reports on these firms were submitted to the War Office.[1]

By May the Board of Trade Survey had covered over 300 firms. It was believed that, while it included a considerable number of shops which, upon inspection, proved useless, it probably took in nearly every firm not already engaged in shell-making, which could without much difficulty be wholly or partially converted to the purpose.[2]

IV. The Co-operative Group for Munitions Manufacture.

What proved to be by far the most important outcome of these activities was the formation of co-operative groups of manufacturers for munitions production. This type of local organisation provided scope for those firms which were not equipped for making complete stores, but at the same time wished to work independently rather than as sub-contractors to the armament firms.

The plan of grouping together small firms which were separately incapable of undertaking a contract for complete articles was not novel. Under the auspices of the Board of Trade, it had been adopted in the autumn of 1914 in the case of certain Army stores other than destructive munitions, and first of all in the saddlery trade. At suitable centres representatives of firms were invited to meetings at which a Board of Trade officer gave information and exhibited samples. Committees were elected to organise the groups, to undertake contracts on their behalf, to purchase and distribute materials, and to collect the weekly output. In the saddlery trade ten such groups were formed.

It has already been mentioned that the application of this system to armament work had been considered in October, 1914, when the Cabinet mission reported on the French organisation.[3] The following is a summary of the information supplied to the British representatives at Paris by General Deville.

Soon after the outbreak of the War,[4] when M. Millerand was Minister of War, the Government had divided France into districts and had conferred with the heads of private engineering establishments (maîtres de forges) in each district. They had put selected employers at the head of each group for the purpose of directing engineering

---

[1] Mr. Davison's report also mentioned the formation of a Co-operative Group at Leicester, which will be described below. L.E. 1965/113A. HIST. REC./R/170/18.

[2] M.C. 428.   [3] See Part I.

[4] The meetings at which these arrangements were made actually took place at Bordeaux on 30 September and 7 and 8 October (Report to the Senate of the Commission on Purchases, No. 284, 1916, p. 8).

energy and plant into the most necessary channels. By this means many private works, which in peace time were producing other things, e.g., automobiles, were now producing ammunition. There had been great difficulty in getting enough skilled workmen, since, when the War began, mechanics specially skilled in the manufacture of munitions had been called up along with the rest ; but they had recalled many of those skilled men. As a result of this policy, munitions were now (October) being turned out by some private firms, and the production would rapidly increase.

General Deville thought that private enterprise might be similarly used for the manufacture of artillery, though some parts of a gun required such delicate adjustment that only a specially trained man could make them. Other parts could be made in private engineering works. If we began now (October) he thought we ought to begin to turn out guns by April, 1915, and the production, once begun, should increase. He said, further, that England had such an immense number of splendidly equipped engineering works, with every variety of machines, plant, and tools, that our situation was, for purposes of rapidly increasing supplies, better than that of France.[1]

As has already been stated, the project of adopting the system in this country was opposed by the expert advisers of the War Office It accordingly remained in abeyance until the end of 1914, when the failure of the chief contractors to redeem their promises again brought to the front the need for further measures to increase output.

Early in January, 1915, the suggestion was revived by Mr. Dumas, the works manager of the British Thomson-Houston Company at Rugby. When the French organisation was first set on foot, Mr. Dumas had assisted a representative of the French branch of his Company in getting together machine tools for the manufacture of the 75 mm. shell. As he now took an active part in promoting at Leicester the first group formed in England for co-operative shell manufacture, through this personal link the system in this country is directly affiliated to the French model.

V.   The Formation at Leicester of the First Co-operative Group.

The movement at Leicester dates from 8 January, 1915, when Mr. P. Handley, manager of the local Labour Exchange, attended a meeting of the Leicester Association of Engineering Employers in

---

[1] The above summary is based on an extract from Lord Reading's Diary and the Attorney-General's Note on the visit to France, which were read to the Munitions of War Committee by Mr. Lloyd George at the first meeting on 12 April, 1915 (M.C.1). A memorandum (dated 15 June, 1915), on the Organisation in France for the Production of Munitions, gives the following additional details. The original number of groups was 9 ; by 15 June, 1915, it had been increased to 15. In most cases the Directors of the groups took charge of the total orders allotted to the locality and divided them amongst sub-contractors. Paris was treated differently, individual contracts being placed with large automobile and engineering firms. Of these, 140 contracted for shell, 240 for gaines.

The Government sent a mission to France in April, 1915, to investigate the French system and its results. A summary of the report by Mr. E. W. Moir is given in Appendix IV.

order to put before them the fresh demand for 30,000 skilled men to be drafted to the armament firms.[1]

Mr. Handley was met by the objection that representatives of armament firms had been in the district as recently as the day before, calling upon engineering employers, making notes of their plant, and inviting them to accept sub-contracts. Many of the firms represented at the meeting had already received large contracts for munitions, and had successfully manufactured and delivered the articles. Among other armament firms who in this way had passed on orders to Leicester, Messrs. Armstrong, Messrs. Vickers, and Coventry Ordnance were mentioned.

Every one of the members present at the meeting had machinery standing idle and was in urgent need of more men to deal with work in hand, the bulk of which was manufacture of boot and hosiery machinery, needle-making machines, and motors, etc, for the Government. It was, in fact, estimated that the engineers of the district were engaged from 80 per cent. to 90 per cent. of their time on manufacture urgently needed for war purposes.

In the course of the discussion, Mr. Dumas described his connection with the French organisation, and pointed out that a group of manufacturers in Paris were at that moment producing large numbers of shell for the French Government. His own company were making shells at their Willesden factory for one of the armament firms, and were preparing to make 4·7-in. shell for the Admiralty at Rugby.

Other speakers also argued that it would be wasteful to remove men and leave the plant idle, while the men would be working under new conditions and on strange machines. The firms could, by readjustment, working overtime, and so on, get some additional volume of work out of their existing staff. It was considered that the best policy would be to distribute the manufacture of Government stores as widely as possible, both from the point of view of safety from raid, and also because men working in familiar surroundings would give a larger and better output.

The meeting passed the following resolution :—

" That the members of this Association, having heard and discussed the request for men by Mr. P. Handley (Board of Trade) for munition purposes, are of opinion that, rather than more men should be taken from this district to work for firms doing Government work, the Government would receive greater benefit by utilising to its fullest extent the facilities already existing in the district, to the extent, if necessary, of arranging for men who have left the district to join His Majesty's forces to return to the engineering works where they were formerly employed."

---

[1] Mr. Handley's Report.   L.E. 1965/76.

On 3 February, Mr. Handley reported further[1] that the Association had sent its President and Secretary to offer its services in any way in which it could be useful, such as advising what classes of work could be undertaken in the district, arranging the distribution of orders, or endeavouring " to organise some scheme whereby the efforts of individual firms could be combined and co-ordinated so as to produce the most satisfactory results." Many members were confident of their ability to undertake almost any class of engineering work. It was anticipated that one of the greatest difficulties would be the inspection of parts at different stages of manufacture ; but it was felt that, in so wide an area as this, inspection could be arranged for, if the Government would fully explain its requirements. The local Association considered that, as a body, they could accept such large contracts as to make it worth while for the War Office to treat with them separately ; while action through the general Federation would entail delay. They proposed that the War Office and Admiralty should send a representative to come to some definite understanding with them. Mr. Handley endorsed this proposal and urged that the Board of Trade should make strong representations to the Departments concerned.

The Divisional Officer, in forwarding this report, remarked that as he understood, Messrs. Vickers' action in going to Leicester to recruit men had " set the local employers ablaze."

The expedient of creating groups for shell-making was also definitely put forward by Mr. Passmore, the Divisional Officer for the Yorkshire and East Midlands Division, in a letter to Mr. Davison on 1 March. Referring to the arrangements then being made for the exhibition of samples and subsequent inspection of firms, Mr. Passmore wrote :— " I gather from information I have received from some managers in engineering centres that many of the small firms will certainly not possess the necessary hydraulic presses. I would, therefore, suggest that some arrangement similar to the grouping arrangement for saddlery might be considered. It would be necessary, of course, for each group to contain at least one firm possessing the necessary powerful hydraulic press. The difficulty would probably arise with the smaller firms in regard to the light hydraulic press (for ' nosing ' the shell body). From what managers in engineering centres tell me, some sort of grouping arrangement will probably be necessary in order to secure the maximum output from the smaller firms."

Mr. Davison replied on 2 March that Major-General Mahon, whom he had consulted on this proposal, saw no objection to the principles involved in such groupings.[2]

On 5 March, Mr. Passmore conferred with four managers of Exchanges in large engineering centres. It was agreed by those present that the whole division did not contain more than six or seven firms possessing the powerful hydraulic presses needed for making shell bodies. If it should be found that these firms were not fully

---

[1] L.E. 1965/76.   [2] L.E. 1965/100.

occupied on Government work, Mr. Passmore suggested that the War Office should give them separate direct contracts for shell bodies. The War Office would thus control the supply of rough shell, which they could then distribute to the smaller firms. These should be organised to do the subsequent processes in groups, each containing one firm with light hydraulic presses.

Mr. Davison informed Mr. Passmore on 10 March that he did not personally think it likely that the War Office would be willing to place one set of contracts with large firms capable of forging shells, and another set of contracts with a sufficient number of small firms for the finishing operations. His own impression was that an attempt should be made to arrange groups which could tender to the War Office for the complete article. The question, however, could be considered later, when offers came in as a result of the exhibitions of samples.

These exhibitions, coinciding with the passing of the Defence of the Realm (Amendment) No. 2 Act in March, gave a fresh impetus to the movement.

At Leicester, the scheme was definitely set on foot at a meeting of engineering employers summoned for 23 March by the Leicester Association of Engineering Employers, acting in co-operation with the local Board of Trade officials. The Central Office of Labour Exchanges was represented by Mr. Davison. The chair was taken by Mr. J. A. Keay, then President of the Association. To his efforts, coupled with those of Mr. Dumas and Mr. Handley, and energetically supported by Mr. Booth, who was then just taking up his new work at the War Office, the successful inauguration of the scheme was chiefly due. As will be seen later, the Master-General of the Ordnance department was at this moment inclined to go back upon the sanction it had given to the principle of co-operative schemes and to revert to the older policy of using the inexperienced firms only as sub-contractors. Mr. Booth, however, procured that Major-General Mahon, who was then engaged in a propaganda for the transfer of skilled men to armament firms, should be present at the meeting. Representatives of some ninety-four firms attended.

Mr. Handley suggested the formation of a group, though he explained that the Board of Trade had not been consulted as to this proposal. He submitted a scheme of co-operation which would embrace every process in the manufacture of certain types of shell, and proposed the election of a Board of Control.

Major-General Mahon said that the War Office intended to support in every way the existing armament firms and other firms which were producing, or could produce, shells. At the same time, the War Office would try to utilise any further manufacturing power that could be found. If the Leicester firms formed a group, they would have to rely on themselves for labour and materials, and for supervision, which, he thought, could not be provided from Woolwich or elsewhere. He thought the War Office would not refuse a small output, provided that no existing plant, material, or men were interfered with. The War Office would appoint an inspector.

The meeting anticipated no difficulty with regard to raw material. Forgings could be produced locally, and little extra plant was needed. It was estimated that about 500 shells, rising to 1,000, could be produced weekly. It was resolved to proceed with the scheme.

A deputation from the new group submitted their proposals to the War Office on 30 March and received their first order for a weekly output of 1,000 4·5-inch shell.

The further developments of the undertaking belong to another chapter in this History. Here it may be noted that the co-operative schemes later set on foot at Hull, Bradford, Leeds, and other northern towns were influenced by the Leicester model. Representatives from these places came to Leicester, and either attended meetings of the Board of Control or were furnished with information.

VI. Change of Policy at the War Office.

The type of local organisation which was first brought into being at Leicester provided a channel for much enthusiasm and energy, which, if this outlet had been denied, would have been chilled and discouraged. The movement was by no means confined to Leicester. After the exhibitions of samples and the passing of the Defence of the Realm (Amendment) No. 2 Act, offers of personal services or of buildings and plant flowed in to the War Office or to the Chancellor of the Exchequer from manufacturers, all over the country, who were eager to take their part.

At this critical moment, on the eve of the decisive meeting at Leicester on 23 March, the Board of Trade suddenly discovered that the attitude of the War Office towards the whole policy had become unsympathetic and even hostile. As the foregoing pages have shown, the original arrangements for the survey and exhibitions had been made in collaboration with Major-General Mahon, whom the Master-General of the Ordnance had designated as the proper authority to sanction the Board's proposals. But on 18 March, when the arrangements for the Leicester meeting were in train, and a representative of the Board requested the War Office to send an expert to attend it, an unexpected check was encountered. Mr. Davison reported his interview with the Director of Artillery as follows[1] :—

> " General Guthrie Smith, Director of Artillery, stated that he was unwilling to send any representatives to Leicester or to any other place where negotiations might be on foot. His reason for this attitude was that it had recently been decided to place no additional orders with any firms for the manufacture of shells until the complete labour requirements of the main armament factories had been met.

> " It was explained that the War Office had originally arranged for this exhibition in order to discover firms which might be suitable to undertake orders. In answer to this, General Guthrie Smith admitted that there had been a recent

---

[1] Memorandum by Mr. Davison (19 March, 1915). L.E. 1965/113A.

change of policy in this respect. The armament firms had undertaken contracts very largely in excess of what they could fulfil. The Government had purchased for them large increases of plant, and it was not intended to place any further orders until labour requirements had been met.

" It was pointed out that the refusal to place any further o ders would not necessarily secure transfer of labour to the armament factories, and that a large amount of productive capacity would thereby be wasted. General Guthrie Smith then stated that, if suitable firms were found and no orders were available for them, it would be possible for the Government to close the works and remove the labour to other districts.

" It is suggested," Mr. Davison continued, " that such a result could hardly be justified in view of the manner in which employers have been approached by the Board of Trade in this matter. It would, moreover, differentiate unfairly between those firms which had showed themselves capable of undertaking orders and other firms which, though not possessing the necessary plant, might still possess the classes of labour required.

" It seems to be necessary at this stage to request the War Office to make no final decision as to the placing of further orders with non-armament firms. If they are unable to place fresh orders, it should still be possible to transfer some of their unfulfilled orders from the main armament firms to any other groups of firms or individual firms who may be able to undertake the manufacture. It also seems to be very desirable that some representative of the War Office should attend the Leicester meeting.

" It should be added that Major-General Mahon has asked the main armament firms to communicate to him the stages of work on shells which they are now in a position to sub-let to non-armament firms which may be found to be suitable as a result of our survey. Experience indicates that such sub-contracts will not easily be arranged with the main contractors without strong action on the part of the War Office. General Guthrie Smith's attitude in this aspect of the case was that he would not be opposed to sub-contracts, but that the transfer of labour to the armament firms was paramount."

The above report was forwarded to the President of the Board of Trade with a strongly worded minute by Sir H. Llewellyn Smith, pointing out that the action of the War Office was " calculated to embarrass us in fulfilling the Cabinet mandate as to armament workers." The President wrote :—" We cannot stop this now, even if we cannot command their expert to go down."

Mr. Davison wrote to Mr. Scott at the Northampton Labour Exchange that he was hoping to attend the Leicester meeting, but that the attitude of the War Office was far from encouraging. " They are now inclined to change their policy and revert to the original idea of removing labour from engineering firms to the main armament contractors. This would, of course, be a very unfortunate consequence of the exhibition of samples which was arranged at the War Office's request, but it shows we must be very careful to give employers no undue encouragement. The War Office are not opposed to sub-contracts being arranged with the main armament firms, but here the difficulty lies in the reluctance of the main armament firms to deal with other manufacturers."[1]

At this moment it seemed as if all chances of further progress were endangered. To promote schemes for spreading armament contracts did not properly fall within the functions of the Labour Exchange organisation. To persist in face of opposition from the Department primarily concerned would have been impossible. Nor was the Central Office of the Labour Exchanges in a position to co-ordinate and direct the efforts of local groups of manufacturers in work of a type which could not be done without a large amount of technical information and assistance.

Much of the ground that had been won by the Board of Trade might now have been lost, had not the direction of the movement been taken in hand with freshness and energy by a new body, which was not only capable of regarding its possibilities with a sympathetic outlook, but at the same time had an official footing inside the War Office. The situation was saved by Mr. Booth and the Armaments Output Committee. It was Mr. Booth who secured the attendance of Major-General Mahon at the Leicester meeting, and carried the negotiations for the first contract with the new group to a successful conclusion.

---

[1] L.E. 1965/110A.

CHAPTER II.

THE ARMAMENTS OUTPUT COMMITTEE.

I. Appointment of the Armaments Output Committee.

The Armaments Output Committee was appointed by Lord Kitchener on 31 March, 1915. The official announcement, which appeared in the Press on 7 April, was as follows :—

" The Secretary to the War Office announces that Lord Kitchener has appointed a Committee to take the necessary steps to provide such additional labour as may be required to secure that the supply of munitions of war shall be sufficient to meet all requirements.

" Communications in regard to this subject should be addressed to

GEORGE M. BOOTH, Esq.,

War Office, S.W."

The names of the members of the Committee were communicated to the House of Commons on 20 April[1] :

Field-Marshal the Earl Kitchener, Secretary of State for War.

Major-General Sir Stanley B. von Donop, M.G.O.

Sir Herbert A. Walker, Chairman of the Railway Executive Committee.

Sir Algernon Firth, President of the Associated Chambers of Commerce.

George M. Booth, Esq.

Allan M. Smith, Esq., Secretary of the Engineering Employers' Federation.

The appointment of this Committee marks the beginning of a central organisation which, in the course of the next two months, was to develop into the nucleus of a Department of State, and finally to be detached from the War Office. The astonishing rapidity of this development, the energy with which the Committee took up, from week to week, and almost from day to day, one new aspect after another of the whole problem of munitions supply, have obscured the fact that the original conception of its scope and functions was, in comparison, extremely narrow. Even at the time, interested persons who had followed the debates on the Defence of the Realm (Amendment) No. 2 Act, or were cognisant of the propaganda carried on by the Board of

---

[1] *Parliamentary Debates* (1915), *H. of C.*, LXXI., 207.

Trade through the sample exhibitions, read with a shock of surprise on 7 April that a Committee was appointed, not to organise the reserve capacity of the Engineering industry, but " to provide such additional labour as may be required " to secure a sufficient output of munitions of war.   The surprise was all the greater among those who knew that the labour in question was labour for the Royal Factories and armament firms, and for them only.   To one who looks back on these first beginnings in the light of the enormous achievement which they heralded, the contrast between what the Committee did and what it was commissioned to do is even more striking.   In order to explain why the terms of reference were so narrow, it is necessary to review the situation which existed when the appointment was first considered in the middle of March.

The new Defence of the Realm Act had become law on 16 March. It has been shown how the original intention of this measure had been to remove certain obstacles to the diversion of labour from commercial to armament work, and so to further the programme dictated by the October policy of the War Office.[1]   In the mind of the Government, this intention had been in some degree transformed and enlarged, so that the measure, during its passage through Parliament, had been described as aiming at a general redistribution of engineering resources. It had been announced that the powers obtained were to be administered through a " Central Committee " at the War Office, and that manufacturers were to be taken into consultation.   Otherwise, the methods to be employed had been left undefined.

This indefiniteness of plan is readily accounted for by a comparison of the dates of the events described in the last chapter.   When the Bill was introduced on 9 March, the pioneer work which the Board of Trade had been carrying on for two months was just on the point of coming to maturity.   The exhibitions of samples were not opened till the following day, and no one could yet estimate either the number of offers that would be made in response, or the value of those offers in terms of actual manufacturing power.   The report on the first results of inspection came forward a fortnight later, on 25 March.   If the Bill could have been delayed till then, it would have been possible at least to indicate a programme of action.   Incidentally, also, the Board of Trade could have been given credit for having opened up the new pathway.   As it was, no reference was made in the debates to this preliminary work, and the unfortunate impression was left on the minds of the House and of the general public that the Government had done nothing towards the organisation of fresh resources—an impression which could not afterwards be removed.

Thus it was not until the last days of March that it became clear what opportunities for immediate action lay before the proposed central committee.   The inspection of works by Board of Trade officials then resulted in a rough classification of firms into four groups. Two of these groups could be fitted into the established system.   The small number of new firms who could take direct orders for complete

---

[1] See Part II., Chap. III

stores could be dealt with by the Contracts department in the ordinary course. The larger number who were willing to become sub-contractors could be put into touch with the armament firms. There remained two classes whose requirements lay outside the field of any existing routine.

In the first place, there were the manufacturers who wished to form independent Co-operative Groups in imitation of Leicester. The movement was young and vigorous ; but at this moment it had received a severe check from the War Office.

In the second place, a large number of manufacturers, stimulated by Mr. Lloyd George's speech on 9 March, and by the exhibitions of samples, were offering to place their buildings, plant and personal services at the disposal of the Government. These offers naturally differed widely in value, and needed to be carefully sifted and followed up by inquiry before they could be either turned to account or declined. The Board of Trade inspectors had already found a certain residuum of works unsuitable for munitions production. These it was proposed to treat on the lines of the new Act by transferring their labour, and perhaps also their machines, to more convenient establishments. The power was vested in the Army Council, and could only be administered through an executive committee.

It was to supplement the normal activities of the Contracts department by dealing with these two classes of firms, that the services of the Armaments Output Committee were required. Its work thus falls into line with both the alternative policies pursued by the Board of Trade—the diversion of labour from unsuitable establishments, and the spreading of contracts by means of co-operative groups. This duality of function is still reflected in the structure of the Ministry, which has always had a Labour department, alongside of the departments of Supply.

Such being the two-fold programme marked out for the new Committee by the earlier course of events, it remains to account for the terms of reference being limited exclusively to one branch of it—the supply of additional labour. The explanation lies in the change of policy at the War Office mentioned in the last chapter. This occurred exactly at the moment when the appointment of the Committee first came under consideration. The interview at which the Director of Artillery explained to Mr. Davison that the War Office still adhered to the policy of October, and was not disposed to go further with co-operative schemes, took place on 18 March, two days after the new Act became law. The Committee was not formed till 31 March ; but Mr. Booth received his first commission from Lord Kitchener on March 18 or 19. The work entrusted to him was the recruiting of labour from engineering shops in London for the Arsenal and for Messrs. Vickers' works at Erith and Crayford. Similar instructions were given at the same time to Sir Percy Girouard to find labour for Messrs. Armstrong in the Newcastle district. The intention of the military authorities at this moment was, in fact, to use the powers just obtained precisely for the purpose that had been in view when it was first proposed to obtain them, namely, the reinforcement of the armament firms at the expense of commercial employment.[1] The terms of reference to the Committee reflect this intention, though, by the time they were made public on 7 April, the Committee had already enlarged its scope to include the other, and much wider, field of activity.

The present chapter will cover only the history of the three weeks from 18 March to 8 April, and of the measures projected in this formative stage. At the beginning of the period, the older policy held the field at the War Office ; by the end of it the Committee had broken free and was launching out upon a campaign of local organisation.

II.   Mr. Booth's London Enquiry.[2]

Mr. Booth had been in touch with the War Office since the previous autumn, when he had been called in as an expert adviser to the department of the Director of Army Contracts.   He undertook his new work of finding labour, which might be drafted from London workshops to Woolwich, Crayford and Erith, at the personal request of Lord Kitchener.   On 19 March, Mr. Runciman gave instructions that Mr. Booth should receive all necessary information from the Divisional Officers, and that the Home Office should be asked to give similar help through the Factory Inspectors.   On 20 March, Mr. Booth had a long interview with Mr. Beveridge at the Board of Trade, and formed his plan of campaign.

On the same day, in collaboration with the Master-General of the Ordnance and Mr. Runciman, he revised a draft letter to be signed by Lord Kitchener, " addressed to employers presumed to have in their employ men suitable for the special needs of the Erith factory." This letter was actually issued in a considerably shorter form on 27 March.[3]   The draft of 20 March will here be quoted, because it shows, even more explicitly than the terms of reference, how the original purpose of the Committee was confined to the diversion of labour from civil employment to war work :—

> SIR,—
>
> I wish to call your careful attention to two extracts from speeches made by myself and Lord Crewe in the House of Lords on 15 March, of which I enclose a copy.
>
> We are in urgent need of certain war supplies, for the manufacture of which the machinery at our disposal is in excess of the available supply of skilled labour.
>
> In order to take immediate advantage of the Defence of the Realm (Amendment) Act No. 2, I have appointed a small Committee, under the immediate control of the Master-General of Ordnance, to take the necessary steps to secure the release, from such civil work as can be postponed, of the skilled labour required for military purposes.

---

[1] See Part II., Chap. III., p. 67, note 3.

[2] Papers relating to the London Enquiry, D.A.O./7B/2016.

[3] For the final form see Appendix V.   This letter and Mr. Booth's letter of 29 March (Appendix VI.) were ultimately issued to employers in other districts besides London.

My Committee will co-operate with the Committee under the chairmanship of Mr. Duke, referred to by Lord Crewe.[1]

I have appealed once for recruits for actual service at the Front, and my appeal has been met with magnificent response. I now make a second appeal to those engaged on work for civil purposes of a nature similar to that which I require for war material, to put themselves at the disposal of the Country.[2]

You will be hearing shortly from the Committee, whose chairman, Mr. George M. Booth, will be in close touch with myself in developing this important subject.

The following is a draft, dated 19 March, of a letter from Mr. Booth,[3] which was to be sent to each employer after he had received Lord Kitchener's letter:—

DEAR SIR,—

You will have just received a letter from Lord Kitchener on the subject of the special need of skilled labour for the increased output of war material. In this connection I should be much obliged if you will please fill in the enclosed form as promptly as possible.

The War Office, while prepared if necessary to make full use of the powers granted by the Defence of the Realm (Amendment) No. 2 Act, is anxious to co-operate as far as possible with employers and workmen. We should be much obliged if you would express your views as to the possibility of continuing your business upon temporarily reduced lines, should it be deemed wiser to recruit a percentage only of the workers under your employ who meet the requirements of the War Office.[4]

You are entirely at liberty to take your workmen into your and our confidence in this matter. We should like them all to know that Lord Kitchener is making this second great appeal to the manhood of England.

Every possible care is to be taken to approach all suitable employers within a certain area, and apply the same principles of recruiting to each and every case. Should any failure in this direction come to your notice, we should value immediate information.[5]

---

[1] This reference to the Defence of the Realm Losses Commission was omitted in the final version. Lord Kitchener had suggested that his Committee should endeavour to settle compensation, and bring Mr. Duke's Commission into the field only in the event of their negotiations breaking down. Mr. Booth, however, was reluctant to touch the question of compensation.

[2] The above paragraph was struck out. In place of it the letter issued has :—
     " The work will be closely co-ordinated with what has been done, and is being done, by the Board of Trade in this direction."

[3] L.E. 1965/170. For the final version see Appendix VI.

[4] In the letter actually issued on 29 March, the above paragraph is reduced to the following :—
     " The War Office, while prepared, if necessary, to make full use of the powers granted by the Defence of the Realm (Amendment) No. 2 Act, is anxious to disturb employers as little as possible."

[5] The last paragraph was omitted in the final version.

Mr. Booth's letter was sent out two days after Lord Kitchener's, on 29 March. The form enclosed in the letter was a questionnaire,[1] which was a modified version of the questionnaire prepared by Mr. Beveridge in January for the projected Survey of Engineering Firms.[2] It contained an inquiry into the nature of the work in hand, to what extent it was Government or private work, and whether the men were working short time, full time or overtime. The numbers of men employed belonging to 23 classes of skilled labour were to be stated, the wages they received, and the percentages engaged on Government or private work. The firms were asked whether they had inspected the samples exhibited at Aldwych Labour Exchange, and what action, if any, they had taken in consequence. Question 6 indicates the measures contemplated by the War Office :

> " (6) Assuming that arrangements for compensati)n in respect of private work postponed could be made under the Defence of the Realm (Amendment) No. 2 Act : (*a*) could you with *your present plant and present staff* do more Government work (1) of the class you are now doing, (2) of any other class ? (*b*) release men for armament work elsewhere ? "

Arrangements for the London Enquiry had been begun on 17 March, when the Master-General of the Ordnance visited Woolwich and gave directions for the preparation of a list of firms in S.E. London who were doing engineering work, and were likely to have mechanics whose services might be taken over. Sir H. F. Donaldson forwarded lists of 94 such firms to the Director of Artillery on 20 March. In the covering letter he wrote :—" I do not know what system it is proposed to adopt to avail ourselves of the powers granted under the latest Defence of the Realm Act ; but it would certainly appear desirable that all the firms on these lists should be visited, in order to see what class of men they have, and how many would be likely to be suitable for our work." He added that he could not allot an officer competent to judge of the men for all the purposes required in the Ordnance Factories, and suggested that the Board of Trade should fill in the numbers of skilled workmen employed by each of the firms.

The Master-General of the Ordnance forwarded the lists to Mr. Booth on 23 March. The total number of skilled mechanics required by the Shell Factory at Woolwich and by Messrs. Vickers at Erith and Crayford, was stated at 1,234.

Seven engineers were appointed as " Armament Committee's Inspectors " to conduct the enquiry. They visited Woolwich on 7 April and Messrs. Vickers' works at Erith two days later. On 12 April, Lord Elphinstone, who was by this time working for the Armaments Output Committee, met the inspectors, Mr. Graves of the Home Office, Mr. Davison, and the London Divisional Officer, Mr. Balaam. The representatives of the Home Office and of the Board of Trade described

---

[1] See Appendix VII. A draft dated 19/3/15 is in L.E. 1965/170.
[2] See Appendix I.

the steps already taken to ascertain what skilled labour and machinery were available. The Metropolitan area was divided into eight districts, corresponding as nearly as possible to the Labour Exchange areas, each under an engineer inspector, who was to report to Mr. Booth. The inspectors were later put in touch with the local Labour Exchange officials and the Factory Inspectors.

On 13 April, Mr. Booth met the inspectors and explained their duties. The North-East and South-East districts were to be visited at once, inspection being confined to firms on Mr. Booth's list.

The inspectors used the collated returns sent by employers in response to Mr. Booth's letter of 29 March. Every firm of note was visited, and reports were presented on the conditions of work and labour.

On 23 April, two of the inspectors conferred with the Defence of the Realm Losses Commission ; but no satisfactory basis of compensation for the transference of labour could be found.

The enquiry ended on May 6. The inspectors' final report[1] stated that 405 firms had been visited, and the consent of the employers had been obtained for the release of 142 mechanics. Of these, up to the present, 30 had been placed at the Arsenal, 10 at Erith and Crayford, 10 had been refused by the Arsenal, 10 had gone, or were willing to go, to other armament factories, and 41 had declined to move.

Nearly all the employers had expressed their willingness to further munitions production by every means in their power. The number of firms wholly engaged on private work was small, and most were working at high pressure with staffs reduced by 20 per cent. to 50 per cent. The number of highly skilled fitters and turners in any one works was usually very small, and the withdrawal of them would entail considerable unemployment. In one case, 900 boys and girls were dependent on the work of 23 mechanics. On the other hand, the employers were anxious to adapt and utilise their machinery for armament work.

Of the firms visited, a large proportion were wholly or partly doing Government work. Small works were making tools, gauges, jigs, and machines for larger firms holding direct contracts for war material. Considerable quantities of shell components, bombs, grenades, cartridge-filling presses, gun sights, and various other articles were being produced. Much work was also being done for transport service, cycle corps, and aircraft factories.

The work was very unevenly distributed ; a number of establishments well equipped for precision work had failed to secure orders. The inspectors believed that, if firms could be properly organised in groups, output could be considerably increased.

Apart from the reasons mentioned by the inspectors, the smallness of the results achieved in the way of actual transfer of men was

---

[1] D.A.O./7B/2027

partly due to the fact that the ground had been thoroughly worked over by the Board of Trade in January. Further, no special inducements to move were offered to the men, and recruiting for the Army was still uncontrolled. In one case a number of men whom their employer had agreed to release for munitions work, were enlisted in the interval before they were called upon for transfer.

In this area, at any rate, the enquiry confirmed the conclusion reached by the Board of Trade that the possibilities of diversion of skilled labour were exhausted.

III. Sir Percy Girouard's Tyneside Enquiry.

Concurrently with Mr. Booth's efforts to secure labour in the London area, Lord Kitchener requested Sir Percy Girouard, who had served under him in South Africa and was now managing director at Elswick, to report what measures he considered necessary or desirable with regard to the supply of additional labour for the armament works on Tyneside.

Sir Percy Girouard interviewed the Master-General of the Ordnance and the President of the Board of Trade on 19 March. Arrangements were made for statistics to be supplied to him by the Board of Trade from the Z8 returns, showing what factories and railway workshops in the Newcastle area were working short time, full time, or overtime, with a view to an estimate of the amount of labour that might be diverted.

On 22 March, Sir Percy Girouard concerted his arrangements with the Divisional Officer of the Scottish and Northern Division and the local Inspector of Factories at Newcastle.[1] He sent to Mr. Booth on 26 March a statement of the labour needed at Messrs. Armstrong's works. Elswick could take from 1,600 to 1,700 hands. Alexandria needed 275 men ; and, as soon as the relaxation of restrictions should admit of the use of unskilled and female labour for shells and fuses, another 275 men weekly for eight weeks would be wanted.[2]

In a report to the Master-General of the Ordnance, dated 25 March, Sir Percy Girouard stated that, in the Tyneside area, the statistics showed that there was a considerable body of labour which, it was thought, might be diverted to Government work from factories not fully employed on such work, or not working full time or overtime. This report also outlined a general scheme of organisation for the distribution of munitions labour throughout the country, which will be considered later.[3]

At Newcastle, the actual work of transfer was done by the North East Coast Armaments Committee, appointed early in April. An account of this Committee will be given in the next chapter.

---

[1] L.E. 1965/126. [2] L.E. 9263. [3] See below, p. 64, D.A.O./Area 1/557.

IV. Other Measures for the Supply of Skilled Labour to Armament Firms.

On 31 March Lord Kitchener wrote to the President of the Local Government Board inquiring whether the local authorities were likely to have in their employ any men, skilled or unskilled, who could be spared to assist in the manufacture of munitions. The Board had already been approached by the Committee of Imperial Defence in January, and had issued a circular to local authorities on 11 March, urging them to release men both for military service and for munitions work. The circular was now followed up by visits of the engineering staff of the Board to some 700 local authorities. By 6 May, lists had been obtained of some 30,000 men who were offered to the War Office.[1] The lists were referred to the Labour Exchange department, who were requested to arrange for the actual transfer to armament firms of such of the men as proved to be suitable It was found that about 84 per cent. were unskilled labourers, for whom it was difficult to find employment.

Lord Kitchener also interviewed the Executive Council of the Amalgamated Society of Engineers at the War Office on 1 April.[2] After explaining the powers conferred on him by the new Defence of the Realm Act and dwelling on the imperative need for increased output, he pointed out that new factories had been built by the armament firms and equipped with machinery, while others were in course of construction. What was needed was a sufficient supply of labour to man these machines.

In his report of this interview, the Chairman of the Executive said that the Council were deeply impressed by the statement. Incidentally, the word " conscription " had been mentioned. Lord Kitchener had remarked that the best way to stave off conscription was to agree to his proposals and to fill the shops with the necessary supply of labour. The Chairman recommended the Society to take a large view and to render all possible assistance.

V. Mr. Allan Smith's Programme.

Meanwhile, on 31 March, the day on which the Armaments Output Committee was appointed, a preliminary meeting, presided over by Lord Kitchener, was held to discuss the scope and methods of its activities. After this meeting, Mr. Allan Smith drew up a memorandum, which was read over at a second conference on 6 April and verbally approved by Lord Kitchener. It will be observed that this document contemplates making a much larger use of the powers under the new Act than the mere transfer of skilled hands to armament firms. It is rather a scheme for that general re-organisation of engineering resources which had been foreshadowed in the ministerial speeches on the introduction of the Bill.

---

[1] Chief Engineer, L.G.B., *Report* (6 5/15). M.C. 405.
[2] A S.E. *Monthly Journal and Report*, April, 1915, p. 22.

The proposals may be summarised under several heads[1] :—

(1) PRELIMINARY INVESTIGATIONS.

A War Office representative was to be appointed for each district, to report on the capabilities of the factories for munitions production, using the help of the Labour Exchanges and Factory Inspectors and keeping in touch with the local Employers' Association.[2]

Returns were to be procured giving detailed information about each factory : (1) the description, numbers, and capacities of the machines ; the general nature of the work turned out ; the extent to which semi-skilled and female labour was, or might be, employed ; lists of machines idle owing to shortage of workpeople or want of orders ; particulars of new installations in progress and the anticipated date of completion ; (2) the number of workpeople of the various classes employed ; (3) whether the factory was at present on short time ; (4) Railway facilities ; (5) the prospect of securing semi-skilled, unskilled, and female labour in the district ; (6) housing accommodation available for labour from outside.

Delays in the erection and equipment of shops for Government work, and transport difficulties, were to be reported, in order that the Committee might take the matter up.

With respect to workpeople, information was to be obtained for each district on the following points : (1) to what extent women and boys were employed in industries other than engineering, and the suitability of such labour for transfer to engineering factories ; (2) whether any difficulties had occurred in introducing semi-skilled, unskilled, and female labour on engineering processes ; (3) the flow of labour to armament districts : what proportion had remained, and for how long ; what proportion had returned or left for other districts, and for what reasons ; (4) the system of payment—time, piece-work, or premium bonus ; (5) to what extent workpeople would be willing to go to war work in other districts. It would be intimated that factories might, if necessary, be closed in order to set free their labour.

Particulars were also to be procured as to the extent to which armament firms had sublet their work ; the names of the sub-contractors ; the nature of the work ; whether the delivery dates had been kept, and the work satisfactorily done.

---

[1] The substance of the document has been freely re-arranged for the sake of clearness. Copy in HIST. REC./R/171/18.

[2] It was presumably with this purpose in view that Lord Kitchener wrote on 31 March to Mr. Runciman : " I want you to find me 10 ' Booths ' or men slightly younger but with his business capabilities and push.   They should have local knowledge of such districts as Sheffield. Birmingham, Coventry, Manchester, Liverpool.   I leave you to add other districts from which it is likely that we can obtain labour.   May I have the names to-morrow, and we will arrange for them to take over the work ? "   On the previous day, Lord Kitchener had asked Mr. Cecil Baring for 50 Booths, and Mr. McKenna for 50 Factory Inspectors to be attached to them.   He was persuaded by Mr. Booth to reduce his demand to 10.

(2)   MEASURES PROPOSED.

(a)   *Factories.*—The memorandum proposed methods of treatment applicable to various classes of factories.

Factories which had been specially equipped for munitions work were to be provided with the necessary complement of labour.

Other factories were to be utilised for munitions work suitable to their machinery, provided that workpeople and superintendents should not be drawn from armament shops without the Committee's leave. The armament firms were to give full information and allow representatives of firms undertaking War Office work to examine processes. Work-people were not to be taken from a factory engaged on war material without the consent of the Committee. Unless the job could be completed in a factory, the parts should be under sub-contract to an armament manufacturer, or co-operation should be arranged in districts, so that the job might be completely finished before it left the district : *e.g.*, aeroplanes at Glasgow ; shells at Leicester ; field carriages, etc., at Barrow.[1]

Where the machinery in a factory was not being used to the fullest advantage, it was proposed that contracts (mainly sub-contracts) for War Office work should be re-distributed among other more suitable factories, and replaced by work that could be more conveniently done.

Factories not on Government work and not convenient for the purpose were to be examined by the War Office representative in the district with the help of a special engineering inspector. If it should be decided to close the factory or any part of it and transfer the labour elsewhere, the inspector, with an accountant appointed in the district by the Committee, was to adjust with the owner the basis of compensation.

(b)   *Contracts for Neutral Countries.*—Particulars of all armaments, munitions and machine and other tools and plant in course of completion for neutral countries were to be obtained. Such work should not be proceeded with except with the consent of the Committee, who might order it to be diverted to any home factory they should indicate.[2]

(c)   *Labour demands* were to be carefully scrutinised.

(d)   *Inspection* was to be relaxed so far as might be consistent with maintaining the necessary quality. Additional inspectors should be appointed. Delays and difficulties connected with inspection were to be reported to the Committee.

(e)   *Supply of raw materials.*—In selected steel works, merchant work was to be stopped, or so restricted as to yield the required supply of ingots and bars. The destination of these products could be settled : *e.g.*, daily or weekly supplies sent to certain factories. This would chiefly affect merchant ship plates, and bridge plates and girders. Slackening of pressure in merchant shipbuilding would also set free some engineers for war work.

---

[1] This is the only reference in the memorandum to the scheme of Co-operative Groups.

[2] It will be noted that this paragraph contains the germ of the schemes of Priority later set on foot.

(*f*)   *Volunteer Industrial Corps.*—It was suggested that a Volunteer Industrial Corps, subject to a certain amount of discipline, should be formed for industrial service in any part of the kingdom.   They would receive their own district rate and also army pay (both on the basis of a full working week), and working-out allowances, if called upon to leave their homes.   Disputes as to rates and allowances could be settled under the Government scheme for settling disputes.

(3)   LOCAL ORGANISATION.

It was proposed that the Engineering Employers' Federation should communicate with their local Associations, referring to the appointment of the Committee and to the provisions of the Defence of the Realm Acts, and asking them to appoint small local committees, representative of the various branches of industry carried on in the district.

These local committees would be available for consultation, to superintend the carrying out of the central Committee's instructions, and generally to assist in matters referred to them and to make suggestions.

Mr. Allan Smith's programme, though much of it was dictated by the new Defence of the Realm Act, in some points resembles a remarkably complete scheme for a central organisation to co-ordinate engineering resources, which had been propounded by Mr. Alfred Herbert, in consultation with Mr. Dumas, five months before.   In particular, both schemes contemplate that the central Committee should work through the machinery of the Engineering Employers' Federation.   Mr. Alfred Herbert's plan deserves some detailed description.   It had been put forward in a letter written on 3 November, 1914, to Sir Arthur Lawton, then Acting Chairman of the Emergency Committee of the Federation.

Mr. Herbert proposed the formation of a small Committee, on which the Federation, the Ordnance Factories, the armament firms, and the Treasury were to be represented.   Its functions were to consist in " co-ordinating the efforts of private engineering firms in such a manner as to best assist the Government Factories and the Armament Companies in increasing the production of war material."

The duties suggested were of a very wide scope.   They covered the supply of raw material, particularly forgings ; the production of gauges and special tools ; securing the necessary machinery ; distribution of Government work to firms not already engaged on such work ; arranging the bases of payment and the passing on of work in various stages of completion from firm to firm ; subsidising firms which did not dispose of sufficient capital ; redistribution of labour ; checking the enlistment of skilled mechanics ; arranging with the authorities for the diversion of work in progress from private or foreign customers to the Government, and for compensation for losses through claims for breach of contract ; promoting relaxation of the Factory Act, to allow longer hours and employment below the present age limit, with proper safeguards ; and framing regulations to facilitate the use of female labour.

The central Committee was to work through the local branches of the Engineering Employers' Federation.

The Federation did not at the time take up this proposal with enthusiasm. Mr. Dumas, however, after the first meeting (8 January) at Leicester,[1] communicated the scheme to Sir H. Llewellyn Smith at an interview on 15 January. His suggestions included the central and local organisation outlined in Mr. Herbert's letter, and he proposed that the Committee should work on the basis of returns furnished every four weeks by firms not wholly engaged on Government work, stating the amount spent during the period on direct labour (a) for Government work and (b) for all customers' orders.

Mr. Herbert and Mr. Dumas, though the machinery of the Employers' Federation was not adopted as the basis of the organisation, foreshadowed to a remarkable extent the functions ultimately to be assumed by the Armaments Output Committee, with which they both co-operated later.[2]

One part of Mr. Allan Smith's programme was at once carried out by the issue, on 12 April, to War Office contractors and sub-contractors of a letter enclosing a form of Return (P.R.1),[3] which they were requested to fill up weekly. The object in view was, not to place contracts, but rather to explore the situation and to remedy any causes of delay in production which the returns might reveal. The form was sent, in the first instance, to 122 establishments. On 13 May about 60 more were added.

The return was to show what proportion of the firm's plant and machinery was at present engaged on production of shells and fuses, or parts thereof, and whether it was being used to the fullest extent ; what surplus there was that could be adapted for such production ; if the plant was not fully employed, whether this was due to shortage of orders, or of labour, or of raw material, with details as to requirements, causes of delay, etc.; particulars as to installation of any new plant and the labour required for it ; and any complaints as to delay connected with drawings, designs, inspection, shipping instructions, etc.

These returns were furnished up to the week ending May 21. After that date, a letter was issued stating that the information supplied had been of great value, and had now served its purpose. The Committee, however, offered to continue the assistance it had already rendered in many cases to contractors in hastening the deliveries of supplies from firms in default.

VI. The Personnel of the Committee and its Work.

On 7 April, the day after Lord Kitchener had approved Mr. Allan Smith's programme, appeared the announcement that the Committee was appointed to " take the necessary steps to provide such additional labour as may be required." The discrepancy between this comparatively small and manageable task and the prospects opened out in the programme might be taken as a measure of the inadequacy of the

[1] See above, p. 11.

[2] Correspondence and memoranda relating to Mr. Herbert's and Mr. Dumas schemes, Hist. Rec./H/1121/1.

[3] D.A.O./7B,2016. Hist. Rec./R/171/4. See Appendix VIII.

Committee to the work required for it, if it were not that the programme itself represents only a part of the problems that crowded in upon Mr. Booth and his small band of assistants in the next few weeks. It is obvious that Lord Kitchener and the Master-General of the Ordnance could not take part in the details of executive work. Sir Algernon Firth co-operated in his official capacity as President of the Associated Chambers of Commerce. Sir Herbert Walker had been included because there had been some suggestion that the Railway Executive Committee, of which he was Chairman, might be federated with the central organisation.[1] Since this suggestion fell through, Sir Herbert Walker was never an active member. The whole burden of the work fell upon Mr. Booth and Mr. Allan Smith.

When a beginning of departmental work was made on 31 March, in order to collate the information supplied by employers in response to Mr. Booth's letter, the War Office had provided neither accommodation nor staff. Mr. Booth borrowed from the Board of Trade a few assistants and a room at the Labour Exchange Central Office in Queen Anne's Chambers. It was not until two days later that a room was found for him at the War Office.[2]

In these circumstances, Mr. Booth, with the small staff he was gradually able to gather round him, had to deal with the information already collected by the Board of Trade and the Home Office ; with the P.R.1. Returns ; and with an increasing volume of correspondence elicited by Mr. Lloyd George's speech of 9 March, by Mr. Booth's own letter of 29 March, and by the announcement of the Committee's appointment.

Offers of services from persons of both sexes and every class ; offers of premises or of machinery ; offers of surplus stocks for sale ; requests for contracts ; descriptions of inventions ; suggestions on every conceivable subject connected with munitions, poured in at a rate which made it impossible even to acknowledge more than a small proportion.[3] All this correspondence was in addition to Mr. Booth's work on the London enquiry, to the programme outlined by Mr. Allan Smith, and to other vital matters, such as the checking of enlistment, release from the Colours, and so on, which soon called urgently for Mr. Booth's intervention. Meanwhile, the employers who had been repeatedly approached and appealed to, were beginning to be impatient of filling up one return after another, and wondering when something definite would be done.

Mr. Booth was, in fine, the first, and perhaps not the least successful, example of a man of business, with no inside knowledge of the methods of government and no staff of experienced civil servants, called in to do, all but single-handed, work which would have taxed the energies of a regular Department of State. His position was exceptionally difficult in that he was not even the independent head

---

[1] This was, for example, suggested in Sir Percy Girouard's Report to the M.G.O. of 25 March.

[2] This room (No. 367) and the adjoining rooms were occupied till the removal to Armament Buildings.

[3] For Mr. Booth's correspondence see Appendix IX.

of an embryo department, but only the chairman of a committee deriving all its executive power from the Master-General of the Ordnance or the Secretary of State for War.

This dependence was still further complicated, almost from the outset, by the creation of yet another body, claiming to direct the policy of the Committee.

VII.   The Munitions of War Committee.

When the Armaments Output Committee had been in existence for barely a week, it became informally, though not technically, subordinate to the Munitions of War Committee (" Treasury Committee "), under the chairmanship of Mr. Lloyd George.

The Prime Minister announced the appointment on 8 April, and the names of the members were given in the House of Commons a week later.[1]

The original members were :—

> Mr. Lloyd George, Chairman,
> Mr. A J. Balfour,
> Mr. E. S. Montagu,
> Mr. G. M. Booth,
> Major-Gen. von Donop,   } representing the
> Mr. Harold Baker,   }   War Office
> Sir Frederick Black,   } representing the
> Admiral Tudor,   }   Admiralty
> Mr. A. Henderson,

with power to add to their number.

Sir H. Llewellyn Smith was co-opted at the first meeting (April 12), and Sir Percy Girouard was added later (26 April).

In his announcement the Prime Minister said :—

" The appointment of such a Committee was decided upon a month ago,[2] and the Departments have been busy preparing the ground for its activities.

" The function of the Committee is to ensure the promptest and most efficient application of all the available productive resources of the country to the manufacture and supply of munitions of war for the Navy and Army.   It has full power to take all steps necessary for that purpose."

It will be observed that these terms of reference covered a much wider field than the instructions originally given by Lord Kitchener to Mr. Booth's Committee, and were indeed wide enough to include any possible measures that might be taken.[3]

---

[1] *Parliamentary Debates* (1915), *H. of C.*, LXXI., 39 (15 April).

[2] *I.e.*, about the time when the Defence of the Realm (Amendment) No. 2 Act was introduced.

[3] Copies of the minutes and other papers printed for this Committee (numbered M.C.1 ff.) are in HIST. REC./R/172/1.

The relations between the two bodies were explained by Mr. Lloyd George, on 21 April, as follows :—

' Mr. Booth . . . is a man of great energy and organising capacity, and his Committee is the executive committee for carrying out the policy which is very largely determined now, under the supervision of the Secretary of State for War, by the administrative Committee of which I am chairman . . . We decide matters of policy ; we cannot undertake executive work. That must be done by the War Office, and they have instructed this Committee, of which Mr. Booth is the great co-ordinating element."[1]

The Munitions of War Committee was, in fact, an overriding committee, which directed the course pursued in the next two months.

The Committee met for the first time on 12 April, and again on 14 April. At these preliminary meetings, its first task was to survey the actual and prospective state of munitions supplies, and to set on foot enquiries into the methods adopted in France and America for increasing output.[2] At four later meetings, held (on 26 April and 7, 12 and 13 May) before the reconstruction of the Government in the fourth week of May, decisions were taken on a number of outstanding questions, which will be mentioned at the appropriate places. The most important act of the Committee was the adoption, on 26 April, of a scheme proposed by Sir Percy Girouard.[3] This finally led to the detaching of the Armaments Output Committee's work from the War Office and the formation of a Ministry of Munitions.

For the moment, it is important to note that the influence exercised by this body on the Armaments Output Committee was from the first in the direction of the Board of Trade policy. In the speech of 21 April above quoted, Mr. Lloyd George described as follows the change that had taken place in the views of the Government since the beginning of the year, and his own attitude towards the main issue :—

" It was discovered in December that the supply would be inadequate—that the contracts would not come up to time. The first effort made by the War Office was to fill up the labour deficiencies in the armament firms, because it is obviously better that you should get your men under the direct supervision and control of those who for years have been undertaking this kind of work. If, therefore, we could enable the armament firms to deliver their munitions according to contract by supplying deficiencies of labour, it was obviously better than giving the work to those who had no experience at all, and who,

---

[1] *Parliamentary Debates* (1915), *H. of C.*, LXXI., 323.

[2] An account of Messrs. Lobnitz and Moir's mission to France is given in Appendix IV. A report by Mr. Wolf on American methods was also printed for the Committee (M.C. 5).

[3] See below, Chap. IV., p. 61.

no doubt, would have made failures at first, and have supplied us with materials which would not have exploded and which might have caused mischief. An effort was, therefore, made through the Labour Exchanges by the Board of Trade to get as many men as we could possibly find to send to these armament firms and sub-contracting firms for the purpose of enabling them to carry out their contracts.

" At first that was very promising. In the first month a very considerable number of men came in. The second month did not look quite so promising ; and by the month of March it was perfectly clear that we could not supply all the deficiencies of labour in these firms.

" That was why we were driven to the other course . . . It would have been better if we had succeeded in obtaining the transfer of men, but that is a matter for the men themselves . . . We went to the utmost limit of the policy of transference of men, and we then came to the conclusion that it would be absolutely necessary to take other steps. And that is why I introduced in this House in the month of March the Defence of the Realm Bill, to equip the War Office and the Admiralty with the necessary powers for taking over engineering works.[1] It was the second-best course, and that was why we hesitated to take it until we found it was inevitable to supply the necessary munitions, not for present purposes, but for the prospect in front of us . . .

" We are, and have been during the last few weeks, proceeding on the assumption that to depend upon those who have hitherto had experience in turning out munitions of war, even by any process of sub-contracting and of pressing labour to go there to fill up deficiencies, will not be sufficient to meet the demands with which we shall be confronted in the course of the next few weeks, and that it is necessary for us to take the risk of organising shops which have not hitherto been employed for this purpose."

In the same speech Mr. Lloyd George referred to the co-operative system adopted by the French, and to the Cabinet mission to France in October, 1914.[2] The only documents prepared in advance for the first meeting of the Munitions of War Committee were an extract from Lord Reading's diary recording this visit and a Note by Sir John Simon on the report made by him to the Cabinet Committee on Munitions when the mission returned. Mr. Lloyd George, in fact, adopted the principle which had already been carried into practice at Leicester.

---

[1] This statement illustrates in an interesting way the change of Government policy with regard to this Act, which, as has been pointed out above (Part II., Chap. III.), was originally designed to further the old policy of transference of labour.

[2] See above, Chap. I., Section IV.

Mr. Booth thus received support from this quarter in the vigorous campaign carried on by his Committee in the month of April for the development of co-operative production.

Nor was it only in this respect that Mr. Booth's position was strengthened by having the Munitions of War Committee at his back. Th · Armaments Output Committee was at first no more than an excrescence on one branch of a single department ; it was not even an integral part of the great War Office machine. As its chairman, Mr. Booth might hope to influence the Master-General of the Ordnance and Lord Kitchener ; but he could not intervene with any independent authority in certain large questions which lay very near the root of his problem. In the first place, within the War Office itself, there was a sharp conflict of interest between the Adjutant-General's Recruiting department and the Contracts Branch of the Master-General of the Ordnance. Every skilled workman enlisted in the new Armies was a man lost, and often irrecoverably lost, to munitions production. In the second place, Mr. Booth had no official status qualifying him to negotiate a reconciliation between the claims of the War Office for recruits and for armaments workers, and the equally urgent needs of the Admiralty for shipyard labour. The two Departments, through their local agencies, were competing in unchecked rivalry, not only with one another, but with the general trade of the country at every important centre of industry. Hitherto, the only authority superior to the Departments, and able to confront their respective claims and adjudicate between them, had been, of course, the Cabinet. Here Lord Kitchener, necessarily and rightly, held a position of unrivalled prestige. His policy was clear : first and foremost, to obtain enough men to fill the ranks of his new armies ; secondly, to enlarge and strengthen the armament firms which were to equip them with munitions. What effect this might have, either on the general trade of the country or on the smaller concerns whose men were to be recruited for the ranks or for the armament firms, it did not lie within his special province to consider.

The Munitions of War Committee, on the other hand, was presided over by a Minister whose primary interest was in munitions production ; and Lord Kitchener was not a member. It could, accordingly, study the whole problem of munitions and man-power from another angle, unbiassed by the legitimate pre-occupations of the Secretary of State for War. Though no one could yet foresee the stages by which this problem would grow and spread until it came to involve, directly or indirectly, the whole fabric of industry and the whole working population of the country, the moment was approaching when the handling of it could no longer be left to the War Office and the Admiralty, Departments whose structure and traditions had taken shape under conditions in which the problem did not exist. The appointment of the Munitions of War Committee marks the moment at which the Government appreciated this paramount fact. The establishment of a Ministry to take independent control both of production and of labour supply for armament purposes was the logical consequence.

To Mr. Booth and his Committee, the shift by which they passed from being an extraneous departmental committee of the War Office

to acting as the executive of this new and powerful Committee at the
Treasury, meant a great increase of authority.   Mr. Booth, as himself
a member of it, could now deal directly, on the one side with the Cabinet
through Mr. Lloyd George, and on the other with the influential representatives of the War Office, the Admiralty, and the Board of Trade.
Left to his own devices in Room No. 367 at the War Office, he might
have beaten his wings in vain.

CHAPTER III.

LOCAL ORGANISATION, 31 MARCH TO 28 APRIL.

I. The Scheme of A and B Areas.

The measures so far described were initiated before the Armaments Output Committee was formed on the last day of March. Its policy, when it was formed, was predetermined by another decisive factor. This was the effective support given to the Board of Trade by Mr. Booth, who realised that the whole problem could no longer be dealt with by the mere diversion of labour from private work, but called for a reorganisation of the industry on a basis acceptable to the manufacturers themselves and adjusted to local conditions.

Addressing a deputation from Manchester on 29 April, Mr. Booth referred to his advocacy of this standpoint in the following words :—

> " Every district will have its own methods. . . . To be purely personal for a moment, the reason that I came here was that I advocated, and persuaded the Government to support my advocacy, that the country should be divided up in this manner—that the big shop was the best, but that the country had thousands of small shops, and that you could not move them more than a certain amount, and therefore you must take the work to them. It is evident, however, that there is a limit of smallness ; but you could take it further than I ever dreamt of."[1]

Mr. Booth, as has been seen, had carried through the negotiations with the Leicester group formed on 23 March.[2] While he was setting about the work entrusted to him by Lord Kitchener, he was at the same time bridging the gulf which had opened between the War Office and the Board of Trade. In concert with Mr. Beveridge, he now devised a scheme which would effect a compromise between the conflicting policies of the two Departments, by delimiting the spheres within which they could be severally and concurrently pursued.

The basis of this compromise was the division of the country into areas of two types, which were designated by the letters A and B.

An A Area was a district within a radius of about 20 miles, measured from any one of the Government Factories or of the recognised armament firms on the War Office List. Such an area was to be

---

[1] A.O.C. *Printed Minutes*, p. 118. Hist. Rec./R/171.

[2] See above, p. 17.

treated as a preserve for the older policy of concentrating the flow of labour upon the armament firms. So long as the machines at the new factories they had erected were undermanned, no new contracts were to be placed with other firms inside these areas.

All other districts where engineering capacity could be found were to be B Areas ; and in these the Board of Trade policy of forming Co-operative Groups was to be permitted, subject to provisions strictly safeguarding the A Areas from any encroachment upon their resources.

The outlines of this treaty were indicated in a memorandum by Mr. Davison,[1] which was sent out to Divisional Officers on 27 March, after it had been approved by Mr. Booth :—

" The War Office have in the last few days agreed to stand by their original proposal to place new orders for the manufacture of shells or fuses with any new firms, or groups of firms, which may be discovered, by means of the exhibitions of samples, to be capable of undertaking this work. At the same time, the War Office are more anxious to increase the supply of labour and material to the existing armament manufacturers than to place fresh orders with firms inexperienced in the work, and they would not consider placing any contract which might interfere with the present output of war material.

" In view of the shortage of labour on existing orders, it also appears unlikely that the War Office will be willing to give out any new contracts in the neighbourhood of the principal armament firms, a list of which is enclosed.[2] It is, therefore, suggested that, for the present, effort should only be made to find new firms or groups of firms outside the radius (say, one hour by train) within which any of the firms on the list are established and might obtain additional labour.

" It should be made clear to any new firms or groups of firms that the work must be undertaken with their existing staff, and that the raw material and any new plant required must be obtained by them from sources whose output is not wanted for existing Government orders. The War Office will require to be satisfied on these points before placing orders."

It was added that, while some firms might be found capable of undertaking orders singly, the group system, just put into practice at Leicester, seemed to be the most promising plan. The War Office would probably accept an offer of as few as 100 shells a week. As a rule, they would consider only offers of complete

---

[1] *Contracts for Shells and Fuses.* L.E. 1965/129.

[2] A revised list, prepared by Mr. Beveridge on 29 March, was issued to the Divisional Officers on 1 April. See Appendix X.

shells ; but, unless the firms were confident that they could make fuses (which the War Office did not expect), they were to apply for orders for shells complete except for the fuse.   Forgings might perhaps be supplied from other Divisions.

" It may be added that firms possessing suitable plant are asked to regard it as their duty to devote their whole resources to this national work, and many engineering manufacturers have already offered to cease all work on private orders for the present.

" Where it appears desirable that a considerable number of firms should combine together, meetings should be arranged under the auspices of the local Employers' Association or the Chamber of Commerce."

In order to make sure that this scheme of compromise had the official sanction of the War Office, Mr. Davison drew up on the same day (27 March) a memorandum of the proposed procedure, which he communicated to Mr. Booth.[1]

This memorandum elicited from the War Office an authoritative statement, which Mr. Booth forwarded to Mr. Davison on 30 March.   It will be quoted at length, since it clearly defines the position of the military authorities at the moment when the Armaments Output Committee was formed.

GENERAL INSTRUCTIONS FOR OFFICERS VISITING DISTRICTS SUITABLE FOR PROVIDING LABOUR FOR ARMAMENT WORK.[2]

Method of increasing output of munitions of war to be adopted for immediate practice.

Method I.—Concentration of labour on any firm already making armaments (and particularly fuses and shells), provided the War Office is completely satisfied that

(a) such firm has the necessary plant available, and needs *labour only* to increase production ;

(b) such firm can supervise properly the increased production that will result from the additional labour supplied.

If these requirements, (a) and (b), are met, the War Office will endeavour to obtain for such firm the additional labour required by getting other firms to release men from employment

---

[1] *Supply of Armaments* (27/3/15).   L.E. 1965/125.
[2] Copy in L.E. 1965/125.

on the production of non-war material, avoiding, if possible, the use of the new powers granted to the War Office under the Defence of the Realm (Amendment) No. 2 Act.

The difficulties of moving labour at all, and the tendency for men to return home, if moved, after a few weeks' work, has led to the decision to confine for the present the work of labour concentration within such geographical limits as will avoid a change of home.

Method II.—The encouragement of fresh production from firms not now making shells and fuses (though probably engaged to a greater or lesser extent on engineering contracts for war materials). Co-operative principles (as in the Leicester proposal) may have an important bearing on this method, which is subject to the following rigid conditions :

Such new firms or group of firms must satisfy the War Office that this fresh production of shells will be produced from

(*a*) material not at present destined for war supplies ;

(*b*) labour not at present employed in the manufacture of war supplies ;

(*c*) supervision not at present employed on the production of war supplies in the same or other districts ; and that

(*d*) no attempt of any sort or kind be made to interfere with or secure the labour, raw material, or supervision of firms in the printed list of Government contractors and sub-contractors which will be attached to any order obtained under the above restrictions.

It was upon the basis of this understanding that the Armaments Output Committee opened its campaign of local organisation.

II. Mr. Booth's Programme of Local Organisation.

The scheme of A and B Areas, like other projects of this crowded period, was short-lived. It governed the operations of the Committee through what may be called the first phase of its existence, that is to say, for about three weeks, from 31 March to 20 April. Then, after the arrival of Sir Percy Girouard at the War Office, it was fundamentally remodelled, for reasons which also led the Committee to enlarge its own scope and functions. In the last ten days of April the Committee was, in fact, ceasing to be a Committee, and beginning to be a department—a transformation which was effected so rapidly that on 22 April Mr. Booth spoke of "the original Kitchener Committee " as if it had been a different body.[1]

---

[1] A.O.C. *Printed Minutes*, p. 45. HIST REC./R/171.

Mr. Booth laid down his programme in a memorandum entitled " *Draft general instructions for prosecuting the special duties allotted to the Executive of the War Office Armaments Output Committee.*"[1]

The main concern of the War Office, at the present moment, was the failure of practically all their contractors to deliver, according to promise, shells, fuses, and guns. The most urgent need was for fuses and shells, particularly 4·5" and 18-pdrs. In order to make the fullest use of the existing skilled labour, two alternative methods were open.

(1) *A Areas.*—" An A Area is a district in which are situated one or more firms already producing shell and/or fuse and/or guns, provided that such factory or factories possess buildings and plant available for immediate use in excess of the labour now engaged." In these districts, in order to ensure that the whole of such existing plant should be fully employed on Government work, it would be necessary to draft in from outside skilled labour employed either on private contracts, or on less urgent armament contracts.

(2) *B Areas* were defined as districts " where at present no direct War Office contracts or sub-contracts from the main War Office armament firms have been placed."[2] Such areas were to be scheduled in respect of suitable plant and labour, and schemes of co-operative production were, if possible, to be developed.

The memorandum proceeds :—

" In order that no time should be lost in pursuing both methods, the particular difficulties applicable to each method should be clearly understood, and the points of contact or similarity between the two methods grasped ; and, in order to make the very best use of both methods, it is held to be essential that in each area there should be established a strong committee representing the facilities required, upon whose judgment, subject always to the final decision of the Committee, the Executive would largely rely for the final course to be pursued. For instance, one district might be able to release a larger number of men for A Areas, while at the same time converting to armament uses a limited amount of machinery and a corresponding amount of labour. Another district might be able to surrender all available men for transfer to A Areas by closing down all

---

[1] Hist. Rec./R/171/16.

[2] It may be noted that this definition, if strictly interpreted, would have excluded almost every centre where suitable engineering resources could be found. At this time Mr. Booth did not realise how extensive were the ramifications of sub-contracting. The definition, moreover, is contradicted by the statement below that the rougher processes of gun-making and the making of carriages, limbers and wagons were " at this moment being done in B Areas." The B Area would be correctly defined as " any district outside a radius of 20 miles from a Royal Factory or armament firm."

non-essential work. Compensation might enter into either of these categories.

" Certain obvious difficulties arise in connection with A, such as housing ; but energetic steps are being taken to make concentration of labour feasible. The greater advantage of the A Area method is the knowledge that first-class production is already coming forward. Supervision is simplified ; also inspection. These advantages may outweigh certain objections of the " too many eggs in one basket " type, and the equally serious objection of over-straining organisations already seriously overtaxed.

" There are equally obvious objections to the B Area method. The finished process in the manufacture of guns and mountings must be ruled out, while the rough preliminary turning and boring of gun tubes, and, of course, the manufacture of gun carriages, limbers and wagons, is at this moment being done in B Areas. The simpler classes of shell are, however, suitable for the method, and it is held that machinery now idle or employed on non-essential work, together with labour which practically could not be moved, may be made available for such production, and that, too, at a very early date, if sufficient assistance is given to the new effort in the way of free inspection of work now being done, with ample samples of the particular shell in question at every stage of its production.

" *Procedure.*—The immediate steps to put into effect the above general instructions are as follows :—

" As rapidly as the Committee can arrange them, meetings are being held at the War Office with representative district Committees. Leicester and Lincoln have already given actual practical assistance, and other districts follow immediately. The information obtained at each meeting will be scheduled and made available for succeeding meetings, and any general lines of advice, as the knowledge of procedure develops, will be submitted beforehand to new districts as they come forward, and, of course, within a very short period the War Office will have at its disposal the complete series of samples that are so necessary for rapid, accurate production."[1]

Such were the main principles followed by the Committee during the first three weeks of April, while it was still under the undivided control of Mr. Booth. This period witnessed the rapid formation of

---

[1] It was explained that a new design of shell, admitting of the use of Basic Steel, was now being prepared, and consequently no samples were available at present. Arrangements were, however, being made with the firm whose work on this shell was most advanced, to place at the Committee's disposal, from stage to stage, the results of its experimental work.

local committees of two types, corresponding to the needs of the two sorts of Area. In the A Areas of Newcastle and Glasgow, Armament Committees were created whose principal function was the transfer of labour to the armament firms dominating those Areas. In B Areas, Co-operative Groups were nursed simultaneously by the Board of Trade, the Engineering Employers' Federation, and the Associated Chambers of Commerce.

In the following sections the history of the two A Area Committees will first be reviewed. Considered as a social experiment, the type of local body they exemplify is of great interest. The North-East Coast Armaments Committee was the earlier of the two in date, and provided the model which was followed at Glasgow. For this reason, and also because it was more effective, it deserves the closer study. The Glasgow and West of Scotland Armaments Committee will be mentioned only in connection with points where the experience and the results were different.[1]

III.   The Armaments Committees in the A Areas of Newcastle and Glasgow.

(a) THE COMPOSITION OF THE COMMITTEES.

The formation of the North-East Coast Armaments Committee arose directly out of Sir Percy Girouard's mission to report on the possibilities of transferring labour within the Newcastle district to Elswick.[2] Captain Creed, who was recommended by Sir Percy Girouard, received instructions from Mr. Booth on 30 March to set about organising the actual work of transfer. In the interval before the Committee was appointed. he started on lines similar to those of Mr. Booth's London Enquiry, the first object being to supply labour to Messrs. Armstrong's works. Since, however, the shipbuilding and ship-repairing work on the Tyne was at least as important as the munitions production, the claims of the Admiralty had to be taken into account. When the Committee was established after a public meeting at Newcastle on 9 April, the Admiralty was represented on it by Captain Power, the Captain Superintendent on the Tyne. The function of the Committee was thus widened to include labour for naval as well as for armament work. The same principle held true of the Clyde district, where the Glasgow and West of Scotland Armaments Committee was set up on 30 April.

Such success as these Committees achieved—though, for reasons to be considered later, it was markedly greater at Newcastle than it was at Glasgow—must be in great measure attributed to the principle of their composition, which was essentially the same in both places. At Newcastle, the Executive Committee combined the representation, in

---

[1] A detailed history of these two Committees is given in Appendices XIV. and XV.

[2] See above. p. 25.

equal numbers, of three elements—Government officials, employers and workmen. The composition was as follows :—

Government officials—War Office	..	..	..	2 representatives	
	Admiralty	..	..	..	2	,,
	Board of Trade	..	..	2	,,
	Home Office	..	..	..	2	,,
Employers	..	..	..	..	..	8	,,
Workmen	..	..	..	..	..	8	,,

This Committee worked through three sub-committees—for Engineering, Shipbuilding, and Ship-repairing—each composed of four, or three, employers and workmen, together with the Government representatives. The first secretary was Captain Kelly, who was succeeded on 5 June by Captain Ross.

At Glasgow the Committee was unwieldy in size, and the official element was considerably weaker. The full committee consisted of 38 members—16 employers, 16 Trade Union representatives, 4 Government representatives, the Chairman, and the Secretary, Mr. Paterson, of the Labour Exchange organisation. The composition of the sub-committees, however, was more like that of the corresponding bodies at Newcastle. They each consisted of 2 employers, 2 workmen, the Government representatives, and the Secretary.

(b) METHODS OF EFFECTING THE TRANSFER OF LABOUR.

Alike at Newcastle and at Glasgow, the Committees tried in succession both the possible methods of effecting the redistribution of labour : first, an appeal to the employers to release their men ; later, an appeal to the workmen to volunteer. The results of the two experiments proved instructive, and had an influence on the policy adopted later in the Munitions of War Act. It was found that the second method was considerably more effective than the first, while both yielded better results than Mr. Booth's London Enquiry. The causes of these differences deserve careful attention.

(1) *The Appeal to Employers.*—At Newcastle, the employers had been approached in the first instance, before the Committee was formed, by means of the letter from Lord Kitchener which had also been issued in London, and the corresponding letter and questionnaire from Mr. Booth.[1] The Committee, on 16 April, decided to issue another form, requiring a return from each firm of the labour employed on Government or private contracts, and of the labour required for acceleration of Government work. Later, the firms were asked to telegraph offers of immediate release.

The Manager of the local Labour Exchange was employed to press the firms to make definite offers of release, and then to interview the men offered and ascertain precisely their qualifications. In order to obviate the skilled workman's prejudice against Labour Exchanges, the men were not required to call at the Exchange, and the Manager was instructed to make it clear that he was acting, not in his official

---

[1] See above, p. 22.

capacity, but as a representative of the Committee. Further, the workmen were informed that their railway fares would be paid from the place of their present employment to the establishment where they were to be engaged on Government work.

It is interesting to compare the preliminary response of the employers at Newcastle with the results of the two similar attempts made in London—the Board of Trade canvass, January 4-23, and the London Enquiry in April.

	Number of firms asked to release men.	Number of men	
		promised for release.	actually transferred.
Newcastle—			
(16-27 April)	300	1,661	—
London—			
Board of Trade (4-23 Jan.) ..	2,619	—	225
Mr. Booth's Enquiry (April–6 May)	405	142	50

It would appear that the readier response at Newcastle was not wholly attributable to differences in local conditions of employment. It may, perhaps, be partly accounted for by the elimination of the Labour Exchange procedure, and by the fact that more pains were taken to approach the men offered for release directly, and not merely through their employers. It may have been due, in a still greater degree, to the weight which the composition of the Committee lent t the appeal. Both employers and workmen were likely to be influenced by the knowledge that their several representatives were endorsing the action of the Government.

The Newcastle Committee, however, were not satisfied with this response. They strained their powers to the extent of issuing a letter calling upon employers to release 25% of their fitters and turners engaged on private work, or to undergo an examination before the Committee upon the reasons of their refusal. Captain Creed and Captain Power wished to go further still, and they applied to the Government for compulsory powers. Captain Kelly also asked for authority to close private workshops, compensation being granted to the employers. About a month later, the Glasgow Committee definitely proposed (among other ways of extending their authority) that the Defence of the Realm (Amendment) No. 2 Act, Section 1 (1) (*d*) should be amended so as to empower, not only the Admiralty and the Army Council, but also their representatives on Armament Committees, to transfer workmen from one establishment to another The refusal of these applications[1] occasioned at Glasgow some loss of prestige to the Committee, which had used a somewhat dictatorial tone towards employers. In both places the Committees had to fall back

---

[1] Captain Power was, indeed, authorised by the Admiralty to demand the release of men on mercantile work for Admiralty work at Messrs. Palmer's, but it does not appear that any general use was made of such authority.

upon their power of persuasion. They frequently encountered the jealousy felt by the outside employer towards the armament firm. Messrs. Armstrong were accused of squeezing their sub-contractors on Government work, and also of such mismanagement and lack of supervision at Elswick that men were often seen asleep on night shifts.

(2) *The Appeal to Workmen.*—In the hope of obtaining better results, the Newcastle Committee made a fresh start. in May, with an appeal addressed directly to workmen, and unanimously endorsed by the trade union representatives on the Committee. They adopted the idea, which had originated in several different quarters,[1] of a " King's Squad or Flying Column of Armament Workers." With the promise that those who enrolled themselves would " earn the same (or more) wages and be under no military restrictions whatever," the Committee called upon workmen to agree to go to any yard or workshop on the N.E. Coast upon receipt of a telegram, stating when and where their services were required. The procedure was simple and direct. The volunteers had only to send in a coupon and act on the telegraphic instructions. Any intervention on the part of employers, Trade Unions, or Labour Exchanges was eliminated until after the man had sent in his name. The employers welcomed the scheme in so far as it saved them from the invidious position of reducing their shareholders' profits by giving up their men ; though there was naturally some resistance from their side, justified in certain cases on the ground that the workmen who had volunteered would shortly be required for urgent Government work. Their reluctance was generally overcome by pressure from the Committee. From the point of view of the Government, the scheme had the merit of ruling out any claims for compensation.

The response of the men was excellent, in respect of both numbers and quality. Whereas the employer, when called upon to release men, was inevitably inclined to part with the least skilful and industrious, the class of men who volunteered was so good that comparatively few were rejected by the employers to whom they were sent.[2] It should be mentioned that what had hitherto been, from the workmen's point of view, the principal hindrance to transfer, had been removed, just before the new scheme was launched, by a satisfactory settlement of the vexed question of travelling and subsistence allowances,[3] and a guarantee that " every workman transferred shall receive the same rate, at least, as in his previous employment." The scheme was in force for about six weeks, from 15 May to 30 June. In this period 5,730 men were enrolled, of whom 1,680 were placed. By 16 June, Captain Ross was able to report that the needs of the large firms were nearly satisfied.

---

[1] A somewhat similar proposal is, for instance, put forward in Mr. Allan Smith's programme of 6 April (above, p. 29). At Newcastle the scheme was advocated and carried through by Captain Kelly.

[2] Under the earlier scheme of the appeal to employers, 521 of the 1,738 men enrolled had been rejected by the armament firms.

[3] See below, p. 49.

The following table illustrates the superior success at Newcastle of the appeal to workmen over the appeal to employers. Allowance must, of course, be made for the fact that the earlier scheme prejudiced the later, so that the superiority is even greater than the difference of the figures.

	Men enrolled.	Accepted by employers.
Appeal to employers (15 April to 15 May)	1,738	290 (270)
King's Squad (15 May to 30 June)		
Week ending 22 May	2,575	476
,, ,, 29 ,, ...	1,007	290
,, ,, 5 June	1,086	356
,, ,, 12 ,, ...	491	204
12 June to 30 ,, ...	571	354
TOTALS	5,730	1,680

A War Squad on similar lines was started at Glasgow early in June. In the first four days 4,500 men were enrolled. Half the applicants, however, proved to be unskilled men. By 15 July the enrolments numbered 9,755, but only 1,320 had been offered to employers, and of these no more than 454 had been accepted—a total less than the number placed at Newcastle in the first week.

The success of the King's Squad at Newcastle influenced the Government in framing the War Munitions Volunteer scheme, embodied in the Munitions of War Act. In this scheme, the Squads at Newcastle and Glasgow were merged, with certain concessions to the established functions of the Committees.

(c) THE COMPOSITION OF THE COMMITTEES AND THEIR EFFECTIVENESS.

It has been remarked that the success of the Newcastle and Glasgow Armaments Committees was principally due to their composition. This statement evidently requires to be justified in face of the fact that, while both were organised by the same man and were similarly constituted, Newcastle was more successful than Glasgow. Glasgow started later, and could take some advantage of the experience gained at Newcastle. It might, therefore, have been expected to do better, instead of worse.

The available evidence seems to show that the inferior achievement of Glasgow was due to external causes, rather than to any internal weakness of the Committee, though the large size of the full body told against its efficiency. The relations between the various elements represented appear to have been harmonious in both places, and the Glasgow Committee was not less active or enterprising. It may be conjectured that its comparative failure was chiefly due to the fact that it was working in an atmosphere vitiated by bad relations between Capital and Labour. From February, 1915, onwards, the unrest and discontent on the Clyde were, both in degree and in kind, exceptional. The rather autocratic attitude assumed by the Committee, and its application for drastic powers of compulsion, were, perhaps, a consequence of this tension.

The principle of the Newcastle Committee's composition was determined primarily by a desire to remedy the conflict of interests and overlapping of activities which had been the subject of much complaint in the district. Different Government Departments had independently called for elaborate returns, now from the employers, now from the Trade Unions ; the Admiralty and the War Office, in competition with one another, had tried to attract men to Government work ; the Recruiting Officer was still enlisting skilled men for the Army ; the employers' interests conflicted with them all ; and the workmen, even apart from considerations of their personal advantage, might well be in doubt to which of these many voices they ought to give ear. In the earlier days of the War, the employers had met the workmen on the old battle-ground of joint conferences, where the public interest was apt to be forgotten, because in normal times it had never been considered. The struggle between Departments, in so far as any attempt had been made to allay it, had been dealt with, not on the spot, but at headquarters, by the necessarily slow, and often ineffective, diplomacies of Whitehall. The best, perhaps the only, chance of adjustment and reconciliation lay in the creation of a local body, acquainted with the peculiar needs and problems of a single district, which could meet round a table to discuss ways and means to a common purpose of national significance, and not identical with the separate aims of any one section.

The presence of the Government representatives proved to be of value in several ways. It necessarily brought about a compromise between the competing claims of naval and armament work, and held the recruiting officer in check. The representatives of the several Departments, with a knowledge of rival needs and of local conditions, were in a position to formulate definite requests to their superiors in London, and to press for the solution of limited problems. In the district itself, their presence was felt outside the Committee, because, though not themselves armed with the powers of the Defence of the Realm Act, they were outposts of the central authorities who held those powers in reserve. Inside the Committee, their influence was still more important. Confronted with employers and workmen, they stood collectively for the public interests of the country, and helped to keep the proceedings from lapsing to the level of industrial disputes.

It would not be fair to ascribe exclusively to this influence the cordial relations which existed, alike at Newcastle and at Glasgow, between the employers' and workmen's representatives. In this respect the success of the experiment surpassed expectations. From the outset, it was agreed at Newcastle that employers and men should not be ranged on opposite sides of the table ; and it was found that on no single issue were they divided by a straight vote. Captain Kelly reported that the Committee, as a whole, was " surprisingly in accord on controversial points." Mr. Hebron, one of the workmen's representatives, said after the dissolution of the Committee : " Confidence between the employers' section and ourselves was growing, mutual understandings were developing, and many positions were adjusted with a maximum of satisfaction and a minimum of friction."

This mutual confidence was strikingly exemplified when, on the issue of an old-standing controversy between the two parties, the men left the statement of their case before Mr. Booth's Committee to a deputation consisting entirely of employers. The matter in question was the travelling or subsistence allowance. The settlement of it deserves more than a passing mention, since it illustrates, under several aspects, the strength and effectiveness of a committee so composed.

(d) Travelling and Subsistence Allowances.

The dispute between employers and workmen over the question of these allowances dated from the beginning of the War.[1] With regard to the terms offered to labour transferred during the emergency of mobilisation, there had been a difference of practice between the War Office and the Admiralty. In both cases, it had been intended that the subsistence allowance should be only temporary. The War Office, whose plans had been laid in view of the mobilisation of the Expeditionary Force, were able to cease paying the allowance after six weeks. The Admiralty, on the other hand, had to reckon with an emergency to which no term could be set. At any moment, after a naval action, there might be large and urgent demands for ship-repairing labour at any of the North Sea ports. They had, accordingly, offered £1 a week for at least three months ; and at the end of this period had continued the allowance, though the bonus was withdrawn.

All the men brought from a distance, whether for the War Office or for the Admiralty, had been taken through the Labour Exchanges. This method obviated any chance of conflict between men coming from other districts on their own initiative and men brought by a Government agency. It did not, however, prevent trouble arising between the imported men and the local workmen, who, of course, did not receive the subsistence allowance or the bonus, and were disposed to agitate for a corresponding increase of their own wages.

The second stage was marked by the joint conferences of employers and workmen held in the winter months of 1914. The employers were then demanding more men both for naval and for private work, and the suspension of demarcation rules. The men replied that plenty of men could be obtained, without a sacrifice of Trade Unions customs, if the employers would offer the Admiralty terms. The established peace-time methods of conducting an industrial dispute were brought into play—proposals and counter-proposals, and a leisurely inter-

---

[1] See Part II., Chap. II., Section VI.

change of correspondence, of a more and more acrimonious tone, between Federations and Unions. Dr. Macnamara's intervention on 15 December resulted in nothing more than a formulation of the opposing views. Neither side would give way, and the matter came to a deadlock.

In February, the controversy passed into the third normal phase, when the Chief Industrial Commissioner and his colleagues of the Committee on Production attempted the method of conciliation. The proceedings opened with the ill-omened refusal of the Employers' Federation to meet the Unions in presence of the Committee. The employers represented that, if they offered the Admiralty terms, it would cause a " general post " of labour. Large numbers of men would gain, merely by removal to another district, an increase of £1 in wages, while there would be no increase of output. All efforts to settle the question broke down, and the Committee on Production was unable to make any recommendation to the Government on this subject.

In this position the matter rested until it was taken up by the Newcastle Committee in April, though by this time some of the large shipbuilding firms had begun to pay allowances. On 23 April, the Committee resolved that men transferred from a distance to Government work should receive either (1) a subsistence allowance, or (2) workmen's fares both ways, together with one hour's travelling time daily at overtime rates. The Government Departments concerned were to be pressed for a speedy decision.

On 29 April, the Secretary reported that the War Office had ruled that subsistence allowance would not be paid by the Government, and had requested the Committee not to take any action that might prejudice the Government in other districts. This brought the Committee's work to a standstill. The local representative of the Amalgamated Society of Engineers maintained that the decision contravened an agreement between Lord Kitchener and his Society that transfers were to be made without infringing trade union rules.

At this juncture, the value of the new machinery was proved. The strength of the local Committee lay in the unanimity of all the three elements in its composition ; for it was on this occasion that the workmen left the statement of the whole case to a deputation of three employers. The Government officials, the employers, and the trade unionists on the spot had been able to thresh out the question and to reach an agreement satisfactory to them all. They had, moreover, in the Armaments Output Committee, a body which would listen to them sympathetically, and was equally anxious to force a way through obstacles. This Committee, when it met the deputation on 30 April, accepted the principle that subsistence or travelling allowances should be paid by the Government Departments concerned.

The workmen's representatives at Newcastle also conferred with Mr. Mosses and Mr. Hill of the National Advisory Committee, on 4 May.[1] They pointed out that workmen and employers were in complete agreement, and merely wanted to maintain local working rules which had been applied to the district for thirty years past.

In the Admiralty representative, the Newcastle Committee had yet another point of immediate contact with the central Government. On 24 April, Captain Power interviewed Sir Frederick Black, who undertook to raise the question on the Munitions of War Committee. The upshot was that this body, on 7 May, endorsed the conclusion of Mr. Booth's Committee that the allowances should be paid by the Government. Five days later, a code of Rules for the transference of men in the North-East Coast district, submitted by Sir Percy Girouard, was approved by the Munitions of War Committee. The same rules were afterwards adopted at Glasgow.[2]

By these means, in less than three weeks, a question which had defied solution under the normal procedure for many months, was settled to the complete satisfaction of all the parties represented in the local organisation.[3]

(e) THE TENDENCY OF THE COMMITTEES TO ENLARGE THEIR ACTIVITIES.

The original purpose for which the Committees at Newcastle and Glasgow were appointed was essentially of a temporary nature. As soon as the needs of the important firms were satisfied, the task of redistributing labour naturally ceased. In the course of July, the weekly numbers of men accepted by employers at Newcastle under the War Munitions Volunteers scheme fell from 416 to 22, and the end seemed to be in sight. At Glasgow, as has been seen, the movement had never had much success. Neither Committee, however, showed any inclination to dissolve itself. Their tendency rather was to seek an enlargement of their functions and a permanent existence. In May and June they were already developing in two directions.

In the first place, as the movement for the concentration of labour approached its natural limit, the Committees began to interest themselves in the reverse movement for the distribution of work. This involved the invasion of the A Area by the other principle of local organisation, which had at first been rigidly confined by the War Office rule to B Areas. The Newcastle Committee had from the first received and registered offers and applications of all kinds from firms or

---

[1] L.E. 1965/221.

[2] The travelling and subsistence allowances were later incorporated as an essential feature in the War Munition Volunteer scheme.

[3] It is a curious fact that, throughout these negotiations, no reference appears to have been made to a pledge given by Mr. Lloyd George on 10 March in the House of Commons : " The hon. Member (Mr. Tyson Wilson) is concerned about workmen who are transferred, under the Bill, from one district to another. The Government are quite prepared to meet the point of my honourable friend by dealing with it on exactly the same basis as they now deal with workmen who are transferred from the Dockyards." (*Parliamentary Debates* (1915), *H. of C.*, LXX., 1459.) In spirit, though not in letter, this pledge appears to be relevant.

individuals who desired to help in the output of munitions. As early as 26 April, when the War Office rule protecting A Areas from the placing of new contracts had broken down, two members of the Committee declared themselves in favour of distributing work rather than concentrating labour ; but the original policy was pursued till there was little more to be done in the way of labour transfer. In June, the Committee were considering schemes for co-operative production within their sphere of influence. This development was cut short by the re-division of the country into large Areas after the formation of the Ministry.

In the second place, thanks to the influence which their composition and internal cohesion won for them in the district, the Committees began, almost from the first, to be looked to as authorities exercising a general supervision over labour questions throughout their areas. At Newcastle, the Committee was called upon by the local Press and by a trade union to take up the defence of the shipyard workmen, when the Federated Shipbuilders accused them of loss of time due to drink, and they conferred on this subject with the Central Board for Liquor Control and with the local authorities. They endeavoured to secure the observance of the Treasury Agreement. They took up questions of railway and tramway services, and co-operated with the local Housing Committee. They took action to check bad time-keeping, prohibited local race meetings,[1] and tried to suppress the Whitsuntide holiday. The Glasgow Committee was equally active in similar ways.

More important than any of these activities was the use made of the Committee as a court of appeal to settle trade disputes. In several cases, Captain Power or Captain Kelly, at the Committee's request, intervened personally with success ; in other instances disputes were brought before the Committee as a whole, and its decisions were generally accepted.

Encouraged by its success in this sphere, the employers' representatives on the Newcastle Committee resolved that Armaments Committees should be empowered to settle trade disputes on munitions work. The Glasgow Committee had made the same request in May, as part of a larger scheme for the extension of their functions. Besides the settlement of differences, they had applied for authority to remove demarcations which hampered output ; to summon before them employers, trade union officials, and others, and compel them to observe the instructions of the Government representatives; to transfer workmen compulsorily ; and to draw labour from other districts.

Both Committees were informed that only the Cabinet could confer such powers ; and their requests were not in fact granted. Sir George Askwith strongly opposed the claim for powers to settle disputes. He considered that the workmen would object to their grievances being settled by members of other trade unions, while employers would not be willing to go before a tribunal of which (as he said) half was frankly

---

[1] Captain Ross notes that this was the first action of the kind to be taken anywhere.

partisan, and the other half would not take a strong line for fear of reprisals.

It may be questioned whether this forecast was justified by the events. Sir George Askwith seems to have overlooked the fact that the Committees were not composed only of employers and workmen in equal numbers—a type of body which is open to the serious objections he put forward. The moderating influence of the one-third consisting of impartial Government representatives appears in fact to have been felt on these occasions. If the first application had been made, not from Glasgow, but from Newcastle, and made three months later, when the Committee could have pointed to a series of successful interventions, Sir George Askwith's judgment might have been modified. On the other hand, it must be borne in mind that, so long as the Committee had no compulsory powers and merely gave its services when they were voluntarily invited, the chances of conciliation were considerably greater than they would have been if it had been empowered to summon the disputants and to enforce its awards upon unwilling parties. Its increasing popularity as a court of appeal depended largely on the fact that, while both sides were sure of a fair hearing, the losing side went away without a grievance.

The two Committees continued in being until they were superseded by the new Area Organisation instituted by the Ministry in August, 1915. Several members of the Newcastle Committee protested strongly against the shelving of a body which had acquired a valuable fund of local experience, and settled down into harmonious relations, both internal and external. They objected to the executive powers being entrusted to three officials. The Labour members were reluctant to remain on a committee reduced to advisory functions, and their dissatisfaction was strongly expressed at the final meeting on 30 August.

IV. The Breaking down of the Distinction between A and B Areas.

No other Armaments Committees on the Newcastle model w.re formed in the remaining A Areas, though early in April it was proposed to treat on the same lines the districts surrounding Barrow, Coventry Ordnance, and the Birmingham Small Arms Co., while London was being dealt with by the methods of the enquiry already described. The principal reason why the system was not extended was that the whole scheme for mutually exclusive A and B Areas was abandoned about 20 April under the influence of Sir Percy Girouard. But even before this date it had become clear that the ring-fence set up round the A Area by the War Office rule of the twenty-mile radius could not be rigidly maintained.

The reason will be evident from a consideration of the following table. The first column shows the Royal Factories and armament firms on the War Office list,[1] grouped according to their localities.

---

[1] See list prepared on 29 March, 1915, Appendix X.

The second column gives the centres of the corresponding A Areas which would result from an application of the War Office rule.[1]

Factories and Firms.	A Areas.
Woolwich Arsenal	
Royal Factory, Enfield	
Vickers, Crayford and Erith	1. London
Projectile Co., Battersea	
London Small Arms, London, E.	
Vickers, Ipswich	2. Ipswich
Vickers, Electric & Ordnance Accessories Co.	
Birmingham Small Arms Co.	3. Birmingham
King's Norton Metal Co.	
Birmingham Metal & Munitions Co.	
Coventry Ordnance	4. Coventry
Armstrong's, Openshaw	5. Manchester
Vickers, Sheffield	
Firth ,,	6. Sheffield
Hadfield ,,	
Vickers, Barrow	7. Barrow
Armstrong's, Elswick	8. Newcastle
Armstrong's, Darlington	9. Darlington
Royal Factory, Greenock	
Beardmore, Dalmuir and Parkhead	10. Glasgow
Armstrong's, Alexandria	
Cammell, Laird, Birkenhead	11. Liverpool
Dick, Kerr, Preston	12. Preston
Greenwood & Batley, Leeds	13. Leeds.

It is immediately obvious that these Areas included a very large proportion of any surplus engineering capacity that could be drawn upon for shell manufacture. Circles of twenty-mile radius drawn round two of these centres alone—Manchester and Leeds—contain nearly all the important towns in Lancashire and West Yorkshire : Keighley, Bradford, Halifax, Wakefield, Huddersfield, Barnsley, Bury, Rochdale, Rawtenstall and Bacup (at each of which a Board of Management was set up before the end of 1915), as well as places of minor importance for this purpose, such as Brighouse, Accrington, Bolton, Oldham, Wigan, Warrington, Stalybridge, Burnley.[2]   What is left of Lancashire and the West Riding is completely covered by the Areas round Barrow, Preston, Liverpool and Sheffield.   If the War Office rule had been strictly applied, there would have been little room left for co-operative schemes, except in South Wales, the Bristol district, and a few outlying centres in the Midlands.

A further difficulty was that eight of the centres on the A Area list—Liverpool, Manchester, Glasgow, Leeds, Coventry, Sheffield, Birmingham and London—were precisely the places at which the Board of Trade, with the approval and co-operation of the War Office, had held the exhibitions of sample shells and fuses, and was at this very time engaged in inspecting the works of firms who desired to

---

[1] The first 10 of these Areas appear on a provisional list of A Areas drawn up at the beginning of April ; and of the remaining three, Leeds, at any rate, was at first regarded as coming under the rule.

[2] At all these places Affiliated Munitions Committees were subsequently set up.

tender for contracts, either singly or in groups. At several of these places the employers were already forming committees, and eager to take immediate action. The Board of Trade was deeply committed, and almost the whole of their work was threatened with stultification. On 8 April, when the Board reported progress to Mr. Booth, they had to point out that the groups which were being arranged at Rotherham, Sheffield, Bradford, Keighley and Leeds all fell under the ban, as well as a number of textile machinery firms at Manchester. The only other groups existing or in prospect at that date were at Leicester, Hull and Lincoln. The Board also furnished at the same time a list of 40 selected firms, of whom the majority offered to machine either 18-pdr. or 4·5-in. shells, while 15 were prepared to make fuses, and four offered forgings. A considerable proportion of these were situated in protected areas. It soon became apparent that the concession obtained from the War Office hardly deserved to be called a compromise. The field it left open to the B Area principle promised only a negligible amount of capacity.

The two policies were, indeed, still unreconciled in practice. The clash between them may be illustrated by the case of Birmingham. Here the local Chamber of Commerce, acting on the suggestion of the Labour Exchange Divisional Officer, had called a meeting, on 7 April, of engineering employers who desired to take up armament work. Several representatives proposed that a group should be formed for co-operative shell production. The idea was opposed by Major-General Mahon, who addressed the meeting on behalf of the War Office. He is reported to have said that the existing sources of munitions supply were sufficient for all purposes, provided that labour to operate the machines could be obtained. He thought it practically impossible to set up, in time to be of service, fresh centres for shell manufacture. After consideration, he had come to the conclusion that the only way of securing improvement was to form a Labour Battalion, which might be sent, as required, to help the armament firms.[1]

This proposal met with no support from the firms' representatives, who had come quite unprepared for the official discouragement of their scheme. Major-General Mahon, in his own report to the Master-General of the Ordnance, wrote :—" So far as my particular object of trying to get assistance to bring together a body of independent labour is concerned, my visit (to Birmingham) is a complete failure. Every man argues that he wants labour and can spare none."[2]

The Divisional Officer was naturally distressed at the apparently hostile attitude of the War Office towards the system of co-operative groups, which had been in the minds of the promoters of the meeting. On 10 April, when his report of the meeting had been received, an officer of the Board of Trade saw Major-General Mahon and ventured upon a remonstrance, which proved effective. Major-General Mahon said that he was not so absolutely opposed to the group system as the

---

[1] Report of Divisional Officer for West Midlands. L.E. 1965/144.
[2] 94/GEN. No./92.

Divisional Officer's report suggested. It might, he admitted, be necessary to approach Birmingham with both possibilities in view.

The advantage so gained was immediately followed up. On 13 April Mr. Booth received representatives from Birmingham, and proposed that contracts should be placed either with a group or with individual firms. It was arranged that a meeting should be called at Birmingham to formulate proposals, and a committee was elected there on 19 April.

It does not appear whether the War Office ever formally withdrew the rule of the twenty-mile radius. But, as the pressure from other centres in the reserved areas became stronger, it soon ceased to be in force. On 16 April Major-General Mahon and Mr. Hanson themselves received a deputation of textile machinery firms from Manchester, and informed them that 12,000 4·5-in. shells would be a sufficient contribution from the textile firms of Lancashire. On the same day, Mr. Davison was able to report that " A Areas, namely 20 miles round armament towns, are no longer regarded as districts in which fresh orders for shells must not be placed."[1]

So, at last, the Board of Trade won back the lost ground, though in the meantime progress had been delayed. For instance, the Sheffield Committee, appointed on 29 March, had been told to suspend its operations except in so far as it could help with labour supply ; and other nascent groups were similarly held in arrest. The barriers were not finally swept away until Sir Percy Girouard's new scheme abolished the distinction between the two types of area.

V. The Development of Co-operative Schemes in B Areas.

In considering the earliest dealings of the Armaments Output Committee with the B Areas, it is important to realise that, although the programme of 6 April above described had on paper a formidable air, the designs of Mr. Booth and Mr. Allan Smith were not really on a very ambitious scale. Apart from the small volume of engineering capacity that was to be found outside the A Areas, there are other limitations to be noticed.

Like the Board of Trade exhibitions, the Committee's operations were confined to the smaller natures of high explosive shell (in particular the 18-pdr., 4·5-in. and 6-in.) and the No. 100 fuse. No other warlike stores came within their commission. Nor were they at first expected to take up the problems of the supply of machinery or of raw materials, though at a very early stage of their enquiries these questions were forced upon their attention. Their first object was to turn to account the resources brought to light by the sample exhibitions and subsequent

---

[1] *Report on Co-operation with Mr. Booth and Lord Kitchener's Committee* (16/4/15). HIST. REC./R/171/17.

inspections. As the reports of the survey were received at the Board of Trade, each firm was entered on a table showing the numbers employed and the proportion of employees engaged on Government work, with a general indication of the firm's capacity for shell and fuse manufacture. Tabulations were also submitted, giving the firms or groups of firms which appeared from the survey to be specially adapted for the purpose and to merit consideration for orders.[1] The function of the Committee was to assist the Contracts department by carrying negotiations with these possible contractors up to the point at which they could make a definite offer of so many hundred shells or fuses a week. The order once placed, the Committee, like the Contracts department in normal times, was not expected to concern itself further with the means and methods by which it would be executed.

The main principle involved was to substitute the placing of direct contracts for complete articles for the old system under which the manufacturers had taken from the armament firms sub-contracts for single processes. The group was simply a composite contractor, a federation consisting of such a number of firms as together, though not individually, possessed the plant required to turn out the forging and machine the empty shell. Such now seemed to be the best method of setting the smaller engineering firms to work.

Mr. Booth was reluctant to put into force the coercive powers obtained under the Defence of the Realm Act. In his letter to employers of 29 March[2] he had stated that the War Office, while prepared, if necessary, to use those powers, was " anxious to disturb employers as little as possible." On 20 April he remarked to a deputation of the Birmingham Committee : " We are very anxious that in no sense should any of these new measures involve compulsion upon anybody. We do not want to adopt violent measures under the Defence of the Realm Act, such as winding up people's shops and taking over the control of them. Our firm belief is that the country will run itself extremely well if it only gets the chance."

There was, indeed, at first some intention of enforcing the Act upon firms in the A Areas, a field in which the application of its provisions, as a means to the diversion of labour, would have been appropriate. But, as the distinction between A and B Areas broke down, the idea, underlying the Act, of the compulsory extinction of commercial work by depopulating or dismantling factories or by " taking them over," faded into the background, where it remained as a bugbear to overawe the recalcitrant employer. In the main, however, employers were anything but recalcitrant, as soon as they were able to obtain a sympathetic hearing of their case at interviews with the Committee, and to formulate proposals compatible with their reasonable interests.

The position, as it appeared to the manager of an important engineering concern of medium size, was stated by Mr. Pybus,

---

[1] L.E. 1965/161.   [2] See Appendix VI.

managing director of the Phoenix Dynamo Company at Bradford, in a reasoned and comprehensive memorandum.[1] The writer pointed out the obstacles which, in districts such as Yorkshire and Lancashire, blocked the A Area policy of concentrating labour. A workman of the best type would not move, even for higher wages, to employment at an armament firm in a congested area. His family, some of whom would be working in mills or factories, could neither find occupation in the new place nor earn enough to live on at home in the man's absence. Men who had left their homes to go to armament districts, had returned disgusted with the high cost of living and the wretched housing conditions, and had deterred others from going. A maximum output from the existing shell-making tools, and particularly from those now on order for the great armament firms, could be obtained only by moving them to the districts where labour was to be found. The railway congestion in armament centres was a further ground for the same conclusion.

There were many objections to the system of sub-contracting. The waste of time and money involved in sub-letting operations on shells to medium-sized firms was illustrated by one instance, which entailed (1) the raw material being sent from the armament works to the sub-contractor for boring and turning ; (2) the rough-turned shell being sent back for the pressing up of the nose ; (3) the shell being returned to the sub-contractor for partial completion ; and (4) finally sent back to the armament firm for finishing. The output under such conditions must obviously be much smaller than it would be if certain key operations, now only done at armament works, could be performed at a central depôt. Further, every department of a well organised factory being interdependent on the others, the whole output would be stagnated, if the full capacity of the one class of tools suitable for armament work were monopolised for that purpose. The work handed out to sub-contractors was of far too limited a range.

Mr. Pybus recommended the grouping of medium-sized firms. For every very large engineering concern in England, there were perhaps ten such firms employing 500 or 600 hands and with an equally good tool equipment. They were usually very efficient. The concern, as a rule, had not passed out of the control of the people who had built it up, and friendly relations between employer and workmen increased output and reduced working costs. The percentage profit was invariably greater than that of the larger firm, though the selling price was commonly less. The percentage efficiency per man and tool must therefore be greater.

The method of organisation recommended by Mr. Pybus was practically that which, shortly after the date of his memorandum, was adopted at Leicester. The functions which he suggested should be exercised by a Board of Control, consisting of one Government

---

[1] M.C. 414. This memorandum was sent by Mr. Pybus to the Treasury on 18 March, and a copy was forwarded by the Board of Trade to Mr. Booth on 31 March.

representative and one representative of each of the co-operating firms, closely resembled the duties later undertaken by the " Board of Management."

Referring to this memorandum in a letter of 5 April to Sir H. Llewellyn Smith, Mr. Booth observed that the writer was very intelligent, and that he was " crystallising in his direction."

Meanwhile, Mr. Allan Smith was setting to work on somewhat different lines. It will be remembered that, in his programme of 6 April, he proposed that the Engineering Employers' Federation should move their local Associations to appoint committees, representing the various branches of industry carried on in the district. These local committees were to have functions different from those of Mr. Pybus' Board of Control. They were not to undertake to execute a contract, but to be available for consultation, to superintend the carrying out of the Central Committee's instructions, and generally to assist in matters referred to them and make suggestions.

Mr. Allan Smith interpreted Lord Kitchener's approval of his memorandum as a commission to take action on these lines through his Federation. The result was that some overlapping occurred at several places, where the Board of Trade was simultaneously organising a committee of the group type. At Leeds, for instance, the first move was made by a deputation of the Engineering Employers' Federation which interviewed the Master-General of the Ordnance on 24 March. They proposed that a central committee of five members of the Federation should be notified by the War Office of any orders that required to be placed, and should hand on the orders to branch committees in localities they thought suitable. On 13 April, the Leeds Engineering Employers' Association appointed the four members of this deputation with one other gentleman a special local committee to deal with the question of munitions production in the Leeds district. On the same day, the Lord Mayor, at the instance of the Labour Exchange officials, issued an invitation to Leeds engineers to meet and consider proposals on co-operative lines. When the meeting was held two days later, the conflict was adjusted by confirming the appointment of the Association's Committee. This Committee saw Mr. Booth at the War Office on 19 April and adopted the co-operative system.

The Federation took similar action at Birmingham, through Mr. Arthur Keen and Captain Hilton ; at Coventry, through Mr. Alfred Herbert ; at Oldham, through the Manager of Messrs. Asa Lees ; and at Sheffield, through Colonel Hughes. Sir Algernon Firth also set in motion the Chambers of Commerce ; but these bodies in most cases made way for the local Engineering Employers' Association, as being an organisation better suited to the purpose. The scheme propounded by Captain Hilton at Birmingham on 11 April was on Mr. Allan Smith's lines. He recommended that the War Office should appoint five Birmingham employers and a War Office official to act for the Department in the district. This committee was to fix prices, issue orders, organise the trades, advise the Armaments Output Committee on labour supply and transfer, and commandeer the output of certain works. The general result, however, was that the co-operative system prevailed, and the machinery of the Engineering Employers' Federation was not adopted as the framework of organisation.

Partly as a consequence of the War Office rule which excluded the co-operative principle from those areas where engineering centres are thickly clustered, the natural geographical unit was at first the town, rather than the larger district. In a place like Leicester, Nottingham, Lincoln, or Hull, a group would be formed by a number of firms, well known to one another and accustomed to mutual dealings, coming together to arrange for co-operation. Four or five members of the principal firms would be formed into an executive. The available surplus of capacity would be represented by a small fraction of machinery and men not already absorbed by Government work ; and an output of 500 or 1,000 shells a week was the most that any of the earliest groups could contemplate at the start.

On 16 April, when Mr. Davison reported on co-operation between the Board of Trade and the Armaments Output Committee, it had been arranged that Mr. Booth should interview, in the course of the next few days, representatives of groups which were being worked up by the Labour Exchange organisation at Walthamstow, Bradford, Leeds, Keighley, Nottingham, Hull, Wakefield, and Rotherham. Other places that have been mentioned were in various stages of advance. The only order that had actually been placed was at Leicester.

If the Armaments Output Committee had continued on these lines, its work might have reached a natural termination in two or three months. By that time, the new contractors would have been organised, the orders placed, and the work begun. The Contracts department could then have dealt with them through the established routine. . It was not long, however, before a much wider prospect opened out before the Committee. In the last ten days of April, the whole plan of operations was remodelled, and the Committee began to assume the functions, and acquire something of the status, of a Department.

CHAPTER IV.

LOCAL ORGANISATION, 28 APRIL TO 26 MAY.

I. Sir Percy Girouard's Scheme for Co-ordinating A and B Areas, and for a Central Department.

About the middle of April, Lord Kitchener sent for Sir Percy Girouard and requested him to advise him personally, in conjunction with Mr. Booth, on the output of munitions.[1] Sir Percy Girouard came to the War Office shortly before 20 April, and resigned his managing directorship at Elswick on 22 April.

Mr. Lloyd George immediately invited him to lay his views before the Munitions of War Committee. He was co-opted to that body on 26 April, and at the same meeting he presented a *Memorandum on the Production of Ammunition*,[2] which he had drawn up in collaboration with Mr. Booth. This document contained far-reaching proposals both for the reconstruction of the whole scheme of local organisation and for enlarging the functions of the central body.

(*a*) In the sphere of local organisation, Sir Percy Girouard attacked the principle of dividing the country into A and B Areas, and the attempt to organise fresh centres of shell production in Areas of the latter type independently of the former. The Government was at present relying for its home supplies entirely upon A Areas. Deliveries were considerably in arrear, but the new equipment of the armament firms was nearing completion and the maximum weekly output promised might be expected in from three to five months, provided that the necessary supplies of labour, machinery, and material were not interfered with. Such interference, however, was threatened by the independent development of B Areas ; the increase of labour demanded by the armament firms would be withheld, and large numbers of skilled men would actually be withdrawn from the most efficient section of our supply. Hitherto, at Newcastle, for instance, labour had been drawn in from the neighbourhood. At Messrs. Armstrong's shell factories the staff had risen from 1,300 to 13,000. But, if independent B Areas were constituted near Newcastle, a proportion of workpeople would be attracted away. There would also be a danger of interference with contracts for machinery or raw material already placed by armament firms for the completion of their works or the

---

[1] As early as September, 1914, Captain Hankey, Secretary of the Committee of Imperial Defence, had suggested to Mr. Churchill that Sir Percy Girouard should be put at the head of an " emergency armament multiplication committee or department, to set on foot and develop the maximum possible output of guns, rifles, ammunition, etc." Hist. Rec./R/170/21.

[2] M.C. 8. Hist. Rec./R/172/1. (23 April, 1915.)

maintenance of their full output. The result would be a diminution of supply, and this must, at all hazards, be avoided.

A further objection was that B Areas, acting independently, would have to face serious experimental difficulties, and could hardly achieve success rapidly unless some central supervision were provided, to guide every operation.

These objections appeared insuperable, and the writer concluded that the two types of Area must be co-ordinated.

In order to provide technical supervision for the co-ordinated Areas, it was recommended that the Government should assume control (nominal in so far as management was concerned) of ammunition factories. The heads of the ammunition departments of the principal armament manufacturers were to be withdrawn from the employment of their firms and taken into temporary public service as Government Superintendents. Besides continuing to control the factories of their companies, they would become supervisors or guides in organising the companies of the so-called B Areas.

The general line of procedure to be adopted would be as follows. Assuming the county as the unit (though this might prove not to be the best unit) the first step would be to form a Committee, whose members would be drawn from the many manufacturing centres which had already sent deputations to the War Office. The new Committee, say in Yorkshire, would be put in touch with the manager of Armstrong's shell factories, now appointed to be a Government Superintendent of Munitions. After visiting the shell shops, they would return to their county to consider the class of work that could best be done in their factories. The ideal to be borne in mind was that each district, or county, or town, which took up the manufacture of ammunition, must be prepared to deliver complete rounds (without propellant or explosives) ; though in certain instances the fuses made in one area might be balanced against the shell or case made in another. The Committee, having thus mapped out the work with the help of the Superintendent, would then nominate managers from the various works to act under the Superintendent and keep the whole area in touch with him.

In order to avoid robbing the armament firms of skilled hands to start the new work, a nucleus of managers, foremen, and skilled workmen should be sent from each factory to be trained at a regular armament works. On their return they would proceed rapidly with the knowledge so acquired. The necessary supply of gauges and tools would be organised, under the Superintendent's direction, so as not to interfere with contracts already placed.

When the Committee could arrive at an estimate of the total output of their district, they would report it to the " central executive or department." The writer believed that, organised in this way, the United Kingdom could yield an output which, supplemented by supplies from the rest of the Empire, would make the country independent of foreign contracts.

(b) On the subject of the "central executive or department" Sir Percy Girouard did not enter into details ; but it is clear that this body was to be both more important and more independent than the Armaments Output Committee. He stated that, in requesting him to appear before the Munitions of War Committee, Mr. Lloyd George had " given him, as a guiding principle, the creation of an organisation in England and the Empire which would fully provide for ammunition requirements, and lead, if possible, to an immediate increase of output." Sir Percy Girouard considered that a " special department " should be organised, which, it was suggested, should " control the whole of our Imperial output." In relation to the local bodies, its function would be to report to the War Office and the Admiralty the offers of prospective output made by the several districts, and to ask for the allocation of these supplies and the distribution of contracts by the usual departments.

The most characteristic feature of Sir Percy Girouard's scheme is the proposed grouping of the new direct contractors under the tutelage and supervision of the Government Superintendent, drawn from the armament firm. In this respect the plan was never put into practice ; indeed, its author had already modified his views before he met the Munitions of War Committee on 26 April, and had come to prefer the method of founding Government factories of a new type.[1] On the other hand, it will be seen that the memorandum summarised above entailed a radical change of policy, and established both the central and the local organisation on a fresh basis. It will be convenient to consider first the new pattern of local organisation, and afterwards to describe the consequential development of the central committee. The bare statement contained in the memorandum can be supplemented from expositions of the scheme given by Mr. Booth and Mr. Allan Smith at a series of conferences with deputations from local committees, held almost daily from 20 April to 29 April.[2] Mr. Booth had spent the whole morning of 20 April with Sir Percy Girouard, and from that time he threw all his energies into the development of the new plan.

II. The Armament Firms and the Minor Contractors.

The negative result established by Sir Percy Girouard's proposals was the total and final abandonment of the distinct A and B Areas which had been the essence of the compromise between the Board of Trade and the War Office. From 20 April onwards, except at Newcastle and Glasgow, where the two Armaments Committees of the A type went on with their work, the terms " A Area " and " B Area " ceased to have any application. This change was no question of mere administrative expediency ; it implied an inroad upon the last defences guarding the privileged position of the armament firm.

---

[1] See below, p. 70.

[2] Printed verbatim reports of these Conferences are in Hist. Rec./R/171.

As managing director of Elswick, Sir Percy Girouard naturally approached the whole problem from the armament firm's point of view, and, as will be seen later, his experience enabled him to put his finger on several weak spots in the earlier scheme. His first commission from Lord Kitchener had been to secure the concentration of labour within the Newcastle district upon Messrs. Armstrong's works ; and in his report to the Master-General of the Ordnance, dated 25 March, he had emphasised the primary necessity of manning the factories laid down by Government under the control of the original manufacturers of munitions of war. To attempt to organise small engineering concerns, in preference to the main factories and at the cost of depleting the competent firms of their supervision, would, he had declared, be suicidal ; though some of the small factories, if almost wholly remodelled, might be organised later. The type of central authority proposed in this report was designed solely to effect the transfer of labour, by correlating the efforts made in the various districts on the lines of his own work at Newcastle. At this date, in fact, Sir Percy Girouard had been, almost without reserve, a supporter of the old War Office policy.

In the first three weeks of April, however, the situation had changed. At Newcastle, the local Committee was beginning to satisfy the immediate labour requirements of the principal Government contractors ; and on the other hand, the Board of Trade and the Armaments Output Committee had pushed forward their work in the B centres to such a point that the claims of this alternative policy could no longer be denied. It has already been pointed out that by 16 April the whole principle of the reserved A Area had broken down.[1] The armament firms were no longer to be protected from the placing of direct contracts in their vicinity.

This really meant a complete reversal of the policy, which had ruled at the War Office since October, 1914, of extending the system of sub-contracting. At the conferences in the last ten days of April, Mr. Booth was explicit on this point. Addressing the Bradford Group on 23 April, he said[2] :—

> " All further sub-contracting through the main armament firms is going to come to an end as far as possible, and to be replaced by direct Government work. The whole producing areas are coming under Government work, including the armament areas themselves. Everybody would have their own contracts : each district would have its own contract, just as the armament areas have their contracts ; so there would be direct touch between the War Office and them."

Again, the following passage occurred at the interview with the Rotherham deputation on 27 April[3] :—

> Mr. Wells (of E. Allen & Co., Tinsley) : " There has been a disposition on the part of Rotherham to assist these large armament firms in turning their shells. I investigated that

---

[1] See p. 53.
[2] A.O.C. *Printed Minutes*, p. 72. Hist. Rec./R/1711.
[3] *Ibid.*, p. 104.

problem thoroughly ; and it appears to me that these large armament firms, in the rates they are paying, are taking the last drop of financial blood from these small contractors."

MR. BOOTH : " There will be no more of that, because it will be arranged through the districts now entirely, and, if we find that there is any question of difficulty, the Government will deal with it on their own account. It may be wiser to let the Government actually do it, though it will be managed by a big local committee. We want to have no one feeling that they are piling up profits for a particular firm. That does not suit anyone. It does not suit the political side of the Government, and it is a very important thing to a man like the Chancellor of the Exchequer, who is having that in hand all the time ; and it does not suit the Labour Party. The armament firms are playing cricket. They are coming in, and they say : ' We do not want any more sub-contracts. Take the whole thing over and run it any way you like ; take our shop and our management over as you like.' Certainly, if any group is asked to help in any way—and your group will be asked to help—you will not be allowed to lose the full credit, the full advantage of the work you have done. There will not be that centralising of huge armament profits for three or four firms that you are thinking of."[1]

In yet another respect the privileges of the armament firms had recently been impaired. From the beginning of April, Lord Kitchener had thrown open Woolwich Arsenal and given instructions that representatives of any of the new groups should be allowed to visit the shops, inspect the whole process of shell manufacture, and receive whatever information and advice they needed. The effect was to break down any barriers of mystery that might have sheltered the expert production of shell, and even the usual reserve of trade secrecy. The armament firms had been accused of trying to keep munitions work in their own hands. Henceforth, the whole resources of expert knowledge were to be thrown into a common stock. The armament

---

[1] The sub-contractor's grievance may be illustrated from a letter sent by a Liverpool firm to the Armaments Output Committee, which stated that for turning 15-pounder shell a sub-contractor had been paid 2s. 8d. per shell. The time averaged 1 hour and 10 minutes. " Is this a fair price for man, machine, overtime, and standing charges ? " From another point of view, the system was unsatisfactory to the main contractors. Mr. G. H. West, of Armstrong's, wrote to Mr. Booth on 12 May that he had continually to send out assistants, whom he could ill spare, to help sub-contractors. He added : " A great deal of harm has been done by the indiscriminate placing of sub-contracts by armament firms."

Sir R. Cooper said in the House of Commons on 23 June : " Rightly or wrongly, an enormous number of business men in this country are suspicious that, if they work for anyone except directly for the War Office or the Munitions Department, they are working for vested interests. . . . There are the prices at which they have worked for armament firms, and the prices for which they themselves in a similar position have done work for the Government direct. There is a 40% margin."—(*Parliamentary Debates* (1915), H. of C., LXXII., 1221-2.)

firms had now nothing to lose by following suit. Messrs. Armstrong consented to open their works in the same way ; and Messrs. Vickers agreed on 20 April. Several others of the chief firms came into line very shortly afterwards. In Mr. Booth's words : " This is a co-ordinated scheme for bringing the whole of England into being on a patriotic basis, and for helping and putting at the disposal of all what have been considered as secrets and special devices—laying them all out flat, so that after the War any big firm would probably be able to make shell."[1]

It was anticipated that the method of sending a nucleus of managers, foremen, and skilled hands from the factories for a period of some eight or ten weeks' training at an armament firm, would be advantageous to both parties. The men who were sent would obviously learn much more than could be picked up merely by visiting the shops ; and the armament firm would get the benefit of having selected men temporarily to man their idle machines. The system was more economical than the earlier notion of mobile labour battalions. Mr. Booth remarked on 20 April : " We do not want to get involved in a large labour-moving problem, with armies of engineers being marched about the country, working where we think it is best. We want to have each area keep its own men."[2]

III. The Number and Size of the Proposed New Areas.

The question of the number and size of the new areas was at first left undecided. At the conferences held towards the end of April, Mr. Booth was feeling his way, and he invited the representatives of the local groups and committees to advise him on this point. On 22 April, he spoke of the intention to start " probably four or five official units "[3] ; and on the following day remarked that it was not desired to have more than six areas in the whole of England.[4] On 29 April he said : " We do not want to start with more than about twelve places, and we want those places large. We shall be forced down to the smaller places gradually."[5]

More important than the number was the principle, or principles, by which the size of a district was to be governed. The notion which had hitherto prevailed, of allowing twenty or thirty small groups, each producing 500 to 1,000 shells a week, to spring up in isolated towns, was now to be abandoned as uneconomical. Sir Percy Girouard contended that it would be impossible to provide the supervision which alone could guarantee effective production ; and that each new centre would bring into the field one more competitor in an unrestricted scramble for labour, machinery, and raw materials. The first point was that the districts were to be larger, not in every case in mileage, but in volume of capacity and output. The units of weekly output were to be, not hundreds, but tens of thousands.

[1] A.O.C. *Printed Minutes*, p. 3 (20 April).
[2] *Ibid.*, p. 4.   [3] *Ibid.*, p. 44.   [4] *Ibid.*, p. 71.   [5] *Ibid.*, p. 104.

Mr. Booth several times mentioned 200,000 shells weekly as the figure to be aimed at for the total production from all the new sources.

The problem of inspection was similar to that of supervision. The congestion at Woolwich had been a serious cause of delay, and, as early as 23 April, the Committee was endeavouring to arrange with Sir Frederick Donaldson that each of the new areas should have a local inspector.[1] They had in view the system adopted by the French Government, which had established local centres in the several districts, where inspection could be carried out from process to process. In this country, only the largest contractors—Vickers, Armstrong, Firth, Coventry Ordnance, and the Projectile Company—had local inspectors. It was purposed to extend the system to the new districts, subject to a final approval by an official of the Inspection Department at Woolwich.

Another canon for determining the size of districts was laid down in the principle, on which Sir Frederick Donaldson had laid stress, that each district should produce the complete round (without explosive or propellant). This ruled out small centres, where a group might be able to muster the lathes for machining the shell, but could not provide heavy presses for the forging. On 26 April, Mr. Allan Smith described as follows the difficulties that had come to light at earlier conferences :—

> " In the first place we have found that, while there is plenty of capacity for machining, there is not the supply of raw material. Then there is not the supply of presses for pressing out the forgings, and we have had a difficulty with the presses for pressing the copper bands on the shells. Again, the shell is not complete without the fuse, and, as the fuse is really a brass-finisher's job, sometimes we have had a difficulty in getting fuses, although we may have no difficulty in getting the machining of the shell done.

> " All these things point to a co-ordination of the various districts, because it is conceivable that one district where there are forges—for example, like Leeds, or Darlington, or Sheffield, which could turn out a large supply of forgings for machining—would be able to co-operate with a district where there are no forges . . . Then, on the other hand, where we have found that in some cases the tools are of a heavy quality, there is not a sufficient supply of small tools for the purpose of turning out the gauges, which are really a conglomeration of small parts. Then we have to go somewhere else to get a district which could co-operate with the other two districts so as to supply the fuses, and so in co-operation produce the finished article."[2]

Considerations such as these led on to the further problem of a more exact balancing of tools within the district, so that, for instance, the unit of production of a forging press working at full power should

---

[1] A.O.C. *Printed Minutes*, p. 68.   [2] *Ibid.*, p. 78.

not seriously exceed or fall short of the unit of the copper-banding and nosing presses or of the machining capacity. It was evidently a matter of great difficulty to delimit areas which would both satisfy this principle without a wholesale redistribution of plant, and at the same time be compact and manageable for the purposes of supervision and inspection. It was proposed to leave the solution of this problem so far as possible to the local committees; but at the same time the purchase and distribution of raw material, machinery, and gauges were matters that called for the exercise of some control by the central organisation. It will be seen later how, under the pressure of these limiting factors, the Committee began to develop specialised departments.

IV. The Constitution of Local Munitions Committees.

The enlargement of the districts entailed the institution of a new type of local munitions committee, more representative than the small groups of employers who had undertaken the earliest co-operative schemes in single towns. Just before Sir Percy Girouard's plan was formulated, the National Advisory Committee had, on 17 April, discussed with Mr. Booth's Committee the danger that local bodies. appointed to organise munitions work might overlap the local Advisory Committees representing Labour. Mr. Booth then drew up *Notes regarding the appointment of Local Committees*, which were printed and circulated by the War Office.[1] It was laid down that the local Advisory Committees " will co-operate with the local committees of employers with the view of settling promptly any questions which may arise, and, failing settlement, will invoke the assistance of the (National) Advisory Committee." The employers and the labour committees were each to nominate five or seven representatives, who were together to form a Joint Committee. The employers were to deal separately with all manufacturing questions; the Advisory Committees of the Unions with all questions affecting their members; the Joint Committees with questions which affected manufacturers and workpeople alike.

The Armaments Output Committee insisted strongly that the co-operation of Labour was essential to their scheme. They pointed out that they were bound to keep within the terms of the Fair Wages Clause in Government contracts, and that this fully recognised Trade Unionism. Mr. Allan Smith said on 26 April: " In connection with the production of these munitions, the Trade Unions have in great measure relaxed their ordinary working regulations, and they are doing things just now that they would not be willing to do in peace times. It is only reasonable, from that point of view, that the employer should do the same thing . . . I am very doubtful if the Committee would feel at liberty to recommend the War Office to agree to the placing of a contract in shops which absolutely refuse to have anything to do with men who are members of Trade Unions."[2]

---

[1] See Appendix XI.   [2] A.O.C. *Printed Minutes*, pp. 86, 87.

The Munitions of War Committee, on 7 May, considered the relations of the local committees to the War Office and to itself. It was decided that the local committees should be responsible to, and take their instructions from, the War Office, and that, in matters of general principle, the War Office might, at their discretion, consult the Munitions of War Committee.

A sub-committee also recommended that all future local committees should be constituted as follows :—

Representatives of Employers.
Representatives of Labour.
A representative of the Admiralty.
A representative of the War Office.
A representative of the Home Office.
A representative of the Board of Trade.

The consideration of this recommendation was adjourned on 13 May, and it does not appear that it was ever approved. It was certainly not put into practice.

In some places, committees with equal representation of employers and workmen were set on foot ; but this was the exception. Owing to the change in the character of the districts under Sir Percy Girouard's scheme, Mr. Booth's regulations above mentioned, which were issued on 21 April, were superseded two days later by a memorandum of general suggestions, which left it to each area to arrive at some arrangement which would be satisfactory to Labour.[1] The ultimate outcome was that, when once an executive Board of Management was appointed, the large local munitions committees, on which Labour had some representation, tended to become obsolete and were seldom called together The Board of Management, except in a few cases, consisted of a small number of employers only, and was thus a body of the same type as the original Co-operative Group. Often it was composed, more or less, of the same individuals.

V. Type of Contract and Prices.

The type of contract which it was at this time proposed to place with the new committees was adapted to the peculiar conditions. It was estimated that it would take eight or ten weeks to instal the machinery and to train the nucleus of workmen. If at the end of this period a committee could begin to produce shell, then for the next ten weeks they would be allowed to increase to any extent the amount produced weekly. After the tenth week they might continue to turn out shell at that maximum rate (but not to increase it still further without permission), the Government having the option of cancelling the contract at any time by giving ten weeks' notice.

Contracts on these terms were proposed to Lincoln, Keighley, and Manchester.[2] In the event, however, no formal contract of this type

---

[1] A.O.C. *Printed Minutes*, p. 74.   [2] *Ibid.*, pp. 24, 85, 122.

was ever actually placed.   Before the new bodies were ripe for that stage, the system had been changed again.

Mr. Booth explained on 23 April that it was intended to fix a uniform price for every article, but to allow an addition in some exceptional cases for extra cost of freight or material.   Under the French system, a fixed price was paid by the Government to the district.   The district management retained a fraction to cover their expenses, and apportioned the remainder among the firms who undertook the several processes.   These might make a profit out of their fraction, if they could. Mr. Booth expressed a preference for leaving the sub-division to be made in this way by each locality.[1]

The prices offered to Groups at this time were[2] :—

H.E. Shell			18-pounder			23s
,,	,,		4·5-inch			£3
,,	,,		6-inch			£4 10s.
No. 100 Fuse (with gaine)						13s.

At Leicester, £3 was offered for the 4·5-inch shell, without nosing, but with the copper-band and base-plate.   The Leicester Committee divided the amount as follows :—For material, 30/- ; for machining, 20/-; for carriage and depôt expenses, 10/-.

VI.   The National Shell Factory Scheme.

The project of uniting A and B Areas into a number of new districts, each under the tuition and supervision of an armament firm and controlled by the manager of its ammunition department, was abandoned after a few days.   The minutes of the meeting, on 26 April, at which it was communicated to the Munitions of War Committee, record that " Sir Percy Girouard explained that, since the report had been written (23 April), circumstances had pointed rather to the setting up of new Government factories than to the formation of co-operative groups."[3]

Sir Percy Girouard afterwards wrote that this change in his views was a consequence of visits paid, between 20 and 26 April, to Leeds, Birmingham, and other places.   The main weakness which he had sought to remedy in the earlier plans for B areas, was the difficulty of providing competent supervision and inspection on a sufficient scale.   His interviews with the committees at Leeds, Birmingham, and elsewhere, appear to have convinced him that the co-operative system was unworkable, and that the problem of supervision and inspection could only be solved by the establishment, in the more important centres, of Government factories of a new type.   His first proposal, though it would have set free a certain amount of expert supervision to guide co-operative effort, would not, in fact, have touched the root of the difficulty, which lay in the dissemination of the work in each place among a considerable number of small shops.   The new suggestion aimed at centralising the whole process of manufacture in single factories specially equipped for it, and so making much smaller demands on the time of supervisors and inspectors.   It involved not merely abandoning the idea of taking

[1] A.O.C. *Printed Minutes*, pp. 75, 120.   [2] *Ibid.*, p. 87.   [3] M.C. 10.

the co-operative group under the wing of the armament firm, but throwing over the co-operative system itself. The other principles laid down in the memorandum—especially the principle of the larger district, self-contained, and producing the complete round—stood unchanged. But it was now proposed that the production should be carried on in new Government factories, in which the resources at the disposal of the local committees were to be concentrated under one roof.

Sir Percy Girouard had arranged that the Leeds Committee should visit Woolwich on 22 April, and a week later they went round Messrs. Armstrong's works under the guidance of Mr. Glynn West.[1] Referring to these visits, Sir Percy Girouard wrote : —" They returned unanimously of the opinion that, in view of the difficulties as to machine tools, supervision, inspection, and control, the best method in a district was to select a suitable factory and concentrate tools, workmen, supervision, and inspection under one management on a non-profit basis, and while the factory was being equipped, to send the management, together with selected skilled workmen, to a properly organised ammunition factory for instruction."[2] Sir Percy Girouard submitted a proposal on these lines to Birmingham on 25 April ; but the scheme was first worked out in detail at Leeds.

On 3 May, the Leeds Committee forwarded to Mr. Booth a draft scheme for the establishment of a National Shell Factory.[3] The proposals were submitted by Sir Percy Girouard to the Munitions of War Committee on 7 May, and in general outline approved.[4]

The main points of the Leeds scheme were as follows :—

(1) The Leeds area was to comprise the district covered by the Leeds and District Engineering Employers' Federation.

(2) The Committee desired power to establish a National Factory, capable of producing at least 20,000 18-pounder H.E. shells weekly from steel supplied to the works, as already provisionally promised, and to increase up to about 40,000 weekly, if required.

The shells were to be supplied at cost price, delivered to Woolwich Arsenal, or elsewhere.

(3) The Factory was to be controlled and directed by a Management Board to be appointed by the Government, consisting of :—

Leeds Engineering Employers, 5 representatives
Trade Unions concerned   1 or 2   ,,

(4) The Leeds Forge Company, Ltd., had, at the Committee's request, offered to place at the disposal of the Management

---

[1] From the date of Sir Percy Girouard's appointment, Mr. West, who was then local Director at Elswick in charge of gun ammunition production, gave expert advice and assistance to the committees at Leeds, Dundee, Bradford and Keighley, though it was not until 21 May that he was formally appointed technical adviser to the Army Council.

[2] Memorandum of 31 May, 1915. HIST. REC./R/200/7.

[3] D.A.O./3/570.

[4] The scheme was printed for the Committee (M.C. 14).

Board for shell manufacture a new building, 280 by 80 feet, self-contained, with electric power and all facilities. The Board desired power to accept the offer of this building at a fair rent, and to make the necessary alterations. The reinstatement at the end of the tenancy to be charged at cost price to the Government.

(5) The Management Board proposed, subject to the general control of the Government, to equip this building with existing machinery from factories within the district.

Action involving questions of compensation, other than reasonable hire or purchase price, was not to be taken without Government sanction. Adjustment of hire or purchase price was not to bar owners of plant or machinery from claiming compensation or consequential loss of profits arising from such hire or purchase. In case of dispute with owners, the Board was to report to the Government what machinery and plant was required and the owners' names ; and the Government was to arrange, if so determined, through the Board, for the transfer under the powers of the Defence of the Realm Act.

(6) The Management Board was to engage the labour and work the plant at the cost of the Government, who would be the owners or lessors of all the machinery, would place the necessary funds at the Board's disposal, and would provide advice and technical supervision. No new buildings or extensions were to be erected without sanction of the Government, who were to arrange for the payment and ultimate disposal thereof, and of the machinery and plant therein.

The Board would engage suitable engineering, administrative, and secretarial staffs, and provide office accommodation.

(7) The Board offered their voluntary services. They were to receive no remuneration or profit as individuals, but out-of-pocket expenses were to be borne by the Government.

(8) The names of bankers and of auditors, to be appointed by, and responsible to, the Government, were suggested.

(9) The Board were prepared, if the scheme were approved, to take up all the work immediately.

This scheme was revised in certain details on 11 May, when Sir Percy Girouard and Sir Algernon Firth conferred at Leeds with the existing Munitions Committee, and afterwards addressed a meeting of engineers in the Town Hall. The principal change made was the omission of the Labour representatives on the Board of Management. The employers stated that at Leeds relations with Labour were easy and old-fashioned, and that there was no evidence that the workmen would insist on, or even desire, representation. As an alternative, it was agreed that a large committee, representing both Employers and Labour, should be formed to secure full co-operation and support for the Factory, and to act as an Advisory Committee to the Board of Management.

The revised scheme came before the Munitions of War Committee on 12 May, and it was then resolved that it should be put into operation at the earliest possible moment.[1] The formal sanction of the Government was obtained on the following day.

On 14 May, Sir Algernon Firth addressed a private circular letter to the members of the Associated Chambers of Commerce, recommending them to get their localities to work on the Leeds lines and to submit definite offers as soon as possible. A description of the Leeds experiment was published in May in a leaflet, entitled, *National Munitions Factories : Working Model.*[2]

VII. The Retention of the Co-operative Group as Alternative to the National Factory.

With the approval of the scheme for large districts and national factories, it appeared as if the group principle, which had undergone so many rebuffs, had now received its death-blow. Its originator and constant advocate, the Board of Trade, requested Mr. Booth to state whether he desired that the co-operation of the Labour Exchange organisation should be wound up. A report was prepared on 26 April, showing the stage which their work had reached at that moment.

The sample exhibitions were still open at nine centres, though the exhibits were not to the latest specifications and 18-pounder shrapnel shell was included. Inspections were being made, and the results, tabulated at the Central Office, were passed to Mr. Booth. The situation of the several groups which had been worked up by Board of Trade officials was as follows. In one instance—Leicester— an order had been placed. Bristol, Bradford, and Keighley had been interviewed by the Armaments Output Committee, and Bristol was awaiting a contract. Halifax, Nottingham, Hull, Wakefield, and Peterborough were ready to send deputations : Rotherham was to wait on the Committee on that day. Cardiff was under investigation.

The Board of Trade asked Mr. Booth whether it was desired that the inspections should continue, and that the Labour Exchange officers should co-operate with the Engineering Employers' Federation in forming fresh groups. The tenor of Mr. Booth's answer was embodied on 4 May in a draft circular to Divisional Officers, which, though it was not issued, illustrates the position at the moment.[3] The circular stated that it would no longer be necessary for the Board of Trade to take the same action as in the past for the engineering survey and the formation of groups. Though the possibility of placing small orders for shells and fuses was not excluded, probably attempts would be preferred to form a limited number of groups, capable of a very large output, in a few chief towns. Hence, while Mr. Booth

---

[1] The revised scheme is printed as an Appendix to the minutes of this meeting of the Committee (M.C. 18).

[2] HIST. REC./R/1121/4.   [3] L.E. 1965/211.

would interview groups already formed, and Divisional Officers should keep engagements for meetings to form groups, they should not open up new ground. The exhibitions of samples were to remain open, but no further inspections were to be carried out in pursuance of these exhibitions. Requests for inspection were henceforth to be referred to Mr. Booth, to whom the reports already made had been forwarded.

On receiving a copy of this draft, Mr. Booth wrote on 6 May, requesting the Board of Trade to postpone action, as " the policy to· be pursued was not yet definitely settled."

This uncertainty suspended progress at some of the centres where groups were becoming ripe for action, and for a short time caused some irritation among employers, who could not follow the very rapid changes of policy at headquarters. A deputation from Hull, which met the Committee on 3 May, recorded, in a letter to Mr. Booth, the impression created in their minds, " that either the statements in the press as to the requirements of the Government in the way of ammunition have been grossly exaggerated, or it is not considered desirable that any more outside firms should be brought into the manufacture of munitions of war."[1]

On the following day the Hull Committee was called together and the members were advised to proceed with their ordinary business. Mr. Booth succeeded in mollifying the Committee by explaining that, just because ammunition requirements were so urgent, it had been found necessary to concentrate on the areas capable of the largest production, while the capabilities of smaller areas were being ascertained with a view to calling upon them later. By "large producing areas " was meant, not only the districts round armament firms, but also large engineering centres like Leeds, where a weekly output of 40,000 shells was contemplated. The Hull Committee declared their willingness to await the convenience of Mr. Booth's Committee, and came to a conference shortly afterwards.

It was partly due to the influence of the Board of Trade, strengthened by the knowledge that they had acquired of the needs and capabilities of the several localities, that the principle of co-operative production was not abandoned, but allowed to stand as an alternative to the National Shell Factory.

Mr. Davison, in a memorandum written on 8 May,[2] criticised Sir Percy Girouard's new scheme, the details of which had not yet been fully disclosed. He urged that " the most effective means of increasing the output of munitions lies in the use and development of existing resources, and not in the substitution for them of completely new centres of production. It is estimated that the new scheme, which involves the moving of labour and of existing machines, the manufacture of new plant, the equipment of new premises, and

---

[1] D.A.O./1/549.   [2] L.E. 1965/218.

organisation of a new staff for each centre, would require at least six months to come into effective operation. During this time no use is to be made of the existing resources of the country, and some men who could be making shell would be engaged in making new machinery. The transfer of labour and machinery on a large scale would be a matter of great difficulty, and would cause dislocation throughout the country. In addition to the difficulties and delay involved, the scheme could not fail to produce considerable ill feeling."

Mr. Davison's main contention was that no uniform scheme should be adopted for the whole country, but each locality should be treated according to its capacity and requirements. The system of giving a joint order to a group of manufacturers met the case of many firms who could spare a margin of capacity for shell manufacture, but could not contribute either men or machines to the proposed new centres without sacrificing their other Government work. In places where the local firms could undertake only some of the processes, the most economical method was to instal in some central depôt the missing plant, which was often only the presses for forging or nosing. This method obviated the necessity for shifting plant and labour on a large scale ; and the groups could be gradually fed with fresh labour and machinery as their power developed.

" It is probable that Sir Percy Girouard's scheme would arouse considerable opposition in the engineering trade generally, and especially among those firms whose plant and labour would be requisitioned for the new centres. It is understood that protests have already been made by group committees in several towns. Accusations will inevitably be made that the armament firms are promoting the present scheme in order to preserve their monopoly of this class of manufacture, since the alternative scheme would be likely to set up serious competitors both during and after the War."

With regard to the problems of supervision and inspection, Mr. Davison estimated that not more than 25 groups of different sizes were likely to be formed. The " mothering system " (which could in any case be retained) would provide for the instruction of their management at the armament firms ; and the experience of the British Thomson-Houston Company and of the Leicester Group showed that the difficulties of shell manufacture had been exaggerated, and that expert advice was needed only in the early stages. Local inspectors could be appointed to the collecting and distributing centres established in each town ; and it should be quite practicable to arrange for frequent Government inspection on the spot.

Finally, Sir Percy Girouard's scheme would involve enormous expense in equipping the new centres and compensating the firms whose plant and labour would be requisitioned. The new factories, moreover, would remain on the Government's hands at the end of the War.

The support given by the Board of Trade to the co-operative principle brought about a compromise, which has become a permanent feature of area organisation.   On 7 May, letters were addressed to the local munitions committees explaining that, while it had been decided in the first instance to concentrate upon the areas capable of a very large production, and to leave in abeyance the districts which promised only a small output, it was nevertheless hoped that every manufacturing centre would form a local committee, if it had not already done so.   Such committees would prepare for any future emergency by acquainting themselves with the resources of their district in labour and machinery.   They would receive drawings and specifications, and also the results of the census made by the Labour Exchanges and by the Home Office.   It was desirable that Labour should be represented.

Another form of letter was addressed to certain committees already in existence, asking whether, if a National Factory on the Leeds model were not found to be suitable to the needs of the district, the Committee could distribute orders for component parts of shells and fuses, assemble these parts in a central factory for finishing and inspection, and form a Board of Management to supervise the execution of their contract.   The following were given as the minimum weekly quantities of shells or fuses that should be offered :—

H.E. Shell	..	..	13-pounders and 18-pounders	5,000, in the proportion of 1 to 5.
,, ,,	..	..	4·5-inch ..	..	1,000
,, ,,	..	..	6-inch ..	..	500
No. 100 Fuse		..	..	..	5,000

On this basis the Armaments Output Committee at last established a policy which was not further modified until after the foundation of the Ministry.   Even then, the changes that were made were rather in the framework of administrative machinery than in the constitution and methods of the local centres.   The Board of Management in some places has controlled a National Factory, in others has acted as a Co-operative Group.   In some instances both systems have existed side by side.   It is not necessary here to pursue the minor variations by which the two types were adjusted to peculiar needs or conditions.

CHAPTER V.

CENTRAL ORGANISATION UNDER SIR PERCY GIROUARD AND MR. BOOTH, 28 APRIL TO 26 MAY.

I. Organisation of the Armaments Output Committee, 20 April, 1915.

The table given below may serve to illustrate the stage of development which the Armaments Output Committee had reached when Sir Percy Girouard's original scheme for co-ordinated Areas under Government Superintendents was in contemplation, that is to say between 20 and 26 April, 1915. The table is, of course, partly designed to provide for the administration of that scheme, which was never in fact adopted ; but in other respects it registers the advance that had already been made in that internal differentiation of function which was beginning to give the Committee the structure of a department. Thus, by 20 April Mr. Allan Smith and Mr. MacLellan were already specialising on the problem of machinery ; Lord Elphinstone was devoting himself to district organisation ; and Mr. Ridpath was concerned with American supplies.

Draft only. TREASURY COMMITTEE.

WAR OFFICE ARMAMENTS OUTPUT COMMITTEE.

Central Committee: Mr. George M. Booth, Chairman.

1. *Supplies—Machinery:* (Technical Department) :
   Mr. Allan Smith ; Mr. MacLellan.
2. *Secretariat:*
   Mr. G. H. Duckworth ; Mr. Arthur Baxter.
3. *Canada and U.S.A.:*
   Mr. E. Guy Ridpath.
4. *Statistics, Finance, Auditing:*
   Auditor.............. ; Mr. E. Guy Ridpath (Advisory)..
5. *District Managers:*
   Lord Elphinstone ; Mr. Follett Holt.
   Government Superintendents of Armament Districts.
   District Engineers, Secretary.
   District Committees (representing manufacturers).

" The Government Superintendent, addressing the District Manager, will report to the Central Committee on the area possibilities, etc.   When he requires to move machinery in the area, he will consult or arrange with the District Committee concerned.   When he requires machinery to be supplied from outside his own district, he will communicate with the Central Committee's Technical Department. He will be the official go-between of the Central Committee and the District Committees."

II. The Appointment of Sir Percy Girouard and Mr. Booth.

The need for a stronger central organisation was urged by several speakers in a debate which took place on 21 April, in the House of Commons, on the following resolution moved by Mr. Hewins :—

" That this House, while welcoming well-considered steps for increasing the mobility and efficiency of labour, is of opinion that it is urgently necessary that the resources of all firms capable of producing, or of co-operating in producing, munitions of war should be enlisted under a unified administration in direct touch with such firms."[1]

The general tone of the debate was not hostile to the Government ; but objections were made to the plan of collecting information and asking advice from local committees, and then proceeding to formulate a scheme.   Mr. Hewins argued that the Government should " begin to organise at the top."   The business community required to have a definite proposition laid before them, framed by some responsible person, " a man of real, concrete, organising ability, who would have the power and the will to decide questions at issue and take responsibility."   He should be assisted by a technical advisory committee, representing the broad divisions of the industries concerned in munitions production, and divided into sub-committees.   The local committees would still be entrusted with the functions of collecting information and organising their districts in the light of their knowledge of local conditions.

Mr. Bonar Law pointed out that neither the Munitions of War Committee nor the departmental committee at the War Office was a " central committee " of the type that Mr. Lloyd George had seemed to foreshadow in his speech on the Defence of the Realm (Amendment) No. 2 Bill.[2]   The problem was much too vast to be met by stretching existing machinery.   The Government must bring in new machinery which should consist of men trained in business, who understood how the industry of the country could be mobilised.[3]

This debate very nearly coincides with Mr. Lloyd George's invitation to Sir Percy Girouard to formulate a plan for " the creation of

---

[1] *Parliamentary Debates* (1915), *H. of C.*, LXXI., 277 ff.

[2] See Part II., Chap. III.

[3] *Parliamentary Debates* (1915), *H. of C.*, LXXI., 329.

an organisation in England and the Empire which would fully provide for ammunition requirements," and Sir Percy Girouard's memorandum was drawn up two days later. The Government, in fact, accepted, and indeed had already anticipated the view expressed in the House of Commons, that the central body needed to be strengthened and placed on a more independent footing.

On 26 April, the Munitions of War Committee, after considering Sir Percy Girouard's memorandum and approving its proposals in general outline, referred to a sub-committee[1] "the question of the constitution of the proposed central department and its relation, on the one hand, to the Chancellor's Committee, and, on the other, to the War Office and Admiralty." The sub-committee reported on the same day that, in their opinion,

> "Sir Percy Girouard and Mr. G. M. Booth should be appointed to give effect to the scheme, with such modifications as should be found necessary, and that they should act in close co-operation with the departments of the War Office, the Admiralty, and other authorities concerned.

> " In the event of any questions arising between them and any Department concerned with the supply of munitions of war or armament labour, these questions should be dealt with by the Chancellor's Committee."

The full Committee was asked to consider what authority should make the appointment ; but it was suggested that, in any case, Sir Percy Girouard and Mr. Booth should probably constitute the channel through which, so far as the scheme was concerned, the Army Council should exercise its powers under the Defence of the Realm Act. The Secretary of State for War would probably have to consider the relation between the administration of the new scheme and the existing War Office Committee on Munitions ; but it was hoped that, whatever might be his decision, the services of individual members of that Committee would still be available.

The sub-committee's report was accepted, and it was agreed that the appointment of Sir Percy Girouard and Mr. Booth should be made by the Secretary of State for War.

Lord Kitchener immediately acted upon this conclusion. Two days later, the following *Notice* was issued at the War Office :—

" *War Office*, 28 *April*, 1915.

" The scheme for increasing the output of ammunition submitted by Sir P. Girouard to the Chancellor of the Exchequer's Committee on Munitions of War on 26 April and recommended by that Committee has been accepted by the Government, and the Secretary of State for War has appointed Sir P. Girouard and Mr. G. M. Booth to carry that scheme into effect, so far as may

---

[1] The sub-committee consisted of Sir H. Llewellyn Smith, Sir Frederick Black, Sir Percy Girouard, Mr. Booth, and Mr. Henderson. (M.C. 10.)

be found practicable and subject to such modifications of details as may be found necessary and expedient from time to time. In matters covered by the scheme, Sir P. Girouard and Mr. G. M. Booth are authorised to act without further reference to the Secretary of State. They will maintain co-operation with all Government departments concerned with the supply of munitions of war or of labour for producing such munitions, and, in event of any difference arising between them and any such department which cannot be mutually adjusted, the instructions of the Treasury Committee on Munitions of War are to be followed."

It will be observed that, although the name "Armaments Output Committee" remained in use, this appointment set the Committee on a new basis. It had hitherto been a departmental committee, with no formal powers, attached to the department of the Master-General of the Ordnance. Henceforth, its two heads were authorised to act, in matters covered by the scheme, "without further reference to the Secretary of State." Nor was the Committee, except in the event of inter-departmental differences, directed to take its instructions from the Munitions of War Committee. Its charter was contained in Sir Percy Girouard's memorandum, which assigned to the "central department," not merely the function of acting as intermediary between the local organisation and the War Office and Admiralty, but also the duty of "controlling the whole of our Imperial output" of ammunition. It is obvious that the setting up of a body with powers so wide, so anomalous, and so ill-defined, could only have been intended to provide a temporary bridge for the transfer of at least the most vital section of munitions supply from the War Office to a Department on a regular footing under a responsible Minister of the Crown. The Armaments Output Committee from this moment falls into no regular category. What is of interest is to observe how, under pressure of the conditions of its problem and in particular of such limiting factors as machinery, gauges, raw materials, and labour, it developed the rudiments of departmental structure.

III. Co-ordination and the Balance of Requirements.

From a very early stage of its operations, the Armaments Output Committee had become alive to certain defects in the system of purchase for Government Departments, which, though in times of peace they may only have led to some extravagance, under the growing stringency of resources in labour, materials, and tools, now threatened to impede and dislocate production.

In the first place, there had been up to this time no machinery to provide for co-operation in this matter between the War Office and the Admiralty. Neither Department possessed such knowledge of the other's operations as would enable it to avoid competition in the same markets and consequent delays. Mr. Booth gave as an instance the case of ammunition boxes. The Admiralty found that the woodwork was ahead of their requirements, but that the supply of hinges was held up. These were made by two or three firms, who probably did not know they were making for the Admiralty. They sold them to an agent, who might be distributing them to the Admiralty, or to the War Office, or for export.[1]

The Armaments Output Committee procured the appointment of a Joint Committee of the two Departments, which it was proposed should also secure priority for the most urgent work.[2]

In the second place, within the War Office itself, several different departments separately bought stores of which the requirements were to some extent interdependent. Thus, while the Master-General of the Ordnance department purchased shells, motor lorries came under the Quartermaster-General, and Military Aeronautics bought everything required for the Flying Corps. There was no means of ensuring that the supplies of shell would not outrun the supply of lorries necessary for its transport. As Mr. Booth remarked on 22 April: " It is going to be a very difficult task for the War Office to see that, in so far as it produces anything in increased quantities, it produces correlatively the high explosive, and the propellant, and the cartridge boxes, and the motor lorries for moving it about. We have got to try and keep a sense of proportion, so that we do not go and make a lot of 4·5-inch shells and get a sort of peak in that line, with a great valley which is not up to date in these other things."[3]

Mr. Booth was here referring specially to the efforts of his own Committee. He had become aware of the danger involved in the very success of the campaign he had undertaken for an unlimited increase of the supplies of a few types of shell and fuse. This was one of the reasons for calling a halt, and suspending the haphazard formation of co-operative groups. " We are here, not now quite so much, as was said in the original Kitchener Committee, to produce shell and fuse, but to organise, through the assistance of really scientific committees in each great area, as well as in each secondary area, our knowledge of what that area can produce best, and then to add it up..... There might be, say, twenty offers of making 4·5-inch shell, ten of which would be eminently suitable, and ten less suitable. To the former we would give 4·5-inch shell, and the other we might put on something else."[4]

As Mr. Allan Smith put it on the same occasion : " The main idea that we have is, taking the information that we procure from the various districts, to see how we can possibly co-ordinate, not only the districts themselves, not only the towns involved in those districts, but the supplies in view of the requirements."

It is clear that, when this point had been reached, the Committee would not long be able to confine itself even to gun ammunition. As early as 27 April, Mr. Booth said the Committee would gradually take over the whole question of the output of motor lorries.[5] It was

---

[1] A.O.C. *Printed Minutes*, p. 18. Hist. Rec./R/171/1.
[2] *Ibid.*, p. 28.   [3] *Ibid.*, p. 44.   [4] *Ibid.*, p. 45.   [5] *Ibid.*, p. 92.

inevitable that the principle of keeping a balance over the whole field of production of inter-related stores should lead still further.

IV. Relations with the M.G.O. Contracts Branch (A 7).

On 22 April, Mr. Hanson arranged with Mr. Booth a procedure to be adopted with regard to offers from firms.[1] It was agreed that, in cases where offers were received, which for any reason it was impossible to accept, the Committee and the Contracts Branch should keep each other fully informed of the objections to acceptance. Mr. Hanson stated that he frequently received proposals from firms who appeared to him to be unable to do much by themselves, but might be useful as members of a Co-operative Group. In such cases, Mr. Booth requested that the Committee might be informed, in order that, where a group was being formed, they might advise their correspondent in the group of the fact that the firm was willing to assist.

After the reconstitution of the Armaments Output Committee, it was agreed on 15 May with Mr. Hanson that all applications for contracts received from new firms by Contracts A 7, other than those relating to rifles, parts of rifles, rifle ammunition, scientific instruments, and explosives, should be referred to Mr. Booth.

V. The Beginnings of the Machine Tool Department.

In a report prepared for the Minister in June, 1915,[2] Sir Percy Girouard wrote :—

" The want of machine tools has undoubtedly been one of the main factors in the failure of the British manufacturers of ammunition to fulfil their promises. Had there been any central authority to indicate to machinery manufacturers the total requirements which would be entailed by the great expansion of munition factories authorised by the Government in 1914, we might have avoided to some extent the delays that followed."

This statement may be supplemented from information supplied by several of the principal firms about the middle of March. The Birmingham Small Arms Company reported that, while they had no shortage of materials or labour, certain milling machines due from the United States in November, 1914, had not yet arrived. Messrs. Harper & Bean and the Birmingham Metal & Munitions Company complained that large numbers of new machines were then from four to six weeks late in delivery. Messrs. Dick, Kerr, were awaiting the arrival of lathes from America. In some instances these delays were due to the congestion of the docks at Liverpool and of the railways. In the case of home supplies, they were partly attributable to the disorganisation of the trade caused by indiscrimate enlistment and other disadvantages common to every branch of engineering. By April these hindrances to supply, coinciding with the large increase of demand, had brought about a stringency which could not be remedied by the violent method of commandeering machines and shifting them from one factory to

---

[1] 94/GEN. No./95.   [2] HIST. REC./R/200/10.

another, but called for a systematic control of orders for new machines and a direction of the supply along channels determined by central authority.

Before the reconstitution of the Armaments Output Committee at the end of April, Mr. MacLellan and Mr. Allan Smith had already begun to investigate the problem. They called in the help of Mr. Alfred Herbert, who was then President of the Machine Tool Makers' Association. Mr. Herbert, as has been mentioned above,[1] had been keenly interested in the organisation of munitions production since the previous year. He offered his personal services on 22 March.

On 21 April, Mr. Allan Smith explained the measures that were being taken as follows :—" We have made a census of the production of all the machine tool people that we can think of. We have now got replies from the majority, and we are getting in the others day by day. Any of that machinery which can be usefully diverted to people making armaments in this country, without interfering with any interests that we desire to protect, will be available straight off.

" We propose to communicate with the contractors as a body, and ask them what machinery they require, what is the class, what are the dimensions, and when they would be ready to instal. Then we can see, from the information we have, the dates when the machinery referred to is to be completed, and, if necessary, we might expedite the particular machinery that was required, and by that means tap a source that is new, and a source which will give us what we desire, without having to wait for the usual manufacturing delays."[2]

The information from contractors, referred to in the second paragraph above, was obtained by means of an advertisement issued on 20 April for insertion in a large number of daily papers.[3]

The Committee soon began to contemplate purchase by the Government of those types of forging and banding presses which the local committees found it most difficult to provide, and the distribution of them by sale or for return.[4] It was proposed to deal in the same way with the shortage of gauges. The Committee intended to purchase 30 or 40 sets of gauges. Each local committee was to receive a master set, which would be used only for checking the working gauges. At the end of April, the Committee was considering whether the Government should take the whole output of the best gauge-makers and prohibit them from accepting private orders.[5] The lack of gauges, indeed, threatened at this time to be the most serious factor in limiting production. The manufacturers were accustomed to turn them out to a high standard of finish in every part. Mr. MacLellan, with the help of Sir F. Donaldson and Dr. R. T. Glazebrook, Director of the National Physical Laboratory, did some valuable work in simplifying the designs so that only the necessary surfaces should be made perfectly true.

The Committee had also begun, before 27 April, inquiries into the export of machinery to the Colonies, the Allies, and neutral countries

---

[1] See p. 29.   [2] A.O.C. *Printed Minutes*, p. 30.   [3] 94/GEN. No./78.
[4] A.O.C. *Printed Minutes*, pp. 25, 65, 104.   [5] *Ibid.*, pp. 98, 109.

The Cabinet had instructed the Committee to give them a controlling answer upon which they might decide to what extent these orders should be stopped or diverted

On 25 April, Mr. Herbert was invited by Sir Percy Girouard to undertake the organisation of the Machine Tool Trade for the War Office. He took up his quarters at Cecil Chambers on 27 April, which may be taken as the date of foundation of the Machine Tool department.

Mr. Herbert's first action was to promote the issue of an order to Machine Tool Makers, containing instructions designed to direct the supply of machine tools in process of manufacture to armament work for this country or for the Allies.[1] The Order was drawn up after consultation with Sir Reginald Brade, Sir Frederick Black, the Treasury Solicitor, and Sir H. Llewellyn Smith. A draft was submitted to the Munitions of War Committee on 7 May, and it was decided that it should be sent out immediately. The Order was issued in the name of the Army Council on 10 May to the firms whose names were attached in a schedule. It is of interest as being one of the earliest attempts to secure precedence for a certain class of Government work, and as having provided a model for later schemes of Priority classification, an account of which will be given elsewhere.

The Order stated that it was necessary that supplies of all machine tools, presses, or other similar appliances in the country should be made immediately available for the manufacture of munitions. To this end, manufacturers were instructed to divide all orders for such articles, whether in progress or on their books, into two classes[2] :—

A. Orders for British and Allied Governments and Armament Companies ; for contractors and sub-contractors to these, where orders were for use on Government contracts or sub-contracts ; and for the Colonies or India, where it was known that orders were for use on munitions work.

B. Orders for Neutral Countries ; for the Colonies or for India, where it was known that the orders were for use on munitions work ; and for British firms, where orders were not for munitions work.

In delivery, preference was to be given to orders in Class A, and, wherever this could be so secured, orders in Class B were to be diverted or suspended without regard to contracts or obligations. Future orders under B were to be accepted only on the understanding that they were liable to suspension, diversion, and delay, and that they could not in any case be executed so long as similar orders in Class A were awaiting execution.

---

[1] M.C. 262. HIST. REC./R/172/16.

[2] It had been decided not to establish orders of precedence inside the two classes, as originally proposed by Mr. Herbert. Mr. Herbert had at first suggested a third class, C : Orders for Norway, Sweden, Holland, and Italy ; but this was considered to be unnecessary in view of the Order in Council of 26 April prohibiting the export of metal-working machinery to certain foreign countries.

Attention was called to the clause in the Defence of the Realm (Amendment) No. 2 Act which gives protection against actions for breach of contract, and to Regulation 8 A, under which the Order was made. On Mr. Herbert's advice, it had been decided not to refer to the Defence of the Realm Losses Commission or to suggest claims for compensation.

Later in May, the department took further steps to extend its control over the supply of machine tools. A letter,[1] over the signature of Sir Reginald Brade, was issued, stating that it was necessary that no orders should be accepted except from the British and Allied Governments, and their contractors and sub-contractors, without the express permission of the War Office. Before proceeding with orders for machine tools for civil work, the makers were to apply for instructions whether such orders might be accepted or not.

A form of fortnightly Return (E.R. 1) was issued at the same time, requiring information as to machine tools already in stock, in progress, or in transit to this country, which were intended for export or for civil work in the United Kingdom. It was proposed to divert such machines to destinations where they would be most useful for munitions production.

From the information obtained and from the large number of applications for licence to export machine tools, the department learned that a considerable amount of work was still going on for neutral countries, which was likely to benefit the enemy. This led to further restrictions. A circular issued in June recommended the makers not to accept orders for neutral countries without reference to the department, which would advise whether the work should be put in hand or not. The firms were also warned not to take orders from merchants without proof that the machines were for munitions production.

The total effect of these successive measures was that the department had assumed a nearly complete control over the destination of the products of this trade before the Machine Tool firms were declared to be controlled establishments soon after the passing of the Munitions of War Act.

VI. Raw and Semi-manufactured Materials.

In peace time, it was no part of the business of any branch of the Contracts department at the War Office to obtain systematic information as to the general state of metal production at any time. Contracts 3 dealt in metals only so far as these were required for manufacture at Woolwich and Enfield, and for the Army Repair Shops. The armament firms, of course, catered for themselves, and to a large extent supplied their sub-contractors with semi-manufactured materials. In the early months of 1915, the Contracts department asked the main contractors

---

[1] 94/GEN. No./109.

to state whether they had any difficulty in obtaining certain materials ; but no general enquiry into the resources of the country was undertaken till the Armaments Output Committee took up the question towards the end of April.

Sir P. Girouard and Mr. Booth, reporting to Mr. Lloyd George at the end of May, wrote as follows[1] :—

> " Hitherto, after placing orders with main contractors, Government Departments had assumed that their responsibility for the materials for manufacture ceased. This, for war purposes, was a grave error. In peace, when military operations are not vitally dependent upon the delivery of munitions, main contractors could have recourse to courts of law in cases where sub-contractors for materials failed. Such a course, in time of war, when the lives of our men are at stake, is inconceivable.

> " The Department,[2] sweeping aside all ordinary considerations, sought at once to obtain information as to the war position in the following basic supplies :—

> 1. Copper Rings.
> 2. Cartridge Metal.
> 3. Brass Rod of high quality.
> 4. Aluminium Rod.
> 5. Lead Bullets.
> 6. Antimony.
> 7. Spelter.

> " The consideration of our position in detail with regard to copper, steel, and ordinary metals was postponed for the moment as being relatively less urgent.

> " The visible supply of these seven semi-manufactured materials is entirely outside the knowledge of any direct contractor, and in no case does a main contractor produce any one of them in sufficient quantity to meet his war requirements. In other words, they form a bottle-neck through which every shell, fuse, and cartridge case, gun and rifle, machine gun and shrapnel bullet, must pass before a complete round, less its propellant and high explosive, can be produced in this country. It was the duty of the Government, not of the main contractors, to enquire into this ; for a contractor could have no possible *locus standi* in any such investigation. Such an enquiry had not been initiated until a month ago, and it is as yet by no means certain that these vital necessities for the output of ammunition under existing contracts can be found in the country, much less the quantities under contemplation by this Department in its short existence."

---

[1] Memorandum of 31 May, 1915. HIST. REC./R/200/7.
[2] *I.e.*, the central organisation under Sir P. Girouard and Mr. Booth.

A memorandum of 15 June adds some further criticisms[1] :—

> " The situation was made worse by the fact that, whereas, in ordering gun ammunition, the Government Department amply covered the requirements of the Royal Factories in respect of raw materials, they yet dictated to the main manufacturers orders on a continuation system, subject to three months' notice on either side. Under such conditions, it was idle to have hoped that the manufacturers would hold in stock or on option supplies materially in excess of what was necessary for three months.

> " It was the pre-eminent duty of the Government in war to schedule the output of raw materials and manufacturers in Great Britain. It should have been a further duty to warn the main contractors that the Government were placing huge orders in America, and to ascertain how far this would affect their sources of supply for raw materials. For, in many respects, British contractors have been largely dependent on foreign sources ; but it is difficult for them to-day to estimate how far these supplies will be forthcoming. Finally, on the top of the British orders, the Russians, the French, and presumably the Italians, have placed immense orders for materials. The position is somewhat deplorable."

The information obtained in April from the deputations of local Groups had made it clear to Mr. Booth's Committee that they would have to assume some responsibility for the supply of materials to the districts. Mr. MacLellan, who studied this aspect of the problem, stated on 21 April that practically every works that could roll round bars or Siemens-Marten acid steel was fully occupied with an order placed by the French Government with some fifteen or sixteen firms for nearly 150,000 tons of steel, due for completion in June. The Committee was prepared, if necessary, to suspend part of this order ; but it seemed probable that 500 tons would cover, up to the end of June, the needs of any districts then starting work. They proposed to arrange for 500 tons to be rolled, and to distribute the quantities required by the local bodies for the experimental stages of their work. Larger deliveries could be arranged for later.[2]

On 22 April, Mr. Steel, of Steel, Peech & Tozer, Ltd., attended with the deputation from Sheffield. He stated that unless the steel makers were given some idea of the amount of steel that would be required for the enormous increase in shell production that was contemplated, the supply would run short. Only two shell makers in the country made their own steel ; and every steel maker was absolutely put to his limit of supply. He suggested that some data should be got together as to the amount of shells that would be turned out by the existing works and the new works, and that the steel makers should, with that information, try to arrange to turn out the steel. It could only be done if the makers abandoned some part of their work and turned over to shell steel. It was practically impossible to-day to get a ton of steel in the

---

[1] Hist. Rec./R/200/10.   [2] A.O.C. *Printed Minutes*, p. 30.

country ; the whole output was taken up. This had nothing to do with shipping.   There was no cover in pig-iron, as there had been three months ago.   They could get as much iron as they wanted.   Even to take the enormous quantities of steel made for foreign Governments would not help to supply the Government with a high explosive steel, under the present specification (which Mr. Steel did not approve of). This was made by practically three or four firms, who could only meet the demand if they could make arrangements months beforehand.[1]

By 29 April, the Joint Committee of the War Office and Admiralty had begun to investigate the sources of supply of the various classes of metal.   These were to be scheduled, so that the Committee might undertake to supply the districts with materials which they could not obtain for themselves.   Every manufacturer and every contractor for the two Departments had been asked to furnish a return of his orders for raw material, the sources from which he was obtaining it, the terms of delivery, and what the weekly deliveries were.   If it should be found that any supplier had overestimated what the Committee believed to be his capacity, they would send down and check it.   They would then try to start fresh sources of supply.[2]

The purchase of raw materials by the Government was not actually undertaken before June.   On 2 June, Mr. Booth informed the Hull Munitions Committee that it had been decided that the War Office should buy all the steel required by the districts and supply it to them at cost price.   Arrangements were then being made to establish a special Raw Materials department.[3]   This was put under the direction of Major Carmichael, of the Engineering department of the Crown Agents for the Colonies, an organisation which had been attached to the Armaments Output Committee since the last week of April.[4]

Sir P. Girouard's memorandum of 15 June,[5] states that a hurried survey of the situation had been made since 1 May, with respect to the more important classes of materials.

Spelter.—Since the beginning of the War, Spelter had risen in price from £30 to above £100.   This material was of the first importance in the manufacture of Brass Rod and Cartridge cases ; though whether it was essential was difficult to determine.   Since the specification had been frequently changed during the War, the principal makers had been brought together in conference.   They had promised to hold stocks which, with those already in the hands of the Committee, would guarantee the position up to the end of the year.

Brass Bar or Rod, and Cartridge Metal.—Several conferences had been held with the Cold Rolled Brass & Copper Association.

---

[1] A.O.C. *Printed Minutes*, p. 48.

[2] *Ibid.*, p. 110.   An account of an Admiralty Sub-committee for advising on purchase of raw materials, nominated on 20 April, is given in Appendix XII.

[3] D.A.O./1/549.

[4] A.O.C. *Printed Minutes*, p. 95.   [5] HIST. REC./R/200/10.

Owing to confusion as to the specification, some had used purer Spelter than was necessary. The pure Spelter should be reserved for cartridge metal required for guns, machine guns, and small arms. The principal Rod Makers had undertaken to increase their plant to meet all requirements.

Copper Driving Bands.—There was a good supply of copper itself. The three chief producers of Copper tubes[1] had been instructed to lay down fresh plant. The increase of output, varying from 100% to 300%, should meet all needs, particularly as the bulk of this rod was required for fuse work, for which it was hoped to use steel more largely, as in France and Russia.

Aluminium Rod.—There were ample quantities of this metal; but there was only one maker, who would be instructed to increase his capacity.

Antimony, used for hardening shrapnel and rifle bullets, had risen in price by leaps and bounds and would rise higher. Certain supplies had been secured, and alternatives were being considered.

High-grade Steels for Cutting Tools, etc.—The high-grade Steels now in use had permitted the speeding-up of all cutting, milling, slotting, etc., machines in the engineering trades from 30 feet a minute to 120 feet. There appeared to be enough machines in this country to turn out the necessary supplies. All the bar and pig required, however, came from Sweden. Any interference with this source of supply would lead to a grave situation. The stocks usually arrived between April and October. Four months' supply was now in existence; and if the supplies came forward as usual up to October, a 12 months' supply would be available in the later months of the year. Manu·facturers were to be impressed with the desirability of spreading out the supply by economy. If the supply were cut off, the most rigid economy would be needed, or alternatives would have to be found But the Swedish ore seemed to have some natural property, lacking in all the substitutes tested.

Steel.—There appeared to be little fear of any serious lack of steel for ammunition. A conference with the steel manufacturers had been arranged for 16 June.

The above-mentioned were the main raw or semi-manufactured materials that had so far been dealt with; but many others would call for investigation.

Co-ordination of Components of Manufacture.—No attempt had been made by the Government to provide a census of the components held by contractors or by the Royal Factories, or to secure a proper distribution by means of exchange. Some manufacturers were heavily overstocked in some things, while others were living from hand to mouth. Every effort was being made to obtain a

---

[1] The Broughton Copper Co., Thomas Bolton & Sons, and the Yorkshire Copper Works, Ltd.

census—in other words, to pool the stocks on paper and thereby ensure a reasonable exchange.

VII. Labour Questions.

(a) ENLISTMENT OF SKILLED MEN AND RELEASE FROM THE COLOURS.

No account of the Armaments Output Committee's activities would be complete without reference to the attempts made by Mr. Booth to secure some settlement of the conflict between the claims of the Army and of the factories, and to introduce some co-ordination among the competing authorities.

One matter which called for his intervention was a case of over-lapping which occurred in the issue of recruiting instructions. The incident may be recorded as an illustration of the extraordinary want of co-operation between the military authorities and the Labour Exchange department, which for the previous three months, had, at the request of the War Office, been steadily supplying labour for armament purposes.

On 31 March, the Director of Recruiting issued a memorandum[1] to all recruiting officers, instructing them to place themselves in communication with all the firms on the War Office list of firms protected from recruiting, and to " do all in their power to obtain suitable men to join those of them who are in want of labour." About the same date, a poster, headed " *The Man the Army wants now*," was published by the War Office.[2] Fitters, turners, millwrights, other skilled workmen, and also unskilled workmen not at present engaged in the production of war material, were invited to volunteer, and to give in their names at the nearest recruiting office, stating what class of work they could perform.

The Board of Trade naturally protested against this usurpation of the functions which had been legitimately exercised by the Labour Exchanges, and, with Mr. Booth's help, they succeeded in procuring the withdrawal of the instructions to recruiting officers, who were now told to refer to the Labour Exchanges any lists of men they had already registered. The Labour Exchanges were then to place the men, if possible, in the ordinary way, after carefully ascertaining that they were not on Government work.[3] The War Office poster had unfortunately not indicated that specially skilled men were required ; indeed, it had expressly invited unskilled men to apply. The result was that the great bulk of the applicants were found to be useless for armament work, and only an insignificant fraction could be placed.

It was no less difficult to establish any concerted policy, within the War Office itself, on the much more serious question of the conflict of interests between the recruiting authorities and the department

---

[1] 2745 (A.G. 2B).   [2] See Appendix XIII.
[3] L.E. Department, C.O. Circ. 1795 (14 April, 1915).

of the Master-General of the Ordnance. In a statement prepared for a sub-committee appointed by the Munitions of War Committee on 26 April to consider co-ordination, Mr. Booth wrote :—

> " The recruiting department at the War Office takes no interest in the troubles of the supply departments. Over 10,000 men were recruited from the engineering trades between 1 January and 28 February, and it is only now that an effort is being made to co-ordinate recruiting for the Front with recruiting for production."

The War Office, unlike most Government Departments, had no single permanent head, superior to the heads of departments. The only person who could adjudicate between rival claims was the Secretary of State, whose time was fully occupied with other duties. This defect of organisation hampered Mr. Booth's endeavours to get the recruiting instructions satisfactorily settled.

Shortly after the issue of the poster mentioned above, Mr. Booth and an officer of the Board of Trade drafted instructions to recruiting officers not to enlist certain classes of men without reference to the Labour Exchanges. Before the printed forms were ready for issue, Lord Kitchener decided that the instructions were to be revised, and that the men should be recruited on the understanding that they might be required to accept employment with a firm doing munitions work. At the end of April, Mr. Booth was trying to get this decision reversed.

The problem of checking the enlistment of skilled men, was, of course, closely connected with the question of Release from the Colours. It appeared to be equally difficult to find effectual means of preventing men from joining the ranks and of recovering them when they had joined. With regard to release, Lord Kitchener had ordered in March that men urgently required for the manufacture of munitions might, in very special cases, be withdrawn from the Expeditionary Force, but every case was to be approved by the Secretary of State on the recommendation of the Quartermaster-General. The men were not to receive Army pay. Many letters were being received from firms and individuals asking for the release of their workmen ; but the Adjutant-General and the regimental officers were reluctant to part with men whose superior intelligence and character made them the best soldiers.

About 23 April, Lord Kitchener took the further step of issuing orders to Commanding Officers, to report by telegram the numbers of men of specified trades (fitters, millwrights, etc.) in certain camps, and to send batches of men direct to some of the chief armament firms. The men were sent without the War Office knowing their names and without any close investigation of their qualifications. They were to remain soldiers and wear uniform, but to receive neither Army pay nor separation allowances, though they might be working away from their homes. The result was that much awkward feeling was created between these soldiers and the regular employees of the firms to which they were sent.[1]

---

[1] L.E. 1965/190.

Anticipating that this system would lead to trouble, Mr. Beveridge drew up on 25 April an alternative scheme for Release, specially designed to secure the return of those men, and only those, who according to their past employer's experience would be of the greatest value for the work required. To avoid difficulties of housing and separation allowances, the scheme provided for the return of men who had originally been enlisted in the districts where they were now to work, so, that they might live at home. Lists were to be obtained by the Labour Exchanges from past employers, not of particular men they wished to recover, but of all men of the classes required for urgent Government work anywhere. These lists, collected and classified, would form a reserve of labour, to be drawn upon as a last resource. They could be compiled in advance for any number of trades when difficulty was anticipated, and the men could be returned only if, when, and for so long as, the difficulty existed. The scheme could be applied, if desired, not only to the large armament firms, but to any employer doing urgent work for the Admiralty or War Office.[1]

The question of release was fully discussed at a conference between the Armaments Output Committee and a deputation from Manchester on 29 April.[2]

One of the employers said that the enlistment of skilled men was still going on. He had applied to the General Officer Commanding the district, who had refused a general exemption, but said that, if the name of any particular man who had enlisted were forwarded, the man should be sent back. The General had not, however, replied to further letters on the subject. It was useless to exempt certain firms, because other firms were indirectly doing war work.

It was stated that Lord Kitchener had said that any man who was wanted might be brought back ; but that he did not want to take out of the Army men who had had six or eight months' training, if the labour difficulty could be met in any other way. Mr. Booth's Committee had then suggested that no further skilled men should be taken.

Lord Kitchener had promised to consider this, and instructions were to be issued to recruiting officers prohibiting enlistment from certain firms and certain classes of employment. There was a conflict of opinion between the Committee and Lord Kitchener. Lord Kitchener held that, if a man were released, he should not leave the Army altogether, but should remain a soldier, subject to recall to the Colours and to some sort of technical discipline, and receive no Army pay for the time being.

Some of the Manchester employers approved of the principle that the men should remain in the Army. It gave a certain hold over the man, and at the same time satisfied his desire to enlist and wear the uniform. Men were refusing to work, if they were not allowed to enlist. It was remarked, however, that the men were going, not from eagerness to enlist, but to escape social persecution.

---

[1] L.E. 1965/190.   [2] A.O.C. *Printed Minutes*, p. 126 ff.

Mr. Booth asked whether the employer's position would be strengthened if the release were for a short period, not to be renewed except on the employer's application. Some of the employers expressed their approval of this plan ; another questioned whether a man could be kept at his employer's request, if he wanted to rejoin. It was also objected that men entered the Army as free individuals, and, if they were released and then sent back to the Army as a punishment, trouble would follow. If all the men were in the Army there would be no difficulty ; but if only a percentage were soldiers and special pressure were brought to bear on them to speed up the factory, things would not work smoothly.

The discussion ended without any conclusion being reached.

On 7 May, Sir H. Llewellyn Smith presented to the Munitions of War Committee a *Memorandum on the Effect of Recruiting on the Supply of Armament Labour.* He stated that all efforts to increase the supply of labour were being counteracted by recruiting in the engineering and shipbuilding trades. In the previous two months, 3,659 men had enlisted from 600 engineering firms which employed 100 men or more before the War. Assuming these results to apply to all the 655,000 engineers in the Kingdom, the total enlisted in these two months would be 8,000, probably as many as had been recruited for armament work in the same period. The corresponding figure for 135 shipbuilding firms, employing 156,000 males, was 1,200.[1]

It was arranged by the Munitions of War Committee that Mr. Balfour should confer with Lord Kitchener on the subject. On May 12, Mr. Balfour reported that he had seen Lord Kitchener, and had been informed that arrangements had been made by the War Office, which would effectively prevent the further drain of men from armament work to the Colours.

The arrangements in question were embodied in a circular memorandum[2] issued by the War Office on 12 May. Lists were enclosed of skilled trades, connected with munitions and Admiralty work, and of selected firms producing munitions of war for the War Office or the Admiralty. All the labour falling within these lists was to be temporarily barred to recruiting. No men enlisted after this date were to be allowed to return to civil work, even on munitions, unless they had had three to six months' training.[3]

It appears that these instructions did not in fact prevent the enlistment of substantial numbers of men covered by them. A table giving the enlistment figures for the three months from mid-April to

---

[1] Tables showing the effect of enlistment on certain industries are given in Part II., Appendix II.

[2] GEN. No. 6/5166 (A.G. 2B). C.O. Circ. 1835 (L.E. 1965/188).

[3] In connection with these instructions a Royal Warrant was issued on 11 May, 1915, granting separation or family allowance to released soldiers.

mid-July shows that in that period another 26,000 men were taken from the metal trades.[1]

Reviewing the situation on 9 June,[2] Sir H. Llewellyn Smith pointed out that the two adverse factors—expansion of demand and enlistment—had far more than counterbalanced any decline in private work. In the engineering trades alone, out of 588,000 occupied males, about 105,000 were stated by their employers to have joined the Forces. Though something like 57,000 not previously employed in engineering establishments had been drawn in, the numbers then working were still 48,000 below those working in July, 1914. In shipbuilding, of 164,000 men, 25,000 had joined the Forces, and 30,000 had been drawn in, so that the numbers actually occupied exceeded the numbers in July, 1914, by about 5,000.

The Armaments Output Committee established in May the nucleus of a Labour department in the form of a section dealing with Release from the Colours. This was at first grouped with the Raw Materials section under Major Carmichael. The Reports of the Intelligence Section from 13 May onwards give figures for releases that had been " arranged for." The total releases " in bulk " for the six weeks ending 29 May are given as 2,694 ; the releases of specified individuals as 276. But no records exist to show what numbers of men were actually released and placed in employment on munitions work before the establishment of the Ministry.

(b) REGULATION OF THE MOVEMENT OF LABOUR : THE PROHIBITION OF ENTICEMENT.

The Munitions of War Committee, besides intervening in matters relating to the supply of men for armament work, also made the first definite move towards securing a control over the movement of Labour.

The particular problem with which it was faced was one which had been brought to the notice of the Board of Trade in January when it began to canvass employers to release their men for armament work.[3] The shortage of skilled men had inevitably led to attempts on all sides to attract labour by advertisement, by canvassing agents, and by offers of higher wages. In the engineering trades men were tempted to leave one firm for another without any regard to the consequent dislocation of work on Government contracts or sub-contracts. The Departments themselves had taken part in the scramble. In January, for example, the Admiralty had put up posters outside an important armament factory in the North inviting fitters and other mechanics to go to the Torpedo Factory at Greenock.[4] At Leeds, Hull, Halifax, Bradford, and Sheffield, the armament firms were advertising in the press that their representatives would attend at the Labour Exchanges

---

[1] See Part II., Appendix II., Table III.

[2] *Memorandum on Labour for Armaments* (9/6/15).   HIST. REC./R/320/1.

[3] See above, Part II., Chap. I.

[4] L.E. 2008 Report of N.W. Divisional Officer.

to select men for employment. The protests of the local employers may be illustrated by a resolution passed by the Halifax District Engineering Association[1] :—

> " At a meeting of the Halifax Association of Engineering Employers held 12 January, 1915, great complaints were made regarding the sending of representatives from Sir W. G. Armstrong, Whitworth & Co., and Vickers, Ltd., to entice the men from our shops. The meeting strongly protests against this unjustifiable means of robbing us of our employees, as practically the whole of the shops in this district are fully occupied on work for war material. The unanimous feeling of the meeting is that the Labour Exchanges are being used for a purpose for which they were never intended, viz., for recruiting centres for armament firms."

In April, the deputations which met the Armaments Output Committee complained that enticement was still unchecked. The Admiralty was offering by advertisement in Birmingham high wages for turners wanted at the Greenock Torpedo Factory.[2] The proposal was made by Mr. Dudley Docker on 20 April that men engaged on War Office work should not be allowed to leave without a certificate from their employer. Mr. Booth was opposed to laying the prohibition on the men, and Mr. Allan Smith thought that the Unions would object to any system of leaving certificates. In illustration of the movement of labour that was going on, Mr. Booth stated that of every 100 men who had gone to Elswick since August, 1914, about 35 had left, so that the permanent increase was only 65% of the arrivals. In three works belonging to Messrs. Vickers, the number of men leaving their employment during April and May amounted to nearly 50% of the number taken on in the same period.[3]

At this time complaints began to be heard also from the men's side. On 18 April, the General Secretary of the A.S.E. wrote to Sir George Askwith that a number of members of that Society who had left employment at Beardmore's (Dalmuir) and Lang's (Paisley) to take work at Fairfield at higher rates, had been discharged on representations made by their previous employers. He added : " You will readily understand the great irritation which is set up by this interference with the liberty of our members to secure work at enhanced rates of pay, and we trust that your Committee (the Committee on Production) will at once issue an instruction with regard to this matter, in order that our members may receive some satisfaction. We shall be glad if you will kindly regard this as an urgent matter, as we understand that much disaffection is rife in these districts owing to the action of the employers."[4]

---

[1] L.E. 1965/29.

[2] This advertisement was still exhibited at the end of May, after Mr. Booth had for seven weeks been trying to persuade the Admiralty to withdraw it (M.C. 492).

[3] A.O.C. *Printed Minutes*, pp. 5, 10.   [4] I.C. 490.

Sir George Askwith reported these complaints to the Board of Trade on 23 April, and suggested that, as the Committee on Production had no authority, the matter should be taken up by the Munitions of War Committee. On the same day, the Board of Trade submitted to the Munitions of War Committee a draft Regulation under the Defence of the Realm Act. The Regulation was promulgated by Order in Council of 29 April. It read as follows :—

" 8 B.   The occupier of a factory or workshop the business carried on in which consists wholly or mainly in engineering, shipbuilding, or the production of arms, ammunition or explosives, or of substances required for the production thereof, shall not, nor shall any person on behalf of the occupier of such a factory or workshop, by canvassing, advertisement or otherwise, take any steps with a view to inducing—

(a) any person employed in any other factory or workshop, being a person engaged on work for any Government Department or otherwise serving war purposes, to leave his employment ; or

(b) any person resident in the United Kingdom at a distance of more than ten miles from the occupier's factory or workshop, to accept employment therein, otherwise than by notifying vacancies to a Board of Trade Labour Exchange ;

and in the event of any person contravening the provisions of this Regulation he shall be guilty of an offence against these Regulations."

The Board of Trade made the following supplementary Regulation under the Labour Exchanges Act (1909) :—

" The Officer in charge of the Labour Exchange in notifying vacancies to applicants for employment, shall during the continuance of the present war give priority to such vacancies as he has reasonable grounds for believing to be on work for any Government Departments or otherwise serving war purposes."

It will be observed that Regulation 8 B avoided the objection raised on the side of Labour to any interference with the workman's freedom to seek higher wages, by laying its prohibition only on the employer. The Order did not forbid either the mere engaging of a workman on the ground that he had just left Government work or the offer of higher wages. It only prohibited attempts, on the part of employers whose business was engineering or of the other kinds specified, to induce men by canvassing, advertisements, etc., to leave Government work or to travel more than 10 miles to apply for work. The check on advertisements and on the use of travelling agents proved beneficial ; but the difficulty of discovering and defining " inducements " was very great.

The Regulation was practically, though not formally, superseded by Section 7 of the Munitions of War Act, 1915, the intention of which was partly to strengthen the Regulation and to bring it *intra vires*.[1]

---

[1] See Part IV., Section VII.

VIII. Conclusion.

The Prime Minister's decision that " a new Department, to be called the Ministry of Munitions," should be created was announced in the Press on 26 May, and on that day Mr. Lloyd George took up his departmental work at Whitehall Gardens.

The Armaments Output Committee had then been in existence for exactly eight weeks. During the first four weeks it had been under Mr. Booth ; during the last four, under the joint control of Mr. Booth and Sir Percy Girouard. So much was done in this short period, so little time was left for making any permanent record, that, with the scanty evidence available, it has been possible to give in the preceding chapters only an imperfect sketch of its activities. Even so, the achievement stands out as remarkable.

When the Committee was appointed, the great bulk of its work fell upon its two active members, Mr. Booth and Mr. Allan Smith, who had to borrow makeshift accommodation and collect a staff as best they could. The pioneer work of the Board of Trade had borne fruit in a single order placed at Leicester for 1,000 shells a week. By the end of May, Mr. Booth and Sir Percy Girouard had under their general direction an organisation which already deserved the name of " central department."[1] One branch, under Lord Elphinstone, was dealing with national manufacture. It was in correspondence with 21 local munitions committees and had placed two direct contracts. It had in view six National Factories and five Co-operative Groups. The total weekly output promised amounted to 38,000 18-pr., 5,000 13-pr., and 37,500 4·5-inch H.E. Shell and 25,000 No. 100 Fuses. A second branch, under Major Carmichael, was in charge of raw and semi-manufactured materials and Release from the Colours. It was exercising control over the Tube Association, the Rolled Brass and Copper Association, and the Aluminium trade. Mr. MacLellan had a section for gauges, presses and steel. Mr. Alfred Herbert, in the Machine Tool Section, had established control over the manufacture in the United Kingdom and the export and import of machine tools. Mr. Chartres had begun to organise an Intelligence Section.

The credit for this achievement must be divided between the Board of Trade, which prepared the ground ; the members of the Committee ; the manufacturers, who responded to the appeal ; and Mr. Lloyd George, who gave publicity to the movement and lent to it the weight of Ministerial support.

---

[1] See Table attached to Sir P. Girouard's memorandum on *The Output of Munitions of War* (31 May, 1915). Hist. Rec./R/200/7.

APPENDICES.

APPENDIX I.

(CHAPTER I., p. 7.)

Survey of Engineering Firms.
Proposed Form of Inspector's Report.

SURVEY OF ENGINEERING FIRMS.

Date.........................

Messrs. ....　　　　Articles normally manufactured:

Address ....　　　　.............................

Questions.	Answers.
I. (a) Is the firm actually at work on a British Government contract or sub-contract? Specify the nature of the order.	
(b) What proportion of the firm's total capacity for armaments is occupied on this Government work?	
II. If the firm is not fully occupied on Government work, have they any machinery on their premises of the classes set out in List A which could be used for the manufacture of any of the articles (or parts of them) set out in List B? Answer here Yes or No, specifying on List A details of machinery.	
III. (a) Does the firm now employ any hands of the classes described in List C? The number of men in each class should be shown on the List and the total, with information as to short time, stated here.	
(b) If these men are engaged on work in connection with private orders, the nature and source of such orders should be specified as accurately as possible. In particular state if any of the work, though not in itself Government work, is required to enable Government work to be performed by other firms (e.g., the making of machines).	

NOTES.

APPENDIX II.

(CHAPTER I., p. 8.)

Home Office Census of Machinery.
Form of Inspector's Report.

Occupier .... District ....

Address......................... Signature ....

Normal Industry................. Date ....

MACHINERY.

| Type. | Total Number. | Number used for. | | | | Where used, e.g., Toolroom or actual manufacturing proces. |
		War Office.	Admiralty.	Allies (state which).	Private Customers.	
Lathes, etc.						

WORKERS.

| Class. | No. of skilled men employed. | | Remarks. |
	On work for Crown or Allies	On private work.	
Foremen, etc.			

Remarks, giving information particularly as to :—

(a) Is the factory accustomed to turn out repetition work of high precision ?

(b) Are they willing to undertake contracts or sub-contracts, and, if so, for what processes and what articles ?

(c) Actual hours of work, to show short time, overtime, night shifts, and week-end work.

(d) Is there surplus of power, and room for additional machinery ?

(e) Any other important points.

APPENDIX III.

(CHAPTER I., p. 9.)

Engineering Survey.

Report for the War Office.

(Form used by Labour Exchange Officers who inspected firms after the Exhibitions of Samples).

Date ....

1. Messrs...

    Address...

2. Articles now manufactured : state if the firm is actually at work on British Government contract or sub-contract.

3. Articles which firm now offers to manufacture :

4. Plant installed of the character described in enclosures to C.O. Circular 1741 :

5. Rate of delivery apart from orders in hand : state date when firm can begin delivery.

6. Wages as compared with district rates :

7. Staff employed in departments likely to be affected by Government contracts :

July, 1914.	Present Time.	Short time, if any, or overtime.

8. Would firm be prepared to undertake new Government work of the above character :

    (a) With their existing machinery ?

    (b) With their existing labour ?

9. Any remarks :

Signature...............................

APPENDIX IV.

(CHAPTER I., p. 11.)

Mr. E. W. Moir's Report on the French Organisation for Munitions Production.

It was decided at the second meeting of the Munitions of War Committee (14 April, 1915) that Mr. Lobnitz should be sent to France immediately to investigate the French system of organisation for increasing output. Messrs. E. W. Moir and Lobnitz arrived at Paris on 16 April, and returned 21 April. They were instructed to enquire particularly as to the manufacture of shells and fuses.[1]

(1) To what extent these were being produced by firms not so engaged before the War, with full details as to the kinds of shell so produced, whether whole shells or parts were made, etc.

(2) As to the administrative methods for outside production, whether mainly by contract with individual firms, or with co-operative groups, and how such groups were organised ; what powers of compulsion the Government possessed ; whether compensation was made for loss of private contracts ; whether private work was allowed ; details as to census of machinery, how prices were fixed, etc.

(3) What special steps had been taken to educate and assist outside firms with regard to supervision, distribution of samples, drawings, etc., payment for experiments, financing new machinery, raw material, inspection and testing.

(4) The supply of labour, wages, discipline, and other conditions of work.

(5) What special steps had been taken to stimulate production in factories previously engaged in making shells and fuses.

Information on similar lines was to be obtained with respect to Field guns ; Field howitzers ; Propellants ; High Explosives (" very little is needed here ") ; Rifles (" very important ") ; and Small Arms Ammunition.

Messrs. Moir and Lobnitz presented a Report to the Armaments Output Committee on 22 April. A less technical Report[2] was circulated to the Munitions of War Committee and considered at the third meeting on 26 April.

The chief points may be summarised as follows :—

1. *General Remarks.*—Approximately 30,000 to 40,000 small calibre high explosive shells per day were being turned out, with the

---

[1] Instructions and Reports, M.C. 212.

[2] M.C. 7, 23 April. Report of 22 April and Minutes of the Armaments Output Committee meeting at which it was discussed, M.C. 212.

necessary gaines and fuses, by new firms. This amounted to about one-half of the total French output.

After the receipt of detailed information and the order to proceed delivery of some shell cases might be expected in from $1\frac{1}{2}$ to 2 months, and an established engineering works could reach its maximum output in from $3\frac{1}{2}$ to 4 months.

No shrapnel shells had yet been made by private firms, but the necessary plant was now being installed by some of the larger producers. Very few shells above 75 mm. had been made by inexperienced firms.

Certain modifications of design, made to facilitate manufacture, had resulted in gun bursts and had been abandoned.

2. *Visits to Works.*—Eleven factories had been visited, ranging from one firm which only produced 25 partly-finished shell cases a day, to Messrs. Renault, who made shell cases, gaines, and fuses complete up to 6,000 a day.

No private firms were making high explosive or propellants. Shells were charged only at Government factories distant more than 100 m les from Paris.

3. *Administration.*—At the outbreak of war the Ministry of War selected one works to be chief of the group of works in each district, and contracted with this chief for supply of shell cases and fuses at fixed prices, uniform for each item throughout the country. The chief sub-let parts of the work to other firms in the group at a slightly lower fixed price. Each member of the group was responsible for the accuracy of his own work. It was now thought that firms capable only of a very small output should be excluded. The Government supplied all raw material and paid for failures due to raw material. No powers of compulsion other than those of the mobilisation laws were needed. Compensation was given for proved loss of private contracts. No private work could be done in factories working on munitions without leave of the Ministry of War. No census of machines or of firms had been taken, but some information as to capable firms was available at the outbreak of war. The inspecting officers distributed drawings and patterns and, at the outset, gave advice and help ; but methods were left free to the manufacturers, subject to the results being satisfactory.

4. *Payments for work done.*—A universal uniform price for each item was undoubtedly the best method.

5. *Financing firms.*—Some firms had received advances amounting to 25% of the value of the order, to be repaid by rebate on price. In one case a large amount was spent on entirely new works and machinery. Many firms, however, had adapted their plant without assistance.

6. *Conditions of Labour.*—Women had been freely employed without friction ; they learnt quickly and worked well. Some men had been recalled from the Colours for munition work. They received the

district wages, becoming soldiers again and reverting to army pay if they left the factory. Wages were paid at pre-war district rates ; but piece-work rates were usually preferred and adopted. The Ministry of War saw that wages were not reduced ; but they had not been increased ; and there was no increased rate for night work, overtime, or Sunday work. One half-day a fortnight was allowed for recreation. There were few absentees. Strikes and labour troubles were unknown. The output per employee was high, running out at from 3 to 4 75 mm. shells per day. Mobilisation would deal with any indiscipline or irregularity.

7. *Increase of Output from existing sources.*—In the National Arsenals a system providing for increase of labour force and for running night and day had been worked out ready for Mobilisation. The Government appropriated all munitions produced by firms working for export in peace time.

8. The Ministry of War thought that rifles, field guns, propellants, and high explosives could not be produced by private inexperienced firms.

APPENDIX V.

(CHAPTER II., p. 21.)

Lord Kitchener's Letter to Employers, 27 March, 1915.

War Office,

Whitehall, S.W.

Sir,

I stated in the House of Lords on the 15th March that we were in urgent need of certain war supplies for the manufacture of which the machinery at our disposal is in excess of the available supply of labour.

It is essential that we should obtain a further supply of such labour. With this in view, I have asked Mr. George M. Booth, acting under my immediate direction, to take the necessary steps to obtain the release from such civil work as can be postponed of the labour required for military purposes. The work will be closely co-ordinated with what has been done and is being done by the Board of Trade in this direction. You will be hearing shortly from the Committee, and I would ask you to do everything you can to help me.

Yours faithfully,

(Signed) KITCHENER.

APPENDIX VI.

(CHAPTER II., p. 21.)

Mr. Booth's Letter to Employers, 29 March, 1915.

War Office,

Whitehall, S.W.

Dear Sir,

You will have received a letter from Lord Kitchener on the subject of the special need of skilled labour for the increased output of war material. In this connection I should be much obliged if you will fill in the enclosed form and return it in the enclosed envelope as promptly as possible.

The War Office, while prepared, if necessary, to make full use of the powers granted by the Defence of the Realm Amendment No. 2 Act, is anxious to disturb employers as little as possible.

You are at liberty to take your workmen into your and our confidence on the subject of this letter. We should like them all to know that Lord Kitchener considers this matter as of the utmost urgency and importance.

Yours faithfully,

(Signed) GEORGE M. BOOTH.

APPENDIX VII.

(CHAPTER II., p. 23.)

Questionnaire accompanying Mr. Booth's Letter of 29 March, 1915.

STRICTLY CONFIDENTIAL.

For the use of the War Office.

ARMAMENT LABOUR RETURN.

M .... Trade.

Locality of Works .... Date.

Question.	*Answer.*

1. Enumerate your various classes of work at present in hand.

2. Are your men working—
   - (a) Short time ....
   - (b) Full time ....
   - (c) Overtime ....

3. Are you engaged on any Government contract or sub-contract ? If the latter, from what firm or firms ?

4. Have you inspected the sample shells, etc., exhibited at Aldwych Labour Exchange, and taken any action in consequence ? If so, what ?

5. If the answer to question No. 3 is " Yes," state—
   - (a) The class of Government work.
   - (b) The percentage your Government work bears to your total work now in hand.

6. Assuming that arrangements for compensation in respect of private work postponed could be made under the Defence of the Realm (Amendment, No. 2) Act—
   - (a) Could you with *your present plant and present staff* do more Government work—
     - (1) Of the class you are now doing ?
     - (2) Of any other class ?
   - (b) Release men for armament work elsewhere ?

7. State the number of men you employ, and the rate of wages paid thereto who may correspond approximately to any of the classes set out below.

Classes of Workmen employed.	Rate of Wages.	No. on War material.	No. on Civil work.	Total.
1. Fitters, Viewers, Markers off				
2. Turners...........................				
3. Horizontal Borers				
4. Gun Borers				
5. Drillers				
6. Gear Millers				
7. Gear Planers				
8. Grinders				
9. Capstans				
10. Millers, Vertical, Universal and Profile				
11. Cross Millers				
12. Planers				
13. Shapers				
14. Slotters				
15. Rifling Lathes				
16. Polishers				
17. Shell Machinists				
18. Rifling Machinists				
19. Lapping Machinists................				
20. Reamering Machinists				
21. Chambering Machinists				
22. Smiths...........................				
23. Hammermen and Stampers				

APPENDIX VIII.

(CHAPTER II., p. 30.)

Form of P.R.1 Return.

STRICTLY CONFIDENTIAL.

P.R.1.

For the use of the War Office.

WAR OFFICE ARMAMENTS OUTPUT COMMITTEE.

ARMAMENT PRODUCTION RETURN.

SHELL AND FUSE PLANT.

Messrs..

Question.	*Answer.*
A. What proportion of your plant and machinery is at present engaged on production of shells, fuses and/or parts thereof ?	
B. Is such plant and machinery being used to the fullest extent, including night-shift ?	
C. What proportion of the remainder of your plant and machinery is suitable or could be easily adapted for production of such work ?	
D. If the plant and machinery at present so engaged is not fully employed as above—	
(1) If you are short of orders, state what proportion of plant and machinery is affected.	
(2) If you are short of labour, state the number of various classes *now* required and the rates of wages offered.	
(3) If you are short of raw or partly manufactured material, state whether the shortage arises from failure to deliver against your orders placed— (a) At home. (b) Abroad.	
(4) Give names of suppliers causing delay.	
(5) Give particulars of delay being experienced in transport— (a) By rail. (b) By steamer.	
E. Give particulars of new plant in course of erection.	
F. Date when completion of installation is anticipated.	

Question.	*Answer.*
G. Particulars and cause of any delays in connection with new installations experienced regarding—	
(1) Buildings.	
(2) Machinery.	
H. Progress since last return as to—	
(1) Installation of machinery.	
(2) Supply of labour.	
I. What arrangements are you making to secure labour for your new plant ?	
J. With regard to the full usage of your new plant do you anticipate any difficulty in obtaining necessary supply of raw material ?	
K. Are you experiencing any delay due to—	
(1) Drawings,	
(2) Designs,	
(3) Inspection,	
(4) Shipping instructions,	
(5) Any other causes ?	

Signature...............................

Date ....

APPENDIX IX.

(CHAPTER II., p. 31.)

Mr. Booth's Correspondence.

The following lists will give some idea of the nature of the correspondence which Mr. Booth had to deal with. The letters were elicited by Mr. Lloyd George's speeches on the Defence of the Realm (Amendment) Act in March; Lord Kitchener's speech of 15 March; the announcement of the Treasury Committee, and the various posters and advertisements issued in May.

It must be understood that the miscellaneous collection from which these specimens are taken does not include the more promising offers of service or of premises, factories, etc., which were classified under districts or filed. Nor does it include the returns sent by employers in response to Mr. Booth's letter of 29 March, or the results of the industrial surveys and census of machinery. The lists are intended merely to illustrate the extraordinarily varied nature of the correspondence and the eagerness displayed by every class in the nation to assist the Government.

(A) OFFERS OF SERVICES.

Applicant.	Work or Position Required.
Engineer's Labourer and handy man.	A vacancy.
Retired Accountant in the West African Civil Service.	Employment in the War Office.
Late Private, Northamptonshire Regiment.	Used to horses and general labour.
Chief Clerk in Paving Contractor's Office.	Light work in evenings at factory or Government Department.
Silversmith	One day a week munitions work.
Manager of a Concrete Company ..	Services.
Old Harrovian with a touring car	To drive Officers.
Foreman Blacksmith	To serve on Armaments Output Committee.
Draper's Assistant	Services in any capacity.
Iron worker from Vancouver ..	Munitions work.
Unskilled Draper	Munitions work.
Silversmith	Supervision.
Clothier, with a fair knowledge of things in general.	Services.
Clerk of Works	Supervision of building construction.
Small Tradesman	Any post.
Employee of London County Council	Services.
Ex-Railway porter, with slight knowledge of the use of plane and saw. Barman.	Munitions work.
Engineer on Indian State Railways	Services.
Unemployed Coppersmith ..	Munitions work anywhere.

Applicant.	*Work or Position Required.*
Educated woman	Filling shells.
Naval Architect	Services of the firm.
Woollen Merchant	Services in procuring clothing materials.
Inspecting Engineer	Post as Inspecting Engineer.
Manager of brick and pipe works ..	To go anywhere.
Commercial Traveller	Inspecting workshops.
Gardener (deaf)	Metal work.
Printer	Munitions work anywhere.
Manager of Furniture - making Association.	Services in any capacity.
Unemployed Compositor	Services in any capacity.
Consulting Engineer	Post as Inspector.
Baker and Confectioner	Vacancy in the Foodstuffs Department.
Compositor	Position of trust.
Belgian refugee, Brass Moulder ..	Munitions work.
Manager of Motor-vehicle works ..	Any vacancy.
Journeyman Cabinet-maker and Trade Union official.	Organising an office.
Repairer of Musical Instruments (deaf).	Any manual work.
Private business in the jig-saw and puzzle line.	Services at usual rates.
Engineer of 20 years' experience ..	Services.
Works Manager of Electro-typing Company.	Services in any capacity.
Ironmonger's Foreman	Munitions work.
Insurance Broker	Transport Officer, Customs Officer, Valuer or Assessor.
Commercial Traveller with knowledge of shipping stores.	Services.
Science Master in County School..	Munitions work.
Storekeeper on South African Railways and Canadian Pacific Railway.	Any position.
Lady (about 60), Music Teacher ..	Clerical work or making ammunition.
Stone-mason..	A job of work at anything in the labouring class.
Engineer, Indian Railways ..	Inspection of munitions works.
Understands thoroughly the handling of barrels.	Suitable work.
Optical Mechanician	Suitable work.
Canadian Engineer in Vancouver..	Instructor or foreman. (Offered to bring Canadian and American mechanics.)
A lady	Offer to organise a party of ladies for armament work.

Applicant.	*Work or Position Required.*
Undergraduate with car　.．　　.．	Unskilled labour in Ordnance works.
Storekeeper, Buenos Aires Harbour Works.	Any suitable position.
Retired business man　　.．　　.．	Services.
Amateur Engineer (Belgian)　　.．	Munitions work or interpreting.

(B) Offers of Premises, etc.

Nature of Firm.	*Offer.*
Hay and Straw Merchants　　.．	Works, to be fitted with machinery.
Farmer　　.．　　.．　　.．　　.．	Some buildings and machinery.
Boiler Works in liquidation　　.．	Premises and machinery for sale.
Ginger-beer Makers　　　　.．	Premises and land for lease or sale.
Cycle and Motor Engineers　　.．	Shop with oil engine and lathe.
Brewery　　.．　　.．　　.．　　.．	Spare power and accommodation.
Engineer　　.．　　.．　　.．　　.．	Small shop and smithy.
Steam Flour Mills .．　　.．　　.．	Empty premises for store or hospital.
Shipbuilder .．　　.．　　.．　　.．	Three shops, to be fitted with machinery.
Potters　　.．　　.．　　.．　　.．	Empty works for storage.
Iron Foundry　　.．　　.．　　.．	To sell or hand over for the War.
Slate Quarries　　.．　　.．　　.．	Works for hire.
Electrical and Sanitary Engineers .	Large workshop and staff.

Several thousands of the more promising offers of premises, machinery, and going concerns were subsequently classified under districts and catalogued.

At the end of May a list of the factories offered to the Government was compiled. Some of the factories included appeared to be fully engaged on Government work ; others of the offers might equally well have been classified as applications for further contracts. In some cases the offer seemed to have been prompted by shortage of labour ; and it was not always possible to make out whether an adequate staff was included in the offer.

The numbers included were as follows :—

London Division　　.．　　.．　　.．　　.．　　.．	21
Birmingham and Midlands Division　　.．　　.．	13
Liverpool and Manchester District　　.．　　.．	11
Leeds Division　　.．　　.．　　.．　　.．　　.．	5
Scotland Division　　.．　　.．　　.．　　.．　　.．	7
South Western Division　　.．　　.．　　.．　　.．	5
Wales Division　　.．　　.．　　.．　　.．　　.．	10

(C) REQUESTS FOR CONTRACTS, PURCHASE OF STOCK, ETC.

Firm.	*Offer.*
Mill and Colliery Furnisher	Large stock of gas, steam, and water tubes, etc., for sale.
Carver and Gilder	Would make ammunition boxes.
Gates and Railings Maker	Any forged iron-work.
Advertising Agents	Office advertisements.
Picture Frame-makers	Two circular saws for hire.
Building Contractors	Large stocks of timber.
Electric Company	Further War Office orders.
Dental Manufacturing Company	Fittings and parts of rifles.
Steam Sawyer	Sawing timber.
Office Fitter	Wood work.
Steam Pumps	More foundry work, forging and machining.
Water Softeners	Purifying water for explosives manufacture.
Not specified	Will produce ten times the amount of shells the army requires, automatically, without engineering appliances.
Maker of Paper-fasteners	Cartridge caps.
Nail Works	Shells, if provided with machinery.
Joiners and Builders	Tent-bottoms.
Iron Works	Iron castings.
Builder	Aeroplanes.
Tailor	Army clothing.

(D) MISCELLANEOUS SUGGESTIONS.

There are seventy to eighty thousand Insurance Agents who might be enlisted and replaced by women.

An Inspector should be appointed to see that unskilled men get a living wage and a war bonus. (Engineering employee.)

In a certain works making machine guns, overtime had been stopped. The men were eager to work longer hours. (Anonymous.)

All the munitions wanted could be obtained, if the shame and degradation of attending at Labour Exchanges were eliminated.

The watch-making district of French Switzerland could produce an immense output of interchangeable parts or complete articles in steel or other metals. (A French Swiss.)

Loss of time could be checked by an agreement between employers and Trade Unions that men who worked shorter hours should be paid at a reduced rate. (Trade Unionist.)

The Chairman of a Company making picketing pegs complained of the waste of labour in polishing the shoes of these pegs to satisfy War Office requirements.

Many men from the Goldsmith and Jewellery Trades could do munitions work. (A goldsmith.)

A certain firm was employing only 10 per cent. of its men on Government work. The remaining 90 per cent. were prevented from seeking employment elsewhere on Government work by an agreement between the Government and other firms on Government work. (A workman.)

Pontoons should be made more roughly and economically. (An engineer.)

Thousands of Egyptian natives could be imported for munitions work.

District Enquiry Agents should be appointed to discover suitable works.

Hundreds of Dutch mechanics could be imported. (A Dutchman.)

There should be a compulsory closing of all workshops in unnecessary branches of metal trades.

Complaints about various abuses at Liverpool in the unloading of vessels, etc.

Parcels to Germany ought not to be packed in tins.

(E) SUGGESTED INVENTIONS.

Innumerable suggestions were received from persons of every rank and class for : the design and manufacture of rifle and body shields for infantry ; armoured cars capable of crossing trenches ; shells made of earthenware, glass, cast-iron, or concrete ; moveable munitions and repair factories for use behind the lines ; various types of shot and shell for destroying barbed wire ; shells containing beer bottles, pepper, poisonous gases, or darts ; respirators ; means of counteracting gases ; automatic carriages to convey bombs to the enemy lines ; periscopic rifle sights ; trench catapults ; automatic aeroplanes ; loopholed sandbags ; poisoned bullets ; discharges of " electric snuff, to make the enemy sneeze " ; rubber tubes to be inserted in the boots, so that the feet could be warmed by the breath ; spraying the enemy's potato crops with sulphuric acid dropped by aeroplanes ; protecting our vulnerable coasts with a line of dummy trenches containing 50 million razor-edged steel man-traps ; training cormorants to attack submarine periscopes and torpedoes ; setting nature students to collect spindle-wood for charcoal, which the writer (a lady) had been informed was a constituent of gunpowder ; and many other more or less practicable devices.

Such suggestions as seemed to deserve attention were forwarded to the proper department.

APPENDIX X.

(CHAPTER III., p. 38.)

Board of Trade Letter to Divisional Officers, 1 April, 1915.

(L.E.1965/125.)

Re Engineering Survey.

On 27 March I sent you a memorandum and a list of the principal armament firms. This list has now been amended by the War Office, and a copy of the revised list is enclosed for your information. As regards the placing of contracts for the manufacture of shells special difficulties are likely to arise within a radius of 20 miles from any of the firms on this revised list.

Enclosure.

LIST OF ARMAMENT FIRMS.

Firm.	*Place.*
Armstrong, Whitworth & Co.	.. Elswick, Darlington, Alexandria, Openshaw, Manchester.
Vickers	.. Erith, Crayford, Ipswich, Barrow, Sheffield.
Firths	.. Sheffield.
Hadfield	.. Sheffield.
King's Norton Metal Co. ..	.. Birmingham.
Birmingham Metal & Munitions Co.	Birmingham.
Electrical and Ordnance Accessories Co. (Vickers).	Birmingham.
Birmingham Small Arms ..	.. Birmingham.
Dick, Kerr & Co. ..	.. Preston.
Cammell, Laird & Co. ..	.. Birkenhead.
Coventry Ordnance Works	.. Coventry.
Greenwood & Batley ..	.. Leeds.
Projectile Co.	.. Battersea.
London Small Arms ..	.. London, E.
Beardmore	.. Dalmuir and Parkhead.

GOVERNMENT FACTORIES.

Royal Arsenal	.. Woolwich.
Royal Factory	.. Enfield.
Royal Factory	.. Greenock.

APPENDIX XI.

(CHAPTER IV., p. 68.)

Constitution of Local Munitions Committees.

(The following Notes were first issued about 21 *April,* 1915.)

WAR OFFICE,
LONDON, S.W.

NOTES REGARDING APPOINTMENT OF LOCAL COMMITTEES.

1. A Cabinet Committee, under the Chairmanship of Mr. Lloyd George, met representatives of the Trade Unions and, amongst other things, appointed an Advisory Committee of the Unions whose function is to deal promptly with all disputes which may arise in connection with the production of armaments and munitions of war.

2. The Advisory Committee, in order to keep in direct touch with questions arising in each district, have requested the district representatives of the Unions to appoint Local Committees who would act, as a medium of communication, with the Advisory Committee as a Central Authority.

3. These Local Committees will co-operate with the Local Committees of Employers with the view of settling promptly any questions which may arise, and, failing settlement, will invoke the assistance of the Advisory Committee.

4. The Local Committees of the Unions will nominate five or seven representatives to confer with the employers locally.

5. In each District employers are setting up Local Armament Committees to superintend the execution of orders which may be placed for armaments and munitions of war, and to secure full and effective co-operation amongst the manufacturers interested, the Factory Inspectors, the Labour Exchanges and others whose assistance would be helpful.

6. These Local Armaments Committees of Employers should also nominate five or seven representatives, who, with the five or seven representatives of the Local Committees of the Unions, will form local Joint Committees representing employers and workpeople, each side having an equal representation.

7. These Joint Committees would be available for discussion of any questions affecting labour.

8. The Employers' Local Armaments Committees will deal with all manufacturing questions, the Local Committees of the Unions will deal with all questions affecting their Members, and the Joint Local Committees will deal with questions which affect manufacturers and workpeople alike.

APPENDIX XII.

(CHAPTER V., p. 88.)

Admiralty Sub-committee for advising on purchase of raw materials.

(*See* M.C.446.)

The Admiralty Restriction of Enemy Supplies Committee in their 48th Report (par. 7) recommended the appointment of a Sub-committee of themselves " to advise as to the purchase of certain classes of raw materials of which the Government and their contractors may be short ; for instance, copper, antimony, tungsten, and spelter."

The First Lord directed the Committee to proceed at once with the appointment, notifying other Departments concerned.

At the meeting of the Committee on 20 April, the following were nominated to serve on the proposed Sub-committee :—

Vice-Admiral Sir E. Slade,
Mr. Gauntlett (Admiralty, Contract Branch),
A representative of the Director of Naval Ordnance,
Mr. H. H. Fawcett (War Office),
A representative of the War Office (Contract Branch),
Mr. Murray (C.I.D.),
Mr. Davis (Colonial Office),
Mr. Chiozza Money,
Mr. Alan Alanson (Board of Trade).

The Board of Trade was asked to inform the Chairman (Sir F. Hopwood) if they desired to nominate a second representative.

After some correspondence, it was agreed between Mr. Runciman and Sir F. Hopwood that the Sub-committee should proceed on the condition that it was purely advisory and that its recommendations should be dealt with by the Board of Trade, War Office, and Admiralty, purchases being made by the Board of Trade or the Department concerned.

The attention of Mr. Lloyd George was called to this Sub-committee on 15 May, and he gave instructions that the matter should appear on the agenda of the Munitions of War Committee's next meeting, notice in advance being given to Sir P. Girouard and General von Donop. The matter appears to have been held up, pending the reconstruction of the Committee and the setting up of the Ministry of Munitions.

On June 11, Sir E. Slade suggested to Sir H. Ll. Smith that the Sub-committee should be transferred to the Ministry. The question was referred to Sir P. Girouard, who recommended that the Sub-committee should cease to act ; but that Mr. Gauntlett should assist the Ministry with advice as to Admiralty requirements.

APPENDIX XIII.

(CHAPTER V., p. 90.)

Poster issued by the War Office early in April, 1915.

(*See* C.O. Circular 1795 (14.4.15) L.F. 1965/154.)

THE MAN THE ARMY WANTS NOW

to provide shells and rifle ammunition required by the Army in the field.

Fitters, turners, millwrights, and skilled workmen, also unskilled workmen not now engaged in the production of war material, can serve their King and Country by coming forward to help in providing the munitions of war of which the Army is in need.

Any volunteers for this service, which is most essential for the successful prosecution of the War, should give their names to the *nearest recruiting office*, stating what class of work they can perform.

No medical examination ; no age limits ; no measurement.

In this way men can serve their King and Country and work for their comrades in the field.

Lord Kitchener calls on all workmen to come forward and help **where** they can.

APPENDIX XIV.

(CHAPTER III., p. 43.)

The North East Coast Armaments Committee.

I. Introductory.

INVESTIGATION OF LABOUR POSITION IN THE
NORTH EAST COAST DISTRICT.

On 19 March, 1915, Sir Percy Girouard was requested by Lord Kitch ner to undertake an enquiry as to the possibilities of transferring labour in the Newcastle area. The district was an A Area dominated by the great armament and shipbuilding works of Messrs. Armstrong. The firm already employed 24,910 workpeople, all on Government work and working continuous time, but in order to man the new plants already constructed or in course of construction an additional 5,000 to 6,000 employees were required, a considerable proportion of whom must be skilled men. At Sir Percy Girouard's request, the Board of Trade supplied statistics dealing with the engineering and railway workshops and kindred firms in the North Eastern district. The statistics covered 54,100 employees, of whom nearly one-half were employed by Messrs. Armstrong. In he district, exclusive of Messrs. Armstrong, there were 44 firms with a total of 28,000 employees of whom 43 % were employed on Government work, and 32 % were working overtime. The remaining 1,300 men were employed by 32 small factories, 25 % being employed on Government work and 14 % working overtime.

In an interim report based on these returns (25 March), Sir Percy Girouard stated that the figures showed that there was " a considerable body of men, even in such a non-engineering district as the North East, who could be made available for munition work." He was strongly of the opinion that the first step in securing an increase of output must be to concentrate effort on the existing armament works. " To attempt an organization " he wrote " of all the various small engineering factories dotted about the North East district in preference to going on with the main factories provided by the Government would appear to be a suicidal policy. The only way it could be done would be by depleting the firms which can turn out in quantity and quality of their supervision."

From this point of view, therefore, the problem resolved itself into providing Messrs. Armstrong with the additional labour they required as soon as possible, 1,600 to 1,700 hands being required at Elswick alone.

On 30 March, Captain Percy Creed, recommended for this work by Sir Percy Girouard, was instructed by Mr. Booth to go down to Newcastle and undertake work of an experimental nature. He was supplied with a list of the factories where, according to the information available, there existed labour of the kind required but occupied at the moment upon civil work as opposed to war material.

Lord Kitchener's letter[1] was sent to each of these firms on 29 March, and followed on 30 March by a second letter, signed by Mr. Booth, informing the firms that Captain Creed had been instructed to call upon them with reference to the special need of skilled labour for munitions, and asking them to fill up a form stating particulars of the labour employed by them, and whether they were prepared to undertake the manufacture of shells, or to transfer labour to armament work.   Captain Creed was put in touch with the Newcastle Committee of the Engineering Employers' Federation (to which most of these firms belonged), with the Divisional Officer of the Labour Exchange Organization, Mr. Paterson, with Mr. Lauder of the Home Office Factory Inspection Department, and with Captain Power, R.N., the Captain Superintendent of contract-built ships (representing the Admiralty in the district) in order " to concentrate endeavours from all points on the one object in view."

At the same time, Sir Percy Girouard was asked to see that Messrs. Armstrong did their utmost to justify the special efforts that the War Office was about to make on their behalf.   There was evidence that their works had grown so fast that the standard of control and supervision was not as good as formerly, and that the new men found the conditions under which they worked at Elswick unsatisfactory. It was said that 80 % of the men moved to Elswick since the beginning of the War returned to their homes after a few weeks.[2]   Every effort must be made to encourage such skilled workmen as could be obtained by the War Office to remain at Elswick over the coming period of pressure.   The Armaments Output Committee wished for an assurance that the output per man and per machine at Elswick was higher than in shops not regularly employed in making munitions of war.

PRELIMINARY WORK IN NEWCASTLE.

Captain Creed arrived in Newcastle on 7 April, and had interviews with Captain Power, with Mr. Paterson, who had come from Glasgow to meet him, and with Mr. Lauder.   He visited Elswick and discussed the position with Sir Percy Girouard and Mr. Marjoribanks, another member of the firm.   He was introduced to members of he Engineering Employers' Federation, and wrote to the local officials of all the Trade Unions concerned in the production of munitions asking them to meet him and discuss the situation.   He proposed later on to make a tour of the factories, taking with him Mr. Lane, the Crown Agents' Inspecting Engineer.

On the following day, 8 April, Captain Creed had an interview with a prominent Trade Union official, Mr. Wile, President of the Federation of Shipbuilding and Engineering Trades, who had been actively engaged in transferring workers of his union

---

[1] See Appendix V.
[2] *Cp.* Memorandum by Mr. P. J. Pybus, above, p. 58.

(the North of England Brass Founders, Fitters, and Finishers' Society) to places where their work was most needed. He promised to do all he could to help. The Newcastle Chamber of Commerce, which had placed its services at Mr. Booth's disposal, was requested to communicate with Captain Creed.

An inaugural meeting held in the Council Chamber on 9 April, was attended by representatives both of employers and of organised labour. The Lord Mayor, Mr. John Fitzgerald, appealed to the " dormant patriotism " of his fellow citizens to accelerate the supply of munitions, and stated that he had been requested by Lord Kitchener to approach the various organisations to ascertain whether any arrangements could be made whereby work of a less vital character could be set aside in order that skilled workmen might be released for the requirements of the Admiralty and the War Office. He proposed that a representative committee, to be called " The City of Newcastle Armaments Output Committee," should be appointed to go into the matter forthwith. The suggestion of Mr. James Redhead, representing the Shipbuilders' Association, that the area to be covered by the work of the Committee should be extended to take in the whole of the North East Coast, and to cover the private and commercial yards on the Wear and Tees and at Hartlepool, Blyth, etc., was opposed by Captain Power. His view was that, though the additional labour required for Elswick might have to be obtained by the goodwill of the employers in Middlesbrough and on the Tees and Wear, it was not necessary for members of those firms to be on the Committee. It was decided, however, that these districts should be included, and the title of " The North East Coast Armaments Committee " was agreed upon.

The Lord Mayor proposed that the Committee should be composed of a representative each from the Admiralty, the War Office, the Home Office, and the Board of Trade, three representatives of employers, three representatives of trade unions, a representative of the Recruiting officer, and a member of the Newcastle Chamber of Commerce. The meeting ultimately decided that the committee was to include seven employers and seven representatives of the men.

The following resolution was carried unanimously :—" Having considered Lord Kitchener's urgent appeal for a greatly increased output of munitions of war, this meeting is of the opinion that everything possible should be done to meet the urgent requirements of the nation at the present time and pledges itself to use its best endeavours to increase the output of war munitions, and towards that end agrees that a repre entative committee to be called ' The North East Coast Armaments Committee ' be appointed from the meeting to go into the matter forthwith under the chairmanship of the Lord Mayor."

Captain Creed thought the widest possible publicity essential to the success of the scheme. He obtained Mr. Booth's sanction to start an advertising campaign in the local press, which began with a full page advertisement in the *Newcastle Daily Chronicle* on April 13.

On 13 April Captain Creed and Captain Power went up to London. to consult Mr. Booth and the Committee with reference to checking the recruiting of skilled men on the North East Coast, to ask for power to put pressure on recalcitrant employers under the Defence of the Realm Act, and to discuss the views put forward by the employers in the engineering trades at a private meeting with the Government representatives on 12 April.

Captain Creed was present at the first meeting of the Committee on 15 April, but went to London and thence to Glasgow, where he organised a similar committee soon afterwards. Captain Kelly, who was sent down to replace him as representative of the War Office, arrived on 17 April.

II. The North East Coast Armaments Committee.

COMPOSITION.

The Committee at its first meeting consisted of twenty-four members : the Lord Mayor, one representative each of the War Office, the Admiralty, and the Board of Trade, two representatives of the Home Office, seven representatives of the workmen, seven representatives of the employers, the Recruiting Officer, the Deputy Town Clerk, a representative of the Newcastle Chamber of Commerce, and an interim Secretary.

Subsequently other members were added : the Sheriff, the Duke of Northumberland, and Lord Durham, together with a second representative of the War Office, the Admiralty, and the Board of Trade, one more representative of the employers, and one more of the workmen. This formed the full Committee, which met on 15 April, 4 and 21 May, 29 June, 27 July, 5, 16, and 30 August.

At the meeting on 15 April three executive sub-committees— Engineering, Shipbuilding, and Ship-repairers—were appointed, each consisting of four, or three, representatives of employers and workmen, together with the representatives of Government Departments. Joint meetings of the sub-committees were held before they met separately, the chairman being Captain Power. After 4 May the joint sub-committees were known as the Executive Committee, and this body did the most important part of the work. Captain Power resigned on 29 June, Admiral Tate being appointed as the Admiralty representative.

At the first meeting, on 15 April, it was agreed that the selection of a Secretary should be left to Captain Creed and Captain Power. Captain Kelly was appointed, and he held office until 5 June, when he left to take up work at the War Office. His place was taken by Captain Ross, who had formerly been Assistant Secretary.

The office staff at Pearl Buildings, Northumberland Street, consisted of the Secretary, an Assistant Secretary, the representatives of the Home Office and Board of Trade, a Labour Exchange Manager, a Labour Exchange Assistant Insurance officer (who was responsible for the subordinate staff and for finance), one Labour Exchange Assistant Manager, one Labour Exchange lower grade clerk, together with two filing clerks, three typists, one telephone operator, one commissionaire, and three boy scouts.

<h3 style="text-align:center">CHARACTER OF THE COMMITTEE.</h3>

The *Newcastle Daily Chronicle* welcomed the representative character of the Committee, which would from its composition be able to form a clear and impartial decision as to how far the continuation on private orders was compatible with the maximum output of war materials. It expressed the hope that there would be no unnecessary secrecy about the proceedings of the Committee[1], and that it would not be hampered by its association with Government Departments.

Captain Creed felt anxious about the attitude of the employers, but reported that the attitude of the workmen was most satisfactory. On 11 April the officials of the Trade Unions in the district had despatched a telegram to the Prime Minister, in which they said : " We do not want any more speeches about the failings of the workers, the employers, or the Government. We want to pull together and get on with it. You may tell Lord Kitchener that we shall deliver the goods. The working man of the North East Coast will do his bit. We hope, for our part, that you may find it possible to be present at the first meeting of the Committee." The Trade Union representatives on the Committee, Messrs. Wile, Rowe, Spence, Gilbert, Ratcliffe, Crawforth, Hebron, and Macpherson fully justified Captain Creed's expectations, and the employers, Colonel Saxton White, and Messrs. Marjoribanks, Clark, Gibb, James, Ropner, and Summers Hunter met them half-way.

A suggestion that employers and men should sit on opposite sides of the table was negatived, and the informal character of the meetings —speakers remaining seated and smoking being permitted—enabled the Committee to get through a large amount of work. The Committee as a whole was reported by Captain Kelly to be " surprisingly in accord on controversial points," and there was a general opinion that " the idea of cordial co-operation between Capital and Labour had been improved by the action of the Government in appointing the Committee."[2] The presence of representatives of Government Departments gave the Committee authority and control of the administrative machinery of the district,[3] and brought employers and men face to face with the vital needs of the situation.

---

[1] The official reports communicated to the Press were scanty, a meeting lasting six hours being summarised in six lines.

[2] *Newcastle Daily Chronicle*, 20 April.

[3] In Captain Kelly's words : " The presence of these accredited representatives of the Admiralty, the Home Office, and the Board of Trade, was of great value, and if, in addition, the Financial Departments had been represented on the Board, a most useful and a unique combination would have been effected."

III. Labour Transfer.

The activities of the Committee with regard to the transfer of labour fall into three periods, the appeal to the employers (15 April to 15 May) the appeal to the workmen (King's Squad scheme) (15 May to 30 June), and the War Munitions Volunteer scheme (30 June to 15 August), which was in the main a development of the King's Squad scheme.

APPEAL TO EMPLOYERS TO RELEASE WORKMEN.

On 16 April the Executive Committee decided that all employers should be required to furnish a return of the labour employed on Government and non-Government work, and of their labour requirements for the acceleration of Government work. Forms were sent out to all the shipbuilding and engineering firms in the district. The firms were later asked to telegraph offers of immediate release.

The firms who made definite offers of release received another letter from the Committee asking for full particulars of the qualifications of the men they were willing to release. The Manager of the local Labour Exchange was instructed to call upon the employers and endeavour to get them to decide immediately which men they were prepared to release. He was then, with the employers' permission, to interview the men individually at the works, and take particular care to secure all essential particulars as to the present and past experience of each workman, where each workman had served his apprenticeship, and, in the case of machine men, the ordinary weekly rate which was then being paid. When interviewing men of the classes required by Messrs. Armstrong, the Labour Exchange Manager (who had been supplied with a list of that firm's urgent labour requirements together with particulars of rates of pay) was to explain fully the conditions of employment and rates of earnings at Elswick, but he was to explain that it could not be definitely stated that they would be transferred to Elswick, as the requirements of the employers engaged on urgent Admiralty work on the North East Coast must be considered. The workmen were to be informed that their railway fares would be paid from the place of their present employment to the employer on Government work to whom they were transferred. The men were not to be required to call at the Labour Exchange, and the Manager of the Exchange, when interviewing individual workmen, was to make it clear that he was acting as a representative of the Committee, not as a Labour Exchange official—the object being to obviate the prejudice of skilled workmen against the Labour Exchanges. Form H.L.E. 11 was to be completed by the Labour Exchange Manager in respect of each of the workmen, and sent forthwith to the office of the Committee. Apprentices were not to be included in the scheme. By 27 April 50 out of the 300 employers appealed to had undertaken to release 1,661 men.

The *Newcastle Daily Chronicle* (23 April) was officially informed that the response of the employers had been " ready and comprehensive," and the later report that the Committee was disappointed with the response of the employers was denounced by the War Office-representative as being " as mischievous as it was untrue."[1]

It is clear, however, that the Committee were not satisfied with the situation. The number of the men released for transfer was small and the difficulties in the way of transferring them to Elswick and elsewhere were great. The efforts of the Committee to overcome these difficulties may be summarised.

(a) Reluctance of Employers to Release.

On 27 April, a letter was sent to the engineering firms pointing out the urgent need for fitters and turners, and urging them to release 25 % of their workmen of these classes engaged in private work before 3 May. The employers were asked, if they were unable to transfer their men, to give their reasons, as to which they would be required to undergo examination by the Committee. The Committee decided that the Government should be acquainted with the necessity of importing from other districts, or releasing from the Army, 300 turners and 650 fitters who could not be supplied on the North East Coast, even when all available men had been taken from private work to armament work.

Already, on 18 April, Captain Power and Captain Creed had asked for authority to compel the employers to release willing men, and Captain Power wrote to Admiral Tudor on 1 May, asking for authority to insist on the release of the 25 % now called for. Captain Kelly's view was that the Committee ought to have authority, if necessary, to compel employers to give up their private work, and he urged that compensation should be given to employers whose standing charges were r ised when their machines became idle by the release of their men. The Admiralty had already authorised payment to the releasing employer of from 50 to 150 % of the men's wages, according to the judgment of the Admiralty representative. He reported that one employer on the Committee, " through stress of financial circumstances," was setting the worst possible example, both on the Committee and ou side.

The Committee empowered Captain Kelly to do his best by personal persuasion to induce employers to release their men. He h d considerable success, but, as he himself pointed out, it was a paper success until the men were actually transferred to the Government work awaiting them.

(b) Difficulties Raised by the Armament Firms.

The attitude of the employers to whom the released men were to be transferred hampered the work of the Committee. At the outset they insisted that the usual Board of Trade employment form of application should be filled up. This difficulty was met with prompt action by the Labour Exchange officials, and Captain Kelly received some of the orms properly filled up by the men before the close of the

---

[1] *Newcastle Daily Chronicle*, 27 April.

committee meeting at which the objection was raised. The minute details required by the Armament firms caused delay which was prejudicial to the success of the transfer scheme.

A very large number of the men offered to them were refused by the armament firms on the ground of age, lack of skill, and so on, 521 men being rejected during the operation of the scheme. It appeared that the employers were releasing an undue proportion of inferior men.

(c) *Subsistence or Travelling allowance.*

This was a more serious difficulty. On 23 April the Committee had decided that men transferred to Government work at a distance from their homes should receive either a subsistence allowance (known locally as "lodging money") or alternatively, workmen's fares both ways, plus one hour's travelling time each day at overtime rates. The Government Departments concerned were pressed for a speedy decision on this point. On 23 April a promise was given, on behalf of Messrs. Armstrong, to provide travelling or subsistence allowance pending the decision of the Government; but on 1 May the firm refused 40 men who were offered on the condition that they should be paid fares and an hour's travelling time only. Owing to this refusal these 40 men had to be passed on to other employers, and the bulk of the other men released either stayed with their former employers, or were taken by Messrs. Harland and Wolff to Belfast, or by Messrs. Parsons to Dumbarton. The attitude of Messrs. Armstrong was particularly unfortunate, in view of the fact that the object of the whole scheme was to obtain more men for their works. Moreover, the Admiralty, Messrs. Palmers, Messrs. Parsons, and Messrs. Harland and Wolff were all paying these allowances. On 29 April, Captain Kelly had to report to the Committee that the War Office had decided that subsistence allowances would not be paid by the Government. The Committee was also requested not to take any action that might prejudice the Government in other districts.

This decision brought the work of the Committee to a standstill. The employers were unwilling to take the men, and the attitude of the Trade Unions, expressed by Mr. Ratcliffe of the A.S.E., was, that the War Office decision was not in accordance with the agreement between Lord Kitchener and the Executive of his Society, to the effect that transfers were to be made without infringing Trade Union rules.

The work of the Committee was suspended, and a deputation, consisting of three employers, Mr. Marjoribanks, Mr. Summers Hunter, and Mr. James, was appointed to lay its views before the War Office Armaments Output Committee, which on 30 April accepted the principle that these allowances should be paid by the Government Departments concerned.[1] The fact that the men were content to

---

[1] M.C. 419.

leave the statement of their case to a deputation consisting entirely of employers is a proof of the feeling of mutual confidence that prevailed in the Newcastle Committee.

On 4 May, Mr. Mosses and Mr. Hill, representing the National Advisory Committee, had an interview with the Labour members of the Committee, and afterwards met the full Committee, the object of their mission being to discover exactly what was required in the way of subsistence or travelling allowances, as the War Office and Admiralty wished to have a uniform system with safeguards to prevent abuse.

On 7 May the Munitions of War Committee decided that subsistence or travelling allowances would be paid by the Government.

Sir Percy Girouard was present at a special meeting of the North East Coast Armaments Committee on 10 May, and, at his suggestion, rules for the transference of men on the North East Coast district were drawn up. These rules were adopted by all members of the Committee except by Mr. Ratcliffe, who thought the men should be treated according to the existing rules of the Trade Unions to which they belonged. Sir Percy Girouard submitted these rules to the Munitions of War Committee on 12 May, and they were approved, subject to the following points[1] :—

1. That the words " Subsistence and travelling allowances will only be paid to men already in employment who cannot be otherwise obtained, and who are transferred to British Government work at the request of the Committee," should be added to paragraph 1.

2. That the War Office be requested to make it clear to the local Committee that the transference of men by the Committee should, as far as possible, affect skilled men and their helpers only.

3. That the fact should be recorded that, in the view of the Committee on Munitions of War, the principle laid down in paragraph 9 of the rules is unsatisfactory, and that it should not be adopted as a model in other cases without reference to the Committee.

The rules thus modified were as follows :—

1. The Committee agree that no workman shall suffer pecuniarily by being transferred to armament work, and that no attempt should be made by, or on behalf of, workmen to derive any actual profit from the country's critical position and the Government's undertaking to pay subsistence allowance, train fares, and travelling allowances as stated below. Subsistence and travelling allowances will only be paid to men already in employment who cannot be otherwise obtained and who are transferred to British Government work at the request of the Committee.

---

[1] Munitions of War Committee Minutes, 12 May.

2. Subsistence allowance, *i.e.*, lodging allowance at the rate of 2s. 6d. per day for seven days per week, will be paid to men brought from a distance beyond that which they can reasonably travel daily, so long as they are in the employment of the firm to which they are transferred. Railway fares will be paid for the men transferred from a distance at the commencement and completion of the work for which they were transferred.

3. When the man is within daily travelling distance, *e.g.*, Sunderland to Newcastle, the man shall receive the value of workmen's tickets and one hour's travelling time per day, at the rate of time and a half, but he should start work at 6 a.m., finishing at 5 p.m. If on night shift he shall start work at 5 p.m. and work until 6 a.m. The Armaments Committee shall take steps where necessary, to secure suitable train or tram service.

4. If, however, a man be living at Newcastle and be working at Wallsend, and he is transferred to a works in Newcastle, the Armaments Committee agree that such man shall only receive his travelling expenses, *e.g.*, tram fare from Byker or Heaton to Elswick or Scotswood, and similar cases will be considered on their merits.

5. The Armaments Committee consider that lodging money should be paid by the firm employing the man to the man, and that it should be paid weekly with his wages.

6. The Armaments Committee consider that a warrant should be issued by them to the firm for each man, stating the nature of the allowance he is to receive and the amount. This warrant should be numbered, and the firm should make a detailed monthly return to the Committee of the men transferred and the amount due to them. The Armaments Committee should certify and forward this to the Government for payment.

7. Men seeking employment in the ordinary way will receive the usual district rates, but are not entitled to subsistence allowance.

8. Should the Committee find that men have been paid off by an employer with the object of having them transferred to another part of the North East Coast district without receiving the authorised allowances, then the Armaments Committee reserve to themselves the right of deciding such a case on its merits.

9. The Armaments Committee undertake that every workman transferred shall receive the same rate, at least, as in his previous employment.

10. All men who are moved will be provided with the certificate or warrant, stating the name of the employer they are leaving and the name of the employer to whom they are going. This warrant should be issued in triplicate, one for the late employer, one for the new employer, and one for the man himself. These warrants will be issued by the Armaments Committee, and will be limited to the North East Coast district.

11. The release is to be for a period not exceeding three months in the first instance, but may be renewed by the Armaments Committee if required, subject to the approval of the Government.

Captain Kelly reported that, in the view of the Committee, the adopting of these rules would remove half the difficulties that had been experienced in getting men transferred.

(d) War Office and the Admiralty requirements.

The clashing of the Admiralty and War Office requirements was a serious difficulty. Captain Kelly suggested it could be met by instructions from the Admiralty to Captain Power to let Elswick be filled first, all surplus men being sent at once to firms indicated by the Admiralty.

Many employers who had men engaged on mercantile work refused to release them on the plea that a surplus must be kept to deal with urgent warship repairs. Captain Kelly suggested that a flying squad of ship repairers should be organised, to be controlled by the Committee and sent at short notice to any firm requiring them for work on warships.

In order to obtain the men required for Admiralty work at Messrs. Palmer's works at Jarrow and Hepburn, Captain Power was authorised by the Admiralty to demand the release of men on mercantile work. The employers were to be informed that the men would be released as soon as the urgent Admiralty work was completed. Captain Power delayed issuing this Admiralty order until he had consulted the Committee. The question was brought up on 13 May, and the general opinion of the Committee was that it was a mistake to call upon the employers to discharge the men until definite arrangements had been made for an immediate start on Admiralty work, as the transfer of skilled men had already thrown a number of unskilled men out of work.

(e) Jealousy between Employer and Employer.

Many of the employers were reluctant to release men for Elswick, as there was much jealousy of Messrs. Armstrong, whose policy with regard to sub-contracting was said to be ungenerous. There were also complaints that the Elswick works suffered from a lack of superintendence, and that men were frequently seen asleep on night shifts.

I-3

KING'S SQUAD APPEAL, 15 MAY TO 30 JUNE.

The King's Squad scheme—a direct appeal to the workmen to leave private work for armament work—was launched by Captain Kelly at the beginning of May. It has special importance as being the forerunner of the general appeal for War Munition Volunteers, which was a development of the idea of the King's Squad.

The first reference to the scheme appears on 17 April, the day of Captain Kelly's arrival at Newcastle, when he urged that the adoption of some scheme of the kind would do away with the chief difficulties met with in the work of labour transfer.

As a preliminary step, Captain Kelly consulted the employers and the local Trade Union representatives, and, having obtained their acquiescence, planned out the details of a scheme adapted to local conditions. A mass meeting was held in the Newcastle Town Hall, at which shop delegates and two workmen from every engineering shop in the North East Coast district were present.

A draft of the proposed appeal to the workmen was approved by the Executive Committee on 6 May. At the meeting on 10 May Sir Percy Girouard stipulated that the scheme must be approved in London, but on 13 May the North East Coast Armaments Committee instructed Captain Kelly to put the scheme into operation, though the approval of the authorities had not yet been signified.

Copies of the King's Squad appeal were distributed by Boy Scouts during the dinner hour on Friday, 14 May, to nearly all the engineering and shipbuilding works in the district. The distribution continued on Saturday and Monday, and at the same time advertisements were inserted in the papers.

The essence of the scheme was to get at the men direct without the intervention either of their employers or their trade unions, though the assent of both to the scheme and a promise of hearty co-operation had been obtained. The employers welcomed the scheme as relieving them from the invidious position of giving up their men and reducing their shareholders' profits of their own accord. If the men threw up their work, the employers would have no option, and the payment of compensation would therefore be avoided.

The campaign was conducted with the object of giving the men the least possible trouble. The appeal provided a detachable coupon for signature, by which the workman undertook to place himself at the disposal of the Committee and go to such place as they might request on receipt of telegraphic instructions. The rules as to subsistence and travelling allowance were printed on the back of the coupon, and were explained to the men by their shop delegates. The appeal assured the men that they would be under no military restrictions, that the rate of wages would be at least as high as they were now earning, and that the appeal was approved by their Trade Union representatives.

As soon as the signed coupon was received by the Committee a telegram was sent to the man accepting him for munitions work and directing him to begin work without fail at a specified works, the name of the foreman and the number of the shop being stated. The man was directed to show the telegram to his employer, to his Trade Union representative, and to the local Labour Exchange manager, in order to get his railway warrant, and then to take it with him to give his new shop foreman. Previous experience had shown the Committee that a telegram was necessary to prevent any flagging after the workmen had undertaken to give up their work.

The response to the appeal was excellent. By 22 May, 2,600 coupons had been returned and 350 men had been placed. The chief difficulties in placing men were the high wages asked for, and the objections raised by some of the employers who had orders for urgent Government work on which their men would shortly be employed. In such cases the Committee solved the difficulty by informing the employers that the men who had volunteered for the King's Squad must be given to the Committee on loan, and be claimed back if the firm were occupied on urgent Government work.

If an employer chiefly occupied on private work was refractory, the Committee put pressure on him by telephone or telegraph, and the case was investigated at the works by Commander Crisp, as representing the Admiralty, together with a Trade Union delegate. On 25 May Captain Kelly reported the names of the employers who had been the most difficult, but stated that hitherto every employer had given way to pressure. The Committee was very anxious to order small private yards where no Government work was done to be closed down and the men transferred ; but, on appeal to the War Office, the Committee was informed (26 May) that it had no such power.

At the date of the King's visit to Newcastle (19-20 May) the success of the King's Squad appeal was assured, and the Committee were congratulated by the King on the success of their work.

The strong point of the scheme, as compared with the former scheme, was the rapidity with which the men who volunteered were placed with the new employer. The class of men volunteering was so good that there were comparatively few rejections by the employers, and on 25 May Captain Kelly suggested the extension of the scheme to other areas.

On 21 May Captain Kelly had reported to the Executive Committee that one firm, Messrs. Armstrong, had made serious mistakes which had occasioned both delay and inconvenience to the King's Squad men coming to take up work with them, and the Committee approved of his action in stopping the supply of men to the firm until they put these matters in order. The men complained also of bad management, lack of supervision, and waste of time at Elswick. Captain Ross, who had succeeded Captain Kelly as Secretary on 5 June, reporting on the work of the King's Squad scheme up to 14 June, stated that the total number of enlistments had been 5,065. Of these, 1,519 were the result of newspaper advertisement, and 3,546 were the result of circulars issued direct to the men. Of the men supplied, about 40% went on ordnance work, and about 60% on Admiralty work.

The approximate average cost of moving the men from their old to their new work, based on the first 600 men moved, worked out at 1s. 8d. per man, while the allowances paid for lodging money, travelling time and daily fares averaged 7s. 1d. per man, owing to the fact that many of the men preferred to claim travelling allowance instead of subsistence allowance.

On ‘16 June Captain Ross reported that the needs of the large firms were nearly satisfied, and that the men they needed were being supplied to the smaller firms.

When the Munitions of War Act had been passed, the King's Squad scheme was merged in the national scheme for War Munition Volunteers.

THE WAR MUNITION VOLUNTEERS, 30 JUNE—15 AUGUST.

The North East Coast Armaments Committee were anxious that their local scheme should not be superseded by the War Munition Volunteers scheme. Their view was that the changes in the conditions of transfer, though apparently slight, would cause complications if introduced in their area.

The changes objected to were as follows :—

(1) The new scheme involved an inquisition as to whether a man would have to keep up two homes.[1]

(2) The new scheme did not provide for the payment in some cases of travelling fares without travelling time.

(3) The new scheme appeared to guarantee that a man should not merely get as high a rate as he was getting before, but as high an actual sum, which would put a premium on slacking in the case of piece-workers.

On 22 June the official members of the Committee asked that the North East Coast area should be exempted from the new scheme. Captain Power went to London to lay the views of the official members of the Committee before Mr. Booth, and reported to the Committee on 29 June that practically a free hand had been secured for the North East Coast district in dealing with its own men. The King's Squad was to be merged in the War Munition Volunteers, but the Committee were to be the agents of the Ministry both for enrolment and transfer. The Ministry reserved the right, in case of an urgent demand, to transfer men from the district to any part of the country, and if desirous of bringing men into the area, the Ministry was to do so through the Committee.

---

[1] This was dropped in accordance with a resolution of the Trade Union Conference, moved by Mr. Wile and seconded by Mr. Hebron (both members of the North East Coast Armaments Committee) on 16 June.

All members of the King's Squad who had not yet been placed were to be invited by the Committee to enrol as War Munition Volunteers, whilst men already placed were to be asked to enrol at the end of their original three months' agreement. All transfers after June 30 were to be made on Munition Volunteer terms.

The transition from one scheme to the other had some disturbing effects in the district,[1] and there was a falling off in the number of men transferred from private to Government work. The employers objected to the obligation to pay a transferred workman the wage he was receiving from his previous firm, if this was the higher of the two. The disturbing effect was only temporary, and in the week ending 10 July, 416 men were transferred, a figure which had only once been exceeded during the existence of the King's Squad.

The uncertainty of the meaning to be attached to the term " rates " of wages in the case of piece-workers transferred from one place to another was brought up by the workmen's representatives on the Committee on 27 July. The Ministry's decision that rate of wages for piece-workers meant piece-rates and not average earnings was objected to by the workmen on the ground that, being transferred to unaccustomed work, they might be unable, through no fault of their own, to secure their usual earnings. The National Advisory Committee to which the matter was referred, decided that any case in which hardships arose might be dealt with by one of the Arbitration Tribunals provided for by Schedule I. of the Munitions of War Act.

Another point raised by the North East Coast Armaments Committee was the payment of differences in wages, where the rate was higher in the district from which the men came than in that to which they were transferred. The Committee was informed by the Ministry that the difference in the rate was to be paid by the employer, but a later Circular stated that the employer was entitled to recover the difference from the State.

By the end of July the transfer work of the Committee was almost at a standstill, as the supply of men on private work available for transfer was falling short. Captain Ross thought that future work in the district would mainly consist in moving men from one Government job to another.

RECRUITING AND RELEASE OF MEN FROM THE ARMY.

At the outset, Captain Creed urged that recruiting in the North East Coast district should be slowed down, and Mr. Booth promised that this should be done. The composition of the Committee, which included a representative of the Recruiting Officer, was some kind of guarantee that the work of getting men for the armament firms would not be hampered by recruiting appeals. Applications from employers for the release of men who had been enlisted without their permission were forwarded through the Committee. The visits of the Prime

---

[1] See the statistics of men transferred, below, p. 136.

Minister on 20 April, and of the King, accompanied by Lord Kitchener, on 19 and 20 May did much to impress the workmen of the district with the paramount necessity of increasing the output of munitions. Recruiting, however, went on vigorously and recruiting appeals were much more prominent in the local Press than the appeals of the North East Coast Armaments Committee. Captain Kelly, therefore, reported on 26 April and 4 May that it was of the utmost importance that the War Office should stop recruiting from among the skilled workmen on the North East Coast, 1,800 skilled mechanics having been enlisted in the Army. The War Office was also asked to instruct the recruiting officers to respect the authorised badges issued by private firms. The Committee was only indirectly concerned with the movement for the release of skilled men from the Army.[1] In July and August a considerable number of released soldiers took up work at Messrs. Armstrong's.

LABOUR STEALING.

During the operation of the various schemes for the transfer of men to Government work the Committee frequently found itself hampered by the labour-recruiting activity of firms situated outside the district. Thus during May there were complaints that Messrs. Harland and Wolff of Belfast were picking up men in the North East Coast district to work in their yards. At the same date men were being asked by Lord Fisher to volunteer for warship repair work at the Dardanelles. Captain Kelly was authorised to telegraph to Sir Percy Girouard protesting against action of this kind, and asking that if men were urgently required, application should be made to the Armaments Committee.

THE THREE SCHEMES OF LABOUR TRANSFER COMPARED.

	Men enrolled.	Accepted by Employers.
1. April 15 to May 15—Appeal to Employers ..	1,738	290 (270)
2. May 15 to June 30—" King's Squad "—		
Week ending May 22..	2,575	476
,, ,, 29..	1,007	290
,, June 5..	1,086	356
,, ,, 12..	491	204
,, ,, 12 to June 30	571	354
TOTAL	5,730	1,680
3. July 1 to August 15—Munitions Volunteers—		
Week ending July 10..	1,211	416
,, ,, 17..	359	168
,, ,, 24..	80	84
,, ,, 31..	24	22
,, August 7..	44	28
,, ,, 14..	21	20
TOTAL	1,739	738

[1] The Committee, however, sent recommendations to the War Office urging the release of skilled men, *e.g.*, North East Coast Armaments Committee Minutes, 23 April.

IV. The Spreading of Contracts.

The Prime Minister, speaking at Newcastle on 20 April, emphasised the fact that the first duty of the Committee was to transfer men from private to State contracts and keep the existing plant running full time on Government work. The second thing to be done was to broaden the basis of production and utilise other works in the production of munitions. From the beginning, side by side with its work of labour transfer, the Committee received and registered offers and applications of all kinds from firms and individuals, who thought they would assist in the output of munitions.

As early as 26 April two members of the Committee declared themselves in favour of distributing work rather than transferring workers, and on 30 May Captain Power asked the Admiralty to place orders with firms whose facilities were not fully occupied, and thus " accelerate output by bringing the work to the men " ; but the official policy was pursued until there was little more to be done in the direction of labour transfer.

On 3 June the employers on the Committee passed a resolution recommending a wider distribution of Government work, and on 17 June a similar resolution was passed by the whole Committee. The organisation of the West Hartlepool district for the production of munitions on a co-operative basis was being considered by the Committee on 9 June, and the Lord Mayor of Hull was consulted.

The formation of Munitions Committees at Blyth and on the Tees was discussed on 17 June, and it was arranged that these committees should be subsidiary to the North East Coast Armaments Committee.

A proposal by the Newcastle Chamber of Commerce to set up a National Shell Factory in Newcastle, to be worked in the main by voluntary labour was discussed by the Committee on 19 July, but the scheme was dropped owing to the difficulty of obtaining skilled supervision and adequate machinery. Arrangements were made to employ on special shifts at Elswick the part-time workers who had volunteered to work in the proposed factory. During August many reports as to the possibility of obtaining supplies of munitions from non-armament firms in the district were sent in by Captain Ross.

V. General Supervision of Labour Conditions.

The composition of the Committee gave it great authority in the district. It was able to put pressure on both employers and employed, and the powers under the Defence of the Realm Act possessed by the Admiralty and the War Office gave quasi-legal authority to the recommendations of the Committee containing their representatives. As time went on, the Committee began to be regarded as having general supervision of labour questions throughout the district, and to its primary work of labour transfer were added the functions of a general Court of Appeal having great local authority. Its activities in this direction must be illustrated rather than described in detail.

RELATIONS WITH LIQUOR CONTROL BOARD.

The indignation aroused in the Newcastle district by the publication of figures given by the Federated Shipbuilders to Mr. Lloyd George about the loss of time due to the drinking habits of the men was reflected on the Committee, one of whose members characterised it as a " most wicked slander,"[1] and the local Press thought one of the chief objects of the Committee was " to send to London a clear and impartial statement as to how far the consumption of alcoholic liquor is interfering with the regular working of the shipyards and factories." The Boilermakers' Society thought the charges should be investigated by the local Armaments Committee—a further evidence of the workmen's confidence in the Committee.

Representatives of the Committee attended a meeting of the Central Board for Liquor Control, in London, on 29 May, and made recommendations as to special facilities for men employed in blast furnaces and rolling mills, the abolition of "treating," and so on, some of which were accepted by the Board. A conference at Newcastle, between the Committee, and the local authorities was held on 14 June, followed by a conference with the Central Control Board on 21 June, which resulted in certain agreed proposals being adopted. On 30 August the Committee reported that the regulations for the North East Coast were causing discontent among the Steel workers, who, in consequence, were working less time.

TRADE UNION RESTRICTIONS.

On 26 April the Committee unanimously decided that all possible efforts should be made to accelerate production, and throughout its existence the Committee acted in the spirit of this resolution, by encouraging the adoption of piece-work, sanctioning the employment on drillers' work of non-drillers, subject to the Treasury Agreement being signed by the firm,[2] and so on. The chief difficulty in the adoption of piece-work was safeguarding the poorer classes of workmen against injury. In the case of the Brass Founders, the Trade Union delegate could not persuade his men to abandon the unwritten Trade Union law known as " shop-figure," and to accept piece-work, but the men expressed their willingness to accept piece-work if they were definitely advised to do so by the Committee.

TRAVELLING FACILITIES.

The Committee did useful work in putting pressure on the railway companies and the Corporation to improve the train and tramway services used by workmen going to and from Government work, and the minutes of its meetings show what was accomplished in this direction.

---

[1] *Newcastle Daily Chronicle*, 20 April, 22 May ; North East Coast Armaments Committee Minutes, 6 May.

[2] The object of the Trade Union officials was to supplement the agreement made with the Chancellor of the Exchequer on 19 March by additional agreements to be entered into by each firm.

HOUSING SCHEMES.

The Committee had close relations with the local Housing Committee, and the problem caused by the large increase in the number of men employed at Elswick during April, May, and June was solved by the use of billets vacated by troops going under canvas, of public buildings, and of houses on the sea coast vacated owing to the fear of naval raids, and by an appeal to local residents to take in lodgers. Accommodation for 7,000 workers was thus provided.

BAD TIME-KEEPING.

The Committee took a strong line on this question. Its recommendations, and the appointment of vigilance committees in the workshops were very favourably received. Captain Power urged the Admiralty to give the Committee power to fine offenders. New rules as to late arrival at work were suggested by the Committee on 27 July.

HOLIDAYS AND RACE MEETINGS.

The action of the Committee in prohibiting local race meetings was unpopular but effective, but its appeal to the workmen and the general public to forgo the Whitsuntide holiday was unsuccessful, in spite of strong support from the local Press.

TRADE DISPUTES.

As early as 3 May it was reported that the Committee was being used as a Court of Appeal to settle trade disputes between employers and men arising in the district. In several cases, when disputes threatened to check the output of munitions, Captain Power or Captain Kelly, asked by the Committee to approach the firms involved, succeeded in settling the question. The Committee was so successful that on 3 June the representatives of the employers on the Committee passed a resolution, which was presented to Sir Percy Girouard by Captain Power, asking that Armaments Committees should be authorised to settle trade disputes in munition work. Captain Power was informed that such powers could only be given by the Cabinet. A number of trade disputes were brought before the Committee during the last two months of its existence, its decisions being generally accepted. On 19 July the Secretary was instructed to inform the Ministry of Munitions that, in the opinion of the Committee, the employer and trade union members of the Committee should be put on the Munitions Tribunals for the district.

VI. Supersession of North East Coast Armaments Committee.

In consequence of the administrative changes introduced by the Ministry early in August, an emergency meeting of the North East Coast Armaments Committee was called on 5 August, and a deputation was appointed to wait on Dr. Addison. A letter was written by the Minister to the Lord Mayor on 10 August, which explained the position, and on 16 August, Mr. McLaren attended a meeting of the Committee to give an account of the intentions of the Ministry with regard to the future organisation of munitions work on the North East Coast. Several members of the Committee strongly deprecated the action of the Ministry in dispensing with the local knowledge possessed by the Committee and in entrusting the executive powers entirely to three officials. The Labour members were reluctant to remain on a Committee shorn of executive, and retaining only advisory functions. The dissatisfaction of the Labour representatives with the new arrangements was still more strongly expressed at the final meeting of the Committee on 30 August, which marked the close of an interesting and successful experiment.

APPENDIX XV.

(Chapter III., p. 43.)

The Glasgow and West of Scotland Armaments Committee.

I. Composition of the Committee.

Captain Creed left Newcastle about 16 April, 1915, to organise a similar Armaments Committee for Glasgow and the West of Scotland. Between 20 April and 30 April he met representatives of the employers and Trade Unions in the shipbuilding and engineering trades and the Committees already appointed by the Glasgow Chamber of Commerce and the North West Engineering Employers' Association. On 30 April the Glasgow and West of Scotland Armaments Committee was established, under the chairmanship of the Lord Provost of Glasgow.

The Admiralty was represented by Captain Barttelot,[1] the War Office by Captain Creed, the Home Office by Mr. Williams, and the Board of Trade by Mr. Cramond. There were 16 representatives of shipbuilding and engineering employers and 16 representatives of the Trade Unions. Mr. Paterson of the Board of Trade was appointed Secretary. The full Committee of 38 members was too large for practical purposes and most of the work was delegated to sub-committees. Each of these sub-committees, of which there were at first two, and finally six, consisted of two employers, two workmen, and the Secretary. All the representatives of Government Departments had the right to sit on the sub-committees.

The Labour Sub-Committee, for " procuring labour for Government work from firms engaged on private work," and the Shell Sub-Committee, to " increase the output of shell in the district," were formed on 3 May, and frequently sat together as the Joint Sub-Committee on Labour and Shell. To these were added, after 2 June, four other sub-committees—for Volunteer Labour, for Trade Disputes, for Finance, and for Business purposes.

II. Labour Transfer.

The work of the Committee in connection with labour transfer followed the Newcastle precedent, but was less successful.

A summary of 20 May showed that in the Glasgow and West of Scotland district there were 73,120 men employed on War Office or Admiralty orders, and 22,751 were employed on private orders. It was estimated that 6,761 additional men were required for Government work, a number which it might have seemed easy to obtain from the large number of men still employed on private work, though the supply of certain classes of labour—plating, riveting, and angle smithing—was already very short.

---

[1] Admiral John E. Bearcroft was appointed as Admiralty representative vice Captain Barttelot on 29 June.

APPEAL TO EMPLOYERS, 3 MAY—10 JUNE.

As at Newcastle, all the engineering, shipbuilding, and boat-building firms in the district were asked to furnish the Committee by 7 May with particulars of the labour employed on Government and on private work. On 11 May, the Admiralty representative, Captain Barttelot, submitted to the Committee a statement of the requirements of those shipbuilding firms to which he wished preference to be given for any labour which might be available. The Committee then ordered that five shipbuilding firms[1] should be called upon to release, within a few days, a definite number of workmen in each of the classes required for the acceleration of urgent Admiralty work. Six other firms were asked to send representatives to appear before the Committee and discuss the position. On 13 May, when the employers appeared, they were told that all their carpenters and iron workers would be required for Admiralty work, and that the foremen were to go with the men whenever possible.

On 15 May a War Office preference list, similar to the Admiralty preference list, was sent to the Committee by Sir Percy Girouard.

The payment of a subsistence allowance of 17s. 6d. a week to all workmen called upon to move to other districts in order to take up Government work had been decided upon by the Labour Sub-Committee on 5 May after consultation with Mr. Mosses of the National Advisory Committee. On 12 May the rules as to travelling and subsistence allowances drawn up by the North East Coast Armaments Committee were communicated to the Glasgow Committee by the Army Council, and were adopted on 14 May, with slight alterations to suit local conditions.

Thus all the machinery for labour transfer was in readiness, but the Committee only succeeded in transferring a very small number of men.[2]

On 16 May the Committee instructed the Secretary to issue requisitions to firms for the labour required, which was to be available at an early date. It was obvious that, if these requisitions were not complied with, the Committee had no power to compel obedience. On 21 May, therefore, a deputation of the Committee, consisting of the Lord Provost, two representatives of employers, and two of workmen, submitted a memorandum to Sir Percy Girouard and the Third Sea Lord, in which wider powers were asked for. With a view to increasing output, the Committee urged that it should be given power to settle trade disputes, remove existing trade demarcations which hampered output, and " to call before the Committee or sub-committee thereof, employers, Trade Union officials, or other persons,

---

[1] Some of these firms were very important merchant shipbuilders, who, in less than a year, were put on the Priority List for Labour. It is, perhaps, fortunate that the Armaments Committee did not entirely disorganise them.

[2] According to the Minutes of the Committee, 82 men had been transferred by 4 June (D.A.O. Area 9 509), but the number transferred by 9 June is given elsewhere as "just over 60 men."

and to compel them to observe the instruction of the Government representatives. . . . . It appears to the Committee that if the necessary statutory authority does not already exist, immediate steps should be taken to secure that the Government representatives on the Armaments Committee are vested with summary powers to deal with such cases, and that these powers be supported by substantial penalties for non-observance."

The Committee also asked that Section I. (1) (d) of the Defence of the Realm (Amendment) No. 2 Act should be amended so as to bestow upon the Admiralty and Army Council and upon their representatives on the Armament Committees, the power of transferring workmen from one establishment to another. This would give legal sanction to the requisitioning of workmen by the Committee, and would protect employers whose workmen were requisitioned from any action or proceedings that might be taken against them for non-fulfilment of contracts.

In addition, the Committee asked for power to draw labour from other districts—Aberdeen, Edinburgh, and the North of Ireland —and to apply the subsistence and travelling allowance rules to apprentices as well as workmen. With reference to finance, the Committee thought that there would be "a good deal of exceptional expenditure which will require to be incurred on short notice, and it does not appear that it will be possible for this to be controlled on the usual Government lines. . . . . It seems that the proper course will be for the Committee to be supplied with funds by, and be responsible direct to, the Treasury."[1]

At the same time, the Committee requested to be furnished with an immediate statement of the requirements of the Admiralty and the War Office for various kinds of shell.

The deputation was unsuccessful. Sir Percy Girouard informed them that the powers they desired could only be conferred by the Cabinet, and that the Committee must not attempt to transfer labour outside its own district.

In the opinion of Sir George Askwith,[2] the suggestion that the Glasgow Armaments Committee should settle trade disputes was "most undesirable, and, if endorsed, fraught with the gravest consequences. . . . . The composition of these Committees is largely partisan, and any question of moment would certainly lead to a taking of sides and to an extension rather than a narrowing of the controversy." He thought that the workmen would not favour their grievances being settled by members of other Trade Unions,

[1] On 23 June it was decided that the past expenditure of the Committee should be audited by Mr. Duckworth of the Finance Department of the Ministry. The expenditure included the payment of two of the representatives of the workmen on the Committee for their services, as they had no time to work at their trades.

[2] Memorandum by Sir George Askwith. (28 May, 1915.) HIST. REC./R/. 1121.32/6.

as was shown by the fact that during the engineers' strike on the Clyde, neither the men nor the officials of the Amalgamated Society of Engineers would allow Mr. Henderson, M.P., Mr. Hodge, M.P., or their own member, Mr. Barnes, to address them. He was also doubtful whether employers would be willing to send questions to these Committees, and go before a tribunal, of which (as he said) half was frankly partisan, and the other half afraid of taking a strong line for fear of reprisals.[1]

With regard to the claim of the Armaments Committee to have settled a dispute at Messrs. Nobel's Explosives Co., Sir George Askwith stated that the dispute in question had subsequently been referred by the firm to the Committee on Production. The handling of industrial disputes should be referred to one Department ; otherwise great confusion would arise. The Armaments Committee would find ample scope for its activity in dealing with " questions of demarcation and the abandonment of Trade Union rules and customs which retard output and limit the application of suitable labour."

On 28 May, the same deputation was received by Mr. Lloyd George. Its report to the Glasgow Committee was that " the result of the interview was disappointing, as Mr. Lloyd George was unable to give any immediate pronouncement other than that he would place the matter before the Cabinet at an early date for their most careful consideration." The Lord Provost took the view that refusal of such powers would entail " a total suspension of the Committee's work, and would create such a want of respect and confidence for the Committee's functions and powers as no subsequent action would remove."

In the expectation of obtaining these further powers, the Glasgow Committee had contemplated closing certain shipyards in order to transfer labour to Government work ; but on 4 June, on receipt of a letter from Mr. Booth, deprecating such action by the Committee, the firms involved were informed that the question of closing their yards was in abeyance for the time.

The Committee did not, of course, succeed in obtaining the powers for which it had petitioned.

WAR SQUAD APPEAL, 10 JUNE.

On 4 June the Committee decided to issue an appeal to workmen to form a " War Squad or Flying Column of Armament Workers " on the lines of the King's Squad formed on the North East Coast. The appeal was slightly amended to suit local requirements, and it was advertised in the Press and elsewhere. As in Newcastle, the appeal was signed by representatives of the Shipbuilding and Engineering Federated Trades Unions. It was issued on 10 June, and 6,500 men were asked for. By 12 June over 2,000 applications for enrolment had been received, and by 14 June the number had risen to 4,500. Half the applications, however, were from unskilled men, while, among the skilled men, there was a surplus of applications from men

---

[1] See p. 52.

in certain trades, and very few applications from riveters, who were urgently required. Though the number of enrolments reached 9,755 by 15 July, only 1,320 were offered to employers and only 454 had been accepted by them at that date.

WAR MUNITIONS VOLUNTEERS, 30 JUNE TO 15 AUGUST.

The Glasgow area, like the Newcastle area, received exceptional treatment under the War Munitions Volunteers Scheme. The Local Committee continued to deal with members of the War Squad who did not wish to enrol in the War Munitions Volunteers, while members of the War Squad who wished to join the National scheme ceased to be under the jurisdiction of the Committee, unless they had already been transferred to Government work.

RELEASE OF MEN FROM THE ARMY.

The procedure to be adopted by employers desiring the release of men from the Army was laid down in a set of instructions drawn up by the Glasgow Committee on 8 June and issued to employers in a circular letter.

III. Organisation of Munitions Production.

THE SPREADING OF CONTRACTS.

From the beginning, the Glasgow Committee took a strong line on the necessity for distributing Government orders among the firms in the district who were capable of transferring their resources to the production of munitions. On 3 May, 14 May, and in their memorandum of 21 May, the Committee had asked for a full statement of War Office and Admiralty requirements for shells, with specifications and, if possible, samples. The Committee was confident that it could bring to the notice of the Government new sources of supply, many firms being dissatisfied with the negative results of offering their facilities direct to the War Office and Admiralty. Many offers from manufacturers and requests for Government orders had been made direct to the Committee, but the Committee had been obliged to refuse them owing to the fact that it had no control over the distribution of Government orders. On 31 May, Messrs. Weir, while announcing that they proposed to devote to the Red Cross all profits from the manufacture of shells under existing Government contracts, had informed the Committee that their shell plant would be available on the termination of these contracts, for the production of shell for the Government at nett cost.

SCHEMES FOR A NATIONAL SHELL FACTORY AND CO-OPERATIVE WORK.

On 21 May Sir Percy Girouard had requested Mr. Rowan Thomson, a member of the Deputation to him, to place before the Glasgow Committee proposals for a National Shell Factory on lines similar to those started at Leeds and elsewhere. The question was remitted by the General Committee to the Shell Sub-Committee who appointed three engineering employers, Messrs. William Weir, R. McLaren and W. B. Lang to investigate and report. Mr. Weir was from the first unfavourable to the scheme. His point of view, as given in a conference with Mr. Stevenson on 25 June, was that, apart from the delay of several months, which must be expected before a National Shell Factory could start production, increased production at firms' own works by putting down further equipment was the best means of organising resources. Most firms in Glasgow were working in connection with Admiralty contracts, but three at least—his own, Babcock and Wilcox, and the North British Diesel Co.—had been turning out and delivering shell since 1914.

At the request of Mr. Stevenson, Mr. Weir immediately after this interview outlined a scheme for production. This scheme definitely rejected the idea of a National Factory and replaced it by a proposal that a local Board of Trustees, appointed by the Ministry, should arrange for the production of 200,000 18-pounders, 100,000 4·5-inch and 80,000 6-inch shell from the area. The work was to be divided among five or six firms ; a price for each size of shell was to be settled by the Ministry and was to include a definite amount per shell for capital expenditure, calculated on the quantities finally ordered from each firm.

Mr. Stevenson met representatives of the Committee at Glasgow on 28 June and discussed the matter. He suggested the possibility, which was favourably received, of an Assembling Factory as a compromise between a National Shell Factory and the extension of direct contracts.

On 1 July a report embodying the main features of this scheme[1] was presented to the Glasgow Committee by whom it was unanimously adopted and forwarded on 2 July to Sir Percy Girouard. Though no action was taken for the moment, these recommendations were not without influence on the subsequent organisation of the area, which was settled after consultation with Mr. Weir, who became Scottish Director of Munitions.

IV. Supervision of Labour Conditions.

Like the Newcastle Committee, the Glasgow Armaments Committee exercised a general supervision over labour conditions in the area. Its minutes record its activity in connection with trade disputes, the aim of the Committee being to act as arbitrator. It succeeded in obtaining the withdrawal of some trade demarcations, which enabled ship-joiners to work as shipwrights, iron moulders to work as brass moulders and brass founders. It drew up a schedule of figures as to the output which ought to be obtained on a ten-hours shift from certain machines ; it urged certain trade unions to allow the introduction of piece-work ; it considered allegations of labour stealing ;

---

[1] The proposal in the Report was for 200,000 6-in. and 200,000 4·5-in. shells.

dealt with the housing difficulty ; issued notices restricting the Fair Holidays, which usually lasted a fortnight, to six days ; considered the Liquor Traffic regulations drawn up by the Central Control Board ; and urged the Glasgow tramways to introduce a universal fare for workmen.

A scheme for punishing bad time-keeping, adopted by the Committee on 14 May and accepted by the National Advisory Committee on 26 May, imposed fines not exceeding £1 for the first offence, £2 for the second offence, and £3, together with dismissal, for the third offence. In the case of trade unionists the fines were assessed by their unions ; in the case of non-unionists, by their employer, with a right of appeal to the Armaments Committee.

V. Supersession of the Committee.

On 28 June, when Mr. Stevenson met the Glasgow Committee, he outlined the scheme of decentralisation then under consideration, and stated that it was the desire of his Department that the Committee should be taken over as the district munitions organisation of the Ministry.

In his letter of 21 June to Mr. Lloyd George, drafting a scheme of Area Organisation to be applied throughout the United Kingdom, Mr. Stevenson had suggested that use might be made of the organisation already in being at Glasgow. "It might, of course, be necessary to extend the existing organisation by augmenting its staff, that is to say, by increasing the number of representatives who will travel throughout Scotland on behalf of the Department in an engineering, inspecting, and information-giving capacity."

During July the work of establishing an Area Office in Glasgow was carried out, and though use was certainly made of the existing administrative machinery of the Glasgow Armaments Committee, its functions tended to become increasingly limited. The premises which served the Committee as offices were adapted to the purposes of the Area Office. Mr. Paterson, their Secretary, was early in July appointed Organising Secretary to the Area, and continued to act in the dual capacity throughout July. Certain other officials too, who had originally been lent to the Glasgow Committee by the Board of Trade, were now transferred to the Area Office.

A letter from Mr. Lloyd George to the Lord Provost on 30 July announced that with the formation of a Munitions Area it would "no longer be necessary to continue the activities of the present West of Scotland Armaments Committee otherwise than as a consultative Committee." The Lord Provost suggested that the Committee should be dissolved forthwith, but was told in reply that Mr. Lloyd George would prefer it to remain as a consultative body, as this would bring the district into line with the rest of the country.

However, with the appointment in September, 1915, of a Board of Management for Glasgow, which was itself purely advisory in character, the last functions of the Committee disappeared and it henceforward ceased to meet.

Reviewing the work of the Committee, it appears that its comparative failure was not due to friction between the representatives of employers and men. What evidence there is points to the existence of cordial relations between them, and the complaint made by the Workers' Union of Glasgow, on 12 August, that, owing to the short notice given of the preliminary meeting, the Committee was not representative, appears to be groundless. Nor was it due to inactivity. The Minutes of the Committee are a record of ceaseless activity in every direction. It intervened in trade disputes, summoned employers and men to appear before it for interrogation and examination, sent deputations of its members to workshops to watch engineering operations and draw up a scale of output, broke down trade demarcations, and so on. In all these directions the Committee had some success at the outset which encouraged it to still greater activity. But when those who resisted the decisions of the Committee discovered that it had no power to enforce them, the prestige of the Committee declined and with it its success. The refusal of the Government to endow it with compulsory powers which would have involved an amendment of the Defence of the Realm Act put an end to the ambition of the Committee to act as a general court of appeal for the whole area.

INDEX.

Contents of Volume I.

Note.—The present issue is subject to revision, and must be regarded as provisional.

HISTORY OF THE MINISTRY OF MUNITIONS

VOLUME I

INDUSTRIAL MOBILISATION, 1914-15

PART IV

THE MUNITIONS OF WAR ACT, 1915

PART IV

THE MUNITIONS OF WAR ACT, 1915

PART IV.

The Munitions of War Act, 1915.

APPENDICES.

INDEX.

(474) Wt. 3643/A.P. 5036 10/18 250 D.St.

PART IV.

THE MUNITIONS OF WAR ACT, 1915.

1. Introductory.

The Ministry of Munitions entered on its legal existence on 9 June, 1915. Before this date the Bill which was to invest it with a large part of its powers was already being prepared. The Munitions of War Bill is defined in its title as a measure " to make provision for furthering the efficient manufacture, transport, and supply of munitions for the present War, and for purposes incidental thereto." Its real purport was more exactly expressed by Lord Curzon, when, in moving the Second Reading in the Upper House, he described it as empowering the Minister " *to organise the skilled labour of the country* for the production of munitions of war."[1] Its provisions are, in fact, directed to the control of labour ; and such disabilities and limitations as are imposed by it upon the employer are to be understood as a means to that end.

The measures that have been described in the earlier pages of this volume fall into two groups, under the headings : (*a*) the supply and movement of labour, and (*b*) labour regulation. To the former group belong the special efforts made to direct the flow of highly skilled labour towards munitions work, and certain compulsory enactments which mark the beginning of Government control over this movement. Under the head of regulation fall the attempts to secure that labour already employed should work continuously and at full power. Here, the two main questions were : the settlement of disputes without stoppage of work, and the suspension of restrictions limiting output. In respect of these, no advance had yet been made beyond the stage of voluntary agreement, reached at the Treasury Conferences in March.[2]

The general purpose of the Munitions of War Act was to carry the progress of Government control over the workman's normal freedom under both heads as far as the exigencies of war production demanded and the state of feeling in the Labour world would allow. In order to measure the step now taken, it will be convenient to review the position already reached and the ways that had led to it.

---

[1] *Parliamentary Debates* (1915), *H. of L.*, XIX., 206.
[2] See Part II., Chap. IV.

B

(a) The Supply and Movement of Labour.

It has been shown that the question of labour supply for armaments and the wider problem of man-power in general had arisen in the winter months of 1914.[1] The two main causes of shortage were the sudden expansion of the demand and the unrestricted enlistment of the very men who were wanted for the new factories. Only the second of these causes admitted of any remedy. There were two possible expedients : to hinder more skilled men from enlisting by giving them the protection of badges, and to recall from the ranks men who ought never to have left the bench and the shipyard. In the absence of a Military Service Act, there was no real power to take effective action in either of these ways. No man could be compelled either to join the Colours or to leave them ; and, so long as the whole matter rested with the War Office, the active propaganda of the recruiting officer went on all over the country, practically unchecked, while the regimental officers could hardly be expected to speed the departure of some of the best soldiers in their battalions and companies. Short of introducing a Military Service Act, which the country was not yet ready to accept, the only remedy was to take Badging and Release from the Colours, so far as possible, out of the hands of the War Office and to transfer the working of both schemes to the new Ministry, which had an interest in making them effective.

The Munitions of War Act (Section 8) empowers the Minister to make rules authorising the wearing of badges. The Act does not deal with Release from the Colours, this being a matter which could not be formally removed from the military authorities ; but the Labour Branch of the Ministry inherited from Mr. Booth's Committee a Section whose duty was to press for the interests of munitions work in this direction. So far as Government control is concerned, no advance was possible while enlistment remained voluntary. Every man retained his original freedom to serve in the Army or in the factory, as he thought best.

The earliest measures of compulsion had been taken in the sphere of the diversion of labour from private work. They were a direct consequence of the Board of Trade campaign carried on for this purpose in the first quarter of 1915, and the need for them had become apparent from the employers' reaction against the appeal made to them to surrender to the armament firms a proportion of their best hands.[2] The two enactments in question are : the Defence of the Realm (Amendment) No. 2 Act of March, 1915,[3] and Regulation 8B (April, 1915), which prohibited the employer from enticing labour from a distance.[4] In each case the form of the enactment somewhat disguises the real intention underlying it. In the Act no mention is made of labour from first to last ; and the Regulation was so worded as to impose its prohibition only on the employer.

Both enactments were designed to regulate the movement of labour, and they restricted the normal liberty alike of employer

---

[1] See Part II., Chap. I.   [2] See Part II., Chap. I.
[3] See Part II., Chap. III.   [4] See Part III., Chap. V., Section VII.(b).

and of employed. They attacked the freedom of the employer to carry on what work he pleased for the greatest profit, and to attract labour by higher wages or other means. They attacked the freedom of the employee to sell his labour at the best price, and to work where and for whom he chose. It is here that Government control begins.

The two measures are complementary. The Act aimed at diverting labour into the channel of munitions production by the indirect method of extinguishing the competition of commercial work. The Regulation, on the other hand, was to hinder labour from moving away from munitions work in one place to work, whether for public or private purposes, in another. Under the Act, labour was to be moved to the place and the type of work where it was most wanted. The object of the Regulation was to keep it there for so long as it was wanted. In both cases, however, besides the indirectness of the method employed, the terms were comparatively mild ; and, in proportion as they proved ineffective, little opposition was aroused.

The sections of the Munitions of War Act which bear on these points are Sections 10 and 7. Section 10 strengthens the Amending Act of March by adding to the power of regulating or restricting the carrying on of work in any factory or workshop, the power to regulate or restrict " *the engagement or employment of any workman or all or any classes of workmen therein.*" This was a move in the direction of the compulsory transfer of workmen from one establishment to another, though no power was taken to assign the men displaced from one establishment to work elsewhere without their own consent. The amendment was also intended to bring Regulation 8 B *intra vires*. But the Regulation itself was practically superseded by Section 7, which provided a more effective means of tying the munitions worker to his employment by the institution of leaving certificates. This was the most drastic restriction of normal liberties contained in the Act, and, while Section 7 has been described as the most powerful instrument of industrial efficiency which the War has produced, in practice it gave rise to discontent which could only be finally allayed by its repeal.

The new Act thus tightened the control of the Government over the mobility of labour, both in the way of directing it to Government work, and of preventing it from moving away again of its own accord.

The Act further facilitates the desired movement of labour by the institution of War Munitions Volunteers. Section 6 provides for workmen entering into a voluntary undertaking to work at a controlled establishment. After giving this undertaking, the man became subject to certain penalties if he failed to carry it out ; but the initial step was a purely voluntary act on the workman's part. As will be seen later, the compulsory enrolment of employees at controlled establishments was at first contemplated ; but this project had to be abandoned before the Bill was introduced.

(b) Labour Regulation.

Up to the passing of the Munitions of War Act no compulsory measures existed to limit the workman's freedom (1) to stop working by a strike pending the settlement of a dispute, (2) to work as few hours as he pleased, or (3) to maintain those restrictive rules and practices which limited output. The Munitions of War Act dealt with all these three points.

(1) With regard to strikes and lock-outs, the first step had been taken by the Committee on Production in February, when labour troubles, which had died down in the earlier months of the War, broke out in a serious form. The Committee procured the issue of the Government *Notice* (21 February) which declared that " no stoppage of work by strike or lock-out should take place on work for Government purposes," and that differences which could not be settled by the parties under existing agreements " shall be referred to an impartial tribunal nominated by H.M. Government for immediate investigation and report to the Government with a view to a settlement." The Committee itself was empowered to act as the tribunal indicated. This *Notice* did not, of course, bindingly prohibit strikes and lock-outs, and no penalty was attached to non-compliance with the direction that disputes should be referred.

In March, Mr. Lloyd George was inclined to take the further step of including in the Amending Act clauses prohibiting strikes, lock-outs, and incitement thereto. It was considered, however, that the time was not ripe for strong measures, and these clauses were struck out in draft.[1] The Government took the alternative way of negotiation with the Trade Unions.

In the Treasury Agreement, the workmen's representatives pledged themselves to recommend to their members that

" during the war period there shall in no case be any stoppage of work upon munitions and equipments of war or other work required for a satisfactory completion of the War."

The Agreement further specified three alternative tribunals of arbitration, to which differences which could not be settled under existing agreements might be referred.

Part I. of the Munitions of War Act covers the same ground as this portion of the Treasury Agreement.

(2) The freedom of the workman to limit the number of hours worked, to refuse overtime, and to stay out whenever he pleased, inasmuch as it was not a matter of organised or collective action, but a purely individual concern, could not be restricted by direct Government intervention without recourse to measures that were likely to be resented as oppressive. Evidence will be produced later to show that the accusations of bad time-keeping freely levelled in the Press against engineering workmen at this time were exaggerated, as well as injudicious.[2] The evil, however, certainly existed, and the only course hitherto open to the Government had lain in an indirect attack upon the various forms of temptation which conduced to it. Under the Defence of the Realm (Amendment) No. 3 Act (19 May, 1915) the

---

[1] See Part II., Chap. III.   [2] See below, p. 45.

Government had taken power to control the liquor trade in any area, on the ground that munitions work was being carried on there. The prohibition of race meetings, football matches, and other distractions, had been mooted from time to time, but no legal powers had yet been assumed for such purposes.

The first sketch of the Bill drawn up at the Board of Trade on 1 June[1] included the suggestion, made by Captain Power of the North East Coast Armaments Committee, that power should be taken " to prohibit the holding of any public sports, races, or other meetings calculated to interfere with the continuity of work for war purposes." It was, however, considered that bad time-keeping could not be effectively checked by indirect methods.

The Munitions of War Act contains the first attempt to deal with the matter directly. The tribunals of one of the two classes set up by Section 15 were principally intended to mitigate this evil. Their powers were, however, limited to the infliction of fines on the employees of controlled establishments.

(3) Trade Union restrictions had the effect of limiting output, in some cases directly, in others indirectly, by the barriers of demarcation or by excluding unskilled labour from the higher forms of work and so making it impossible to supplement by " dilution " the depleted ranks of the highly skilled. In the engineering industry, the old method of joint conferences had led to some measure of success in the Shells and Fuses Agreement of March.[2] With the appointment of the Committee on Production the second stage—Conciliation—was reached, and at this point the counter-demand of Labour for the limitation of employers' profits emerged. In the retrospect, it appears unfortunate that the question of excess profits should have been thus closely linked with the suspension of restrictions. Probably it would now be universally admitted that the taxation of war profits ought to have been dealt with at the outset on its own merits and applied at once to every form of what is now called profiteering. The opportunity was lost owing to the acute anxiety of the Government to accelerate the production of munitions. Since it was only in the field of War Office and Admiralty work that the suspension of restrictions was immediately desired, and only in this field could there be any question of " taking over " the establishments concerned, the limitation of profits came to be looked upon as a *quid pro quo* and confined to the same class of work. The pledge embodied in the Treasury Agreement of 25 March with the Amalgamated Society of Engineers ran as follows :—

> " It is the intention of the Government to conclude arrangements with *all important firms engaged wholly or mainly upon engineering and shipbuilding work*, under which their profits will be limited, with a view to securing that benefit resulting from the relaxation of trade restrictions or practices shall accrue to the State."[3]

---

[1] *Heads of Labour Policy* (1/6/15), HIST. REC./R/300/38.
[2] See Part II., Chap. II.   [3] See Part II., Chap. IV.

In June, this pledge had not yet been redeemed. After prolonged negotiations with the armament firms it had been discovered that there was no legal power to redeem it.[1]

Part II. of the Munitions of War Act was designed to provide the necessary powers and to sanction the rest of the bargain struck at the Treasury Conferences. It creates the " controlled establishment," which is essentially an establishment within which the terms of the Treasury Agreement, including the suspension of restrictions and the employers' guarantee to restore them at the end of the War, are enforced, together with the limitation of profits. The control exercised over labour under the provisions relating to controlled establishments, which include power to make regulations " for the general ordering of work " therein, with a view to efficiency and the due observance of rules, depends on the willingness of the workman to enter into an undertaking to work there. No man could be compelled to take employment at a controlled establishment, unless he had already given this voluntary undertaking.

II. Sections 1-3. The Settlement of Disputes.

Part I. of the Act provides for the settlement of labour differences, for the prohibition of strikes and lock-outs in certain cases, and for arbitration, which on certain conditions is compulsory.

The understanding reached at the Treasury Conference with regard to stoppage of work had remained to a large extent a dead letter. This failure was attributed to the fact that the Agreement was only an expression of opinion—a recommendation—not a definite instruction entailing penalties for non-observance. The machinery for the settlement of disputes had been destroyed by war conditions ; and it was considered that the time had come for the Government to lay down rules binding on employers and workmen.

It was reported in June that stoppages were by no means of rare occurrence and threats of stoppage were common. The following instances were quoted from a large number.[2] An important firm of explosives manufacturers stated that during the last five months the number of strikes and threatened strikes had averaged two a week. The men had struck on the ground that they were being hustled by their foremen, and had threatened to strike because a foreman examined some work under protest, and again because an attempt was made to improve time-keeping. The ironworkers were on strike on two vitally important vessels at Grangemouth Dockyard in spite of the instructions of their Society and of the recommendation of the Committee on Production. The Amalgamated Society of Engineers, in pursuance of a dispute with the Iron Founders' Association, had called on their members employed by Messrs. Brown, Duncan & Co. to strike, and had refused arbitration, though the

---

[1] See Part II., Chap. III.

[2] *Memorandum on the position leading up to the introduction of the Bill.* Hist. Rec./R/221.1/6.

Iron Founders' Association were willing to accept it. A dozen small strikes were reported by the Shipbuilding Employers' Federation as having occurred in the last two months.

In so far as strikes were occasioned by the refusal of demands for higher wages, the attitude of the workmen was admitted by those who knew the facts to be, in general, not unreasonable. The case was plainly stated by Mr. Hodge in the Second Reading debate.[1]

> " In the early days of the War, trade unionists declared that, so far as they were concerned, they would raise no new questions during its continuance. That declaration was made in the belief that other sections of the community would act as patriotically as they were anxious to do. But, unfortunately, the price of food rose by leaps and bounds, and the price of every necessity of life increased in the same way. . . . Notwithstanding the pressure that we endeavoured from time to time to place upon the Government to control prices, they almost did nothing in that direction. As a result of that, the standard of living for the workers was so much lowered that it became absolutely essential that they should ask for some increase in the wages to meet that additional cost of living. In most cases that assumed the phase of a war bonus, and as soon as the War terminated the men would be required to give it up. If it was generally agreed that the prices of the necessities of life should be limited, I am quite convinced the workers of this country during the further continuance of the War would not seek to exploit the nation's necessities as the holders of food and other commodities have done, but they would be contented to go on as they are."

On the strength of his experience as a member of the Committee on Production, Sir George Gibb wrote[2] at the beginning of June that experience had confirmed the views expressed in the Fourth Report of that Committee.[3] Labour unrest would continue and would increase so long as efforts were made to limit the natural increase of wages, due to shortage of labour supply and to the high cost of living, without concurrent efforts to deal with profits, either by limiting prices or by drastic taxation of war profits. The Trade Union leaders acknowledged the need for removing restrictions, but they wanted assurances, followed up by Government action, that the concession would not simply swell employers' profits. The taking over of armament firms, though the Government had announced the intention, had not been carried into effect. The Trade Union leaders and the workmen were watching and wondering as to the reasons of the delay.

Sir George Gibb added that workmen generally could not be charged with having taken advantage of the shortage of labour to

---

[1] *Parliamentary Debates* (1915), *H. of* C., LXXII., 1512.
[2] *Memorandum on the Labour Situation* (3/6/15), M.W. 9279.
[3] See above, Part II., Chap. III.

enforce by strikes, accompanied by refusals to submit to arbitration, excessive demands for higher wages. Except in a few districts and in a few classes of labour, mainly in shipyards, workmen, while maintaining for the moment established trade union customs, had worked exceedingly well, and had been content to accept, under agreement or arbitration, increases of wages based on figures considerably below the actual increase in the cost of living.

Mr. W. L. Hichens wrote[1] : " There has been a very rapid rise in wages since the beginning of the War, and there is every indication that it will continue. It is true that the Government have stated that there must be no stoppage of work over wages disputes and that such questions must be arbitrated upon. Usually, though not always, this procedure has been followed ; but the arbitrators have been given no definite principles to work upon in making their award, with the result that their findings are often conflicting and unsatisfactory. Moreover, the employers are largely to blame ; for, in their desire to get men, they have offered bonuses in individual cases, which naturally tend to become general. The men, on their part, would be more than human if they did not sometimes restrict output with a view to improving piece-work rates. And it would be unfair to blame them for trying to make the best terms for themselves that they can ; and so long as they see certain men, or certain classes of men, getting bonuses, they naturally think they are entitled to look after themselves.

" In discussing wages questions, too, the point has sometimes been put to the employers that it is unreasonable on their part to refuse an increase, because, after all, it is the Government that pays, and, as Mr. Lloyd George said, the Government purse is bottomless. There is more truth, indeed, in their contention that the employer need not refuse an increase in wages than appears at first sight. Many Government contracts are now given out on a percentage basis— that is, the Government pay the actual cost of labour and material, plus a percentage for profit. Obviously, therefore, the higher the labour bill is, the greater will be the profit.

" All this has an important effect on output, for three reasons : (a) We find by experience that the existence of a dispute tends to make men less keen on their work. (b) The restriction of output, whether conscious or unconscious, to show that existing piece-rates are inadequate, tells its own tale. (c) With certain classes of men it is a fact that the more they earn, the less work they do. The instinct for saving being undeveloped, they naturally require leisure in which to spend all earnings above the subsistence margin."

Mr. Hichens observed that demarcation disputes were a frequent cause of strikes. Under the ordinary industrial system there was much to be said for the principle of demarcation ; but in its results it was obviously wasteful. " That urgent work should be held up when suitable

---

[1] *Memorandum on the Influence of Drink on the Production of War Materials.* HIST. REC./R/345/2. Mr. Hichens was Director of Messrs. Cammell, Laird & Co.

men are available, simply because they are not fully qualified members of a certain trade, is a disgrace in war time. And yet the demarcation disputes are as frequent to-day as in peace time, and strikes, owing to the attempt of some employer to turn on men outside the trade, are common occurrences. Here, again, the men are not really to blame. They think—and in the light of the history of industrial disputes the thought is not without justification—that the employer will use any relaxation of the present rigid system to break down the barrier between trade and trade. They think too that the employment of large numbers of outsiders will tend to build up a black-leg reserve, who will be employed as strike-breakers after the War. The Government has promised, in general terms, to safeguard their position after the War, but the undertaking is too vague to be convincing, and moreover there is no machinery for stopping demarcation disputes or enforcing an award. The effect of these disputes and restrictions on output is too obvious to need further explanation."

Mr. Hichens recommended (among other remedies) the appointment of a central committee, under the Minister of Munitions, representing both employers and workmen, with full powers to deal with all labour questions. There should be similar local committees, under the central committee, for local questions. No increases of wages, not justified by the rise in the cost of living, should be granted ; and all increases should be settled by the central or local committees, who should also decide demarcation disputes.

On the other hand, the Government should impose limitation of profits, not merely on a few firms, but in the form of a heavy super-tax on all firms earning more than a certain rate of interest on their share capital. They should also limit prices, so as to keep down the cost of living.

Sir George Askwith's view of the situation and his proposals for remedy were communicated to the President of the Board of Trade in a Memorandum[1] dated 1 June. The following is a summary.

There were indications that some further action would shortly be needed to prevent the occurrence of labour disputes. It was doubtful if the rank and file of Trade Unions, or even some of their leaders, had accepted the spirit of the Treasury Agreement of 19 March. The Committee on Production had already given nearly 40 decisions on wages questions, covering directly some 750,000 work-people and involving very large additions to the wages bill. Such a process could not be again followed without serious difficulty, and it was necessary to consider carefully what course should be followed.

The present London Tramway strike indicated how many of the men viewed the position. It appeared to be, not a sudden outbreak, but a deliberate revolt, engineered by the leaders of one of the two Unions so as to look spontaneous. It was intended partly to force

---

[1] *Industrial Disputes : Power to investigate prior to stoppage of work.* HIST. REC./R/180/33.

the London County Council to make concessions, partly to attract the men into one Union at the other's expense. The trouble in the cotton trade had come to such a pass that it was hard to see how widespread stoppage could be averted.

The position in the engineering trades was even more serious. In the last four months, every engineering district in the United Kingdom had agitated for, and received, by agreement or (in most cases) by arbitration, advances in wages reaching in the aggregate to a very large amount. A movement was now beginning (particularly on the Clyde, where the agitation had been most pronounced in February and where there had been a serious strike) for a further advance of wages ; and if this movement gained headway, it would rapidly grow into another wave of demands for higher wages throughout the country. The local leader on the Clyde had not concealed his determination to exploit to the utmost the national needs, and, in view of his recent successes, his example might be followed elsewhere. The new claims would, of course, be resisted by the employers, and the result, sooner or later, would probably be strikes. Even if the arbitration procedure under the Treasury Agreement were followed for a time, the men, if their demands were disallowed, would be disposed to stop work.

Besides the more general movement, there were many cases (particularly on munitions work) where sudden stoppages took place, or were threatened ; and in such cases the employers were giving way on the best terms they could obtain to avoid interference with output. The continued rise in food prices was likely to be used as a cover for exercising the power which, owing to labour shortage, was now in the hands of many Unions.

The writer thought that the more responsible Union leaders would welcome any remedy ; and it was for consideration whether measures to prevent the occurrence of disputes should not be initiated. The possible steps were :—

(1) The total prohibition of strikes, and compulsory arbitration. This method, while it would entail a considerable organisation for arbitration and invite a flood of applications for settlement, could be largely simplified if it could be established that pre-war controversies (e.g. recognition of Unions), must not be raised.

(2) Some measure like the Canadian Act, which prevents strikes and lock-outs pending investigation by an independent authority, with recommendation of terms of settlement. This would obviate all sudden strikes.

(3) To make it a condition of employment that one month's notice must be given before work could be left, with penalties for breach. This would really be an extension of the Conspiracy and Protection of Property Act, 1875 (Clause 4), which protects gas and water undertakings from sudden strikes, and could be made applicable to irregular attendance.

The first method (with the provision against raising pre-war questions) would at this time be preferable ; but the other alternatives might be considered.

The Canadian Act[1] embraced three fundamental principles :—

(a) Restrictive measures prohibiting strikes and lock-outs, pending investigation ;

(b) Authoritative investigation, with public recommendation of terms of settlement ;

(c) The exercise, during such investigation, of conciliation with a view to settlement.

Under normal conditions, and particularly having regard to the special nature of our industrial organisation, the writer had recommended that the restrictive measures were unnecessary, but that the remaining principles should be adopted here. In a state of war, however, more was necessary, and, if the Government took this course, the restrictive measures should be included. The investigation authorised under the Act would include power to summon witnesses, administer oaths, and call for books, documents, etc., for confidential use. The latter power would enable enquiry to be made into profits, and so help to meet the workmen's suspicions that exorbitant profits were being made.

If the proposal could be made statutory under the Defence of the Realm Acts, it could be promulgated forthwith ; but if legislation were necessary, a short Bill on the lines of Clause 6 of the Draft of an Industrial Agreements and Inquiries Bill prepared early in 1914,[2]

---

[1] Sir George Askwith and Mr. Mitchell had been sent to Canada in the autumn of 1912 to study the Lemieux Act and its working. In their Report (*Parliamentary Paper* Cd. 6603) the opinion was expressed that an Act which embodied those portions of the Canadian Act which give power to conciliate in a dispute and, if necessary, to make recommendations for a settlement, but which omitted the restrictive and penal clauses, would be suitable and practicable in this country, and would be valuable alike to the country and to employers and employed. The proposals of the Report were taken up by Sir Stanley Buckmaster in January, 1914, and led to the drafting of an Industrial Agreements and Enquiries Bill (30 March, 1914), designed to enlarge the powers already possessed by the Board of Trade under the Conciliation Act, 1896. (Copy of this draft Bill in HIST. REC./R/221/22.)

[2] This is the draft Bill referred to in the previous Note. Clause 6, which was based upon the Canadian Act, provided that—

" Where a difference exists or is apprehended between an employer or any class of employers and workmen, or between different classes of workmen, the Board of Trade shall have power, in addition to the powers which they may exercise under section two of the Conciliation Act, 1896, to direct, if they think it expedient in the public interest, a formal inquiry under this Part of this Act into the causes and circumstances of the difference."

The persons holding the enquiry might be directed to act as conciliators under the Conciliation Act. They might summon witnesses and examine them on oath, and require the production of books and documents for confidential use. Failure to comply with any summons or requisition was to be subject to a fine.

Under these provisions the initiative lay with the Board of Trade, not (as in the Munitions of War Act) with the parties to the dispute. But, beyond this power of directing an enquiry, there was no interference with the ordinary course of trade disputes, and no provision for a binding award.

with such additions as were needed to incorporate the restrictive and penalising features of the Canadian Act, might be passed as an emergency measure.

The remaining alternative was to extend Clause 4 of the 1875 Act to all works and services engaged in supplying Government requirements, with the addition that an implied condition of employment on such work was that one month's notice must be given before work could be left. The aim would be to prevent sudden strikes and absences from work without good cause. Sir George Askwith concluded by again expressing his preference for the first method proposed.

On 1 June, Sir H. Llewellyn Smith wrote to the President of the Board of Trade, expressing his concurrence in Sir George Askwith's conclusion. He believed that nothing short of an absolute prohibition of strikes, coupled with compulsory arbitration, would meet the present needs, at all events in munitions industries. He also expressed the opinion that the time was ripe to prohibit restrictions on work and output in these industries, and that this should probably be done by amending the Defence of the Realm Act rather than the Conciliation Act. He believed that drastic legislation would be really welcomed by the Union leaders, though they would not dare to admit it. It was further recommended that the penalty to be imposed on persons guilty of resorting to a strike or lock-out, or of leaving work without a month's notice, should be imprisonment up to three or six months, fines being useless. The President, on 5 June, gave instructions for an " Amended Bill " to be drafted.[1] The Draft was to include the necessary provisions for limiting the profits of contractors.

In a *Preliminary Note on Labour Policy* (4 June)[2] Sir H. Llewellyn Smith sketched the outline for the Draft of the Bill, following as closely as possible the lines of the Treasury Agreement, but including the limitation of profits and provisions for a " King's Munition Corps."

It was proposed that the prohibition of stoppages of work and the enactment of compulsory arbitration, where other methods of settlement without stoppage failed, should be universal.

This proposal did not go beyond the intention of the Treasury Agreement, which laid down in the first place that during the War there should " in no case be any stoppage of work upon munitions and equipments of war or other work required for a satisfactory completion of the War." This absolutely ruled out stoppage on war work, but only on war work. The other two provisions covered all the trades represented at the Conference (a very wide field, including occupations only remotely connected with munitions production), and laid down that questions arising out of the War should be settled, without stoppage, by arbitration ; and that questions not arising out of the War should not be made the cause of stoppage during the War. The

---

[1] It was proposed at this time that the Bill should take the form of an Amended Defence of the Realm Bill.

[2] HIST. REC./R/221.1/17.

phrasing was not meant to be legally exact ; and it is clear that the intention was that there should be no stoppage of work in any trade whatever that could be brought to adhere to the Agreement.

The proposal to make the prohibition universal merely removed the question from the region of voluntary agreement into the region of compulsion. It was, however, modified in the first Draft of the Bill (12 June). Clauses 1 and 2, which prohibited strikes and lock-outs, subject to notice being given by the Minister of Munitions, were confined to work " on or in connection with the supply of munitions of war." On the other hand, Clause 4 of this Draft, which enacts the compulsory reference of disputes to arbitration, was not so limited, but extended to all employment, subject only to the provision that notice should have been given, prohibiting a lock-out or strike, or the continuance of a lock-out or strike, in connection with any such difference. The scope of these clauses was the subject of much subsequent discussion, and was substantially modified.

This first Draft did not leave to agreement between the parties the choice between three alternative methods of arbitration, as laid down in the Treasury Agreement. Differences were, on the application of either party, to be referred to an arbitration tribunal appointed by the Board of Trade, whose award was to be binding under penalty of a fine.

One of the three alternatives in the Treasury Agreement was a court of arbitration on which employers and labour were to be equally represented. The following general criticism of bodies so constituted was put forward in a memorandum by Mr. I. H. Mitchell, of the Chief Industrial Commissioner's department, and deserves to be quoted :—" The policy during the past few months has been to leave the solution of many of the labour difficulties in the hands of Committees largely composed of employers and Trade Union officials. Frankly, I do not think the best results will follow. It would be as reasonable to expect good temperance results from a licensing authority composed of publicans and total abstainers. Trade Union officials are pro-Labour ; they are elected because they are more pro-Labour than any of their shopmates ; they cannot go further in the direction of giving judicial decisions than those who elect them will allow ; in most cases they cannot go so far, as, in their anxiety to retain the confidence of those they represent and keep off ambitious rivals, they must show by their actions that they are the best champions the men can possibly have. They are, therefore, in an extremely difficult position, when called upon to judge fairly upon questions affecting Labour ; and, with a few honourable exceptions, they seldom try to be anything but candidly pro-Labour, irrespective of the merits. The employers also are not free from bias ; so that to expect a fair and just solution from such bodies is likely to lead to grievous disappointment. A much better way is for the Government to departmentally collect the facts and then to act accordingly."

The three alternative courts of arbitration were, however, subsequently embodied in the Bill (Schedule 1). This was agreed to by the Minister at a conference with Trade Union delegates, which was called to discuss a synopsis of the Bill on 16 June.[1] At this meeting the general sense appeared to favour the prevention of all strikes and lock-outs universally. It was, however, pointed out that employers might take advantage of the prohibition of strikes to refuse to consider petitions from the men, and that power should be taken to make bodies of employers come together for that purpose.

SECTION 3.   DIFFERENCES TO WHICH PART I. APPLIES.

In studying the provisions of this First Part of the Bill, as introduced and modified during its passage through the House of Commons, it will be convenient to begin with Section 3, which defines the differences to which Part I. applies.

These differences are divided into two classes :—

(a) Differences arising in employment " on the manufacture or repair of arms, ammunition, ships, vehicles, aircraft, or any other articles required for use in war, or of the metals, machines or tools required for that manufacture or repair (in this Act referred to as munitions work) "[2] ;

(b) Differences arising in employment " on any other work of any description, if this Part of the Act is applied to such a difference by His Majesty by Proclamation on the ground that in the opinion of His Majesty the existence or continuance of the difference is directly or indirectly prejudicial to the manufacture, transport, or supply of Munitions of War."

Further, this Part of the Act may be so applied to such a difference at any time, whether or not a strike or lock-out has occurred.

It will be observed that under (b) the method of Proclamation is substituted for notice given by the Minister prohibiting a strike or lock-out, as the condition which would bring differences in other than munitions work within the scope of this Part. With reference to this provision, Sir John Simon pointed out that this was not a Bill for compulsory arbitration over the whole field of labour.

" The Bill is so drawn that, if it is to be extended at all in case of need by Proclamation, the extension is not to be to a new trade or to a new field of labour ; the extension is to be to the specific difference or dispute which calls for such intervention. . . . It is not our intention, automatically, to bring in large additional classes of labour merely because in a given case we have to use the machinery of the Bill."[3]

The miners and the cotton operatives could not be induced to assent to compulsory arbitration being applied to their industries.[4]

---

[1] HIST. REC./R/300. See below, p. 36.

[2] This definition of munitions work is less comprehensive than that contained in the Ministry of Munitions Act.   The words " aircraft " and " metals " were added in Committee. (*Parliamentary Debates* (1915), *H. of C.*, LXXII., 1980, 1982.)

[3] *Parliamentary Debates* (1915), *H. of C.*, LXXII., 1541, 1543.

[4] *Ibid.*, 1199.

The Minister held three conferences with the Executive of the Miners' Federation of Great Britain on 24, 25, and 28 June, with the object of securing means, if not by the Bill, then by agreement, of preventing the disturbance of industry. Mr. Lloyd George had informed the miners' delegates at the outset that, while the Government much desired that the miners should come under the Bill, he would bring no pressure to bear upon them and would accept their refusal. Mr. Smillie pledged the Miners' Executive, of which he was President, to do everything possible to maintain the output of coal ; but stated that the Executive, after full discussion, had been unanimous against coming under the Bill. The miners were accustomed to settle small disputes with the colliery manager ; but if a dispute had to go before a court, " the whole colliery would be out, because they resent very much any outside interference."

At the conference on 28 June, the Executive proposed, if the South Wales dispute were settled shortly, to give the following guarantee :—

> " That, in order to prevent strikes by miners during the War, we are prepared to enter into an arrangement with the coalowners in every district, by which all disputes can be settled by the representatives of the owners and the workmen, and in the case of the two sides failing to settle any dispute, an independent chairman be called in with full powers to settle."

The Minister pressed for the inclusion of these terms in a special clause of the Bill without any provision for penalties. The Executive resisted this suggestion on the ground that the miners, if they were brought under the Bill, would refuse to join in the movement which was being promoted by the Executive for increasing output. The conclusion reached was that the miners were to be excluded from the Bill, but the Executive agreed to give a guarantee to set up machinery on the lines of the resolution above quoted.

Mr. Henderson and the President of the Board of Trade met the cotton operatives,[1] who also contended that their industry was so well organised that any method of preventing stoppage which their Union advocated would be effective. They passed a resolution substantially to the same effect as that of the miners.

At the Committee stage, on the motion of Mr. Lloyd George,[2] the following paragraph, which had been accepted by the Labour leaders, was inserted in Section 3 :—

> " Provided that if in the case of any industry the Minister of Munitions is satisfied that effective means exist to secure the settlement without stoppage of any difference arising on work other than on munitions work, no proclamation shall be made under this section with respect to any such difference."

A further addition was made to the Section, embodying a principle which had been agreed upon between the Minister and the Trade

---

[1] *Parliamentary Debates* (1915), *H. of C.*, LXXII., 1576.

[2] *Ibid.*, 1989.

Union leaders.   Mr. Hodge[1] in moving the insertion of the clause, explained that the object was to provide for cases where civil or commercial work was being carried on side by side with munitions work in a controlled establishment.   The employer might claim that Trade Union rules should be relaxed for the commercial work in the same way as for the munitions work.   The amendment was to secure that such changes should not take place till an agreement had been reached.   It ran as follows :—

> " When this Part of this Act is applied to any difference concerning work other than munitions work, the conditions of labour and the remuneration thereof prevailing before the difference arose shall be continued until the said difference is settled in accordance with the provisions of this Part of this Act."

Section 1.   Settlement of Differences.

The classes of differences to which the Act applies having been thus defined in Section 3, Section 1 provides the machinery for the settlement of disputes arising within those limits.   It enacts :—

(1) That any difference to which the Act applies, whether existing or apprehended, may, if not settled by the parties or under existing agreements, be reported to the Board of Trade by either party[2] ;

(2) That the Board shall consider the difference and take any steps that may seem expedient to promote a settlement, and may, if they think fit, refer the matter for settlement either in accordance with the provisions of the First Schedule (which enumerates the three arbitration tribunals provided for by the Treasury Agreement), or to any suitable existing machinery for arrangement ;

(3) That where undue delay occurs in settling a matter referred by the Board under (2) to existing machinery, the Board may annul the reference and substitute a reference to a court of arbitration under Schedule 1[3] ;

(4) That the award shall be binding on both parties, and may be retrospective.   Contravention or non-compliance is an offence under the Act.

Section 14, which deals with penalties, provides for this offence a fine not exceeding £5 for each day or part of a day during which the offence continues, and, if the offender is an employer, for each man in respect of whom it takes place.

---

[1] *Parliamentary Debates* (1915), *H. of C.*, LXXII., 1996.

[2] In this clause " may be reported " was substituted for " shall be reported " in the original draft.   The clause became permissive.

[3] This sub-section was added in Committee (*Parliamentary Debates* (1915), *H. of C.*, LXXII., 1958).

SECTION 2. PROHIBITION OF STRIKES AND LOCK-OUTS.

Section 2 contains the prohibition of strikes and lock-outs. A strike or lock-out on munitions work or occasioned by a difference which has been proclaimed, is legal under the Act only if it satisfies the condition that the difference shall have been reported to the Board of Trade and the Board shall not have referred it within twenty-one days[1] for settlement.

The penalties for contravention are laid down by Section 14. For lock-outs the penalty is a fine not exceeding £5 in respect of each man locked out, for each day or part of a day during which the offence continues ; for strikes, a fine not exceeding £5 for each day or part of a day.

The terms " lock-out " and " strike " are defined by Section 19.

The Act contains no prohibition of incitement to strikes or lock-outs.[2]

III. Section 4. The Controlled Establishment.

It has been seen that Part I. of the Act was based on those paragraphs of the Treasury Agreement which provided against stoppage of work. The main purpose of Part II. is to give legal sanction to the remainder of the Agreement and to ratify the bargain that Trade Union restrictions which tended to limit output should be suspended, provided that employers' profits were limited and that the restoration of conditions after the War should be guaranteed.

Section 4 enacts that, " if the Minister considers it expedient for the purpose of the successful prosecution of the War that any establishment in which munitions work is carried on should be subject to the special provisions as to limitation of employers' profits and control of persons employed and other matters contained in this section, he may make an order declaring that establishment to be a controlled establishment." Any part of an establishment in which munitions work is not carried on may be treated as a separate establishment.

---

[1] " Twenty-one days " was substituted for " a month " in Committee (*Parliamentary Debates* (1915), *H. of C.*, LXXII., 1973).

[2] A prohibition of incitement had been included in the synopsis of the Bill discussed with the Trade Unions on 16 June. A motion to omit the words was defeated by 37 votes to 21 ; but as this was the only point on which a serious cleavage of opinion was evident, the Government decided to drop it out of the Bill. A provision against incitement was afterwards inserted in D.O.R. Regulation 42 : " If any person attempts . . . . *to impede, delay, or restrict the production, repair, or transport of war material, or any other work necessary for th successful prosecution of the war*, he shall be guilty, etc."

Upon such order being made, several provisions are to apply to the establishment[1]:—

(1) The profits are to be limited in accordance with the provisions of Section 5.

(2) Rates of wages, salaries, etc., are not to be changed without authorisation.

(3) Rules, practices, and customs tending to restrict output or employment are to be suspended, with penalties for incitement and a provision for arbitration in cases of dispute whether a rule, practice, or custom is restrictive or not.

(4) The employer is to be bound by the guarantee of restoration, the clauses of which are set out in Schedule II.

(5) The employers and persons employed are to comply with regulations made for certain purposes by the Minister, with penalties for non-compliance.

(6) The owner is empowered to comply with the provisions of the Section, notwithstanding other obligations, and required, subject to penalty, to comply with any reasonable requirements of the Minister as to information or otherwise for the purposes of this Section.

Certain points in connection with these provisions call for remark.

(1) The limitation of profits will be considered below, in connection with Section 5.

(2) This sub-section prohibits unauthorised changes in the rates of wages, salaries, or other emoluments "of any class of person employed in the establishment, or of any persons engaged in the management or the direction of the establishment." The intention was that the excess profits payable to the Exchequer should not be diminished by any undue increases of these emoluments. A further safeguard was afterwards added by Rule 9 (f) of the Munitions (Limitation of Profits) Rules, 1915, which provides against increases being made after the end of the standard period and before the beginning of the control period, in anticipation of the declaration of control.

At the Committee stage the following qualification was added[2]:—

"(other than changes for giving effect to any Government conditions as to fair wages or to any agreement between the owner of the establishment and the workmen which was made before the twenty-third day of June, nineteen hundred and fifteen)."

---

[1] It will be noted that, as all these provisions come into force together and only from the date of control, the limitation of profits is not retrospective, and profits made before that date cannot be touched. This fact seems not to have been understood when the Bill was before the House of Commons, even by some members of the Government. Mr. Henderson said in the Second Reading debate : "Members . . . will find that under these clauses very considerable amounts of the profits that have been made are already assured to the Treasury." · (*Parliamentary Debates* (1915), *H. of C.*, LXXII., 1578).

[2] *Parliamentary Debates* (1915), *H. of C.*, LXXII., 2031.

A clause was also added,[1] making it an offence for the owner or any contractor or sub-contractor employing labour in the establishment to make such changes without submitting his proposal or when ·consent had been withheld. The penalty under Section 14 (e) is a fine not exceeding £50.

(3) The sub-section dealing with the suspension of " any rule, practice, or custom not having the force of law which tends to restrict production or employment," did not undergo any important amendment.

(4) The provision for the employer's undertaking to carry out the provisions of Schedule II., was amended in Committee[2] by the addition of words making it an offence under the Act to break, or attempt to break, such an undertaking. The penalty is a fine not exceeding £50 [Section 14 (e)].

This addition is to be read in connection with Section 20 (2) where it is provided that the Act " shall have effect only so long as the office of Minister of Munitions and the Ministry exist,"[3] but that " Part I. of this Act shall continue to apply for a period of twelve months after the conclusion of the present War to any difference arising in relation to the performance by the owner of any establishment of his undertaking to carry out the provisions set out in the Second Schedule to this Act, notwithstanding that the office of Minister of Munitions and the Ministry of Munitions have ceased to exist." This clause also was added in Committee.

Both these additions were made because it had been pointed out that the Bill in its original form provided no legal sanction for the employer's undertaking and no machinery for enforcing its fulfilment. Section 20, however, provides only for the continuance of the system of settling differences established by Part I. ; it does not provide for the perpetuation of Munitions Tribunals—the only courts before which a fine is recoverable under this Act (Section 14 (2)). The Act accordingly appears to make no provision for the punishment of an employer for the offence under Section 4 (4) at any time after the Ministry shall have ceased to exist. Nor was it made clear how the penalties for offences under Part I. were to be inflicted during the year after the conclusion of the War, if the Ministry should in the meantime have ceased to exist.[4]

---

[1] *Parliamentary Debates* (1915), *H. of C.*, LXXII., 2033.   [2] *Ibid.*, 2040.

[3] Clause 6 of the Ministry of Munitions Act, 1915, enacts that " the office of Minister of Munitions and the Ministry of Munitions shall cease to exist on the termination of a period of twelve months after the conclusion of the present War or such earlier date as may be fixed by His Majesty in Council."

[4] The Amending Act, 1916, repealed the words " Part I. of " in Section 20 (2), thus providing that the other relevant clauses of the Act should continue, for a year after the end of the war, to apply to this class of differences.

The Minister, in introducing the Bill, once more pledged the Government to see that the undertaking was carried out :—

"The second thing is the removal of all regulations and practices—or rather, I would not say removal, but suspension —during the War, on the honour and pledge of the nation that things would be restored exactly to the position they were in before."[1]

Mr. Pringle prophesied that, after the War, the masters, who would have realised an increase of output by the suspension of restrictive rules, would argue that a reversion to the old system would be economically bad for the country. The conclusion of the War would bring a reversal of the conditions that now prevailed between Capital and Labour. The demand for labour would be small ; the supply would be large. Prejudiced by this change, the Trade Unions would not be in a strong position to resist the plausible representations of employers that a restoration of hampering rules and customs would injure trade, and that workmen would be foolish to exact a fulfilment of the pledge.

The clauses of the employers' undertaking, as set out in Schedule II., are substantially identical with the form of guarantee embodied in the Treasury Agreement.[2]

At the Minister's meeting with Trade Union delegates on 16 June,[3] to discuss the provisions of the Bill, it was pointed out that firms which did not come under the Act as controlled establishments, but continued to do commercial work, might take advantage of the withdrawal of their skilled men to introduce less skilled labour. In such cases there would be no guarantee that the *status quo* would be restored after the War. The Minister was asked whether the Government would put pressure on these firms to restore pre-war conditions. Mr. Lloyd George replied, in the first place, that, since the statutory obligation to suspend restrictions was confined to controlled establishments, the statutory obligation to restore them must be similarly limited. If, however, a dispute arose in the case of an uncontrolled establishment, the arbitrator might make any conditions he chose with regard to the settlement. "He can say : Owing to the special conditions of the War, you must allow these regulations to be suspended for the time being ; but it is on the express condition that you return to the *status quo ante* after the War."

---

[1] *Parliamentary Debates* (1915), H. of C., LXXII., 1199.

[2] See above, Part II., Chap. IV. The only important change is in paragraph (4), which provides that where semi-skilled men replace more highly skilled workers, "the *time and piece* rates paid shall be the usual rates of the district for that class of work." The words "*time and piece*" were inserted in Committee. The National Advisory Committee had been informed that some Birmingham employers had insisted that the corresponding paragraph in the Treasury Agreement should not apply to time rates ; whereas the original intention had been that this paragraph should safeguard the time rates, and paragraph (5) the piece rates. In making this intention clear, the amendment incidentally introduced an anomalous expression, since, except in shipbuilding, there are no district piece rates. Paragraph 9 of Schedule II. contains a drafting error : "the fourth paragraph" should be "the third paragraph." The correction was made by Section 19 of the Munitions of War (Amending) Act, 1916.

[3] Hist. Rec./R/300/5.

(5) This sub-section contemplates the making of regulations " with respect to the general ordering of the work in the establishment with a view to attaining and maintaining a proper standard of efficiency and with respect to the due observance of the rules of the establishment."

Contravention or non-compliance is an offence, punishable under Section 14 (d) by a fine not exceeding £3.

The object was explained to be " to establish discipline in the workshops," and in particular to enforce better time-keeping. The original draft of the Bill had provided for the establishment of a " King's Munition Corps " and it had been proposed that discipline should be enforced in the controlled establishment by a " Munitions Officer " or commandant, armed with quasi-military authority. As will be seen later, the negotiations with the Trade Unions before the Bill was introduced resulted in the substitution of a scheme 'for enrolling Munitions Volunteers, and the consequent disappearance of all features of a military character connected with this body. Sub-section (5) was correspondingly altered, and the Munitions Tribunal of the second class (under Section 15) became the authority to enforce compliance with the regulations.

(6) This sub-section relieves the owners of a controlled establishment from obligations " in any Act, Order, or deed under which they are governed," which might prevent compliance with the provisions of the Section, and requires them to produce information reasonably demanded by the Minister. The refusal of information is an offence, and the giving of false information is punishable under Section 12.

This sub-section underwent no amendment.

In Committee the question was raised, what classes of firms it was intended should be controlled. Sir John Simon replied that he could not say more than that " every patriotic firm which seeks to do useful work, and would like to be controlled, has only to apply to the Minister of Munitions." He would not say that every firm making munitions would be controlled, " but inasmuch as it is highly desirable that we should get the Ministry of Munitions in close connection with the work of making munitions, it will be obvious that this is not intended to apply merely to cases here or there, but an attempt to make munitions, partly by controlling labour and partly by controlling profits, within such limits as will enable munitions to be produced as rapidly as possible. I do not think I can give an answer more specific than that."[1]

IV. Section 5. The Limitation of Profits.

When the Bill was being prepared, some objections were raised to confining the limitation of profits to controlled establishments. The Director of Naval Contracts, in a Note forwarded to Sir H. Llewellyn Smith on 5 June, had pointed out that, if armament and

---

[1] *Parliamentary Debates* (1915), *H. of C.*, LXXII., 2020.

shipbuilding firms alone were taxed, invidious questions would arise. These firms had made special efforts, while collieries, millers, metal manufacturers, and others had made money with no effort. Further, armament firms might expect to suffer after the War, and, in any case, a too severe limitation would discourage much zeal that was being shown.

On similar grounds, Mr. Terrell, at the Committee stage, moved to omit all the provisions for limitation of profits. He said :—" There are a great many other classes of individuals in the country who . . . most of us have pretty good reason to suspect are making great profits out of the War, and I do not for the life of me see why they should be let off and only these particular establishments, which are doing a special service to the State, be singled out."[1]

' It was, of course, impossible to introduce into the Bill provisions for a universal tax on war profits ; but, in pointing this out, Sir John Simon observed that the case for such a tax was in no way prejudiced by this partial application of the principle.[2]

It has already been remarked that the real cause of the restriction lay in the circumstances which had led to the bargain with the Unions at the Treasury Conference. That the provisions of Sections 4 and 5 constitute, even in a legal sense, a bargain, was the view taken by the Speaker and the Chairman of Committee in the House of Commons. At the Committee stage, Mr. J. M. Henderson asked for a ruling on the question whether these clauses were not taxing clauses, and could, therefore, not be entertained except under a Resolution in Ways and Means. The Chairman, after consultation with the Speaker, ruled that this was not the case. He said :—

" I think it may be described in this way : that these two clauses contain an arrangement by which certain persons who receive certain benefits in the way of relaxation of customs and rules will, at the same time, surrender certain financial advantages which would otherwise accrue to them ; therefore it is in the nature of a contract, in other words, a *quid pro quo*.

" Secondly, I think it may be looked at in this way : that the State proposes to give to certain establishments orders for war materials, and the limitation of the profit to be obtained by means of these orders is what, in Committee of Supply, we call an Appropriation-in-Aid—that is to say, that any amount beyond a certain produce shall come back to His Majesty's Government. That, I think, is the correct way of looking at the procedure of this Clause."[3]

Later experience has justified the critics who urged that the taxation of excess profits should have been handled first on general principles, before Labour was asked to make serious sacrifices whose immediate effect would be to increase profits. The following words are quoted from a memorandum written in April, 1917 :—

---

[1] *Parliamentary Debates* (1915), *H. of C.*, LXXII., 2007.
[2] *Ibid.*, 2015.   [3] *Ibid.*, 2005.

"There is no doubt that of all the factors that have been contributing to the difficulty in handling the labour problems in this country, the most formidable has been what has been called ' profiteering by contractors.' Experience entitles it to be said ; and it is likely that, if from the outset of the War there had been automatic provision preventing individuals from profiting by the War, labour difficulties, both sentimental and actual, might have been in part, if not wholly, avoided. It must have followed that, if the workmen had realised that the employer had forgone all material advantage, he on his side might be asked to forgo certain of his rights. The ultimate limitation of profits and the heavy Excess Profits Duty, while to a certain extent efficacious, never entirely removed the first and abiding sting of the sight of huge profits being compiled. Of all the conclusions that one is entitled to draw, none emerges with greater certainty than this : that compulsion in dealing with private profits is the fundamental method of grappling with all labour difficulties from the outset."[1]

Under Section 4 (1) " any excess of the net profits of the controlled establishment over the amount divisible under this Act . . . . shall be paid into the Exchequer." Section 5 defines the divisible profits as " an amount exceeding by one-fifth the standard amount of profits," and contains the supplementary provisions for the ascertainment of the standard amount. The basis of these provisions was that which had been laid down in the negotiations with Messrs. Armstrong and Messrs. Vickers in March.[2]

This Section underwent several important changes.

(1) The main principle that " the amount of profits divisible under the Act shall be taken to be an amount exceeding by one-fifth the standard amount of profits " remained unchanged.

An amendment was moved by Mr. Terrell[3] to the effect that the profits should be ascertained by the Commissioners of the Inland Revenue, on the ground that the Commissioners already possessed the necessary evidence, which, being private, could not be communicated to the Committee which Sir John Simon had stated would be appointed.[4]

It was objected, however, that, as the Treasury had an interest in the profits, it would not be right for the Commissioners to assess them, and the amendment was withdrawn.

(2) The definition of the standard amount of profits in Sub-section (2) was modified. In the Bill as introduced it read :—

"The standard amount of profits for any period shall be taken to be the average of the amount of the net profits for the

---

[1] *Notes on Labour Problems in War Time*, by Mr. U. Wolff, Hist. Rec./H/300/2.

[2] See above, Part II., Chap. III., Section VII.

[3] *Parliamentary Debates* (1915), H. of C., LXXII., 2046.

[4] The reference is to the Committee under the chairmanship of Sir H. Babington Smith, referred to below.

two *corresponding periods* completed next before the outbreak of the War."·

In Committee, on Mr. Lloyd George's motion, the words "*financial years of the establishment*" were substituted for "corresponding periods "; and the words "*or a proportionate part thereof*" were added at the end.[1]

(3) This Sub-section provides for certain cases in which it may appear or be represented to the Minister that the standard as above defined is in some way not fairly applicable to a particular establishment. Three types of cases are given :—

(*a*) It may appear or be represented " that the net profits *or losses* of all or any other establishments belonging to the same owner should be brought into account." The words " *or losses* " were added in Committee.[2]

(*b*) It may appear or be represented "that the average under this section affords or may afford an unfair standard of comparison."

(*c*) It may appear or be represented "that the average under this section . . . affords no standard of comparison." It was pointed out by Mr. Duke[3] in Committee that in the case of a new business there would be no standard of comparison, and these words were added at the Report stage.[4]

It is provided that in these cases " the Minister may, if he thinks just, allow those net profits or losses to be brought into account, or substitute for the average such an amount as the standard amount of profits as may be agreed upon with the owner of the establishment."

The Minister " may, if he thinks fit, *and shall, if the owner of the establishment so requires*, refer the matter to be determined by a referee or board of referees appointed or designated by him for the purpose, and the decision of the referee or board shall be conclusive for all purposes." The words in italics were added in Committee.[5]

(4) This Sub-section provides that the Minister " may make rules for carrying the provisions of this section into effect."

In Committee[6] Mr. Lloyd George moved to add the following words :—

" and these rules shall provide for due consideration being given in carrying out the provisions of this section as respects any establishment to any special circumstances such as increase of output, provision of new machinery or plant, alteration of capital or other matters which require special consideration in relation to the particular establishment."

---

[1] *Parliamentary Debates* (1915), *H. of C.,* LXXII., 2059.
[2] *Ibid.,* 2120.   [3] *Ibid.,* 2066.   [4] *Ibid.,* 2120.
[5] *Ibid.,* 2064.   [6] *Ibid.,* 2064.

This important addition became the basis for Rule 10 of the Munitions of War (Limitation of Profits) Rules, made under this Sub-section on 15 September, 1915. Rule 10 provides for allowances, in addition to the standard amount of profits, to be made in respect either of increased capital or of increased output.

The purpose of this addition was explained by Sir John Simon in Committee.[1] He gave two illustrations to show that a too rigid application of the main principle upon which the divisible profits of a controlled establishment were to be ascertained, might have the effect of discouraging efforts to increase output.

(a) Suppose two businesses, each of which before the War had an output represented by a turnover of £100,000 a year, and earned a profit of 10% on that turnover (£10,000). If one of these factories were controlled and threw itself into munitions production to the extent of doubling its shifts and incurring expenditure which might not be permanently remunerative, and thereby doubled its output and increased its turnover to £200,000, its divisible profits under the principal rule, being fixed with reference only to its past performances, would be £10,000 plus one-fifth, i.e. £12,000. Supposing that the other business remained uncontrolled and only increased its efforts to the extent of raising its turnover to £120,000, a profit of 10% would yield as much as would be allowed to the controlled factory. It was evident that some adjustment was needed to avoid penalising the establishment which made the greater effort.

(b) The second case was the business which had made no profit, or only a very small profit, before the War. If that became a controlled establishment and its capital began to make a large return, it would not be fair to allow no profit.

Sir John Simon announced that such matters would be referred to a small, impartial Committee of Referees under the chairmanship of Sir Henry Babington Smith.

V. Provisions for the Supply and Movement of Labour.

Three important Sections (6, 7, and 10) of the Act may be considered together, being all concerned with control over the supply and movement of labour. They represent all that was left standing of a much larger scheme, and lie nearer to the central purpose of the measure than other more prominent features. The Act is to be understood as having been designed to go as far in the direction of industrial compulsion as the Trade Unions and their members could be persuaded to move. The history of these parts of it can best be approached by starting from the ideal extreme of compulsory service. It will be seen how, as the preliminary negotiations went forward, one after another of the more unpopular features of this ideal were abandoned, until the Bill finally came before the House as a measure agreed with the Trade Union leaders.

---

[1] *Parliamentary Debates* (1915), *H. of C.*, LXXII., 2015.

In some circles, compulsory military service was at this time put forward as a short and sufficient remedy for all the labour difficulties that hindered the production of war material. Under a Military Service Act the Government would have been armed with powers, at least in theory, to allocate man-power to the Army and to the factories, to distribute labour among the various classes of work, and to enforce discipline by military methods ; though conscription by itself would not have provided an administrative organisation capable of handling the whole problem on a comprehensive plan.

The Liberal Government which held office until the end of May was known to be averse from compulsory military service. On 20 April, Mr. Lloyd George, in reply to a question in the House, said : " The Government are not of opinion that there is any ground for thinking that the War would be more successfully prosecuted by means of conscription " ; and added that the Secretary of State for War was " very gratified with the response which has been made to the appeal to the country for voluntary enlistment."[1] The advocates of conscription at this time could not, in fact, point to any deficiency of numbers. It was notorious that tens of thousands of men had been recruited, whom it was impossible to equip even with Service rifles and bayonets. The complaint was rather that the young unmarried men were not coming forward. But it was believed, not without reason, by the Labour world that conscription was really desired, not to secure any " equality of sacrifice," but as a means to industrial compulsion.

This motive was indeed avowed by some supporters of the proposal. Sir F. Banbury, criticising the Amending Bill for the control of the liquor trade, said on 10 May :—" Supposing that the Government were to bring in conscription, it would be perfectly open to them to say, if a man were losing time : ' You will have to join the Forces.' . . . I would also remind the Chancellor of the Exchequer of what the French Government did in the railway struggle some years ago. Having conscription, they embodied the men and ordered them to do certain work."[2]   Sir F. Banbury, at a later stage, moved for a new Clause in the same Bill embodying his suggestion :—

> " It shall be lawful to enlist men compulsorily for any work that may be required for the defence of the Realm and to bring such men under military discipline."[3]

Shortly before the reconstruction of the Cabinet, the milder suggestion of a National Service Register came to the front. This was recommended, for instance, on 19 May, by General Sir Ivor Herbert, who explained that he had " generally been in opposition to those who represent the views of what we call the National Service League." He considered that the object of such a Register would be " to bring home to every man and into every home that there is work of some

---

[1] *Parliamentary Debates* (1915), *H. of C.*, LXXI., 173.
[2] *Ibid.*, 1387.   [3] *Ibid.*, 1575.

sort for every man to do, whether it is military service or whether it is not."[1]

With the formation of the Coalition Government, it was commonly supposed that the partisans of conscription had received an accession of strength. This impression appeared to be strikingly confirmed by the speech delivered by Mr. Lloyd George at Manchester on 3 June, the day on which the Ministry of Munitions Bill was introduced. After referring to the French system of organisation, Mr. Lloyd George dwelt on the need for equality of sacrifice. It was not fair that one employer should give all his machinery, another do nothing to help. The Defence of the Realm Act provided a means for jogging the laggards. He then touched upon the question of compulsion for labour.

" To introduce compulsion as an important element in organising the nation's resources of skilled industry and trade does not necessarily mean conscription in the ordinary sense of the term. Conscription means raising by compulsory methods armies to fight Britain's battles abroad. . . . If the necessity arose, I am certain no man of any party would protest. But pray do not talk about it as if it were anti-democratic. We won and saved our liberties in this land on more than one occasion by compulsory service." France and America had done the same. But it would be a mistake to resort to it unless it were absolutely necessary. He would, however, say to those who wished to dismiss conscription : " You are not getting rid at all of the necessity for the aid which compulsion would be in mobilising the industry and strength of this country." Compulsory powers had already been taken to mobilise employers' workshops and machinery, to save time that would otherwise be lost in persuasion.

For labour two things were essential : to increase the mobility of labour, and to secure greater subordination to the direction and control of the State. In France, owing to National Service laws, all labour was at the disposal of the State. Labour could be moved where it was wanted. Our voluntary army had taken ten months to enlist : we could not afford another ten months to enlist an industrial army. Men who were wanted at home had enlisted. We needed compulsion to prevent this. In the Army there were no Trade Union restrictions.

He added later that workmen on Government work should be protected by a badge or uniform, and that release from the Colours would be much easier if we had conscription as it existed in France.

This speech gave rise to a question in the House on 7 June[2] : " Whether the statements made by the Minister of Munitions at Manchester indicate that it is the intention of the Government to introduce a system of compulsory military service or of compulsory labour." The Prime Minister replied that the response to the latest appeal for recruits had been satisfactory, and that an announcement of the Government's policy would be made shortly.

---

[1] *Parliamentary Debates* (1915), *H. of C.*, LXXI., 2397.
[2] *Parliamentary Debates* (1915), *H. of C.*, LXXII., 81.

Two days later, in the House of Lords debate on the Ministry of Munitions Bill,[1] most of the unofficial speakers argued in favour of compulsion, whether military or industrial or both. Lord Joicey supported conscription. Lord St. Davids, who warmly defended workmen in general against the current charges of idleness, forecasted that it would nevertheless be necessary to " requisition labour by force." Earl Stanhope said : " It does appear to us that men who refuse to work should be made to fight. The man who refuses to do his duty in the workshop should be sent to the Front." Lord Stalbridge considered that the Minister of Munitions would have a very difficult task in organising the men in the workshops " unless he can have them under some discipline and say that they have to work so many hours a day." Lord Curzon, who was in charge of the Bill, recognised certain echoes of earlier speeches of his own, but declined to follow their Lordships on to this ground.

It is interesting to note that none of the speakers showed any consciousness of one principal ground of the workman's objection to conscription for industrial purposes. This was that the employers were still free to make unlimited profits, and it was well known that in some quarters these profits were enormous. Mr. Wilkie put the point clearly in the debate on the Second Reading in the House of Commons :—

" Our difficulty with our workmen is this : ' I am quite willing to do the behest of the Government, volunteering for war work or anything else, going to the front and sacrificing my life ; but I am not going to do it to allow a fellow-citizen to make a profit out of my sacrifice.' "[2]

The most that the Government was even pledged to do was to limit the profits of the " most important " engineering and ship-building firms, which in practice meant some forty firms on the War Office and Admiralty lists ; and, when the above-mentioned speeches were delivered, even this had not been done. Labour regarded the whole propaganda with inveterate suspicion, as aiming at striking every weapon out of the workman's hands, while no actual measures had yet been taken to control profits and prices.[3] The atmosphere so created was not favourable to the success of the Munitions of War Bill which, on the one hand, made no provision for limiting every sort of excessive war profits, and, on the other, restricted the only means by which workpeople can at any time protect their standard of living.

---

[1] *Parliamentary Debates* (1915), *H. of L.*, XIX., 25 ff.

[2] *Parliamentary Debates* (1915), *H. of C.*, LXXII., 1586.

[3] At the Minister's conference with Trade Union Delegates on 16 June, one speaker said : " Can we have any declaration from the Government or from you of the policy in regard to conscription ? Or will it be possible for you to take some advantage of the Trade Unions having given up this power (of striking) which they have threatened several times to use against conscription and to introduce conscription, knowing that we had given away this weapon ? " In reply Mr. Lloyd George said that he could see no necessity for military conscription so long as tens of thousands of recruits were still unarmed. " As far as I can see, there is no immediate danger of conscription, and I shall be very surprised if we do not get through without it." (HIST. REC./R/300/5, p. 34).

VI. Section 6. War Munition Volunteers.

Section 6 provides that—

" (1) If any workman, in accordance with arrangements made by the Minister of Munitions with or on behalf of trade unions, enters into an undertaking with the Minister of Munitions that he will work at any controlled establishment to which he may be assigned by the Minister, and be subject to the penalty imposed by this Act if he acts in contravention of or fails to comply with the undertaking, that workman shall, if he acts in contravention of or fails to comply with his undertaking, be guilty of an offence under this Act."

The offence is punishable, under Section 14, with a fine not exceeding £3, recoverable before a Munitions Tribunal of the second class, as instituted by Section 15.

Sub-section (2) makes it an offence for an employer to dissuade a workman from entering into such an undertaking or seek to retain him in his own employment.

This purely voluntary scheme was the outcome of negotiations carried on with the Trade Unions in the first three weeks of June. In order to appreciate how widely it differed from what was projected at the outset, it is only necessary to compare it with the first sketch of the Bill drawn up at the Board of Trade on 1 June.[1] The proposal to establish some sort of military organisation and discipline for workmen is there put forward in two forms.

(1) It is suggested that all armament and shipbuilding establishments whose war profits were limited should be " mobilised." Certain provisions of military law (for discipline, etc.) should be applied. In each establishment there was to be a military commandant. After seven days' notice, every man should be compulsorily enrolled. The men were to wear uniform, and receive a medal for good service and a war bonus.

(2) All other skilled workmen in engineering and shipbuilding, who were willing to go anywhere and accept this discipline, were to be voluntarily enlisted and to undertake to come when they should be called up. They were to receive a subsistence allowance of 17s. 6d. a week if they were removed to a distance from their homes, and perhaps to wear a badge, but not uniform. It was proposed that they should be called up only if they were engaged on private work.

Under the first head, various proposals were drafted for empowering the commandant to declare all persons employed in the establishment to be subject to military law, and otherwise for forming an industrial army serving under conditions more or less similar to those prevailing in the army in the field.

---

[1] *Heads of Labour Policy.* HIST. REC./R/300/38.

Mr. I. H. Mitchell, in a memorandum[1] recommending the idea of national service, wrote as follows : " Every man up to the age of thirty (the age could be extended as found necessary) should be required to register himself at, say, the Labour Exchange, so that whatever type of men were needed, in whatever numbers, whether for the field, the workshop, or the sea, they could be called upon at once under military conditions to perform what was required of them. Under this system I see no reason why thousands of young men now serving, but not required at the front, could not return to their work, put in some time each week at drill and firing and be ready to take the field immediately they were required.

" Under this system the mechanics required for quick transfer from place to place could be at once drafted under military conditions. The system would avoid the worst features of conscription, as those registered would not know whether they were wanted for civil duty in a workshop or military duty in the field, until they were actually called on. It would not interfere, and might be expressly explained as not interfering, with the present voluntary military method, which would go on as usual. If the voluntary method proves sufficient, all is well ; if not, the men required would be there ready, and, in any case, the mechanics required for transfer would be obtainable at once."

The effect of Mr. Lloyd George's Manchester speech on 3 June, of the House of Lords debate already mentioned, and of the campaign for conscription carried on in certain middle-class newspapers, was such that it soon became clear that proposals of this kind would meet with strong opposition. The following paragraph from the June Report of the Executive Council of the Amalgamated Society of Engineers may be taken as a typical expression of the attitude of Labour :—

" There is a feeling abroad that the underlying objective of the Coalition is to force military conscription on the country. The numerous organs of the Northcliffe Press are carrying on a vigorous agitation in favour of compulsory military service, and some folks are actively advocating industrial conscription. However, the Government has made no pronouncement, therefore we are unable to say what their views are on the question. Compulsory Service, military or industrial, is alien to the spirit and tradition of the British people, and any attempt to force this pernicious system on the nation would create serious difficulties for the Government."

In consequence of this state of feeling, the notion of enforcing military law upon the compulsorily enlisted employees of " mobilised " establishments was dropped. It remained to try a scheme of the second type—a Munitions Corps, enrolled under a voluntary agreement. The model followed was not the Liverpool Dockers Battalion, which was organised as a military unit and subject to the Army Act, but

---

[1] HIST. REC./R/180/37.

rather the " Flying Squads " at Newcastle and Glasgow,[1] with the addition of commandants wielding disciplinary powers.

In his *Preliminary Note on Labour Policy* (4 June), Sir H. Llewellyn Smith suggested that a " King's Munition Corps " should be established under the Act, whose members would take one of two pledges : either (*a*) to work anywhere within a certain radius, or (*b*) to work anywhere, with a subsistence allowance if they were required to remove to a distance. The second class would form a special Flying Corps, perhaps with a uniform. The whole Corps would have a badge or brassard. The Corps might be raised by the Minister on a territorial basis. The members would be pledged to obey the commandant, and to do any work of which they were capable for the current rates, probably with a safeguard for their existing standard: The local commandants should, preferably but not necessarily, be officers of naval or military rank. They should be attached to districts, or even to great armament establishments, not as superseding the business management, but as autocratic referees, by whom cases of bad time-keeping, disobedience, drink, and other disciplinary offences, would be summarily dealt with. It was questioned whether the commandants should have any direct power of imprisonment for disciplinary offences against the employer ; but it was to be an offence punishable by imprisonment to disobey the commandant's orders.

In the first Draft of the Bill (12 June), Section 7 (1) empowered the Minister to " arrange for the constitution of a King's Munition Corps by means of voluntary enrolment [through the agency of trades unions or otherwise] of persons undertaking to comply with the rules of the corps."

(2) The Minister might make rules for the regulation of the corps and the conditions of service, and in particular—

(*a*) for placing the corps and any divisions thereof under the control of munitions officers and officers subordinate to them ;

(*b*) for securing obedience to such officers and defining their powers and duties ;

(*c*) for the reference of any question of non-compliance with the rules to the munitions officer in command, and for the procedure to be followed ;

(*d*) for the wearing of a badge or uniform ;

(*e*) for the dismissal of any member by the munitions officer in command, with or without appeal.

(3) The work of the corps and its members was to be available for munitions supply either in controlled establishments or, subject to conditions determined by the Minister, in other establishments.

(4) The members of the corps might be billeted like soldiers.

---

[1] See Part III., Chap. III.

Such were the schemes in contemplation when negotiations were opened with the Trade Union leaders. The Minutes of the National Advisory Committee for 9 June record that, in consequence of certain representations which had been made to the Committee on the previous day by the Minister of Munitions, the object of which was vastly to increase the output of munitions of war, it was decided to convene a meeting of representatives of the trades who had attended the Treasury Conference of 17-19 March, with a view to reaching an agreement resulting in such a reorganisation of labour as would ensure a maximum output. The Committee drew up and submitted to the Minister a scheme to be handed to the delegates at the meeting.

The Committee's Memorandum[1] stated that the serious situation of the British and Russian Armies in consequence of shortage of munitions, as laid before them by Mr. Lloyd George on 8 June, demanded that all the resources of labour should be brought into play. The Trade Unions were responsible to the country for helping to secure a sufficient increase of output ; and the Government was responsible to the Unions and to the workers for safeguarding their established position and their interests by controlling profits and the prices of the necessaries of life.

There was no time either for a scheme of national registration, or for the extensive training of unskilled or semi-skilled workpeople. It must therefore be considered how the available resources could be effectively applied " without having to resort to any form of compulsion, even as a temporary expedient. The application of any form of compulsion to workmen concerned in the manufacture of munitions of war, except as a last and unavoidable resource, would be so disturbing as to defeat the object in view."

Accordingly, in order to give the fullest trial to a voluntary system of transfer of workmen from one shop or locality to another, the Committee suggested :—

(1) That the Minister should state the kind of munitions required, the area where they could most readily be manufactured, and the class and number of men necessary ;

(2) That in those areas the required workmen at present on private work should be invited to volunteer for service in controlled establishments ;

(3) That a list of volunteers should be submitted to their present employers, and to the Trade Unions, who should report to the local Munitions Committees as to the suitability of the workmen for the class of work proposed ;

(4) That the lists should be closed within seven days of the issue of the invitation.

It was provided, further, that rules for transference (subsistence allowance, etc.) similar to the Newcastle rules should be applied.

---

[1] *Acceleration of Supply of Munitions ; the Organisation of Labour.* HIST. REC./R/221.1/6. See Appendix II.

The Trade Unions were to assure the Government that any of their members selected by any local Munitions Committee for war work should be at once placed at the Government's disposal, at the rates of wages and allowances decided upon by that Committee. Such men were to continue at work at the factory or yard appointed by Government, and not to change their employment without the local Committee's consent. Men who refused to abide by these conditions were to be dealt with on lines agreed to by the local Committee.

Skilled workmen might be brought back from the Colours and less skilled and female labour used on minor operations in accordance with the Treasury Agreement, which was to be strictly observed.

The meeting of Trade Union Delegates was held on 10 June at the Offices of the Board of Trade. Mr. Lloyd George, who was accompanied by Mr. Arthur Henderson and Sir H. Llewellyn Smith, addressed the meeting.

He explained the need for a greatly increased quantity of high explosive shell for attacking trenches. The deficiency was attributable to two causes.

First, orders had not been spread widely enough. That was now to be remedied by taking every engineering shop that was engaged on unnecessary private work. The powers conferred on the Minister would be used to bring compulsion to bear on employers. But this would not meet the needs of the next few months, during which a delay must occur in turning over to the new work.

The second difficulty concerned labour. Unskilled labour would not suffice. More skilled men must be found and restrictions must be suspended. Employers were hindering by bringing pressure, which it was very hard to detect, on their skilled men not to leave their employment. To obtain the necessary labour, one course was to rely on voluntary methods, but he wanted some guarantee from the Unions. He wished to be able to requisition from a Union (say) the 75 mill-wrights who were then wanted to set up some machinery at the Birmingham Small Arms Factory. It was " not a question of universal conscription or of universal compulsory labour." The Government would prefer to use the Trade Union machinery ; only they wanted to be sure that a requisition would be honoured. He suggested that the requisition should be backed by an order compelling the recalcitrant employer to release men who were needed.

Another thing that must be stopped was the stealing of labour.

There was a considerable amount of bad time-keeping. The Trade Union leaders had exhausted every art of persuasion, but had not been able to remedy it. He did not propose that the employers should have power to deal with bad time-keeping. " It would be very much better for the men themselves that you should have somebody sitting with representatives of the Trade Unions, with powers to deal with people who habitually absent themselves from their work. We would submit the names of those who would adjudicate on the cases, and you

I-4   D would nominate your own men to sit with them. It is not a question of martial law ; it is not a question of magistrates ; it is rather a question of setting up a tribunal, after we have put the names before you and heard what objection you have to them. They would be men in whom you would have confidence that they would deal fairly, and the representatives of the Trade Unions would sit with them as assessors."

Finally, it was proposed to prevent stoppages of work ; and he was going to put this to the employers on the following day.

After the Minister had retired, the National Advisory Committee's statement was put before the meeting. The following resolution was passed :—

"That we accept and endorse the scheme of the National Advisory Committee, and further agree to empower the Committee to accept such extension of the proposals contained in these suggestions as may be necessary to provide a full supply of the necessary munitions required for the speedy termination of the war."

An amendment to omit " and further " to the end, was rejected by 53 votes to 16 ; and the motion was carried with seven dissentients.

It was further proposed that the main provisions of any Bill to be introduced to give effect to the scheme and suggestions outlined in Mr. Lloyd George's speech should be the subject of a further conference.

On 14 June, the Executive Council of the Amalgamated Society of Engineers addressed a letter[1] to the Right Hon. Arthur Henderson, on the transference of workmen from civil to munition work. After referring to the conference with Mr. Lloyd George on 10 June, the letter continued :—

"The Executive Council of the Amalgamated Society of Engineers, representing 186,000 workmen, while accepting the memorandum of the National Advisory Committee on War Output submitted to the above-mentioned conference, place on record their entire opposition to any compulsory powers being adopted by the Government for the transference of workmen from commercial to munition work. The Executive Council further place on record their entire opposition to any system of fining as a result of loss of time, feeling sure that, so far as our members are concerned, they are working at the utmost extent of their powers.

"The Executive Council, having regard to the urgent demands of the nation and the consequent need for securing the utmost mobility of labour, are prepared to recommend their members to accept the following scheme :—

" 1. That members of the Amalgamated Society of

---

[1] A.S.E. *Monthly Journal and Report*, July, 1915, p. 9.

Engineers now employed on work other than that of munitions
of war shall be strongly recommended to offer themselves for
voluntary removal from civil to war work, provided—

(a) that their consent is first obtained ;

(b) that their rates of pay, if in excess of the standard of
the district to which they are transferred, shall in
every case be fully guaranteed ;

(c) that no member shall at any time receive less than
the standard rates of pay for the district to which
he is removed ;

(d) that all railway fares shall be guaranteed from Government sources ;

(e) that a subsistence allowance of 17s. 6d. per week shall
be paid to all men transferred to a district from which
they cannot daily return to their homes ;

(f) that in the event of the workmen being able to return
home each day, their travelling expenses shall be
guaranteed and time occupied in travelling be paid
for at least at the rate they are at the time receiving.

" 2. That the foregoing proposals shall operate for a
period of three months in each case ; all volunteers under this
scheme to have the right to renew the agreement for additional
periods of three months, should the needs of the nation still
require it.

" 3. Any person or persons who shall endeavour to
bring force to bear upon workmen to prevent them from volunteering or those who for family or other reasons cannot volunteer
under this scheme shall be immediately reported to the Local
Armaments Committee, whose duty it shall be to at once
forward the complaint to the Minister of Munitions'Department,
Whitehall.

" 4. The Minister of Munitions shall have power to deal
with any firm offending against clause 3."

At a meeting of the National Advisory Committee on 15 June
it was stated that the Minister of Munitions had requested that a
Delegate Meeting be held on the following day, to consider the draft
proposals upon which a Bill was to be based to increase the output
of war munitions by a system of transference of workmen, on the
basis of the speech he had delivered to the Trade Union representatives
on 10 June. The Societies represented at the Conference on that day
had been summoned. A memorandum containing the outline proposals
for legislation was considered by the Committee. The Committee
later interviewed Sir John Simon with regard to the form and
regulations to be used for the enrolment of volunteer workmen willing
to go from private contract to Government work.

The Conference with Trade Union Delegates was held at 6 White-hall Gardens on 16 June. With Mr. Lloyd George, Mr. Arthur Henderson, Sir H. Llewellyn Smith, Mr. William Brace, Mr. Beveridge, Mr. Wolff, and Mr. Davies were present.[1]

The Minister in his opening speech called attention to a Synopsis of the Bill, which was distributed to the meeting.[2] He pointed out that all the provisions applied only to controlled establishments, except those which referred to stoppage of work and arbitration, and the clause restricting the movement of men from one factory to another (Section 7).

He then propounded the scheme for Munition Volunteers. Copies of the schedule containing the form of undertaking to be given by the volunteer, and the conditions of employment, were in the hands of the meeting. It was explained that men already engaged on Government work would not be allowed to leave it under the scheme, though they might be skilled men doing unskilled work.

Mr. Lloyd George said that this scheme was " purely an attempt to avoid compulsion . . . It is an experiment, which, if it fails, will bring us face to face with compulsion. I think it would be a very good thing if the workmen knew that . . . If we cannot get workmen . . . then there is only one way of doing it, and that is by laying it down as a principle that every man during the War must render the service the State thinks he can render. But we will try this experiment first."

After a long discussion, the Minister retired, and the meeting considered the memoranda submitted.

A motion that the prohibition of strikes and lock-outs should apply only to munitions manufacture, was defeated by 54 votes to 16 ; and it was resolved, with 11 dissentients, that the prohibition should apply to all work and all trades during the present crisis.

It was agreed that the conditions for munitions work and private work should be identical. A proposal that restrictions should be relaxed on munitions work only was defeated.

The National Advisory Committee's proposal that all disputes should be dealt with under clause (2) of the Treasury Agreement was accepted. It was also agreed that arbitration under any of the three alternative methods should be speedy and compulsory.

The National Advisory Committee was empowered to carry through certain suggested amendments and additions to the Munitions of War Bill.

The outcome of these negotiations was the disappearance from the Bill of every feature suggestive of compulsion or of military

---

[1] Report in HIST. REC./R/300/5.   [2] HIST. REC./R/221.1/6.

organisation and authority in connection with the Munition Volunteers.[1] The Section was reduced to a provision binding the workman who volunteered to work in a controlled establishment, to keep his undertaking, and prohibiting employers from hindering volunteering.

The Volunteer scheme was introduced in the first instance as a temporary measure. The week beginning 24 June was set apart for the enrolment. It was understood that, if at the end of that time enough labour had not been obtained, the Minister would be free to propose other methods, including possibly industrial conscription. To this extent the scheme was analogous to the Derby scheme of enlistment as an alternative to military conscription. In fact, however, although the full numbers were not forthcoming in the stipulated time, it was not found possible to resort to compulsion.

In introducing the Bill on 23 June, Mr. Lloyd George[2] said that in the course of frank discussion with the Trade Unions he had been " bound to point out that, if there were an inadequate supply of labour for the purpose of turning out the munitions which are necessary for the safety of the country, compulsion would be inevitable." The Unions had said that, if in seven days they could not get the men, they would admit that their case was considerably weakened. If any members of the House were opposed to compulsion, the best service they could do to voluntaryism would be to make this army a success. " If we succeed by these means, ... then the need for industrial compulsion will to that extent have been taken away."

At a later stage of the debate, the Minister, in reply to a speech made by Mr. J. A. Pease, said : " I certainly had not in my mind anything of the nature of a threat, but I am bound at the outset to say that if we cannot, by voluntary means, get the labour which is essential to the success of this country in a War upon which its life depends, we must use, as the ultimate resort, the means which every State has at its command to save its life."

These expressions appear to have revived some of the apprehensions felt by the Labour leaders. A deputation of the General Federation of Trade Unions, consisting of Messrs. O'Grady, Bell, Gwynne and Short, waited on the National Advisory Committee on 24 June. Mr. O'Grady stated that the impression prevailed that if, after seven days, during which Munitions Volunteers were called upon to enrol, the required number had not been obtained, industrial compulsion would be resorted to. The words used by Mr. Lloyd George in introducing the Bill seemed to justify this opinion, though the terms of the Bill itself did not.

Mr. Henderson pointed out that the Bill made no provision for compulsory service, which would require the assent of the Cabinet and fresh legislation.

It was decided that Mr. Henderson should draw up a statement for issue to the Press, to make this point clear and also the salient

---

[1] Including the provision for compulsory billeting. Mr. Lloyd George pointed out on 16 June that this would involve putting the men billeted under discipline.

[2] *Parliamentary Debates* (1915), *H. of C.*, LXXII., 1201.

features of the circular drawn up by the National Advisory Committee and submitted to the Delegates' meeting on 16 June. The manifesto appeared in the Press on 28 June. It was endorsed by the Parliamentary Committee of the Trade Union Congress, and the General Federation of Trade Unions.[1]

In the Second Reading debate, the Bill was supported by the leading members of the Labour Party. No amendments to Section 6 were moved in Committee and the Clause went through without alteration.

VII. Section 7. Leaving Certificates.

Section 7 (1) reads as follows :—

"A person shall not give employment to a workman, who has within the last previous six weeks or such other period as may be provided by Order of the Minister of Munitions as respects any class of establishment, been employed on or in connexion with munitions work in any establishment of a class to which the provisions of this section are applied by Order of the Minister of Munitions,[2] unless he holds a certificate from the employer by whom he was last so employed that he left work with the consent of his employer or a certificate from the munitions tribunal that the consent has been unreasonably withheld."

Sub-section (2) provides that a certificate may be granted by a munitions tribunal on complaint made by any workman or by his trade union representative that the employer's consent has been unreasonably withheld.

Sub-section (3) makes it an offence for any person to give employment in contravention of these provisions. The penalty under Section 14 (e) is a fine not exceeding £50.

This enactment was proposed as a means of checking the constant drifting of labour in the direction of higher wages—a tendency which not only interfered with regular work, but was likely to cause a general rise of wages. Cases occurred where men left skilled work to go to unskilled work on higher wages ; where men were drawn from permanent work of national value to temporary employment at higher rates ; and where men were finally lost to some industries by drifting into temporary employment, at the end of which they were taken for the Army.

One method of dealing with this problem is to equalise the rates of wages. This does not seem to have been contemplated, and, indeed, the attempt to introduce uniformity into the endless variety

---

[1] *Parliamentary Debates* (1915), *H. of C.*, LXXII., 1514.

[2] It is an important point that the provisions of this section, though it stands in Part II. of the Act, are not applicable only to controlled establishments. It is doubtful whether this fact was fully understood by the House of Commons.

of wages paid would have been to attack the question on its most intricate side. The first expedient to be adopted had been the prohibition of enticement by Regulation 8 B (29 April, 1915), of which an account has already been given.[1] The difficulty of proving enticement had made this measure ineffective. The next expedient was to tie the workman to his work by requiring a leaving certificate.

The advisability of this method had been under consideration in April, when Regulation 8 B was being framed ; and the draft of this Regulation submitted to the Munitions of War Committee on 23 April[2] actually contained a provision for a leaving certificate. It prohibited the occupier of a factory or workshop engaged in munitions work or shipbuilding from inducing " any person employed in any such factory or workshop in the United Kingdom to leave his employment *without the previous written consent of his employer."* The words in italics were, however, cut out of the draft. It was argued that the condition requiring the employer's consent would be much resented and would be difficult to control.

When the draft was submitted to the Treasury Solicitor, he expressed the opinion that neither the provisions of the Defence of the Realm (Consolidation) Act, 1914, nor those of the Amending Act of March, 1915, extended to enable the Army Council to make the proposed Regulation. It was, however, decided to leave open the question whether it was *ultra vires,* and to proceed in the hope that the Order would have a moral effect.[3]

A defect of Regulation 8 B was that the prohibition was laid only on " the occupier of a factory or workshop, the business carried on in which consists wholly or mainly in engineering, shipbuilding, or the production of arms, ammunition or explosives, or of substances required for the production thereof." There was nothing to prevent employers whose business was of any other kind from enticing labour from one another or from munitions and shipbuilding work.[4] Section 7 does not formally supersede Regulation 8 B or amend this defect. It attacks the problem in another way. But it is not itself open to a corresponding objection, since it provides that no person whatsoever is to give employment to a workman who has left munitions work without a certificate.

Before the end of May, another draft Regulation, embodying the principle of leaving certificates, had been prepared by the Board of Trade. This draft, dated 22 May, read as follows :—

" 8 C (1) The occupier of a factory or workshop the business carried on in which consists, wholly or mainly, in

---

[1] See above, Part III., Chap. V.   [2] M.C. 6.

[3] Correspondence in E.27867 (Board of Trade).

[4] Thus, at the Minister's conference with the Manchester Board of Management on 10 August, 1915, the representative of a Lancashire firm doing munitions work complained that a company manufacturing concrete was attracting away his labourers by offering an extra 1d. an hour, and that Regulation 8 B gave no protection.

engineering, shipbuilding, or the production of arms, ammunition or explosives, or of substances required for the production thereof, shall not, nor shall any person on behalf of the occupier of such a factory or workshop, engage or employ any workman who is, or has within the last preceding six weeks been employed on work for any Government Department or otherwise serving war purposes, unless the person by whom he is or was so employed gives or has given his consent in writing to the workman leaving such employment, which consent shall not be unreasonably withheld.

" (2) Where a workman in an insured trade employed on work for a Government Department or otherwise serving war purposes leaves such employment without the consent of his employer, the employer, in lieu of returning his unemployment book to the workman in accordance with regulation 5 (1) of the Unemployment Regulations, shall send the book to the local office of the Unemployment Fund with a statement of the reasons why he withholds his consent to the workman leaving his employment.

" (3) Any question between a workman and an employer as to whether the consent of the employer to the workman leaving his employment is unreasonably withheld under this regulation shall be determined, in accordance with rules made by the Board of Trade, by the authorities constituted to deal with questions in connection with claims for unemployment benefit under Part II. of the National Insurance Act, 1911.

" (4) If any person contravenes any of the provisions of this regulation he shall be guilty of an offence against these regulations."

The draft Order containing this regulation was never issued. It was decided to incorporate the required provision in the Act.

In introducing the Bill, the Minister referred to this Section in the following terms[1] :—

" The third thing is the prevention of the practice which has done more to destroy discipline in the yards than almost anything—that is the practice of employers in pilfering each other's men.   It is absolutely impossible to obtain any discipline or control over men, if a man who may be either slack or disobedient to a reasonable order is able to walk out at the moment, go to the works which are only five or ten minutes off, and be welcomed with open arms without any questions being asked. That must be stopped.   It is a practice for which the employers are responsible far more than the men."

This passage reveals that the purpose behind this enactment was really different from that of Regulation 8 B.   The original complaint

---

[1] *Parliamentary Debates* 1915), *H. of C.*, LXXII., 1199.

had come from employers whose men were being enticed to Admiralty or munitions work, especially by the large armament firms, to the prejudice of other Government work.[1] It was a question of the distribution of the available labour supply. In Section 7 the method is d fferent : " discipline "—or rather the retention of labour where its services were most needed—is to be secured by taking away the workman's normal freedom to leave his employer on any ground that seems to him sufficient, without having to prove its sufficiency before a tribunal. This is a totally different matter from the pilfering by employers of one another's men by the offer of higher wages—a practice which can correc.ly be described as one for which employers, rather than workmen, are responsible. Section 7 is only in form a prohibition laid upon employers. In substance it limits, not the employer's freedom, but he workmen's, and it actually invests the employer with new and irresponsible powers.

On the Second Reading, Mr. Hodge[2] said that the Labour Party thought it unfair that, while the workman could not leave his employment without a certificate, the employer was left free to dismiss him. They considered that there ought to be more equality of treatment ; and objections had also been raised to the period being as long as six weeks.

Mr. Pringle[3] maintained that Section 7 virtually extinguished the market for free labour. It amounted to this, " that there is no competition for labour, the only commodity which the worker has to sell, whereas there is open competition for every commodity which he has to buy." He claimed that, before the representatives of the workmen consented to these sacrifices, they were entitled to a Parliamentary pledge from the Government that there should be tribunals for fixing rents, and some means of regulating the prices of commodities.

In order to give effect to the objections felt by the Labour Party to inequality of treatment, Mr. Hodge[4] moved in Committee the following amendment :—

" At the end of Sub-section (2), to add :—

" Any person who is employed working in or about a controlled establishment on munitions work shall not discharge or suspend any such workman without the previous consent of the Munitions Tribunal."

Mr. Lloyd George opposed the amendment on the ground that it would subvert discipline, and that, labour being so scarce, men were not likely to be dismissed unless the case were overwhelming. The amendment was withdrawn.

The actual working of the measure, however, proved that the Labour Party were not wrong in anticipating that trouble would arise.

---

[1] See Part II., Chap I., Section VI.
[2] *Parliamentary Debates* (1915), *H. of C.*, LXXII., 1519.
[3] *Ibid.*, 1600, 1601.   [4] *Ibid.*, 2071.

It was not long before complaints were heard that the workman could not leave his employment on grounds judged to be insufficient by his employer or by a tribunal, on pain of six weeks' unemployment ; but a manager or foreman could dismiss a man on grounds which seemed frivolous or unfair to the man or to his fellows. The onus lay on the man to convince a tribunal that the employer was unreasonable. Even if he succeeded in doing so, the employer was liable to no penalty, however unreasonable his refusal of a certificate might have been,[1] while the man was unjustly punished by being debarred from obtaining other employment during the interval before his claim was vindicated. The natural remedy of a strike was forbidden by the Act. The total effect was to arm employers, managers, and foremen with arbitrary powers that were certain to be abused in unscrupulous hands.

The reality of such abuses was acknowledged by the Government when it provided safeguards against them in the Amending Act of 1916. Although by that time Section 7 had acquired in certain quarters an unpopularity which no concessions could eradicate, these amendments went far to remove the reasonable grounds of complaint. The essential principle of the leaving certificate might be justified by the argument that, in the interests of rapid and regular production, it was necessary to impose some check on the drifting of labour, and that this could not be done without a serious curtailment of normal liberty. The defenders of Section 7 might urge that, in resenting restriction upon his freedom of movement, the workman was simply rebelling against an inevitable consequence of war conditions. The final repeal of the Section left the problem unsolved, and it was found necessary to aim at securing the same results by methods less direct and no more popular.

VIII. Section 10. Restriction of Employment.

Section 7, as has been seen, was designed to prevent workmen from leaving munitions work without their employers' consent. Section 10 is a complementary provision intended to compel workmen to leave private work without either their employers' or their own consent. It is a further step in the direction of the compulsory diversion of labour from commercial to Government work,[2] though the powers obtained have not actually been used for that purpose.

This Section amends the Defence of the Realm (Amendment)

---

[1] An amendment empowering a Munitions Tribunal, when it granted a certificate, to direct the employer to pay compensation to the workman, was moved by Mr. King. Mr. Lloyd George opposed it on the ground that the workman would be still employed, since his appeal was against a refusal to let him leave his employment. The amendment was withdrawn. (*Parliamentary Debates* (1915), *H. of C.*, LXXII., 2071.)

[2] It was reported in June that in the engineering trade 233,000, or 43% of the persons occupied, were still engaged on private work. (Memorandum on *The position leading up to the introduction of the Bill*, HIST. REC./R/221.1/6.)

No. 2 Act (March, 1915), Section 1 (1) (*d*), by adding the words in italics.[1]   It empowers the Admiralty and the Army Council

> " (*d*) to regulate or restrict the carrying on of any work in any factory, workshop, *or other premises, or the engagement or employment of any workman or all or any classes of workmen therein*, or to remove the plant therefrom with a view to *maintaining or* increasing the production of munitions in other factories, workshops, *or premises, or to regulate and control the supply of metals and material that may be required for any articles for use in war*."

The effect of the addition in the earlier part of this paragraph was to restore its provisions to very nearly the same form as they had taken in the first draft of the Amending Act of March.[2] The paragraph had originally read as follows :—

> " (*d*) to *prohibit* or restrict *the employment* in any factory or workshop *of any workman or class of workman whose services may be required* for the production of war material."

These words had been struck out before the Bill was introduced, because it was feared that the explicit avowal of an intention to extinguish employment on commercial work in this way would be resented by Labour. The substitution of the words, " the carrying on of work," disguised this intention, and, incidentally, so weakened the powers obtained that the prohibition of enticement under Regulation 8 B proved to be *ultra vires*. Section 10 brings that regulation *intra vires ;* but its main purpose was to facilitate the compulsory displacement of labour, so as to make it available for munitions work.

An application for powers of compulsory transfer had been made on 1 May by Captain Power, the Admiralty representative on the North East Coast Armaments Committee. In a letter to the Admiralty he wrote :—" The Prime Minister told me the other day[3] that the Admiralty have full authority to use, under the Defence of the Realm Act, compulsion in withdrawing men from private work for Government work, and said that, as Admiralty representative, I had that authority also. I shall be glad to hear from you whether the exercise of such authority on my part would be approved by their Lordships in case such a course becomes necessary. The difficulties of getting labour for our urgent work without using some form of compulsion are very great, and until such compulsion is put in force I see no prospect of getting any adequate increase. One plan that suggests itself to us is to order all or any firms to discharge forthwith, say, 25 per cent. of the men employed on private work, who would then be mobilised by their Trade Union delegates, and drafted in accordance with the order of the Committee."

The Admiralty representatives on the Munitions of War Committee raised this question at its fourth meeting. In a memorandum

---

[1] A few verbal changes of no substantial importance are also made.

[2] See Part II., Chap. III., Section II.

[3] Presumably 20 April, the date of the Prime Minister's visit to Newcastle.

submitted to the Committee on that occasion, the opinion is expressed that the powers under the Act and the corresponding Regulation 8 A (b), " to regulate or restrict the carrying on of any work in any factory or workshop . . . . with a view to increasing the production of war material in other factories or workshops," appeared to cover an order to an employer to restrict part of his work by ceasing to employ a number of men. The men, however, could not be compelled to go to other work. It was suggested that a formal order, specifying the nature of the restriction, would be necessary. Possibly a threat to use the power might be preferable to an actual exercise of it.

The legal point was referred on 3 May to the Treasury Solicitor, who was asked to state an opinion on the following points[1] :—

" (1) Assuming that an order were made by the Army Council, could it direct the release of men without reference to the work on which they were engaged ?

" (2) If this is not possible, would it be necessary to make an individual order in each case ?

" (3) Assuming that an individual order would be necessary, would it be possible to avoid the great practical difficulties that this would involve, by attempting to arrive at an amicable arrangement with the firms, using as a lever the power given by the Regulation (8 A (b)) to close down factories altogether ? "

The Treasury Solicitor held (1) that, since war production in other factories could not be increased by mere restriction of work, but only by freeing labour or plant or possibly raw material, the Regulation must be taken as giving power to make an order for the reduction of labour in a factory, either by a certain percentage or by a certain number. Such an order should be addressed to each manufacturer concerned, and should specify both a date for compliance and the factories in such a way that they could be identified. (2) An individual order would, he thought, be necessary to the extent above indicated. He advised that strict legality should be observed. In the present case, the order might be in a general form, requiring, for instance, the reduction of employment of hands of a certain character by a certain percentage ; but the circumstances of firms might differ too much for this to be practicable.

It appears to have been considered advisable to strengthen paragraph (d) in such a way as to make it indisputably legal to prohibit the employment of any particular man in any particular shop, and so make him available for service elsewhere. No power, however, was taken to transfer the labour so displaced to munitions work.

This Section passed through the House of Commons without attracting much attention. The only amendment made was the addition of the final words, giving power to regulate and control the supply of metals and material.[2]

---

[1] The reference and the Treasury Solicitor's opinion were printed for the Committee. (M.C. 12.)

[2] *Parliamentary Debates* (1915), *H. of C.*, LXXII., 2074.

IX. Sections 14 and 15. Penalties and Munitions Tribunals.

Section 15 lays down the constitution and powers of Munitions Tribunals.

A Munitions Tribunal is to be constituted as and when occasion requires, and to consist of a person appointed by the Minister (or by the Admiralty for offences in docks declared to be controlled establishments), sitting with two or other even number of assessors, chosen in equal numbers from two panels constituted by the Minister, the one representing employers, the other workmen.

The purpose which lay behind this institution was explained by Mr. Lloyd George as follows[1] :—

"If you have a voluntary army of workers, there must be a means of enforcing contracts. It is no use having 20,000 or 30,000 men who say, ' We will go anywhere we are told,' if, when the time comes, they refuse and you cannot compel them. They volunteer to enter into this contract, but once they enter into it, it is a contract and it must be enforceable. . . . .

"The other point of the Bill is that we take power to establish discipline in the workshops. Here, again, we discussed this matter with the Trade Union representatives, and we are not going beyond the agreement we have entered into. They admit that, where men who voluntarily go into this army habitually absent themselves and make bad time when they know that the work is very urgent for the country, there ought to be some means of enforcing better time. It is proposed that there should be a Munitions Court set up with an employer and a Trade Union representative sitting upon it as assessors, and a president appointed by the Government. They will decide in these cases where a man has a reasonable excuse for absenting himself habitually, and they will have the power of inflicting a penalty." The Court was also to decide when a leaving certificate had been withheld unreasonably.

The history of the Bill shows that the principal function for which the Munitions Tribunal was designed was to check bad time-keeping. In ordinary circumstances, if a man keeps bad time, the employer has the simple remedy of dismissing him. Under war conditions, the extreme shortage of labour had made this impossible, since the man dismissed knew he could at once find work elsewhere. It was therefore considered necessary to strengthen the employer's position by instituting some system of " discipline."

A considerable body of evidence bearing on the extent of bad time-keeping had been collected in April in a White Paper.[2] The great bulk of this evidence referred to the shipping areas, and it was collected with a view to illustrating the influence of drink. Little more

---

[1] *Parliamentary Debates* (1915), H. of C., LXXII., 1202.

[2] *Report and Statistics of Bad Time kept in Shipbuilding, Munitions, and Transport Areas* (1 May, 1915).

than one page out of thirty dealt with armament works. Here it was stated that the reports received indicated that " much time was avoidably lost in certain works," but that " the great majority of the workmen were above reproach and their action was praiseworthy."

Reference has already been made to Mr. W. L. Hichens' Memorandum on this subject.[1] He stated that, on the whole, time-keeping was better than before the War, but not so good as it should be. Employers were asking too much, and getting too little. Men could not work overtime and on Saturday afternoons and Sundays continuously. Yet an employer who did not offer overtime, which carried higher rates of pay, risked losing his men. The men preferred to work for double pay on Sundays, and stay out some other day ; and many would only work till they had made enough money for the week. The result was that the hours worked were irregular generally, and in some trades inadequate. The irregularity threw out of gear the delicate machine of industrial organisation. If regular hours were worked, he believed that overtime would not be necessary, or indeed possible, save on exceptional occasions, while output would be greatly increased.

Mr. Hichens thought that the influence of drink had been over-rated. In his own experience there was less actual drunkenness than before the War, though there appeared to be a good deal of heavy drinking in some parts. He recommended that opportunities for drinking just before working hours should be universally removed by closing orders.

Mr. I. H. Mitchell, in a memorandum written at the beginning of June[2] stated that Government Arsenals and Dockyards were practically free from all the troubles that hampered private firms. " The restrictive rules are reduced to a minimum in Government shops[3] ; irregular attendance does not exist ; there is no drink problem among the mechanics ; strikes and lock-outs are almost unknown." He suggested that all these evils could be remedied by assimilating private armament works to Government establishments, beginning with the curtailment of profits.

When the Bill was drafted, the notion was to assimilate munition works not so much to the Arsenal as to the Army. Bad time-keeping was to be dealt with by a system of discipline resembling as closely as possible that which prevails in a military unit. This part of the Act took its colour from the ideal of industrial conscription.

In the original draft, the Minister was authorised to appoint Munitions Officers and assign to them such duties and districts as he might determine. Such officers were to be empowered to hold command in the proposed Munition Corps ; to issue orders to its members ; to take cognisance of questions referred to them of non-compliance with the rules of the corps ; to dismiss members of the

---

[1] See above, p. 8.   [2] HIST. REC./R/180/37.
[3] So far as Woolwich Arsenal is concerned, this statement perhaps needs qualification.

corps with or without appeal ; and to give or withhold consent to proposed changes of wages, etc., in a controlled establishment, or to require that such proposals should be submitted to a referee. Apart from the last-mentioned function, the authority explicitly assigned to the Munitions Officer was confined to the members of the corps, who might be only a portion of the employees in any establishment. As this first draft did not contain the Penalty Section, it is not clear what authority it was then intended should enforce compliance with the provisions of Part II., though penalties of a fine were attached to certain of these provisions. The fines would presumably have been recoverable in the ordinary courts of law.

The disappearance of the Munitions Officer followed upon the abandonment of the idea of a Munitions Corps. This entailed two changes made in the Bill as introduced.

In the first place, the penalties for offences under the Act were collected into one Section (Section 14 of the Act). These offences were of two classes :—

(1) (a) Contravention of, or failure to comply with, an 'award ;

(b) Contravention of the provision prohibiting lock-outs ;

(c) Contravention of the provision prohibiting strikes ;

(e) Contravention of, or failure to comply with, any other provision of the Act.

In each of these cases the penalty was a fine to be inflicted *on summary conviction*, and therefore recoverable in the ordinary courts.

(2) (d) Contravention of, or failure to comply with, any regulations in a controlled establishment or any undertaking given by a workman under Part II.

In this case the fine (not exceeding £3) was to be recoverable only before a Munitions Tribunal.

In the second place, the necessary tribunals were provided, to take the place of the Munitions Officer, who had now been eliminated. The tribunals were to take cognisance of the offences under (d), and to inflict fines (which might be deducted from wages), but not imprisonment. They could also hear complaints from workmen under Section 7 and grant leaving certificates. Thus, apart from leaving certificates, their functions were originally confined to enforcing the regulations in controlled establishments and workmen's undertakings under Part II. The figure for the maximum penalty under (d) was fixed at £3 because this was a usual figure for fines connected with matters of domestic discipline between a Trade Union and its members.[1]

On the Second Reading, Mr. Duke made an important speech dealing with the constitution and powers of the tribunals. He admitted that the proposed tribunals would be dignified and would carry weight throughout the country. But it did not follow that such a body would carry weight in a particular factory. He suggested

---

[1] *Parliamentary Debates* (1915), *H. of C.*, LXXII., 1550 (Sir John Simon).

that the confidence reposed by organised Labour in the Government and in Parliament might well be repaid " by enabling the men who are concerned in the class of cases to which reference has been made, to themselves nominate a tribunal to deal with matters of this kind." He thought that a domestic court consisting of workmen belonging to each factory might be able to remove many small causes of friction, which might otherwise ripen into a strike.[1]

At the Committee stage, Mr. Henderson[2] said that the Government desired to follow Mr. Duke's suggestions as far as possible, and to have all the offences enumerated in Section 14 dealt with by what Mr. Duke had called a " domestic court." Mr. Henderson accordingly moved a series of amendments. These left untouched the class of tribunal already provided for in the Bill, which was still to have jurisdiction over the offences under (d). The effect of the amendments was to add a new class of tribunals (afterwards called General Munitions Tribunals) which were to deal with all the offences under (a), (b), (c), and (e). These offences were thus removed from the cognisance of the ordinary Courts of Justice ; and all fines for offences under the Act now became recoverable only before a Munitions Tribunal of one or the other class.

Mr. Henderson explained that it was intended that the new (General) tribunals should be smaller than those of the other (Local) class ; and that where a General Tribunal had been set up, a Local Tribunal would not be required. There might be ten or a dozen of the former ; and perhaps sixty or seventy of the latter.

It will be observed that this change did not really give effect to Mr. Duke's proposal that the men of each factory should themselves nominate a tribunal of their fellow workmen, and that " where there is organised labour, the men who are going to pay penalties, if they have to pay them, shall be judged by their comrades, who shall be assessors." Whether such a plan would have worked well or ill is a question that cannot be answered since the experiment was not made. Under the Act, every tribunal consists of a person appointed by the Minister, sitting with assessors chosen by the Minister, from two panels constituted by the Minister. The amendments were, however, welcomed by the Labour Party as at least an improvement on the method of assigning the jurisdiction over these offences to the ordinary courts.

X. Minor Provisions of the Act.

The most important provisions of the Act have now been reviewed. It remains to record some minor enactments which have not yet been noticed.

SECTION 8 empowers the Minister to make rules with regard to the issue of badges, and to prohibit unauthorised badges.

The Section was introduced by Mr. Lloyd George at the Committee Stage.[3] He pointed out that the absence of a systematic

---

[1] *Parliamentary Debates* (1915), *H. of C.*, LXXII., 1520.
[2] *Ibid.*, 2077.   [3] *Ibid.*, 2088.

system of badging had been responsible for the loss to engineering production of many indispensable men ; and that unauthorised badges had been issued to persons who ought not to have been protected.

The intention was to issue badges only to men genuinely engaged on Government work.

SECTION 9 provides for the application of Part II. to Admiralty Docks.

The addition of this clause was made at the request of the Admiralty. No question arose as to the applicability of Part I., which could be made to apply to strikes and lock-outs in the docks, if necessity arose.

The possibility of including hands employed on ships hired by the Admiralty for transport service was also considered ; but difficulty was felt about defining the undertaking of which the profits were to be limited. Further, the clause suggesting alteration of wages was inapplicable, as it was proposed that all employment on these ships should be under an agreement lasting for the duration of the War and admitting of no change of wages.[1]

SECTION 11 requires the owner of any establishment to furnish information, if so required, as to

(1) The numbers and classes of persons employed ;
(2) The numbers and classes of machines ;
(3) The nature of the work on which workpeople or machines are engaged ;
(4) Any other matters about which the Minister might require to be informed.

SECTION 12, in the Bill as introduced, made it an offence

(1) For employers, owners, and workmen to make false statements, give false certificates, etc.

(2) To wear a badge in a manner calculated to deceive.

(2) was cut out in Committee.[2]

SECTION 13 provides for the payment of travelling and other expenses incurred by members of arbitration tribunals, munitions tribunals, referees, and officers required in connection with such tribunals. It was passed without alteration.

SECTION 16 empowers any company, association, or body of persons to carry on munitions work during the War, notwithstanding anything contained in any Act, order, or instrument, by or under which it is constituted or regulated.

The Section was introduced in Committee.[3] It was pointed out that some companies desirous of making munitions had been prevented by the fact that their objects did not include such work.

---

[1] HIST. REC./R/221.1/7.

[2] *Parliamentary Debates* (1915), *H. of C.*, LXXII., 2075.   [3] *Ibid.*, 2112.

E

SECTION 17 deals with procedure in regard to laying before Parliament rules made under the Act. It was added at the Committee stage.

SECTION 18 applies the Documentary Evidence Act, 1868, to the Ministry of Munitions.

SECTION 20 (1) gives the short title ; (2) provides that the Act shall have effect only so long as the Minister's office and the Ministry exist, except that Part 1 shall continue to apply for 12 months after the conclusion of the War to differences arising in relation to the carrying out of the Employers' Guarantee of Restitution (Schedule II.).[1]

NEW CLAUSE.—At the Committee stage a new clause was brought up :

" *Transfer of Powers.*—As soon after the date of the passing of this Act as may be found expedient all powers at present exercised by the Ordnance Department of the War Office in respect to the supply of munitions of war shall be transferred to the new Ministry of Munitions."[2]

This motion was made the occasion of an attack from the front Opposition bench on the Ordnance Department, the Master-General of the Ordnance, Lord Kitchener, and the War Office in general. Mr. Lloyd George deprecated these attacks, and stated that he preferred to build up the Department gradually, and then apply for powers to take over War Office functions. The clause was withdrawn.

XI. Conclusion.

The main provisions of the Munitions of War Act were shaped at private conferences with the Trade Union representatives. In the process of bargaining and compromise, the bolder features were softened or obliterated, the clauses became complex, and, without the closest study, it was not easy to measure the extent, or to forecast the operation, of the powers it conferred on the Government and the employer. Presented to the House of Commons as an agreed measure, the Bill escaped public criticism from the accredited guardians of the workman's interests. It was supported by the leaders of the Labour Party, and no other group of members had any motive for opposition.

Only a single day was given to the debate on the Second Reading. In spite of Sir John Simon's lucid exposition, it is evident that the House was unable to take in all the significance of the measure. Mistaken statements about the effect of its provisions were made even by Ministers, and passed without challenge. The only serious criticism came from two speakers : Mr. Snowden, who was afterwards rebuked by the Labour Party, and Mr. Pringle, who spoke at a late hour and was heard with impatience. Amendments of great importance were passed in Committee, some of which left flaws in the measure

---

[1] See above, p. 19.
[2] *Parliamentary Debates* (1915), *H. of C.*, LXXII., 2090.

such as could not have survived the scrutiny of any competent lawyer, if time had been allowed to consider their bearings.

The Bill passed through all stages in the House of Lords in two days, and, after a nugatory discussion in that chamber, became law on 2 July. Together with the Ministry of Munitions Act and the Order in Council defining the duties and powers of the Minister, the Act constituted the charter of the new Department.

This is neither the time nor the place to offer any general verdict on the policy embodied in a measure whose merits and defects are unhappily still involved in a cloud of controversy. It may, however, safely be described as a bold attempt to solve the problem of the control of labour, which must confront any Government waging war with the whole industrial resources of the country. The extent to which control could be carried at any given moment without exciting reasonable or factious opposition to a dangerous point, has throughout the War depended on numerous psychological factors which no Government could gauge with any certainty beforehand, and which in the event have constantly taken even well-informed observers by surprise. Control has sometimes been accepted with unexpected docility, sometimes resented with unexpected violence. That the inevitable sacrifice of private liberty to public interest must occasion many troubles in a country which entered the War profoundly attached to individual freedom, could easily have been foreseen by anyone who even dimly discerned how radical a readjustment of all English ideas would be entailed by the magnitude of the struggle. In a field where too rapid and sudden advances would have meant irremediable disaster, the Government had no alternative but to feel its way along the path of negotiation, bargaining, and timely concession. The spirit in which Ministers and Labour leaders co-operated weathered the critical points where a failure of tact or goodwill on either side might have shipwrecked the State. That the State has not been shipwrecked is in itself a strong answer to those critics of the Act and of the Labour department which administered it, who are disposed to magnify the troubles that attract public attention and to ignore the immense volume of work that has all the time been going forward without friction and without pause.

APPENDICES.

APPENDIX I.

Munitions of War Act, 1915.

[5 & 6 Geo. 5. Ch. 54.]

ARRANGEMENT OF SECTIONS.

An Act to make provision for furthering the efficient manufacture, transport, and supply of Munitions for the present War ; and for purposes incidental thereto.

[2nd July, 1915].

BE it enacted by the King's most Excellent Majesty, by and with the advice and consent of the Lords Spiritual and Temporal and Commons, in this present Parliament assembled, and by the authority of the same, as follows :—

PART I.

1.—(1) If any difference exists or is apprehended between any employer and persons employed, or between any two or more classes of persons employed, and the difference is one to which this Part of this Act applies, that difference, if not determined by the parties directly concerned or their representatives or under existing agreements, may be reported to the Board of Trade, by or on behalf of either party to the difference, and the decision of the Board of Trade as to whether a difference has been so reported to them or not, and as to the time at which a difference has been so reported, shall be conclusive for all purposes.

(2) The Board of Trade shall consider any difference so reported and take any steps which seem to them expedient to promote a settlement of the difference, and, in any case in which they think fit, may refer the matter for settlement either in accordance with the provision of the First Schedule to this Act or, if in their opinion suitable means for settlement already exist in pursuance of any agreement between employers and persons employed, for settlement in accordance with those means.

(3) Where a matter is referred under the last foregoing subsection for settlement otherwise than in accordance with the provisions of the First Schedule to this Act, and the settlement is in the opinion of the Board of Trade unduly delayed, the Board may annul the reference and substitute therefor a reference in accordance with the provisions of the said Schedule.

(4) The award on any such settlement shall be binding both on employers and employed and may be retrospective ; and if any employer, or person employed, thereafter acts in contravention of, or fails to comply with, the award, he shall be guilty of an offence under this Act.

2.—(1) An employer shall not declare, cause or take part in a lock-out, and a person employed shall not take part in a strike, in connexion with any difference to which this Part of this Act applies, unless the difference has been reported to the Board of Trade, and twenty-one days have elapsed since the date of the report, and the difference has not during that time been referred by the Board of Trade for settlement in accordance with this Act.

(2) If any person acts in contravention of this section, he shall be guilty of an offence under this Act.

3. The differences to which this Part of this Act applies are differences as to rates of wages, hours of work, or otherwise as to terms or conditions of or affecting employment on the manufacture or repair of arms, ammunition, ships, vehicles, aircraft, or any other articles required for use in war, or of the metals, machines, or tools required for that manufacture or repair (in this Act referred to as munitions work) ; and also any differences as to rates of wages, hours of work, or otherwise as to terms or conditions of or affecting employment on any other work of any description, if this Part of this Act is applied to such a difference by His Majesty by Proclamation on the ground that in the opinion of His Majesty the existence or continuance of the difference is directly or indirectly prejudicial to the manufacture, transport, or supply of Munitions of War.

This Part of this Act may be so applied to such a difference at any time, whether a lock-out or strike is in existence in connexion with the difference to which it is applied or not :

Provided that if in the case of any industry the Minister of Munitions is satisfied that effective means exist to secure the settlement without stoppage of any difference arising on work other than on munitions work, no proclamation shall be made under this section with respect to any such difference.

When this Part of this Act is applied to any difference concerning work other than munitions work the conditions of labour and the remuneration thereof prevailing before the difference arose shall be continued until the said difference is settled in accordance with the provisions of this Part of this Act.

PART II.

4. If the Minister of Munitions considers it expedient for the purpose of the successful prosecution of the war that any establishment in which munitions work is carried on should be subject to the special provisions as to limitation of employers' profits and control of persons employed and other matters contained in this section, he may make an order declaring that establishment to be a controlled establishment, and on such order being made the following provisions shall apply thereto :—

(1) Any excess of the net profits of the controlled establishment over the amount divisible under this Act, as ascertained in accordance with the provisions of this Act, shall be paid into the Exchequer.

(2) Any proposal for any change in the rate of wages, salary, or other emoluments of any class of persons employed in the establishment, or of any persons engaged in the management or the direction of the establishment (other than a change for giving effect to any Government conditions as to fair wages or to any agreement between the

owner of the establishment and the workmen which was made before the twenty-third day of June, nineteen hundred and fifteen), shall be submitted to the Minister of Munitions, who may withhold his consent within fourteen days of the date of the submission :

Provided that if the Minister of Munitions so directs, or if the Minister's consent is withheld and the persons proposing the change so require, the matter shall be referred for settlement in accordance with the provisions of the First Schedule to this Act, and the consent of the arbitration tribunal, if given, shall in that case have the same effect as the consent of the Minister of Munitions.

If the owner of the establishment or any contractor or sub-contractor employing labour therein makes any such change, or attempts to make any such change, without submitting the proposal for the change to the Minister of Munitions or when the consent of the Minister has been withheld, he shall be guilty of an offence under this Act.

(3) Any rule, practice, or custom not having the force of law which tends to restrict production or employment shall be suspended in the establishment, and if any person induces or attempts to induce any other person (whether any particular person or generally) to comply, or continue to comply, with such a rule, practice, or custom, that person shall be guilty of an offence under this Act.

If any question arises whether any rule, practice or custom is a rule, practice or custom which tends to restrict production or employment, that question shall be referred to the Board of Trade, and the Board of Trade shall either determine the question themselves or, if they think it expedient or either party requires it, refer the question for settlement in accordance with the provisions contained in the First Schedule to this Act. The decision of the Board of Trade or arbitration tribunal, as the case may be, shall be conclusive for all purposes.

(4) The owner of the establishment shall be deemed to have entered into an undertaking to carry out the provisions set out in the Second Schedule to this Act, and any owner or contractor or sub-contractor who breaks or attempts to break such an undertaking shall be guilty of an offence under this Act.

(5) The employer and every person employed in the establishment shall comply with any regulations made applicable to that establishment by the Minister of Munitions with respect to the general ordering of the work in the establishment with a view to attaining and maintaining a proper standard of efficiency and with respect to the due observance of the rules of the establishment.

If the employer or any person so employed acts in contravention of or fails to comply with any such regulation, that employer or person shall be guilty of an offence under this Act.

(6) The owners of an establishment shall have power, notwithstanding anything in any Act, Order, or deed under which they are governed, to do all things necessary for compliance with any provisions of this section, and any owner of an establishment shall comply with any reasonable requirements of the Minister of Munitions as to information or otherwise made for the purposes of this section, and, if he fails to do so, shall be guilty of an offence under this Act.

Where in any establishment munitions work is carried on in some part of the establishment but not in other parts, the Minister of Munitions may, if he considers that it is practicable to do so, treat any part of the establishment in which munitions work is not carried on as a separate establishment, and the provisions of this Act shall take effect accordingly.

5.—(1) The net profits of a controlled establishment shall be ascertained in accordance with the provisions of this section and rules made thereunder and the amount of profits divisible under this Act shall be taken to be an amount exceeding by one-fifth the standard amount of profits.

(2) The standard amount of profits for any period shall be taken to be the average of the amount of the net profits for the two financial years of the establishment completed next before the outbreak of the war or a proportionate part thereof.

(3) If in any case it appears or is represented to the Minister of Munitions that the net profits or losses of all or any other establishments belonging to the same owner should be brought into account, or that the average under this section affords or may afford an unfair standard of comparison or affords no standard of comparison, the Minister may, if he thinks just, allow those net profits or losses to be brought into account, or substitute for the average such an amount as the standard amount of profits as may be agreed upon with the owner of the establishment.

The Minister of Munitions may, if he thinks fit, and shall, if the owner of the establishment so requires, refer the matter to be determined by a referee or board of referees appointed or designated by him for the purpose, and the decision of the referee or board shall be conclusive on the matter for all purposes.

(4) The Minister of Munitions may make rules for carrying the provisions of this section into effect, and these rules shall provide for due consideration being given in carrying out the provisions of this section as respects any establishment to any special circumstances such as increase of output, provision of new machinery or plant, alteration of capital or other matters which require special consideration in relation to the particular establishment.

6.—(1) If any workman in accordance with arrangements made by the Minister of Munitions with or on behalf of trade unions enters into an undertaking with the Minister of Munitions that he will work at any controlled establishment to which he may be assigned by the Minister, and be subject to the penalty imposed by this Act if he acts in contravention of or fails to comply with the undertaking, that workman shall if he acts in contravention of or fails to comply with his undertaking be guilty of an offence under this Act.

(2) If any employer dissuades or attempts to dissuade a workman in his employment from entering into an undertaking under this section, or retains or offers to retain in his employment any workman who has entered into such an undertaking after he has received notice from the Minister of Munitions that the workman is to work at some other establishment, that employer shall be guilty of an offence under this Act.

7.—(1) A person shall not give employment to a workman, who has within the last previous six weeks, or such other period as may be provided by Order of the Minister of Munitions as respects any class of establishment, been employed on or in connexion with munitions work in any establishment of a class to which the provisions of this section are applied by Order of the Minister of Munitions, unless he holds a certificate from the employer by whom he was last so employed that he left work with the consent of his employer or a certificate from the munitions tribunal that the consent has been unreasonably withheld.

(2) If any workman or his trade union representative complains to a munitions tribunal in accordance with rules made with respect to those tribunals that the consent of an employer has been unreasonably withheld that tribunal may, after examining into the case, if they think fit, grant a certificate which shall, for the purposes of this section, have the same effect as a certificate from the employer.

(3) If any person gives employment in contravention of the provisions of this section, he shall be guilty of an offence under this Act.

8.—(1) The Minister of Munitions may make rules authorising the wearing of badges or other distinctive marks by persons engaged on munitions work or other work for war purposes, and as to the issue and return of any such badges or marks, and may by those rules prohibit the use, wearing or issue of any such badges or of any badges or marks indicating or suggesting that any person is engaged on munitions work or work for war purposes except as authorised by those rules.

(2) If any person acts in contravention of, or fails to comply with any such rules, he shall be guilty of an offence against this Act.

9. This Part of this Act shall apply to any docks used by the Admiralty for any purposes connected with the war as it applies to establishments in which munitions work is carried on, with the substitution in relation to any such docks or persons employed in any such docks of the Admiralty for the Minister of Munitions.

PART III.

10. The following paragraph shall be substituted for paragraph (*d*) set out in subsection (1) of section one of the Defence of the Realm (Amendment) No. 2 Act, 1915, and shall be deemed to have been contained in that Act, namely :—

(*d*) to regulate or restrict the carrying on of any work in any factory, workshop, or other premises, or the engagement or employment of any workman or all or any classes of workmen therein, or to remove the plant therefrom with a view to maintaining or increasing the production of munitions in other factories, workshops, or premises, or to regulate and control the supply of metals and material that may be required for any articles for use in war.

11.—(1) The owner of any establishment in which persons are employed shall, if so required by the Minister of Munitions, give to the Minister such information, in such form and in such manner, as the Minister may require as to

(*a*) the numbers and classes of persons employed or likely to be employed in the establishment from time to time ;

(*b*) the numbers and classes of machines at any such establishment ;

(*c*) the nature of the work on which any such persons are employed, or any such machines are engaged, from time to time ;

(*d*) any other matters with respect to which the Minister may desire information for the purpose of his powers and duties ;

and the Minister may arrange with any other Government department for the collection of any such information.

(2) If the owner of any establishment fails to comply with this section he shall be guilty of an offence under this Act.

12. If any employer, or the owner of any establishment or any workman, for the purpose of evading any provision of this Act, makes any false statement or representation, or gives any false certificate, or furnishes any false information, he shall be guilty of an offence under this Act.

13. There shall be paid out of moneys provided by Parliament to any person being a member of an arbitration tribunal, munitions tribunal, or board of referees under this Act, or being a referee under this Act, and to any other officers required in connexion with any such tribunal or board, such remuneration and travelling or other expenses (including compensation for loss of time) as the Minister of Munitions or Board of Trade, as the case may be, with the sanction of the Treasury may determine.

14.—(1) Any person guilty of an offence under this Act—

(*a*) shall, if the offence is a contravention of or failure to comply with an award, be liable to a fine not exceeding five pounds for each day or part of a day during which the contravention or failure to comply continues, and, if the person guilty of the offence is an employer, for each man in respect of whom the contravention or failure takes place ; and

(*b*) shall, if the offence is a contravention of the provisions of this Act with respect to the prevention of lock-outs, be liable to a fine not exceeding five pounds, in respect of each man locked out, for each day or part of a day during which the contravention continues ; and

(*c*) shall, if the offence is a contravention of the provisions of this Act with respect to the prohibition of strikes, be liable to a fine not exceeding five pounds for each day or part of a day during which the contravention continues ; and

(*d*) shall, if the offence is a contravention of or failure to comply with any regulations in a controlled establishment or any undertaking given by a workman under Part II. of this Act, be liable in respect of each offence to a fine not exceeding three pounds ; and

(*e*) shall, if the offence is a contravention of or failure to comply with any other provisions of this Act, be liable in respect of each offence to a fine not exceeding fifty pounds.

(2) A fine for any offence, under this Act, shall be recoverable only before the munitions tribunal established for the purpose under this Act.

15.—(1) The munitions tribunal shall be a person, appointed for the purpose by the Ministry of Munitions, sitting with two or some other even number of assessors, one half being chosen by the Minister of Munitions from a panel constituted by the Minister of Munitions of persons representing employers and the other half being so chosen from a panel constituted by the Minister of Munitions of persons representing workmen and the Minister of Munitions may constitute two classes of munitions tribunals, the first class having jurisdiction to deal with all offences and matters under this Act, the second class having jurisdiction, so far as offences are concerned, to deal only with any contravention of, or failure to comply with, any regulation made applicable to a controlled establishment or any undertaking given by a workman under Part II. of this Act.

The Admiralty shall be substituted for the Minister of Munitions under this provision as the authority to appoint and choose members of a munitions tribunal to deal with offences by persons employed in any docks declared to be controlled establishments by the Admiralty.

(2) The Minister of Munitions or the Admiralty shall constitute munitions tribunals as and when occasion requires.

(3) Rules may be made for regulating the munitions tribunals or either class of munitions tribunals so far as relates to offences under this Act by a Secretary of State, and so far as relates to any other matters which are referred to them under this Act by the Minister of Munitions, and rules made by the Secretary of State may apply, with the necessary modifications, any of the provisions of the Summary Jurisdiction Acts or any provisions applicable to a court of summary jurisdiction, which it appears expedient to apply, and any provisions so applied shall apply to munitions tribunals accordingly.

In the application of this provision to Scotland the Secretary for Scotland shall be substituted for the Secretary of State, and in the application of this provision to Ireland the Lord Lieutenant shall be substituted for the Secretary of State.

(4) A person employed or workman shall not be imprisoned in respect of the non-payment of a fine imposed by a munitions tribunal for an offence within the jurisdiction of a tribunal of the second class, but that tribunal may, without prejudice to any other available means of recovery, make an order requiring such deductions to be made on account of the fine from the wages of the person employed or workman as the tribunal think fit, and requiring the person by whom the wages are paid to account for any sums deducted in accordance with the order.

16. Any company, association, or body of persons shall have power, notwithstanding anything contained in any Act, order, or instrument by or under which it is constituted or regulated, to carry on munitions work during the present war.

17. Any rule made under this Act shall be laid before each House of Parliament forthwith, and, if an Address is presented to His Majesty by either House of Parliament within the next subsequent twenty-one days on which that House has sat next after any such rule is laid before it praying that the rule may be annulled, His Majesty in Council may annul the rule and it shall thenceforth be void, but without prejudice to the validity of anything previously done thereunder.

18. The Documentary Evidence Act, 1868, as amended by the Documentary Evidence Act, 1882, shall apply to the Minister of Munitions in like manner as if that Minister were mentioned in the first column of the Schedule to the first-mentioned Act, and as if that Minister, or a secretary in the Ministry or any person authorised by the Minister to act on his behalf, were mentioned in the second column of that Schedule, and as if the regulations referred to in those Acts included any document issued by the Minister.

19. In this Act, unless the context otherwise requires,—

(a) The expression " lock-out " means the closing of a place of employment, or the suspension of work, or the refusal by an employer to continue to employ any number of persons employed by him in consequence of a dispute, done with a view to compelling those persons, or to aid another employer in compelling persons employed by him, to accept terms or conditions of or affecting employment :

(b) The expression " strike " means the cessation of work by a body of persons employed acting in combination, or a concerted refusal or a refusal under a common understanding of any number of persons employed to continue to work for an employer in consequence of a dispute, done as a means of compelling their employer or any person or body of persons employed, or to aid other workmen in compelling their employer or any person or body of persons employed, to accept or not to accept terms or conditions of or affecting employment.

20.—(1) This Act may be cited as the Munitions of War Act, 1915.

(2) This Act shall have effect only so long as the office of Minister of Munitions and the Ministry of Munitions exist :

Provided that Part I. of this Act shall continue to apply for a period of twelve months after the conclusion of the present war to any difference arising in relation to the performance by the owner of any establishment of his undertaking to carry out the provisions set out in the Second Schedule to this Act notwithstanding that the office of Minister of Munitions and the Ministry of Munitions have ceased to exist.

SCHEDULES.

Schedule I.

1. Any difference, matter or question to be referred for settlement in accordance with the provisions of this Schedule shall be referred to one of the three following arbitration tribunals :—

(a) The Committee appointed by the First Lord of the Treasury known as the Committee on Production ; or

(b) A single arbitrator to be agreed upon by the parties or in default of agreement appointed by the Board of Trade ; or

(c) A court of arbitration consisting of an equal number of persons representing employers and persons representing workmen with a chairman appointed by the Board of Trade.

2. The tribunal to which the reference is made shall be determined by agreement between the parties to the difference or in default of such agreement by the Board of Trade.

3. The Arbitration Act, 1889, shall not apply to any reference under the provisions of this Schedule.

SCHEDULE II.

1. Any departure during the war from the practice ruling in the workshops, shipyards, and other industries prior to the war, shall only be for the period of the war.

2. No change in practice made during the war shall be allowed to prejudice the position of the workmen in the owners' employment, or of their trade unions in regard to the resumption and maintenance after the war of any rules or customs existing prior to the war.

3. In any readjustment of staff which may have to be effected after the war priority of employment will be given to workmen in the owners' employment at the beginning of the war who have been serving with the colours or who were in the owners' employment when the establishment became a controlled establishment.

4. Where the custom of a shop is changed during the war by the introduction of semi-skilled men to perform work hitherto performed by a class of workmen of higher skill, the time and piece rates paid shall be the usual rates of the district for that class of work.

5. The relaxation of existing demarcation restrictions or admission of semi-skilled or female labour shall not affect adversely the rates customarily paid for the job. In cases where men who ordinarily do the work are adversely affected thereby, the necessary readjustments shall be made so that they can maintain their previous earnings.

6. A record of the nature of the departure from the conditions prevailing when the establishment became a controlled establishment shall be kept, and shall be open for inspection by the authorised representative of the Government.

7. Due notice shall be given to the workmen concerned wherever practicable of any changes of working conditions which it is desired to introduce as the result of the establishment becoming a controlled establishment, and opportunity for local consultation with workmen or their representatives shall be given if desired.

8. All differences with workmen engaged on Government work arising out of changes so introduced or with regard to wages or conditions of employment arising out of the war shall be settled in accordance with this Act without stoppage of work.

9. Nothing in this Schedule (except as provided by the fourth[1] paragraph thereof) shall prejudice the position of employers or persons employed after the war.

---

[1] " Fourth," a drafting error for " third," corrected by the Amending Act, 1916, Section 19.

APPENDIX II.

Memorandum by the National Advisory Committee.

ACCELERATION OF SUPPLY OF MUNITIONS.

THE ORGANISATION OF LABOUR.

The serious position of the British Army in Flanders and of Russia in consequence of an inadequate supply of munitions—especially shells and fuses—was the subject of an interview between the Minister of Munitions (Mr. Lloyd George) and the National Advisory Committee on Tuesday, 8 June.

The statements made by Mr. Lloyd George clearly indicated a situation that was both grave and menacing, and demonstrated the essential importance of bringing home to the skilled and organised workers not only its extreme gravity and danger, but also its supreme urgency.

The extent of the nation's requirements, which Parliament has charged the Minister of Munitions with supplying with all possible speed, is such as to demand that the entire organising capacity of the nation be concentrated upon it.

In this effort, which may mean the saving of the nation, organised labour can and must take an essential and indispensable part, for with enthusiasm and unselfishness it can render invaluable service in a great national crisis.

If the world of industry is to be changed and adapted to meet the clamant and paramount need of the hour, it must be obvious that something more is required than the transfer of a few men here and there. It means that all our available resources of skilled, semi-skilled, and unskilled labour (male and female) must be utilised.

To enable this to be done speedily and efficiently there are two points that must be considered, both of primary and essential importance :—

1. The responsibility of the Trade Unions to the country for so increasing, by their assistance, the production of munitions of war as to place the issue of the war beyond all doubt or uncertainty.

2. The responsibility of the Government to the Trade Unions and the workers generally for preventing their established position from being prejudiced, and in safeguarding their social and economic interests by eliminating the element of excessive profits or exorbitant prices of the necessities of life.

The Trade Unions have the best machinery of registration, especially as concerns the skilled trades immediately concerned with the output of munitions. This machinery, worked in conjunction with the Returns made voluntarily by employers to the Board of Trade, which if thought desirable could be made universal, could with the least possible delay place the Minister of Munitions in possession of the best information as to the resources available for his purpose.

Regard must be had to the extreme urgency of the problem, and the small amount of unemployed labour available either at home or in the oversea dominions.

We cannot afford the time that would be unavoidably occupied were the Government to embark upon a scheme for the national registration of the names, addresses, age, and occupation of all workers, who might be called upon for some form of service in the making of munitions of war. It must also be recognised that, as time is so important an element, the training of semi- or unskilled workers cannot be accomplished on any extensive scale.

We are forced, therefore, to consider whether the available resources can be efficiently and effectively applied so as to increase the production of munitions to meet the demands of our own country and any of the Allies without having to resort to any form of compulsion, even as a temporary expedient. The application of any form of compulsion to workmen concerned in the manufacture of munitions of war, except as a last and unavoidable resource, would be so disturbing as to defeat the object in view.

In order that a voluntary system of transfer of workmen from one shop or locality to another be given the fullest possible trial, we request :—

1. That the Minister shall state the kind of munitions required, the areas in which their manufacture can be most readily carried on, and the class and number of men necessary.

2. That in these areas the workmen required, and who are at present engaged on non-Government work, be invited to volunteer for service with such firms as are or may be engaged in the manufacture of war munitions, under Government control, and whose profits will consequently be restricted.

3. That a list of volunteer workmen shall be submitted to their present employers, and to the Trade Unions representing each particular trade, who shall report to the Local Munitions Committee as to the suitability of the workman for the particular class of work which it is designed he shall be called upon to do.

4. That the lists of volunteer workmen shall be closed within seven days of the issue of the invitation, and a completed list, when vouched, shall be lodged with the Local War Munitions Committee, who shall immediately report to the Ministry of Munitions.

Any transference of labour shall receive consideration in respect of fares and subsistence allowances in accordance with the following conditions[1] :—

1. No workman shall suffer pecuniarily by being transferred to armament work, and no attempt shall be made by or on behalf of

[1] NOTE.—The rules for labour transference are those which were drawn up by the North East Coast Armaments Committee and approved by the Munitions of War Committee on 12 May, 1915. (See Vol. I., Part III., App. XIV.).

workmen to derive any actual profit from the country's critical position, and the Government's undertaking to pay subsistence allowance, train fares, and travelling expenses as stated below. Subsistence and travelling allowances will only be paid to men already in employment who cannot be otherwise obtained, and who are transferred to British Government work at the request of the Local Munitions Committee.

2. Subsistence allowance, *i.e.*, lodging allowance at the rate of 2s. 6d. a day for seven days per week, will be paid to men brought from a distance beyond that which they can reasonably travel daily, so long as they are in the employment of the firm to which they are transferred. Railway fare will be paid to the men transferred from a distance at the commencement and completion of the work for which they were transferred.

3. When the man is within daily travelling distance, *e.g.*, Sunderland to Newcastle, the man shall receive the value of workmen's tickets and one hour's travelling time per day, at the rate of time and a half, but he should start work at 6 a.m., finishing at 5 p.m. If on night shift, he shall start work at 5 p.m. and work until 6 a.m. The Armaments Committee shall take steps where necessary to secure suitable train or tram service.

4. If, however, a man be living at Newcastle and be working at Wallsend, and he is transferred to a works at Newcastle, such man shall only receive his travelling expenses, *e.g.*, tram fare from Byket or Heaton to Elswick or Scotswood, and similar cases will be considered on their merits.

5. Lodging money shall be paid by the firm employing the man to the man with his weekly wages.

6. The Armaments Committee shall issue a warrant to the firm for each man, stating the nature of the allowance he is to receive and the amount. This warrant to be numbered, and the firm to make a detailed monthly statement to the Committee of the men transferred and the amount due to them. The Committee shall then verify and forward this to the Government for payment.

7. Men seeking employment in the ordinary way will receive the usual district rates, but are not entitled to subsistence allowance.

8. Should the Committee find that men have been paid off by an employer with the object of having them transferred to another locality without receiving the authorised allowances, then the Armaments Committee shall reserve to themselves the right of deciding such a case on its merits.

9. The Armaments Committee shall undertake that every workman transferred shall receive the same rate, at least, as in his previous employment.

10. All men who are moved will be provided with the certificate or warrant stating the name of the employer they are leaving and the name of the employer to whom they are going. This warrant to be issued in triplicate, one for the late employer, one for the new employer, and one for the man himself. The Armaments Committee will issue it.

11. The release is to be for a period not exceeding three months in the first instance, but may be renewed by the Armaments Committee if required, subject to the approval of the Government.

The Trade Unions assure the Government that any of their members selected by any Local Armaments Committee for war work shall be immediately placed at the disposal of the Government on the rates of wages and allowances decided upon by the Local Armaments Committee. Such selected men shall continue to work at the factory or yard appointed by the Government, and shall not change their employment without the consent of the Committee. Workmen refusing to abide by these conditions shall be dealt with on lines agreed to by the Local Armaments Committee.

In view of a continued shortage of men, skilled workmen who are at present serving with the colours may be drafted back to the workshop and less skilled and female labour shall be used on minor operations connected with munitions production in accordance with the Treasury Agreement, the whole of the provisions of which must be carefully observed.

The National Advisory Committee rely upon the Government realising their responsibility, referred to previously, for preventing the established position of the workmen from being prejudiced and for safeguarding their social and economic interests by eliminating the element of excessive profits or exorbitant prices of the necessities of life. The Committee also rely upon the whole of the organised machinery of the Trade Unions being placed at the disposal of the Government in their endeavour vastly to increase the output of war munitions, and the Committee appeal with confidence to the organised workers to assist to the utmost extent of their powers to this end. The National Advisory Committee, in conjunction with the Local Advisory Committees, will be prepared to co-operate in this work in every way open to them, either by the distribution of literature or addressing public meetings.

ARTHUR HENDERSON (*Chairman*).

J. T. BROWNLIE.

JOHN HILL.

FRANK SMITH.

ALEX. WILKIE.

C. W. BOWERMAN.

WM. MOSSES (*Secretary*).

10 *June*, 1915.

INDEX.

Contents of Volume I.

NOTE.—The present issue is subject to revision,
and must be regarded as provisional.

27766455R00311

Printed in Great Britain
by Amazon